FARRAR
STRAUS
GIROUX

BECOMING

MODERN

THE LIFE OF

MINA LOY

BECOMING

MODERN

THE LIFE OF

MINA LOY

CAROLYN BURKE

Farrar, Straus and Giroux

New York

Published simultaneously in Canada by HarperCollinsCanadaLtd
Printed in the United States of America
First edition, 1996

Library of Congress Cataloging-in-Publication Data
Burke, Carolyn.
Becoming modern: the life of Mina Loy / Carolyn Burke.—1st ed.
      p.   cm.
Includes bibliographical references and index.
1. Loy, Mina—Biography. 2. Women poets, American—20th century—
Biography. 3. Modernism (Literature)—United States.   I. Title.
PS3523.O975Z58   1996   811'.52—dc20   [B]   95–13118   CIP

FRONTISPIECE
"Dusie" (Mina smoking), Paris: photo by Stephen Haweis, c. 1905

Introduction

I FIRST HEARD of Mina Loy when I was living in Paris twenty years ago. A fin-de-siècle English painter, she had made her name, quite unexpectedly, as a writer of *vers libertine*—the sort of free verse that in the 1910s seemed to lead to free love. To the modernists, she was the first to chart the sensibility of the "new woman." Ezra Pound praised her intellect and her refusal to traffic in sentiment, the staple, he judged, of women poets. (Her poems bristled with such intelligence that Pound coined the term "logopoeia" to describe them.) William Carlos Williams, Hart Crane, and E. E. Cummings all learned from her example. In the 1920s she was as well known as Marianne Moore, the other female modernist with whom she was frequently compared.

In her many years abroad, Mina Loy also befriended Gertrude Stein, John Reed, Djuna Barnes, James Joyce, Brancusi, Peggy Guggenheim, Tristan Tzara, Natalie Barney, Ford Madox Ford, Marcel Duchamp, and Man Ray, to name a few of her "crowd." She makes brief, brilliant appearances in expatriate memoirs: one catches sight of her in New York during the Great War, in the hectic avant-garde of postwar Berlin, at the opening of a risqué Paris nightclub or a clandestine Surrealist film showing in the twenties. By the mid-thirties, however, she had disappeared, and her poems were out of print.

Mina Loy was forgotten, Kenneth Rexroth thought, because her poems were unlike those of any other woman poet. Indeed, they defied the category. Subordinating the pleasures of lyricism to wit, irony, and a fierce sense of justice, she forced readers to think—whether they liked it or not. Now, when poetry reflects concerns with sexual difference as well as the relations between language and perception, she seems decades ahead of her time. Although *Lunar Baedecker* [sic], her first book of poems, has been a collector's item since its publication in 1923, the voice that speaks from its pages is decidedly that of a modernist; her poems see art, love, sex, and childbirth from the perspective of a new woman. Yet she had adopted this perspective through an effort of will, just as she had taken her name.

Mina Loy was born Lowy in 1882, a time of overt anti-Semitism in England, to a Christian mother and a Jewish father. She adopted "Loy" for her first painting exhibition in Paris: the name, which suggested French antecedents, hinted that she would be a law (*loi*) unto herself. But "Loy" was only the first in a series of verbal disguises. Her name changes would mark reformulations of identity. The anagrammatic shifts of Lowy into Loy and later Lloyd symbolize her attempts to resolve personal crises. In this book, she is Mina—the name that stayed fixed as her surname varied. (Even "Mina" by itself could be volatile; in some moods she announced contrarily that it was pronounced "miner," British style.)*

A poet's poet despite the academy's dismissal of her as "minor," a pun she would have enjoyed, Mina was rediscovered and reforgotten for decades. The recent revival of her work owes much to Rexroth, who carried on a one-man campaign to make it available. "There is no question but what she is important and should be reprinted," he argued in 1944. "No one competent and familiar with verse in English in this century would dream of denying it." In the 1960s, when Rexroth's friend Jonathan Williams mentioned his limited edition of her poems to Pound—by then immured in the silence of his Venetian years—the old poet opened up and talked for hours of the free-verse wars, the *Little Review* scandals, and Paris in the twenties. Mina Loy was the key that unlocked his memory.

For us, decades later, her name opens the door to an era of spirited exchanges between American and Continental vanguards. It conjures up smoky art classes in prewar Montparnasse, costume balls at Mabel Dodge's Florentine villa, Futurist soirées where enraged audiences hurl vegetables at the stage, Dadaesque poetry readings, gossipy visits with Gertrude Stein and Alice B. Toklas, dinners in Brancusi's studio among half-finished blocks of marble—all scenes that reveal the shapes of the modernist imagination. Her life, that of a woman peculiarly responsive to the social and artistic movements of her time, allows us to look more deeply into the self-constructing strategies of the international avant-garde.

But as her title *Lunar Baedecker* suggests, Mina Loy also saw herself as a cartographer of the imagination—at a time when terms like "expatriate" and "exile" held somewhat different meanings than in ours. This biography

---

* It was curious to experience the continual mix-up between Mina Loy and Myrna Loy while I was working on this book. Rexroth, who knew both women, told me that the actress, née Williams, named herself after the poet, but efforts to have this story confirmed went unrewarded. Myrna Loy's account of her name change is nonetheless compatible with Rexroth's. In the 1920s she took "Loy" at the suggestion of a friend, "a wild Russian writer of free verse," who surely knew Mina's reputation.

follows her on voyages of many kinds, tracing her development from a repressive London childhood in the 1880s to art studies in fin-de-siècle Munich and Paris, the Florence of Futurism, and New York in the days of Dada, to revolutionary Mexico (with Arthur Cravan) and postwar Europe (after his disappearance), then back to the United States, where she spent the rest of her life. Her transits describe not linear progress but a series of motions like the epicycles on the celestial maps in which she sought inspiration—travel as an elliptical form of quest.

Leaving England at the turn of the century meant escaping from the repressive forces embodied by her mother: the complacency of British culture, its contradictory goals for daughters, the constraints of London in the 1890s (the time of the Oscar Wilde trial and public condemnation of "immoral" art). In Munich, Paris, Florence, and New York, Mina was able to turn her back on the class system that had put her at a disadvantage. And while she longed to get free of all that England represented, she also yearned to find in the community of "geniuses" an alternative home.

Yet in some ways, despite her residence in these centers of modernism, she remained a late Pre-Raphaelite whose artistic voyages were shaped in reaction to a fin-de-siècle aesthetic. Mina spent much of her life critiquing the values of art-for-art's-sake, eventually finding the means to dethrone assumptions about the superiority of "fine art." Anticipating the Surrealists in her appreciation for the underside of high culture (the flea market castoffs dignified by others as *objets trouvés*), she gave her lowly discoveries new life in the form of lamps, collages, constructions, and a variety of poetic décors—all "applied" arts of unusual and fragile beauty. Her travels and her assemblage of art from shards are related: their metaphors of waywardness and fixity, fragmentation and wholeness, hint at her movements toward a state of grace. For her life is also the story of a soul's progress.

Mina's "memoirs" are fragmentary and incomplete. Though I had expected more coherence from her autobiographical writings than finally emerged once they were collated, I have nonetheless been guided by *her* perspective on her development—from repressed oldest child of a troubled family to timidly rebellious art student to promising artist whose early recognition was eclipsed by marriage and the accidents of so-called private life. Other patterns have also emerged to suggest that her lifelong tendency to blame others, starting with rage at her mother, did not abate. The tenor of this particular prose is so wrathful that its anger still crackles, just as some of her poems all but bite the reader.

In the end, Mina did not achieve her goal—recognition as one of the "geniuses"—and she came to see this goal as misguided when its achievement set one apart from others. What she *did* achieve was the considerable goal of seeing her life as expressive of a time and place—a late-Victorian social milieu seething with the prejudices that distorted relations between the sexes and the possibility of self-affirmation for women. As she understood, hers was a life at the intersection of public and private, one that illuminates the concerns of its era. Mina was, in some ways, her era's poetic consciousness—as Harriet Monroe (editor of *Poetry*) called her, its "guide to the moon."

I have tried to give the feel of Mina's inwardness by making use of her own metaphors of self-discovery. If maps and Baedekers symbolize the quest that shaped her transits through the modernist landscape, the image of the book expresses her enigmatic spiritual searching. In childhood, when she learned to regard the Bible as the vessel of truth, books became doorways through which to take imaginary voyages. A book was an object inhabited by and inhabiting space. For this reason, no doubt, *Lunar Baedecker* streamlines the language of Genesis and Revelation. Ideally, its images should be lit from within.

In some ways, Mina put poems together as one would assemble a stained-glass window: her true self is found in the shimmer of light on color. She loved reflective materials of all kinds—translucent or opalescent glass, fabrics like moiré, satin, and velvet, butterfly wings and gemstones. In them she saw an animate presence at play in matter. Her vision of fulfillment is also suggested in the many poetic images assembled from fragments—a method of construction that gave body to the developing modern consciousness while carrying private meanings at once erotic, aesthetic, and spiritual.

"I never was a poet," she declared in the 1950s. (T. S. Eliot said that it was hard to evaluate her because she lacked an "oeuvre," an anachronistic demand for a woman of her time.) She has been neglected because she paid no heed to the requirement for consistent self-presentation in an age that, increasingly, valued professionalism and its external sign, the career. Over the course of her long life, Mina acted, wrote feminist and utopian tracts, explored occult religious and spiritual practices, and made a haphazard study of what turn-of-the-century intellectuals called the New Thought—including everything from Nietzsche, Bergson, and Freud to Vedanta and Pragmatism. (She also had two husbands, four children, and several complicated love affairs.) We see her as an innovative poet with her roots in art; she saw herself as a painter called to language. Yet her life was more varied than these labels imply, and its variety attests to the abundance of impulses behind modernism. It may be that in her multiplicity, Mina speaks to us now, in the era of the postmodern, *because* she followed no one path and did not present a unified body of work.

This temperamental stance has made the reconstruction of her life all the more challenging in that biographical narrative relies more on chronology than "assemblage"—a principle in some ways better suited to Mina Loy, if not the reader. But if biography eschews the strategies of modernist juxtaposition (even though, like this one, it works with fragments), it may nonetheless acknowledge its subject's love of the world's, and the self's, variety. I have come to feel that Mina lived her trajectory, her spiritual zigzags, in full awareness of her contradictions, and that she cherished them all as facets of her "genius."

This book relies on Mina Loy's "subconscious archives," the trove of her lightly veiled fiction and autobiography constituting her memoirs. I have approached this rich storehouse with empathy and with caution, aware that the woman who wrote to make sense of her life also did so to justify herself. Moreover, I have become acutely aware of the biographer's tendency to identify with the subject, to whom she is drawn by some mysterious affinity. (Resurrecting another's life may become a calling, as the current owner of Mina's Florence house observed.) Because Mina's memoirs include everything from after-the-fact noting of dialogue to settling of accounts, I have sifted through them with a set of variable meshes, seeking consistency, plausibility, and externally verifiable information. This process came to resemble the psychic activity she called "silting the appraisable"—letting the weightier elements sift through the mesh of interpretation as the rest volatilizes.

If Mina *had* completed the autobiography she drafted for decades, she might have chosen to call it *Being Geniuses Together*, the ironic title her friend Robert McAlmon gave his account of their group's adventures. But she kept rewriting her life from different angles. In the end, all of them nourished, troubled, and informed my version—which I have called, with a similar sense of irony, *Becoming Modern*. For just as Baedeker offered Victorian travelers guidance, so Mina Loy provides us with a Baedeker of modernism—a guide to the imaginative landscapes created and inhabited by this quirky new woman.

Contents

BECOMING

MODERN

THE LIFE OF

MINA LOY

Prologue

The Modern Woman

(NEW YORK, 1916)

TRAVELERS ARE OFTEN awestruck on their first sight of New York Harbor. In the decades before planes, however, they had time to let their impressions take shape. Passengers arose at dawn—when most steamships entered the harbor—and went on deck in a dream. After weeks of pitching and tossing, seasickness, and the ordeals of steerage, Manhattan looked like paradise. The long-awaited arrival, an observer noted, "was the nearest earthly likeness to the final Day of Judgement." On that day, however dispiriting the voyage, they tried to make a good impression: the few women traveling alone took care to be deemed worthy—as housemaids, seamstresses, or some suitable occupation. Often their only welcome came from the female figure that greeted ships on their approach. "I felt grateful the Statue of Liberty was a woman. I felt she would understand a woman's heart," recalled a traveler about her arrival in 1916, when German warships on patrol intensified the hazards of transatlantic passage.

That year, on October 14, Mina Loy saw Manhattan for the first time. At dawn, after a perilous trip past the mines and submarines that lay along its path through the Mediterranean and across the Atlantic, her ship—the *Duca d'Aosta*—entered the harbor. The Statue of Liberty was invisible beneath the fog. Mina peered through the dim light with the other passengers, mostly Italians. Her fashionable coiffure—her long black hair was parted in the middle and twisted in a low chignon—her intricate tortoiseshell earrings, elegant dress, and willowy figure set her apart. Unlike these immigrants come to begin new lives, she traveled alone. Judging by her accent and her woolen cloak, a cross between a cape and a poncho, an observer might have placed her as a member of some artistic British family long resident in Italy who had unaccountably sailed to New York at the height of the Great War.

Mina, too, thought that New York looked like paradise—but paradise imagined by a Cubist or a Futurist. As the famous skyline emerged through the mist, its buildings floated above their foundations like ladders reaching to heaven. Soon thousands of windows shone like colored glass. Although these glistening towers reminded her of medieval spires, the most beautiful Italian buildings were dwarfed by comparison. Then, as the mist evaporated, the air brightened and the city woke up. Watching its skyscrapers sharpening their angles, she composed a mental picture of Manhattan's vast cityscape. But not everything was designed on such a scale. "No inordinately elongated gulls flew out of the office windows," she noted wryly. Soon Wall Street began looking "like a monstrous progeny of England's cliffs."

European artists arriving in New York during the war were often met by reporters inviting their opinions on art, the New World, and the future. In the wake of the scandalous 1913 Armory Show, their views were thought newsworthy, and although some Americans resented the attention paid them, many looked to these "invaders" for new ways of understanding their homeland. New York journalists had rushed to interview abstract artists Albert Gleizes and Marcel Duchamp, who came to sit out the war in America: while Gleizes compared the Brooklyn Bridge to Notre Dame Cathedral, Duchamp claimed to prefer New York's skyscrapers to Europe's finest monuments.

Mina, not yet discovered by the press, was happy to see a young American woman waving to her from the pier. Her friend Frances Stevens had come to meet the ship. Three years earlier, when barely nineteen, Frances had traveled by herself to Florence, where she rented Mina's spare painting studio and enlisted her as her chaperone. Although Frances became an active member of Mina's Anglo-American expatriate circle, she also cultivated the Futurists—that group of Italian activists gathered around Filippo Tommaso Marinetti, the self-styled "caffeine of Europe." Attracted by Frances's blond good looks, Marinetti brought the Futurists to her studio, where he met Mina, and soon found that he preferred Mina's fin-de-siècle grace and whimsical high spirits. In 1914 Frances and Mina accepted his invitation to show their paintings in the first international Futurist art exhibit, as the sole representatives of America and England. Following the outbreak of hostilities, Frances returned to New York and Mina spent the early years of the war in Florence, becoming more entangled with and disentangled from the Futurists and, rather unexpectedly for a painter, writing poems, plays, and manifestos. It had been too difficult for her and, above all, too dangerous to make the trip to New York until 1916, following the Kaiser's temporary suspension of attacks on neutral shipping.

Mina waited her turn to go through immigration with the first- and second-class passengers. At that time, a middle-class woman, even one possessed of an independent spirit, would not have lowered herself (literally or figuratively) to travel in steerage. Consequently, having sold nearly everything in order to sail in relative comfort, Mina was spared the trials facing the steerage passengers, who clutched their trunks and carpetbags as they lined up to be ferried to Ellis Island. While she and Frances waited for her luggage, Mina asked for news of their mutual friends from Florence and of Frances's career. Mabel Dodge, who often entertained them at her villa, had abandoned the radical salon she presided over after her return to New York: she was dividing her time between her psychoanalyst and her love affairs. Carl Van Vechten, another American friend, had become a fashionable New York critic. As for herself, Frances had recently had her first one-woman show: in the catalogue the gallery director noted that while he did not understand her art, he thought it should be shown, and Frances explained the Futurists' passion for modern life. The most enthusiastic response had come from the IRT subway's chief engineer. After comparing her painting of his powerhouse to the original, he declared that her painting had taught him to see.*

Finished with the formalities of arrival, Mina pondered the contradictions between the Old World's view of modern life and the New World's inability to understand itself. As Frances drove through lower Manhattan, the heavenly skyscrapers she had spied from the ship proved to be topped with ill-assorted final stories in imitation Egyptian or Gothic. Nor did the neat rows of Greenwich Village brownstones impress her: they looked too much like the London streets where she had taken endless walks with her nannies. What she wanted was life on a different scale, a break with Europe and all it stood for.

Within days of her arrival, Mina learned that her reputation had preceded her. In Florence she had had little idea of the controversy her poetry aroused when it first appeared in *Rogue* and *Others*, the vanguard literary reviews that featured her. The New York critics, *Others* editor Alfred Kreymborg recalled, had "shuddered at Mina Loy's subject-matter and derided her elimination of punctuation marks and the audacious spacing of her lines"—those aspects of her work that fascinated him because they translated into English the aesthetics of Apollinaire and Marinetti. In his view Mina had "simply transferred futuristic theories to America, and in her subject-matter had gone about expressing herself freely." But as far as the public was concerned, this sort of poetry—*vers libre*, or free verse—was preoccupied with sex and devoid of thought. Parodies of Mina's poems had appeared in the newspapers, and for the past year the columnist Don

* Stevens's *Dynamic Velocity of Interborough Rapid Transit Power Station*, her only surviving painting, is in the Arensberg Collection, Philadelphia Museum of Art.

Marquis had poked fun at *vers libre*: "Not only do we understand the New Verse," he claimed, "but we are the only person who does understand all of it."

By November 1916 Mina's name was so suggestive of artistic and sexual license—or nonsense—that the young reporter Djuna Barnes slipped it into her New York *Morning Telegraph* account of the up-to-date Greenwich Villager's décor: "A touch of purple here, a gold screen there, a black carpet, a curtain of silver, a tapestry thrown carelessly down, a copy of Rogue on a low table open at Mina Loy's poem." (She illustrated the article with a drawing of a woman whose dark hair, dangling earrings, and worldly gaze suggest a caricature of Mina.) That same month, *Poetry* magazine published an "imaginary conversation between two lady poets": "Said Mina Loy to Muna Lee, / 'I wish your style appealed to me.' / 'Yours gives me anything but joy!' / Said Muna Lee to Mina Loy."

The poem that had outraged one and all was the first of Mina's "Love Songs"—better known as "Pig Cupid":

> Spawn   of   Fantasies
> Silting the appraisable
> Pig Cupid   his rosy snout
> Rooting erotic garbage
> "Once upon a time"
> Pulls a weed   white   star-topped
> Among wild oats   sown in mucous-membrane
>
> I would   an   eye in a bengal light
> Eternity in a sky-rocket
> Constellations in an ocean
> Whose rivers run no fresher
> Than a trickle of saliva

Readers of Victorian poetry were unprepared for such visceral evocations of love. A letter to the editor denounced *Love Songs* as "swill poetry" or, more succinctly, "hoggerel." What Kreymborg called Mina's "utter nonchalance in revealing the secrets of sex," some saw as lewd and lascivious writing—in the same class as Margaret Sanger's birth-control pamphlets and Emma Goldman's talks on free love. Most agreed that "to reduce eroticism to the sty was an outrage, and to do so without verbs, sentence structure, punctuation, even more offensive," but Kreymborg thought that readers were offended because the author of "Pig Cupid" was female. Contributors to *Others* were in awe of Mina *because* she had expressed herself on the subject of a woman's desire. William Carlos Williams spoke for the moderns when he recalled, "Never shall I forget our fascination with Mina's 'Pig Cupid, his rosy snout rooting erotic garbage.' "*

Mina kept busy that winter, finishing a play, preparing the full se-quence of thirty-four "Love Songs," designing "art" lampshades to sup-plement her savings, and, in her spare moments, painting the occasional picture. Through Frances Stevens she met the couple she would call the most civilized people she had ever known, Walter and Louise Arensberg —at whose West Sixty-seventh Street duplex a cosmopolitan group of artists and writers gathered nightly to gossip, play chess, analyze each other's dreams, and consume the quantities of alcohol that nourished these prac-tices. In this stimulating atmosphere, where the emphasis was on the new—whether it was psychoanalysis, free verse, free love, or Cubism— Mina came to know Arensberg's French friends, including Marcel Du-champ, Albert Gleizes, and Francis Picabia, as well as Kreymborg, Williams, and other American poets with whom she appeared in the little magazines. Throughout the winter they flirted with new ideas and each other.

By 1916, an equally *épater-le-bourgeois* approach had erupted among the artists, radicals, and "drinking intelligentsia" who gathered downtown in Greenwich Village. In November the Provincetown Players staged two one-acters: *Suppressed Desires*, a satire of the vogue for psychoanalysis written by George Cram Cook and Susan Glaspell, and *Enemies*, written and acted by the husband and wife team Neith Boyce and Hutchins Hapgood. Fol-lowing these quasi-Freudian dramas, the Provincetown's December pro-duction of Kreymborg's play *Lima Beans* was a surprise. Starring William Carlos Williams as the husband and Mina as the wife, this free-verse romp sent up the whole idea of marriage. But at a time when nonconformists were being pressured to support the idea of intervention in the war, the play's antibourgeois sentiments seemed unpatriotic. Progressives and pac-ifists alike began to feel powerless against the increasing tide of militarism.

By the new year, American involvement seemed inevitable. On January 13, Arthur Cravan, poet, boxer, draft evader, and one-man scandal, arrived in Manhattan on the same ship as Leon Trotsky, a few weeks before the Kaiser announced the resumption of attacks on steamships. On January 23, Duchamp climbed Washington Square Arch to declare the independence of Greenwich Village—a gesture that typifies the agitation of the months just before the American declaration of war. In the opinion of Hutchins Hapgood, a progressive journalist as well as playwright, "much of the expression of those explosive days was the same, whether in art, literature, labor expansion, or sexual experience." The New Art, the New Psychology, the New Politics, and the New Woman were all related. From this per-

---

* Conrad Aiken, a contributor to *Others*, nonetheless advised lovers of poetry to "pass lightly" over "the gelatinous erogenous quiverings of Mina Loy."

spective, Kreymborg was right: Mina's poems provoked outrage because they challenged artistic and sexual propriety. Her writing embodied the attitude that journalists called modern, modernist, or futurist—as if these were all variations of the same impulse—and what was worse, it spoke in a woman's voice.

At that volatile moment, some even claimed that "women are the cause of modernism, whatever that is." Alert to the latest trend, the *Evening Sun* told its reporter to find out "who is she, where is she, what is she—this 'modern woman' that people are always talking about." The obvious place to track down one of these controversial females was Greenwich Village, the haunt of Duchamp's friend the alarmingly modern Baroness Elsa von Freytag-Loringhoven: she had recently been sighted wearing black-and-purple anklets, a postage stamp on her cheek, and a purple wig tied on her head with shipping cable, in place of her usual headgear, a coal scuttle. But the Baroness had been done.

Someone suggested, "Try Mina Loy; you know she writes free verse and things like that. If she isn't the modern woman, who is?" Loy was known to live uptown and to dress with a less unconventional sense of personal style than the Baroness. Although her opinions might be odd, her portrait could appear on the women's page, and her list of credentials sounded unassailably modernist, whatever that was. She wrote free verse, designed lampshades, made her own street and stage clothes, and could tell *Sun* readers "why futurism is and where it came from." Mina Loy was, without doubt, a presentable "new woman."

The interview appeared in February 1917 under the arresting title "Mina Loy, Painter, Poet and Playwright, Doesn't Try to Express Her Personality by Wearing Odd Looking Draperies—Her Clothes Suggest the Smartest Shops, but Her Poems Would Have Puzzled Grandma." The unnamed reporter found Mina at home in her West Fifty-seventh Street apartment. As she worked on a painting, Mina traced the outlines of her artistic development, beginning with her early training in England, residence in Italy, and acquaintance with the Futurists. She was scathing on the education of Italian women, like the immigrants with whom she had traveled to New York: society had granted them only the most childlike images of their potential. But primarily Mina presented herself as a woman determined to create her own image. To do so meant to reject passé ways of thinking, the mental corsets that constrained consciousness. Only then could one begin to live like a modern and not "as your grandmother thought you ought to . . . according to the rules."

Instead, Mina asserted, "the modern flings herself at life and lets herself feel what she does feel; then upon the very tick of the second she snatches the images of life that fly through the brain." During her first concert at Carnegie Hall, she explained, images came to her that inspired her latest poem—as strange as this might seem. The "modern way," she went on, meant not caring if you transgressed familiar categories: "If you are very frank with yourself and don't mind how ridiculous anything that comes to you may seem, you will have a chance of capturing the symbol of your direct reaction." While the reporter was doubtful about this "Freudian" approach to inspiration, she wanted to learn more about Mina's methods, since her poems "were the kind that people kept around for months and dug out of corners to read to each other."

The tone of this article suggests that the reporter may have remained a bit skeptical, despite Mina's energy, certainty, and glamour. The interview rings with conviction, nonetheless, and it underscores Mina's belief that "no one who has not lived in New York has lived in the Modern world." The reporter closed with the observation that although this sophisticate was "always half-way through the door into Tomorrow," it was to her credit that she chose to explore the future not in Europe but in the United States. New York might not be paradise, but Mina Loy *was* the modern woman.

Yet in the process of explaining how one went about becoming modern, Mina omitted any discussion of those vexing issues—family, marital status, children, and finances—as if the new woman were exempt from such concerns. She avoided the subject of her London childhood and ultraconservative parents, who would also have been shocked by her poems—had they known about them. Similarly, the interview fails to mention the demise of her marriage and the suspicion among Anglo-Florentines that given her husband's departure and her relations with Marinetti, she had forfeited her status as a "lady." Nor does it refer to Mina's two young children, left with their nurse in Florence, or to the financial support required for the new woman to keep flinging herself at life.

Perhaps these day-to-day concerns seemed less pressing at a time when the headlines warned in extra-large bold type, "Decision to Arm U.S. Steamships May Bring Speedy Clash at Sea." If one reads between the lines, the reporter's views fall somewhere between those of the traditionalists, who thought modernism an assault on society, and those of the progressives, who believed in its transformative powers. Arriving at a moment when these contradictions were at their height, Mina was fortunate in her welcome by a group of free spirits who saw her not as an outcast but as a cartographer whose poems mapped the modern woman's psyche.

As the interview makes clear, Mina was at home in exile. It would not always be so for her over her long life. There were to be many countries, many exiles. While the interview stressed her exuberance, the accompanying photograph shows her gazing into the unknown. Among the many things she did not reveal to the reporter was her neurasthenia—the dark side of her ebullient moments. Nor did she let on that in her emancipated verses she was sounding her "subconscious archives"—the layers of memory that surface as one moves into tomorrow.

—PART I—

THE

SUBCONSCIOUS

ARCHIVES

Everything has already taken place . . . our personality or destiny, like a roll of

negative film . . . is unrevealable until it has found a camera to project it and a

surface to throw it upon.

—MINA LOY, *Islands in the Air*

We were the last group to grow up under the formidable discipline of the

nineteenth century, whose effect, however much we resented, cannot be entirely

eradicated from our systems.

—BRYHER, *The Heart to Artemis*

1

The Bud beside the Rose

(LONDON, 1882–97)

A DOORWAY FIGURES in Mina Loy's earliest memory, of a time when she found herself among strangers. Too young to know why she had been brought to this large, dark house full of people she did not recognize, she knew that she wanted to go home. One afternoon they bundled her into her winter clothes; then someone picked her up and began carrying her down a flight of stairs. There was nothing familiar about the man who held her in his arms. Suddenly something flashed above the doorway at the bottom of the stairs. Colored lights dazzled her eyes. She blinked and stared at the fiery reds and yellows, barely making out the colored bottles that stood in a row behind the fanlight. The sun was shining through layers of glass and straight at her, as if she had caught fire, as if shards of color had entered her body. But as she stretched her arms toward this brilliance, the force that gripped her like a clamp kept on going down the stairs. The colored lights vanished when they went out the door.

In this first memory, something precious is lost, and something else —which we might call self-consciousness—is gained. Trying to analyze this moment decades later, Mina could still feel its power over her in middle age, as she wrote and rewrote the many versions of her autobiographical fiction. First impressions of this kind were unconditional, she wrote: such experiences could "print pictures, even maps, which are not, as it were, taken 'off the press' until years later."

But as a child, Mina could interpret neither this first "map" nor her feeling of having been "so lately embodied." In adolescence she learned from a chance remark that she had been sent to stay at the family doctor's house during her sister Dora's birth one month before her own second birthday. When she remembered being carried downstairs to go home, she understood that the doctor's professional grasp had been the clamp that held her: "The entire event emerged quite clearly. I was staying with the wife of our family doctor to be 'out of the way' while my younger sister was born."

Mina returned to this memory as an adult because she wanted to grasp its meaning. She had yearned to become one with the glow, she thought, since an infant, "conceiving no distinction between the thing to be known & the knowing of it . . . becomes in turn everything it encounters." In that moment her precocious aesthetic sense had been "quickened by that fundamental excitement combined of worship and covetousness, which being the primary response to the admirable very likely composes the whole human ideal." The memory also crystallized the time just before self-consciousness. "My conviction of having been everywhere-at-once while definitely aware of my *self* survived my discovery that something I since have known as space intercepted my relation to other contents of the nursery." This "first concrete impression" underlay her efforts to map her inner world.*

Yet it stayed "on the press" for reasons other than those revealed in her autobiography—even when she saw the difference "between the thing to be known & the knowing of it." The intensity of her focus on this first memory also suggests a disturbance in the little girl's passage from her parents' house into the world.† The image of the door is charged with ambivalence—on neither side can she regain the comfort of her mother's arms. At the onset of self-consciousness—she is not quite two—the child finds herself in the grip of a stranger who, rather than giving her what she wants, carries her off in the opposite direction. She must forgo the blazing reds and yellows and return to the house where she is always "in the way."

For the young Mina Loy, the discovery of self was linked not only with the enchantments of light and color but also with the loss of "home." The memory stages embodiment as a shock. She is exiled first from her mother, then from the colored glass. Although her yearning is displaced onto the glowing shapes, this consolation proves inaccessible and, for that reason, all the more fiercely desired. (In memory, the blaze of colors signals pain as well as wonder: gazing up at them, she is "riddled with splinters of delight.") Like a palimpsest or a pentimento lying beneath the "homes" she created in verse and on canvas, this first impression maps the space

---

* Loy's ideas about the infant's sense of identity anticipate those of Marion Milner, who states that painting, an art "concerned with the feelings conveyed by space," takes up "the problems of being a separate body in a world of other bodies."

† Winnicot's idea of creative play as transitional space between periods of fusion with and separation from the mother help explain Loy's enduring rage: her efforts to deal with the loss of emotional security during this period of "exile" would have been disrupted, particularly by the "doctor's grip," a symbol of masculine authority.

where Mina felt that she had been cast out from paradise; its component parts—the door, the colored glass, the flash of illumination, the sense of embodiment—recur in her art like sudden glimpses into her imagination.

By reflecting on such memories, Mina hoped to write her way to self-knowledge: "Far from being fantastic interpretations of half forgotten infantile responses," she believed, "these analyses are as painstaking in their accuracy as a blueprint." For this reason she kept analyzing her life in poems, fiction, and lightly veiled memoirs. This unfinished "autobiography" is voluminous but fragmentary, as if her experiences as she traveled from the Victorian era into the modern world were too diverse to be woven into a single narrative. Yet certain threads recur. Rage against her mother runs like the weft through her tales of childhood, and a sense of herself as the family outcast interlaces her later forays into modernism. Taken together, these stories comprise the materials for an autoanalysis carried out on the page, and only in part, since they bristle with unassuageable anger at her mother as the cause of her difficulties and internal divisions. Yet to a sympathetic reader they also suggest that without this adversary, Mina might never have been driven to compose her own story.

I

She was born Mina Gertrude Lowy, the first child of Julia Bryan and Sigmund Lowy, on December 27, 1882. Anxiety about the family name, which sounded unmistakably Jewish to British ears, would inspire in both mother and daughter a variety of strategies for dealing with the awkwardness it inevitably provoked. But Mina never guessed at the equally embarrassing circumstances that preceded her birth, nor did she realize that her mother had been seven months pregnant at her wedding. Had she known the reasons for this unlikely marriage, they might have given her greater insight into what she saw as her mother's innate dislike of her firstborn. About this union, only the date and place are recorded: whether the delay reflected the Bryans' concern over Julia's marriage to a man who was both a foreigner and a Jew, or whether there was little love between the couple, is not known.

What *is* known about Mina's grandparents is suggestive. George Bryan, a carpenter and, later, cabinetmaker, lived with his wife, Ann, in Bromley, a village southeast of London where, in the second half of the nineteenth century, Evangelical and Nonconformist chapels outnumbered Anglican churches. As the daughter of an artisan in this area, Julia was presumably raised as a Baptist, a Congregationalist, or in one of the Methodist denominations. Consequently, even if her parents respected Lowy's skill as a tailor, they could not have helped thinking him an unusual choice for her hand. While forced marriages were not unusual, mixed ones were: a Jew was foreign to their experience except as a descendant of the Old Testament Hebrews.

There were many secrets in the Lowy household. Mina had no idea that her mother had married Sigmund, who was twelve years her senior, to avoid disgrace. Nor did she know what had attracted her to this handsome foreigner in the first place. But she was aware that, for her mother, life with a man who clung to his faith and his profession, and who could not—or would not—lose his accent, was a trial. In Mina's view her mother tried all her life to conceal both her husband's religion and the source of his income. Although Julia sometimes let it be known that he was "connected with trade," no one was allowed to mention what he did. Mina was surprised to learn in later years that he began as a tailor.

Haunted by the contradictions of her family life, Mina wrote and rewrote her autobiography—first as the modernist verse epic "Anglo-Mongrels and the Rose" (1923–25), then in the many prose versions that constitute her fictionalized memoirs. While this writing brims with the sensuous immediacy of childhood, it is also shot through with the analytic insights of adulthood, in nearly the same proportion in which physical exactness and intellectual acuity combine in her poetry. She rarely recorded sensory memories without commenting on them or trying to interpret their meaning; returning to the same incidents from different angles, she kept trying to grasp the emotional dynamics of her childhood and its effect on her imagination. It is difficult to see beyond her perspective—both because it is so persuasively presented and because there are no sources other than her autobiographical writing for most of her life. Yet it *is* possible to evaluate the plausibility and consistency of these accounts, as well as their confirmation in her art and adult experience.

In one version of her childhood, the free-verse autobiography Mina wrote in her forties, she and her father are "Anglo-Mongrels" and her mother the "English Rose"—a blossom "self-pruned" yet bristling with "the divine right of self-assertion." Once Sigmund decided to follow Jewish custom by assigning the spiritual education of his girls to their mother, Julia could bully the family in the name of religion; in Mina's view, her mother's delicate coloring concealed a self-righteous determination to have her way. Julia probably believed that children were born not in innocence but in sin, and that girls had to learn to suppress their natures through self-denial. Like most Evangelicals, she was undoubtedly raised to think that the slightest indiscretion paved the road toward depravity. If Julia resented her firstborn as intensely as Mina's memoirs suggest, it was because her daughter was a daily reminder of her own lapse from rectitude.

But Mina came to suspect that her mother's religion was based less on theological principles than on her concern with other people's opinions. For those of uncertain social status like the Lowys, genteel affectations and censorious cant justified their claims to middle-class respectability, especially at a time when "not only were the middle classes drawing away from the poor, but each stratum within the bourgeoisie was drawing away from the stratum next below it." And as the Lowys moved up the social ladder, trading the lower-middle-class standing of small shopkeepers for the more middle-middle rung of the merchant and professional classes, Julia's enhanced respectability only partly concealed the insecurities of her position. Lacking self-assurance as well as an education, she paid close attention to the codes of propriety—a practice which complemented her religious belief that stringent rules applied to the least acts of everyday life.

Julia may have also shared the widespread Victorian belief that parents should repress young children for their own good. Reflecting in middle age on her "inner necessity to escape from the Victorian era," Mina was thinking of her own childhood, but also more generally of the sternness with which childish attempts at self-expression were usually met. Although Julia maintained only a slightly exaggerated version of common practice, Mina came to see her mother's tyrannizing as the domestic version of imperial rule: just as Britannia had taken for granted her right to govern the uncivilized peoples over whom she held sway, so her mother believed it her duty to encourage the repression of her daughter. While one could not overemphasize the inhibiting force of Julia's views on Mina's temperament, one could also say that this oppressive force may also have served to strengthen her resolve and focus her imagination.

In "Anglo-Mongrels" Mina's father appears as the Jewish tailor "Exodus," a touching figure who bows to the will of his British wife, while in one prose version of her life he is "Mr. Israels." As Mina understood it, the Lowys had been wealthy members of the Jewish community in Budapest for more than a century before her birth. After giving part of his fortune to build a synagogue, Sigmund's grandfather had disinherited his son Adolph—Sigmund's father—for marrying a working-class woman who came there to worship. Their son—Mina's father—was born in 1848, a year of anti-Semitic riots following the granting of civil rights to Hungarian Jews. Adolph Lowy named the boy Sigmund Felix in honor of the composer Felix Mendelssohn, who had died the year before and was a relation of the Budapest Lowys. Sigmund's father transferred to his son his own frustrated ambitions, making sure that the boy learned Hebrew along with German and Hungarian. But after his father's early death, Sigmund's mother married a man from her own class who disparaged his stepson's cultural interests and forced him to learn tailoring. Although Jews were granted political rights in 1867, when Sigmund was nineteen, they were denied religious equality, and anti-Semitism persisted among the Hungarian bourgeoisie. After his apprenticeship Sigmund emigrated to England, where, it was said, Jews prospered.

Lowy soon became the highest-paid tailor's cutter in London. A handsome man who carried himself well, he painted delicate studies of English flowers or strolled around London on his days off. Once Lowy acquired fluency in business English and began to dabble in stocks, he was ready to go into business and start a family. But he was of a sensitive nature, preoccupied with his health and social status, especially at a time when

17

Jewish tailors were associated in the public mind with the East End sweat-shops.* Although the marriage brokers introduced him to a number of eligible Jewish women, he could not interest himself in their charms. On a holiday in a country village near London, he met the pink-and-white hedge rose who, he decided, would initiate him into Englishness. Wondering (in "Anglo-Mongrels") how such an unlikely match was made, Mina thought that her father believed he had found "Albion in female form" and would "unite their variance / in marriage."

Their variances were so great, however, that once united, the Lowys shared little more than their three daughters and their common interest in marking out their superiority to those beneath them on the social ladder. When Mina was born, Lowy had already established himself as a merchant rather than a man who worked with his hands and put considerable distance between his Gracechurch Street office and the squalid East End. Having suffered from both social rigidity and religious discrimination in Budapest, he was happy to find that in London, being a tailor (or a draper as he now called himself) could be socially acceptable provided one made a great deal of money, and being a Jewish tailor might be overlooked provided one made even more. By the time Mina's sister Dora was born in 1884, her father had joined the ranks of the highly skilled "English" tailors, who made clothes for the upper classes; judging by his own manners and appearance, he could have been taken for one of his clients. But he was never to accumulate the great wealth that might have opened the doors of society.

When Mina came into the world, so precipitously after her parents' wedding, the Lowys had not yet consolidated their social position. Since Lowy had no time to find new lodgings, Julia joined him in his boarding-house in Hampstead, a comfortable North London suburb where many successful English Jews lived, as well as a number of writers and artists. He may have hoped that Julia would feel more at home in countrified Hampstead than in the center of the city. In any case, their anomalous marriage would seem less unusual there, and the location—a short walk to Hampstead Heath and the station where Lowy caught his train to the City—was convenient. Not only would his new family enjoy the better air and green expanses, but their position would be enhanced by life far from the center of commerce.

Yet one could not claim middle-class status simply by living in a place like Hampstead. Others had to behave as if they, too, felt you belonged. Sigmund was confident of his position as a merchant and a family man, however suddenly this had come upon him, but Julia was unsure of herself. Suspicious of strangers and hostile to foreigners, although (or because) she had married one, she tended toward anti-Semitism as well. Even though

---

* In the 1890s, with the influx of immigrants, most Jewish tailors either made shoddy imitations of fashionable clothing or "clobbered" secondhand garments for resale in the East End.

Lowy had already joined the better class of tailors, a certain taint of exoticism clung to him, and Julia was dismayed by his refusal to adopt either her religion or her prejudices. Within a few years, energized by the self-righteousness of her faith, she began to domineer over her husband despite his superiority in years and worldliness. Julia maintained her advantage in the face of all arguments: she was British and Christian, while he was foreign and Jewish. By the 1890s—Mina's teenage years—Lowy had withdrawn into hypochondria. Julia's attitude remained that of her lower-middle-class origins, where support for the British Empire often joined with virulent jingoism and anti-Semitism. Under these circumstances Mina's emotional life became a battleground of contradictory loyalties.

In the process of writing "Anglo-Mongrels," Mina managed to reach some understanding of her mother's situation. Realizing that Julia saw her as her father's child—the trick he had played upon her and the cross she had to bear—she could all but put herself in her mother's place:

> To the mother
> the blood-relationship
> is a terrific indictment of the flesh
>
> under cover
> of clothing and furnishing
> "somebody" has sinned
> and their sin
> —a living witness of the flesh
> swarms with inquisitive eyes

But although she had almost grasped the reason why she had always felt "overshadowed / by the mother's aura / of sub-carnal anger," this insight did not release her from her rage against the parent who, she believed, had never really loved her.

Lowy made occasional attempts to intervene in his wife's methods of child-raising, but gradually concluded that he could do little to alter the social equivalent of Julia's austere theology—the doctrine of what is and is not "done." This highly coded set of rules governed behavior, since to flout its expectations meant to risk disgrace. From Julia's perspective, their mixed marriage was a blot to be overcome with unfailing attention to external forms. As the Lowys were both impeccably dressed and could soon afford servants, appearances were maintained, but not without considerable anxiety. For Mina was always about to do something that would reveal the true nature of things. Their recently acquired middle-class standing was like a new suit of clothes that might come apart at the seams to uncover the family's secrets.

Because Mina Loy's accounts of early childhood recall its colors, textures, and atmospheres so vividly, they are more painful to read than if her memories had faded. Interwoven with an unusual number of very early yet clearly focused memories is a litany of complaints against her mother, relieved only by infrequent attempts to see Julia as a woman of a certain class and generation. Since the same incidents are examined from slightly different perspectives, it is likely that these events took place much as Mina remembered them. But the emotional distress coloring her interpretations of them suggests that while she gained some understanding of their relationship, she never forgave Julia for withholding "the intuitive value every true mother sets upon the babe she treasures."

An unusual number of scenes from childhood open the door to her imagination. Like the first impression of colored bottles, another early memory connects her attraction to light with childish play, bodily fragmentation, and separation from her mother. As a very young child, perhaps no more than two, Mina was waving her arms about with one of her set of dominoes clenched in her fist. Suddenly the little block flew off in the direction of a large illuminated surface, which shattered in pieces on the floor. Then "words instead of sailing off to unknown destinations descended stinging me with a vocal shrapnel." Her mother swooped down at her, shrieking about damnation: Mina had broken a windowpane. She was to contemplate her wickedness while everyone had tea. Trying to understand the meaning of these words, she gazed up at the window and became "tremendously engrossed with that placard of light set in the air . . . It was the being there of its not being there that intrigued me." When her nurse comforted her by calling it an accident, the word took on a mysterious meaning. Mina later wondered whether emotional balance depended on one's having a sense of proportion and supposed that her own had been injured in this "accident." In a stinging critique of her mother's taste and judgment, she recalled her sense that a home should offer reassurance, and her realization that "a room composed in a quarrel of display and thrift could not hold out the arms of its walls to gather me in."

As a child Mina learned to comfort herself by taking refuge in her imagination. She remembered watching pixies appear and disappear among the patterns of her mother's bed and talking to the childish figures who stepped off her nursery wallpaper. By concentrating her imaginative powers upon objects or sensations, she could feel them "coming alive" and, by this means, blot out her mother's tirades. Hearing a march played on the piano, she could see toy soldiers parading across her carpet; walking across a colored print of a meadow placed on the floor, she found herself in the country. But while her imagination provided escape from the constraints of childhood, it also caused her to be reprimanded for "making things up." Like most Evangelicals, for whom the imagination was a source of sin, Julia distrusted her child's ability to invent. Not only was Mina guilty of a crime she could not fathom, but her chief refuge, her imagination, provoked repeated threats of impending disgrace.

By November 1884, when Mina was staying at the doctor's house, the Lowys had moved to more spacious lodgings in Bloomsbury. They did not find permanent accommodations until Mina was four and Dora two, when they moved back to North London and settled at 17 Greville Place, too close to working-class Kilburn and too far from prosperous Hampstead to allay Julia's anxieties. For their girls, however, returning to the suburbs meant a stable middle-class existence, with a nursery, a succession of nannies, and daily lessons in proper behavior. Family photographs taken at this time show a wistful Mina, with her dark hair cropped like a boy's, and a sulky Dora, with long blond curls. Between them stands their mother, whose firm mouth belies a certain wariness in the eyes: placing her arm around Dora to support her on her perch, Julia turns her back on her elder daughter.

Once a nurse was engaged, her mother made fewer appearances in Mina's domain. Since the Lowys had decorated the nursery with a wallpaper by their Hampstead neighbor Kate Greenaway, Mina spent hours bringing to life the beautifully dressed, well-behaved little children on her walls, who also seemed to inhabit her picture books. These pleasant images offered a vision of a life without tension, where little Phyllises and Belindas took tea in their garden while their friend May Blossom lolled under the apple tree. But the charming melancholy of the Greenaway girls must have had a depressing effect over time, since these idealizations of a simpler age are strangely lacking in energy. Like most middle-class parents, the Lowys probably expected daughters who never soiled their sashes or crushed their bonnets. Mina's imaginary friends were models of a demure goodness that she could never quite manage when making up games with Dora: compared with the urchins she saw in Kilburn during their walks, they seemed unsuited for life outside the world of her imagination.

As for the grown-up women who dominated daily life, they looked to her like "armored towers" in their whalebone corsets. Moving through the house as if on the warpath, Julia seemed propelled by "the irate dignity innate to her, her abdomen steering her fine draped dress." Julia did her best to embody the feminine ideal of the eighties—two cage-like shapes connected by a waist so small that a man's hand could encircle it with his fingers. But rather than suggesting vulnerability, Julia's hourglass figure reminded Mina of "a corset-busk giving out ominous creaks as if nursing resentment for some secret affront." (What she could see of her father resembled "two tubes rattling coins in their summits, magical sources of the houses and provisions that poured from them.") Much later Mina depicted her mother as one of the many women of the eighties who bristled with the resentments of emotionally repressed lives, while also sardonically pointing out the resemblance between her mother's contemporaries and their overstuffed furniture.

When the Lowys engaged nurses for their daughters, Mina began to see that there was another class of women, often more pliant than the armored towers. The first in a series of substitute caretakers was Lilah, who had understood that her charge's crimes were accidents. Mina responded to Lilah's gentleness, her violet eyes, and her one treasure, a brooch of coral rosebuds that Lilah let her touch. She listened attentively to Lilah's stories about Hungary, where she had worked for a Jewish family, and to her reassurances about the one person who always understood little children, the gentle Jesus, who died for their sins. Mina yearned for the Saviour to come to her house. He would convince her mother that she was a good girl and let it be known that "for every infantile / indiscretion / there is absolution."

Hearing of her child's spiritual disposition, Julia instructed the nurse to read to her daily from *The Peep of Day, or A Series of the Earliest Religious Instruction the Infant Mind is Capable of Receiving*. In the first chapter of this terrifying evangelical tract, the Infant Mind is told "how easy it would be to hurt your poor little body! If it were to fall into the fire, it would be burned up. If hot water were to fall upon it, it would be scalded. If it were to fall into deep water, and not be taken out very soon, it would be drowned." Adam and Eve's expulsion from the Garden into a place full of weeds and thistles seemed harsh punishment for their mysterious sin, yet in keeping with what Mina already knew about the administration of justice at the hands of her mother. Lilah always reminded her of God's kindness in sending His only son into the world and assured her that release from its perils would come at last, when "God will burn this world we live in . . . and make another much better than this." Years later, Mina wondered at the contrast between what people like her mother, "while proclaiming the ineluctable purity of Christ, made of the merely annoying brat I may actually have been, and His 'suffer the little children to come unto me' with its implication that children alone were fit for His company."

Although Lilah was sure that God would spare them from the torments of hell, Mina fretted over the question "Whom will he save?" What if her mother was right and she was to be numbered among the damned? To make matters worse, Mina woke up one morning to learn that Lilah had been sent packing. When Julia said that her nurse had not been useful, Mina decided she "was never going to set any store by useful things again." Soon Mina had a new nurse named Queenie, who took her on endless walks around the newly developed streets of South Hampstead: "All the streets were the same—bare and buff. Sometimes a richer house would have pillars painted a dull red. The more streets they saw—the less they had to say." Queenie, though good-natured, had few stories to tell and offered no visions of a happier existence. Soon she, too, went the way of

Lilah: just when Mina became accustomed to a new nurse, Julia would find fault with her and she would be dismissed.

Under such circumstances Mina developed a lifelong interest in underdogs. Once she noticed that the right side of things was always favored at the expense of the left, a childish sense of justice urged her to make up for this inequity: "I would pick up the left hand side with my sensibility and nurse it in my astral arms like a doll, croon to it and make ugly faces on its behalf at the aristocratic right that gave itself such airs." One day she was standing at the top of the stairs while performing an expiatory ritual that consisted of wearing her left shoe on her right foot to punish it for its pretensions. Swinging the right foot back and forth while humming a sort of incantation, she was so absorbed in her ritual that she failed to notice the housemaid replacing the rods on the stairs below. When Mina inadvertently kicked her in the eye, the maid screamed and sent her to her mother for punishment. Mina could not understand the reason for their rage. Still preoccupied with the problem of injustice in the world of left and right, she could not fathom "the mystery of how innocence may at any time and unwittingly change into guilt."

Another memory symbolized for her the emotional dynamics of her childhood. Mina discovered a basket containing some Japanese paper fish, whose unexpected colors and textures delighted her. Her father explained that she was to be given these fish later on and told her not to spoil the surprise by mentioning that she had already seen them. Proud of their secret, she accompanied her father to the drawing room. When he asked her whether she had looked into the basket, she said no, only to be pounced upon by her parents. In front of the guests they called her a liar: "If I did not remind him that he had asked me not to tell," she recalled, "it was because I succumbed to their necessity to make something out of me that they knew how to 'deal' with. (Does not society create its own criminals?) Or rather because their animosity always stabbed me in the solar plexus, causing a knotted agony that paralyzed self-defense." Years later, Mina concluded that her role in the family had placed her in a psychic double bind. But at the time she took the only escape open to a child—running away. Outside in the street, the fresh air and the lilac trees' perfume banished her unhappiness, until she was caught and taken home: "They *did* want a liar."*

Throughout her childhood Mina took refuge in "curative colour," in the reaches of her imagination, or in moments of natural beauty, all private "places" where she could be alone. Although the street was forbidden territory, she loved the back garden, where she could play by herself. Not long after the incident of the Japanese fish, she was playing alone in the

---

* This section of *Islands*, entitled "Ethics and Hygiene of Nightmare," reads like one of British therapist R. D. Laing's case studies in *Family Life*.

garden when she suddenly felt in touch with the great world around her. "Illumination," one of the few non-satiric poems in "Anglo-Mongrels," evokes this moment when

> *The high-skies*
> *have come gently upon her*
> *and all their*
> *steadfast light is shining out of her*
>
> *She is conscious*
> *not through her body   but through space*

She cherished the memory—"this saint's-prize / this   indissoluble bliss / to be carried like a forgetfulness / into the long nightmare."

But most expeditions out-of-doors were taken under the supervision of her nurses. She and Dora left the house each day on "walks in glum streets between semi-detached façades in paralysed regimentation . . . like soldiers on the march." Expeditions to the Maida Vale sweetshops at the end of the street provided tantalizing glimpses of forbidden licorice strings, iced biscuits, and sugar mice—all reserved for the "common children," according to the nurse. They sometimes walked as far as the populous streets of Kilburn, which Mina understood as "kill-burn"—a paved lid over the fires of hell and a premonition of her own damnation. Although the nurse drew her skirts back from the crowds—mainly Jewish or working-class—Mina was fascinated by the "common" children's accents and pastimes. One day when she was peering with concern at a girl her own age, whose foot was stuck in an iron grating (perhaps an entrance to hell), she heard her nurse chide, "Hold up your chin . . . you begin to walk like a horrid ragamuffin." The outcast's freedom began to seem appealing: although one wore rags, one was given, as compensation, the daily muffin.

As Mina grew older, she met people in whose presence she felt more relaxed than at home. "Aunt Mary" Gunne, a ladies' companion hired to help Julia with the ways of being a middle-class matron, made a handy addition to the Lowy household, since she lived nearby with her elderly mother. Of a happier temperament than Julia, Aunt Mary believed in brightening the children's days by behaving whenever possible as if fairy tales might come true. She made up stories, produced surprises like the ill-fated Japanese fish, and welcomed Mina to her home. The next time Mina ran away, her destination was Miss Gunne's house. Enchanted by old Mrs. Gunne's intricate lace cap and white corkscrew curls, she was pleased to be allowed to trace the delicate patterns on their antique china. Although Mina was nearly always out of sorts at home, Miss Gunne's easygoing ways made her happy. But like Lilah and Queenie, Aunt Mary was soon banished over a difference of opinion about the proper methods for disciplining young children.

To escape these disappointments, Mina visualized the land of her dreams. "A peculiar land I could see distinctly," it held only "two trees like planed poles, each bearing its single enormous fruit, the one a pear, the other an apple," whose symmetry promised some kind of knowledge other than that mentioned in the Bible. She realized only in adulthood that these dream images had been adapted "from the rosy branches of fruit dividing vignetted groups of Kate Greenaway figures in the night nursery." Although she later dismissed such images—"the hot-house purity / essence / of English childhood"—she remembered her ardent desire to escape into that promised land, envisioned as "a musical-box / of colored glass / growing like gilly-flowers / and Phlox / with butterfly-winged / cherubim / warbling in / low-branched fruit trees." There, fruit hung from the trees for little girls to enjoy, and colored glass glittered—within arm's reach.

Although her grandparents might also have provided alternatives to the atmosphere at home, Mina remembered only one visit to the Bryans in Bromley. They were well-meaning but ineffectual presences who seemed to shrink from contact. As if he feared to grow fond of Mina, her grandfather contented himself with a "timid benevolence." She was particularly interested in his craft and the variety of tools in his carpenter's shed, where, "understanding that all operative objects have magical properties for small creatures like myself, he show[ed] me an enormous magnet." But her grandmother had no such secrets. Thinking back on Mrs. Bryan's one visit to the Lowys', Mina guessed that this modest woman must have felt ridiculous perched on a gilt chair in their showy drawing room. When her grandparents died within the year, Mina was full of grief at the idea that her magical powers had proved fatal: shortly before their deaths, she had reached for a white weed during a walk with the nurse, only to hear that if she picked that flower, her mother would die. Since Mina had cried out that her grandparents should die instead, she was horrified to learn that they had done so. She must be truly wicked, as her mother said.

When Sigmund's aged grandmother paid a visit from Budapest, she reminded Mina of the fairy godmother in the Christmas pantomime. This apparition in black silk and lace took her great-grandchild on her lap, cried over her, and choked out *Mein schönes Kind* as if it were a blessing. Mina remembered feeling swathed in the unconditional love of her great-grandmother's adoration—like her illumination in the garden, an experience of bliss that later seemed a "spiritual orgasm, the mystic's admittance to cosmic radiance." But since Julia wanted to minimize contact with foreigners, especially Jewish ones, she vetoed plans to have Mina visit her father's family.

Through her precocious discovery of books, Mina learned that "there are many thresholds that may be crossed . . . into non-existent sanctuaries." Education was one of these doors opening onto new prospects, which, on closer inspection, concealed fresh disappointments.

At three she crossed a new threshold when she discovered what she took to be a small door lying on its side: it opened to reveal "an infinite succession of white, four-cornered flaps . . . covered with linear conundrums." This sanctuary proved to be a book, like her beloved *Peep of Day*. Mina begged for one of her own: "As the result of many inquiries I gathered at last that such doors as these open onto the contents of time; that behind them is stored the composite brain of humanity as if preserved in microscopic slides." A book might offer "the final answer to the whole question" of her being. Once she learned to read the alphabet book her parents gave her, she felt that she was "holding the doors of the universe ajar": each letter had meaning, its thickness and heft, and in the company of its fellows lived a life of its own. But rather than praise their daughter's precocious knowledge, the Lowys called her a show-off—an opinion echoed by the alphabet itself, which accorded the letter *X* to Xantippe but remarked of Socrates' wife that she "was a great scold." This condemnation of strong-minded females put a stop to her quest for knowledge, which did not, after all, provide the answer.

Mina still clung to the idea of divine forgiveness, since, at least in God's eyes, she was innocent. One day her mother would show her the love she craved. Julia was quite capable of playing the doting parent in public, where she appeared to cherish her daughter's beauty and intelligence. Mina saw that some parents appreciated children despite their sinfulness when she came across one of the few nonreligious books allowed into the nursery—a cultural version of the earliest instruction the infant mind is capable of receiving, entitled *Chaucer for Children*. This new door opened not onto eternity but onto British history and culture, and its author, a Mrs. H. R. Haweis, had dedicated her book to her four-year-old son. More than her bowdlerized versions of Chaucer's tales and flat, Pre-Raphaelite-style illustrations, it was the author's estimate of her child's mind that impressed Mina. She envied the young boy in the dedicatory portrait and wondered at his cleverness as he sat reading the stories that his mother had provided him.*

Her own found fault with her on most occasions. As she grew, Mina began to think of Julia not so much as an armored tower but, rather, as "the Voice," the overwhelming force that invaded her thoughts. When her mother's threats about God's seeing her evil ways collapsed into what

---

* Mina may also have been struck by Master Haweis's "aesthetic" costume, long curls, and soulful expression, which made him look like a little girl.

seemed like an uncanny ability to reach into her daughter's mind, Julia became the embodiment of "the parental, or counter-will" which "awaits the convenience of seizing its opponent on common territory." One morning, when Mina hurt her hand searching for her mother's smelling salts, she uttered a childish imprecation. Suddenly "that dreaded voice leapt out of the thick air conserved by heavy curtains so like a lash it almost whipped me off my balance." Julia chastised her for using bad language and rehearsed her future as an outcast. To clinch the point, she shrieked, "You're just like your father."

Decades later, Mina tried to understand Julia's background in her efforts to gain relief from the self-critical part of herself—the internalized mother or "the voice that edits private history." She came to think that if her peace of mind had been shattered by the impact of the Voice, it was because her mother was herself the product "of a class whose loud self-assertion lifts them above the manual clatter of their lives, whose heritage it is to lack the mental leisure which alone, of all conditions, allows for the culture of such superficial graces as amenity, the expression of affection or the tempered rebuke—a class for generations so hard-driven they had no time for loving their offspring." But as a young girl she could neither understand her mother's animosity nor ward off her tirades. She often stood mute until Julia told her to get out of her sight, since she did not like what she saw (of herself?) in Mina's eyes.

Coming across her own image in a full-length mirror had a strange effect on Mina's imagination. On a visit with her father to one of his colleagues when she was nearly seven, she wandered through his shop while the men talked. "Before that winter evening my being alive had consisted entirely of a narrow variety of intensive emotions," she recalled. "I had no identity, until, wandering into a deserted fitting-room, I came upon my appearance in a triple mirror. Drenched in those depths and distances of interreflected glass which are endless in having no existence . . . I found my covered image surmounted by my naked face." She was stirred by the shock of seeing herself not as her mother saw her but as an imaginary friend: "My own face filled me with the instant sympathy one might feel for an exile . . . 'That's me,' I thought, 'and it's got such a "different" expression.' The unreal distance between myself and 'it' disquieted me." Once again fascinated by absence—"the being there of its not being there"—she wondered whether a part of herself had gone into the mirror.

Soon a Miss Ware, known as a strict disciplinarian, was hired to curb Mina's imagination while giving her lessons. She learned the rudiments of grammar, arithmetic, and English history, which consisted mostly of kings and queens. But as welcome as it was to have work to do, the penalties for mistakes were hard to swallow; Miss Ware believed in "punishment bread"—one dry whole-wheat slab for each error. Under her care, Mina went into a decline that no amount of tonic could cure. In consultation with an eminent physician known to attend Queen Victoria, the Lowys learned that their child was in danger of contracting tuberculosis, for which the specialist prescribed immediate removal to the country. When they ignored his advice, Mina decided to hasten her decline by pouring cold water over herself under her nightgown. After several attempts at finishing herself off, she decided to get well. Soon Miss Ware, too, was sent packing, along with her punishment bread.

Julia's opinion of her daughter was confirmed by Mina's accidentally acquired "sex-enlightenment" at the age of eight. When she repeated her mother's stinging-nettle theory of her origins to her new friend Evangeline, the girl hooted at her ignorance. Passing quickly over the initial phases of procreation, Evangeline explained: "The woman gets most terribly ill and writhes in agony for nine months and then the doctor comes to cut her open and takes 'it' out. But it hurts so badly that she almost always dies before he has time to sew her up again." This information, acquired shortly after her mother's third pregnancy and the birth of her baby sister, Hilda, in 1890, made Mina so nervous that her parents asked what was wrong. "Alas, I had given my mother the opportunity to draw herself up to the very pinnacle of her superb morality. 'Now you are like a leper,' she told me." What Julia called her disgusting secret meant that "behind the ominous creaking of those busks" lay "a relentless machinery, involving myself."

Julia's attempts to repress all references to procreation—a common strategy in middle-class households—had the effect of driving the subject deeper underground. Mina had two recurrent nightmares that express her confusion about the nature of sexuality. The first dream began to haunt her after her mother took her to see one of the earliest electrical power plants, whose "weird sparks and flashes flying from the slip and clang of enigmatic engines" made her uneasy. That night she dreamed: "I drag at my mother's towering skirts to entreat her to come away—she takes no heed— Suddenly this dream mother comports herself in the wildest way— She is flinging her arms up, and at once they become steely arms." Her mother is turning into a sort of dressmaker's dummy: "There, where the skirts should have been, all that upholstery dissembling the site of sin, is a forbidding cage of iron wire." The mother's hand rasps the fingers "that have clutched at it for protection, a protection I now require against itself, the very author of my being, being author of my fear." The grimacing mother spins faster and faster until she dissolves, and the nightmare ends.

In the second nightmare, Mina is crossing a bridge over a terra-cotta–colored sea. From the water there arises a totem pole from which the heads of bearded patriarchs stare at the terrified child: "All prophesying at once, they conjure me to some enterprise that is obscure to me." For a long time she was afraid of falling asleep, because the patriarchs returned when the light went out. Much later, she connected them with her father's lectures to the nurse on the continuity of Jewish history. While he evoked "the priestly glory of his ancestors," Mina would tell herself that the patriarchs were "only dead men's heads in a dream." Sometimes this nightmare took another form. Walking in a shed with an earthen floor, she would come upon a bearded old man buried up to his chin: "Not so much coming out of the earth as sinking in, my English grandfather tries to convey some duty—as though he were drawing me into the ground with him." She would awaken at this point, desperate to escape from the demands of the patriarchs whose claim on her was impossible to grasp. It is hard to know which nightmare was worse, since each reveals the fault lines in her emotional ground, her relation to her parents.*

IV

In 1892, when Mina was ten, Sigmund Lowy purchased his own home in a newly developed part of West Hampstead, between Finchley Road and West End Lane. This large, semidetached brick house at 68 Compayne Gardens, which the Lowys named Clinton, was one of the newest three-story homes in an area designed to express the prosperity of its residents. The unified character of the neighboring streets proclaimed the homeowners' membership in the "middling" middle classes, families that kept three or four domestics but could not aspire to a carriage. Despite their pretentious names, these double residences were far less grand than the costlier individual homes east of Finchley Road or the glamorous Norman Shaw houses on Fitzjohn's Avenue; and they were still too close to the crowded working-class districts just beyond West End Lane. Their status had been concretized in an exact social geography: Compayne Gardens lay "at the western foot of the Hampstead heights whose elevation stood always close at hand as a visible reminder of where social superiority resided," and just a few blocks east of Kilburn's "populous vulgarity." While Sigmund was satisfied with their proximity to the Finchley Road and the West Hampstead station, Julia's anxiety increased as they moved up the social ladder.

Mina was struck by a detail in the doorway of their new home—"this papered & enamelled container prepared for my adolescence." Patterned after the wealthier houses of Hampstead proper, their development featured "aesthetic" touches like Dutch gables, terra-cotta ornaments, and imitation stained-glass panels. Some of the more ornate single houses on the slight rise to the west also had Victorian Gothic or Classical details applied to their façades as decorative afterthoughts. Standing at the threshold, Mina touched an apple-blossom branch in the *faux*–stained glass beside the front door as if it were a talisman: "On touching that pane of glass I

---

* When her parents took her to see the freaks in a circus sideshow, these "human accidents dependent on the indelicacy of a crowd" aroused equally nightmarish feelings, and she felt a "sickening pity" when shown the Siamese twins. Similarly, a visit to the "Venice" exhibition left a terrifying impression of dead men's souls imprisoned in mummified legs—her baffled response to Scottish bagpipes.

turned into a commonplace person with average expectations, agog with the expectancy of normal life. Of the Cosmos of infancy the Voice alone survived."

At first, she recalled, daily life at Clinton "seem[ed] to consist in my being flapped in and out" on a series of walks around the streets of West Hampstead. Mina's "brick box" was distinguished from the others primarily by the tense atmosphere within, which seemed to stifle her as soon as she entered: "Day by day, drifting from room to room seeking for something to do," because she had no governess and hence no occupations, she began to feel "like machinery working full blast on the production of nothing." Like many of her background, Julia believed that stitching, embroidery, and other forms of fancy "work" provided sufficient occupation for a young lady: did not *The Young Englishwoman* advise readers to pass their time in the manufacture of such items as embroidered handkerchief boxes, ornamental pincushions, and crocheted garters?* Although she did learn to sew, Mina preferred reading to work of this kind and begged to be allowed to start her education.

Soon after their move to Clinton, Julia engaged Miss Nickson, the one governess with whom she was never to quarrel. Pleased that Mina's religious training had begun with *The Peep of Day*, Miss Nickson prescribed as the next step a program of biblical study, confined to the New Testament. "Hour upon hour we looked up texts, compared references under the awning of her white eyelashes," Mina recalled. This grounding in the practice of citing chapter and verse backfired, however, by producing in her the desire to be irreligious, if to be pious meant to resemble Miss Nickson. It did not help matters that her governess looked like a pig in a woolen dress, or that her habit of breathing down her neck as Mina bent over the Bible made her nauseous. Nor did Miss Nickson's morning prayers aid in her charge's daily struggles with lumpy porridge, or her nightly Bible reading outside the nursery door help in the process of falling asleep. Their governess, Mina believed, had been brought into the household as Julia's ally, "to insure a silence in which no original sin could rise to the surface."

The spare diet of pious texts, monotonous prayers, and lumpy porridge did little to purge Mina of her imagination. One day when Miss Nickson was too busy to keep close watch over her charges, Mina investigated the Old Testament. Pondering the long series of "begats" and the suggestive "he went in unto," she concocted a scenario in which a lion would go in unto Miss Nickson, who would then beget cubs in keeping with her tawny mane and freckles. She respected her governess on one score only: Miss Nickson was sometimes seen to sharpen her pencils to a fine point in order

---

* During this period, the novelist Elinor Glyn did not consider writing to be "work": "for her, 'work' meant fancy embroidery . . . as it did to most Victorian women." The remarkable number of pincushion patterns devised in this period attests to the need to occupy adolescent girls.

to draw exquisitely shaded narcissi, a skill for which Mina expressed her admiration, for she, too, liked to sketch. Miss Nickson's talent was, however, an anomaly. She often glared at Mina, who was turning into a very pretty young girl, and told her that beauty was to be regarded as a delusion: Mrs. Nickson, a good Christian woman, never cared what her children looked like as long as they had the right number of fingers and toes.

Mina's aversion to her governess's physical presence extended to her pious lessons as well. She had become a precocious atheist not long before Miss Nickson's arrival at Clinton. In defiance of her mother, Mina decided to behave as if God did not exist. Although she "could not be *sure* that the everlasting flame was bluff," she wrote, "I decided to risk eternal torture rather than resemble the people He approved." This decision also seemed like a step in her father's direction. Even though he had given up attendance at synagogue, he refused to join his wife and daughters at church. Although Mina was unsure what it meant to be Jewish, her father's religion did not seem to confer the right to tyrannize others. But she may also have wondered whether he had abandoned the attempt to give her a religious education because she was female and could not, for that reason, learn Hebrew. Although he often showed Mina the affection she craved, he also teased her and called her "Goy," which she took to mean that she was different from him despite their obvious likeness.

Lowy nonetheless cherished the idea that his girls might excel, since Mina showed artistic talent and Dora was musical. Dora would study both voice and piano, he declared, and Mina would be allowed occasional bursts of self-expression. What he had had to renounce when forced into apprenticeship in Budapest he would cultivate in his daughters, in the hope that their worldly glory would crown his success by attracting desirable suitors. But his belief that artistic refinements were an ornament ran counter to his wife's desire to school the girls in self-denial. When Mina produced a poem on the marriage of a daisy and a gnat, her mother declared that she had the mind of a slut. Clearly she was doing this to get round her father. " 'Where on earth's your modesty,' she shrieked. 'You certainly never got such ideas from me. Nice girls never think about weddings until after they're married.' "

Mina's "nasty" poem is of particular interest because it prefigures sections of "Anglo-Mongrels," on the subject of the parents' marriage. In "Nat and Daisy," the lowly Nat flies higher than his station when he asks the white Rose to marry him, just as in "Anglo-Mongrels," Exodus proposes to the proud English rose whose thorns hide under the hedgerow. Nat is more fortunate than Exodus, however: once his Rose has scorned him, he wins the heart of the humble Daisy. In Mina's nine-year-old romance, she identifies with both the gnat who yearns for beauty and the lover brought low by the rose's disdain—as in later years, she would identify with the father whose higher instincts seemed to have been crushed by the weight of Julia's disapproval.

Given her own religious upbringing, Julia could not help seeing Mina's attempts at self-expression as proof of her depravity, and she lashed out at her whenever she got hold of her drawings or poems. During the reign of Miss Nickson, Mina observed, her mother was calmer, because she had an ally. Together they would attempt to drive out some "evil, originated, I felt, in my father," and Miss Nickson would purge her of her disgusting secret. But when the pious governess left Clinton after two years' service, Julia's calm shattered. She insisted that they replace Miss Nickson with someone of equal rectitude. When Sigmund announced that he planned to send Mina and Dora to school rather than engage another governess, renewed hostilities broke out between their parents.

v

Asserting his prerogative as head of the family, Mr. Lowy enrolled the girls in a progressive school in Hampstead, where the children of that suburb's elite, both gentile and Jewish, were known to study. Mina was overjoyed at the idea of becoming a scholar, until Julia struck back by insisting on increased surveillance. In retaliation for her daughters' new freedom, she refused them any opportunity for privacy by hiding the door keys and, worse, by screaming about blasphemy when they tried to do homework. Thus, Mina noted, "in the sheltered homes of the nineties, daughters were bullied to maturity subject to prohibitions unmodified since babyhood. Their only self-expression: to watch and pray." She saw going to school as a form of defiance, akin to her decision not to believe in her mother's God. Anticipating that as a schoolgirl she would be "joining an opposition club of youth combatting the mother-myth," she looked forward to exchanges of confidence about the terrors of domestic life.

Her first attempts at friendship produced the realization that not all households resembled her own, since not all mothers were at war with their daughters. When she asked another girl whether she loved her mother, the child responded, "But of course," and stared at Mina disapprovingly. Rethinking the incident, Mina recalled the girl's "formal curls . . . tied up with love," a contrast to the "crippled knot in which some random hairs of my culpable head were caught." Her first lesson had made it clear to her that a gulf existed between children whose appearance showed a loving hand and others, like herself, "whose covering is not civilized with the detail of affection." Tellingly, she called the institution the Chaucer School, a wistful allusion to the affectionate mother-child relations she had glimpsed in the dedication of *Chaucer for Children*.

Like other women for whom a daughter's maturation provokes a crisis, Julia resented Mina's adolescence. As a girl, Mina had already wondered why "nobody took action when we grew out of our clothes or boots." When she complained that a pair of boots bought the previous winter pinched her feet, Julia accused her of ingratitude. Faced with a daughter whose figure was developing, she resorted to a familiar strategy, denial of the truth. She dressed Mina in childish flat yokes, scolding her as she pinned the offending bodice: "How can I fit you? You nasty girl. Do you think at your age it is decent to have a figure." Perhaps seeing in her daughter her own story, Julia shrieked, "Your vile flesh, you'll get no good out of it. Curse you. Curse your father."

School offered respite from the Voice, but this form of escape had come too late. Thinking back on her three years there, Mina wondered, "Original sin, where does it lie, in the logical process of thought? The problem wearied my mind to the exclusion of all further operation." Well trained in the forms of self-suppression thought appropriate by women of her mother's temper, Mina had become a demoralized, anxious adolescent—whose very existence, or so she believed, provoked her mother's ire. Even though she could escape into books, the beauty of art or nature, or her own imagination, the certainty of her future disgrace had undermined her self-confidence. Between the tensions of home and her inability to concentrate at school, her lessons were nearly wasted. And in any case, since middle-class girls were educated to become decorous wives, their lessons rarely went beyond a superficial knowledge of arithmetic, English grammar and history, art, and religion.

Mr. Lowy did what he could for Dora and for Mina—the English, or "goyish," version of himself, especially once she took up drawing. The Lowys had musical evenings in their grand reception rooms, where Dora sang and had her voice recorded on an early gramophone. (They thought Dora far more talented than the other Jewish girl who won the school music prizes, whose name was Myra Hess.) Although Dora blossomed under the general approbation, Mina felt confused by visitors' inquiries about her artistic skill, such as whether or not she could do a faithful representation of a cork. Still, her father brought home reproductions of the pictures in the annual Royal Academy exhibitions and took both girls shopping whenever he noticed that their clothes were shabby. He even sought Mina's advice "as to what could be done" in the face of Julia's opposition to his plans for their futures: rather than address Julia directly, her father took Mina aside to plan strategies for a more harmonious home life. Although he maintained that, with some coaxing, Julia's anger might abate, Mina boldly suggested a separation or some other way of living apart from Julia. But Mr. Lowy could not think of such a step. "No daughter should ever leave her mother's side," he insisted. "It's *so* beautiful, the bud beside the rose; men like it."

Mina had to resign herself to the idea that following her last year at school she would take up the role of the grown-up daughter at home. There were moments when she longed to tell her mother that there was really nothing wrong, that they *could* be happy. But, if Mina's memoirs may be trusted (even assuming they exaggerate her grievances), Julia found it impossible to sympathize with her daughter. They grated on each other's nerves until the inevitable eruptions took place. Not only was Mina a reminder of Julia's lapse from propriety, but she had entered the stormy stage of adolescence. She was a foreign element, like her father.

A state of war prevailed between mother and daughter which neither understood. While Mina was developing a mind of her own, Julia came up with an unbeatable way of getting what she wanted. At the height of an argument she would swoon and fall to the floor by the firescreen. These dramatic faints came to seem predictable, but it was frightening to see her lying unconscious on the rug. Mina's feelings combined the suspicion that her mother had an unfair advantage and the fear that she might one day cause the death of which Julia spoke so often. And it was just as disturbing to see her father being gradually reduced to obsessive concern with his own health, even though the Harley Street specialist assured him that there was nothing wrong.

A full-length portrait taken in a commercial photographer's studio at this time, when Mina was fourteen or fifteen, shows a demure young girl who does not realize she is about to become a beauty. She stands before a studio backdrop representing a carefully tended park or garden—some secluded space where feminine virtue, flower-like, can be sheltered until wedlock. The photo is a cheap variation on what was by this time an artistic convention enshrining the middle-class female's sexual purity. But in place of the white lilies or roses which, in pictures of this kind, suggest the young lady's purity, the photographer has placed some inexpensive daisies in a pot at her feet, in a halfhearted gesture at tasteful composition.

Yet his subject seems oblivious of both the perfunctory setting and her aesthetic props, the Chinese parasol in her left hand and the three flowers in her right. Her dark hair is loose in a girlish coiffure: it cascades over the elaborate tucks, frills, and ruching of the starched white shirtwaist, which contrasts in its fussy detail to the severe plainness of her three-quarter-length dark skirt. The darker stockings and childish shoes complete a costume that presents her as dutiful daughter—the bud beside the rose. Although Mina's gaze avoids any recognition of the photographer's presence, her thoughtful expression betrays her awareness that this portrait has been staged: she is playing her part in a conventional drama.

2

The Worst Art School in London

(1897–99)

THE LOWYS, who held opposing views on most matters, agreed that their fifteen-year-old daughter presented a problem. She had completed her education but seemed unsuited to the role of young lady. Should she remain at home to adorn the parlor? Should she be sent to finishing school in preparation for her future as a wife and mother? Or should she be allowed to do as she wished, to attend art school? While Mina's sketching seemed innocent, her mother was opposed to her actually *studying* art. The aura of sinfulness that clung to the art world had only been enhanced by the recent trial of Oscar Wilde, whose life illustrated the common belief that artists were degenerate. Her daughter's place was with her. If she must do something artistic, she might embroider to her heart's content.

Mr. Lowy, aware that modern girls often pursued some form of higher education, took a more enlightened view. Mina might study painting as long as she did not become "strong-minded," like the girls whose self-assertive ways were deplored in the newspapers. Mr. Lowy's position was that of the self-respecting bourgeois, for whom a daughter's accomplishments increased her marriageability. As Virginia Woolf—Mina's exact contemporary—observed of the middle-class girl in their era, "It was with a view to marriage that she tinkled on the piano, but was not allowed to join an orchestra; sketched innocent domestic scenes, but was not allowed to sketch from the nude; read this book but was not allowed to read that."

From this perspective, most agreed that a girl could sketch as a way "of recalling to her remembrance and that of her friends, pleasurable scenes and lovely landscapes enjoyed long ago"—provided, of course, she did not aspire to professional status. Watercolor was thought an appropriate medium, since its misty effects etherealized everyday life and pointed the artist's thoughts toward higher spheres. As for girls who insisted on working in oils, their paintings were more likely to win praise if they were quaint, in the style of Kate Greenaway, or fanciful, in the Pre-Raphaelite manner of many contemporary women artists. Whichever genre they chose was to be handled in a feminine way, which meant that their work would be small in scale, emphasize the picturesque, and forgo displays of originality.

By 1897, when the Lowys were discussing Mina's future, English art schools were full of young ladies from the middle and upper-middle classes. Because their talents were cultivated according to the strictest notions of sexual propriety, they were often dismissed as "lady amateurs." Even though women studied at the Royal Academy during the nineties, most felt handicapped by family pressures, social expectations, and their inferior education. Teachers often assumed that women preferred the minor genres—watercolors, still lifes, portraits, and miniatures—to the strenuous demands of oil painting and sculpture—for which they were, in any case, unsuited, because they lacked the knowledge of the classics thought necessary to these genres. Their situation is summed up in the remarks of the journalist who noted ironically, "In these happy times every young lady learns to dabble in paint."

The fashionable art schools that proliferated during the last decades of the century were not taken seriously except as an answer to the question "What shall we do with our daughters?" Critics assumed that women could not learn "the royal road to art," as one of them declared, since in classes for women, "sentiment and effect are the qualities most eagerly sought and certainly most easily gained, thanks to a clever dodging of the real difficulties of art." Women would always be second-rate, it was thought, because they lacked creative genius: in the opinion of the influential writer George Moore, "women have created nothing," but they have done so "charmingly."

But the Lowys were concerned less with artistic achievement than with social propriety. Once Mr. Lowy managed to convince Julia that it would be preferable to have Mina out of the house, he had to find a school where her reputation would not suffer. He was unwilling to let her attend courses in the more disreputable parts of London, where she might be mistaken for an actress or, worse, a "professional." There were several possibilities. She could attend the National Art School in South Kensington, where students learned the principles of industrial design. The nearby Hampstead International College offered comparable preparation, but its commercial emphasis implied that its students came chiefly from the working class. Similarly, at Mrs. McIan's Female School of Design in Bloomsbury, students were prepared to support themselves by designing silverware, pottery, fabric, lace, or book illustrations. One could assume that they were reduced gentlewomen or the daughters of tradesmen who had seen better days:

the North London School of Drawing and Modelling, for example, actually stated that its students would acquire the means of obtaining an income.

Mina's parents had no such aims. They no doubt agreed with the correspondent to *The Englishwoman's Journal* who declared, "My opinion is that if a woman is obliged to work, at once (although she may be Christian and well bred) she loses that peculiar position which the word lady conventionally designates." Taking up the applied arts meant either that she was unlikely to marry or that her father could not provide for her. Since it was unthinkable for Mina to enter any situation that hinted at such circumstances, the schools of design were out. The art establishment itself looked down on "the lesser territories of design, those which were universally recognized as being entirely humble, the door knobs, the antimacassars, the applied arts generally." (It was part of Mina's complaint against her parents that she received no consistent education: in her attempts to earn a living, she regretted the lack of practical training that such schools could have offered.)

Acceptable alternatives were not lacking. Mina's father admired the "Olympians," the Royal Academy painters whose artistic achievements were crowned with social success. To attain to the ranks of genius, as they had done, was the secular equivalent of being "chosen." Artists like Lawrence Alma-Tadema and Frederick Leighton had received the full range of academic honors, and their historical allegories and classical scenes had become widely available in the form of the engraved copies that adorned the homes of the cultivated middle class. During visits with Mina to the annual Royal Academy exhibitions, Mr. Lowy applauded their glory, as if social preeminence (and high prices) established the indisputable correctness of their art. Lord Leighton's recent elevation to the peerage confirmed the value of the academic system, just as his claim that art provided moral uplift suited the Lowys' requirements for Mina's education.

Her parents looked with favor, consequently, on the private art schools which prepared for the Royal Academy, where women could matriculate even though they might not become full-fledged members. Of these, Cope's in South Kensington was too far away, the Leigh Studio in Great Ormond Street had a raffish Bloomsbury location, and Heatherly's, near Oxford Street, sounded suspicious, since the masters taught in the French manner. Similarly, the Slade School was out of the question because it was known to be "advanced." Mr. Lowy settled upon the St. John's Wood School on Elm Tree Road: it combined the advantages of proximity, respectability, and solid connections with the Royal Academy schools. Mr. Ward, the principal, assured them that, as their youngest pupil, Mina would be chaperoned and that the "Wood" had a special entrance for ladies.

Mina could walk or bicycle to school or, in cold weather, take a bus down Finchley Road in the direction of St. John's Wood. From there it was a short walk past the Hampstead-style cottages of this prosperous area to the Wood. Since its founding in 1878, the school had traded on its association with the artists who lived nearby. On Grove End Road, students could admire the Dutch-inspired mansion of James Tissot, the popular chronicler of Victorian society, and the Pompeian palace of Sir Lawrence Alma-Tadema, whose visits to the school were emphasized in its brochures. They could also hope to emulate the careers of the St. John's Wood Clique, a group of Royal Academy artists esteemed for their illustrations of scenes from Shakespeare and English history: it was whispered that their paintings sold for as much as a thousand pounds. And unlike the Pre-Raphaelites, these painters were received in society.

Mina was safe at the Wood, her parents concluded. She might even hope to be among the eight or ten women accepted each year at the Royal Academy School, where St. John's Wood students invariably outnumbered those from other schools. They did so well, in part, because the Wood modeled its course of instruction and methods on those of the Academy schools. Men and women worked together in the Antique and Still Life classes, but were separated when it came to drawing from the nude. Reassured on this score as well, the Lowys concluded that Mina's training would be rigorous and her situation correct.

The course of instruction reflected the same spirit of rectitude that Mina's parents admired in Mr. Ward. New students began in the Antique Room, where they were to copy ornamental patterns on casts of classical bas-reliefs and friezes. From there they went on to draw casts of hands, feet, and heads from the best examples of Classical sculpture, and finally, if successful at these portions of the anatomy, the full torso. Only once they had followed this fixed progression were they allowed to draw from life. Each stage took months, as students learned to fill in their outlines with the tight, highly stippled shading favored by the Royal Academy—a technique resulting in something like a photograph. By 1897 this method had already been abandoned in the more progressive schools, like the Slade, where Mina's contemporaries Wyndham Lewis, Augustus John, and his sister Gwen, later her acquaintances in Paris, were learning a freer and more constructive approach to draftsmanship.* To those who were knowledgeable about art, the Wood's approach was out of date.

But if Mina knew that her new school enforced this painstaking discipline, it did not disturb her. She accepted without question that she would spend her days at a place she later judged "the worst art school in London." The night before she was to begin, she was so excited that she could hardly sleep. Lying in bed, she tried to visualize the scenes she would paint in

---

* At the Slade, students were encouraged to draw from life. The first drawing master, Alphonse Legros, had initiated a respect for the masters—Raphael, Rembrandt, Ingres, and Delacroix. Students studied the relations of light, shade, and half-tone, then built up solid forms with cross-hatching. Although still somewhat academic, this method was an improvement over the tight stippling favored by the Wood. Under the Slade's next drawing master, Henry Tonks, students learned to reveal an object's inner form through the representation of contours. This approach became the standard in British art schools within ten years.

the approved manner, as soon as they taught her how: "Having seen little except for machine made furniture, the subjects I found appropriate to art were cupids, peacocks, cypresses, and swans." She had in mind a pair of canvases that would win immediate acclaim: the first depicted a cupid reposing on the white feathers of an ethereal swan, the second "a 'bronzed' cupid, his curls and eyes of ebony . . . against the outspread fan of a peacock glowing with unsullied color straight from the tube."* But as she fantasized about her work's elogious reception, she became anxious about her ambitions. "I automatically reproached myself for my presumption," she recalled, as if her mother had been reading her mind.

When Mina was ushered into the Antique Room the next morning, she experienced a shock. Rows of students sat perched on high stools, working in silence as they drew from soiled plaster casts of Classical or Renaissance sculpture. They looked to her like so many chimney sweeps in their grimy aprons. She had imagined art as "an aesthetic leap at the superlative," but she was to take her place among "rows of miners in the galleries of ignorance." Students were to reproduce each feature of a particularly distinguished head, which, the monitor explained, was that of Michelangelo's *David*. Mina was to begin with the nose. She set to work on the wing of his left nostril, sharpening her Conté crayon to a fine point, then speckling the pores of the Whatman paper and softening these specks with an eraser. After weeks of work on the nose, she learned how to "stipple it up" by smoothing out the whole drawing with wads of blotting paper or bits of dry bread. Her dreams of impossibly white swans vanished amid the reality of charcoal smudges and bread crumbs.

Nonetheless, the social pleasures of the Wood made up for its pedestrian teaching methods. As the baby of the school, Mina was often invited to tea by her fellow students and their teachers. On her first day, an instructor asked over cakes in her private studio whether Mina felt unhappy away from home; everyone burst into laughter when she replied innocently, "How should I among such charming people." After blurting out her fear that she could never learn to paint beautiful pictures from soiled plaster casts, she was relieved to learn that she would find what she needed in the evening life classes. At another tea in the Antique Room, behind the giant statue of Hermes, she heard the headmaster expound the theory that everything—Hermes, the teatray, they themselves—was composed of atoms. "Nothing is solid," he insisted, "each atom is surrounded by space."

But Mina was again disappointed when the downtrodden life class model failed to inspire a sense of mystery, and she felt unable to transform his dispirited pose into an arrangement of atoms. While the professor directed the class to sense "the bony structure beneath the masses, noting

---

* Typically, Mina's description of this vision emphasizes an oppositional schema—the "pure" white cupid vs. the darker one—and while it evokes the "glowing" colors of her first memory, it also internalizes her mother's role as censor.

how the leaning torso sagged into the pelvis," she recalled, she could only stare at the diaperlike swath of drapery concealing his parts. (The Wood followed the 1893 Royal Academy directive authorizing female students to draw the male model undraped, "except about the loins." "The drapery to be worn by the model to consist of ordinary bathing drawer," it continued, "and a cloth of light material 9 feet long by 3 feet wide, which shall be wound round the loins over the drawer, passed between the legs and tucked in over the waist-band; and finally a thin leather strap shall be fastened round the loins in order to insure that the cloth keep its place.") Art was little more than technique and composition, and its tools, sandpaper, dry bread, and house paint. Yet even though the Wood's aesthetics failed to inspire her, the school—a "haven of disappointment"—offered escape from home.

Mina accidentally found the cure for her disappointment in a review of an influential book entitled *Degeneration*. The author, a self-styled sociologist named Max Nordau, whose slashing critique of modernism had just been translated from German, took delight in denouncing all the geniuses of the modern movement—from Wagner and Nietzsche to the Pre-Raphaelites, Impressionists, and Symbolists. Not only did their works demonstrate nervous exhaustion, he claimed, but they were themselves symptoms of the diseased state of contemporary life. To support his claims, Nordau applied the vocabulary developed by Krafft-Ebing and Lombroso in their studies of the criminally insane to the works of representative modern artists, with Oscar Wilde as exhibit A.

Since its publication in 1893, *Degeneration* had been cited as gospel throughout Europe, in large part because its prose bristled with phobias, manias, and other newly coined scientific terms. Dante Gabriel Rossetti's use of the poetic refrain proved the point, Nordau believed: his rhyming "echolalia" demonstrated the artist's mental debasement.* Nordau's attack on Rossetti brought Mina to life, aesthetically speaking. Showing an independence of mind that owed much to her horror of being criticized, she took Rossetti's side. "Not seldom an aesthetic springs from the spirit of contradiction," she later reflected. She identified with Rossetti not only as underdog—taking his part "in the manner in which I had espoused the cause of the inferiorised left hand"—but also because of his name: it was as pleasing to her ear "as to the nose an orange stuck with cloves to temper dried rose petals." Yet at the time she knew little more than that she must defend him: "How could a man named more ornately than all other men be mad?"

Mr. Lowy indulged Mina's passion for her new hero by bringing home Rossetti's complete works and reproductions of his paintings, along with

---

* Following the 1895 publication of *Degeneration* in English, G. B. Shaw had written a defense of Rossetti entitled "The Sanity of Art: An Exposure of the Current Nonsense about Artists Being Degenerate," in Shaw, *Major Critical Essays* (London: Penguin, 1986).

his sister Christina's poems bound in red morocco leather. Upon inspection of Rossetti's portrait on the frontispiece, Lowy observed that he must be a poor artist, judging by the way his trousers bagged. Yet by this standard as well Rossetti was Mina's kindred spirit. How could such an ardent temperament prosper in the mildew of British culture? Even though he had expressed himself in an alien tongue, adapting his "passionate brush to tentative British technique," she wrote, his "luscious gloom" expressed the state of her soul. From then on, whenever she felt trapped at home, Mina recited Rossetti's "echolalic" refrains inwardly, like prayers or mantras. Thus protected against antagonistic vibrations, whether emanating from her mother or from Nordau, she felt soothed: "This psychic retreat, this area of perfectability hitherto stored with emptiness, Rossetti filled for me."

Gradually, Mina gathered that alternatives to both home and school could be found in the art of Rossetti and his brother Pre-Raphaelites. "Under his influence," she recalled, "I began to 'furnish' England with a small pattern, an incipient rhythm, a wisp of Folk-lore[,] a poppy head, a knight errant." In her imagination, if not in actuality, her surroundings were furnished with "art" work in muted colors—wallpaper and fabric patterns, hangings and tapestries—designs resembling the work of William Morris, whose stylized floral patterns and dreamy medievalism offered a private world in contrast to the garishness of Compayne Gardens. Liberty silks in yellows and greens seemed morally superior to her mother's stiff brocades, and the painted wooden furniture she saw at advanced shops like Heals preferable to her parents' upholstered armchairs.

Although Morris's gospel—"Have nothing in your house that you do not know to be useful or beautiful"—had many devotees in Hampstead proper, it had not made much headway in West Hampstead. If the eighties craze for "art" decoration had taken place chiefly in higher circles, where interiors like the Lowys' were seen as vulgar, members of their class in turn looked with suspicion on both the "aesthetic" furnishings inspired by Morris and the artists who made them. The spindly art furniture of fashionable Hampstead sitting rooms showed no regard for the human anatomy, and in any case, the Lowys were proud of their overstuffed chairs and horsehair sofa. In their view, the reception room's gilded mirrors, satin draperies, and display of ebony, gilt, and alabaster reflected their position.

Reasoning still according to the principle of contradiction, Mina concluded that the goal of art was to evoke a more spiritual existence; for this reason, it must avoid the contamination of daily life. Some months later, she discovered in the work of Rossetti's fellow Pre-Raphaelite Edward Burne-Jones her ideal of artistic purity. Her favorite painting, his enigmatic *Love among the Ruins*, showed a pair of lovers apparently so overcome by thoughts of mortality that the woman, although clinging to her love, turns away and stares into space. As if he had read her mind, Burne-Jones's yearning, nostalgic melancholy perfectly expressed Mina's disdain for Victorian values. Had he not defined art as "a beautiful romantic dream of something that never was, never will be—in a light better than any light that ever shone—in a land no one can define or remember, only desire"? At the same time, her affinity with the Pre-Raphaelites also provided the solution to the soiled casts and bony models. "Love being the mechanism of talent," she observed, "I discovered that if my powers of concentration flagged with a model before me, I could draw anything I longed to see provided I had nothing to look at."

Mina won a coveted school prize for the first of these visionary compositions. From then on, she was considered one of the Wood's outstanding students, and by the end of the year, she recalled, became particularly adept at drawing imaginary women in whose pale Celtic features shone an "egoless purity." Although her otherworldly beauties suggested a solution to the problem of female self-assertion, paradoxically they also attracted the attention of her peers and teachers. Enjoying the "liberation of my self confidence," Mina went on, she nevertheless became nervous when a visiting Royal Academy artist lingered so long over one of her beauties that he "practically licked his chops."

Noticing Mina's new air of self-assurance, Julia resumed her complaints about the art world's depravity. Confirmation of her suspicions materialized in Mina's latest drawing, a naked Andromeda lashed to a rock: her daughter was a "vicious slut," Julia shrieked, and ripped up the drawing. Henceforth, Mina was to submit all her drawings and poems for inspection. Julia's objections focused on the fact that Andromeda's nudity revealed her creator's ill-gotten knowledge—the knowledge that sex existed. In her view, the nude was objectionable both on moral grounds and as a violation of social propriety, which required the denial of any "impurity."* This widespread attitude further complicated the predicament of women art students, who considered the nude an important part of art training. "It was almost a crime to mention the word nude," recalled one of Mina's contemporaries. "Although acquainted with our personal anatomies, we were supposed to accept the conventional point of view that women had no legs. They had heads, arms and feet, apparently linked together by clothes," she went on. "However beautiful the body might be, it was to be hidden as a thing of shame."

Once Mina began to censor her work in anticipation of Julia's criticism, she found that she could no longer retreat to her imagination: the Voice followed her there. She had been put in another demoralizing double bind. At school her drawings won praise, while at home the same drawings earned increased surveillance. She sometimes went to the extreme of ruining a particularly good drawing in order to avoid either praise or blame, she recalled in her memoirs, since the former seemed to guarantee the

---

* In a sense Julia was right: the Andromeda theme was an occasion to show women in bondage—a scene conducive to much sexual fantasy.

latter. Her inability to mention her mother in this passage, along with the knotted quality of her writing, conveys the anxiety that she often felt about her talent: "The interference in my work took the form of violent depression, and soon, of terror, on receiving praise, of never being able to produce anything again that could merit praise." She could not express what she felt, which was tremendous anger.

In this scheme of things, being a good artist meant that she was a bad girl, the next thing to a fallen woman. But in addition to the paralyzing effects of her mother's belief that art was immoral, the art world itself placed a woman artist in a strange position. Women, naked or clothed, were the subjects of most successful paintings, whether the frigid allegories of Lord Leighton, the Roman fantasies of Alma-Tadema, or the wan re-creations of the Middle Ages produced by the many latter-day Pre-Raphaelites. The females in such paintings included alarming femmes fatales and languorous, self-absorbed sufferers, but there were few images of real women, like Mina and her classmates. How was she to present herself to the world, or to the students who wished her to sit for them, and furthermore, what subjects should she paint now that the very subject matter of art, the female body, had been contaminated by her mother's allegations? It had become more difficult to convey the "egoless purity" of her ideal image.

Mina continued to model her subjects and herself after Burne-Jones's females, whose listlessness expressed her emotional impasse. These passive heroines, who often wait at doorways as if immobilized in the space around them, looked as if all they could do was yearn for "something that never was, never will be." Mina had already concluded with some irony that, in life as well as in art, "the highest function of a maiden is to yearn, of a young man also if he can be brought to it." Trapped between her urge to rebel and her fear of the consequences, she was drawn to the emotional temper of Burne-Jones's imagination—"a world in which no violent emotions exist, in which everyone is quietly and decently sad," notes critic Quentin Bell, "a lovely pensive existence amidst Italianate scenery peopled by graceful persons whose soberly coloured robes echo faintly the realities of Marshall and Snelgrove [a fashionable department store]." Yet at the same time, this mournful aesthetic also produced "an overwhelmingly prurient effect," Bell observes, in large part because Burne-Jones was so anxious to avoid vulgarity. From her own perspective, Julia had detected this note of prurience.

At sixteen Mina knew little more about sexual matters than she had learned from her friend Evangeline eight years earlier. When Evangeline came to stay with the Lowys again for the summer, their lessons resumed. As soon as the bedroom lights were out, Evangeline began to explain what married people did on their honeymoon: all women yearned for the bliss revealed on that occasion, a pleasure so intense that it was "just like being in heaven." While "Evangeline prattle[d] on of ways and means," Mina glided off into a trance. She imagined bodily contact as a transformation, like something that happened in fairy tales. Perhaps the ecstatic expressions of Rossetti's women and the world-weary look of Burne-Jones's heroines revealed their knowledge of this bliss. Although her father destined her for marriage, Mina worried that no suitor would present himself because of her social standing. And as an art student she might be mistaken for a bad woman, one of the courtesans known to live near the Wood or, worse, one of the "professionals" she had noticed in Piccadilly. Although it offered the prospect of indescribable pleasures, being female also seemed to bring trouble no matter what one did.

The constant focus at the Wood on the differences between the sexes, especially in life class, made it impossible to forget the subject of sex. Male students struck up what seemed like harmless conversations while appraising Mina's work, but when they asked her to sit for a portrait, she told them that she could not do so without a chaperone. It was not clear to her whether they were lingering over her drawings or her person. By the end of the year, she decided that men were not an ever-present danger. Most students assumed that they were above the prudish suspicions of those who warned that men and women could not be left alone together. Mina began to relax with her male classmates, whose friendship opened still another door to freedom. "A little breathless with escape, a girl in their company achieved an illusion of sharing in that liberty," she noted. "It seemed so clear that life for them entailed no anxieties."

Under the auspices of the school's sketching club, Mina received her parents' permission to go on excursions to Kew to paint the gardens or to Frensham to sketch in the country lanes. Everyone enjoyed the easy camaraderie of these expeditions, especially when their teachers strolled off in another direction. The men regaled the women with tales of evenings at the music halls, places with exotic names like the Tivoli, the Pavilion, and the Metropolitan, where ladies could never be seen. The most that they might hope for was a meal together at the Café Royal or the other French restaurants fashionable among artists, where they sometimes met the notorious "Sladers." But as far as Mina was concerned, the best times were their escapes to the country, when they were left alone to sketch with a degree of freedom that she had not until then experienced. She never entirely escaped from the Voice, which returned to plague her once they were in the classroom.

Students at conservative art schools like the Wood were aware that the Sladers took for granted both drawing in mixed company and mixed company itself. Women had been admitted since the Slade's founding in 1871. Just as their independence from the Royal Academy system encouraged artistic innovation, the Sladers' familiarity with life class also produced a more relaxed atmosphere, as if the free and lively line with which they learned to draw carried naturally into their social lives. In their rented rooms at the northern edge of Soho, they lived as a group apart, even if their independence sometimes meant, as in the case of Gwen and Augustus John, sharing rooms and "subsisting, like monkeys, on a diet of fruit and nuts." The Slade girls' high-spirited "new woman" behavior was at odds with their bohemian costumes of loosely draped fabrics and muted hues. The men showed a similar disregard for convention by designing their own clothes, including old-fashioned knee britches and velvet tunics in peacock blue lined with emerald green. Students from the Wood, who envied the Sladers' flamboyance, exuberance, and apparent disregard for convention, gossiped about them from a safe distance.

A genius had appeared among them, it was said, in the person of Augustus John. At nineteen he had attracted the attention of John Singer Sargent, who "exclaimed when he visited the Slade Augustus's drawings were beyond anything that had been seen since the Italian Renaissance." After that, John's classmates took to saving the sketches that he threw in the wastebasket. It was generally agreed that "not only were his drawings of heads and of the nude masterly; he poured out compositions with extraordinary ease; he had the copiousness which goes with genius, and he himself had the eager understanding, the imagination, the readiness for intellectual and physical adventure one associates with genius." Already the hero of the art students, he was on the way to becoming a notorious, yet successful, nonconformist. But in the nineties, when John's golden earrings, red beard, and amorous successes were as well known as his artistic ones, few young women risked making his acquaintance. Their lives were to follow the path toward marriage, provided appropriate suitors could be found.

Looking back on the nineties, Mina concluded that, unlike her own, most English families "functioned contentedly within the boundaries of their domestic interests." Which seemed to leave them "uniformly flat." "What imagination, emotion, apprehension they could generate, they summoned solely for Birth and Marriage and Death," she went on, forgetting for the moment her mother's vivid imagination for Sex, Sin, and Downfall. No doubt recalling her own experience, she lamented those households where "girls were torn with anxiety between the appeal of a sole liberation and the paralysing certainty that the very torture of their isolation rendered marriage unattainable."

Anxiety on the part of marriageable daughters was particularly intense in families with mixed backgrounds. The Lowys' twin humiliations, Sigmund's Jewishness and Julia's humble origins, made it pointless to aspire to the rituals they read about in the illustrated weeklies—the annual round of tea parties, regattas, formal dances, and receptions at which young women of good family met prospective suitors. By this point Julia had succeeded in banishing her husband's Jewish friends, some of whom had become wealthy enough to merit titles. Since few people lived up to her standards, callers were rare at Compayne Gardens. Yet Mr. Lowy had not altogether abandoned hope for his artistic girls. They might still "appear," since genius was the one category (in addition to great wealth) that occasionally opened the doors of society.

Suitors could be found, her father supposed, if only something could be done about Mina's appearance. Although it was in bad taste to mention the subject on everyone's mind, she overheard him muttering, "Sixteen and as thin as a rail." "I gathered that were I not 'dressed,' " she noted, "I should resemble 'bad women.' Unless I turned out to be a genius I would never 'appear.' That were I to express an opinion, I should fail to find a husband." As fashionable dress emphasized her willowy figure and she already had her share of opinions, her only hope was to become a genius. But in the meantime, premature efforts to "appear" would redound against her: "All spectators of that suspect showpiece, myself, must inevitably receive impressions to my disadvantage."

More disconcerting than these criticisms, which had the merit of familiarity, were the unexpected reactions that Mina evoked outside her family. When new acquaintances stammered, "You're the loveliest thing I've ever seen," she assumed that, given her slender form, they must be joking. And since the clinging maiden in Burne-Jones's *Love among the Ruins* was her private standard of beauty, it was impossible to take such declarations seriously. Had these new friends been speaking the truth, she reasoned, her "induced complex of culpability" would have caused her to feel guilty about their admiration. She had so thoroughly internalized her parents' perspective, she later wrote, that she was unable to take at face value other, more favorable evaluations: "The insidious element in rebellion against parents consists in your inability to detach yourself completely from the basic substratum of their ascendency."

As soon as Mina's rebellious feelings rose to the surface, well-trained emotional responses tried to suppress them. At sixteen she felt incapable of defying parental authority (which she imagined as "an omnipotent adult of dual embodiment—female . . . with a divine right to insult me, male . . . with a similar right to ruin me"). Years later, looking back on her parents'—and the period's—obsession with "that somewhat unformulated concept, sex," she concluded that by "putting it into words," the postwar era allowed people to concentrate on other things, incidentally reducing the amount of cruelty directed at marriageable daughters. But during her years at art school, she recalled, "the extremes which marked my to & fro between world and home were those of a pendulum endowed with consciousness swinging beyond a calculable range."

By her second year at St. John's Wood, Mina no longer felt like the baby of the school. She made friends with Eva Knight, an art student with whom she had an immediate understanding. They discovered their bond when each admitted an intense dislike of her mother. Mrs. Knight was a stickler for morality of the narrowest kind, her daughter explained. She had prevented Eva's marriage to the man she loved on the grounds that her daughter was committed to her tennis partner, whom she accused Eva of "leading on." Despite their obvious animosity, mother and daughter continued to live together for lack of an alternative.

Mina explained her own entrapment in a situation that made it impossible for her to express her wishes when they ran counter to her mother's. Although this predicament was of Julia's making, she believed, it made her feel guilty, especially when Julia resorted to swooning: "Seeing my mother fall by the fender purposely, hearing her sob at will, served merely to render more complex the initial imposition of filial duty. Behind her tantrums loomed the collective maternal heart given into the keeping of the doctor of that era. He pronounced it so weak the slightest emotional stress must cause a devoted mother's instantaneous decease."

And when Julia was in good health, she was capable of a cruelty rivaling Mrs. Knight's. Mr. Lowy had concluded that given the overt anti-Semitism of the English, it was in his daughters' interest to change their name. Julia refused to go along with his plan, Mina wrote (although this explanation seems excessive), because of "the joy she extracted from even our minor nuisances such as my name on the roll-call of a Protestant bible class eliciting laic giggles." Her mother's solution to the embarrassment caused by their Jewish surname was to slur over it—as if her husband's origins could be elided as easily as the *w*. Keeping the name, moreover, allowed her to present herself as "the right side of a mésalliance."

Seeing herself as the prisoner of her parents' contradictory obsessions, Mina imagined "*man*, the scarecrow on the parental landscape, in the ingratiating guise of an Evangelist."* Engagement to an acceptable young man offered the only possible escape. She resolved to comply with her father's wishes by choosing a fiancé from among her classmates at the Wood. "In the jocular prelude to conscious adolescence one not [i]nfrequently falls in love with something 'funny.' I picked my young man," she explained, "because he smoked a curved pipe which hanging over his long chin made him easy to caricature, having first consulted with my girl chum before clenching my choice." Above the pipe Lucas (she did not supply his surname) was equipped with good bone structure, and he was always well dressed, unlike the prototypical artists whose baggy trousers her father deplored. Once they had become friends, Lucas showed his respect for Mina's opinions by dressing in brown to match his hair. Like many sixteen-year-olds, Mina believed that conformity to a visual ideal was what made one attractive.

Although Lucas qualified on this score, he was neither an inspired conversationalist nor a latter-day Rossetti. When they managed to steal away from life class to the fields of Primrose Hill, Mina assumed that he

---

* Mina's choice of names suggests an intriguing association: just as "Evangeline" had informed her about the sexual act, which she understood as a kind of transcendence, so man "the Evangelist" would lead the way to another sort of liberation.

would take the lead. But all he could manage was to put his arm around her while they huddled on a damp bench, staring into the fog. "There were no primroses," Mina recalled. As Lucas sat "hunched in inhibited ardor, paralyzed with 'respect,' " she suggested that he think of Rossetti's wooing of Elizabeth Siddal. The poet was probably just as paralyzed as he once his fiancée was sitting beside him, Lucas replied. Their relations continued for some time in this farcical manner. Striving to resemble artistic ideals did not make intimacy any easier, nor did life class carry over into real life. Mina "yearn[ed] for concrete experience before it should be too late."

Her parents found Lucas an acceptable suitor, especially after learning of his parents' wealth and position. They had no objections to Mina's seeing him in Devon, where "through arduous plotting," she recalled, they persuaded both families to spend their holidays. Once again having little to say when they found themselves alone, Lucas read aloud to Mina from *Lorna Doone*. Occasionally they progressed to philosophical discussions on such topics as "whether all human beings had souls," or more "advanced" ones such as whether most English people "would even want to do 'it' if they had not been told they mustn't." But when Lucas offered to take Mina rowing on the lake, her sister Dora was sent along as chaperone and performed her duties as suspiciously as if she were Julia. As soon as Lucas put his arm around Mina's waist underneath her cape, Dora uncovered the offensive gesture.

Although Mina detected progressive attitudes in Lucas, she thought him "unlikely to grow in poetry" and broke off the engagement. Lucas was good enough to draw but not to marry. It was no use choosing a fiancé to please others, and in any case, Mina had her eye on someone else, although she did not want to admit it. "Unsuspected an inner self," she wrote, "unhampered by that programme of the practical, began to have its subconscious reactions"—to the appearance at the Wood of a very different kind of man, whose poetic mien distinguished him from inexperienced art students. Mina first caught sight of "Holyoak" (no Christian name is given in her memoirs) on the school tennis court—"a pale stranger broad-shouldered, narrow-hipped, lifting his arms in a white shirt"—whose silhouette suggested the image of "a lily on the air of spring swaying from a dark stalk."* Holyoak embodied her artistic ideal. Stirred by the look of benevolent amusement in his sad gray eyes, she took in his "ethereal" height, his air of "someone soaring in an [u]nattainable beyond."

The next time she saw him, again reaching heavenward, she felt drawn to Holyoak "as if to a fount of compassion"—she might have been the cat he was rescuing from a tree in his front garden. Holyoak had been an actor

---

* Mina may have chosen this name to suggest her friend's unconventional ways because of the contemporary reputation of George Holyoake, author of *The Origin and Nature of Secularism* and a well-known anti-church intellectual.

before taking up his current profession, "art" photography. Mina joined the more bohemian students at his studio near the Wood. She noted his "look of mystic dissipation" and "condemnatory sniff: his comment on life in its essentials." Holyoak was just the sort of freethinking aesthete to whom her parents would have objected, had they known anything about him.

In his company, Mina felt, she entered another psychic refuge: "Across the threshold of that little house, through a glass door, I passed into my 'other life.' " Soon she and Holyoak were constant companions: "Except for the blank intervals when he disappeared into his darkroom, his nearness made the light grow lighter." As Mina watched him posing the actresses Marie Tempest and Constance Collier, two celebrities of the day, she passed judgment on their showy charms as disdainfully as if she had been her mother: these professional beauties "appeared" on stage and in the newspapers, but such fame as they enjoyed was tawdry, in keeping with their artificial complexions.

It was not long before Holyoak asked Mina to pose for her portrait. At seventeen, she had the willowy grace of her Pre-Raphaelite models, as well as their yearning expression. Holyoak arranged her against a dark background in three-quarter profile and gave her an iris to hold: her downward gaze, rapt focus on the flower, and velvet gown all mark her as an aesthetic subject, to be admired by people of taste. But while Mina was delighted with this new image of herself, Julia became so irate upon seeing it that she demanded an appointment with Mr. Ward. (The principal assured her that even though Mina's bare shoulder showed, the picture was a simple study in drapery.) Compared with her parents' taste in portraits, Holyoak's was "art."

Mina was only half aware that her friend's aesthetic principles bore some relation to the Aesthetic Movement of the eighties. The poetic gloom and picturesque melancholy to which their circle aspired were throwbacks to the decades before they were born. Although they continued to paint wistful ladies in medieval settings, Mina and her friends were far more energetic than their subjects. The girls rode bicycles, played tennis, and took long walks up and down the Hampstead hills. Yet they continued to droop like Pre-Raphaelite heroines at social gatherings, as if trying on new aesthetic strategies with their clothes. Slender as any Burne-Jones maiden, Mina looked best in the loose, light, and rather old-fashioned dresses modeled after those worn by the women of the Aesthetic inner circle. Holyoak's house was itself an Aesthetic-revival cottage, with all the props of artistic good taste; like others near the Wood, his studio had the countrified charm of the Queen Anne revival. Mina felt the contrast between his airy quarters and her parents' dark interiors each time she passed into her "other life," where dreams and intuitions were respected.

When Holyoak asked her why she was unable to concentrate on her drawing, Mina was at a loss for a reply. Even when she blurted out the story of her mother's role as censor, he thought she must be exaggerating. "You seem to be waiting for something to happen," he remarked. "Let me assure you, dear, nothing ever happens." But once Holyoak met Dora and their father, who accompanied them to a Royal Academy ball, he understood, she felt, that she was not simply the spoiled child he had thought her. Mina had decorated Dora's ballgown to show off her sister's complexion and introduced her to her friends from the Wood. When Dora took it into her head that the best way to behave was to maintain a haughty silence, her partners decided it would be more amusing to waltz with Mina. Overhearing Mr. Lowy scold Mina for taking away Dora's partners, Holyoak began to understand Mina's scapegoat role in family dramas.

Once Holyoak expressed his sympathy, she felt implicit trust in him. Whenever they walked to his studio after classes, he behaved perfectly although they were unchaperoned. During these dreamy strolls, they told each other what they saw in the patterns of the clouds, a pastime that Mina found enchanting: "I was exalted by my first intimacy with anyone who ever looked up at the sky." And while primroses had failed to bloom with Lucas, they blossomed with Holyoak. One spring afternoon, after they had lingered under an apple tree laden with flowers, Holyoak led Mina to his music room. "On first arriving, as if the apple blossom showered over a wall," she wrote, "he covered my face with rueful kisses, then dashed to the organ and began to play music I could not yet interpret." These chaste kisses inaugurated a new stage of intimacy. They talked of everything and anything. In his presence, she exulted, "surroundings resumed their erstwhile aspect of the miraculous." But this time it was no joking matter. He was neither a subject for caricature nor a social convenience.

Holyoak's domestic arrangements were hard to fathom, except that he shared his house with an actor and his wife, a Mr. and Mrs. Peck. When the Pecks rented a place in the country for the summer, Holyoak invited some of the students from the Wood to bicycle out for lunch. Stopping to rest in a pub along the way, Mina was somewhat surprised to find herself in this grimy establishment. But Holyoak's company transformed their surroundings: "The confining expanse of marbled yellow wall-paper, the vinegar moat of a glass fly-trap became Empyrean whose sublimated glow gilded an all inclusive precinct of quietude." She had forgotten her self-consciousness, her depression, the internalized Voice.

Soon after their arrival, Mrs. Peck flew into a rage after noticing that Mina was wearing a cobalt bead that Holyoak had given her, one of a number of relics that a friend had brought back from Egypt. Mina could not comprehend the woman's outburst, which resembled her mother's tirades, until Holyoak's brother took her aside and explained the situation. Holyoak was not a free agent. After nursing him through a difficult illness, Mrs. Peck had become Holyoak's mistress, while Mr. Peck, who believed in letting everyone live their lives, shared the house "for the sake of appearances." His brother had tried but failed to disentangle himself from this relationship. Surprised to learn that "men also to a certain degree could be ruined, by getting too inextricably involved with another man's wife," Mina went home in a state of confusion.

She did not see Holyoak again until she ran into him by chance near the Wood. Because she believed unwaveringly in their "affinity," she had not felt jealous. Consequently she was shocked when, "looking as if he had by superhuman ordeal recreated the world," Holyoak announced that he had broken with Mrs. Peck. Overcome by a sudden feeling of modesty at the thought of a declaration, Mina replied as primly as if her mother had written the script, "But that is of no interest to me." Holyoak stared at her in amazement, and Mina fled. Once she reached home, she understood his response to her unexpectedly demure behavior. He had taken her to mean that she didn't care whether he was free. "Remorseful as a pugilist who should unwittingly hit below the belt," she recalled, "I decided in a flash of anticipatory feminism to make amends." After confiding in Eva, Mina saw that she must tell Holyoak that she loved him. But it was difficult to make contact, since Mrs. Peck's presence prevented her from getting word to him.

When Mina returned home from one of her attempts to reach Holyoak, she found the house in turmoil. Julia was dangerously ill, the result of a miscarriage brought on by her latest swoon. The girls were not to leave the house until she recovered her health, which was complicated by a case of peritonitis. Even though her father had hired a complement of nurses, Mina was to sit at her mother's bedside. When she implored the doctor to tell Julia that no good could come of these falls, he replied frostily that she was unable to appreciate her mother. Mina distracted herself with the novels of Ouida, a popular writer whose sensational tales of peasants and aristocrats offered an escape from middle-class morality. But as soon as Julia heard of her interest in this author, she had Ouida's books placed under lock and key. A widowed lady's companion, a Mrs. Rayburn, was hired to chaperone the girls even though they were not to go out. There was no escape from family life, paradoxically dominated by her invalid mother.

In this atmosphere, her father's state of mind had coarsened, Mina thought, "reflecting the unexpected agony of his respectability & an increasing obtuseness to any sensitivity but his own. This craven neurotic," she continued, "was almost impossible to relate to the glorious enthusiast I had glimpsed in my babyhood." Nevertheless, Mr. Lowy roused himself to take advantage of Julia's convalescence: "His opponent actually prone, Father gathered what wits remained to him, in a supreme effort to save me from 'those good-for-nothing artists.' " If she must study art, let her do so at a women's academy, far from temptation and, if possible, from home. Paris, the repair of the demimonde and the déclassé, was out of the question. She would attend classes at the Women's Academy in Munich.

After writing to the British Consulate for the names of families that took paying guests, he received the address of a baronial couple and wrote to them. Mr. Lowy pictured Mina launched at last into good society, while she worried that, like her mother, the Baroness would find her unacceptable.

Her father's solution was to send Mrs. Rayburn as well. The presence of a chaperone would convince anyone that she came from a good family. She was to set off in time for the autumn term, become accustomed to her surroundings, and learn German, a language of which he approved. Mina was unhappy that she had not managed to see Holyoak, let alone explain her feelings. Although she vowed to remain faithful and sort things out on her return, she never saw him again: "Holyoak's front door closed on that period in which Nature allows innumerable maidens some inviolable appeal, inspiring men to crown them with a healing devotion."

3

Jugendstil

(MUNICH, 1900)

THE CHOICE OF MUNICH was not as arbitrary as it seems. The Bavarian capital was known throughout Middle Europe for its first-rate university, cultural life, and status as an art city second only to Paris. And in Mr. Lowy's view, the "Athens on the Isar" was preferable to the French capital. The Munich Künstlerinnenverein—the Society of Female Artists' School—was, he gathered, a respectable institution with ties to the Munich Academy of Fine Arts, whose annual shows at the Glass Palace dwarfed even the vast Royal Academy displays. Since Munich had become an artistic center under the aegis of the Bavarian royalty, this was art with an official seal of approval. Mina would learn something of the old ways, and a year's stay with a baronial family would set her on the right path.

Keyed up about her new life as well as nervous about the impression she would make, Mina set off with Mrs. Rayburn. When they had rested from the train trip, the Baron, a tall, excitable man with an impressive beard, took them on a walking tour of the city, which turned into a lesson on the Bavarian nobility. Although he pointed out the neoclassical monuments and Baroque churches, most important in his view was the vast Residenz of the royal family. Discoursing on the lineage of a prince whose palace they were approaching, he asked Mrs. Rayburn about Mr. Lowy. Her cautious response—he was a man of importance, with numerous subordinates—failed to satisfy their curiosity and the Baroness pressed for details. He was a tailor who dealt in wholesale cloth, Mina replied, adding nervously that her mother did not allow the subject to be mentioned. The Baroness produced an elegant explanation: one would take his daughter for a princess, so Mr. Lowy must be a purveyor to the Queen. Mina accepted the compliment with misgivings.

Once Mina had said goodbye to Mrs. Rayburn, she began to feel more at home. Munich's wide white avenues were nothing like the sordid streets of London. Here, one could walk freely all over the city, she discovered, since the family's entertainment seemed to consist of daily strolls. In contrast to her constricted life at home since Julia's illness, Munich felt spacious. In Schwabing, the artists' quarter, students strolled about in nonchalant attitudes and called gaily from their studios to friends in the streets and cafés. Music wafted from open windows in a permanent rehearsal, while groups of models in peasant costumes posed in front of the Academy of Art. In the shops, one saw a startling variety of beautiful objects, copies of Italian sculpture, modern Madonnas with disturbing expressions, vases in iridescent blues and purples, art embroideries with fantastic floral designs, and bronze nudes all tastefully arranged for the discriminating buyer. The bookshops were full of works on the arts-and-crafts movement and magazines with titles like *Kunst für Alle* (*Art for All*). The whole city was on display, its different quarters like so many stage sets.

In his role as Mina's protector, the Baron approved of her plan to enroll at the Künstlerinnenverein. This institution combined culture and social propriety, and a number of its students came from noble families. But given his conservative outlook, the Baron no doubt shared the common prejudice against women artists, said to be of two kinds: "the ones who want to get married and the others, who also have no talent." Determined to paint in spite of their exclusion from the official art academies, the women of the Künstlerinnenverein had founded their own school the year that Mina was born. Several distinguished German women began their training at the Women's Academy, including Käthe Kollwitz and Gabriele Münter, who was enrolled for a few months during the time that Mina was a student. Impatient with its old-fashioned teaching methods, Münter left to study with Kandinsky, but Mina, inured to an academic approach, stayed on.

She later insisted that she had learned the essentials of draftsmanship in these segregated classes. Her first instructor was Maximilian Dasio, well known at that time for mythological paintings. His students looked forward to one day painting the Muses and Bacchantes, as he did, but for the time being they had to content themselves with drawing "heads" from the model, often for weeks at a time. Although Dasio was uninspiring, he taught discipline and respect for draftsmanship. Mina was soon promoted to Angelo Jank's class, which she found more stimulating because of the opportunity to draw the whole figure. Jank acclaimed her as a budding talent. But as at the Wood, the approved technique required laborious interior shading rather than quick sketches. It was painstaking work, and after a few months Mina, too, grew impatient.

What went on outside the Women's Academy was more inviting. As soon as she had enough German, Mina tried to read *Jugend* [*Youth*], the leading cultural weekly, as a guide to Schwabing. The curvilinear aesthetic of the art objects she had noticed in the shops was called *Jugendstil*, she learned, after the magazine: this playful "youth-style" flaunted its sinuous swirls in opposition to the sobriety of classical Munich. In exhibition posters and art galleries, in the many displays of the arts-and-crafts movement, she saw the same rhythmic lines and broad planes of color playfully combined. It was an art devoted to the pleasures of the senses. The students went to study the quintessential *Jugendstil* building, August Endell's new Hofatelier Elvira, whose free-form exterior decoration swirled across the façade as if Endell were thumbing his nose at official Munich. It was hard to know what to make of a style that ignored the claims of tradition. Mina was uncertain whether the new architecture was an elaborate joke or a new form of art.

Within a short time, she felt uncertain about her new family as well. Once the Baron and Baroness settled down to their domestic routines, it became clear that their own façade was in need of maintenance. They had several anemic children and not enough money. And despite his appearance, the Baron's only strong points were his Vandyke beard and volatile temperament. Just the same, the Baroness, a placid blue-eyed woman with a crown of "mouse colored" braids, seemed eager to bestow affection. Mina was to call this large woman Mammalie, as if she were her daughter. The Baroness let Mina do as she pleased, cooked her favorite treats whenever she wished, and was bent, Mina thought, on spoiling her.

Soon they were exchanging confidences. When Mina told the Baroness of her difficulties with her mother, Mammalie clucked over Mrs. Lowy's obsession with Mina's impending downfall. Women, in Mammalie's view, had little to look forward to: there was no such thing as conjugal bliss. She baffled Mina with a story of a lady who sampled illicit love, only to exclaim, "Why, it's just as dull as marriage." This response did not jibe with Evangeline's descriptions of love's delights, nor with what Mina thought of as appropriate conversation for a chaperone. Still, it was a change to be treated as a grownup. In her role as confidante, Mammalie showed Mina the letter she received from Julia, who set out the details of Mina's "strongheadedness" and exhorted the Baroness to "exercise the utmost severity" should she go against her wishes, especially with regard to the opposite sex. This news was not reassuring: despite Mammalie's affectionate ways, Mina thought, the letter "placed me unconditionally at her disposal." When she made a point of mentioning her devotion to Holyoak, Mammalie wagered that she would forget him.

Mina wondered what had happened to the "old ways" and what vision of her future the Baroness could be imagining. When her classmates pointed out the notorious Gräfin Franziska zu Reventlow, who was both a countess and a fallen woman, she became curious about the life of this Schwabing heroine. After leaving her aristocratic family at twenty-one, the Gräfin had been disowned, tried unsuccessfully to become an artist, and now managed to support herself with her writing.* Fanny was to be seen everywhere in Schwabing, at the cafés and in the studios, usually with a number of lovers and admirers. And although she had a child, she refused to identify the father. Studying her erect bearing and impeccable manners, Mina concluded that her irregular way of life only enhanced her charm.

The other topic of gossip at the Women's Academy concerned the artists who founded the Munich "Secession" in 1892, when they broke from the official Artists' Society. Snubbing its overwhelming exhibitions at the Glass Palace, the Secessionists had organized their own, to which they invited some of the most innovative artists in Europe. By the turn of the century, the Secession had attracted a number of imaginative foreigners, like Paul Klee and Vasily Kandinsky, and created an audience for the decorative work of the English artists Mina admired. The barriers between the "fine" and "applied" arts were already breaking down. Important art galleries showed *Jugendstil* embroideries as if they were paintings; Secession shows featured work by Fabergé, Lalique, and Tiffany. By 1900, art objects and furniture of all kinds were shown along with the "higher" forms, and Mina looked with particular interest at the many imaginative lamp designs in iridescent or opaque colored glass.

Yet while women artists were particularly active in the new decorative movement, here, too, as in England, the dominant figures were male. Once men took an interest in the applied arts—known as *Kunst in Handwerk*—their status improved, provided that someone else did the actual "handwork." Men often conceived of the decorative projects, but women did the stitching. In a few years' time at the Salon d'Automne in Paris, Mina saw the beaded handbags and appliquéd wall hangings designed by Kandinsky but sewn by Gabriele Münter. Given that her father had, for many years, been a tailor, it was unclear to Mina whether fashion, in which she was deeply interested, could be considered an art, or whether it was the sort of humble occupation of which her mother disapproved, a trade.

It was known that one member of the Künstlerinnenverein had made her mark in the applied arts: after achieving success at the Paris World Exhibition, Margarethe von Brauchitsch set up a school in her Munich studio to teach the principles of design. Known for her support of the "reform clothing" movement,† which aimed to do away with corsets, von

---

* In her 1913 *roman à clef* of artistic Munich, *Herrn Dames Aufzeichnungen*, Fanny called Schwabing a "spiritual movement, a niveau, a direction, a protest, a new cult or much more, the attempt to win once again out of ancient cults new religious possibilities." In this period, the gospel of free love was also preached in the circle around the Von Richthoven sisters—Else, later the mistress of Max Weber, and Frieda, later the wife of D. H. Lawrence—whose shared lover, psychoanalyst Otto Gross, claimed that marriage repressed the erotic impulses.

† Apostles of the *Reformkleid* movement treated clothing design as an art with a purpose, that of liberating women from the constraints of fashion. Corsets were discarded as unnatural and unhealthy; the wasp waist of the previous century was permitted to expand to more normal proportions. The light silk tunics worn by Isadora Duncan in this period are another expression of contemporary interest in allowing women greater freedom of motion.

Brauchitsch designed loosely fitting garments with a high sash under the bosom, often in shades of iridescent gray with shimmering silk appliqués. These *Jugendstil* dresses seemed more modern than the nostalgic Liberty gowns that Mina had favored in London, yet it took a certain daring to wear them. Still unsure of herself at seventeen, Mina studied "new women" like Fanny and Margarethe from a distance.

She was beginning, nevertheless, to form her own opinion on the subject of emancipated, or fallen, women—it amounted, she believed, to nearly the same thing. Was not society, and, more precisely, the family, responsible for their situation? Her parents had warned repeatedly that "a girl who mislaid her maidenhood was promptly let out on the streets." What else could one do but walk these same streets after such rejection? She sympathized with all women who had broken with society, whether by choice or by constraint: "Inwardly I was evolving a weird strictly personal form of feminism of which the militant aspect consisted in being peculiarly benign to any woman who had been 'pushed.' " Recalling the expressionless gaze of a Piccadilly prostitute who had shocked her into compassion, she concluded (somewhat illogically) that the irregular lives of the Schwabing women were also the result of social "pushing"—an idea tinged with defiance as well as ambivalence about the fate for which her mother had destined her. Each day on her way to school she measured the distance between the Germanic version of propriety and Schwabing's improper bohemia.

Yet things were not what they seemed in the Baroness's household. Mina's chaperones showed no inclination to introduce her into Bavarian high society and kept bringing her together with a series of strange men. When a young diplomat appeared at dinner, Mina assumed that he, like herself, was a paying guest. But he acted peculiarly. After his first visit he sent Mina a note asking her to meet him at a restaurant. When she showed the note to the Baroness, Mammalie muttered, "Bad move. Too fast a worker." Mina remained in the dark until the next guest, a Dutch law student, explained that he had come to dinner after reading a suggestively worded newspaper advertisement offering an English miss along with the repast: Mina was the bait to lure paying customers. This explanation made sense of the baronial couple's habit of leaving her alone with their guest. She was lucky to have as company a man of honor like himself.

Mina continued to worry about the aura of naughtiness with which her chaperones surrounded her. There were other mystifying examples of unorthodox behavior. On walks or at restaurants, the Baron, after clicking his heels, would introduce Mina with a wink as *Die Miss*, to which his friends replied, as if she were a well-known courtesan, "But surely this is Cléo de Merode or Liane de Pougy?" As the family seemed set on turning her into a femme fatale, she became increasingly suspicious of their sense of decorum.

Her foreboding increased when the whole family boarded the train for the Bavarian Alps—although they obviously could not afford such an excursion. When the Baron told the other passengers that she was English, their references to the Boer War added to her discomfort. Once settled in the hunting lodge, Mina learned to her dismay that their daily recreation consisted of long hikes with the neighbors in search of local beer halls. Whenever she could get away, she took walks in the fields, stopping to draw. Her self-consciousness left her, she recalled, as she sketched the wildflowers, "the heraldic curves of giant dandelions, the crowded constellations of the umbel," whose spirals she preferred to the curves of *Jugendstil.*

But the Baron was intent on showing Mina the sights. While they consumed large quantities of sauerkraut washed down by the local Pilsener in a terraced restaurant overlooking the Starnburger See, Mina tried to imagine the flamboyant Bavarian king Ludwig II sailing around the lake on his luxury boat. Watching the water turn from sapphire blue to opalescent brilliance in the afternoon sun, she managed to ignore both the lunch and the appetites of her companions—until the Baroness interrupted her thoughts with comments about Mina's "successes" with their neighbors at the hunting lodge.

Her alarm deepened during their outing to a remote mountain valley, where the party was to spend the night before ascending the Grottenkopf with two friends from the area. When they arose at four the next morning to get an early start, the Baron suddenly changed his mind about going and announced enigmatically, *"Es ist erreicht"* (It has been arranged). The Baroness announced that she, too, would remain behind and pushed Mina out into the dark with their acquaintances. Although all three felt this to be a peculiar situation, the men were considerate, and the sight at the top of the mountain made up for hours of embarrassment. Amazed to see range after range of icy peaks glittering in the light, Mina imagined that the mountains were alive. On the way down, the men became formal and, on parting, bowed and kissed her hand, as relieved as she was, Mina supposed, to have survived the climb uncompromised. Such a situation was unthinkable in England. She could not grasp the Baroness's intentions.

Mina felt ill at ease as they set off for Oberammergau on another early-morning expedition. Serene despite the failed "arrangements," the Baroness explained to Mina her good fortune. She had picked the right time to come to Munich, since the Passion Play was performed only every ten years. She would see the results of years of preparation, when the "volkish" inhabitants of the village carved wood, prepared sets and costumes, and restored their open-air theater. But while Mina admired the decorative painting on the wooden chalets, the play itself was preposterous, she recalled, evoking her personal dismay along with her artistic disappointment. The policeman's rattle used to break the bones of the crucified thieves with vigorous realism looked like something from a cheap bazaar. Similarly, the much-vaunted "truly German" theater resembled a pen for tourists, and the villagers lacked dramatic talent. Only Judas declaimed with enough energy to match the sudden windstorm. And although she never mentioned the fact that her father was Jewish, the Baroness's anti-Semitic remarks did not improve her mood. By the end of the afternoon, she felt completely alienated from the family and their idea of German culture.

They spent the night at a guest house whose host was suitably impressed by the Baron. Since the actors in the Passion Play were dining there as well, the host presented them to the family. Mina felt as if she had stepped into an Old Master painting. A row of ruddy medieval faces gleamed out from the chiaroscuro of the oil lamp: "Leaning this way and that, spontaneously biblical in composition, they ate at a long narrow table. The parting above Mary's brow lay quiet as if smoothed by hands in prayer. Christ Jesus shred an onion with the gesture of sacrament. Above a virgin beard rested the saintly eyes of St. John the Baptist in humble tranquillity. Deftly handling their peasant knives, they might have been hewing out of themselves cathedral monuments of those they represented." They had been ennobled. Studying their unself-conscious "composition," Mina forgot the ambiguities of life with her protectors.

They returned to Munich with her honor intact. By February, when preparations were under way for Fasching, the Carnival season, Mina made friends with the paying guest who had explained her role in the Baroness's advertising schemes. Although Alexander appeared to be a man of the world (a matter of good tailoring, she thought), his ideas were unconventional. His compassion for fallen women resembled her own. Yet despite his sympathy for the outcast, Alexander placed Mina in the other class of females, those who were "angels." He was happy to watch over her, he insisted; she was quite as intelligent as any man.

As they raced around the streets during Carnival, Mina wondered how she came to be doing exactly the opposite of what her parents had told her. The cafés were full of masqueraders throwing confetti; the cold clear air crackled with excitement. One evening, as Mina gazed at the showers of confetti dotting the newly fallen snow, Munich looked like a Pissarro painting. The Carnival had provided a subject suitable to his technique. But how could one capture the flamboyance of Fasching? Everything familiar was turned upside down. To look at them, she and Alexander had exchanged sexes: he had on a Neapolitan woman's costume with a velvet hood, and she wore black velvet knickers and had her hair cut short like a medieval page's. Skipping down the broad white avenues, Mina was free. Everyone welcomed them. In the beer halls people stood on tables, one group sang to another, even the shopkeepers joined in. She had never seen anything like it.

Toward the end of Fasching, having spent most of it with Mina at street celebrations and in the cafés, Alexander invited her to the Vier Jahreszeiten, an elegant restaurant far from confetti throwers. He wanted to talk about her future. She should not return to her impossible home life or endure any more of the shabby treatment he had witnessed at the Baron's house. Later that evening, as they returned to the Café Luitpold, Carnival headquarters, Alexander grew increasingly serious. When he asked her to marry him, she said that while she could not possibly accept, she felt honored. She returned to the Baron's house, subdued in the midst of the turbulence.

Mina's uncertainty about the reasons for Mammalie's behavior was resolved after a letter came from her father. He wondered why she had written nothing but nonsense about the Alps and Oberammergau; he was cross with her for failing to mention the three hundred pounds he had sent at the Baroness's request. Why had she not described her new gown and the social season? Suddenly Mina understood the mysterious improvement in the family fortunes: the sum intended for her ballgown had gone to finance their vacation. But what did that have to do with her being thrown together with a series of men? After thinking it through, Mina confronted Mammalie, who hinted that the three hundred pounds had purchased her freedom. Mammalie had hoped she would compromise herself and leave before the fraud was discovered: "If only she had reflected that no financial complications whatever could have induced me to cut short my year's respite from the Voice." Dismayed at first to admit that their protectorship was an illusion, Mina shrewdly turned the situation to her advantage: she would go along with their deception in order to stay in Munich. She ended the interview with a request for a key to the front door. At eighteen she could make her own "arrangements."

Mina's situation struck her as comical. She was unprepared to go in for naughtiness yet generally perceived as a femme fatale. In order to appear "voluntarily unseductive," she decided to disguise herself as an eccentric. This process of self-transformation began with the purchase of a clay pipe adorned with an albino fly: "I preferred to appear as an amateur lunatic rather than an amateur baggage." Strolling about Munich with the penny pipe in her mouth, she soon attracted attention; those who did not laugh wanted to make her acquaintance. It was not as hard to "appear" as she had thought, provided one's appearance was arresting. Suddenly she was meeting the extremes of society. A countess decided that she was worth cultivating; the "geniuses" at the Künstlerinnenverein asked her to their parties. She had become a character in the drama of Schwabing, where, in an ironic reversal, someone from her parents' world or that of the Baron would have been out of place.

For the first time in her life, Mina forgot "the done thing" and felt free to be herself, at least the new version of herself that she was inventing. At school she was drawn into a cosmopolitan set of courteous German men and dashing Russian women who were "chastely advanced." Some had titles, but these, she noted, "they subordinated to their intellects." They dined late in the evening under the chestnut trees at the outdoor cafés or went to see the shows at the *tingel-tangels* (low music halls)* and cabarets, then at the height of popularity with artists. Although Mina's new friends retained the good manners of their traditional upbringing, their conversation was worldly, and they seemed more knowledgeable about contemporary art than her "shadowy Pre-Raphaelites" in London. She made friends with an anarchist who had been bold enough to make the first move with her working-class lover. Mina wondered whether the pale anarchist intended to live on love, since she regularly skipped lunch to draw. Free love required financial backing if it was going to succeed.

Alexander had seen her as an angel; the Baroness, now reduced to the status of landlady, had taken her for an apprentice courtesan. Her scene-painting classmates, however, chose Mina to play the Virgin Mary in an improvised *tableau vivant*. Reflecting on the paradox of the courtesan as Madonna, she sat holding a wooden Christ Child whose divine light was to illuminate her gaze with the help of a lamp tied at her waistband. Suddenly the lamp burst into flame, and her classmates ran from the room; the janitor cut her free and hurled the lamp into the courtyard just before it exploded. Reflecting on her "extraordinary calm in this and other tight corners" some years later, Mina supposed that "as the breaking up of the normal condition, which for the average person is security, occasions shock, so for the habitually scared, real danger in shocking them *out* of their usual condition acts as a calmative." Her self-consciousness evaporated in an instant, when it was miraculous to be alive.

From then on Mina stopped worrying about other people's opinions and enjoyed life in Schwabing. At the cafés, everyone felt that the future was being decided on the spot. Some, in defiance of Nordau's thesis, argued that a new harmony would emerge after a period of decadence. Others maintained that art's role was to mock high culture and the good burghers who supported it. Still others worried that the bourgeois were incapable of understanding Schwabing: "If only the Munich bourgeoisie would realize what is happening here, and see that the first act of the drama of the art of the future is being played out here—the art that will lead from applied crafts to sculpture and further to painting." Like those who believed their social experiments as important as their aesthetic innovations, Mina felt that she too was taking part in the drama of the future.

Discussions raged about articles in *Jugend*, whose program to renovate the arts extended to social criticism: the magazine called for "a rejuvenation of the liberal middle classes not just politically, but also psychically and aesthetically." Some had as their goal the transformation of the whole human environment, especially the home and the objects in it. In practice, however, *Jugend* concentrated upon the arts and *belles lettres*, leaving social and political satire to the other weekly, *Simplicissimus*. Even with her im-

---

* The most popular *tingel-tangels* featured suggestive songs performed by lightly clad young women.

perfect German, Mina could understand its cartoons, which took aim at both the self-satisfied bourgeoisie and the posturing artists. (Bruno Paul, a *Simplicissimus* contributor, mocked the fashions worn by artistic women: his "Munich Fountain of Youth" showed ladies with the erect carriage and conventional fashions of the Victorians stepping into an Art Nouveau structure and emerging on the other side in a series of contorted poses and fantastic garments.) The artists did not take themselves so seriously that they could not laugh at their own excesses.

The Schwabing avant-garde was a group apart. Many were in the process of cutting their ties to a mother country; their imaginative freedom seemed linked to their rootlessness. They painted, performed, and wrote for each other. But at the same time, they depended upon the bourgeoisie to buy their paintings: they were "advanced" only in relation to their less advanced audience. Debating their peculiar status in society, they held long discussions on the meaning of the term "decadence." Some, following the example of the English decadents, struck world-weary poses, while others took the view of *Jugend*, that a revival of youthful energies could regenerate society. It was hard to follow but exciting to be included. Although Mina felt too unsure of her German to venture into these debates, she was pleased when her new friends bestowed a teasing nickname upon her: they called her "Dusie," a name composed of the two pronouns (*Du* and *Sie*) between which she always hesitated.* She was one of them. She felt more at home with these easygoing foreigners than she had ever felt in London.

They also gossiped about local celebrities like Franz von Stuck, said to be an authentic genius.† During the past decade he had been knighted, named director of the Munich Academy, and paid enormous sums for his paintings—a success story like those she had heard in London about Alma-Tadema and Leighton. Like them, Stuck had a classical villa and designed each element—lighting, ornaments, and furniture—down to the last detail. The decorative allegories that had made him famous were, for the most part, titillating female nudes, with titles like *Sin, Vice, Sensuousness*, and *Medusa*. During Mina's year in Munich, Klee and Kandinsky attended Stuck's classes, but women were not admitted. While their male companions talked admiringly of the Decadents, their own art classes continued along traditional lines.

Opposition to the Schwabing spirit became apparent when issues of *Simplicissimus* suddenly disappeared from the newsstands: government officials had them seized on charges of libel, sacrilege, and obscenity. Catholic moralists, political conservatives, and anti-Semitic pressure groups saw both *Simplicissimus* and *Jugend* as advocates of the hedonism they identified

---

* Mina may not have noticed that her nickname was an emblem in miniature of the many internal divisions underlying her anxiety when speaking to strangers.

† Students knew Stuck as a Secessionist who achieved fame at twenty-five by winning a gold medal at the Glass Palace. At thirty-two, he was named director of the same academy he had challenged a few years earlier.

with modern art, as practiced in Schwabing. For the past decade, both modernists and conservatives had been following the central government's debates over the Lex Heinze (Heinze Law), a proposal to include in the definition of obscenity all depictions of the nude. And although this proposal had begun in a drive against prostitution, this social problem had been linked by the law's supporters to the idea of indecency in the arts, as practiced by foreign, particularly Jewish, artists—all those whose work was "not truly German."

By March 1900, when the bill came up for debate, intense opposition to the Lex Heinze had focused in Munich. Throughout the month, crowds met in protest, including prominent representatives of both the modernist and traditionalist camps. "Under the rule of the Lex Heinze," their joint resolution argued, "our Munich would cease to be a center of artistic and intellectual life—indeed, it would cease to be 'Munich.' " Soon the Bavarian regent himself was speaking against the proposal. Clauses implying cultural censorship were removed before the passage of the bill, leaving only the original provisions against prostitution. "In spite of the boisterous celebrations and sighs of relief in Munich's cultural community," notes an observer, "many artists realized that they had won a pyrrhic victory."

By April, however, the politics of art had given way to the easygoing rhythms of the Bavarian capital. One festival succeeded another; a continual celebration seemed to be in progress. Soon after Fasching came to a close, people talked of Maibock and planned trips to the country. There, even the poor dressed gaily and decorated their wooden houses with floral patterns in primary colors. It was not surprising that a tradition of decorative arts and crafts had developed in Munich. The spring *"Kunst im Handwerk"* exhibition went up at the National Museum, where a variety of objects from furniture to light fixtures seemed to have been inspired by the new curvilinear style. In the cafés some praised the beauty of form without content, while others insisted that form was successful only when it embraced function. Whatever one's belief, the distinctions between "high" and "low" art had collapsed with the triumph of *Jugendstil*. Soon Kandinsky was announcing in *Kunst fur Alle* that a new exhibition society called Phalanx would feature the young artists, those who were associated with neither the Academy nor the Secession. Submissions would be sent and judged anonymously, a principle that even the most progressive found "hypermodern."

Mina's new social life continued in a dreamy round of visits to outdoor restaurants, music halls, and rooftop studios. The advanced students all went sketching in the country, where they painted each other's portraits *en plein air*, in the French fashion. One evening at sunset, she recalled, they were ferried to a party on an island, on a barge hung with Chinese lanterns and brocaded draperies. Among their company that night, Mina recognized Fanny zu Reventlow, "the fair gräfin, superbly wan, bearing back to the barge at dawn her love-child asleep against [her] shift of red 'art muslin.' " Admiring this "notorious nymph-heroine" from afar, Mina also noted, as she later recalled, Fanny's crimson shift trailing "sodden in the mud."

Despite attempts on her own reputation, Mina had, by contrast, remained "chastely advanced." When she thought about Munich in later years, the Baron and Baroness had decreased in importance, *Jugendstil* had been absorbed into Art Nouveau, and Alexander was little more than a sympathetic suit of clothes. Yet her German year had contributed to her sense of herself—in the form of the nickname by which she was known for the next decade, and in her vision of a different family, the cosmopolitan artists with whom she had played at being modern. In her most telling memory, of a performance "at one of these art cabarets producing the compositions of the ultra modern," the year is condensed into a single image—a fallen woman singing a risqué song:

> I was a slip of fifteen years
> The most faultless, purest, ripest child
> When for the first time love beguiled me
> Learn how sweet his pleasures are.
>
> He took me in his arms and laughed
> Then whispered to me oh what bliss
> And then so gently lowered he
> My head toward the pillow's kiss.
>
> Now ever since I love you all
> My life is bright and brave.
> But when I can no longer please
> I'll turn to seek the grave.

Through Mina's association of the "art" cabaret with the prostitute, one glimpses not only the Baroness's attempt to compromise her but also the Schwabing debates on the new woman, the Lex Heinze, and the meaning of decadence.

"Safely unchaperoned," Mina concluded this section of her autobiography, "my year in Munich drew to a close." She had avoided love's beguilements, whose consequences, even in Schwabing, meant that a woman like Fanny, especially one with a love child, had to earn her own way. She considered the alternatives on the train to Ostend. This time she was traveling alone, her father having decided that she might do as she pleased. Although a small victory compared to the deal she had struck with Mammalie, it was a real one. But the velvet knickers and the penny pipe stayed where they belonged—in Munich.

— PART II —

BECOMING

MINA LOY

All I get out of life is the sensation of looking for something which has a
flavour of eternity.

—MINA LOY TO CARL VAN VECHTEN

Why should we look back, when what we want is to break down the mysterious
doors of the Impossible? . . . We already live in the absolute.

—F. T. MARINETTI, *The Founding and Manifesto of Futurism, 1909*

4

La Ville Lumière

(PARIS, 1900–3)

IF THE IMAGE of the fallen woman epitomized turn-of-the century Munich, an outrageous specimen of the opposite sex came to symbolize Mina's student years in Paris, which followed soon upon her return to London. Writing about Montparnasse decades later, Mina saw it as the domain of the art student she called Esau Penfold, whose style and affectations she had found disturbingly seductive. In reality, Esau Penfold was Stephen Haweis, a young English painter who, like herself, was bent on becoming a genius.

She saw him for the first time at art school. Shorter than average, Haweis compensated for his lack of stature with a peculiar intensity. To a contemporary observer, his "flashing black eyes, olive skin, and glossy dark hair, hanging down like a curtain about his head, gave him the appearance of a young Italian who had stepped from a picture of Raphael." This self-consciously arty young man not only wore his bangs cut straight across the brow like a girl but draped himself in scarlet sashes and amber necklaces—an unlikely costume even for a painter. Moreover, Haweis seemed to prefer the company of women.

While his cultivation of an androgynous modernity attracted notice, his behavior struck many as forced. Haweis (pronounced "Hoyes") flaunted his eccentricities, people said, because he had to live up to the reputation of his father, a fashionable London preacher of the last century. Despite his excesses, this strange little man piqued Mina's curiosity: here was an example of pure British privilege who deliberately defied convention. She could not ignore him. Watching Haweis labor over his drawings and listening to his cultivated voice, she tried to dismiss him as a poseur. But something about him preyed on her mind. "He had a famous name from his parents," she recalled in old age, when she spoke disdainfully—as if she still saw him hunched over a drawing—of her troubled relations with "this dark-haired little dwarf."

I

Of the years between Munich and Paris, Mina observed ironically, "I went home to England and stayed there for a few minutes." Munich had been an initiation into the avant-garde, the world of the déclassé, cosmopolitan artists who welcomed her once she took up the pipe, and had provided a set of images to try on like so many costumes; during her year there, she had been a fallen women, a femme fatale, a gamine, and a madonna. But in London she was again expected to play the dutiful daughter.

Mina was surprised to feel like a foreigner on her return. The brick mansions of Compayne Gardens looked unfamiliar, her parents' décor all the more ornately Victorian. What was worse, daily life was restricted to their corner of West Hampstead. A door key was out of the question. Julia, on holiday in the country, had left instructions that Mina was to remain in the morning room, where Ouida's novels were still locked away in the bookcase. The dense fog and the thick rows of trees outside the windows were her mother's allies, she thought. Everything, including the furniture, conspired to ensure her isolation: "An invalid chair in the corner, left over from Father's convalescence, had like himself still more broken down."

Within a short time Mina reverted to her familiar swings between listless passivity and energetic defiance. Disturbed by the change in her father, whose health had deteriorated during her year abroad, she feared that he had lost his zest for life as well as his appetite. He was so wraithlike that he appeared to be withdrawing from the material world. Yet while Mr. Lowy no longer envisioned brilliant futures for Mina and Dora, he was still obsessed with their reputations. Each day he told the same cautionary tales about "bad women."

Mina tried to make him see life from her new perspective. The prostitute played a part in the social system, she argued; it required her services as an outlet, "a sort of moral sewer." But rather than judge society, she believed, her father referred all such arguments back to herself. Attributing his attitude to his Jewish upbringing, Mina supposed that thinking of women as "unclean," her father feared that she would soil her reputation through her unfortunate new tendency toward strong-mindedness.

Soon after Julia's return, Mr. Lowy's nervous condition worsened. No matter how much the doctors reassured him, he continued to believe that his health was failing. Hypochondria had become a form of self-protection. Domestic tensions flared whenever Julia interpreted Mina's desire to pursue an occupation as proof of her selfishness. Mina, in turn, became enraged to find herself cast as the "disturbing element"; on occasion, her suppressed anger broke through her depression. Within a short time the independence of mind with which she had judged life abroad evaporated. "Since my return to my mother, the aching fog muffling my perceptions having a good deal lifted towards the end of my stay in Munich had settled in a permanent density," she observed of these years. "It was impossible for me to associate any event with what I thought of it," she went on. The old feelings of powerlessness engulfed her.

Mina began suffering from nerves, in sympathy, no doubt, with her father, as well as in response to domestic restraints. The diagnosis, neurasthenia—a catch-all term for a variety of psychosomatic complaints suffered by artistic or intellectual women and a few sensitive men—did little to alleviate, let alone cure, the condition. Outwardly Mina was plagued by headaches, respiratory problems, and generalized weakness, while inwardly she raged at the constraints of home. In later years, she would see conditions like her own as somatic responses to the "subliminal poison of the maladjusted home," but at the time the aching fog enveloped her.

Occasionally she roused herself from self-pity: "As sometimes neglected illness will put an end to itself, at intervals the sheer desperation of my being alive abated," she remarked, "clearing the way for spells of apparently rootless courage; when they occurred I became indiscriminately militant on behalf of myself or my sisters." During one of these spells, she persuaded her father that her sisters' schooling was inadequate, and he agreed to transfer them to an establishment that was not only coeducational but numbered among its pupils the children of well-known artists. Although at eighteen she was too old to attend herself, Mina chose her sisters' new school as if it could solve her own problems: "It recommended itself to me as likely to combat my parents' obsession [with] the peril of confronting the sexes, provid[e] topics of conversation other than my original sin, [and] cure my sisters' aesthetic of our 'interior.' " Delighted when Dora was chosen as the head pupil, Mina felt "certain that in [Dora] my father's vision would materialize." She imagined her sister "passing from the suburbs of the incognoscenti whose self respect is suspicion of one's fellows into that illuminated core of a metropolis." Somewhere in London there were people whose thoughts on social intercourse were as advanced as their taste.

But if Mina could imagine a brilliant future for Dora, she doubted that ten-year-old Hilda would defy parental and social pressures to grow up "normally British." Although she and Dora understood each other's devotion to art, to their baby sister Mina felt merely "related." Hilda had been born at a time "when already our queer urges toward occupation had convinced my mother we were socially hopeless," she noted, and Julia had barred Mina from playing with her baby sister, to save her from "moral contamination." While she could see the advantages of growing up with no goal beyond marriage, she still nourished the thought that somewhere there was "a world which unlike mine did not exist incognito."

Mina's London life was so uneventful that she began to feel as if she were immured in a cloister—"with a Voice which substituted speech for an absolute lack of knowledge." She yearned for more stimulating company. When Dora brought her favorite teacher to tea, Mina was delighted to meet this intelligent, well-spoken woman. Although the teacher's trained mind made Mina wince at her own inadequacies, she jumped at the chance to accompany her to a meeting of a philosophical society, where the ideas of Auguste Comte were to be discussed. Once there, she felt even more inadequate: she had never heard of Positivism, let alone suspected that there were different schools of thought on the subject. Yet another teacher took her remarks seriously. Her idea of the philosophical, she recalled, "that of remaining calm under an annoyance, was put to a severe test when I found it unavoidable to be seen home by this professor." Fearing the exposure of both her own ignorance and her parents' décor, she failed to invite him inside.

For the next few years Mina felt trapped between her desire to frequent the cognoscenti and her aching sense of inferiority. When her father's collapse left her without an ally, she became even more resentful of her family. In time, lacking occupation and believing herself unable to effect any change at home, she no doubt became the "disturbing element" that Julia took her for. After a period of unusually fierce hostilities between mother and daughter, Mina won the right to board with Mrs. Knight and Eva, her friend from the Wood—presumably Mr. Lowy's way of keeping mother and daughter from each other's throat. Mrs. Knight fussed about the proprieties nearly as much as Julia but, after seeing Mina's drawings, relented to the point of tolerating Mina's new distraction, cigarettes: "It may be right for anyone who can do anything so wonderful to be *allowed* to smoke." During this time, according to family legend, Mina studied with Augustus John, who by the 1900s had married, attracted critical praise, and opened a school in Chelsea.

Despite her father's anxiety about her lack of suitors, Mina believed that he still cherished the thought of her recognition as a genius. Seizing on this last hope for a life of her own, she begged to be allowed to study art in France. Everyone agreed that this was the only way, since English art schools did nothing to encourage individuality, particularly in women. Full of ambivalence, Mr. Lowy accepted the unthinkable—he would allow Mina to join Mrs. Knight and Eva in Paris. This decision suggests both his desperation and his courage in the face of Julia's objections. "In the first years of the twentieth century," a contemporary noted, "to say that a lass, perhaps not out of her teens, had gone prancing off to Paris to study art was to say that she had gone irretrievably to hell."

But hell was—from Julia's perspective as Mina understood it—where she and her father belonged. To some extent, she came to identify with him, especially in later life, when it was obvious that her talent as a designer of hats, clothing, lampshades, and a variety of inventions drew in some way upon his skills. She saw that, without his encouragement, she would have had neither the art training nor the compelling desire to identify with beauty, which also suggested his influence. Yet the nature of her emotional pact with him, the ways in which she was playing out his blocked ambitions, never became clear to her, no doubt because of the intensity of her animus against, and emotional ties to, her mother. It would not be an exaggeration to say that her character was shaped by the painful division between her paternal heritage, inescapably alien in the context of her upbringing, and her mother's evangelical perspective, in which anything foreign was to be cast out.

The Lowys said goodbye to their difficult daughter at the train station. Despite Julia's parting remark to Mrs. Knight—"Don't let her *speak* to a man!"—Mina imagined the romantic vision of Paris as represented in the illustrated weeklies—"flocks of fascinating women dressed by 'Worth,' a champagne music on the air . . . Brilliant acquaintances hailing us with a debonaire camaraderie." These daydreams occupied her during the journey to Dover, the Channel crossing, and the long ride to the Gare Saint-Lazare.

II

Soon they were driving past the Opéra, the Louvre, and across the Seine. Mrs. Knight had contracted for a furnished flat in Montparnasse, the new artists' quarter on the Left Bank: they were to reside on the boulevard Edgar-Quinet. While the location was convenient, the building's sooty gray façade proved something of a disappointment. In Mina's mind, Paris looked more like the "opalescent palaces" of fairy tales or pageants. "In my ignorance of history and architecture," she wrote, "my expectation of Beauty [was] still coloured by the 'transformation scene' whose civic parallels I was never to find until I had forgotten I had ever sought it." Having envisioned Paris as "a shimmering transformation pretty much like the epilogue of a pantomime," she found herself living opposite a cemetery.

Mrs. Knight's presence as chaperone no doubt had as much to do with Mina's disappointment as the blank walls across the street and the gray Parisian skies. Women artists were already studying there in increasing numbers, and many lived alone without outraging public opinion. Of this relatively new phenomenon a British journalist noted: "That the life they lead there differs from that led by their male companions, both as regards its freedom and its strenuousness, goes without saying; but it is sufficiently Bohemian for the most enterprising feminine searcher after novelty." Mrs. Knight's role was to serve as a reminder of the Lowys' opposition to the novelties of bohemianism.

Although many female art students boarded in family-style pensions, the more emancipated found their own apartments—like the spirited American painter Alice Woods, soon a friend of Mina's, who rented a large studio in order to work at home. But few could afford to hire models or had room for them to pose in their cramped living quarters. Most young women rented rooms in the studio complexes around Montparnasse and set up housekeeping on a modest budget. For the Lowys, such arrangements were out of the question for their nineteen-year-old daughter.

The English, basing their ideas of Paris on popular novels of *la vie de bohème*, generally imagined the French as a nation of seducers. Books like George Moore's *Confessions of a Young Man* and similar stories of free love warned of the dangers lurking in artistic surroundings. Moore's praise of Montmartre—"an exquisite mistress in whom I find consolation for all the commonplaces of life"—was just the sort of thing that worried respectable people. It did not matter that across the Seine female art students were leading disciplined lives: in the public's opinion they were little better than the prostitutes depicted by Toulouse-Lautrec. Years later, the painter Romaine Brooks, another of Mina's friends, recalled her adventures in turn-of-the-century Montmartre, where her attempts to earn a living included stints as an artist's model and a brief career as a music-hall performer—at that time the profession of the French writer Colette following her divorce. Artistic women left to their own devices had few choices once their financial support ran out.

Montmartre might be off limits, but Montparnasse looked safe enough. Although their neighborhood would soon be urbanized, in 1902 it was still a pastoral outpost on the edge of the city. Mina and Eva caught glimpses of the few remaining farms and vineyards near the Luxembourg Gardens, and even closer to their apartment, on the rue Delambre. Cows mooed at the traffic, a goatherd walked his flock through the streets each day, and grass grew between the paving stones. Montparnasse still kept many traces of the peaceful country life of the previous century, when Latin Quarter students first went there to refresh themselves at the rural restaurants.

The area would soon undergo rapid transformation. Work had just begun on the extension of the boulevard Raspail all the way to the Vavin crossroads, and the houses and shops of what had been a village were being replaced by multistoried modern buildings and artists' studios. Still, amid the construction, traces of village life survived. Just outside their door trained goats and dogs performed along with human entertainers at the outdoor market. A short walk up the boulevard Raspail, at the place Denfert-Rochereau, a fantastic population of animal trainers, sword-swallowers, and popular singers gathered in a permanent carnival. Wherever they walked, there were people quite unlike those one saw in London: artists sat on the pavement to draw with colored chalks, acrobats performed their feats, and laborers thought nothing of breaking into song. Of the Parisians' lack of reserve an art student noted, "There's a childish joy in living, in letting oneself go the way nature seems to like it best, without much concern about whether it is good or bad."

After a few days in Montparnasse, they explored the Right Bank, walking from "grands boulevards" behind the Opéra all the way to Montparnasse. The wide streets were dense with animated shoppers; the long vistas of the boulevards culminating in a variety of civic monuments formed an outdoor theater for the drama of Parisian life. The new Métro looked exciting, particularly when compared to the cavernous London Underground, since its tunnels were full of stylish posters. In the midst of the crowd, Mina found herself alone with her thoughts, free of the internalized Voice. "Walking along the street is for many the only assumption of freedom," she observed, "releasing us from our circumstantial identity when we 'go out' on the Boulevards."

The following weeks found her crossing and recrossing the Seine, watching the moiré shimmer of autumn light on the water and the subtle shades of gray playing across the wintry sky. She spent hours gazing at the trees lining the riverbanks, the intricate choreography of the boat traffic, the ferries with their varied cargoes, and the leisurely couples strolling by the Seine. She thought she would never tire of Paris. The nuances of light, shadow, and color that she observed on these daily explorations interested her more than the monuments: these new "impressions" held out the promise that she would be able to paint again.

The spectacle of Paris also included the picturesque subjects who crossed her path daily—the chimney sweeps, tinkers, scissors grinders, and glaziers passing through Montparnasse, each with his instruments and particular cry. People called out their readiness to mend dishes and cutlery, cane chairs, or show the latest in lampshades, while others begged to clean your windows. Their cries mingled with the songs of the artichoke woman, the purveyor of French fries, the herb vendors and fishmongers, which had been passed down for generations. One could find everything in the streets, from dog barbers to umbrella salesmen.

To those who knew how to look, the commercial posters, shop signs, and painted walls brought the gray streets to life. A walk through the more heavily populated areas offered an education in the latest products and styles. Brightly colored images proclaimed the virtues of mineral waters, tea biscuits, and digestive liqueurs or announced a range of events from the Winter Circus to the "Salons"—the official art exhibits held each spring at the Grand Palais. The most prominent poster style was called Art Nouveau or, more popularly, *style nouille* (noodle style), which Mina saw as a variant on *Jugendstil*. Its limp curves adorned Métro stations, restaurants, and the posters of Alphonse Mucha, whose perpetual springtime decorated wintry Paris in attempts to sell everything from soap to Sarah Bernhardt's *Hamlet*. (Struck by the magic of these "vermicellian Sarahs" as well as the actress's panache in a man's role, Mina "venerated Bernhardt as she turned on her ascent of a marble stairway to intone 'Etre ou ne pas être.' " By 1902 Art Nouveau was already in decline: anyone could adapt its floral aesthetic to the purposes of advertising, as Mucha demonstrated in his popular design classes. It was time to enroll at a school, to learn to paint some of the sights she had been absorbing.

III

Mina had arrived in Paris just a few years after it became possible for men and women to work together in any class, let alone in life drawing—where the question of the nude was on everyone's mind. Students and teachers still recalled the battles of the nineties, between the female artists seeking access to the academic art system—state-sponsored art classes, prizes, and exhibitions—and the male artists who resisted their advance. Although Frenchwomen already attended the Ecole des Beaux-Arts, they were still barred from competition for the Prix de Rome, the coveted award that assured official recognition following a year in Italy. In 1903, when they finally won the right to compete for this fellowship, foreign art students (who could not participate) rejoiced at the news. Not all Frenchwomen welcomed this opportunity, however. A successful academic painter doubted that "the female student who was kept at a distance from real art because of the nude model would accept the shared life of the Villa Medicis with young men" and declared, moreover, that no French mother would allow her daughter to be exposed to such a situation.

Foreign students usually enrolled in the popular art academies of the Latin Quarter or Montparnasse, where no entrance exams were required and women could choose among a variety of classes. All followed a similar pattern: an instructor known as the *maître* visited to give critiques, and a student monitor called a *massier* chose models, collected fees, and saw to the details of daily life. At the Académie Colarossi in Montparnasse, classes had been integrated for several years when Mina arrived, while the more conservative Académie Julian offered separate instruction for women, with three different studios "arranged to satisfy different sensibilities—one for drawing from the nude model, one for working from a draped model, and a third with a separate entrance and staircase, for those amateurs who did not even wish to glimpse a nude model." But the more experienced women artists felt that access to the male model, draped or nude, was not the most important issue: only their full participation in the academic system through membership on the salons' selection committees would put an end to hostilities between the sexes.

Since the general public remained uncertain about the motivation of women who asserted themselves, female art students met with considerable ambivalence despite, or perhaps due to, their victories. The controversial topic of women in art schools soon inspired a popular melodrama, *La Massière*, about the adventures of a female monitor whose *maître* fell in love with her. When a painting student at the Académie Julian was hired to play the leading role, caricatures of the piquant *massière* appeared in all the papers. The play ended predictably with the romance of the *massière* and the maître's son: her talent would stay in the family. Although women painters had won a more equitable status, their success was thought to depend upon their social standing. As in London, women were seen as amateurs who would either marry or become teachers.

The choice of an art school meant a great deal, since it put the painter who was not herself the daughter or wife of an artist in touch with her future mentors. Of the private schools, the Académie Julian reproduced most faithfully the discipline of the Beaux-Arts. If one wanted access to the most successful artists of the day, it was the place to enroll. The school's brochure prided itself on its segregated classes, where in "an atmosphere of impeccable character and advanced technical values," a woman could acquire "a professional attitude which, quite unlike the plague of 'amateurism,' has made these women's classes successful." But to a more advanced eye, it seemed that the women at Julian's painted "as if they hadn't seen anything that had been done since Courbet." Increasing recognition for women had come just as the academy system began to seem irrelevant.

Whistler's classes offered an alternative, provided one did not mind the adoration which prevailed there. His students not only copied the Master's work but dressed in his favorite hues—cobalt blue, yellow ocher, or Venetian red—gathered before Whistler's portrait of his mother as if in church, and murmured about its "mystery of color and line, exquisite maternity, charming conception, [and] quaint execution." Occasionally they amused themselves in parodies of fashionable attitudes: at a mock-decadent *bal d'ennui*, everyone wore sackcloth and ashes. Alice Woods loved to gossip about the excesses of Whistler's monitor, Miss Bates. The story went round Montparnasse about the day the Master's handkerchief dropped and a new student pointed to it with her paintbrush. Miss Bates retrieved the handkerchief and scolded the student: surely she had not expected the Master to stoop. Only the faithful felt at home in this rarified atmosphere.

Mina and Eva chose the Académie Colarossi for its informal tone, convenient location, and modest fees. At Number 10, rue de la Grande Chaumière, above a rabbit warren of studios, Colarossi's was open from six in the morning until ten at night. In the morning, students drew or painted the models who posed for genre paintings; in the afternoon, they practiced the quick, frequently changed sketches called *croquis*. Classes in watercolor, decorative art, and sculpture were also available, and these offerings could be supplemented with free instruction in anatomy at the Beaux-Arts.

English art students agreed that instruction in these academies surpassed anything at home, since the *maîtres* who critiqued their work did so chiefly to enhance their reputations. Colarossi students particularly admired Raphael Collin, whose allegories of subjects like *Music* or *Dreams*—classically draped females gazing heavenward—had earned him many state commissions. Much praised by his contemporaries, Collin was thought a genius. "His force and exaltation of temperament impresses one as being the rare gift or the finer inflorescence of character," wrote an admirer.

75

Other Colarossi masters included two students of Gérôme—the Orientalist artist Louis Girardot and Gustave Courtois—as well as the Czech Alphonse Mucha, who taught decorative arts, and the Norwegian Christian Krogh, known throughout Montparnasse as the tolerant husband of the emancipated Oda Krogh, a portrait painter.

In practice, Colarossi's was distractingly cosmopolitan. The Italian director, a former artist's model who had taken over the old Académie Suisse, where Courbet and the Impressionists studied, tried to maintain a certain tone: he cultivated the appearance of an aristocrat. Like the students at Whistler's, Colarossi painters dressed the way people imagined artists to dress. So many men sported long hair, velvet suits, and fluttering cravats that the swarthy little Englishman whom Mina noticed the first day took pains to distinguish himself from the rest with his sashes and beads. The women, dressed primarily in shirtwaists and plain skirts, concentrated on their coiffures: like Mina, many wore their hair parted in the middle and pinned in graceful chignons at the nape of the neck.

Although some students posed almost as much as their models, good-natured horseplay prevailed. Classes often ended with conversations in six or seven languages, imitations of cocks crowing, and mutual bombardments with the bread crusts used as erasers. Compared with the seriousness that prevailed in Munich, the atmosphere at Colarossi's was amateurish, Mina thought—a state of affairs that had a great deal to do with barely suppressed excitement over the presence of both sexes. Since the men's conversation often revolved around the topic of whether or not various women were *gentilles* (sexually encouraging), the initiation of a *nouvelle* (a new female student) involved considerable innuendo in the guise of advice. On her first day, one young woman was startled to find several men around her easel whispering "things you do not learn chez Berlitz." Trying her best to ignore their efforts to live up to their ideas of *la vie de bohème*, another noted, "What seems simply rowdy in the men immediately appears unattractive in the girls," before adding, "We do have it harder." It was especially hard to concentrate in life class, where the model posed "without as much as the grace of a gee-string." But Mina would not give up the freedom of these classes. Intent on coming to terms with "the liberative wickedness of the Ville Lumière," she found it "concentrated in the masculinity of the model in the 'cour de croquis.' "

Soon she began attending the night drawing class, where the level of accomplishment was said to be higher. The room stank of fresh paint, perspiration, damp raincoats, and unwashed feet, but the students worked tirelessly despite the unbearable heat. The reputation of the class quickly drew even greater numbers, as well as a higher quotient of eccentric behavior. Among the regulars in the crowded, stuffy atelier, Mina noticed Haweis, the little man who dressed so peculiarly but spoke with the most refined Oxbridge accent. He presented himself to the world as "the exotic, the blasé, the ever mysterious artist," she thought, but to her he was "the horror of the night class."

One evening when she could bear the atmosphere no longer, Mina splashed her face at the sink and dried herself with the one clean towel. Suddenly men were rushing past her to summon their friends, and crowds chattering in a variety of languages gathered around her: "It did not occur to me that this had to do with my cooling off until I learned that all the habitués of the night classes had been betting on whether my face was painted." Another student remembered her complexion as "so perfect that the students betted [sic] upon its truth and could not believe their eyes when a scrub of the studio towel left it . . . perfectly white." After this episode, Mina could no longer concentrate on her drawing, believing that she must be in the wrong for attracting so much attention.

Anatomy classes at Beaux-Arts also produced difficult emotions. The school's classical façade and solemn atmosphere dampened the Colarossi students' high spirits while they lined up outside the crowded amphitheater. Everyone watched attentively as the professor demonstrated the articulations of the bones with his plaster casts, skeletons, and the occasional cadaver. Their studies progressed by stages: one began with a cast of the knee, moved on to the professor's bone collection, and finished with the classical expression of anatomical correctness, a cast of a Dying Gladiator. The professor also demonstrated the science of physiognomy by explaining the contortions of the facial muscles which produced emotions such as terror and ecstasy.

Since Eva had warned Mina that the most disturbing aspect of this class would be her first glimpse of a corpse, she felt more than usually anxious as she made her way into the classroom on the day scheduled for this part of the program. She was stunned to learn that what she had taken for a wax model was actually the cadaver—"It was hung from an iron hook fixed in its cranium to a seated posture on a rickety chair," she recalled, "when the lecturer hurrying across the platform to specify a muscle lifted its arm and, on being dropped, that arm slid off the dead man's thigh." She steeled herself for their trip to the morgue, where students went to supplement anatomy classes. The corpses, mostly fished out of the Seine, "seemed still to balloon under a dim water" behind the protective sheet glass. Those who had read the poetry of the nineties opined that art was linked with mortality, but Mina did not share their taste for the macabre.

As in Munich, one could learn as much outside classes as in them, but the most interesting discussions took place in the cafés, where Mina was not to venture unchaperoned. The solution was to visit other students in their studios, since this kind of interchange was less likely to incur criticism. At first she met only a few British and Americans, among them Wyndham Lewis and Alice Woods. Occasionally they gathered at the inexpensive restaurants catering to art students, the Crèmerie Charlotte opposite Colarossi's and the Crèmerie Leduc on the boulevard Raspail. Such places had sand on the floor, warm stoves in the center of the room, and long tables where everyone ate together. Each had its habitués, who came not only because they could eat on credit but because they felt at home: the proprietors were waiters, cooks, and substitute parents. But for the most part, Mina put up with Mrs. Knight's approximations of English home life. From a distance she read about the glittering social whirl of the Belle Epoque. Of her first years in Paris she noted, "We lived on those extraordinarily unrevealing strata of a city open to those who have no 'connections.' "

IV

In time, Mina—at twenty already a great beauty—attracted the attention of the group she called "the British intelligentsia of Montparnasse." However contradictory her feelings about this privileged set, she was pleased to have been noticed. These Oxonians dressed in the "aesthetic" styles of the nineties—corduroys, flowing ties, and berets—and espoused the ideas of Oscar Wilde, as if a mild "dandysme" could erase their middle-class backgrounds. A Miss Benson at Colarossi's, who expressed her sympathy on learning of Mina's social disadvantages, invited her to meet Geoffrey Kane, the leader of their group. After the conversation turned to modern writers and Mina praised Robert Louis Stevenson, Kane sprang up from the divan on which he had been lounging to dismiss Stevenson as bourgeois. Miss Benson did not fail to report that while Kane thought Mina's was "one of the two most beautiful mouths in the world," he also thought her "an abysmal ass." The intelligentsia could rest assured that she was not worth knowing.

Some of this group amused themselves by dabbling in the occult. The most daring sought out Aleister Crowley, a member of the esoteric Order of the Golden Dawn and a self-appointed magician who roamed Montparnasse in search of recruits. That he had been disavowed by the London Golden Dawn chapter and dismissed as "an unspeakably mad person" by one of its most distinguished members, William Butler Yeats, only enhanced his prestige, since playing at black magic was an exciting way to defy one's parents without incurring much danger. To their interest in the black arts they added a slight knowledge of Bergson, tinged with an even slighter appreciation of Nietzsche. The result, colored by British snobbery, produced what Mina called "their somewhat sinister conviction of being supermannish." When Crowley began gossiping about his desire to know Mina, she feared the loss of her reputation—it was said that "no young thing could remain alone in the same room with him in safety."

For all their emancipated airs, it was clear that among her compatriots some standards were to be maintained. Mina's beauty was proving to be a handicap, and her sense of inferiority made her ill at ease. But if a woman was to achieve recognition, she had to be noticed by the all-male selection committees and art critics. Even if she had been bold enough to seek out those artists who were already rejecting the academic system, she could have shared in their camaraderie only in the most limited way. Like other middle-class women unprepared to defy convention, Mina found the interchange of artistic life in Paris largely inaccessible. She contented herself with secondhand accounts of what went on in the cafés, where the men met regularly to gossip and argue.

The heart of Montparnasse was the Café Dôme, at the corner of the boulevard Raspail and the boulevard Montparnasse. Although artists and foreigners were looked on with suspicion in the rest of Paris, the Dôme welcomed them. One could keep warm there when inadequate heating made it impossible to work at home, find friends more easily than by going to their official addresses, learn who was showing in which salon, as well as who was keeping company with whom. Reputations were made there during the ongoing discussions about the respective merits of the academies, teachers, models, and patrons.

Painters also devoted a large part of their conversation to the topic of women, who knew that during their rare appearances at the café they would be scrutinized from head to toe. Women, Mina learned, could be classified according to their headgear. The more complicated their hats, the more lavishly bestowed with veils and ribbons, the more bourgeois they were, and, for that reason, unobtainable. A woman whose head was uncovered was out of place there, since a female whose hair was loose was informing the world that she was available. It was a complicated code. On the one hand, the popular images of Mucha's posters proposed flowing lines as the ideal silhouette, while on the other, respectability required hats and high starched collars.

Fortunately, there were more relaxed forms of social interchange. On Sundays, especially in good weather, mixed groups from Colarossi's went boating on the Seine or the Marne, stopping to sketch in country villages and at outdoor restaurants. In nearby parks like the one at Sceaux, they could paint the yellow-gray reflections of the tall poplars lining the waterways and enjoy the peacefulness of the countryside just outside the great city. At the Luxembourg Gardens, a few blocks from the art schools, couples held hands on the benches around the central fountain or under the chestnut trees, and groups of artists sauntered along the formal paths, gazing at the palace, where they hoped that one day their own work would be shown.

As in Munich, there were parties in the studios, evenings when, more than the wine, youth and spring fever contributed to the high spirits. Often someone played a guitar or a mandolin while the costumed students waltzed in rooms lit by candles and Chinese lanterns or decorated with comic versions of the Classical scenes they had learned to reproduce for the academy. When the weather was fine, the party might continue out-of-doors, as at Mardi Gras, when Pierrots and Columbines bombarded each other with confetti, which lay on the paving stones like colored snowflakes.

There were also public concerts, which even Mrs. Knight could not declare off limits. Everyone went to hear the military bands in the Luxembourg Gardens. On the grassy slopes of the nearby Montsouris Park, free Sunday concerts drew crowds of workers, whom the art students sketched when they felt ambitious. In the relaxed atmosphere of these old-fashioned suburbs, they wandered past windmills and vegetable gardens, outdoor stalls and ambulatory merchants selling cheap food like mussels and French fries—the Parisian equivalent of fish and chips in London.

But most of all, Mina loved the concerts and dance halls of Montparnasse and Montrouge. Sometimes she went to the Cabaret Rouge on the rue de la Tombe Issoire, where the walls were painted a brilliant red and the garden planted with clematis. She preferred the Bullier dancehall at the place de l'Observatoire, the meeting point of the Latin Quarter and Montparnasse just opposite the famous literary café, the Closerie des Lilas. At the Bal Bullier's weekly *grande fête*, artists, students, and workers flocked through the huge Art Nouveau entryway into the illuminated groves and dancehall. White gravel walks led through the gardens to an artificial grotto where a statue of Venus was half hidden by the cascading water and colored lights flickered over the outdoor proscenium. In spring, the art students paraded there in their costumes all the way from Beaux-Arts, and on summer evenings, the dancehall resembled a Renoir painting, one of them recalled: "students and artists, handsome and merry in their stunning velvet suits and floppy slouch hats, and with their girls, some in their cycling bloomers, others in silk robes, and still others in summer blouses." The atmosphere was so contagious that Mina forgot herself and joined in the dance.

V

Another respectable English "girl," Madeline Boles, made overtures one day as she and Mina were leaving Colarossi's. Madeline came of a large ecclesiastical family and appeared to practice the Christian virtues. Studying her simple compositions, Mina concluded that her new friend was as straightforward as her paintings. Soon Madeline was explaining that better models were available than those who repeated the same poses at Colarossi's. She invited Mina to paint the model she had hired to pose in her meticulous studio. Another student would join them, and they would split the fee in thirds.

Mina was beginning to feel at ease when the third person burst in and flung off a long black cape. It was the horror of the night class. Although Mina found him physically repugnant, Stephen Haweis spoke beautifully. "It was almost as if a disinterested ear had listened for an English as it would speak itself, unmodified by any individual voice," she observed.

Stephen and Madeline, who knew each other through their families, liked to invent sacrilegious parodies while they painted. When Madeline intoned, "And the Lord spake unto Moses," Mina's self-consciousness returned. "To make mock & relieve myself of my strange pain, strange in that it functioned according to some cerebration of its own in my abdomen," she recalled, "I would, now & then, amuse my companions with my spontaneity in the woeful exclamation 'God forgive me for being alive!' " Excruciatingly aware of her hybrid background, she felt that while they could make fun of religious orthodoxy, she could only mutter excuses for her existence.

Stephen had noticed Mina's nervousness as well as her looks and talent. It soon became apparent that in the company of their compatriots, she also lacked confidence. As if she had no choice, she let herself be drawn into his circle—an unlikely blend of British dabblers in black magic, spinsters, and elderly ladies. Although she claimed to take no pleasure in these new acquaintances, she went along with their plans as if she had no will of her own: "Associates, like parents, were the appointees of fate. Fatefully they must seek me out and I defer to them gratefully for not having snarled at me." Apart from Madeline and herself, Stephen's lady friends were not an attractive lot. Because he "served as 'token' masculinity in their lives," Mina wrote, they did not see in his relations with them what she later called his "parasitic drawing-out of one's vitality to recharge, as it were, his own deficient battery of life."

Madeline surprised Mina by asking her to look after Stephen. It was her Christian duty, she insisted, since he could thrive only in the company of understanding females. Many found Stephen irritating because of his attempts to ingratiate himself with those whose allowances permitted a more luxurious standard of living. In *Edges*, Alice Woods's contemporary account of art students in Montparnasse, two women meet a man very much like Haweis: before striking up a conversation, they notice his amber beads, scarlet sash, and black bangs. Intrigued to learn that he prefers their company to that of his own sex, one of them accepts his invitation to tea because she is curious about men who go in "for making a decorative appearance." Although this may be a composite study of a Montparnasse type, it suggests that by the time Mina arrived Haweis was already known as a poseur.

Despite her aversion to the idea of looking after him, Mina went along with the plan. When Stephen wasn't making fun of religion or charming ladies who received monthly allowances, he held forth on "worldly success" and "sex." Chiding Madeline for her lack of sophistication, he expected more from Mina because of her year in Munich, yet despite his diminutive stature, she thought, he managed "to condescend to his listeners from a height." Madeline sent him off to accompany Mina when she did her shopping. Soon he was borrowing small sums of money from her: since she had promised to look after him, she observed years later, it did not occur to her to refuse. Moreover, Madeline was always proposing visits to Stephen's studio, of which she spoke with awe. As if it were out of her hands, Mina's social life soon revolved around Stephen. While the other British students now regarded her as one of his set, she persisted in thinking of their relations as accidental. "I began to be pressed by chance into my unfounded relationship with a mannikin," she noted. When Stephen invited her to his "dressing-gown party" (a current fad), Mina wore her real dressing gown, an aesthetic Liberty-blue robe that made her "look like a shadow among the oriental trappings of the other guests." No one had explained that this was another kind of costume party. After telling one of the Oxonians that his embroidered robes made a decorative background for their group photo, she worried that she had offended him. Ill at ease with her compatriots, especially those of privileged backgrounds, she seemed inevitably to say the wrong thing.

Stephen invited her to his studio as if bestowing an honor. It was one of several in a courtyard off the rue Campagne Première, a few minutes away from Colarossi's. When Mina recognized the courtyard as the site of her inept visit to Geoffrey Kane, who had dismissed her as an ass, her feelings of inadequacy deepened. She walked nervously down the stone stairway to the basement section of the cottage where Stephen lived. Her first impression was of polished wood floors and gleaming antique furniture.

Stephen began opening drawers full of family treasures. These relics were mementos of his mother, whose death seemed not so much a disappearance from his life as a dematerialization. There was the sleeve of the strawberry satin dress his mother had worn when presented to Queen Victoria, the train of which now lined Stephen's cape. There were place cards from his mother's dinner parties, inscribed with the names of important Londoners. Not only had Stephen saved his mother's clothing and amber beads (the ones he always wore), but he also venerated the objects that she had treasured. There were sewing boxes full of tiny heirlooms, mother-of-pearl daisies wound with silk thread, miniature patchwork quilts, embroidered baby clothes, a great-great-grandfather's copy book, an hourglass, and the leather hood that had once adorned the family falcon—with a wisp of gray feathers still clinging to its surface. Mina recoiled from the plaster cast of the hand of an uncle who had died in infancy and the Etruscan vase containing the ashes of his mother's dog. When he took out ancient balls of twine and started demonstrating arcane versions of cat's cradle, Mina felt as if she were attending medieval kindergarten.

But who was his mother and why did Stephen cherish her memory? Mary Eliza Haweis had been an arbiter of fashion during the 1870s and '80s. The daughter of Thomas Joy, a court painter, and the wife of the well-known Reverend H. R. Haweis, whose sermons at St. James Marylebone drew admiring crowds for decades, Mrs. Haweis had been one of the cognoscenti. Her magazine columns on interior decoration and fashion had offered sound advice for the aesthetically confused: she counseled readers to reject both the worst in Victorian fussiness and the silliest of the new "Art" furniture, in favor of simple, harmonious domestic settings. She had also tried to help the uninitiated adapt in their own dress the best aspects of the Aesthetic Movement. Her suggestions were practical, and her books—*The Art of Beauty* and *The Art of Decoration*—well illustrated with her adaptations of Pre-Raphaelite and Aesthetic designs.

Mrs. Haweis was also known for her literary adaptations. Stephen spoke admiringly of *Chaucer for Children*, in which his mother had retold and illustrated Chaucer's tales to make them suitable for Victorian readers. She had always been proud that, despite her earnings, she retained the status of a gentlewoman. Browning had come to call, as had Oscar Wilde. In the midst of Stephen's stories about his mother, Mina realized that she had once read Mrs. Haweis's Chaucer and envied the little son to whom it was dedicated—with whom she was now engaged in a *tête-à-tête*.

Mina was not impressed with Stephen's own talents. His latest portrait of a woman looked commonplace in its antique frame. "Her stiff white shirt-waist and tie, the neckless face forced into formless shoulder," she wrote, "compared too unexpectedly with the miniature beauties of the inherited trifles he had just been showing me." Yet she felt guilty about her critical judgment and, to compensate, promised to "be kind" after Stephen begged her not to abandon him. Taking her hands, he hinted at emotional frailties with damaging consequences. Stephen's constant dwelling on his psyche seemed to draw her into his vision. "He had nerves of steel, the steadfastness of the non-neurotic," she observed much later, realizing that, at the time, she had underestimated him. What was more, Stephen was his own favorite topic of conversation: he "liked to invent himself as languourously devastating," uttering such pronouncements as "I am a man who, should love come to him, would kill that love." Because she did not understand that he was only repeating the sentiments of the nineties, Mina "supposed his eccentricity to be the cause of his isolation."

Once they began to be seen together, Mina noticed a falling off of other invitations. Apart from his harem of spinsters and Madeline, whose visits became infrequent, he had few friends. Stephen thought most men unworthy of acquaintance with his mother's treasures, and they were, moreover, deaf to his requests for small sums of money. Mina told herself that it was her fate to be cut off from others because of her friendship with Stephen—"after those evanescent, invisible disgraces that all my life had attached to me at home."

By summer, Stephen had borrowed so much that her allowance nearly ran out before she could work up the nerve to ask him to repay her. One warm evening she crossed the boulevard Raspail and walked the block to his studio. When she explained why she had come, Stephen glowered, as if her request were proof of a base spirit, then taunted her with the gossip about her rendezvous with Aleister Crowley. Although Mina protested that she had never met him, Stephen kept repeating, "Whether you are lying or not, when a woman's reputation goes, everything goes." Then, changing his tone, he implored her forgiveness, a tactic that threw her off guard.

Paralyzed by Stephen's about-faces, which reminded her of her mother's emotional gambits, Mina found herself responding to his appeal for sympathy. Changing the subject again, he disclosed his family's secrets as the reason for his ostracism. The Haweises were not the pure Anglo-Saxons they appeared to be. One of his father's forebears, he told her in the racialist language of the period, had married a Hindu dancing girl in India, thus diluting their blood. During Stephen's adolescence, moreover, his parents' marriage had broken down. While posing as the model of rectitude to his admiring congregation, the Reverend Haweis had been leading a double life, and the mother of his illegitimate offspring had blackmailed him for years. Stephen shared his mother's sense of disgrace following his parents' separation.

If Mina was emotionally bound to Julia through the dynamics of their estrangement, Stephen was equally tied to his mother through his sympathy for her as an artist and a victim. Although her will left everything to Stephen, his father had forced him to make over a portion of this legacy. Stephen linked his emotional problems to these family dramas, which, he felt, caused his excessive sensitivity. He had already consulted an English doctor about an unnamed malady, which he took to be a kind of bisexuality: so great was his appreciation of the arts and matters generally reserved for her sex that he considered himself half man and half woman.

While Stephen went on with his self-absorbed explanations, Mina felt "as sullenly involved as with my mother's sadistic hysterics." She listened passively while he lit some incense and settled close to her, she recalled. Remembering her promise to be kind, she felt confusedly that "below this bona fide motive the habit of my mind, in spite of its unformed preferences, was seeking an excuse to slide relieved back into the deepened 'rut' of doing what it most disliked to do." The seduction scene that follows in her memoirs is lurid and self-exculpating: it reads like a chapter from one of the novels locked in Julia's bookcase.

Mina believed that she fell into a hypnotized state while Stephen read to her. Awakening the next morning, she found herself half undressed and Stephen naked beside her. He was a normal member of his sex, it appeared, and most anxious to demonstrate his virility. Afterward, she recalled, she felt nothing but grief. What she had been taught to fear as the worst thing that could happen had finally taken place. Since adolescence she had imagined the specter of lost virginity as painted by Rossetti—"a repudiated head-hanging female, creeping alone forever in the shameful shadow of a rainy wall, on the outside of the human confines." Walking home past the blank walls of the Montparnasse Cemetery, she felt like the incarnation of that image.

At home, Mina peered at herself in the mirror. She thought she saw an older woman with a deadened expression. On learning where Mina had been, an outraged Mrs. Knight threatened to pack their belongings and return at once to London, while Eva protested that she should not have to leave Paris just because Mina had spent the night with a "homosexual," and Mina worried that her parents would cut her off without a farthing. She wondered how she could live, whether she could bear to pose as a model. She would have to get her money back from Stephen, since it was he who had caused her disgrace.

When she saw him next, Stephen was in command of the situation. He could not repay her, and if she attempted to earn her living, she would sink even lower in the eyes of those who mattered. Didn't she understand that she had a stake in his future? The longer she listened to his account of their relations, the more Mina felt that they were bound together in mutual dependence. Stephen proposed that they follow the example of the Russian students in Paris, who often formed platonic unions (though theirs could no longer be quite that) in order to evade parental control. They could then lead separate lives, he continued.

On Mina's arrival in London for the August holiday, she was swept up in family drama. Dora had lost her confidence and become depressed. Her voice was failing, she believed, and she could no longer play the piano. Mina came up with a plan: Dora should leave home and earn her living by singing at private receptions and teaching piano. Dora's music teachers were enlisted in her attempt to make her sister see that domestic tensions were the cause of her depression. But Julia would not hear of another daughter leaving home. Soon Dora, too, was insisting that her problems "had nothing to do with her home life—it was physical . . . merely nerves." Following this burst of energy on her sister's behalf, Mina realized that she was not feeling very well herself. But when her father proposed a rest cure at home, she insisted on returning to France: "The physical horror of [Stephen] did not compare with the mental horror of that family life." Mr. Lowy gave her a floor-length fur coat and told her to look after herself.

Mina realized in Paris that she might be "enceinte" (the term used in her memoirs, as if it was as improper to say "pregnant" as to be in that condition). When a doctor confirmed her fears, she saw no alternative to Stephen's plan. But while she saw herself as the victim of circumstances, her autobiography also suggests a glimmer of self-knowledge. "Thus it came about that this weakened creature actually united in wedlock to the being on earth whom she would least have chosen," she wrote. "The marriage lasted for many years—a lasting arena for my efforts to be rid of him," the passage continues. "It seemed that what in others would have been normal resistance to objectionable events to me sunk even beneath the subconscious to an almost hysterical 'sporting interest' of getting out of impossible situations as if I had brought them upon myself in bursts of helplessness only to be matched by bursts of incredible and abstruse determination [to] dissolve them." It concludes thoughtfully: "If light and shadow are a law—I can fancy—the incredible depths of gloom I was forced into must be balanced by sparks of light—comparatively brighter than those experienced by the normal run of people."

When the Lowys arrived in Paris to meet Mina's fiancé, whom she described as the son of the distinguished clergyman, Stephen came to the station without his sash and beads. He had no intention of doing anything to provoke his father-in-law's opposition, and could not have guessed that Mr. Lowy was already predisposed in his favor—since, in his view, Mina was almost an old maid.

Mr. Lowy came to an understanding with his prospective son-in-law. Impressed with Stephen's faith in his future, he promised the financial backing needed to launch him once he was ready and, in the meantime, income. But this generosity came with a warning: "If we did not make out well together," Stephen recalled his saying, "this was the last chance he was giving his daughter, who had been a source of much trouble and anxiety to him." Taking Mina aside, Mr. Lowy informed her that since it was clear that no other woman would want Stephen, he would hold her accountable for any difficulties. If the marriage foundered, he would indeed cut her off without a farthing. Mina could not conceive of explaining the reason for her marriage. She had brought this upon herself in a characteristic burst of helplessness.

Even taking into account the natural desire to see one's motivation in the best light, there is something both incredible and credible about Mina's description of her relations with Stephen, the seduction scene, and her subsequent behavior. While she may well have become pregnant after one night in his studio, her complicity in the affair is not mentioned in her memoirs, which emphasize her status as one who was "pushed." Mina chose to believe that Stephen had taken over where her parents left off. "If anyone I disliked insisted upon my doing anything I was averse to," she wrote of herself at this time, "I would automatically comply, so systematically had they obfuscated my instinct of self-preservation." Rather than the plucky seventeen-year-old who had obtained her own front door key, Mina saw her twenty-one-year-old self as someone who was powerless to account for her actions. Yet her "bursts of helplessness" also served her purpose. By marrying, Mina arranged to jettison the past, and however odd their union, Paris with Stephen was preferable to life as an old maid —or an unwed mother—in London.

Mina told the story of her marriage quite differently in old age, this time emphasizing her agency and volition. In order not to go back to her "horrible parents," she explained, she had "arranged with this little dwarf, this dark-haired dwarf, the son of the parson, that we would get married but not *be* married." Although he accepted these terms initially, she continued, he changed his mind later, insisting that "if I didn't really belong to him he wasn't going to go on with the joke." In this account, a virginal

Mina makes all the arrangements, and it is her husband who lacks potency: "He had to try and possess me, but he couldn't do it." Their roles are reversed.

While it is unclear whether this later version sprang from a desire for revenge, a more mature but still partial understanding of her character, or from her dotage, it may be that the truth lies somewhere between these two very different fantasies—in her characteristic oscillation between passivity and control. What is clear is that both spouses entered into a marriage where each thought to have the upper hand. Neither would prevail.

5

"Café du Néant"

(PARIS, 1904–7)

THE WEDDING TOOK PLACE at the Mairie of the Fourteenth Arrondissement on the last day of 1903. It was a strange start for the new year: Mina
had just turned twenty-one, and she was four months pregnant. Without
knowing it, she was repeating her mother's story. Yet if everything had
happened as in a nightmare, she would have her freedom—at the cost of
sharing her life with Stephen, who no longer wished to treat their union
as a marriage of convenience. Proud of having captured such a beautiful
wife, he would not dream of going his own way. Mina liked to think that
Stephen had meant to ensnare her, as if her beauty, talent, and income
could make up for his deficiencies, and his snobbery played into her image
of herself as victim. While outwardly Stephen gave her to understand that
he did her the honor by bringing her into an old and illustrious family, he
was extremely proud of his "radiant, beautiful wife, who had been assid-
uously wooed by every man who ever saw her," he noted in his memoirs.

Things went badly from the start. Arriving in Brussels late at night in
a downpour, they found that the hotel at which they had planned to spend
their honeymoon no longer existed. Stephen was also disappointed to learn
that despite Mina's condition and her year in Munich, she behaved "as
though made immaculate by the power and care of some British middle-
class guardian angel." They were awkward with each other, and their
marital relations were unfulfilling. By the time Stephen learned something
about "this sex-business," he recalled, "the wear and tear on my wife's
nerves had tarnished the glamour." The other art students thought them
mismatched. "When she married, her husband, following past tables of
diners, often heard a soon-familiar whisper, 'And that's what she MAR-

RIED!" Stephen recalled ruefully. "I know that full well," he went on, "for I was her husband."

Mina spent her confinement in the basement studio on the rue Campagne Première. She continued to draw and paint, but persisted in her low opinion of Stephen's talents: she was not impressed by his skill as a copyist, the result of a training that emphasized Old Masters. His imitations of Watteau and Chardin were too ethereal, she thought, and his drawings, which reminded her of Beardsley, were tantamount to plagiarism. That her resentment of Stephen made it hard to judge his work objectively did not occur to her. Everything about him seemed diminished. Sketching his profile, she saw "the head of a sallow crow"; looking back on their marriage, she remembered feeling "as an eagle might feel impressed into service in the secret storehouse of a jackdaw." She had let herself be drawn into his world, which was being sustained by offerings from her own.

Stephen's opinion of their marriage was quite unlike Mina's. Years later, he still recalled "several amazingly beautiful girls in our Paris of the early 1900's"—Gudrun from Sweden, Signe from Norway, and Martha from Hungary. But Mina, whom he described as "half English, half Jewish-Hungarian," was by far the loveliest: her complexion was perfect, "her mouth was an incredible wonder and almost plum coloured." Still trying to fathom the contradictions of their marriage, he mused: "I married the most beautiful woman I ever saw, with fine ideals, a fine mind, one who could be a quite delightful companion—when she chose. But I have often wondered since if I ever was in love with her," he went on, "or whether I was only fascinated by her beauty, even more than by the charm of her conversation."

However mixed his motives, Stephen admired Mina's originality almost as much as her looks. "Of course there are always beauties where many young people of different nationalities are gathered together," he wrote, "yet some remain like planets among the stars, more radiant than others." To his mind, Mina had been a "planet," as notable for her imagination as for her talent. "It is not only for their beauty that these girls are to be remembered," he went on, "nor for their talent, though some of them were talented and one [Mina] was a genius. They marked the end of an era and created a new one."

In Stephen's view, Mina played a role in the invention of modern fashion, which, like modern art, started in Montparnasse. "The move towards simple clothes," he claimed, "began in the Quarter, and began chiefly because good corsets were very expensive, and the fashionable clothes of the time were not adapted to the life our girls led in the studios." Mina's particular genius was shown in her dress patterns, which helped inaugurate the new silhouette. Soon after coming to Paris, she rejected the hourglass figure of high fashion in favor of her own designs, made up in printed fabrics that draped softly over the uncorseted body (and were no doubt inspired by the "reform clothing" movement of Munich). Rather than wasp waists, lacy frills, and elaborate ruching, Mina's designs featured natural lines in daring colors—reds, oranges, and purples instead of the pastels of turn-of-the century good taste. These simple dresses in turn influenced designers like Iribe and Poiret. Others copied her in the meantime: "There were lovely girls in 'Poiret' dresses for a couple of years before Poiret risked any capital," Stephen recalled. "His first creations were to me recognisable as . . . Mina's last year's frocks."

While Mina waited for spring, when she would give birth, Stephen prepared for the April Salon, organized by the Société Nationale des Beaux-Arts but called (after its former exhibition grounds) the Salon du Champs de Mars. Like their counterparts in Munich, the modern French artists had formed this exhibition society in protest against the official Salon, administered by the Société Nationale des Artistes Français. By 1904, the new Salon listed some of the most interesting modern artists among its members, including Auguste Rodin, Eugène Carrière, John Singer Sargent, Maurice Denis, Aristide Maillol, and Jacques-Emile Blanche.

During the 1900s, artistic success came chiefly through exhibition societies and their salons. These organizations provided artists with the opportunity to be shown, make contacts, and eventually achieve recognition. After several years of showing at one salon, one might be made a *sociétaire* (permanent member) and have work hung without its having to be chosen by a committee. Although Mina did not fully understand the selection process, Stephen did. He knew which were the popular genres: allegorical female nudes, domestic scenes, historical subjects, or Spanish, Italian, and Oriental studies. By 1904, however, the importance of the decorative arts had begun to blur these categories, and the more radical artists rejected genres altogether.

Mina's stylized drawings would be well received at the new Salon, Stephen thought. But nothing seemed to matter to her now that she was growing slower in her movements. Stephen, who was more ambitious and more worldly than Mina acknowledged, intended to keep in touch with those who could help him. Before they met, he had studied with Mucha when the Czech artist was at the height of his fame. His ubiquitous posters were the best advertisement for the "Cours Mucha" at Colarossi's—a course of applied composition where students learned to adapt Mucha's techniques to media like stained glass, ceramics, goldsmithing, and jewelry. Mucha had chosen Stephen as his *massier* and later recruited him to help teach his summer courses in Brittany.

By the time Stephen married Mina, he knew his way around the art world well enough to imagine ventures of his own. He chose a different medium, which was not yet recognized as one of the fine arts. With another Englishman, Henry Coles, Stephen took up photography—an art form that had fascinated him since childhood, when a print by his parents' friend Julia Margaret Cameron hung in his nursery. Coles's training in chemistry provided the technical knowledge, to which Stephen added his Art Nouveau aesthetic. Working under artificial light and retouching prints with a brush, he produced dreamy portraits and romantic landscapes. The firm's lucky break came when Stephen obtained an introduction to Auguste Rodin.

By the 1900s, magazines throughout Europe and America had publicized the sculptor's prodigious personality on such a scale that Rodin became the world's most famous living artist. He was also a worldly success. Society figures and heads of state flocked to his studio, and the Master was surrounded by admirers, as well as the many artists hoping to profit by the connection. (With less than his usual shrewdness, Rodin had been so moved by a sonnet of Aleister Crowley's on the sculptor's bust of Balzac that he invited Crowley to write a poem for each of his masterpieces.) Rodin distrusted art dealers but sometimes allowed photographers to help sell his work; he had recently granted Stephen permission to photograph his latest sculptures.

Between 1903 and 1904, the firm of Haweis and Coles produced over two hundred photographs of Rodin's work. In December 1903, a few weeks before his wedding, Stephen was already showing some of these studies, along with his woodcuts, at the English Church bazaar, while still others hung at the Berlin Secession. Soon journalists began taking an interest in Haweis and Coles. Not only was Stephen's portrait of Rodin "the most exquisite study that has yet been done of the great sculptor," according to the *Pall Mall Gazette*, but the Master himself likened it to a Tintoretto and judged it as fine as the work of the American photographer Edward Steichen. Haweis and Coles used only the most costly printing techniques, Stephen told the reporter, in order to produce photos with "something like the quiet harmony and balance of Whistler's painting." "I want a man to come to have his photograph taken in the same spirit (and be prepared to pay a good price for it)," he added hopefully, "as he does when he is having his portrait painted."

To some, the Haweis and Coles photographs of Rodin's sculpture were even better than Steichen's. An agent for the newly formed Pathé film company urged Stephen to devote himself to the "kinematograph"; the Paris *American Register* reported that the firm had "aroused the enthusiasm and interest of both critic and public." Continuing in the overwrought style thought appropriate to art criticism, the reviewer gushed, "The Camera is as pliable as the brush in their practised hands, and the secrets of light and shadow are to them as accessible as the colours on the painter's palette." In their Rodin portrait, one saw "light and shadow manipulated after the metier of Rossetti or Burne-Jones and approaching remotely, yet distinctly, the manner of Rembrandt." A portrait of "Miss L"—surely Mina—also won praise, as did photographs with Whistlerian titles like *White Fan* and *Crépuscule*. The writer predicted that society ladies would soon seek out the rue Campagne Première studio.

It became common practice to distinguish the work of Haweis and

Coles from standard reproductions of Rodin's sculpture by calling them *photographies d'art*. Stephen often photographed at dusk in Rodin's garden in Meudon or created lifelike effects by shooting a sculpture detached from its base, as if the form were about to spring into life. Typically, in his photograph of Rodin's *Walking Man*, taken slightly off-center, the statue seems to be striding through the night. He also painted misty aureoles around the works in the manner of Eugène Carrière—a source of inspiration for both the Master and his pictorialist photographers.

Stephen's hopes were buoyed by his unexpected success with Rodin and his circle. The dancer Loie Fuller took his photographs to New York for an exhibit of Rodin's bronzes; the Master planned to include Stephen's work in an article devoted to his work by *Paris Illustré*. Stephen soon devised his own plan for a "poetic and photographic exhibition" in Paris, to include his best Rodin photographs and Crowley's poems. By 1904, the art photography of Haweis and Coles was so well launched that viewers were unsure whether they were seeing original works or reproductions.

When not engaged with the Master, Stephen liked to photograph his beautiful wife. His portraits of Mina were every bit as aesthetic as Holyoak's five years earlier but decidedly more commercial. During the early years of their marriage, she grew accustomed to striking poses: he photographed her as a painting come to life. The most dramatic of these studies, taken in 1905, shows her in an old-fashioned dress with leg-of-mutton sleeves trimmed with lace. Mina leans toward the camera, as if about to swoon or fall from the barely glimpsed Art Nouveau chair on which she sits. Her hands are clasped in meditation, her eyes closed as if to shield her from the spectator. The pose evoked the Pre-Raphaelites, while implying that a photograph with the harmony and balance of fine art was, as Stephen had said, worth a good price.

Mina became her husband's favorite model. Several photographs taken in their studio show her as a work of art—a Symbolist painting or a Rodinesque sculpture. In one, in which she wears a simple peasantlike costume, she leans forward in three-quarter profile with a small Rodin sculpture in her hand; in others, her eyes are modestly cast down, in variations on the Pre-Raphaelite pose. Stephen kept two rather surprising portraits for his private contemplation. The first, a languid profile, shows Mina smoking—a provocative gesture for a young married woman in this period. The second is even more surprising: it shows her entirely naked, although demurely photographed from behind. In the hip-shot pose of classical statuary, Mina stands slightly off-balance on a Persian rug, her left side framed by richly patterned draperies and the cascade of her thick black hair—the unseeing center of an artful composition, a studio nude.

Mina's silence on this aspect of her life with Stephen is intriguing. She may have been so absorbed in pregnancy that she took little interest in his career. Possibly she was envious and not a little annoyed at his success. Probably she resigned herself to her role as beautiful object, the subject of portraits but not the maker. The belief that through marriage she had won some measure of independence proved illusory. She became increasingly dependent in the later stages of pregnancy, while his contacts multiplied.

The more progressive British artists often turned up to visit Stephen and his beautiful wife. George Moore appeared with Walter Sickert to take the couple to dinner. Moore, who had known Manet and Degas as an art student, had tried to enlighten the British establishment about French art but met with little success—particularly once his first novel, *A Modern Lover*, had to be withdrawn from circulation. The Haweises treated Moore with respect. "He was a celebrity," Stephen wrote, "but some of us rather enjoyed the off-hand, friendly contempt with which Walter Sickert treated him." Sickert, who had also studied with Degas, warned young artists against the reverse snobbery of the art world. "With his loud checked sporting clothes, and a small, ridiculous bowler hat, greenish with age," Stephen recalled, Sickert "looked far more like a bookmaker than an artist." Stephen was aware, nonetheless, of Moore's status as a critic and of Sickert's influence in the New English Art Club, the only London gallery to sponsor French-influenced art.

Before he married, Stephen had also met a number of prominent Belle Epoque figures—the people whose exploits were described in the illustrated weeklies. Santos Dumont, an aviator who became the toast of Paris, showed up to have his portrait taken, as did French aristocrats like the Princesse de Breuilly and her dandified friend, the Vicomte d'Humières. They in turn brought the writer Willy and his wife, Colette, already known for her scandalous Claudine books—for which Willy took credit. Willy looked like a caricature of the stage Frenchman, Stephen recalled, while Colette was "the most vitally alive woman it was ever my privilege to see." Colette's name was already synonymous with "naughtiness" because of the play made from her books in 1902: Claudine had been played by the half-Algerian actress Polaire, who dressed like Colette's twin—a publicity stunt concocted by Willy in order to spread rumors about the supposed relationship between his two "girls." When Colette invited Stephen to a party where "half naughty Paris was gathered" and introduced him as Polaire's brother, he felt out of his depth in such sophisticated company.

At Rodin's Stephen met a man named Meyer, who said that he, too, took photographs and asked to visit his studio. When Mr. Meyer showed up at the rue Campagne Première and bought a photograph, Stephen wondered about him, since his clothes were too shabby for a man who could buy what he pleased. Mina insisted that he must be "someone." "Coming to a studio in this quarter is 'slumming' to him," she exclaimed. "The clothes were suitable to the occasion but you never saw boots like that on a photographer!" She was not surprised when he proved to be Baron de Meyer, a society figure and patron of the arts, who would soon prove useful to Stephen.

Stephen felt honored when Rodin gave him a letter of introduction to his friend Carrière, whose portraits of his wife and children were considered masterpieces of tender feeling. Rodin and Carrière often sought inspiration in each other's work: Rodin's *Mother and Dying Child* sculpture echoes Carrière's numerous *Maternité* paintings, where, typically, a mother gazes sorrowfully at her child in anticipation of some disaster she is powerless to prevent. Stephen studied the expressive atmospheres that had made Carrière's name and worked to refine his own depiction of form, which, Carrière explained, must be painted as if "entirely surrounded with liquid air." Stephen did not take Mina to meet these giants of the art world but let it be known that she, too, had an unusual ability as an artist.

Although less sentimental than the English, French critics responded to displays of tenderness toward the weaker sex. Women were more likely to achieve recognition if they produced specimens of *la peinture de femme*, although it was not clear what constituted this feminine mode of painting. Subject matter alone did not indicate the artist's sex, as Carrière's studies of women and children seemed to demonstrate. Carrière's genius was evident in his paintings of his wife and children, Rodin believed; motherly love "was all he needed to be sublime." But while a man who painted motherly love might be called a genius, such sentiments were seen as the natural outcome of the female temperament.

Moreover, the critics admired women painters who used Impressionist technique to depict domestic life. A female neo-Impressionist had shown the influential critic Roger Marx "how well the very principle of Impressionism responds and adapts itself to the basic inclinations of the feminine temperament," he explained. But what defined the feminine temperament? It arose, another critic argued, from "a vision of the world that we feel is quite distinct from our own, lighter, more flowing, more gentle, such as it must exist, more or less, in the eyes of a woman"—such as one saw in the paintings of Berthe Morisot. Only a woman could practice pure impressionism, the critic continued, since "the essence of woman is not to bother herself with the deeper relations of things, [but] to apprehend the universe as a graceful, moving surface with an infinite number of nuances, and to give way inwardly to the adorable succession of her fleeting impressions." It was unfortunate, he concluded, that in later life Morisot had "tried to give to her figures the outline and the energy that she admired in the works of the masters." Judging by the terms of this "definitive" account of Morisot's art, Mina's willed passivity was a posture which the art world encouraged in women artists.

Mina had also heard of Elizabeth Nourse, an American painter who not only achieved official recognition but, unlike Morisot, managed to support herself. Although Nourse's genre scenes were regularly shown at the new Salon, the *New York Herald* described these highly professional products as "intimate little scenes" painted "with an emotion that is always true and which communicates itself perfectly naturally"—because the artist was female. But despite her success, Nourse was not a model for those who were alert to the artistic currents of the 1900s.

Confined to the studio and the rue Campagne Première, Mina drew what she found around her. She painted the domestic furniture in studies entitled *Objects* and *La Guitare*, as well as the domestic climate and her own self-absorption in *La Dispute*, *Devant le miroir*, and *La Mère*, possibly a self-portrait. Throughout the year, she concentrated on studies of women in interiors, reflecting on her restricted place in the world. Perhaps this was a difference between a *peinture de femme* as practiced by women: a woman's eyes might look with empathy upon the female figures of their studies, while male artists more often saw them as set pieces that might or might not arouse their desires. A man might see the model as his possession, while a woman was more likely to see her as someone like herself. Such issues, implicit in the idea of a *peinture de femme*, were ones to which she would return a decade later in both poetry and painting.*

In April, when the baby's birth was imminent, Stephen was more than usually busy. Some of his latest Rodin photographs were on display at the Master's gallery, and more were being sent off to Düsseldorf. He was also preparing for the new Salon at the Grand Palais, where his oils and engravings would be hung. With Rodin and Carrière among the founding members, it was important to make a good showing. Stephen came home from the opening full of gossip. He admired Carrière's most recent portraits of mothers and children, and several of their neighbors from the rue Campagne Première also had work on display: François Boquet showed a case full of decorative *objets d'art*, rings in the shape of astrological signs and glasses decorated with mythical creatures, and Rose Fuchs exhibited an embroidered tablecloth, ceramics, and hand-painted fans. But most of their friends thought the applied arts demeaning. Their neighbor Eugene Ullman, who had married Mina's friend Alice Woods, continued to show his oils and was now a member of the Salon's selection committee for paintings.

As Mina awaited the day when she would actually experience motherhood, Stephen's praise of Carrière's *Maternités* may have seemed ironic. Following a painful labor that lasted through the night, she gave birth to a girl on May 27. Stephen took no interest in the event, she believed. Whatever actually took place, she never forgave him for visiting the woman she took to be his mistress while she suffered through labor. A decade later, after she began to publish poetry, her analysis of this experience in "Parturition" was seen as shocking, no doubt because its rhythms recreated the contractions and expansions of childbirth:

* This view supposes a degree of identification that a woman artist might not always feel. On occasion, Mina also used historical or regional costumes to emphasize her separateness from her subjects. A definitive account of her artistic practice during this period will have to wait until the many drawings and paintings listed under her name in Salon d'Automne catalogues are recovered.

> *I am the centre*
> *Of a circle of pain*
> *Exceeding its boundaries in every direction*
> *The business of the bland sun*
> *Has no affair with me*
> *In my congested cosmos of agony*
> *From which there is no escape*

Between contractions, the woman ponders the man's indifference: "The irresponsibility of the male / Leaves woman her superior Inferiority." In the final stages her resentment evaporates: "something in the delirium of night hours / confuses while intensifying sensibility / Blurring spatial contours . . . pain surpassing itself / Becomes exotic." Unexpectedly, labor becomes the process of "knowing / All about / Unfolding," and the moment of birth, an "elusion of the circumscribed . . . a leap with nature / Into the essence / Of unpredicted Maternity." But it would take years to give shape to the idea of childbirth as orgasmic, a "lascivious revelation."

There were practical matters, such as naming the baby. While a son would have to carry on the Haweis tradition, they could be more original with a girl. Stephen chose Oda Janet, which was unconventional enough for both of them. For the foreigners of Montparnasse, this name evoked the Norwegian painter Oda Krogh, the wife of Christian Krogh—the Kroghs had a studio a few streets away from the rue Campagne Première, and Christian was one of the most popular instructors at Colarossi's. Oda was even better known than Christian. Her husband did not interfere in her love affairs because he believed that women should have the same rights as men. "Oda" hinted that this child would be brought up in the spirit of Montparnasse, while "Janet" made a slight concession to propriety.

For some time Mina was overwhelmed by the birth and all that had led up to it—her peculiar relationship with Stephen, the way in which she backed into marriage, and the months of sluggish domesticity that followed. At first she adapted her life to the baby's. By late summer, when Oda's schedule had settled into a predictable pattern, Mina again felt strong enough to paint. The few hours she had free between feedings, naps, and strolls in the Luxembourg Gardens helped to organize her time. Stephen encouraged her to prepare for the Autumn Salon, where Carrière would preside. He planned to try his luck there and urged her to do the same.

Because the art dealer had not yet come into being as such, the Salon remained the most important artistic institution, especially for a foreigner —for whom recognition in Paris enhanced one's reputation at home. But acceptance by a Salon often meant that the artist had internalized the academic system and its institutional approach to art. When the Salon National des Beaux-Arts broke away from the official Salon in the nineties, it did so to offer an alternative to this perspective. But already by the 1900s, the new Salon seemed tied to the old ways of doing things. When the next new Salon—the Salon d'Automne—opened its doors in October 1903, it appeared to be thumbing its nose at the two spring Salons. The respected critic Elie Faure applauded its rejection of genres and bold espousal of "the confused order of life." The Salon d'Automne was, he wrote, "a spiritual garden, where all the mingled flowers had the natural harmony that light, space, and the secret rhythm of things bestow on the street, the sky in motion, the monotonous plains, the sea, the crowds." Through the practice of yearly retrospectives, its organizers honored their predecessors—experimentalists and "primitives" like Stephen's new idol, Gauguin, whose retrospective was held in 1903. Stephen liked to think that he and Mina were part of this fresh new approach.

Once Mina resolved to enter the Salon d'Automne, there was the question of her name. Should she show as Lowy, take Haweis, or adopt a different surname? Some years later, Mina claimed that she had chosen Loy rather than Haweis "in a spirit of mockery, in place of that of one of the oldest and most distinguished families of England." This account disguises the fact that she had been uncomfortable with the name since childhood. Since her mother already slurred their name to make it less foreign, Mina simply elided the telltale *w*, a move that simultaneously protected her against anti-Semitism and provided a cover. In another account of this name change, Mina told her daughters that she first thought of using Loy in Munich, where she had seen the name on a shop window: in Paris, she was now asserting, however ironically, that she would be a law (*loi*) unto herself.* She would soon invent another version in which the letters *L*, *O*, and *Y* formed her insignia and, throughout her life, would rearrange this self-appellation in anagrams and other verbal disguises. Like her nude image in Stephen's portrait, this surname suggests the tension Mina felt between concealment and revelation of her innermost self.

The Salon d'Automne exhibited six of her watercolors, including one entitled *The Mother*, under her new name. She was no longer one of the "incognoscenti." She had begun to "appear." Having her work shown at the newest Salon brought Mina out of her self-absorption; the other foreigners took a renewed interest in her. She had taken the first step toward recognition.

However odd they might appear as a couple, she and Stephen became intent upon establishing themselves as "fine" artists. Apart from the Kroghs, their few married friends did not frequent bohemian circles. Unlike their friend Eugene Vail, an American whose wife's income allowed him to dress well and maintain bourgeois standards, the Haweises went out of their way to be noticed. A French friend recalled being astonished by them "because they dressed so differently from other people and were still under

---

* She may have also been thinking of Charles-Auguste Loye (1841–1905), who was well known in England for his drawings and watercolors.

the influence of Oscar Wilde." Stephen looked like a dandy, Mina wore clothes "that were going to be in fashion a little later on, as one would see in *Vogue*." Her father's daughter in that she believed in the importance of good design, Mina appeared at openings in her graceful Poirets, antique beads, and fanciful hats trimmed with flowers or feathers. "Because of her elegance," their friend observed, "she was someone you simply could not fail to notice."

That autumn Stephen became even better known as a photographer. The Salon d'Automne showed his portraits in a special section devoted to this new form, while at the same time others were on display at the Galerie Moderne. Mina's time was divided between her duties as the wife of the young artist-photographer who was herself a talented painter and her private life as a mother. A sketch of her drawn at this time (perhaps a self-portrait but more likely done by Stephen) shows a confident woman facing straight ahead, her eyes wide open: at that moment she seemed to know where she was going. The following year, Mina had two watercolors accepted by the 1905 spring Salon des Beaux-Arts, which took only one of Stephen's paintings, and she enjoyed appearing at the glittering Grand Palais.

She was surprised that she cared so much for Oda. As the baby grew, Mina came to love her as she had never loved anyone—as if she could make up for the love she had not received from her mother by lavishing affection on this tiny version of herself. She was a graceful child with huge violet eyes. Mina studied her movements: "She had a way of making shadows dance upon the wall by turning the exquisite wrists of her outspread hands—watching them gravely as if to time them to some eternally remembered measure." (The "hidden blood" of Stephen's ancestor had resurfaced in their child, she believed.) When Oda became ill, Mina worried but believed that she would recover. She felt increasingly helpless as she watched the little girl grow worse. Oda died of meningitis two days after her first birthday, and Mina nearly went mad with grief. Yet her response to the death of her daughter leads one to speculate about the meaning of motherhood in this period—about her absorption in her own highly aestheticized sensibility.

Mina later told a friend that she had stayed up all night after Oda's death, pouring her grief into the dark-toned composition that she called *The Wooden Madonna*. This tempera painting, now lost, showed two very different women with their infants, an angry figure and a serene Madonna—a "foolish-looking mother holding her baby, whose two small fingers are raised in an impotent blessing over the other anguished mother who, on her knees, curses them both with great, upraised, clenched fists, and her own baby sprawling dead with little arms and legs outstretched lifeless." In its refusal to take comfort in orthodox piety, the painting was a bold reply to the fatalistic *Maternités* of Carrière. Characteristically, Mina structured her composition around a tension—between the promised consolations of divine motherhood and the pain of her loss. At the same time, her painting transformed Oda's death into a representation of her psyche.

Mina's health was particularly bad in the months that followed; she may have suffered a nervous collapse. It did not help matters that Stephen had to disband his partnership about that time. According to their contract, Haweis and Coles were to have their prints stamped by Rodin's official photographic agency, to whom they paid a commission on top of Rodin's royalties. To show a profit, they had to sell photographs at ten francs, a high price in an uncertain market. They had accepted these terms in hope of future benefits, but by 1905 their earnings came to less than one franc per print. Despite their critical success, the contract proved so onerous that they could no longer stay in business.

Mina and Stephen lived modestly on her income from her father and concentrated on work for the next Salon d'Automne. Disillusioned about his future as a photographer, Stephen intended to perfect his printmaking. When Mina felt stronger, she forced herself to concentrate on her draftsmanship, to keep from thinking of Oda. Apart from what she had expressed in *The Wooden Madonna*, she could deal neither with the pain of mourning nor with her knotted emotions.

The politics of the art world offered some distraction. In September a delegation from the Société Nationale des Beaux-Arts tried to have the Salon d'Automne ejected from the Grand Palais. When Carrière, who belonged to both groups, threatened to resign from the older society if its members kept harassing the "radicals," the conflict was settled. But the controversy over the 1905 Salon d'Automne had just begun. At the opening visitors were scandalized by the raw colors and throbbing brushstrokes of the oils in the central room. One observer called these paintings—the work of Matisse, Derain, Van Dongen, Rouault, and Vlaminck—"a riot of color—sharp and startling, drawing crude and uneven, distortions and exaggerations—composition primitive and simple as though done by a child." Because a neo-Renaissance sculpture stood in the middle of the room, the critic Louis Vauxcelles quipped, *"Donatello chez les fauves"*—implying that classicism had fallen among the wild beasts. Crowds gathered before two portraits by Matisse, all but unknown at the time: one showed a man with a blue beard and a yellowish complexion, and the other a woman in a large black hat shot with oranges and greens. (In the sea of people, Mina may have noticed the Americans Leo and Gertrude Stein, who stood gazing as if transfixed at Matisse's portraits.)

It was a strange moment. The so-called Fauves had not planned an assault on tradition. At a time when many were searching for alternatives to academicism, their new perspective had appeared almost by accident. It did not matter to Mina that her own submissions looked tame by comparison. She had become engrossed in her rivalry with Stephen, which was exacerbated when the committees announced their selections. Stephen had three paintings and three etchings accepted, while Mina showed four drawings, all portraits of women. Worse, her drawings went unnoticed, while *Art et Décoration* praised her husband's "reminiscences of Whistler . . . exquisite little variations, in antique rose, gray and celadon blue."

Since Coles was to keep the rue Campagne Première studio following the dissolution of their partnership, Stephen and Mina had to find a new home. She was not sorry to leave the basement studio. They found lodgings near the Kroghs on the other side of the boulevard Raspail, which brought them closer to the Dôme, Colarossi's, and the hub of Montparnasse. But by this time the Haweises had little in common except the life of the Quarter and their professional ambitions.

The strains in their marriage became more pronounced with each Salon. As if in reaction to the Fauvist riot of the previous autumn, Whistler's influence pervaded the 1906 Beaux-Arts spring Salon; strolling through the Grand Palais, one saw numerous studies of feminine figures shrouded in mist and small, harmonious landscapes with musical titles. Again, the critics called Stephen's work "Whistlerian," an epithet that did not displease him, while they failed to notice Mina.

She finally caught the attention of the critics in the 1906 Salon d'Automne. The *Gazette des Beaux-Arts* singled out "Mlle Mina Loy who, in her uncommon watercolors where Guys, Rops and Beardsley are combined, shows us ambiguous ephebes whose nudity is caressed by ladies dressed in the furbelows of 1855." What set her apart from the ubiquitous "Whistlerians" was her original use of a subject and style derived from the decadents of the nineties—their suggestive sexual ambiguity and their love of detail. The critic was particularly taken by the work entitled *L'Amour dorloté par les belles dames* (later known as *Love among the Ladies*). In this sophisticated, ironic composition, Love is an effete Pre-Raphaelite who swoons in the lap of a fashionably dressed woman. She in turn bends over him in a pose that parodies the traditional Madonna and Child, since here the Infant is equipped for adult male sexuality. Yet despite his anatomy, Mina's Love also suggests the androgynous figures of Burne-Jones and depends quite literally upon the woman for support. Three other "ladies" surround the central group: on the left, the one kneeling above them shows a sharp Beardsleyesque profile. A fourth woman, turning away from this scene, sits with her arms folded on an intricately patterned ball which resembles a globe, a world on which she meditates while this ambiguous reversal of sexual roles takes place behind her.

While *L'Amour dorloté* satirizes the conventions of Mina's art training, it does so in ways that contemporary critics were not prepared to recognize—despite its obvious reversal of the sexual dynamics of Manet's *Déjeuner sur l'herbe*. (Similarly, her poetry would employ the very conventions which she sought to critique.) Here, instead of offering the female body as the site for the deployment of male fantasies, as artists had always done, a defenseless male body is displayed—for the contemplation of the "ladies" within the composition and those outside. And it appears that Love is losing strength in the company of these solicitous females. One is tempted to guess that it was Mina's reversal of sexual roles which the *Gazette*'s critic found "uncommon," given his enthusiastic response to Carrière's latest *Enfant malade*. "One feels a sort of élan which is held back by a maternal tenderness that is even stronger than her anxiety," he gushed. The idea of a love so strong that it could suppress its own fears was more reassuring than Mina's subversive approach to the subject.

When the Salon d'Automne closed, Mina received an invitation to become a *sociétaire* of the drawing section. Membership not only meant that she could exhibit without having to submit her work to the selection committee: she could also join this committee, attend annual meetings, and consider herself to have been accepted by her peers. She was elated. Although she still felt at a disadvantage intellectually and socially, this vote of confidence was an exceptional mark of recognition for an unknown Englishwoman of twenty-three.

At this point, had her life not taken a different turn, Mina might have gone on to establish herself as a minor Post-Impressionist whose drawings showed a distinctively witty approach to artistic tradition. But her spirits soon followed the familiar pattern. Once their Montparnasse acquaintances began talking about her success, self-doubt returned to plague her. Perhaps she had not deserved the honor, perhaps she would never do anything as good. Moreover, her health was far from robust. The damp climate aggravated her respiratory condition, and the constant irritation of life with Stephen told on her nerves. The doctors explained away such conditions by saying that neurasthenia was the lot of artistic women.

Thrown back on herself, Mina turned increasingly to her self-presentation—to the creation of a mannered self-image corresponding to the stylization of her art. For his part, Stephen took to behaving in public as if he were a figure out of Baudelaire or Swinburne, or from one of his own etchings, recently described as "mysterious and perverse." Mina dealt with her emptiness by dressing as exquisitely as she could. Both had internalized Wilde's notion of the genius and adopted the veneer of sophistication expressed in his famous *mot*—"I would rather be a work of art than own one."

Looking back on their marriage, Stephen saw that his fascination with Mina's beauty had not provided a basis for understanding. To a mistress with whom he had a more satisfactory sexual relationship he confessed that he and Mina had been incompatible from the start: "With you I was not the failure I had been with my poor, over-inhibited, unprepared spouse who had been neither told nor taught anything." In 1906 Stephen and Mina agreed to live apart in order to keep their marriage from degenerating into what Stephen painfully recalled as "an estate of wholly acrimony." He went to live with his mistress while Mina maintained appearances in the studio.

These marital arrangements contrasted with the free-love credo of couples like the Kroghs and the nonconformist household of Augustus John, who had settled in Paris. John lived with his two wives—Ida, the legal spouse, and Dorelia, the third member of their *ménage à trois*—and their many children, all apparently cohabiting in harmony. "There was no wrangling and jealousy between those two beautiful ladies," Stephen observed. "They had the supremest indifference towards what anybody thought of their domestic arrangements." But Mina was not indifferent, nor would she have dreamed of living as poorly as Augustus's sister, Gwen, who remained in Paris as a model after falling passionately in love with Rodin; she wore her poverty proudly, "like a wreath which gave the finishing touch to her costume," Stephen noted. But this was not a costume that Mina could see herself wearing.

About this time she met the flamboyant Bulgarian artist Jules Pascin, who was said to have learned to draw by sketching prostitutes. When not at Colarossi's, Pascin could be found at the Dôme, thinning his colors with seltzer water and darkening them with coffee grounds. He lived intermittently with the illustrator Hermine David—who would become one of Mina's closest friends—in the sort of free union that the French called a *collage* or a *ménage à la colle.** While everyone in Montparnasse accepted the couple, Mina could no more see herself in a relationship that had been "pasted" together than garbed in poverty. Nor could she forget that she must maintain the façade of marriage in order to receive her income.

During her separation from Stephen, she nevertheless drifted into a relationship with Henry Joël Le Savoureux, the sympathetic French doctor who treated her for neurasthenia after the death of Oda.† Attracted to the informality of foreigners, this young man had often visited the Haweises on the rue Campagne Première. Since he, too, possessed an artistic temperament, he took "art" photographs of Mina, Stephen, and their friends, and they traveled to the Alps together. Mina continued to see Le Savoureux, especially in times of crisis. In the autumn of 1906 their relationship grew more intimate. They became lovers.

Although their liaison resembled Stephen's, Mina worried that her husband would not agree to a separation. Divorce was out of the question, since any impropriety meant the end of her income. An oblique passage in Stephen's memoirs evokes the bitterness he felt about the doctor's attentions. "As I recall the names of French artists, or indeed artists of good standing of any nationality, I do not seem to remember many that were

---

* In *Collage,* Harriet Janis and Rudi Blesh explain the term as follows: "The word collage is derived from *coller* (to paste or glue) and means pasting and, by extension, that which is pasted. The name, like the pictures, had carried a shock, the word collage having the slang meaning of an illicit love affair."

† Le Savoureux, born January 5, 1881, was the son of Joël Le Savoureux, a former French consul. Le Savoureux was on the staff of several Paris hospitals and contributed to both medical and literary journals.

conspicuous for their dissolute life," he began. "In their youth artists may be a little wild, but probably even their youth compare favourably with the youth engaged in other professions," he went on. His anger surfaces in the following sentence: "Medical students who become the guardians of our wives and babies as soon as the magic formula of doctorhood has been pronounced over them have a reputation for wildness, and I do not know why the godly should pick on artists for their sins."

To complicate matters, Le Savoureux, who had no money of his own, was engaged to a woman who had been chosen by his parents and whom he felt obliged to marry. Mina had reached a dead end: the romantic vision of her art-student days had proved to be an illusion. A bitter poem entitled "Café du Néant"—which was not published until 1914—hints at her state of mind eight years earlier. In the imaginary café where the poem is set, lovers gaze at each other over tables that resemble coffins, their eyes "telling of tales without words / And lies of no consequence." At the center of the composition sits a woman who "As usual / Is smiling as bravely / As it is given to her to be brave." Both the subject matter of the poem and its composition, with its strident hues—"the blue powder edge dusting the yellow throat"—suggest the melancholy, enervated vision of Degas.

Despite her election to the Salon d'Automne, Mina was deeply discouraged. At openings she studied the splendid clothes and self-assured manners of the *beau monde* figures who entered the Grand Palais as if the huge glass structure, the artworks, and the artists were all part of an enormous stage set. She read about people Stephen had known, Baron de Meyer, Rodin, and Colette, who had left Willy and was now acting in vaudeville. She may also have heard about the Saturday evenings at the home of Leo and Gertrude Stein, where one saw Matisse and Picasso along with people of all nationalities, but she would not meet this eccentric pair for another five years. She would never become "known" in Paris, yet she was too much her father's daughter to abandon her hopes.

The winter was cold and depressing. Little sunlight found its way into the studio, and Mina's neurasthenia worsened. When she realized that she was expecting her lover's child, she gave way to despair. Stephen "presented himself as an outraged husband," she recalled, "to whom I owed immeasurable amends." She offered him half her income in return for a divorce; he threatened to inform her father of the truth if she left him. Stephen finally wore down her resolve, she wrote: "He had one weapon for which there was no possible shield. Any allusion to the dead child, the child he had scarcely noticed, revived that kind of madness her death had brought me to—making my mind more cruelly confused." Guilt combined with self-pity tortured her like "some terrible Golem of doom shattering my aspirations." Stephen could not do without her two hundred pounds, he insisted. Rather than separate, they would resume their marriage as if nothing had happened. Once he declared himself ready to recognize the child, Mina knew that she was trapped. "Society accepts any child born in wedlock so long as it is not repudiated by the husband," he told her. Despite Le Savoureux's willingness to abandon everything, she was caught between Stephen's resolve and the "determining impasse of the financial situation."

The façade of respectability was more easily maintained by putting Paris behind them, Stephen believed. They would settle in some place where his name was known. He had long had in mind the idea of moving to Florence, where the English residents were people of taste who appreciated fine art. Life in Italy would combine the highest social and artistic standards with a favorable exchange rate, and the climate would be better for Mina's health. Besides, no one in Florence knew their history. When a friend told Stephen that he could have her small villa outside Florence for the remainder of the lease, he made plans to leave as soon as possible.

6

Anglo-Florence

(1907–10)

AS IN THE PREVIOUS CENTURY, travel to Mediterranean parts resolved a variety of dilemmas. Families needing to flee from scandal, wards whose guardians opposed their wishes, couples wishing to fudge the dates between marriage and childbirth, all sought refuge in Italy, where in time their faults could be expunged. One could remake one's reputation there; a prolonged immersion in Renaissance culture was seen as purifying. And while these unwitting colonists often re-created expatriate versions of England, they also became more tolerant of deviations than they might have been at home. Eccentricity was admired in Florence—provided it showed the mark of a cultivated mind.

Like most English people, Mina imagined Italy bathed in a golden light, as depicted in the murals at the restaurant above the Gare de Lyon, where she and Stephen awaited their departure. But when she awoke the next morning, what she saw through the train window bore no resemblance to the rose-colored scenes of the restaurant. A blanket of snow covered the ground all the way from Milan. Arriving in Florence, they found it colder than Paris.

The station buzzed with confusion, like a badly directed play with a cast of liveried servants and disgruntled travelers. Once Stephen and Mina had retrieved their possessions, a horse-drawn carriage bore them through the city, across the Arno, and beyond the walls to their villa in Arcetri. Mina was dismayed to learn that they were to live in the country: the Villino Ombrellino might have been in Switzerland. From their windows one saw villas hidden behind high stone walls, olive trees bordered by dark cypresses, and in the background, the mountains to the south. In their little villa, whose distinguishing feature was its tower, Mina felt like a princess imprisoned in a turret—with her husband as jailor.

Her first concern was how to keep warm. Florence was unusually cold that winter, and Arcetri offered no neighborhood cafés. Ladies did not venture into such places, although they often met at the tea shops on the via Tornabuoni. English visitors often found the heating worse than inadequate. Inefficient braziers were expected to warm the large, empty rooms of Florentine buildings. On days when the *tramontana* wind seemed to blow through the walls, servants brought *scaldapiedi*—brass foot warmers filled with embers—but these did little to throw off the chill.

Life in the Anglo-Florentine community resembled an endless round of tea drinking. Mina tired easily during pregnancy, and she was reluctant to accompany Stephen on visits. Here, everything seemed to happen more slowly and at a greater distance than in Paris. Arranging Stephen's furniture in the vacant rooms, she recalled their cramped quarters in Montparnasse. The Tuscan light might be preferable to the grayish air of Paris, but their *villino* symbolized her removal from civilization to solitude. Only the daily procession of donkey carts winding their way down the hill reminded her that Florence was nearby.

Fearing that Mina might go back on her decision and bolt, Stephen watched her closely. He tried nonetheless to modify his tone now that he had the upper hand. Some very nice people would take an interest, he assured her, if she would make herself known to them. He began a series of visits to his family connections, who proved to be artistically inclined Englishwomen of independent means. Their patronage would help Mina as well if she wanted to show her work. But whenever she accompanied him, her self-consciousness returned, as well as her resentment at having to listen to the same anecdotes about Stephen's parents. At twenty-four, she found it maddening to be put in the position of a child: new arrivals were to wait until residents passed judgment on them. In the cold *villino*, Mina pieced together a mental map of Anglo-Florentine geography, which featured not so much the monuments as the impressive villas inhabited by the expatriates.

Florence had long been known as "the only Italian city with a strong English accent," noted Harold Acton, himself a resident. During the previous century, travelers from Paris had called it "an entirely English city, where the palaces have almost the gloomy darkness of London and everything seems to smile on the English." Specialized guidebooks listed English bankers, doctors, churches, and tea shops, as well as resident British artists. The English were so much a part of Florentine life that "the term *Inglese* [sic] was applied to foreigners in general," Acton recalled. "A hotel porter would say to his manager, 'Some *Inglesi* have arrived but I haven't yet discovered if they are Russians or Germans.'" Although Florence was known for its international art colony, the English claimed the city as their own.

Mina and Stephen were taken up by the imposing Mrs. Ames-Lyde, who lived in one of the Arcetri villas that Mina studied on her walks. An amiable woman whose girth was emphasized by her silks and laces, Ethel Ames-Lyde, it was said, looked very much "like a fat, old George Sand." Six months in Florence nourished her for winters in England, where she made wrought-iron objects in her foundry. A woman of strong passions for food and friendship, Mrs. Ames-Lyde enjoyed the company of artists, especially if they had good manners. But while Stephen told her tales of life in Montparnasse, Mina kept silent, not knowing what to make of a woman who was a blacksmith half the year and a giver of tea parties the other half. Mina's self-absorption kept her from enjoying these visits. In Florence, she believed, her disadvantages glared more obviously than in Paris—particularly under the scrutiny of those whose pedigrees excused their peccadilloes.

Stephen's ideas of their new life blended his mother's recollections of the Brownings with Victorian poeticizing about the Renaissance. He and Mina would begin over again in more favorable circumstances. They would become another celebrated couple, burning with the hard, gemlike flame thought appropriate to aesthetes. On a more practical note, Stephen had heard of the growing influence of Bernard Berenson, the Anglophile American connoisseur who lived in the Villa I Tatti, on the road to Settignano. And there were other well-to-do residents whose pursuit of art might extend to encouraging artists like themselves. His adaptations of the Old Masters would strike the right note in a milieu where distinctions between the *trecento* and *quattrocento* were of the utmost importance.

The foreign colony at that time resembled a costume party where everyone tried to look like a famous painting. Even those of modest means contrived to look picturesque. The new century had not yet taken hold there, Acton observed: "An atmosphere of Ouida lingered, and the Guelphs and Ghibellines had been replaced by rival schools of art-historians." The scandalous Ouida, whose novels Mina had been forbidden to read, was recommended as a guide to the secret spell of Florence. To be accepted as a person of taste, one had to demonstrate one's susceptibility to this spell, since unlike the Parisians, who loved everything modern, the Anglo-Florentines worshipped the past.

Only very occasionally was their nostalgia criticized. When the novelist Arnold Bennett visited Florence at this time, his compatriots' attitude disgusted him. Dismayed by "the[ir] sublime, unconscious arrogance," he mocked the residents' desire to "possess themselves of another age and genius, and live in it as conquerors, modifying manners, architecture, and even perhaps language!" For such people, he wrote, "Florence is a museum and nothing but a museum." The rest of Florence had "not occurred to them." For relief, Bennett turned to the opera, the cafés, and the pleasure of watching the noontime spectacle of shopgirls, children, and street hawkers. Like Bennett, Mina thought it foolish to treat the city as a museum.

The lively, pleasure-loving Italians were too interesting in their own right to be regarded collectively as servants or peasants.

Yet a sense of the past was useful if one wanted to understand the present. Here, too, Ouida offered guidance. Newcomers learned that *Friendship*, her *roman à clef*, explained the feuds of expatriate Florence in the nineties—which were still simmering a decade later. The hateful "Lady Joan" of Ouida's novel was Janet Ross, Ouida's rival for the affections of a Florentine nobleman. Still a powerful force in her seventies, Mrs. Ross had been the muse of the writers George Meredith and Arthur Symonds. Moreover, her artistic credentials were nearly as good as Berenson's, a status which helped her to traffic in "Murillos" and "Peruginos." An astute businesswoman who marketed her homemade vermouth in the best London shops, she also applied modern theories of viniculture on her estates. In the midst of these activities, she published art books, memoirs, and a collection of her cook's recipes. Like Mrs. Ames-Lyde, Janet Ross struck the note of energetic eccentricity admired in Anglo-Florence.

Mina also heard a good deal about Lady Paget of Bellosguardo, the inspiration for several of Ouida's heroines. Lady Paget was a woman of sharp intelligence and commanding social presence. Having restored her own villa, she too was writing her memoirs. Like Janet Ross, she was remarkably energetic, dividing her time among the study of Theosophy, her tapestries, her dachshunds, and her activities as a cobbler: she was known for her medieval-style slippers of silk and velvet, the sort of footgear appropriate to someone who called her autobiography *In My Tower*. Lady Paget reigned over Anglo-Florence like a remote dowager in an inaccessible fortress.

One also heard stories about recluses in the hill towns. Violet Paget, a writer who wore her gray hair cut short above a collar and tie, was called the duchess of her district—perhaps to distinguish her from Lady Paget, to whom she was not related. Under the name Vernon Lee, Violet had published *Studies of the Eighteenth Century in Italy* and *Miss Brown*, a satiric novel on aesthetic circles in London. Currently at work on a theory which explained the difference between the Good and the Beautiful, she offered to teach Stephen to write. When he called at her villa, he found her "surrounded by a somewhat terrifying company of ladies"—her acolytes, often seen in "more or less Botticellian poses, all breathing an aura of acute Renaissance." New arrivals were also told about the owner of the Villa Gamberaia—the Princess Giovanna Ghyka, who lived in seclusion with her companion, Miss Blood. Miss Blood might be "brutal and vulgar and wicked," Berenson was heard to observe, "but she isn't commonplace." One might do anything, provided one was not commonplace.

Florence was also a refuge for those with something special to hide. Following the Oscar Wilde trial, Stephen noted, "it acquired an unenviable reputation through the influx of many who thought themselves in danger, and anybody was liable to the suspicion of what the French call 'moeurs un peu spéciales.' It was often asked of the newcomer if he was . . . or was not," he continued. "I heard one lady describe a man as 'perfectly all right,' and prove it by saying that not only had he been married, he had even run away with another man's wife!" People told stories about the two Reggies—Reggie Temple, who copied the paintings in the Uffizi, "even putting in the blemishes, the flyspecks and the wormholes," and Reggie Turner, who was such a good mimic that when he repeated Wilde's bon mots, "it was as if Oscar's spirit had taken possession of him." Although both Reggies dressed conservatively, the more outré Gino Sensani appeared in public with his face painted green, a habit that did not deter an English spinster from installing him in her palazzo, where, Mina noted, "they gathered round them a scattering of expatriated bachelors deeply attached to their furniture." In this atmosphere, it was understood that "he who treads tactfully may keep one foot in society and one in Fairyland."

Most refugees from the Wilde scandal avoided Sensani's flamboyance. Reggie Temple complemented his pale-gray shirts with Florentine handkerchiefs in mauve or lavender and bound his books in rose-colored chintz. "One would have thought him all sensibilities and delicacies," a contemporary remarked, "but his extreme sensitiveness ran off into its opposite." Given Reggie's mildness, Mina was surprised by the cruel tales he told about his aunts, whom he kept "on his well-dusted anecdotal shelves, like china effigies." Although he mocked the race of aunts as enforcers of prissiness (as would E. M. Forster), Reggie was not immune to snobbery. Writing him up as "Bertie Lavender" in her portrait gallery of residents, Mina noted that despite his low opinion of Queen Victoria, he boasted about the aunt who had been her lady-in-waiting.

Residents with modest means imitated the eccentricities of these social arbiters. Nearly every English resident planned to write a book on Tuscany, and many did, although, as Acton observed, most were "naïve priggish volumes." Few English residents adapted to local customs. Having learned only the rudiments of Italian, they made it bend to their needs—just as they taught their Tuscan gardeners to grow English flowers among the formal box hedges. In the same way, rambling roses were made to appear among the wisteria, and wicker chairs were planted upon the lawns, as if Edwardian England had been imported wholesale. When Mrs. Keppel, King Edward VII's mistress and a longtime resident, announced to her gardener *"Bisogna begonia!"* (the two words pronounced to rhyme), he did his best to cajole the English flower into an expatriate life among her flower beds. By the time the Haweises arrived, many residents on reduced incomes were painting, writing, and gardening in their *villinos*. The modestly endowed felt fortunate when invited to tea at the grand villas, where one enjoyed exquisite pastries, gossip, and exchanges of information on antiques, all going on amid the appreciation of the "view."

Mina rarely appreciated such occasions. She could not stop thinking about Le Savoureux, who continued to write, or tormenting herself about her acquiescence to Stephen. She missed the Paris cafés, the openings, the stimulating life of the great capital. She longed for the democracy of the art studios and the ease with which she had come and gone. To make matters worse, Stephen rarely left her alone. Self-pity mingles with rage in her account of this period: "Deprived of her art, her sex, her maternity, her intellect, and her comfort, Ova [Mina], an artificial monument of neurosis erected upon his nothingness, rose before him in the inertness to which he had reduced her—and he found her ripe for the imprint of his peculiar mastership." She had ceased to be Mina Loy; she had been reduced to being Dusie Haweis. Her career was finished, the fabled charm of Florence left her unmoved. Not only would she not "appear," she was receding into the background of her own life.

When the intense cold gave way to spring, Mina took a halfhearted interest in the scene around her. Stephen had found a studio for rent on the Costa San Giorgio, a bracing walk down the hill into a densely populated area of Florence called the Oltr'arno. From his studio it was a short walk across the Ponte Vecchio into the heart of town. While most English residents could be found having tea at Doney's or Giocosa's—Ouida's favorite haunts—artists and intellectuals of all nationalities gathered a few streets away at the Caffè Giubbe Rosse, where Stephen took Mina on occasion. The café's antique mirrors, fin-de-siècle murals, and spirited conversations in a dozen languages reminded them of Paris. They often caught glimpses of the Florentine writer Giovanni Papini, known as a *stroncatore* —a polemicist who pulled other people's opinions to pieces. At the café, the unofficial headquarters of his newspaper, *Leonardo*, one saw him engrossed in discussion with contributors. Although this group exchanged a few words with foreigners, it was hard to find subjects of mutual interest.

The Haweises had more in common with other English residents who preferred town to villadom. One of the first people they met at the Giubbe Rosse was the stage designer Gordon Craig, better known in Florence as Isadora Duncan's lover. When Craig settled in Florence, he had thought the inhabitants "serious—much at ease, they seemed, not earnest, not enthusiastic—just serious, quietly learning each one his craft or art and talking very little about it." In this disciplined atmosphere, he believed, he would find the respect for the arts lacking in London. Of all the artists who frequented the café, Stephen seemed the most interested in his idea of a radically new theater. Soon they were comparing notes about the lives they had left behind. Craig boasted of his successes at the Hampstead Conservatory and the Shakespeare plays he had staged for his mother, the actress Ellen Terry. Still angry that these artistic triumphs had been commercial flops, he raged against the philistinism of the British.

That spring, while Mina suffered through her pregnancy at home, Stephen often walked along the hill roads to Craig's villa in San Miniato. Craig had enlisted him in the effort to illustrate his idea of a new theatrical space with movable screens in place of stage sets—a concept which, in Stephen's view, might take shape in a series of etchings; for this reason, he was initiating his new friend into the subtleties of drypoint. In June, Craig moved to a nearby villa on the via San Leonardo, where he planned to build a model stage, and often sought Stephen's help with the plates for his new drama magazine, *The Mask*.

Mina found Craig's relations with Isadora Duncan far more interesting than his plans to modernize the theater. Their affair, begun three years earlier, had so far weathered Isadora's dance tours, Craig's temper tantrums, and his marital dramas. Separated from his previous companion, with whom he had several children, Craig had promised marriage to a second woman, with whom he had three more, when Isadora, too, became pregnant. Although Isadora was supporting him with the proceeds from her tours, Craig showed little interest in their daughter, Mina felt. He took it for granted that women would look after him. His mother had kept him and his various children for years, and it seemed natural that others should do the same. When Isadora failed to provide the large sums he needed for his theater, he treated her coldly: Isadora had come to Florence only to find her lover so distant that she left the next day. Mina distrusted Craig —in her view, the greatest egotist she had ever met—but admired Isadora, whom she would later portray as the representative modern woman artist.

Through Craig, Stephen learned of another center of Florentine culture, the Gabinetto Vieusseux, a private lending library within walking distance of the Costa San Giorgio. This elegant library specialized in foreign-language books, and foreign residents took advantage of its stock of modern literature. Among the regular borrowers were Stephen and Mina, Craig, and members of Gertrude Stein's extended family who summered in Florence. One saw Papini there, as well as Roberto Assagioli, the young doctor said to be specializing in the new science called psychoanalysis. But the expatriates and their Florentine counterparts rarely mixed. When the sculptor David Edstrom, a friend of the Steins, met Papini there, he was surprised to see the writer's glare give way to an enchanting smile yet felt uncomfortable with the intensely intellectual Papini group, whose enthusiasms ranged from William James and Henri Bergson to the occult arts and spiritualism.

The only Florentine in whom foreign residents expressed an ongoing interest was the swashbuckling poet Gabriele D'Annunzio, whose "aura of moral sultriness" spiced tea-party gossip. "There was no limit to the length to which popular belief would go when it concerned D'Annunzio's power and fascination over women," Stephen recalled. "He was never popular among married men, and when he left Italy for Paris before the war, men said that he was finished; that he must needs seek strange and exaggerated vices in the depraved French capital."

Craig also introduced the Haweises to his American benefactor, Charles Loeser, in whose villa he had found the peace of mind needed to begin

111

his model theater. This unassuming patron of the arts was almost profligate in his generosity. He had offered to support his friend George Santayana while he studied philosophy and now thought nothing of providing a home and a Stradivarius for the Lener Quartet. Loeser's generosity seemed all the more admirable because it was disinterested. What was more, he was known for his Cézannes—an unexpectedly modern taste in this Renaissance city—and his artistic connoisseurship put him in a class with Berenson.

When Craig's painter friend William Rothenstein visited Florence that year, he found it still inhabited by warring factions. "But the fighting was far less bloody," he observed, "concerned as it was with attributions rather than Ducal thrones." While Rothenstein frequented the rival camps without getting caught in the crossfire, like Craig, he felt more at home with Loeser. "I was thankful to see anything so fresh and vital as a Cézanne painting in an Anglo-American-Italian interior," he wrote. "The palatial rooms in which the scholar-aesthetes lived," he continued, "their massive Italian furniture, their primitives, bronzes, wood-carvings and Venetian stuffs which one was expected to appraise, wearied me."

Stephen was amused by these rivalries among collectors, "each of whom made 'finds' which he exhibited to his friends as Michelangelos, Leonardos, or, if very old and dirty, Carpaccios." But the feud between Loeser and Berenson was no laughing matter; its effects were felt daily. If one was close to Loeser, one was unwelcome at I Tatti; if one believed in Berenson, then one must avoid the man he called his "enemy-friend." Although it was hard to avoid being labeled a partisan of either side, the lines were sometimes redrawn. Amused by Craig's flirtation with her American guest, the writer Neith Boyce, Mary Berenson stage-managed their rendezvous at I Tatti, insisting to friends that "nothing" would happen. What did or did not happen was often the subject of discussion the next day.

Religion was an equally lively topic of interest. Many foreign residents followed unorthodox practices, ranging from Christian Science and Theosophy to yoga and vegetarianism. The Papini circle was immersed in both occultism and Pragmatism, and Bergson was read by "advanced" thinkers. The one religion that excited gossip was Judaism: it was an acceptable indoor sport to speculate about who was, and was not, Jewish. Berenson had taken pains to suppress his Jewish origins, people whispered. Baptized Episcopalian in his twenties, he had recently succumbed to the lure of Italian Catholicism. By the time he settled in I Tatti, Berenson disdained anyone who was too obviously "commercial," that is, Jewish, unless, of course, he might be seen as a future client.*

---

* As a young Boston aesthete eager to distinguish himself, Berenson had described the Jews as a race whose "character and interests are too vitally opposed to our own to permit the existence of that intelligent sympathy between us and them which is necessary to comprehension"—an act of self-denial in which the Jews are allotted a collective personality opposed to the sensibility of the essayist.

Loeser posed problems for Berenson on this score as well. Not only was he a connoisseur; he was candid about the source of his income—his father's department store in Brooklyn. Loeser disclosed his Jewishness with what Santayana called "a rare and blessed frankness that cleared away a thousand pitfalls and insincerities." With a glance at Berenson, Santayana noted that many Jews "wish to pass for ordinary Christians or ordinary atheists." "Not so Loeser," he went on. His friend did not try "to manage things for other people, or to worm himself into fashionable society." "Somehow I felt more secure under the sign of Loeser," he concluded.

While Mina and Stephen also felt more secure under the sign of Loeser, Mina's ambivalence about her mixed background kept her from being candid until she knew that she was dealing with a "modern" thinker. It was not an easy subject to broach, nor could she feel, as she had in Paris, that it was of little account. In a place like Florence, where everyone examined his neighbors' behavior through a lorgnette, to expose one's difference was to become vulnerable. She did not belong to villadom, yet lacked the assurance to ignore its prejudices. Infractions of the social code, a resident recalled, were "discussed and rediscussed at countless tea tables in that town, where so little actually happened, and where the laws were as those of the Medes and the Persians." While Craig might enjoy breaking the rules, Mina could not imagine herself behaving with his abandon now that she was once again under the surveillance of her compatriots.

A fresh scandal erupted in April, when the weather became unseasonably warm. Craig and his guest, the English composer Martin Shaw, stripped off their clothes and went out to sunbathe. This experience was so enjoyable that they began taking al fresco showers. "We both had somehow got into our heads the erroneous notion that it is only in England that convention exists," Shaw recalled. "We had quite thought that we were living in a golden age of innocence," he went on, "and the idea that Italians would feel shocked caused us surprise." When Loeser told the men that their behavior was inappropriate, Craig replied by flinging off his clothes and exclaiming, "But is it not beautiful?" The story made the round of the tea tables, and Craig moved to another villa. He had gone too far.

Mina was just as uneasy with Craig and his friends as with the arbiters of villadom. Of this period she observed, "My confusion resulted in feeling sullen over the accident of my presence—anywhere." When she accompanied Stephen to bohemian gatherings, she took little pleasure in listening to "the peculiarly unanalyzable conversation of second-rate artists." At one of these parties, which had turned into an occasion for self-promotion, she recalled, her emotions fluctuated between her "Jewish" desire to assert her intelligence and her "Christian" sense of inferiority.

That evening she met the person who was to change her feelings about Florence. "Kashof," the fictional name she gave one of the resident Russians, had invited the Haweises to see his portrait of Papini. Although the writer was said to be the ugliest man in Italy, Mina did not find him unattractive. When Kashof had Papini stand next to his portrait, she studied him. His haughty slouch was appealing, his hazel eyes astonishing, and his mouth, she noted, that of "an impertinent gamin." She wanted to befriend him. In some way, they resembled each other: Papini's features expressed her state of mind, the anguish beneath the mask of her beauty. But she was too much in awe of him to speak. Their acquaintance— they acknowledged each other on such occasions and at the Giubbe Rosse—would continue for years until they met again under other circumstances.

After Papini's departure, Mina found herself being drawn into the artists' social maneuverings. The Russian was presenting his canvases of apples painted "in deference to Cézanne," he explained, while hinting that Stephen might use his influence to have them hung at the Salon d'Automne. Kashof would do better to ask his wife, Stephen replied, since she was a member of that Salon and he was not. Stephen was willing to draw attention to her in order to embarrass their host, Mina thought. His attentions were often of this kind. She caught him watching her with a peculiar expression as she tried in vain to draw. "I wonder, you do not work, after the *very great honor* the Salon has done you," he observed sardonically. A shadow seemed to have fallen across her imagination.

Stephen had also taken to carrying a pistol, which compensated for his height, she thought, and gave him an advantage. Irritated by her restiveness, he tried even harder to assert his dominance, often covering her approach with the pistol as she entered the room. Mina recalled the later stages of her pregnancy as a time when she was under a surveillance as intense as any she had experienced in her parents' house. Stephen had replaced Julia as her judge, guardian, and censor.

Although Mina's account of this period may seem exaggerated, one incident in particular suggests her state of mind. When Craig appeared one day to work with Stephen on *The Mask*, Martin Shaw accompanied him. Mina felt comfortable with the composer, a cockney who dressed unpretentiously and was as modest as Craig was conceited. While Mina had been at the Wood, it turned out, Shaw had been working with Craig in Hampstead; they might have crossed paths. She decided to do the composer's portrait, in part to annoy Craig—*he* was said to be extraordinarily good-looking and Shaw had a disfiguring birthmark. But Craig looked to her "like an old lady—his famous drifting hair, moth-eaten," while Shaw made her think of a medieval Dutchman.

Mina arranged Shaw in a pose showing his "good" profile. During a break he picked up Stephen's pistol, aimed it at Mina, and pulled the trigger. When the bullet skimmed past her temple, she was shocked but not surprised, she recalled, since she had been expecting something to happen. Stephen rushed into the room to find her quite calm. He was annoyed with Shaw for usurping his rights, she believed: the powers conferred upon him by the weapon were not to be invoked by another. From then on, Stephen kept the pistol within eyesight and rarely left her side.

Mina lived through the final stage of pregnancy in extreme discomfort exacerbated by insomnia. "When my body lay down," she wrote, "it was given up entirely to the growth of invasion." The new life felt like an intruder "endeavoring to unbundle itself from the tissues enfolding it." Imagining the child moving through the stages of evolution, she noted how a "fist would land its muffled blow, an aimless foot [would kick] as if to walk through the flesh." At times, the intruder seemed to threaten her existence.

When the *villino's* lease expired, they moved to the Costa San Giorgio just as the city succumbed to summer. Nighttime became "a long semi-asphyxiation" in the stuffy rooms of their new apartment. When she awoke at night, Mina rushed to the window for air. Gazing down, she found a confirmation of her state of mind: the cobbled road "deserted but for the central row of refuse heaps awaiting the morning sweeper with his wheel-barrow and broom." Still, although this arid vision could not compare to Arcetri, she was not sorry to have come down to earth, "where the effluvia of a lovely Italian slum left little freshness." In the morning the neighboring houses came alive; during the day the cries of the artisans and peddlers kept her company. The rubbish heaps lining the Costa were, she wrote, the signs of their common humanity—"the scattered litter cast from windows before they closed in that sleep inanimate dwellings share with the living."

Her peace evaporated as soon as she came to breakfast, where she found Stephen occupying his position as head of the household at their long Florentine table, his hand on the pistol. He had been lying in wait for her and demanded to know why she would not eat. Realizing at last that their mutual suspicions, combined with the heat, did not provide a suitable atmosphere for her delivery, they left Florence for Bagni di Lucca, a nearby mountain resort where Mina could breathe more freely.

Since the beginning of the previous century, a sizable English colony had visited this watering spot, where the temperature was fifteen degrees cooler than in Florence. Older residents still talked about the days of James III, who had kept a villa in Bagni di Lucca, and retold the local adventures of Ouida, the Brownings, and both Byron and Shelley. The resort had an English library, an English church and cemetery, and the settled habits of English life. Each summer a committee organized dances, costume balls, and tennis tournaments—rituals which the residents performed as if they were in some English watering spot, with the advantage of being in Tuscany. Although Bagni di Lucca was old-fashioned, for many this was its charm.

The town, set on a hill in the middle of chestnut forests, consisted of a piazza surrounded on three sides by the Stabilimento di Bagni (Bathing

Establishment), shops, and houses. Estivants spent their time reading or gazing across the wooded ravine from their balconies, while their servants looked after daily life. The waters of the area were said to be as beneficial as those of Aix-les-Bains, and refreshing excursions could be made to the neighboring hills or, for the more energetic, to Volterra, Viareggio, or Carrara. Berenson's friends, Neith Boyce and her journalist husband, Hutchins Hapgood, found the spot remarkably peaceful. Not even Gertrude Stein, who visited them there, could interfere with the flow of daily life, although she had insisted on sitting outside at noon, when everyone closed their shutters.

Mina's condition made it difficult for her to enjoy Bagni di Lucca. Exhausted by the tensions of life with Stephen, she was about to give birth in a foreign country, without family or friends. When a girl was born on July 20, Stephen acknowledged her as his own. She was to be called Joella Sinara, he decided, the second name pronounced with the second syllable accented, like *Cynara*, the muse of Ernest Dowson's famous poem "Non Sum Qualis Eram." Taken together, her names evoked the fin-de-siècle atmosphere of artistic London and Paris, and to those in the know, they hinted at her paternity—since "Joella" recalled Le Savoureux. Stephen's ambiguous role in the affair was also implied in the lament with which Dowson's poem concludes:

> But when the feast is finished and the lamps expire,
> Then falls thy shadow, Cynara! The night is thine;
> And I am desolate and sick of an old passion,
> Yea hungry for the lips of my desire:
> I have been faithful to thee, Cynara! in my fashion.

It was a provocative name for a baby girl, and one that covertly acknowledged their respective infidelities.

They returned to Florence at the end of September and engaged domestic help. Mina devoted herself to Joella, a golden-haired baby who proved to have a sunny disposition, and for a time she forgot the awkwardness of her situation. If Joella lived through her first year, Oda's death might cease to haunt her. The calm ministrations of Giulia, the nurse, and her sister Estere, the cook, were reassuring. Life took on the semblance of stability.

In Stephen's view, while they had been through a difficult time, their relations might improve. Mina promised to make up for her lapse "by giving me another child," he noted in his journal. A few months before Joella's first birthday, Mina became pregnant. When a boy was born on February 1, 1909, Stephen named him John Stephen Giles Musgrove Haweis. Giles, as he was called, would carry on the family tradition. He was a happy child and soon his sister's eager playmate, but Mina had little to do with him, as it appeared that Joella's legs were not developing properly. She was late walking, having had a form of infantile paralysis which caused her muscles to atrophy. When she became ill and lay in a coma, Mina was terrified that Joella, too, might have meningitis.

In desperation Mina turned to Mrs. Morrison, a Christian Science practitioner with a following in the artistic community—even though she knew little more about this religion than the fact that its leader was a woman. Begging Mrs. Morrison for a miracle, she promised to follow "Science" if it proved successful. Mrs. Morrison's treatment, combined with orders to feed the child beef broth and donkey's milk, produced some improvement, and Mina became convinced that practitioners performed miracles. From then on she went regularly to the Christian Science church, where one saw a number of artists and advanced thinkers.

After three years in Florence, her life had stabilized. Because Mr. Lowy had promised to buy the couple a house once they were ready to settle, they looked for one that was large enough for the children and their painting studios, yet close to the center of town. When a small three-story house on the Costa came up for sale, they decided it would do. Oltr'arno was less expensive than villadom, and it suited them. This part of Florence was a city within the city, where one found the artisans whose skills were needed for the restoration of both houses and paintings. On the Costa, a street full of gilders, carpenters, carvers, and stucco experts, their status as *Inglesi*—bourgeois as well as fine artists—set them apart. The deed was drawn up in Stephen's name, in accordance with tradition.

Joella's health still required her removal from Florence at the first sign of summer. As toddlers, the children spent two months in the mountains followed by two months at Forte dei Marmi, by the sea, where they took a comfortable house with a garden, while Mina stayed part of the time in Florence. In Joella's earliest memories, her mother was "a tall very slim woman in flowery clothes [and] large hats who would swoop down on us or through the house like a whirlwind." But to the little girl, "the comfortable everyday presences were Giulia, the nurse I had since I was one year old with her starched white blouses and long black skirt, always calm, always soothing, and her sister, the quick-tempered cook, Estere." With both parents given to displays of temperament, the children understandably clung to their nurse.

Once it was clear that they were well cared for, Mina stopped going to Forte de Marmi. Children should be brought up by the servants, she believed; their ways of thinking resembled those of the young. Once they were of an age to benefit from their parents' perceptions, they could be introduced to adult conversation. It did not occur to her to doubt the British view of Italians as closer to the instinctual responses of the unrepressed, nor did this self-serving theory of child-rearing appear to be at odds with

Mina's critique of her own childhood.* Such views were the norm in the circles to which she and Stephen aspired and may have seemed to Mina —who never forgave her mother for her surveillance—to be preferable. Under this system of benign neglect, children could enjoy themselves.

Despite their comfortable home and devoted servants, the basic incompatibility of the marriage remained. As a child, Joella sensed how dissimilar her parents were: "My mother, tall, willowy, extraordinarily beautiful, very talented, undisciplined, a free spirit, with the beginning of too strong an ego; my father, short, dark, a mediocre painter, bad tempered, with charming social manners and endless conversation about the importance of his family." The servants often overheard rows, and Stephen sometimes behaved harshly toward Giles, who had inherited his looks and temper. Almost as soon as Mr. Lowy bought the house, they began building two studios on the top story, with an outdoor stairway and a roof terrace. Mina had her own bedroom and bath, and the children their sitting room, where they dined with Giulia. While Stephen became one of the most sought-after members of the tea-table set, Mina looked for some source of inspiration to take her out of herself.

It is possible, although uncertain, that during her long periods of introspection she began writing the poems that quite unexpectedly saw their way into print within the next few years. (She began dating their composition in 1914 but did so inconsistently.) What *is* certain is that Mina saw her first years in Florence as a time of creative, emotional, and intellectual doldrums.

* At this time, when Mina was learning the Mensendieck System of Functional Movement (an orthopedic method of body-shaping and strengthening), her carriage improved so noticeably that she came to resemble the straight-backed Edwardian ladies with whom she socialized. Yet it did not occur to her to have Joella taught this innovative method, which might have helped the little girl's legs after her bout with infantile paralysis.

7

Delightful Dilettanti

(FLORENCE, 1910–13)

TO AN ACQUAINTANCE who asked about her life in Florence, Mina called it a time "of shilly-shallying shyness—of an utter inability—to adjust myself to anything actual." She saw herself as a recluse, "a sort of hermit crab occasionally lured to expansiveness under the luxury of Mabel Dodge's flowering trees." The considerable drama in which she was engaged during the next few years occurred mainly in the entourage of Mabel Dodge, the rich American who became her closest friend. Through Mabel, Mina met the American artists and intellectuals—chief among them, Gertrude Stein —whose enthusiasm for new forms of expression would turn her sights toward the New World and inspire her to write. With Mabel, she read Freud, Bergson, and other pioneers in the New Thought; together they investigated a variety of spiritual practices. But Mabel offered more than stimulating company and inspiring books. To Mina their friendship was "a great salvation," and Mabel "the most ample woman-personality alive."

I

When Mabel and her architect husband, Edwin, came to Arcetri, she looked forward to a life of "grandeur." In flight from nouveau-riche America, Mabel was, she recalled of herself at this time, "greedy of significance." Pronouncing the Villa Curonia significant enough to own, Mabel began turning her palatial new home into a setting where she could be "both majestic and careless, spontaneous and picturesque, and yet always framed and supported by a secure and beautiful authenticity of background."

To reach the Villa Curonia from the Costa San Giorgio, one walked up the steep road to Arcetri, and from there, still higher to an avenue of cypresses leading up to the hilltop villa. From this vantage point Florence was so many splotches of pale color; across the city to the north, the Apennines formed a purple-gray mass. The Medici had built the Villa Curonia for their physician, it was said; when Edwin uncovered a fifteenth-century courtyard next to the entrance, Mabel declared it the work of Brunelleschi. She spent the next few years in an orgy of decorating.

To provide Mabel with the grandeur she required, Edwin added a ninety-foot *salone* with French doors opening onto a terrace. Hung with brocades and furnished in the Renaissance style of Anglo-Florence, this spacious sitting room combined grandeur with intimacy. Mabel was particularly pleased when Berenson declared of the *salone*, "Ah! No one can build rooms like this anymore!" A soothing atmosphere inhabited this large, inviting space, Mabel believed, "so reassuring, so loving, so embracing, and so alive like a womb" that she spent much of her time there gazing soulfully at her visitors. Although Mabel was short and dumpy, her enigmatic air reminded the portrait painter Jacques Emile Blanche of "a fleshy odalisque, worn out by the heavy perfumes of the harem."

Under Lady Paget's sponsorship, Mabel staged her first "at home" as theatrically as if it were a Medicean feast. The *salone* tables were laden with flowers, the French doors flung open, and the torches lit just as the light began to fade. Watching her guests strolling in the twilight, Mabel pronounced the effect "Tintorettish." But while she considered her debut a success, some in Florence disagreed. Janet Ross dismissed the Villa Curonia as "absolutely hopeless and uninhabitable, all their improvements terrible and they themselves the commonest people she had ever known," and Mary Berenson noted, "Mabel Dodge made friends with all the people in Florence whom we consider peculiarly undesirable."

Visitors with greater tolerance for Americans than the Anglophile Berenson camp were flattered by the attention that Mabel focused on them from the depths of her velvet couch. Lulled by the voluptuous atmosphere, guests often found themselves relating the details of their amorous contretemps or marital stalemates. Mina let down her guard with this seductive new friend soon after they met. She told Mabel about her mixed background, inadequate education, hasty marriage, and paralyzed ambitions—unaware that Mabel had also invited Stephen's confidences.

When Mabel visited them in the Oltr'arno, Mina felt as if she were receiving a duchess. Mabel swooped into Stephen's studio, glanced at the paintings Mina despised, and pronounced him a genius. Soon she was inviting them to dinner parties with a variety of the older residents. Their adoption by the Dodges marked the beginning of Mina's "expansion" into the circles gathered around these tolerant, unexacting, but gossipy Americans.

As far as Mina could tell, her new friend had settled in Florence with the usual ambitions. Mabel's villa, "stuffed with things bought in the flurry of a woman with taste and scattered around in the harmonious untidiness of temperament," Mina observed, gradually became "an ordered setting for what was most durable in her personality." Different rooms corresponded to her moods, different outfits to each part of the day. When Blanche arrived to paint her portrait, Mabel met him wearing a Poiret, but offered to change. "I can be a Manet or a Berthe Morisot," she told him, "anything you like except an American." One morning Mina watched Mabel throw her Paris frocks on the bedroom floor because they lacked "emotions." Bored with *objets*, Mabel began collecting "impecunious types" like the Haweises, and Mina obliged her by accepting a few Paris rejects.

While Mabel liked to think of herself as a seductress, she considered Edwin "matter-of-fact." He was too prosaic to use the rope ladder she had installed for him to descend into her bedroom from the floor above. Mabel had already made up for Edwin's lack of imagination by initiating a platonic affair with a latter-day Medici, a find even if his homosexuality had made him an outcast. (When Mabel dropped him, her friend committed suicide—since the one person who cared for him had cut him dead in public.) She had also fallen in love with her chauffeur, an infatuation which ended when she tried to kill herself by eating figs stuffed with broken glass. Mabel's constitution was so strong that she recovered and resumed her role as femme fatale. "As a substitute for love," Mabel believed, "the ascendency over the desires of others" would do.

So happy to have an intelligent female friend, Mina did not see that Mabel cultivated an ascendency over the desires of others in most relationships. They bestowed nicknames on each other—Mina, still called "Dusie," became "Doose," and Mabel was "Moose"; Mina chose her as Giles's godmother and gave Mabel several of her delicate watercolors. At the Dodges', Mina's circle widened. She met Loeser, the wealthy artist Sir Arthur Acton, Paul and Muriel Draper, the socialists George Herron and Carrie Rand, the eccentric Braggiottis, and the extended Stein family. Mina often lingered in Mabel's rose pergola, watching the peacocks strut in the garden and the mountains deepen from mauve to purple. Of herself at this time she observed: "Ova's [Mina's] consciousness expanded with this first impetus towards liberation—here was an adoptable standard—easy and the mind was free of the middle-class god."

Once Mabel had attained her goals she no longer thought them worthwhile. "Having exhausted this marriage and the social prestige in Palms [Florence] as inspirational agents," Mina wrote, "she flopped herself on the chaise longue." Within a short time Mabel turned inward—to the New Thought, a movement comprising everything from tarot and spirit readings to Vedanta and Theosophy. Like many of her circle, she had already tried various forms of spirituality. Such experiences seemed as valid as Freud's new science, which left no room for the spirit or for creative inspiration. Mabel was reading Bergson when she first met Mina, who recalled of her friend's studies, "She had the divine female quality of lending to every

latest science or philosophy no matter how mathematical or how austere
—a ribald flavour of lubriciousness." When Mabel recommended Bergson
to friends, her expression seemed "to assure them that Being was indeed
as they had long suspected—an infinite orgy."

In some ways, Bergson's thought applied to Mina's situation. If reality
was something like a rope of beads—"strung on the continuous flux of
Being," as Mina saw it—then introspection might show her the way past
the painful inner divisions of which she was so conscious. In the realm of
pure duration, perhaps, the contradictions between being Christian and
Jewish, British and foreign, respectable and commercial, might dissolve.
And if, as Bergson claimed, the self could know its essence as perpetual
becoming, then the past could be set aside and the self remade.

It was thrilling to discuss the idea of cosmic consciousness while gazing
down on the ancient buildings, Mina recalled, yet "after some time of
communion [my] expanding understanding—that unfortunately fed itself
fatter than the food it flourished on—came to a new barrier." Compared
to Mabel, Mina felt uneducated and wanted to know things "that the
educated are educatedly contented not to know. The trained mind has this
advantage over the untrained," she continued, "that it has been held in
pious reverence of its own limitations." After floundering in "waste lands
of formless metaphysical speculation," she came down to earth each time
she went home.

While Mina studied Bergson with Mabel, Stephen's relations with their
friend were taking a different turn. Although Mabel did not mind buying
his paintings, she warned him not to rely on her: "Any day you give out
in amusement," she told him, "I will have you returned home marked
'empty'!" For this reason, he took care to amuse her with tales of his
mother's salon, his parents, and their famous guests. Mabel did not think
him attractive—"He was a *penguin* type," she wrote, "diminutive, black as
a beetle, and very, very inky"—but enjoyed their flirtation. "I used to play
cat and mouse with Stephen and get him to tell me all his little magical
secrets," she added. He brought her presents: a painted silk fan, a watercolor, his latest poem. One day he arrived with a self-portrait in the style
of a Persian miniature. Certified by the connoisseur "BB" as "A Genuine
work by Amico di Mabello di Arcetri," it showed the "Artist in search of
a crutch . . . the Poet Stefin Hafiz who flourished about the middle of the
last three weeks."

But most of all, Mabel liked to hear of his relations with women other
than his wife. Stephen boasted about a young friend of Mrs. Ames-Lyde
who had fallen in love with him, then killed herself, and told of his affair
with an ascetic painter, who later informed Mabel that after her capitulation
Stephen rejected her. Mabel derived nearly as much amusement from her
friends' dramas as from her own. In this way she could interfere in marriages while maintaining close relations with both sides.

The residents prided themselves on their sense of the past: it was the index of one's spiritual sensibility. In reality, experts like Berenson acquired prestige not only because of their highly developed responses to art but also because they were building up valuable collections. Lesser connoisseurs demonstrated their respect for the past in the zeal with which they purchased *objets d'art*. "Everyone played with the past in Florence," Mabel recalled. "Everything in the Florentine life was minutely seen, known, and named," she continued: in a place where pictures mattered more than people, "the only people who counted, who were visible to the trained eyes of the Florentine world, were those who resembled works of art." Lady Paget looked like a Gothic queen, and Mina was "as lovely as a Byzantine Madonna" or, in her modern moments, "a painting by Augustus John."

Such idolatry of the past suited Stephen. In Florence it seemed only natural to allude to the time when his family name counted. Soon everyone knew of his father's fame and his mother's reception by Queen Victoria. When Mina asked him why he continued to paint, he replied candidly: "In pretending to the Arts I am received by Society, whereas were I a bankclerk, I should be definitely out." Although his Whistlerian studies found their admirers, Mina dismissed him as someone who saw "the Art Market in the light in which the middle-class regards court etiquette."

While Stephen stood to profit by maintaining Anglo-Florentine codes of behavior, Mina had less of an investment. In London, as a half-Jewish woman of lower-middle-class origins, socially speaking she did not exist. Consequently, in Florence she could not help feeling some satisfaction in her altered status—as the wife of the "charming Stephen Haweis," she was received by social arbiters who would not have known her at home. Fully aware of the "restorative" aspect of residence abroad for those whose reputations were not *comme il faut*—through the circumstances of birth or some peccadillo—she understood that, in time, most lapses were redeemed. Those who settled in Florence because they could live well on reduced incomes were "almost hysterically grateful that they could now afford such spacious dwellings," she noted. Due to the exchange rate, she went on, "the Anglo-Saxon religion of ancestral halls revived in the bosoms of poor relations among these towering pillars and vaulted ceilings carved with other people's coats of arms."

During her years there, Mina watched the Anglo-Florentines rebuild their lives "upon the prejudices they had only momentarily mislaid." Through prolonged residence abroad, they came to believe that "the aesthetic tumulus of the Renaissance had in bulk become an official preserve"—for their benefit. Mina suspected that the worship of the past concealed a brisk traffic in the antiquarian market, where "big critics attributing big things to the big masters prospered on the percentage for their guarantees." Similarly, marveling at the number of certified "Della Robbia" Madonnas being shipped to America, she studied the pecking order among the dealers. Such persons conducted business by seeking to "fasten their right to exist upon the battered figurines of the Catholic past." Ironically, her critique of expatriate Florence is tinged with the prejudice against trade with which Julia had tormented Mr. Lowy.

As a fine artist, Mina wanted to think that she stood outside the system, yet as the protégée of the wealthy, she was implicated in the structure she claimed to despise. Since she also wanted to think that her friendship with Mabel was free of such considerations, it took her many years to grasp the emotional gambits by which Mabel practiced her ascendency. What Mabel wanted from others was to tap the source of their fascination: "When we see a man or a woman whose power rises in him like the water in a spring, we are immediately attracted to it," she observed; "we cannot resist trying to tap it, somehow, to get it for ourselves." New acquaintances were a means to satisfy her desire for plenitude, and social intercourse a substitute for the intimacy that Mabel often promised but rarely saw to completion.

The repressed sensuality that Mabel brought to social life also rose to the surface in orgies of art appreciation. "It's almost like a love affair, the drama over the antique," she recalled. "We were always talking trecento, quattrocento, cinquecento or discussing values—(Berenson's 'tactile values'), lines, dimensions, or nuances in knowing phrases." Like Mabel's attempts to tap the springs of power in others, Berenson coveted a source of energy he located in art. "We must look and look and look till we live in the painting," he explained; "a work of art is like a woman; 'il faut coucher avec.' " The aim was to achieve rapturous communion. Visitors, wondering about the propriety of discussing such theories in the presence of the young, were heard to titter at the thought of becoming one with a work of art. Artistic communion, Mina suspected, was a substitute for a more direct encounter with life.

III

Through Mabel, Mina also met the most uninhibited family in Florence, the Braggiottis. The Braggiottis were unusual not only because they had seven children. "The parents were musical vegetarians of tangled origin, Turkish and New England on the father's side, French and German on the mother's," Harold Acton recalled. "They believed in and practised a Rousseau-istic return to Nature," he went on, "and produced a prodigious progeny on a diet of nuts, fruit and vegetables." A Bostonian whose father conducted an export business, Isidore Braggiotti had put his operatic training to use as a singing coach. When he and his wife, Lily, bought a villa on the outskirts of Florence for their Scuola del Canto, they created a concert room by roofing over the patio, where weekly concerts were held beneath the two-story glass roof. As it was said that he could "place" good voices, Braggiotti's pupils did not mind paying the large sums he charged them.

Mina took Joella and Giles to play at the Braggiottis' even though their child-rearing practices were as unorthodox as their diet. The children often went without clothes. "Self-expression was encouraged so that they sang, danced or played a musical instrument in public as easily as they removed their garments," Acton noted, "without the slightest taint of affectation." Clothed, the children worked in the fields with the *contadini* (sharecroppers) because Lily believed in the benefits of fresh air and exercise. The other residents were both amused and scandalized by Lily's theories. Everyone heard about the unsuspecting English ladies: arriving at teatime, they were greeted by three Braggiotti children who were entirely naked except for the leaves decorating their suntanned bodies. Distressed by the idea of children playing "naked devils," the ladies barely held on to their teacups when they caught sight of the twigs stuck into the children's bottoms as tails.

At the time that they befriended Mina, the Braggiottis also practiced unconventional forms of spirituality. By the 1910s, Mabel recalled, they were "far gone in Theosophy and were always having psychic things happen in their house." Lily furnished the villa and dressed the children according to her beliefs about color—her favorites were blue and gold, for the Italian sky and sun. She wore loosely pleated Fortuny gowns rather than the tightly cinched fashions of the 1900s because her theories about dress were as important to her as her ideas about religion or food.

A happy mixture of Braggiotti self-confidence and enough money to keep sixteen servants produced a life that Mina could admire only from afar. When she joined Mabel at one of the Braggiottis' musicales, she met the third member of their circle of artistic exiles, Muriel Draper, whose husband, Paul, was studying with Braggiotti. Muriel had a New England pedigree but limited means. Possessed of "an infinitely elegant and royal air that permitted her any license of speech or gesture," Muriel wore her one lace-trimmed dress with a queenly air, and her self-assurance effaced any embarrassment over her being four months pregnant although just married. The Drapers and the Dodges became intimates, but when Mabel took over Muriel's role as Paul's muse, relations cooled and the Drapers announced their intention to settle in London.

In time, most women of their set tired of the genteel Anglo-Florentine life. "One was always 'visiting,' " Mabel wrote, "people, paintings, architecture, scenery, palaces, villas, museums, gardens, and galleries." They were all ripe for extramarital affairs or the more esoteric satisfactions of spirituality—unless, like Mabel, they craved both. Years later, when she composed a verbal portrait gallery of these "delightful dilettanti," Mabel observed that most people lost their verve if they stayed too long in Florence.

Stephen held Mabel's interest nonetheless. She thought him clever, "often amusing; playfully so, with the affectionate condescension that a much larger, older man might display successfully." As for Mina, she was beautiful but lacking in "sap," and while she was gifted, her talent expressed itself "in an unhappy, morbid way." Her unhappiness had much to do with the fact that she hated her husband, Mabel thought, "with a profound, convinced detestation," an emotion which caused her "to grow dry as the years went on. It was not Stephen's fault, although perhaps he was difficult to live with after one outgrew the taste one had for him," Mabel concluded. Her retrospective account of these years reflects Mabel's change of heart once she put Florence behind her—as if the Haweises stood for everything she rejected once she made up her mind to return to America.

IV

By 1910 it was clear to both Mina and Stephen that they were losing touch with the art world. Mabel's observation that neither had enough to do was correct. Sending a few canvases to the Salons each year did not suffice: one needed to be in Paris to keep in touch. They no longer knew what people thought of the Fauves or the new group called Cubists. Agreed for once, they decided to try for exhibitions in London, where work by British expatriates was welcomed and Gordon Craig's connections could do them some good.

Through the offices of Craig's friend Rothenstein, the New English Art Club accepted *Jemima*, one of Mina's portraits,* for their summer exhibit. The New English, founded in the 1880s as an alternative to the Royal Academy, had been at its height when Mina left for Paris. Although the society had now reached artistic middle age, the London papers praised the summer show, especially the contributions of Sargent and Max Beerbohm. The critics were so taken by the caricaturist's wit—"the hors d'oeuvres in the New English Art Club's ample feast"—that both *Jemima* and the canvases of Gwen John went unnoticed, most likely because they were hung in the same room as Beerbohm's drawings. While it was a tame show by Continental standards, *The* (London) *Times* called the summer exhibition "the seed-plot in which the English art of the twentieth century is to take root, grow and flourish."

In December news of a more controversial exhibition filtered back to Florence. "Manet and the Post-Impressionists," Roger Fry's exhibition, had foisted Van Gogh, Gauguin, and Cézanne on the London public. While the critics pronounced it anarchist, degenerate, pornographic, or mad, Brit-

---

* *Jemima* may have been a self-portrait, since Mina often used this name for herself in her autobiographical writing. From her biblical studies, she would also have known that Jemima was the first of Job's three daughters, born after the return of his fortunes, as well as one of his heirs—contrary to contemporary usage.

ish artists were divided. Fry's supporters praised the show, but those with ties to the older generation thought it in bad taste. Fry's friend Virginia Woolf, who liked the exhibition, went so far as to claim that human character changed that December—because the exhibition forced England to recognize the Continent.

Since few Londoners shared Bloomsbury's Francophilia, most saw the show as an attack on tradition. Taking the xenophobes to task, Arnold Bennett observed scathingly: "London may be unaware that the value of the best work of this new school is permanently and definitely settled— outside London." Similarly, Stephen's friend Sickert was pleased that the Royal Academy would now be forced to respect foreign art. In his view, the national taste either broke the spirit of those who cared for modern art "or compel[led] them to toe the line." "The young English painter who loves his art ends by major force," he continued, "in producing the chocolate-box in demand." Sickert's analysis was apt. Stephen charmed potential patrons with chocolate boxes in the form of Persian miniatures or painted fans.

When another Post-Impressionist exhibit was held in Florence that year, discussions of its merits divided along similar lines. Loeser was pleased, but the more conservative protested. While Mina bemoaned her increasing isolation, Stephen turned to the example of Gauguin, who had sought in the "primitives" of the South Seas new sources of inspiration, and he urged Mina to follow up on her contacts with the New English Art Club, which looked with favor on Post-Impressionists like themselves.

Although Fry's term had been chosen to designate the art that followed Impressionism, his coinage soon acquired other meanings. To its supporters, it meant emotional liberation and intellectual freedom; to its detractors, it meant nonsense: "a widespread plot to destroy the whole fabric of European painting" or, worse, "the rejection of all that civilisation has done." "The Post-Impressionists are in the company of the Great Rebels of the World," declared a reporter for the London *Daily Herald*, for whom the only serious political movements were women's suffrage and socialism. "They are both Post-Impressionist in their desire to scrap old decaying forms," she went on. Books appeared in Post-Impressionism's defense, one dedicated to "the rebels of either sex all the world over who in any way are fighting for freedom of any kind," another praising it for "inviting the pilgrim who is casting off the burdens of mere representation."

As Fry later saw, those who denounced Post-Impressionism did so for social rather than aesthetic reasons. His exhibition had seemed revolutionary, not because it abandoned form, but because it unsettled people whose ideas about art formed an important part of their identities. "To be able to speak glibly of Tang and Ming, of Amico di Sandro and Baldovinetti," Fry thought, "gave them a social standing." Faced with a Matisse, the British art lover took offense: "At a time when formality in dress and behaviour sustained a man's or a woman's position in life, the informality of these paintings looked shockingly subversive." Like brazen upstarts, these canvases threatened the smooth surface of Edwardian life.

To Mina and her contemporaries, the spirit behind the new painting paralleled the quests that some were making in spiritual realms. All were "communicants" in a new vision of the spirit inherent in matter, "pilgrims" casting off the burden of tradition. From this perspective Stephen argued that Gauguin's rejection of European art had begun with "a revolution in his soul." "He was like a missionary going out to seek the poor heathen in himself which he had been taught to despise," he wrote, "only to realise suddenly that the poor heathen in him was the strongest and best part of him." But while Stephen dreamed of reclaiming his own inner heathen, neither he nor Mina was ready to ignore their circle.

Mabel's account of the couple's artistic doldrums is malicious but shrewd. Stephen was, she wrote, "quite a little alchemist in paint and had an extraordinarily fine color sense. . . . Of course he did imitate Charles Conder somewhat," she continued, "but he knew how to mix paint though he was essentially dark in his nature." Mina's work showed a lesser talent: "She painted small, cynical pictures, picturesque and delicate, of ladies' tea parties, of half-fantastic scenes from a fabulous world where her mind dwelt customarily in a perpetual half-tone, poetic and depressing." Mina was, she concluded, "dissatisfied through some lack in herself."

Judging by the titles of Mina's work from this period (all of it lost), Mabel's observations were not inaccurate. Mina may have been trying to produce the chocolate boxes of which Sickert spoke: her titles suggest a faded charm. Several series on related topics evoke the ennui of life in Florence: a group of *Ladies at Tea* was followed by a similar series, including *Ladies Watching a Ballet* and the somewhat surprising *Ladies Fishing*. Another group dealt ambiguously with romance: in one drawing, young ladies disposed of the hearts they have captured, while another showed love for sale at a *Heart Shop*. Her subject matter seems as restricted as her life, which offered only the occasional stimulation suggested in *The Little Carnival* and *Voyageurs*. It is tempting to speculate that the decadent veneer of this work concealed some satire but impossible to know until it is recovered.

Stephen painted more salable subjects, in keeping with his practical approach. In 1911 he began negotiations with the Baillie Gallery, to which Craig had provided an introduction: Stephen's Italian studies fit nicely into their roster of Continental and exotic landscapes. He was given a show in December to which he sent Florentine and Venetian scenes, floral studies painted at the Villa Curonia, and a number of Whistlerian *Songs without Sound*, which met the criteria of mainstream British taste. After making £200, he contracted for a second show in 1912 and, most likely, handled negotiations for Mina's first one-woman show—at the Carfax Gallery, which favored artists whose work showed Continental influence but was neither difficult nor too obviously Post-Impressionist.

V

Earlier that year Mabel had returned from Paris with news of Leo and Gertrude Stein, whose collection people went to see because it was full of Post-Impressionists: like Mina, she had heard of this pair but had not yet made their acquaintance. Every Saturday evening in their studio, Leo discoursed about his discoveries, Matisse and Picasso. He believed in a new kind of art, based not on the balanced harmonies of the previous century but on the expression of tension, and he argued so persuasively for the need to look beyond representation that Mabel had come away a believer. Once one understood Picasso, she observed, the world looked different— "and the more difference there is, the more life there is."

Moreover, Leo's sister, Gertrude, was "prodigious." Mabel had never met anyone who seemed so happy with her bulk, "pounds and pounds and pounds piled up on her skeleton—not the billowing kind, but massive, heavy fat." Mabel not only warmed to Gertrude's bulk, she also admired her spirit. Although Alice Toklas had begun the gradual process by which she would replace Leo in the household, Mabel believed that she and Gertrude "had taken to each other." She could hardly wait for their arrival in Florence.

The Steins had been summering in Tuscany for a decade, along with their brother Michael, his wife, Sally, and an entourage of family and friends. By 1911 their domestic arrangements reflected new alignments in the household: Gertrude was to stay with Alice in Fiesole, where formerly she had lived with Leo. More than ever, Mabel felt that Gertrude looked "richly attractive in her grand *ampleur*," but Leo complained that his sister was growing increasingly helpless while Alice made herself indispensable. "He had seen trees strangled by vines in this way," he told Mabel.

Meeting Gertrude for the first time at the Dodges', Mina, too, felt an affinity with this large, intelligent woman. It was not until she received a formal letter of introduction from Alice Woods Ullmann, their mutual friend, that she wrote to invite the Stein household to the Costa San Giorgio. Since Leo was busy, Gertrude and Alice Toklas came without him. Recalling the day with pleasure, Toklas noted that "a friendship with her commenced that lasted over the years." Mina regained her high spirits in their company: she was, Alice wrote, a charming companion, "beautiful, intelligent, sympathetic and gay." On another occasion, when Mabel asked Gertrude, Alice, and Mina to dine with André Gide, Alice watched their hostess drape herself on the chaise longue to converse with the Frenchman while Mina, "who thought this highly ridiculous," danced behind them with an imaginary partner.

Gertrude later recalled that the Haweises were "among the very earliest to be interested in the work of Gertrude Stein." Although she had published *Three Lives* in 1909, the book sold poorly, and so few readers had responded positively to *The Making of Americans* that Gertrude noted, "I am writing for myself and strangers." When Stephen pleaded for the insertion of commas in her long, unpunctuated sentences, Gertrude replied that "commas were unnecessary, the sense should be intrinsic and not have to be explained by commas and otherwise commas were only a sign that one should pause and take breath but one should know of oneself when one wanted to pause and take breath." Following this mimetic demonstration of her principles, Gertrude added that while she had granted Stephen two commas in exchange for a painting, on rereading the manuscript she took them out. The passage concludes: "Mina Loy equally interested was able to understand without the commas. She has always been able to understand."

Mina was, it seemed, one of the strangers for whom Gertrude was writing. Although *The Making of Americans* began as the study of two families (the Eastern and Western branches of the Steins), it had already left the track of narrative to encompass a series of psychological studies of what Gertrude called people's "bottom nature." During the years she worked on the book, she became "enormously interested in hearing how everybody said the same thing over and over again with infinite variations until if you listened with great intensity you could hear it rise and fall and tell all that there was inside them." The result was a novel in name only.

Intuitively Mina understood Gertrude's attempts to place individual temperament within the overlapping contexts of personal and social history. Her new friend's manuscript stimulated her to think that she might do the same with her own background—analyze its effects on her through the act of writing. (It would take more than a decade for her to prepare for "Anglo-Mongrels," the long autobiographical poem one might retitle "The Making of British Expatriates.") Mina was astounded that Gertrude brought into writing the habits of mind she had struggled to learn in her study of philosophy. In their different ways, Henri Bergson and Gertrude Stein both seemed to say that one could get at the truth through introspection.

Mina also admired Gertrude's lack of concern with taste as defined in Florence. She responded directly to people and paintings, Mabel believed: "I remember she was the first one—of all those sophisticated, cultured people I had grown accustomed to—who made me realize how nothing is anything more than it is to oneself." Gertrude enjoyed the trifles sold to tourists on the Ponte Vecchio—mosaic brooches and miniature fountains—and never worried whether they were "good." Such insouciance was a revelation.

Equally charmed by Gertrude's devotion to female saints, an interest that was an alibi for visits to out-of-the-way churches with Alice, Mina took Gertrude shopping. Wandering about the Oltr'arno inspecting ceramic Madonnas, they made an odd sight—Mina so willowy and Gertrude so massive. One day, noticing an unusual black Madonna and Child in Mina's studio, Gertrude declared them finer than the set she had just purchased.

After her departure Mina mailed the figurines to Paris with an affectionate note, which began: "Dear Gertrude Stein—as the generic term 'Miss' cannot be applied to the unique. I don't know why but your black Madonna is on a cabinet in my studio," Mina continued. "I hope you will not allow the absolute vacancy of her white eye to debar you from appreciating her intrinsic worth—eight & forty centessimi." In the package she included a ceramic gendarme "to keep watch in case of attempted theft."

Gertrude's interest in Catholic folklore was even more intriguing when one knew that she had not only read psychology with William James but had nearly completed medical studies. She was the first woman Mina had ever met who had the kind of intellect that she associated with being Jewish. Unlike Berenson, Gertrude made no attempt to hide her origins. Although she had grown up with a strong attachment to Judaism, she too felt some ambivalence about her identity: as she revised *The Making of Americans*, the characters were identified in successive drafts as "Jewish," as "German," and, finally, as plain "middle-class."

Leo and Gertrude generally impressed acquaintances not as bourgeois but as wealthy eccentrics. They strode about Florence in sandals—normally worn only by peasants—Leo declaiming on the genius of Cézanne and Gertrude "walking as it were roughshod over the aesthetic interests that were in vogue there." While his sister analyzed her subjects' bottom natures, Leo investigated the nature of consciousness—his own—in an effort to achieve serenity. He had, for a time, practiced awareness of his digestive system by "Fletcherizing" his food—chewing each mouthful thirty-two times. When Fletcherism offered no solution, he took up Freud. Of his latest enthusiasm he explained, "I have not gotten religion, nor found a newer doctrine, nor an unknown light that never was on sea or land, nor last and briefest am I drunk. No, that which I have sought and found is simpler far than these: it is only the goal of the quest psychoanalytic." And this, he emphasized, was no "Christian Science fairy tale."

Despite Leo's disdain for Christian Science, it was an acceptable alternative to traditional religions, especially among Jews. Less unorthodox than Bahai, which flourished in Paris, or Vedanta, which was winning adepts in Massachusetts, the emphasis on science made Mrs. Eddy's religion sound modern. Because the shifts in consciousness were as great whether one was straining to grasp Post-Impressionism or the new religions, those who were spiritually inclined rarely distinguished between aesthetic and spiritual seeking. In the Stein circle, these two concerns overlapped. Gertrude's sister-in-law Sarah, a student of Matisse's, often lectured on the spirituality of modern art at her salon; when she transferred her interest to Christian Science, her entourage found themselves pressured to do the same. The Stein family attended the Christian Science church in Florence, where Mina, too, sought solace in the one spiritual practice that promised to bridge the gaps between mind and body, Judaism and Christianity, the commercial and the saved.

VI

By 1912 Mabel was so restless that she agreed to accompany Edwin to Boston. Social calls there soon became as tiresome as in Florence. Out of curiosity she attended lectures at the Vedanta temple, where Swami Paramananda, a handsome young Indian in apricot robes, was having an astonishing effect: his presence was "like a light, conveying the strength and beauty and peace for which her whole being yearned," a member of the audience recalled. Mabel, already "in the mood to be assuaged by a swami," found that his intoning produced the release she had longed for. Thinking that it would be "lovely to have him around making that comforting atmosphere where all the knots of the heart are untied," she invited him to stay at the Villa Curonia that summer.

Paramananda's understanding of Mabel's invitation was characteristically generous. Once settled in Arcetri, he told his followers that he had been offered the use of the villa to further his work. Shortly after his arrival, however, Mabel changed her mind. Despite the white robes and turban she had bought for the occasion, her efforts at meditation were in vain. She could hardly wait until Paramananda's bedtime to light up a cigarette; she no longer needed his comforting atmosphere. But how could one dismiss a swami who had come all the way from Boston?

Sensing that the Braggiottis might take him off her hands, Mabel invited the family to Arcetri. They not only fell in with her plans by asking the swami to accept their hospitality but offered the use of their villa as a center. Of all their friends, Stephen expressed the keenest interest in meeting Paramananda. In his youth he had known Paramananda's master, Swami Vivekananda, whose integrity and intellect had made a profound impression. In July, Mina and Stephen began attending the weekly services in the Braggiottis' music room. They listened carefully to Paramananda and reflected on what he said.

His words were "falling on good soil," Paramananda believed. Things were going so well in Florence that another permanent center seemed likely. The young guru quickly adopted local customs: his sandals and loose brown robe made him look like an Indian monk or a relative of the Steins. He was, moreover, enjoying a social success. Although the Princess Ghyka begged him to stay at the Villa Gamberaia, he said that he could not forsake the Braggiottis. Of Lily, who considered him the Messiah, Paramananda observed, "Her feeling for the work and teaching is very beautiful."

Throughout September and October, crowds gathered to hear him. Stephen, who was studying the Bhagavad Gita, concluded that since Paramananda praised chastity as a path to spiritual development, he might do as Mina wished and forgo sexual relations for the sake of her nerves. Abstinence was not a virtue per se, Paramananda explained, but a path toward enlightenment and, eventually, nirvana—a state of mind that appealed to Mina. With such a receptive audience, Paramananda noted, "those who are ready will feel the living quality just from the presence without words." But after his return to Boston, he saw that he could not keep two centers going at once. Lily Braggiotti tried to make the best of it, telling herself and their friends that the swami's work was for the whole world. The interest he had awakened in Anglo-Florence was, she noted, developing in many hearts in addition to her own.

While Lily made every effort to go on living as one of the enlightened, the Braggiotti children, who had been made to minister to the guru's needs, were relieved to see the last of him. (One of them was heard to protest, "I don't want to wash God's feet, Mamma!") Paramananda represented "the life" for spiritual seekers like Lily, but others found it hard to remember exactly what he had said. Mina returned to Christian Science, and Mabel forgot her attraction to Vedanta's atmosphere.

What Mabel desired at this point was not enlightenment but greater intimacy with Gertrude Stein. Following her visit to the Villa Curonia the previous summer, Mabel had wooed her by mail: "*Why* are there not more real people like you in the world?" she wrote. Spending time with Gertrude felt like "drinking champagne." Mabel's flattery comforted Gertrude at a time when publishers showed no desire to rush her work into print. She and Alice returned from Spain to an avalanche of letters asking them to prolong their summer holiday at the Villa Curonia. They decided to accept.

Gertrude sensed that their hostess found her person as attractive as her writing and soon learned what a tease Mabel was, especially in Edwin's absence. Not only was she flirting with her son's tutor, but she had given Gertrude the bedroom next to her own. Tensions developed. It was obvious to their friends that Gertrude enjoyed Mabel's attentions. "One day at lunch," Mabel recalled, "Gertrude, sitting opposite me in Edwin's chair, sent me such a strong look over the table that it seemed to cut across the air to me in a band of electrified steel." Alice's campaign to turn Gertrude from her began that afternoon, Mabel believed.

Things were worse than Alice suspected. Mabel had already tried to enlist Gertrude in her marital dramas. After Gertrude's return to Paris, Mabel begged her to come back to Florence to help sort out her future. Unable to decide whether to return to America with Edwin or to spend the winter in Paris, Mabel kept repeating Edwin's observation that she had a crush on Gertrude. One can infer from Mabel's departure for New York that Alice's campaign was successful. But Alice's victory was Mina's loss: her closest friend was leaving Florence.

Gertrude soon put life at the Villa Curonia to good use. For some time she had been composing portraits of her acquaintances—"to find out inside everyone what was in them that was intrinsically exciting." She began writing one about their seductive hostess. "The Portrait of Mabel Dodge at the Villa Curonia" asserts innocently that "the days are wonderful and the nights are wonderful and life is pleasant," but its evocations of the pleasant life at Mabel's are full of innuendo:

So much breathing has not the same place when there is that much beginning . . .
All the attention is when there is not enough to do . . .
There cannot be sighing. This is this bliss . . .
There is that desire and there is no pleasure.

Mabel's portrait ended on a note that recognized Alice's victory: "That is what is done when there is done what is done and the union is won." Pleased with her portrait nonetheless, Mabel had it printed, bound with Florentine paper, and sent to her friends like a press release.

Gertrude had also completed studies of numerous friends, including Matisse and Picasso, which were about to appear in *Camera Work*, the avant-garde art review edited in New York by Alfred Stieglitz. Before leaving Florence she promised to send copies of the magazine to Mina and Stephen, who had observed the dramas at the Villa Curonia with interest. But when *Camera Work* arrived, they were unprepared for what they read. "Matisse" meandered from its subject's lack of self-assurance to an ambivalent appraisal of his importance, while "Picasso" emphasized both its subject's charm and his erratic nature. Whatever Gertrude's intentions were, her portraits of these little-known artists re-enacted, through their halting, meditative rhythms, the moments of crisis in artistic creation.

Stephen conveyed to Gertrude his "thanks from both of us for the charming Matisse & Picasso volume which we have both reread and studied with great pleasure." Although he found her writing difficult, it was having an effect on him: "The New Movement in Art has produced a distinct change in me though it has not percolated through to my work." Next he told her to prepare for a shock: "I have made up my mind to go to the South Seas islands [for a] change of air early next year," he announced. "I propose to paint, write, and (have you got tight hold?) lecture!" he continued. Just as Mabel said, Gertrude made one see life anew.

In time (it is impossible to date the moment at which Mina, too, began writing of their friends' "bottom natures"), Gertrude's example would percolate into Mina's work as well. Gertrude would nonetheless have been shocked by her portrait of Mabel. "To Gloria" [Mabel], she wrote, "life, if only she could get her fingers under the crust, was a pie, probably sweet—she wanted to stir and dip into it with her fingers—and pull out a plum." As deftly as if she were drawing, she evoked Mabel's character: "She reached out for attitudes and rid herself of them with the self-same amplitude . . . The assurance of her states of mind came to her with lightning certainty," Mina continued, "when she was bored she was bored." But where Gertrude limited herself to innuendo, Mina was explicit: "More organically conscious than most women," Mabel longed "to stuff everything into her vulva to see what marvelous creative modification it has undergone in the process." Understandably, this portrait of Mabel has never found its way into print.

Since her move to Florence, Mina had been storing up observations about men and women, the British and the Italians, and the sharply drawn social distinctions that dominated all their lives. Although she kept her jottings to herself during this period of gestation—the internal censor was not easily defied even at this distance from London—they would soon bear fruit in her unexpected turn from art to poetry.

VII

In 1912, while Gertrude's example was bringing a change of air, the Haweises' marriage entered a new phase. That spring Amelia DeFries, an Englishwoman with literary connections who was interested in the "moderns," called regularly at Stephen's studio. As well as admiring his work, she sympathized with his personal frustrations. After Stephen asked her to sit for her portrait, Amelia became his confidante. Their affinity soon took a more physical turn, and she became his mistress. Stephen would undoubtedly earn his place in the ranks of artistic genius, she assured him in a series of "notes to my beloved"; he was, in the words of Carlyle, a "Messenger from the Great Unknown with Tidings for us." Physical stature—a subject that continued to distress him—was unrelated to artistic genius, Amelia insisted. Both Wagner and Beethoven had been "very short men."

Stephen took their affair far less seriously than Amelia did. By the time she returned to London, she was convinced that they shared a great love. Stephen's genius would at last be recognized under her guidance—provided he won the freedom for which, he assured her, he greatly yearned. Amelia began advising on strategies for obtaining a divorce, and members of her family were given to understand that she was engaged—to an artist whose life she could not yet share, because both were penniless.

Alarmed, Stephen replied that he had never imagined, let alone proposed, marriage, yet he did not break off their correspondence. Asking Amelia to think of their relations as a "deep friendship," one that could transcend passion, he kept on writing. (He told her of his commitment to an enlightened way of life, including meditation and sexual abstinence.) Amelia was more than a little surprised to learn of Stephen's efforts to attain serenity. While her love could follow him into this Beyond, she replied, she did not believe one must renounce the senses to get there.

That autumn, inspired by Paramananda and the Bhagavad Gita, Stephen put his vision into words. He was his father's son in spite of himself—he kept falling into biblical cadences—yet the non-Christian content of the tract he called "The Seven Ages of God" would have startled Reverend Haweis. Stephen identified a non-dualistic Deity with the cosmos. "Man and mammal, bird or fish, flow through the veins and channels of His being as blood corpuscles in the bodies of men," he declared. "Towns and great cities are like cells of energy in a mighty brain which is now slowly awakening to a newer consciousness," he went on. To prepare for the new age, he recapitulated the growth of the idea of God, from "the age of Primal Life . . . before the son was completely separated from the Mother," through the Ages of Knowledge and Fear to the era of sexual romance, which offered man "the adorable shape of woman." But like other images of the divine, this goddess proved unsatisfactory. "Sweet things cloy upon the tongue," he noted, perhaps thinking of his own situation. Freedom would reward the man "who hath ceased to heed or need either mistress or master." It was a summation and farewell to the conventions—social, artistic, and spiritual—in which he had been raised.

When Stephen wrote to Amelia of his desire to follow Gauguin, he included a copy of his pamphlet. Disturbed by what she read, Amelia begged him to come to London instead: he could rent a studio and remake all the contacts he had forsaken. She would introduce Stephen to people of influence, and while they could not live together, they could frequent society as friends, just as Ford Madox Ford and Violet Hunt were doing. Since "people who like artists don't mind where they live," she wrote, they would be invited to her friends' country houses. And she teased him about the idea of marriage—she was not so easily had.

Amelia had in mind a brief waiting period, followed by Stephen's brilliant success and their equally brilliant union. The model of Ford and Violet kept recurring in her letters. But the issue of divorce was problematic. According to an 1857 law still in force, a husband could sue on the basis of adultery, while a wife had to prove that her husband had not only committed the act but that it was "intolerable"—accompanied by bigamy, incest, sodomy, desertion, or rape. Since 1906 the Divorce Law Reform Union had been advocating the extension of these grounds to include insanity, cruelty, desertion, drunkenness, and penal servitude. Although a Royal Commission recommended in 1912, the year of Stephen's affair with Amelia, that wives be allowed to sue on adultery alone, the terms of the law would not change until 1923. If Mina tried to divorce Stephen, she would have to prove that he had committed "intolerable adultery," while he had only to claim that she had been unfaithful. Stephen was loath to risk the scandal, and, more important, unwilling to forgo the income from Mr. Lowy.

Amelia saw that she would have to do the work. After obtaining the names of solicitors, gathering information about the relative cost of divorces in London (eighty pounds) and Paris (less), she suggested that Mina bear the expense. She proposed two solutions: either Stephen could leave Mina, whereupon she could claim adultery without naming the lady in question, or he could sue Mina for the loss of conjugal rights. Either was acceptable, she insisted, "nor will any right thinking person think the worse of you."

Amelia was also doing her best to make contacts for Stephen. Her acquaintances in the literary reviews would be useful in the campaign to bring him into the public eye; she suggested that he write letters about modern art to the editors of the better newspapers. When Stephen's 1912 exhibition opened at the Baillie Gallery in October, she praised it to her friends and took them there herself to point out the beauties of Stephen's panel paintings. Although he remained in Florence and seemed determined to sail to the South Seas, she still assumed that he would eventually come round.

While Amelia tried to manage Stephen's affairs in her own interest, she was also falling in with Mina's plans. Watching Mabel manipulate others over the years, Mina had picked up some idea of how it was done. Amelia did not know that Mina had all but pushed Stephen into the affair with her or that she already knew a good deal about it—in part because she had retrieved the incriminating letters, which Stephen habitually tore in pieces but did not destroy. Mina hoped that he would go along with Amelia's plans for the divorce since, however it was done, their correspondence would be useful. It proved adultery, if not the intolerable kind.

Things became more complicated when Amelia learned that Mina, rather than Stephen, would come to London that autumn for her one-woman show at the Carfax Gallery. Obliged to maintain the fiction of friendship with both Haweises, Amelia attempted to drive a wedge between them by aggravating their professional rivalry, since their shows were up at the same time. Whenever she took prospective buyers to see the work of both, she did so with the understanding that they should declare their preference. These judgments were then reported to Stephen: one of her titled friends had declared Mina's work clever but one-sided, while his was clearly of greater importance.

The peculiarities of this triangular rivalry were enhanced when Mina arrived in London after a stop in Paris to help select the drawings for the 1912 Salon d'Automne, where one hopes that she found time to visit Gertrude. Following this brief stay in the city she loved, Mina was in good spirits. Amelia kept her promise to introduce her to the Duchess of Rutland and other important people, performing these duties with her own ends in mind. (To the Duchess she wrote: "Mrs. H. is charming and very clever but of course her husband is the genius.")

During their visits, Amelia wondered why Mina kept bringing the subject round to Stephen. Speculating about how much Mina "knew," she begged for Stephen's permission to mention their plans for the future. Mina had already told her that they had never been in love, that he had married her for her income, and that they had already discussed divorce. And while she made it clear that she would not stand in Stephen's way once he made up his mind, she would prefer a French divorce, to minimize scandal. Comically, while both women were on the verge of admitting what they "knew," the rules of polite society made this disclosure unthinkable. Amelia veered between the desire to stay on good terms with Mina in order to further her plan and the impulse to denigrate her work to those who mattered.

The Carfax's reputation had changed since Mina left London. Established at a time when British xenophobes spurned French art, the gallery had bravely shown the work of Rodin, Augustus and Gwen John, Sickert, Beerbohm, Roger Fry, and William Rothenstein, as well as the Camden Town Group. Yet while Robert Ross, the director, favored a Continental approach, he had gone on record in opposition to the Post-Impressionists: "The emotions of these painters (one of whom, Van Gogh, was a lunatic)," he wrote, "are of no interest except to the student in pathology, and the specialist in abnormality." Ironically, Ross may have been receptive to Mina's decorative approach because it recalled that of his friends—the decadents of the nineties. Membership in the Salon d'Automne and residence abroad were also in her favor, but what mattered most was that her drawings were neither disturbingly foreign nor offensively modern.

Her work attracted critical attention. The *Studio's* review was favorable although somewhat ambivalent: "The Directors of the Carfax Gallery have, during the past month, introduced to the public an artist who is quite unusually gifted as a colourist—Mina Loy (Mrs. Stephen Haweis), who descends artistically from Beardsley and Conder," it began. "Her work, which has many limitations," the review continued, "is carried through to success in the strength of a fine imaginative feeling for pattern and an indisputable sense of colour." As if prompted by Amelia, the *Morning Post* praised Stephen's panels ("both dainty and strong"), then added: "While Mr. Stephen Haweis is exhibiting at the Baillie Gallery, Mrs. Haweis (Mina Loy) shows a collection of drawings at the Carfax. It is difficult to find for these any common denominator save in their quaintness—though 'quaint' is not precisely the term." *L'Amour dorloté par les belles dames*, the canvas that had won praise at the 1906 Salon d'Automne, struck this reviewer as one of her best designs, along with the "dainty conceit" of a drawing entitled *Ces Coeurs*, in which young ladies were shown emptying captured hearts into a wheelbarrow. Because the whole *Ladies at Tea* sequence resembled old-fashioned cartoons, he concluded that Mina would make a talented illustrator. While these notices were positive, "quaintness," "cleverness," and "subtle coloration" were the familiar stereotypes of feminine painting. And were they judging her as Mina Loy or as Mrs. Stephen Haweis?

Mina decided to stop seeing Amelia once she had dropped enough hints about being cooperative in the event of a divorce. After the doldrums of Florence, it was exciting to be invited to parties where one "met bigwigs in quantity," and to be cultivated by the Duchess of Rutland. The years of taking tea with wellborn Anglo-Florentines had taught her how to behave on such occasions. Mina boasted to Stephen about her social life and told him that she might have some book illustrating to do. Stephen relayed the news to Mabel—by then in New York—that Mina "sailed into lunch with a duchess by herself half an hour late without fainting—lost a good many things—sold her clothes, went to theatres and generally had a very good time." One assumes that she also took the time to visit her family and let them know that, contrary to expectations, she *had* amounted to something.

In 1912 Mina might have managed to re-establish herself in London—provided she maintained the connections that she and Stephen had made through their British friends in Florence. The New English Art Club and the Carfax Gallery provided excellent credentials. Either Gordon Craig or Augustus John could put in a word with Rothenstein, who advised galleries and exhibition societies, and through Mabel's friend J. E. Blanche, they could obtain introductions to painters in these circles.* If things went well, she might have been asked to show at Vanessa Bell's Friday Club, a Post-Impressionist stronghold where the decorative potential of Matisse and Gauguin was being explored. But following up on these contacts required a self-assurance that Mina could tap only inconsistently when faced with the class distinctions of British life. She felt more comfortable with Americans like Mabel and Muriel Draper, for whom such distinctions did not seem to matter, than with her own compatriots.

By 1912 Mina had lived abroad for more than a decade. Muriel, who had become one of London's most celebrated hostesses, was the one friend there with whom she could be herself—particularly since Muriel entertained, Mabel recalled, "as one is seldom entertained on this earth." Muriel's all-night parties made the Villa Curonia look tame. Her salon began late in the evening, when the best musicians in London, Arthur Rubinstein and Pablo Casals, arrived from their performances. Muriel had remade one of her two small houses into a modernist version of the Braggiottis' music room, with walls stripped to the bricks, a skylight, and a Bechstein piano; champagne suppers appeared at midnight, followed by scrambled eggs at dawn. Muriel's wit had established her as the most original woman in London.

When she and Mina received copies of Gertrude's "Portrait of Mabel Dodge" from its subject, they were amused by the contrast between the antique floral cover and the ultra-modern prose. Muriel told Mabel, "Ducie Haweis & I wanted to wire from London, 'We understand *the cover*(!) We *know* that.' " The three women were all engaged in the process of self-transformation, which called for something more than what was known or familiar.

The most important artistic event while Mina was in London was Roger Fry's second Post-Impressionist exhibition. An occasion to judge how far London had come in its belated acceptance of European painting, the show featured Bonnard, Cézanne, Matisse, and Picasso, along with the British "Post-Impressionists" including Vanessa Bell, Duncan Grant, Wyndham Lewis, Spencer Gore, and Stanley Spencer. Mina did not find this group impressive, except for Lewis, whom she had known in Montparnasse. He

---

* About this time Mina must have met C. M. Pearce, a minor Post-Impressionist and friend of Blanche who later served as her London representative.

was "a marvellous draughtsman," she wrote, "of the Picasso school—in method—but himself alone in vision." Stunned by his *Timon of Athens* illustrations, in which hard-edged geometrical figures are propelled through space as if in an explosion, she considered his approach the only one to make inroads on the unconscious.

Although Mina could not, at this point, conceive that her own art might transcend the conventions of representation, Lewis's use of vigorous semiabstraction succeeded in stripping figurative art of the excrescences that had accumulated over the centuries. His armored men struggling across a battlefield as if they found themselves in an electric storm were recognizable as soldiers, yet they seemed to have been abstracted from historical time into some other realm. And although she could not draw that way, she understood his wish to depict a world composed of clashing forces and energies. Lewis's vision struck her as more forward-looking than Picasso's: it pointed a way beyond linearity.

Amelia's plans for Stephen to "push" his work in London had accelerated his desire to set sail for Australia. Of her scheme for him to live in the studio she had found, he protested, "Nothing will induce me to live in England until I have plenty of money. I am perfectly sure that you and I could never get on together under any but very favourable circumstances." In desperation Amelia wired that she would accompany him on his trip, but in her next letter made it clear that she had resigned herself to more distant relations. If she was not to be his companion, she might at least act as his agent. She had already negotiated favorable terms with the Baillie Gallery for future exhibitions and distributed "The Seven Ages of God" to a number of important people, including G. B. Shaw. Couldn't he sail from England, she pleaded; couldn't they meet once more as friends with "no thought of sex in either head"?

In November Mina returned to Florence to find Stephen's preparations under way. When she objected to his plans to have her cable him money at regular intervals, Stephen let slip the fact that Mabel had not only encouraged him to go but warned him that Mina would object, just as she was doing. Even though Mina was angry at the thought of their plotting, she could not bring herself to put all the blame on Mabel. "What on earth do you mean by enthusing Ste to go to Australia," she scolded. "It's a most expensive 'idea' this one," she went on. "I wish I could shove all the responsibility of the consequences on your charming shoulders—I wish I had seen Edwin. I would have bewitched him off to Greenland." On the one hand, she welcomed Stephen's departure, but on the other, she was anxious about the long period during which their marital status would remain unclear. And because she was far from London, she feared that nothing would come of her fragile connections to the art world, the book-illustration scheme, or her friendship with the duchess. Since Mabel was at least partly responsible for her fate, she asked her "whether there is any dealer in America who would give me a show & whether you would help this lonely widow—with a family growing up—by advising me *which one?*" Her elation over her London successes gave way to a depression which deepened in the gloom of Florentine winter.

At the same time, Stephen became exceptionally energetic. Busily selling paintings and studying taxidermy in order to prepare museum specimens on his travels, he was also preparing a series of talks on modern art. He would lecture "not to the savages—but to the next best, to the Australians," he told Gertrude, and asked her to send lantern slides of the best modern art, since he wanted to say "what Matisse & Picasso would like said of themselves." He might prepare the way for a big exhibition in Australia before settling in Fiji, where he intended to "declare to these people the will of the Gods of Montparnasse." Anticipating objections, he added, "I know you think me old-fashioned, bridgeless, hopeless, nevertheless I feel blindly sympathetic. Having no bridge for myself," he continued, "it has occurred to me that I may be myself a bridge unto Beyond-Art for some even more rudimentary souls in the sorrow of unenlightenment." He closed on a note which Gertrude would appreciate: "I feel a real need to go away from old masters and candelabra, and the placid docility of Mabel's tiger rug is beginning to give me a pain."

Yet Stephen still needed Mabel, who in her role as promoter of the spirit was arranging a joint exhibition for him and Craig. She had begun discussions with Martin Birnbaum, one of the few New York dealers who liked modern art, but when Birnbaum insisted they pay for shipping and insurance, Stephen told Mabel to drop the negotiations. He hoped that something could be arranged instead for Mina: "I would like Dusie to have a show in America as I'm sure she would do well with it—for myself I'm in a wave of not caring if anybody sees my work." Enclosing his visionary pamphlet, he asked whether he might dedicate "The Seven Ages of God" to Mabel. Talks were being conducted with a London publisher through "an agent," the long-suffering Miss DeFries.

In a burst of sympathy of the kind one feels before departures, Stephen was concerned about Mina, who was suffering from headaches. In December she took to her bed, where the doctor told her to remain "without even reading or being spoken to," Stephen noted. When she failed to improve, the doctor decided that she was suffering from "suppressed influenza," the source of the pain that moved all over her body. Three weeks of bed rest failed to bring any improvement. Mina spent her thirtieth birthday in bed. She had little to do but ponder the collapse of her marriage, combined with the prospect that her artistic career would not progress under the circumstances.

Stephen took her to Forte dei Marmi to convalesce early in the new year. Despite their differences, she let him take care of her: she took walks on the beach and collected seashells as if she were one of the children. Stephen did not even seem to mind when his London publisher finally rejected "The Seven Ages of God" as likely to do more harm than good. He felt the need to put Europe and its disappointments behind him. Explaining to Giles and Joella that he would be gone for a long time, he filled a large wooden box with their Christmas ornaments and the colored beads with which he planned to amaze the natives. In February, when Mina's health seemed better, he informed Mabel that he was about to leave his "deserted wife & poor fatherless children." Once he set sail, Mina's desperation grew. She went back to bed in her darkened room while the household tiptoed around, whispering about a nervous collapse.

8

Risorgimento

(FLORENCE, 1913–14)

ALTHOUGH MINA'S RESPONSE to her situation was dramatic, she was not the only member of their group to succumb to malaise. Having "done" the Renaissance, Mabel was seeking fresh sources of power in America, and Gertrude was freeing herself of Leo's influence in favor of Paris, Picasso, and Alice, while her brother turned to psychoanalysis. In a similar spirit, Gordon Craig was drawing up plans for the theater of the future as Stephen traveled in search of the primitive nature beneath his layers of civilization: he saw himself, like Gauguin, as an explorer "painfully seeking simplicity" along with a change of air. That winter, only Mina had nowhere to turn.

I

Sometimes it seemed that both her debility and her neurasthenia were disguised forms of spiritual longing. She had been too preoccupied with her own misery to notice the changes in Stephen. Now she felt abandoned despite her efforts to be rid of him. A peculiarly unfulfilling dependency had developed between them. Signs of spring appearing in the market— the wild irises, tulips, and tuberoses—did not refresh her spirits, and Christian Science brought no comfort.

Whenever Mina roused herself sufficiently to think about the future, it was Mabel's ability to listen that she missed. Despite Mabel's faults, she was the one person who could help her to think through her predicament. Mabel's letters were full of news about the upheavals in consciousness taking place in the New World, where people spoke of mind cures and the most advanced planned to try psychoanalysis. Mina had already forgiven her for her role in Stephen's departure. Although she did not feel well enough to work, she hoped to make a name for herself in New York with Mabel's help: her spirits lifted when she thought of Birnbaum's gallery. Promising Mabel that she would paint some new tea parties, Mina asked to have her exhibition postponed. She did not feel equal to the task of recovery.

During her weeks in bed, Mina reread Mabel's letters and thought about their talks at the Villa Curonia. To complement Freud's idea of the subconscious, her friend had proposed a superconsciousness. Something of this sort was needed, Mina wrote to Mabel, to account for the imagination: "Freud who seems to have been a sort of wet nurse to sub-c[onscious] would not leave much room in it for evolving creative inspiration." While the subconscious sounded like "a dumping ground for cast off impressions," she went on, "if you accept the superc[onscious]—there is no limit to possibility." She and Mabel were still trying to make contact with a higher realm, the "possibility" beyond the borders of mundane reality.

On her return to America, Mabel had been so disoriented that she, too, suffered a nervous collapse. When she persuaded the well-known neurologist Bernard Sachs that Edwin was the cause of her depression, Dr. Sachs told him to leave and prescribed a nourishing diet and long walks for Mabel. She now lived in the social limbo of those who, like the Haweises, had separated "for health reasons" but had not divorced. Since the doctor emphasized physical strength at the expense of spiritual insight, Mabel had begun a self-directed reading program on the nature of consciousness.

While Mina repined in Florence, Mabel immersed herself in the thought of the British scholar Frederic Myers, a founder of the Society for Psychical Research and the author of a study proving that the spirit survived after death. At the time, Myers's theories struck many readers as more complete than Freud's, which offered no consolation on spiritual matters. After poring over *Human Personality and Its Survival of Bodily Death*, Mabel posted the two heavy volumes to Mina, who, she thought, would appreciate Myers's interest in clairvoyance. The notion of a "subliminal" self had come to him during experiments with automatic writing—when this part of the psyche seemed to dictate the events that resurfaced.

To spiritual seekers like themselves, Myers was more uplifting than Freud. The subliminal self lay hidden below the threshold of awareness, he believed, but often emerged in the "uprush" of artistic genius. Artists were more permeable than other people: their creativity sprang from "states in which some rivulet is drawn into supraliminal life from the undercurrent stream." What was more, in his view artistic genius played a role in evolutionary progress. Myers's theories seemed to justify Mabel's yearning for a higher stage of consciousness, and his terms for the subliminal—"gold"

144

amid "detritus," the "uprush" of fresh waters, an "intensified glow" of the visual spectrum—joined poetry with science.*

But Mina was less interested in the latest theory, however stimulating, than in finding a way of joining Mabel. If Stephen could ship himself off to Australia, surely she could cross the Atlantic. Like divine providence, Bergson had just arrived in New York to deliver a series of lectures. There was an *élan vital* at work in the world, Mabel believed, and she had a role to play in its unfolding. Having banished Edwin, Mabel had hastened the process of personal liberation by bobbing her hair and decorating her home in white, for a fresh start. Next she invited all the modern thinkers to her soirées. A new energy would start to flow, she wrote, once "all *sorts* of people could meet under one roof and talk together freely on all subjects." By 1913, the most diverse groups came to Mabel's salon: "Socialists, Trade-Unionists, Anarchists, Suffragists, Poets, Relations, Lawyers, Murderers, 'Old Friends,' Psychoanalysts, I.W.W.'s, Single Taxers, Birth Controlists, Newspapermen, Artists, Modern-Artists, Clubwomen, Woman's-place-is-in-the-home Women, Clergymen, and just plain men."

Soon Mabel was boasting to Mina about her latest project. The Association of American Painters and Sculptors was preparing an exhibit of modern art to be hung at the 69th Regiment's armory rather than at a museum. Not content to flout tradition in this way, they also planned to bring most of Fry's 1912 Post-Impressionism show, which was sure to provoke a scandal. As the subject of Gertrude's "Portrait of Mabel Dodge," Mabel had acquired a name in artistic circles and was, for this reason, asked to join the organizing committee of what would soon be called the Armory Show. She had adopted the exhibition, she wrote: "It became, overnight, my own little Revolution."

In her role as revolutionary, Mabel felt revitalized. The Armory Show would awaken the consciousness of all those who had been asleep, she believed: "What is needed is more, more and always more consciousness, both in art and in life." As examples of awakened consciousness, Gertrude's portrait of Mabel was to be distributed before the show along with a special issue of *Arts and Decoration* including Mabel's recent article about Gertrude. The armory was mobbed on opening night; by the end of the month, over 100,000 people had seen the notorious paintings. A parody of Marcel Duchamp's infamous *Nude Descending a Staircase* appeared in *The Evening Sun* under the title *The Rude Descending a Staircase, or Rush Hour at the Subway*, and New Yorkers were asking, "*Who* is Gertrude Stein? *Who* is Mabel Dodge at the Villa Curonia?" Gertrude was, the editor of *Arts and Decoration* explained, "the only woman in the world who has put the spirit of post-

---

* Myers's idea of creativity manifested as "a rush upward of a subaqueous spring" bears comparison with William James's notion of the stream of consciousness. Of Myers, Samuel Hynes observes, "For all the scientific gestures, psychic research appealed to a need that was essentially religious."

impressionism into prose," and Mabel "the only woman in America who fully understands it."

Mina read Mabel's article, "Speculations, or Post-Impressions in Prose," the moment it arrived. Addressing their shared sense of spiritual urgency, Mabel declared, "This is an age of communication, and the human being who is not a 'communicant' is in the sad plight which the dogmatist defines as a condition of spiritual non-receptivity." To illustrate the point, she continued, "Gertrude Stein is doing with words what Picasso is doing with paint." Her method, she explained, was to wait for words "to rise from her sub-consciousness to the surface of her mind," an approach to composition which Mabel considered "a working proof of the Bergson theory of intuition."

Mina replied at once. "Your article excited me immensely," she told Mabel. It was as if their conversations had been put into print. "You said just what had to be said," she went on. "It probed so well that even to the 'non-communicants' it must convey the certainty that your conception of the thing was entirely fertile." Those who insisted on remaining unconvinced were nonreceptive philistines. Thanking Mabel for keeping her informed, Mina continued, "This is the first time I've felt enough joy in me to write about anything that matters—remember that any news you send me will be a real tonic . . . What fun you are having," she added wistfully.

By this time Mina had consulted the young psychiatrist Roberto Assagioli. Doctors in the United States and Europe generally believed that women were prone to nervous disorders such as neurasthenia and prescribed bed rest, sensory deprivation, and a regimen of forced feeding to strengthen the patient. Unlike most of his colleagues, Assagioli liked and respected women. Mina responded to his treatment, which included daily rest in a dark room and vapor baths followed by cold compresses, and, when she felt better, visited Assagioli, whose presence was itself soothing.

Assagioli, who came from a cultivated Jewish family, was well known in Florence and had written papers on both medical and literary subjects. A friend of Papini, Assagioli was also widely read in philosophy and Eastern religions, but his manner was as gentle as Papini's was fierce. While at medical school, where he studied psychoanalysis, Assagioli had contributed to Papini's magazine as well as to the official psychoanalytic journal. Jung had recognized him as one of Freud's most promising disciples. By the 1910s he was formulating his own approach, which he would call psychosynthesis.

Like Myers, Assagioli thought that the unconscious was balanced by another dimension, a "superconscious," where one's soul experiences the desire for transcendence. And while Freud saw religion and art as sublimations, Assagioli considered them pathways to this higher self. Like Freud, he believed that we suffer from the repression of our instincts, but he also felt that we suffer as much from the repression of the sublime. Assagioli was particularly sensitive to the spiritual concerns of women: he was perhaps the only man in Italy interested in Christian Science, meditation, and his mother's new faith, Theosophy. To Mina he was above all a reassuring friend and counselor. One could effect change by becoming aware of the will, he explained, as well as by imagining what one hoped to bring about—a technique now known as "visualization." And he, too, believed in spiritual evolution, a possibility that Mina found reassuring.

She also turned for advice to Mabel's friend George Herron, a deposed American minister whose radical interpretation of Christ's word had led him in the direction of utopian socialism. Herron's messianic outlook accorded with her own, and his philosophy—an applied Christianity resembling an idealized socialism—opposed the "will to love" to the much-discussed "will to power." Herron and his wife, Carrie Rand, were the sorts of outcasts with whom Mina could sympathize. After the scandal of Herron's free union with Carrie, which died down only when she made over her fortune to his first wife, they had settled in Fiesole, where he expounded the need for a socialism based on spiritual ideals: his habit of applying biblical exegesis to political realities no doubt brought to mind Mina's childhood hope to see the kingdom of heaven on earth. God was Love, in this literal reading. What Mina lacked was nourishment for the spirit—which would be found, she believed, in Manhattan, among the communicants.

While news of the Armory Show and her friends' counsel improved her spirits, Mina did not feel up to painting. (Presumably she also wondered whether "tea parties" would do in such volatile times.) That spring she barely managed to interest herself in daily life. The children were well looked after, there were visits to the Braggiottis', afternoon teas at Giacosa's or fruit ices at Doney's, Sunday walks to the Boboli Gardens, and soon the household's annual departure.

The only news concerned Gordon Craig's attempts to demonstrate his genius. Several years earlier he had discovered the Arena Goldoni, an open-air theater in Florence where he hoped to establish his School for the Art of the Theatre. These plans materialized in 1913, when Craig secured financial support and began to attract pupils. Despite his reputation abroad, Anglo-Florence thought him ridiculous. Harold Acton remembered Craig "with his flowing hair and velveteen clothes, driving his school, a bevy of Kate Greenaway girls, round the city in a Dickensian stage-coach." Unlike his many female devotees, Mina scoffed at his floating hair, and Mabel thought he looked like "Mother Goose drawn by Arthur Rackham." One day when Craig was complaining that they did not take him seriously, Mabel had proposed the idea of turning present-day Florence into a pageant: everyone would dress in Renaissance robes, eat Renaissance dishes, and sing Renaissance music. Craig had taken her at her word. He would abandon his contract with the Moscow Art Theater if she would devote herself to the plan. But Mabel had no intention of working with him and dropped the project.

Since Craig's move next door to Mina on the Costa, she had observed him at close range. He suffered from the belief that he had not done as well as Isadora, who not only had her own school but was living in Parisian splendor with Deirdre, their daughter; Paris Singer, her wealthy new companion; and their son, Patrick. In April, while Deirdre, Patrick, and their nurse were being driven home from Isadora's studio, their car rolled into the Seine and all three drowned. Craig observed calmly to Mina, "You have your children, I have my children, Isadora *has* no children." Too self-absorbed to attend Deirdre's funeral, he remained, in Mina's view, a vain aesthete left over from the nineties.

By contrast, Mabel's efforts to dynamite New York had not only shocked her out of depression; it had made her reputation. She was now, she believed, an "instrument of the times." She had created the one place in New York where people whose ideas were as different as their backgrounds could talk freely about everything from psychoanalysis and birth control to the IWW,* anarchism, and the Mexican revolution. Following her success at the Armory Show, she was being asked to support innumerable causes. After hearing IWW leader Bill Haywood describe the silk workers' strike in Paterson, she proposed to dramatize their struggle in Madison Square Garden—Craig's loss would be the IWW's gain—and dropped everything to work with a committee including Haywood, Margaret Sanger, the stage designer Robert Edmond Jones (known as Bobby), and the journalist John Reed, who was to write and direct the show.

In June thousands of workers converged on Manhattan to see the pageant. Jones's enormous silk-mill set loomed over the action; the street-wide processional aisle running through the hall to the stage created such solidarity between actors and audience that, Mabel recalled, "for a few electric moments there was a terrible unity between all those people." Despite the pageant's success, ticket sales fell short of expenses, and the demoralized workers ended the strike. By the end of the month Mabel was more interested in Reed than in the brief unity of the people. She saw herself as his muse: "I felt that I was behind him, pouring all the power in the universe through myself to him."

II

With such things going on in New York, Florence seemed more of a backwater than ever. After packing the children off for the summer, Mina counted the days until Mabel's return. Following her "honeymoon" with Reed in Paris, Mabel returned to Florence in the guise of a radical. She wore her hair in a pageboy and claimed to prefer shapeless dresses of pale

---

* The IWW (Industrial Workers of the World), a revolutionary socialist union founded in 1905 by Eugene Debs and William ("Bill") Haywood, numbered about 100,000 members—the often jobless and unskilled "Wobblies."

crêpe de chine to her Renaissance robes. She had shed the weight of the past along with Edwin.

As soon as Mabel was settled at the Villa Curonia, she invited Mina to meet her guests. Dreamy Bobby Jones, whom Mabel had installed in her Fifth Avenue apartment after their work on the pageant, derived a vicarious thrill from watching the progress of Mabel's affair with Reed. Their love, he told her, was godlike. Mina also met the tall, blond, and dandified journalist Carl Van Vechten, who looked to Mabel as the worldly woman he needed to complete his education. "She had some bad qualities and the worst one was what made her great," he wrote. "She adored to change people." At first, Van Vechten had been happy to have her change him. *The New York Times* had sent him to interview her at a time when she needed amusement, and he had introduced her to the most stimulating people in Manhattan in return for instruction in the finer things—art, wine, and sophisticated conversation. Bobby and Carlo, as they were called at the Villa Curonia, had their work cut out for them—they were to entertain their hostess.

Reed's role was different. Mabel was so proud of her young lover that she pressed copies of his writing on her friends, as she had done with Gertrude's portrait. And when she installed him in Edwin's bedroom, the silken rope ladder was at last put to good use. Their affair was often stormy. Reed wanted to learn about Italian politics and history, but Mabel resented his interest in anything besides herself. "I hated to see him interested in Things," she complained. If he visited churches, she worried that he had forgotten her. When he decided that Italy was beautiful but "so *old*," she felt reassured. Yet whenever his attention wandered, she feared she was losing him.

Although Mabel's emotions were too volatile for discussions of spiritual matters, Mina had not had such a good time since her visit to London. She often spent the night in Arcetri rather than go down the hill to the Costa. Mabel had also invited Muriel Draper, who arrived with her husband and members of their circle, including Arthur Rubinstein, Muriel's lover. The close proximity of these two sets of self-dramatizers produced a comic-opera atmosphere, Muriel recalled, where "almost everyone was in love or in hate." Carlo sulked whenever Rubinstein took his place at the piano and quarreled with Bobby about his increasingly bizarre designs for Muriel's costumes. (Bobby added ostrich feathers to her multicolor turban as the perfect complement to a long yellow dress and bright blue bodice stitched with scarlet beads.) Several members of the party gave way to hysterics following the return of the Villa Curonia ghost.

Soon Mabel was again trying to entice Gertrude to Florence. "*Please* come down here soon," she begged, "the house is full of pianists, painters, pederasts, prostitutes, and peasants . . . Great material." Although Gertrude failed to take the bait, several guests began to draw on this provocative "material." Reed, for whom life at the villa offered "a real picture of ultra-modern, ultra-civilized society," was writing a play about how difficult it was to reconcile his political beliefs with his new life. This skit included Haywood and the strikers along with an account of God's attempt to create the modern woman. Reed's recipe sounded as if it would produce Mabel Dodge: "figure that will stand a Greenwich Village Uniform; thorough comprehension of Matisse; more than a touch of languor; a dash of economic independence; dark hair, dark eyes, dark past." The play also included the Voice of Leo Stein, Gertrude, and three Fairy Godmothers, choruses of pederasts, Pierrots, and Pierrettes, and a special part for Mina as a dragonfly. But Mabel failed to see its humor. By August Reed was composing verses on the "smothering silky death" of the villa's atmosphere.

When not quarreling with the others, Van Vechten was also writing about his Italian holiday. *Peter Whiffle*, his 1921 bestseller, would portray Mabel as Edith Dale, "the amalgam which held the incongruous group together." All that summer he took notes on their conversations, which formed the basis for the symposia on modernist aesthetics in his novel. One evening a visitor announced that art was a cross between style and black magic. Struck by the vehemence of Mina's reply, Van Vechten wrote it down: "Each artist is protesting against something," she insisted, "Hardy, against life itself; Shaw, against shams; Flaubert, against slipshod workmanship; George Moore, against prudery; Cunninghame Graham, against civilization; Arthur Machen [an English author of supernatural tales], against reality; Theodore Dreiser, against style." Since Mina also imagined a new kind of novel, to consist of "two hundred thousand words about the events of an hour," Van Vechten later claimed, rather inaccurately, that stream-of-consciousness prose had been invented at the villa, "before the day of Dorothy Richardson, James Joyce, and Marcel Proust."

While Mina was pleased by his enthusiasm for new writing, she was even happier to hear about his recent visit to Gertrude. After reading her portrait of Mabel, he had written a piece called "How to Read Gertrude Stein," explaining in Stein-inflected prose that she "has really turned language into music, really made its sound more important than its sense." In May he had made a pilgrimage to the rue Fleurus, where they began a lifelong friendship. While Gertrude would become the most famous of the many distinguished women with whom Van Vechten associated himself, his interest in Mina grew once she let slip that she, too, wrote but was reluctant to show her work.

By September Mabel's guests were all gone except for Reed, whose illness delayed their departure. Feeling more secure with the power on her side, Mabel promised to do what she could for Mina on her return. In the meantime, she counseled, Mina should concentrate on making money for her passage. Mabel's financial independence made it hard for her to imagine having to live under constraints, but she sympathized with Mina's aversion to business—the belief that "trade" meant the demise of one's position.

Under the circumstances, the only solution was to take a paying guest, someone she could chaperone without loss of status.

III

Mina agreed to the plan. Within the month Stephen's studio was rented to a young American named Frances Simpson Stevens, who had come to Florence that autumn to complete her art training. She hoped to make contact with the Futurists, a group of cultural revolutionaries said to worship change. Shocked that Mrs. Stevens had sent her twenty-year-old daughter to Italy unchaperoned, Mina could not help thinking of her year in Munich under the tutelage of the Baroness, whose position she now occupied. Yet the difference in their ages—Frances was twelve years younger—did not seem important. Her boarder was a Christian Scientist, she had studied with the modern American painter Robert Henri, and her work had hung in the Armory Show. Although she could not replace Mabel, Frances was good company. Her spirits buoyed by the presence of this self-confident young woman, Mina completed a painting and three drawings for the 1913 Salon D'Automne.*

The two women made a striking pair. Frances, a talented equestrienne, had an athletic stride and a mane of blond hair which she draped around her head like a crown. The coloring and manner of each set off the other, and it was not long before they attracted the attention of the Papini group at the Giubbe Rosse. When Frances made the acquaintance of the Florentine painters Carlo Carrà and Ardengo Soffici, who, with their friend Papini, had joined forces with the Futurists earlier in the year, they began turning up at the Costa San Giorgio in the hope of enlisting her in the movement.

Futurism had spread swiftly under the aegis of its leader, Filippo Tommaso Marinetti. Since 1909, when Marinetti published the first Futurist manifesto, this well-publicized movement had exploded all over Europe in a series of exhibitions, proclamations, and performances. Marinetti's incendiary rhetoric had inspired a number of painters, sculptors, and musicians to join him. Disgusted with the nostalgic stance of European culture, they urged the destruction of artistic tradition. Why, in the age of the airplane, the wireless, and the automobile should artists restrict themselves to classical antiquity or romantic love? "Burn the museums," they cried. "Let's murder the moonlight!" Instead of art for art's sake—for the enjoyment of the cognoscenti—they envisioned art as a public happening, the overflow of their energies into the world.

Although the Futurists were responding to the becalmed situation of European culture in the 1900s, when cultivated people claimed to abhor modernity, the intensity of their program derived from the particular sit-

---

* Mina's entries included an oil painting, *La Machine à coudre*, and three drawings, *Le Cirque hagenback à Florence*, *Le Petit carnaval*, and *La Grotte de Cythère*, none of which have been located.

uation of Italy. "Futurism could only have been born in Italy, a country absolutely fixed on the past, and where only the past is newsworthy," explained one of the movement's founders. Insisting that the only way to break with this mindset was to "spit on the Altar of Art," they kept improvising new forms of scandal. At the height of their campaign, Marinetti had climbed the clock tower in the Piazza San Marco and showered the square with 800,000 copies of his speech against "passéist" Venice.

Looking back years later, the Italian theorist Antonio Gramsci emphasized Marinetti's foresight. The Futurists had understood that the age of industrial capital required *"new forms of art, philosophy, behaviour and language,"* he argued, at a time "when the Socialists were not even vaguely interested in such a question." In the field of culture, they were revolutionaries. But whatever one thought of his politics, Marinetti liked being a Futurist because it was shocking. To a new recruit he explained, "You must convince yourself that the revolutionising of *forms* prepares and assists a fundamental revolution." Then, with his gift for the unexpected, he added, "I have noticed that when I wear my fur coat, my girlfriend is a shade conservative."

Marinetti combined the skills of a propagandist and a tactician. Beneath his bravado lay the idea that culture should be treated as a political field. Both the canons of artistic decorum and the conventions of the past century were bankrupt, he believed. European standards were all *passatista*—backward-looking, outworn, passé. Rather than rehash the classics, the Futurists would depict modern life: "We will sing of great crowds excited by work, by pleasure, and by riot," they wrote. "We will sing of the multicolored, polyphonic tides of revolution in the modern capitals; we will sing of the vibrant nightly fervor of arsenals and shipyards blazing."

In Marinetti's view, the art of the past was dead. "Admiring an old picture," he argued, "is the same as pouring our sensibility into a funerary urn." What was worse, art as currently practiced mirrored the complacency of the middle classes. When Boccioni, Carrà, Russolo, Balla, and Severini —some of the best Italian painters of the day—converted to the cause, they adopted Marinetti's tone in their manifestos. "All is conventional in art," they proclaimed. "What was truth for the painters of yesterday is but a falsehood today." They intended to paint the world around them. "We would at any price re-enter into life," they proclaimed. "We would that art, disowning its past, were able to serve at last the intellectual needs which are within us." To begin afresh, they would have to unlearn "all the truths learnt in the schools or in the studios."

The painters recognized, nonetheless, that they faced an impasse, since Western art emphasized the moment—the subject caught or posed like a still life. How were they to express "our whirling life of steel, of pride, of fever and of speed"? To begin with, by abolishing the practice of painting from the model—in their view little more than "an act of mental cowardice." They proposed instead to render "the *dynamic sensation*, that is to say, the particular rhythm of each object, its inclination, its movement, or to put it more exactly, its interior force." They would show the object—animate or inanimate—not abstracted from the world but within "its surrounding atmosphere," its "emotional ambience."

The example given in the painters' manifesto was of particular interest. Rather than follow the laws of perspective, a painting of a woman looking out from her balcony might "render the sum total of visual sensations which the person on the balcony has experienced; the sun-bathed throng in the street, the double rows of houses which stretch to right and left, the beflowered balconies." This arresting image described one of Boccioni's recent paintings, *The Noise of the Street Penetrates the House*, which transcends the limits of classical perspective by breaking the barrier between the woman's domestic space and the scene she sees from the balcony. And it was not by chance that the subject was a woman: the painting illustrated the Futurist credo that art had to begin from "the starting point of an absolutely modern sensation."

Frances and Mina studied these manifestos as if they were news from the front. A painting that opened the window onto a noisy city was particularly challenging to Mina, since its title hinted at erotic freedom. While Frances was stimulated by the thought of paintings in which the mechanical forms of modernity seemed to throb and vibrate, Mina responded to the Futurists' call for change. The idea of the artist's participation in the painting was inspiring: rather than trying to paint objectively, they proposed "to insert ourselves into the midst of things in such a fashion that our 'self' forms a single complex with their identities." In this view, one's empathy with the world could infuse the onrushing quality of life into the canvas.

Frances found these ideas so exciting that she began translating the manifestos. With Mina, she discussed the meaning of Futurist "dynamism." Marinetti had recently begun to illustrate this idea in his *parole-in-libertà*, a kind of "liberated" poetry that went beyond free verse. Dynamism was best evoked by the infinitive, he claimed, because this verbal form evokes "the continuity of life and the elasticity of the intuition that perceives it." To the painters, the term meant something similar: unlike the Cubists, they aimed to show objects in motion. In addition to these technical meanings, dynamism also proclaimed the Futurists' desire to participate in, and to shape, the limitless world unfolding before their eyes.

That fall, when Marinetti was racing all over Italy like a one-man propaganda machine, he spent several weeks in Florence. In a typical Futurist amalgam of street theater, showmanship, and provocation, he often roared through the narrow city streets in a fast sports car while tossing manifestos out the window. His latest manifesto urged the modernization of the country's most *passatista* cities—Rome, Venice, and Florence—condemned both the Church and socialism, called for "the economic defense and patriotic education of the proletariat," and exalted progress, heroism, and physical force. Mina finally had a chance to meet the man who called himself "the caffeine of Europe" when Soffici and Carrà brought Marinetti to meet Frances. He took one look at the young woman, turned to Mina, and asked her to give herself to him—a *coup de théâtre* for the benefit of his comrades, she decided.

Marinetti was one of the most theatrical people Mina had ever met. Dressed like a bourgeois, he exuded the confidence of a millionaire; once he began to speak, he became a man of explosive energy. Moreover, Marinetti seemed not to converse but to speechify. "Each one of us," he declaimed, "has a cemetery within ourselves—but that cemetery must be reduced to a minimum." Although it was clear to her that he had used these lines before, they made an impact. When he boasted of his affairs with a number of foreign women, however, Mina bristled. "It's not *done*," she scolded. "If you must bawl about them, you're going to omit their names." Marinetti was quite pleasant once he stopped trying to impress her, she observed. He began dropping in whenever he came to Florence, and she noted down their conversation as if they were characters in a novel. "When are you coming over to meet Marinetti?" she asked Mabel. "His conversation is disgusting—he is so nice."

Marinetti's seductive maneuvers were such good literary material that she was soon composing a *roman à clef* about their relationship. When they met again, Marinetti asked whether Mina knew of his literary fame (he had published Symbolist-inspired verses in French, a language he spoke fluently). She knew only that his recent novel, *Mafarka*, a Nietzschean pastiche in which the hero gives birth to his own son, had been seized in Italy and judged pornographic. In her reconstruction of this conversation, Marinetti promised to send it to her, scoffing at the verdict and roaring that his novel was *"the greatest masterpiece extant."* Mina replied demurely, "Now you shout it as loudly as that, I know it must be." She was having such a good time teasing him that she did not bother to take his ideas seriously. It was too much fun playing along with his script and seeing where it took her.

When the Futurists brought their latest convert, Papini, to Frances's studio, Mina again felt the inward sympathy he always produced in her. After some initial hostility, he had voiced a reserved solidarity with the movement in his new journal, *Lacerba*. "Futurism has made people laugh, shout, and spit," Papini wrote. "Let's see if it can make them think." Mina watched him as he studied Frances's depiction of *Lacerba*'s typographic dynamism, "his restless silence in that uproar a volcano dormant among . . . petty explosions." She still recalled the shock of seeing him "like a tramping prisoner between close grey walls" one day when their paths had crossed on the road from Arcetri: "It was in some way to Sophia [Mina] as if she had passed her own self."

Yet Papini seemed unsuited to the Futurists' habit of noisy self-celebration, and Mina wondered how he managed to tolerate Marinetti. Their alliance rested on a shared desire to shake up Italian culture and politics, but while Marinetti was happy to make use of *Lacerba*, he did not think much of its editor. Marinetti observed in private that the Florentine had neither the physique nor the voice for Futurist rallies: he was monotonous, myopic, and lacked the stamina of a revolutionary. Papini was equally suspicious of the boisterous, privileged Milanese; Marinetti boasted of staying up all night on the trains he took from one end of Europe to the other while composing his speeches, while Papini compensated for his lack of vigor with slashing verbal attacks on his enemies. As the title of his magazine implied—it was a deliberate misspelling of *l'acerba*—his intellectual posture was that of an acerbic, bitter man. Yet as she watched the two sparring, Mina again saw something in Papini that touched her.

I V

In November the Futurists devoted their collective energies to the art exhibit touted in *Lacerba* as "the most important, the most modern, and the newest that has ever been put on in this medieval city." Because Boccioni, Balla, Carrà, Russolo, and Severini were, the article continued, "the only young Italians truly concerned with reviving painting and sculpture in our great country," theirs would be "the most important demonstration of Italian art since Michelangelo." Visitors were advised to come "free of any silly traditional and academic prejudice," and with some "basic notions of the development of modern and ultra-modern painting outside Italy."

Just as the organizers hoped, a mob awaited them on opening night. The crowd stormed into the dark, narrow rooms, stared at the paintings, and pelted the artists with questions. When the crush receded, Mina brought Giles and Joella into the gallery. Although they were only four and six, the children gazed at Boccioni's *The Farewells* as if looking through a window. When someone asked what they saw, they said without hesitation that it showed a train rushing into the night. People exclaimed at their cleverness. The picture's swirling composition of dark shapes beneath superimposed lines—couples embracing before boarding the train—made sense to children but baffled adults. (In the other paintings of this triptych, *Those Who Stay* and *Those Who Go*, Boccioni had infused Symbolist emotion into his slumping figures—those who are left behind—and the fleeting glimpses of the travelers.) But if one's eyes were accustomed to classical painting, it was no easy thing to step into these scenes of modern life.

Mina was surprised to see how well the Florentines rose to the challenge. The exhibition quickly became a *succès de scandale*. People who had never shown an interest in modern art came to gape at the artists, although many simply wanted to corner a Futurist and make him explain himself. She was completely unprepared for the violence of the public's response to Marinetti's next performance, a Futurist *serata* [soirée] planned as a cross between a theatrical event and a riot. On December 12 an overflow crowd gathered at the Teatro Verdi armed with eggs, dried pasta, and rotten fruits and vegetables. As the huge mob entered the theater, their pent-up energies exploded. The organizers had created a nightmare: "Things were said that cannot be repeated, much less written," one of them recalled.

Marinetti took possession of the stage. His first words produced applause, insults, clapping, and obscenities, followed by a tumult of boos and hisses and a shower of vegetables aimed in his direction. Catching an egg in the palm of his hand, Marinetti awed the crowd into silence. "Your frenzied behavior gives me pleasure," he shouted. "The only argument the *passatisti* have," he added, "is a horde of dirty vegetables." After declaiming his latest example of "words-in-freedom" at the top of his voice, he declared another triumph for Futurism.

Next, Papini took the stage to denounce Florence. The ancient city had become a museum devoted to the amusement of foreigners, he scolded. To regain their vitality, Florentines had to renounce their worship of the past. "In a city like this one, imbued with, marked by the past as by a disease," he chided, "the fresh air of Futurism is needed to remind those who make their living from the oppressive trecento that we are in 1913." Only when they had rid Florence of Dante specialists and "other disgusting passé-ists who make their home here," he went on, "will the city cease to be the charming medieval city beloved of snobs." The evening ended in applause, and Mina observed to Frances "that she felt as if she had benefited by a fortnight at the seashore."

Lacerba's next issue proclaimed a victory. The Futurists had produced feelings of shame in the public, joy among their ranks, and countless conversions to the cause. Not only had they held the stage against five thousand hostile spectators, the article claimed, but they had transformed the crowd's "overflowing vulgarity, personal hates, posthumous resentments, drunken frenzy of being many against few, [and] raging stupidity" into "a magnificent spectacle."

When Marinetti next appeared at the Costa San Giorgio, Mina was feeling the effects of the *serata*. Confused by her susceptibility to "this bombastic superman," she adopted an ironic tone. He did not really exist without a crowd, she teased. "Even there you are a spurious entity," she went on, "drawing 'something' out of an audience to give back to them in your superb pretentiousness as yourself." Trying to get the upper hand, he declared that henceforth she was not to attend his performances. "I will rely on myself not to allow you to give me the same emotion twice," she replied, relishing the twists and turns of their verbal combat.

Marinetti brought the conversation around to the subject of "woman." When Mina objected to his *disprezzo della donna* [scorn for woman], he claimed that by this slogan he intended a critique of bourgeois culture, which depicted women as femmes fatales or madonnas and turned art into a corrupt posturing before an effeminate ideal. His scorn was directed not at individual women, he explained, but at woman conceived "as the divine reservoir of *Amore*." He had made his meaning clear in his latest manifesto, a satire entitled "Down with the Tango and Parsifal," which warned his cosmopolitan lady friends—like herself—against love as envisioned in D'Annunzio's plays, in the "musical neurasthenia" of Wagner's operas, and in "the effeminizing poisons of the tango," which was currently turning men into "gelatine." Love was not an "epidermic oscillation," he continued. It was "an exciting, strengthening, muscular dance."

Moreover, his painter friends had made the point in their public stance against the nude in painting. Like himself, they did not scorn flesh-and-blood women, nor were they concerned with immorality. They objected to the nude as a genre and urged a ten-year moratorium simply because "artists obsessed with the desire to expose the bodies of their mistresses have transformed the Salons into arrays of unwholesome flesh!" Marinetti and his collaborators called for the end of all cultural forms based on "a sentimental, decadent, paralytic Romanticism toward the Femme Fatale of cardboard."

Mina was not so easily convinced. His point of view was too masculine, and his opinion of woman too appallingly low. And it did not help to be treated as an exception to the abasement of her sex. But she was having such a good time playing cat and mouse with him that she let down her guard. As re-created in her *roman à clef*, at this point he took her in his arms—"His tactile adroitness equaled his conversational celerity," she wrote—and demanded proof of her affection.

"You can have me," she agreed, "some other time."

"No," he insisted. "Now."

"I prefer to put you to a little more trouble," she replied. Standing a little apart from herself, she realized that "she was watching a spectacle she had never seen acted that way before."

While Mina admired Marinetti's bravado, she had doubts about his intentions. "I am in the throes of conversion to Futurism," she told Mabel, "but I shall never convince myself. There is no hope in any system that 'combat le mal avec le mal,'" she continued, "& that is really Marinetti's philosophy—though he is one of the most satisfying personalities I ever came in contact with." It was hard to explain his effect on her. "I have torn up at least half a dozen letters I wrote you," she added, "as being already outworn in conception half an hour after I wrote them." Since Marinetti had just hopped on a train to Russia, it would be some time before she could make up her mind. She was "coming to life again, but don't feel the risorgimento will be complete."

By winter the rhetoric of Futurism colored her thinking. Her revival from depression was a *risorgimento*—a resurgence of energy, an uprising against internal doubt and division. Consorting with the Futurists had proved to be the best antidote to low spirits. Since their onslaught on the city, Florence had become quite lively. Right-wing groups had raided Assagioli's office, she told Mabel, "& there is every semblance of an explosive atmosphere here—only if you stop for one moment you find there is nothing to explode." To pay for her trip to New York she planned to sell Stephen's antiques, a form of revenge that had the merit of sounding practical. Her social life already presented ambiguities: some of Stephen's female friends had dropped her, and Carrà was courting her. "He's a dear scrubby little person—about 3 years old," she wrote, "who invited me to matrimony," an offer she declined. "Everybody I know at present is trying to forget what a complicated affair life has been mistaken for," Mina continued. "We are all busy re-simplifying ourselves—I am 29—next year I shall be 28."

In addition to simplifying her age (she was thirty-one), Mina chose an unexpected means to complete her *risorgimento*. Energized by Marinetti's assault on language and freed, to some extent, of her subservience to villadom, she attempted a number of prose and poetic forms, including rhymed verse, prose poetry, aphoristic statement, and an idiosyncratic version of Marinetti's favorite genre, the manifesto. If she could not paint her way out of her depression, she might write her way out, as Mabel had done.

In these exercises, the earliest evidence of her turn from art to literature, Mina was also parsing the contradictions of Christianity—its unkept promise that "the last shall be first." A prose poem entitled "The Prototype," perhaps her first writing from this period, rings with the messianic socialism of George Herron: its vision of the Duomo on Christmas Eve depends on the contradictions between religious ideals and social realities on which much of Mina's poetry, as well as her art, would be structured. Rather than worship a statue of Christ, the poem's speaker prays to the sickly infant of a poor woman beside her: "And I who am called heretic am the only follower in Christ's footsteps among this crowd adoring a wax doll. For I alone am worshipping the poor sore baby—the child of sex ignorance & poverty." In the speaker's appeal "to humanity's social consciousness," Mina's old outrage at her mother's God combined with her newly energized social awareness and the desire to see *passatista* convention overthrown. But to one who knew her state of mind, "The Prototype" also voiced Mina's ambivalence at being thought a "heretic," a status that filled her with anxiety and pride.

Mina sent "The Prototype" to Mabel for an issue of *The Masses* she was to edit. But in her new role as progressive spokeswoman, Mabel chose not to publish her friend's critique—perhaps because of its sentimentality. This prose piece is of interest just the same, because of the conclusion's unexpected turn. After pointing out the contrast between "perfection" and the "inconsistencies of life," the speaker shifts to an almost unpunctuated free verse:

Blow out the candles—
Throw away the wax-baby

Use the churches as night-shelters
Come into the Daylight & preach a New Gospel

To preach a more democratic gospel, she told herself and potential readers, institutions like the Church had to be reinvented, and new forms of expression had to be forged.

Of the other writing that Mina sent to Mabel during this period, two poems on messianic themes, "The Beneficent Garland" and "Involutions," also remained unpublished—no doubt because their rhymed verse made them sound old-fashioned to one whose ears were attuned to Post-Impressionist cadences. Mabel thought well enough of one of Mina's poems, however, to send it to Alfred Stieglitz for *Camera Work*: the colloquial tone and compression of "There Is No Life or Death" gave it an urgency that Mabel admired. Trying to impose her new perspective onto an older form, Mina had scraped it clean of sentiment. The result, something like a crossing of Emily Dickinson's spatial sense with Marinetti's immediacy, might have been punctuated by Gertrude:

> *There is no Life or Death,*
> *Only activity*
> *And in the absolute*
> *Is no declivity.*
> *There is no Love or Lust*
> *Only propensity*
> *Who would possess*
> *Is a nonentity.*
> *There is no First or Last*
> *Only equality*
> *And who would rule*
> *Joins the majority*
> *There is no Space or Time*
> *Only intensity*
> *And tame things*
> *Have no immensity.*

(In the manuscript the first two stanzas are unpunctuated, but light punctuation marks, dashes and a full stop, reappear in the final stanzas—a compromise between old and new.)

While Mina's writing moved back and forth between tradition and experiment, she also found the energy to begin painting again. The Friday Club, which had ties to the Bloomsbury group, accepted two of her portraits—*Woman's Head* and *Maria con Bruno*—for their 1914 exhibition. Other artists shown included Mark Gertler, C. R. W. Nevinson, David Bomberg, Paul Nash, and Nina Hamnett, among the most innovative London artists. But one had to be on the spot to make something of such connec-

159

tions. Mina was proud that Lord Henry Bentinck, the brother of Ottoline Morrell, had bought one of her paintings, yet inwardly she did not think much of her artwork. "I painted one good picture," she told Mabel, "but I have not evolved beyond post-impressionism."

More than recognition by the London art world, Marinetti's optimism was the tonic she needed. And although she could not bring herself to convert, as she put it, Futurism was doing more for her than any medicine. She was intrigued by Marinetti's *parole-in-libertà*, or words-set-free, a poetic form, he claimed, which liberated language from the patterns of linearity. She found herself responding to his writing's dynamism now that she knew what the term meant. Wildly different typefaces and sizes jostled each other, phrases ran in all directions, and boldface headlines caught one's attention. Treated this way, words all but jumped off the page.

As a stage in her personal *risorgimento*, Mina also composed the piece entitled "Aphorisms on Futurism." This idiosyncratic manifesto adapted Futurist practice to a form that was, in essence, a dialogue with herself. Although she could not quite accept the all-out warfare prescribed by Marinetti, these pointed aphorisms on psychic liberation ring with his defiance:

YOU *prefer to observe the past on which your eyes are already opened.*

BUT *the Future is only dark from outside.*
Leap *into it—and it* EXPLODES *with* Light.

FORGET *that you live in houses, that you may live in yourself—*

FOR *the smallest people live in the greatest houses.*

BUT *the smallest person, potentially, is as great as the Universe.*

WHAT *can you know of expansion, who limit yourselves to compromise?*

Once the mind was set free, she told herself (and the internalized censor), everything would be found there: "YOU cannot restrict the mind's capacity."

By adopting the Futurists' oppositional stance—the heroic "we" addressing its adversary—Mina was staging the conflicts of her psyche. But while she could now voice her desire to repudiate *passatismo*, her mind was still inhabited by the internalized "you" with whom she argued:

LOVE *of others is the appreciation of one's self—*

MAY *your egotism be so gigantic that you comprise mankind in your self-sympathy*

THE *Future is limitless—the past a trail of insidious reactions*

LIFE *is only limited by our prejudices*

DESTROY *them, and you cease to be at the mercy of yourself*

One accomplished this process by changing one's perception of reality. "Today is the crisis in consciousness," she wrote, for herself and for her generation.

In this view, geniuses like Stein and Marinetti were already inventing the new forms that would literally change the minds of those who paid attention. "CONSCIOUSNESS cannot spontaneously accept or reject new forms as offered by creative genius," she continued. "It is the new form, for however great a period of time it may remain a mere irritant—that moulds consciousness to the necessary amplitude for holding it." Her own was being reshaped as she compressed her thoughts into a form, the aphorism, that mimed self-enclosure while imitating the dynamics of expansion and release. As a group, her aphorisms enact the mind's concentration on a problem, followed by its explosive letting go.

Relations with the Futurists were stimulating in other ways as well. Although Marinetti's program included *azione femminile* (a "feminine action" unrelated to the suffragists' struggles), it was not clear whether any women played a part in the movement. The only one associated with it thus far was the French writer Valentine de St. Point, whom Marinetti put in charge of his nonexistent female cadre after she wrote two spirited manifestos in reply to his "scorn for women." Although she was writing in the years of suffragist agitation, St. Point rejected feminism as a political mistake. Her "Manifesto of the Futurist Woman" spoke of virile heroines purged of sentimentality, and her "Futurist Manifesto of Lust" argued that the new woman would come into being through her conscious use of sensuality. "Lust, like pride, is a virtue urging one on," she insisted; lust was to the body what transcendence was to the spirit.

Once Marinetti had publicized her manifestos, St. Point renounced Futurism, and she had no successors—perhaps due to the common belief that a female Futurist was a woman of easy virtue. *The Diary of a Young Futurist Woman*, an amalgam of words-in-freedom and pornography published in 1914 as the work of the mysterious Flora Bonheur, was undoubtedly meant as a satire. For several years no self-respecting woman, Italian or foreign, would find the cause sufficiently enticing to enlist. Marinetti was not the only Futurist for whom discussions of "woman" provided the occasion for banter; invitations to matrimony were the standard line of approach to anyone they thought interesting, especially if unencumbered by a husband. Thus far, Mina had enjoyed her bouts with Marinetti and Carrà's good-humored attempts at seduction. Papini was another story. Said to be happily married, he was more than wary around intellectual women.

Papini let down his guard when Mina asked him to sit for his portrait. Despite his reputation as the ugliest man in Italy, he enjoyed the interest artists took in him: "Having had to accept this face himself, he was impishly pleased for others to share in the nuisance." Mina saw that Papini had no idea how expressive he was. "His mass of curly light brown hair shot up from the deeply lined enormous forehead in a tall surprise," she noted. "The lower muscles of his cheeks were so developed they reminded one of how Demosthenes filled his mouth with pebbles, and when he spoke it was indeed as if those muscles muffled his languorous yet, at the same time, blustering voice." (His mouth was that "of an impertinent gamin.") An odd mixture of mental vigor and sulky sensuality, Papini struck her as the other half of her divided self.

During the weeks she worked on his portrait, Mina read Papini's autobiography. *Un Uomo finito* (*A Done-for Man*, translated as *The Failure*) is the confession of an autodidact who hoped to become a genius. In his youth Papini had studied the ancients in his desire to become the spiritual leader of his generation. Now he wanted to throw off his erudition—"the cloaks of religion, the cassocks of philosophy, the shirts of prejudice, the ties of ideals, the shoes of logic, and the underwear of morality"—to become as naked as Adam in the Garden of Eden. But as things stood, his desire to revert to radical innocence could have no outcome other than "four, eight, sixteen pages of printed paper—the usual journal" of the kind he published.

Moved by the book's emotional and spiritual inebriation, Mina felt it offered a glimpse into his soul. By the time his portrait was completed, she had guessed at much that Papini kept hidden. He had not overcome his defensiveness about his modest social background, which rankled whenever he spoke of Marinetti's fortune, nor did his intellectual daring fully mask the frustrations of the autodidact, for whom the acquisition of culture had meant years of sacrifice. And although *Un Uomo finito* revealed the sensitivity which Papini omitted from his polemics, he had not been frank about the issue that rankled most: just before the book went to press, he had deleted his confession that he had always known he was ugly. In some moods he philosophized about the influence of facial features on destiny. In others he made a virtue of necessity. "My own ugliness pleases me," he claimed. "To it I owe the encounter with my wildness, the greater isolation and sense of superiority of the solitary spirit." More telling than these rationalizations was the passage that Papini often quoted from Rémy de Gourmont: "Ugliness makes for timidity in the affairs of the heart, and timidity wreaks its vengeance when it turns itself into intellectual aggressivity."*

Despite—or perhaps because of—his complicated psyche, Mina was fascinated by Papini. He lacked the seductiveness of the Latin lover, and he remained silent when others boasted of their adventures. Yet he had written for all to see, "I too have been in love . . . I was not born impotent," he went on, "nor did I ever choose to become a eunuch." Neither in casual affairs nor in marriage had he found what he wanted. He had yet to meet

---

* De Gourmont, one of Papini's idols, was a provocative and much admired French literary figure and recluse who suffered from a disfiguring disease, lupus.

his Beatrice, "the woman who can take her place in the spiritual history of a soul."

In reality, Papini was gun-shy. He had recently ended an affair with Sibilla Aleramo, a well-known novelist of feminist inspiration. In 1912, after Papini encouraged Aleramo to explore the personal strain in her writing, they had a brief affair, which he broke off with excuses about his family. "It was one thing to talk about anarchy and free love over a glass in the Caffè delle Giubbe Rosse," a critic observes, "but in practice these ideas had intolerably disquieting results." Aleramo had her revenge by publishing a story in the form of an unmailed letter to Signora Papini—which had delighted the regulars at the Giubbe Rosse.

Mina could not help feeling that in Papini she had found her mate. Surely if she approached him with tact, his suspicions would relax. Yet after an awkward flirtation, she found that she could not break through his reserve. Although Papini used the same excuse with her as he had with Aleramo, he could not, however, put the beautiful Mrs. Haweis out of his mind. For some time his friend Soffici had been writing a running commentary in *Lacerba* on life at the Giubbe Rosse, where Mina and Frances were often to be found: it was jarring to see their most recent conversation with Soffici and Papini reprinted there verbatim. The two women had been saying that life just then was a sad affair. After a winking Papini claimed that Futurists were always in the best of spirits, Soffici agreed, maintaining a solid front with these "beautiful lady friends." For Papini, Futurism was often little more than an occasion for prankish displays. But by then Mina was too infatuated to notice.

In the meantime, Stephen was making inroads on her resources. Having completed the education of the South Sea natives, he had sailed to San Francisco, where the art world welcomed him as a follower of Gauguin. He was a "very modern Englishman," the *San Francisco Examiner* explained, "whose London and Paris career has attracted a great deal of attention." Within a few weeks Stephen provoked a controversy by denouncing the city's preference for nineteenth-century art. In response to the "Savonarola from Tahiti," a local art critic remarked that despite his claim that art must be the vital expression of its time, Stephen's own painting showed the influence of earlier artists, especially Whistler. Bored with provincial art politics, Stephen told Mina to wire him the money for his trip to New York.

Soon after his arrival there in March, Stephen called on Mabel. He showed her Mina's letters and asked what she thought of their references to Futurism. Mina had no doubt meant to be reassuring when she told him that she was "not intellectual enough to become a futurist—but am intelligent enough to have given up everything else." And although she could do nothing without his consent, Stephen was alarmed by her plans. Full of mixed messages, Mina's letters expressed the volatility of her emotions during the process of *risorgimento*. After informing him of her latest solution to their financial problems—renting rooms to foreigners—she teased, "The lodgers are good looking & I am very worried by them—their mothers have *no* sense of responsibility—or they would not have left them with me—they can argue me into anything." The letter was signed, "Yrs faithfully ta femme incomprise."

Had he known what she was up to, Stephen would have been even more concerned. Soffici had invited Mina and Frances to show their work in the First Free Futurist International Exhibition, to be held in Rome that spring at the Sprovieri Gallery. He hoped that they would join him, Marinetti, and the others at the opening. It was hard not to take the offer seriously: Mina would represent England in the first gathering of Futurist-inspired art. And since Papini was spending March in Paris, she could concentrate on getting her work ready. But the trip would cause gossip. People would think that she *had* converted.

When Marinetti returned from Russia with news of his successes, Mina had not decided whether to go to Rome. She must stop worrying, he told her. She was neglecting the present for what she called her inner life. "You are a busy little mystic," he scolded, pursuing "an enigma that isn't there." The unconscious, the superconscious, and the subliminal self were illusions. When Mina protested that he took everything at face value, he replied that there *was* nothing more. Any other view was a sham. Her family, her education, the awkwardness of her status—none of it mattered. Marinetti, who was trying to yank her into the present, began to seem like a modern-day Aladdin with a new kind of lamp.

Mina set to work on a series of Futurist portraits of this mental conjuror. The next time he called, she wondered why—given his well-known misogyny—she was susceptible to his influence: "Here she was with the horrid man she ethically despised feeling thoroughly comfortable." "His proximity was in a manner thermal," she noted. Marinetti possessed some quality to which she could not help responding. "He had the right stuff to give," she continued, "& he flung it about this liveness of his careless of who picked it up." What was more, he knew how to bolster her while leaving her free to make her own decisions: "Raw from her enforced intimacy with mollycoddles & her aborted love for Joannes [Papini], she felt the salutary jar of being lifted up & let down." And doing things his way had something to be said for it. "After all it had its beauty, rushing through life like an express [train] with the flair for congealing in a moment what it took others three quarters of a century to overlook."

In exchange for lessons in taking life at face value, she would give him what he wanted. She would go with him to Rome.

9

Futurist Wars

(FLORENCE—ROME—FLORENCE,

1914–16)

I

While Mina saw this adventure as the start of her *Vita Nuova*, she knew that she was taking a risk. Wealthy Americans like Muriel and Mabel might travel with their lovers and not suffer the consequences, but someone like herself would pay a price. The foreign residents would find out; Stephen would be informed. Still, it seemed better to run that risk than to stagnate in Florence.

When she met Marinetti at the train station, Mina was so embarrassed that she hid her head in a newspaper. Once settled in their compartment, her doubts gave way to the physical comfort of his presence. She felt herself slipping into his world, she recalled, "where everything seemed to be worked by a piston." Hiding away from the past in his jacket, she continued (speaking of herself in the third person), "she was caught in the machinery of his urgent identification with motor-frenzy." Time and space rearranged themselves for this man, whose essence "lay not in arrival, but in activated suspension"—the rhythm of the railroad linking the successive moments in the perpetual motion of his life.

They arrived in time for the opening. Giuseppe Sprovieri, a young

Roman who hoped to combat the provincialism of Italian art by devoting his gallery to Futurism, expected to provoke a scandal. The French had failed to jump on the Futurist bandwagon, but the participation of the Russians, Americans (Frances), and English (Mina) demonstrated the movement's growing influence. Whereas Frances's most recent paintings, entitled *Dynamism of a Market, Dynamism of Pistons*, and *Typographic Simultaneity of "Lacerba,"* were all orthodox Futurist subjects, Mina's were more unusual. Along with three portraits of Marinetti—two "dynamisms" and a "facial synthesis"—she had sent a "dynamism of the subconscious," no doubt an attempt to blend what Marinetti called her obsession with the inner life and her current flirtation with Futurism. The Russian section included paintings by Alexander Archipenko, Alexandra Exter, Nicolai Kulbin, and Olga Rosanova, at that time unknown outside their country. Sprovieri also included Marinetti's efforts, a three-dimensional self-portrait and a collaboration with the playwright Francesco Cangiullo, both composed of objects. It was a daring show, Sprovieri observed, one which people came to see out of curiosity.

Mina stood next to the piano and talked to the Futurist musician Pratella, who explained that only the most original, courageous, or violent canvases had been chosen. Pleased with this estimate of her work, she could not help wondering whether her association with Marinetti might have influenced the process. As Pratella played his compositions faster and faster, she began feeling overwhelmed by the "dynamisms" and "decompositions" on the walls: the paintings seemed to whirl around the room in a frenzied demonstration of Futurist theory.

Most of the guests were sympathizers. Under the impression that Mina was a Futurist, an enthusiastic woman hailed Marinetti as the prophet of a new religion. Just as Mina started to object that his work was pornographic, the discussion turned to Papini's latest diatribe in *Lacerba*, a bitter, almost hysterical call for the suppression of women. Marinetti seized the occasion to harangue the group on the difference between Futurist obscenity and Papini's foray into the genre. Papini had reduced woman to her sexual organ, he bellowed: "a urinal of flesh that desire represents to itself as the chosen recipient." This ugly attack was a blow to Futurism, he went on; it would alienate the movement's best propagandists, the women. *"Woman,"* he roared, "is a wonderful *animal*, and when I put into print any part of her body I choose, it is in purest appreciation." When the crowd became silent, he continued: "I do not admit that I can write about a fondant [a creamy confectioner's base used in candy-making] which gives me some pleasure—& not about a vagina which gives me infinitely more. This is a beautiful word, it means what I say."

In her reconstruction of the scene, Mina emphasized her awe: "He had said one word—distinctly, unaffectedly; & it had crashed down the barriers of prudery. Such primordial pokes of simplicity," she wrote, "might re-direct the universe." Papini's rage resulted from his failures with women,

Marinetti believed. Glancing at Mina, he decried the Florentine's ugliness: "It is a physical commotion to sit in the same room with it." But Mina had already forgiven Papini. Eventually, she told herself, her affection would bring him round.

Another *serata* was about to begin. Having just penned a manifesto on public speaking, Marinetti enacted the principles of declamation as "lyrical sport." In the old oratory, he insisted, the speaker resembled "a marionette parading on the stage of a farcical puppet show." The Futurist orator aimed to transcend the merely personal by evoking cosmic energies: he tried, Marinetti went on, "to metallize, liquefy, vegetalize, petrify, and electrify his voice while merging it with the very vibrations of the subjects treated." Whether or not the audience grasped the meaning of his gestures—"a synthetic creation in space of cubes, cones, spirals, and ellipses"—they were mesmerized by the amount of noise he made.

Next, the Futurists joined their leader in a performance piece enacting the obsequies of a *passatista* philosopher. Cangiullo, its author, played a funeral march while the defunct—a clay head stuffed and garlanded with rotten vegetables—was paraded about with mock solemnity. Marinetti's funeral oration concluded with some words-in-freedom intended to hasten the process of decomposition: the old philosophy was rotting from the inside out, and the Futurists were finishing it off. As in the Dada evenings anticipated by these Futurist soirées, the participants were moved by a mixture of revenge and generation murder—as if the old order would simply die of ridicule.

A few days later, Marinetti announced that he was taking Mina to the seaside. She was having such a good time that she agreed to do whatever he wanted. At lunch by themselves in the dining room of the empty hotel—in the off-season they had the place to themselves—she found herself again becoming Marinetti's audience. He warned her not to look at another man. But Mina took pleasure in teasing him: she *had* looked at Papini, she told him, and entertained thoughts of marriage. Did he think Papini could fall in love? Marinetti scoffed at the idea. Papini was, he shouted, "a man who could never love anything but the publicity of attaching a distinguished woman." Mina wondered whether she could carry off this adventure. Nothing would go wrong, she noted, "as long as I have got tight hold on myself." But it was one thing to hide away in Marinetti's jacket and another to maintain this outlook in Florence.

II

After her return from Rome, Mina's moods swung between elation and depression. Marinetti was to lecture in England and could not say when they would meet again. She had initiated the affair as a cure for low spirits, she told herself, and she had always known nothing would come of it. Marinetti hadn't time, and she didn't trust him. But there were moments when this perspective deserted her. Hinting at the situation to Mabel, she wrote: "I cannot tell you anything about myself—without telling you *all*—which is impossible." "Even if the old values are gone," she went on, "& my roots . . . being tugged out—for experiment—in exquisite & terrific anguish," her new life was "interesting." Nevertheless, she wondered where they were all going ("ma *dove* si va?").

Marinetti always said that the destination did not matter; what counted was to go. But while *he* could hop on the next train to London, she was not free to join him. News of his exploits filtered back to Florence in the London papers. On April 28 he recited his war epic, "Zang-tumb-tumb," with the help of the English artist C.R.W. Nevinson, who banged drums offstage to simulate the noise of battle. Wyndham Lewis, in the audience that night with most of the London avant-garde, described the event as proof of "what Marinetti could do with his unaided voice" and some years later remarked that a day on the Western Front was nothing compared to Marinetti's oratory. Although he would soon reject Futurism, at this point Lewis considered Marinetti one of the age's most forceful personalities, "an intellectual Cromwell."

In May, Marinetti raced to Naples for another exhibition, then returned to London to finish the manifesto he was writing with Nevinson. "Vital English Art," their collaborative effort, proposed to purge English art of *passéism* by denouncing not only the Royal Academy but also "the commercial acquiescence of English artists," the public's thirst for "the pretty-pretty, the commonplace, the soft, sweet, and mediocre"—the Pre-Raphaelites and the Aesthetic Movement—and a host of attitudes that made the English see art as "a useless pastime, only fit for women and school-girls." For an artist schooled in this tradition, this manifesto had the effect of a cold shower. Even if one agreed that English art lacked vigor, its call for work "that is strong, virile and anti-sentimental" went too far in the opposite direction. Soon after Nevinson declared himself a Futurist—the only British one apart from Mina—his fellow avant-gardists denounced the new "ism" as a vulgar Italian product and of no importance to Vorticism, the new movement they were hatching.

But Mina was too far from London to follow these controversies, and she was more interested in what was happening in New York. Resettled into the routines of expatriate Florence, she slipped into such *passatista* states of mind as self-doubt and depression, especially after Frances became engaged to a wealthy nobleman, the Marchese Salimbeni. Asking for Papini at the Giubbe Rosse, Mina learned that he had been in poor health since his return from Paris. And from what she could glean in conversation, the tensions that had always existed between the Florentine and Milanese branches of Futurism had revived.

Soon after the Teatro Verdi *serata*, Papini began to chafe at the demand that all Futurists endorse certain principles—opposition to the past, words-in-freedom, dynamism in the arts, and Marinetti's political program. He voiced his concerns in *Lacerba*: these principles encouraged imitations of reality and cultural activism as an end in itself. Against his attack, Boccioni defended the movement as a "superior barbarism, through which the Futurist artist proceeds into an unfamiliar world"—a reply that all but threatened Papini with excommunication. Papini's countercharge insisted on his rights: "absolute freedom, risk, a hazardous quest without any rules, contempt for all mythologies, total atheism, immoralism, cynicism." Given the all-or-nothing claims of Marinetti's program and the chip on Papini's shoulder, no compromise seemed possible.

In March, while Papini, Carrà, and Soffici were fighting fresh artistic battles in France and Marinetti was dashing from Moscow to Rome, what looked like a stalemate became a wary truce. The three Florentines traveled to Paris for the opening of the Salon des Indépendants. Although they claimed that the best modern art was Futurist-inspired, no one in Paris agreed. Their efforts to win respect for the movement, related in *Lacerba*, included expressions of respect for the exploits of one Arthur Cravan, an unusually tall boxer and poet whose writing had the impact of his punches. "The artistic and literary world is turned upside down because of *Maintenant*," Papini wrote, "a magazine where this same Cravan has the courage to put into print the filthy gossip that circulates surreptitiously just about everywhere." Papini printed Cravan's name in capital letters—a tactic he would employ in his own campaign of self-aggrandizement.

Mina finally saw her own name (Loy, not Haweis) in print when *Camera Work* arrived in June. "Aphorisms on Futurism" was the central literary text in an issue including excerpts from a play by Gertrude and an art review by Mabel. Mina had made her literary debut in the company of friends, yet she was also set apart as that mysterious thing, a Futurist. For some time American readers had been curious about Futurism, which they tended to confuse with all art that looked outlandish: the *New York Herald* called Futurism the attempt "to disintegrate things seen into their emotional constituents" resulting in "frantic network[s] of form and color." Mina's use of "the new form . . . that moulds consciousness" spoke to an audience eager to learn about her subject.

To readers unfamiliar with Futurist typography, the look of her writing produced a shock. The first word of each aphorism was printed in bold capitals, as if she were shouting at the reader. Sentences ran as one line to emphasize the final word, or spilled over so that both the last word of the line and the initial word of the next stood out in the white space around them. And although she had used dashes to create reflective pauses, no punctuation connected the successive aphorisms, which floated in the void of the page. Few readers saw that these expressive uses of typography depicted the "fallow-lands of mental spatiality," as she put it—the tabula rasa of the imagination.

Since the author of these aphorisms was a woman, many found her tone as disturbing as her punctuation. Whoever Mina Loy was, she had gone beyond the conventions of womanly feelings: women could not forget that they lived in houses in order to live in themselves, nor would they seek to express "egotism . . . so gigantic that you comprise mankind in your self-sympathy." And how could a woman endorse the aggressive Futurist call to "arrive at respect for man as he shall be"? Although Mina would soon acknowledge the price paid by women who identified with Futurism, she began by seeing acts of will, courage, and deliberate creation as imbued with an energy that was masculine. By aligning with the Futurists to this extent, she could exteriorize her psychic struggles. She was surprised, nonetheless, by the daring look of her words upon the page.

Yet when Mina ran into Papini again, she did not feel particularly daring. Their mutual friends knew that she had gone to Rome for the Sprovieri exhibit, but it was unclear from Papini's brusqueness what he knew of her relations with Marinetti. She invited him to bring his daughters to tea with Giles and Joella, a gesture that could hardly be construed as antagonistic. They met again, alone. Despite her Marinettian "cure," her feelings for Papini remained, and she noticed that he kept bringing the conversation around to Marinetti. Not only were they rival leaders of the new generation, but Papini could not suppress his resentment of Marinetti's advantages. She would have to find a way to take their relations back to where they had been in January, when she was painting his portrait. Yet Marinetti always seemed to get in the way. When she pointed out the lack of logic in Futurist theory, he accused her of bad faith. Whatever Marinetti's shortcomings, Papini was certain that he had had won her with his energy.

Increasingly, Papini voiced hostility to his rival in *Lacerba*. Asserting his right to publish whatever he chose, he argued that just as the artists who showed at the Paris Indépendants insisted on absolute freedom, so did the Lacerbiani, and he stressed his dislike of those who were all of a piece or lacked imagination—in sum, of people unlike himself. "My own spirit is like a cinema where the program changes hourly," he boasted. Others required consistency in order to "catalogue us once and for all, to know where we stand, as friends or as enemies." He rejected such demands. "I hate all fixed doctrines—all closed sects—all immovable 'movements,' " he declared. Since there was no such thing as true friendship, it was better for false friendships to erupt into enmity.

III

While these veiled threats appeared in *Lacerba*, Papini was spending the summer in the mountains, Marinetti was recovering from his London skirmishes, and Mina was waiting for Mabel, who arrived at the Villa Curonia toward the end of July. She was accompanied this time by her son, Neith Boyce and her children, and a nurse. Van Vechten was to join them shortly, and Reed was expected in August.

Although the newspapers spoke of trouble between Austria and Serbia, Neith and Mabel were too tired to pay attention. When Mina came to Arcetri to meet her, Neith noted, "Mrs. Haweis looking like a Futurist poster—pretty and very talkative." (Mina designed her own versions of the fashionable new skirts that bared the wearer's ankles while binding them so tight that she could only hobble.) Neith listened as Mina explained the intricacies of her situation: "She relates her affair with Papini, from whom she is taken by Marinetti, her present lover," Neith observed in her diary. Although she was not sure about the details, she gathered from this conversation that Mina was involved in an awkward triangle with the two Futurists, and that, as a result, the men were estranged. They also gossiped about Frances Stevens's engagement to the Marchese Salimbeni, who seemed loath to set the date. The women decided to escape the summer heat in Vallombrosa, a mountain resort two hours from Florence. Van Vechten, Leo Stein, and his companion would join them.

Van Vechten arrived from Paris on July 31. In France, he explained, the train stations were full of soldiers, and everyone was talking about war. When he added that Jaurès, the socialist leader, had been assassinated, Mabel became alarmed. Van Vechten wanted to know where the Futurists stood. Leo Stein argued that the movement should be seen as "the protest of Milan, the machine city of dynamic force, against the museum cities, in which there is little industrial activity." Marinetti did not understand music or painting, but endorsed the work of his collaborators, Leo thought, provided they kept "to the expression of the dynamic, which is symbolized by the automobile or the airplane . . . He loves noise and he loves war because it is noisy," he concluded.

Mina was particularly critical of the Futurists' misogyny, and she ridiculed Marinetti's desire to bear his own children. Despite these reservations, Van Vechten, who was interested in Marinetti's call for a virile modern art, asked Mina to lend him copies of the official Futurist publications. His appetite whetted for aesthetic novelty spiced with gossip, he also asked about Papini, wondering at Mina's affection for this "strange and very ugly youth, who mingled his dreams and his politics, mixing mysticism and propaganda until one became uncertain whether he was seer or socialist." Only Mabel felt certain of imminent catastrophe. While her friends debated the merits of Futurism, she kept repeating, "Just think, the world will never be the same again."

On August 2 Germany declared war on Russia. What would Marinetti say now that he had what he wanted, Mabel asked. On August 3 the Germans invaded Belgium—a de facto declaration of war on France—and the Italian government announced its neutrality. Life at the villa was finished, Mabel wailed. "I'm glad I don't want *this* any more," she went on. "I've made a perfect place of this and now I'm ready for whatever will come after the war." But while she was prepared to renounce private property in the future, Mabel wired Reed to bring gold. The war would finish Cubism and Futurism, Leo declared. "After the war," he went on, "there will be no more of this nonsense."

The mood was sober on the train to Vallombrosa. Uncharacteristically, Mina paid no attention. Her nose buried in *Trend*, the new literary magazine Van Vechten had brought from New York, she forgot to look out for the station where they were to catch a connecting train. Fearing that they would be trapped in the mountains after the outbreak of hostilities, Leo returned to Florence, and Carl became so nervous that Mabel sent him back as well.

Once they were in Vallombrosa, the cool mountain air and pleasant quarters at the Albergo Paradisino revived the remaining party. Other guests at the inn, a former monastery, included a number of English convalescents and Roman matrons—members of the grande bourgeoisie who dressed in black enlivened by diamonds and seemed more preoccupied with their daughters' matrimonial prospects than with the crisis. Mina and Mabel were set apart by their unusual clothing and manners—they smoked in public. From her isolated position as a foreigner, Mina observed the differences that placed her outside both cultures and began drafting "July in Vallombrosa," the poem that would become the first in a series of "Italian Pictures." Contrasting the desiccated English invalids with the spirited Italian matrons, she eavesdropped as they discussed "the better business of bed-linen."

Within days of their arrival, Europe was in turmoil. England, France, and Russia had declared war on Germany, rail and postal services were interrupted and currency of all kinds in short supply. Although there were rumors of engagements in the Mediterranean between the English and the Germans, the Italian press was so severely censored that it was impossible to know what was happening. They were cut off.

While Mabel's group debated a variety of scenarios, Mina remained calm. She found a cottage in Saltino, a nearby hamlet, for Frances, Giles, Joella, and herself. Soon Mabel and Carl, who had reappeared in Vallombrosa, were proposing to rent a house where they, too, could wait out the war. Before a peasant would rent his house, Mina explained, one would have to build him another; village life was conducted on such economic principles that houses never sat empty. Although she had managed to rent her cottage from its absentee owners, Van Vechten disapproved on aesthetic grounds. It had been sent from Sweden in sections and set up here, "entirely out of harmony with the landscape," he noted. Shocked into practicality by the circumstances, Mina hired a cook, began stocking flour, beans, and oil, and inquired about rooms for her friends. True to her taste for luxury, Mabel remained at the Paradisino.

By the second week of August, Mina began to worry. There was no news from England, and cash was running low. The Marchese arrived to see Frances, bringing provisions in case of a siege. He offered the party the use of one of his more remote castles. Because it could be reached only by donkey cart, they might winter there in safety. Frances and Mina were planning to volunteer as nurses, but Neith noted that after two weeks in close quarters, they were getting on each other's nerves. Elated by a letter from Marinetti, who planned to form a foreign legion if Italy remained neutral, Mina announced that there had been uprisings in Milan. "She says he believes in Italy as religiously as the Kaiser does in Germany," Neith noted in her diary, "that he is a born leader." Mina also managed to find the latest *Lacerba*, with much of its pro-war rhetoric blacked out by the censors. If Papini and Marinetti agreed on little else, both supported immediate intervention.

The war was sure to reach Italy by September, people said. "We are doomed," Mabel moaned, "our pleasant useless civilization effete and worn-out—the goths are upon us." The Chinese would invade Europe and the Americans would be dragged into the ultimate world war. In this state of mind, Mabel could not bear Van Vechten; she muttered about "his 'great stupid eyes' " and his "solemn greed," while he blurted out his resentments to Neith. Mabel was "a perfect tyrant," he complained, "and the most jealous person alive." Worse, she was neglecting her appearance.

Since there was little to do but stroll through the forest, Carl joined Mina on her daily walks to the post office. A few years later, he published a cameo of her "as she tramped along the dusty roads of Vallombrosa, enveloped in a brown cloak trimmed with variegated fur, scarcely able, thanks to her tight skirts, to move one smartly shod foot in front of the other." With a characteristic touch of venom, he recalled that, however bad her nerves, Mina took pains with her toilette:

She made an unforgettable figure with her grey-blue eyes, her patrician features, her waved black hair, parted in the centre. Tall and slender, her too large ankles were concealed by the tight hobble-skirts she wore. Her dresses, of soft dove-coloured shades, or brilliant lemon with magenta flowers, or pale green and blue, were extremely lovely. Strange, long earrings dangled from her artificially rosy ears: one amber pair imprisoned flies with extended wings.

A crisis was no excuse for a lowering of standards.

While Mina tried to plan her future in Florence, Neith and Mabel kept discussing the likelihood of revolution at home. They would all have to work, Mabel thought, but could "get jobs from the labor leaders and adopt the Revolution." "These days," Carl recalled, "were very comic opera."

Mina had not told Carl about her affair with Marinetti, the person whose letters she was watching for at the post office. Between engagements he took the unusual step of having himself driven up to Vallombrosa to see her. He began by boasting about his conquest of London, thinking in this way to impress her with his influence in her homeland. When this tactic failed, he told her that she was unlike other women. "You've got a wonderful brain," he cried, "but it's like a gimlet. I wonder it doesn't hurt you!" Mina must renounce her "mania for the Absolute" and enjoy what he had to offer. "It would do you so much good if only you could stop thinking," he argued.

As they strolled beneath the cathedral ceiling formed by the pine trees, Marinetti unexpectedly dropped his bluster. Suddenly he was making a declaration of love. "He offered himself as a poor thing but a genuine article," she recalled. It was hard to take him seriously. Although he swore he had been faithful since their trip to Rome, Mina feared that he would soon treat her as one more conquest. His scorn for women made her distrust him. "I have quite a few sympathies with my sex," she explained. As he drove off full of plans to rally volunteers, she analyzed their relationship. She had begun the affair "to save her equilibrium," she told herself, and he had turned to her to soothe his vanity. But "two necessities need never make one love."

The comic-opera aspect of their stay was enhanced when hundreds of peasants in costume came down from the mountains on August 15 to celebrate Assumption. Hearing that tickets to New York could be had for passage on an emigrant ship leaving Naples in a week, Mabel's party hurried to Florence in time to get the last four berths—despite the fact that this "one-class ship" was a kind of cattle boat. When Mina joined them in town for a few days, she related the news from Marinetti, who had reached Paris. The French were "fighting like wolves," he wrote, and the city was deserted. Since Reed was also in Paris, Mabel decided to forgo the cattle boat and join him. In an abrupt about-face, Mina admitted that she did care for Marinetti. Her plans, Neith noted dryly, were "to go to Milan and get a child by him before he goes to war—she says there is nothing else for women to do in war-time." Neith was delighted to be leaving Florence, "the same gossipy parochial little place—people and everything on a small scale—everybody having an affair and rather sordid."

But unlike her friends, Mina had nowhere to go. She decided to stay in the mountains until the end of summer, since Marinetti might reappear between attempts to organize his foreign legion. Before leaving Florence she took the precaution of letting her house and taking a small flat nearby, on the via dei Bardi, where Papini lived. With her friends she pondered the crisis. Workers who had been employed in France were flooding back to Italy. The Marchese was concerned about his *contadini*. He had no work for them and no way to feed them. "There will be a peasant uprising this winter," he predicted, "unless we go to war!" Only the Braggiottis remained calm. They had plenty of money due to their habit of hiding gold pieces and, being vegetarians, required very little. Less optimistic souls were laying in stocks by the hundredweight.

Sigmund Lowy,
London

Dora, Julia, and Mina Lowy,
London, c. 1886

Mina Gertrude Lowy,
London, c. 1886

Mina Lowy,
London, c. 1897

"Dusie" (Mina nude), Paris: photo by Stephen Haweis, c. 1905

Stephen Haweis and Mina Loy, Paris:
photo by Henry Le Savoureux, c. 1905

Stephen Haweis:
drawing by Mina Loy

Stephen Haweis, Paris:
photo by Henry Le Savoureux, c. 1905

L'Amour dorloté par les belles dames: *drawing and gouache by Mina Loy, 1906 (Collection of Roger L. Conover). Commenting on the effect of* L'Amour dorloté *and its companion piece,* La Maison en papier, *at the 1906 Salon d'Automne, a Paris art critic called them a singular outgrowth of Decadent art*

Consider Your Grandmother's Stays: *drawing by Mina Loy, 1916*

La Maison en papier: *drawing and gouache by Mina Loy, 1906*
(Collection of Michael Duncan)

Gertrude Stein in birdbath,
Tuscany, c. 1910

Mabel Dodge in lotus position,
Arcetri, c. 1913

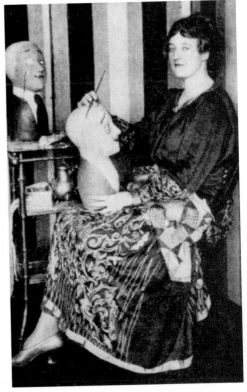

Frances Simpson Stevens
in her New York studio,
c. 1916

Filippo Tommaso Marinetti, 1910

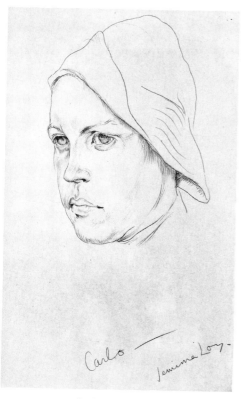

Carl Van Vechten:
drawing by Mina ("Jemima") Loy,
c. 1913

Giovanni Papini, 1910

Mina and Joella,
Forte dei Marmi, c. 1909

Joella and Giles,
Florence, c. 1911

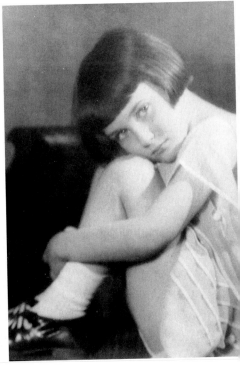

Giles, Giulia, Fabienne, and Joella
on the roof of 54, Costa San Giorgio,
Florence, 1920

Fabienne: photo by Man Ray,
Paris, c. 1924

Marinetti by analyzing it. He had urged her to take her life seriously, encouraging her to think that she might defy her upbringing without dying of shame. Despite his misogyny, he had helped her to see what self-respect could mean to a woman.

Mina began to take her poetry more seriously as well after receiving a copy of *The International*, a left-leaning review to which Carl had sent her "Café du Néant." Its publication in the August issue, along with poems by the Indian mystic Tagore, marked her debut as a poet. Set in the Paris of the 1900s, "Café du Néant" evokes a Symbolist atmosphere in order to transcend it. As carefully as if she had painted the scene, Mina arranged her verbal composition to spotlight the central figure, a woman who, like herself, had been in thrall to the myth of love:

> *There is one*
> *Who*
> *Having the concentric lighting focussed precisely upon her*
> *Prophetically blossoms in perfect putrefaction.*

This decadent ideal is undercut by the poem's mannered rhetoric and onomatopoeia, which are both supplanted by the conclusion's gesture toward freedom: "Yet   there are cabs outside the door." "Café du Néant" bade farewell to the past as if already looking back from the future.

Shortly after his return to New York that autumn, Carl put Mina's avant-garde connections to good use. As the new editor of *Trend*, the little magazine that published such New York moderns as Walter Arensberg, Djuna Barnes, Mabel Dodge, and Wallace Stevens, his editorial policy was to give "the younger men free reign to experiment with new forms." As if to prove the point, he added disingenuously, "In this number we introduce to American readers Mina Loy, who is in sympathy with the Italian school of Futurists." Reading the contributors' notes—also by Carl—Mina learned that she was "a painter of international fame" who "has interested herself in the Italian Futurists, led by F. T. Marinetti, and for them has renounced the brush and taken up the pen."

Of the work that he had taken to New York, Carl chose for Mina's debut in his magazine "The Costa San Giorgio," a poem with a strong affinity to Futurist painting. If "Café du Néant" is a melancholy interior, "The Costa San Giorgio" is a bustling street scene—the one Mina saw from her window—written from the perspective of an Englishwoman for whom Italians were at once more vital and more disorderly than her compatriots. What seemed Futurist-inspired to Carl was not only the poem's subject matter but also the way it looked on the page. Capital letters called to the reader like street signs; irregular lines and spacing transcribed the dynamism of the Costa's "life-traffic":

We English make a tepid blot
On the messiness
Of the passionate Italian life-traffic
Throbbing the street   up   steep
Up   up   to the porta
. . .
Oranges half-rotten are sold at a reduction
Hoarsely advertised as broken heads
BROKEN HEADS   *and the barber*
Has an imitation mirror
And Mary preserve our mistresses from seeing us as we see ourselves

Van Vechten may not have noticed that this kaleidoscope of details also makes an implicit social comment. The maids' prayer to the Virgin implies that things are not what they seem; other female eyes watching from behind their shutters can only

Mingle eyes with the commotion

For there is little to do
The false pillow-spreads
Hugely initialed
Already adjusted
On matrimonial beds.

Their pillow shams are false, their initials—their claim to identity?—are exaggerated. Although these women's lives are far from tepid, the poem hints, they unfold within confines that constrain self-knowledge.

Wondering what *Trend's* readers made of her, Mina teased Carl about his efforts as publicist: "I am so interested to find that I am a sort of pseudo Futurist. Couldn't I become an absolutist or something as I evolve?" To make him understand that she was "in no way considered a Futurist by Futurists," she explained, "If you like you can say that Marinetti influenced me—merely by waking me up." But she withheld comment on Carl's mischievous publication in the same issue of her husband's recent letter to a New York paper. "Man can manage everything best entirely alone," Stephen had written. "We 'antis' proudly point to Europe and its little health-giving squabbles; or perhaps the war was due to votes for women accorded in Finland, in which case it is a disaster."

Fencing with the Futurists had already reawakened Mina's interest in the "woman question." In Vallombrosa, when Marinetti had insisted that his scorn for woman did not apply to her, his bad faith enraged her. He supported the suffragists, whose efforts, he wrote, would free woman from "her actual state of intellectual and erotic slavery," but maintained that whatever came of their crusade, the average woman would continue to

178

exist within the "closed circle" of femininity, "as a mother, as a wife, and as a lover." And the alternative proposed by Valentine de St. Point—a woman along the lines of Futurist man—seemed too self-serving. As another exception to the rule, Mina felt compelled to write "an absolute resystemization of the feminist question" in the form of a manifesto, her opponents' weapon of choice.

However uncertain Mina may have felt in private, her "Feminist Manifesto" is confident. It reads like a continuation of her long-standing debate with Marinetti. She began by rejecting reformism. "The feminist movement as at present instituted is *Inadequate*," she declared. "No scratching on the surface of the rubbish heap of tradition will bring about *Reform*, the only method is *Absolute Demolition*." The goal of equality between the sexes was illusory, she argued: women should "leave off looking to men to find out what you are *not* [and] seek within yourselves to find out what you *are*." As things stood, men and women were enemies, "with the enmity of the exploited for the parasite, the parasite for the exploited . . . The only point at which the interests of the sexes merge," she concluded, "is the sexual embrace."

Mina's cures for this situation were drastic. They included the surgical destruction of virginity at puberty, woman's right to sexual experience and motherhood regardless of marital status, collective resistance to the misleadingly "advantageous bargain of marriage," and new social attitudes toward love. "The realisation in defiance of superstition that there is *nothing impure in sex*—except in the mental attitude to it," she argued, "will constitute an incalculabl[y] wider social regeneration than it is possible for our generation to imagine." But to effect this regeneration, "sex or so called love must be reduced to its initial element, [and] honour, grief, sentimentality, pride & consequently jealousy must be detached from it." Only then would women find themselves ready to exert "intelligent curiosity & courage in meeting & resisting the pressure of life."

Mina posted her manifesto to Mabel and asked what she made of feminism: "Have you any idea in what direction the sex must be shoved —psychologically I mean?" She was eager to know more about Mabel's new friend Margaret Sanger. For months, Sanger had been embroiled in legal battles over the publication of her magazine, *The Woman Rebel*, following the American postal authorities' condemnation of its articles as "obscene, lewd and lascivious." Frances Stevens, who had informed Mina of the Sanger scandal, wrote to say that "there are some of us over here . . . who won't believe that '*thats*' all Love is," Mina told Mabel, adding that Frances was having "virginal hysterics." "Of course '*thats*' all nothing and yet '*thats*' all it is," Mina observed. Anything more was "spiritual effervescence." While Sanger might eventually put "that" in perspective, Mina was not optimistic about feminism's current direction, since "slaves will believe that chains are protectors."

As for herself, she complained, "I haven't a wise companion for the

moment—entirely dependent on myself for everything." Marinetti's courtship had ceased once he devoted himself to politics, his allies were "fighting
him to the death," she added, "& he's getting fat & his eyes are brutalised."
While Mina agreed that Futurism had to become a political party to survive,
she also feared the effects of modernization. "Italy won't be half as de-
lightfully human when it gets a modern move on it," she wrote. "One's
almost inclined to hope its apathy will survive all shaking—although
personally—I am indebted to M. for twenty years added to my life from
mere contact with his exuberant vitality."

V

Throughout the autumn, Papini maintained a shaky alliance with the Futurists. Although he shared their intoxication with war as the solution to
Italy's problems, most important for him, intervention offered his compatriots the chance to recognize her national genius—in himself. Imagining
war as an apocalypse, Papini hoped that it would realize the "empire of
the spirit." Even before the outbreak of hostilities, he had argued that
progress required sacrifice. "Blood is the wine of strong peoples," he insisted. "Blood is the oil for the wheels of this great machine which flies
from past to future." *Lacerba's* tirades continued to unleash his dreams of
fusion with the Zeitgeist, that great machine that flies from past to future.

Although Mina paid little attention to Papini's apocalyptic language,
she could not help noticing the absence of Marinetti's name or any account
of his political activities in *Lacerba's* pages. Papini claimed that the Futurists'
propaganda did not warrant attention: instead of noting Marinetti's growing
influence, Papini dismissed his "little Milanese demonstration" and ridiculed Balla's "inopportune and empty manifesto on neutralist clothing."
In Papini's view, *Lacerba's* pro-war efforts were more intelligent than anything concocted by the Milanese.

The spirited independence of Mina's "Feminist Manifesto" could be
maintained as long as she did not have to test it. Once Papini returned to
Florence, it became more difficult to separate "sex or so called love" from
the other emotions with which it often becomes entangled. Pondering ways
to repair the damage to his pride caused by her affair with Marinetti, she
determined to create "a loophole whereby Geronimo [Papini] could return,
with honour, to the point of departure." This was best done in writing,
his own medium for action. "Finally I managed a concoction of skits of his
literateur's [sic] attitude," she recalled, "a parody attempting to make this
unconscious man conscious of an opportunity to forgive me!"

Mina was thinking her way through a dilemma that was thoroughly
literary. By dramatizing the sexual politics of Futurism and her "current
obsession the sex-war," she would show Papini how to turn the tables on
his antagonist. Her "Futurist Dialogue," written at this time and as yet
unpublished, restaged their encounters the year before in Frances's studio,

180

when Marinetti's boasting had startled Mina and embarrassed Papini. The byplay among the characters—Tea Table Man, Don Juan, Futurism, and Love (Mina's part)—made clear how little she thought of "crude virility" as proof of manliness. But one needed a dash of feminism and a sense of humor to enjoy her parody of masculine posturing, both characteristics in which Papini was lacking.

Life was not a play that could be rewritten with a clever last act, and in any case, the main character kept inventing his own dialogue. Throughout the winter Papini was preparing his farewell to Marinetti. The December issues of *Lacerba* brimmed with hostility. In his retrospective account of the Florentines' ties to Futurism, Papini claimed that he had allied himself with Marinetti despite misgivings. He had labored to offer the Futurists a theoretical basis for the construction of "a truly modern aesthetic," he went on, despite a leadership which went in for "mere charlatanism and theatrical clowning." In this view the Futurists got more from the deal than the Lacerbiani. They had gained "the support of learned men, who could with all the more reason despise the past because they had studied it," Papini wrote, and who could express the inchoate desires of their comrades. This was a low blow. Long before joining forces with Papini, Marinetti had reinvented the practice of polemical prose, the "art of making manifestos."

Papini's animosity also resurfaced in his chronology of disagreements. By the spring of 1914, he claimed, the Milanese had become "a school, a sect, a church whose recognized high priests alone had the right to give out the formulas and show the way," and Futurism itself little more than a "brand name." As one historian has observed of his attack, "Powerful as this indictment may sound, much private disappointment and rancor went into it." In New York, Cook had gotten the essentials of the story right. Papini's emphasis on ideological differences rationalized strong personal dislike: the first conflict had erupted at the start of Marinetti's affair with Mina. When Papini finally called on her in mid-December, he was still obsessed with his rival.

Once settled in the little salon where she had imagined their reconciliation, Papini told her angrily that he *had* been in love with her earlier that year, that he had felt an affinity between them. His love had evaporated when he learned of her "betrayal." After some arguments about who was to blame, Papini condescended to make love to her—as if to even the score. This stage of the affair—more a matter of searching discussions than of passionate lovemaking—brought Mina little satisfaction. Continuing to tax her with "infidelity," Papini insisted that she had been attracted to Marinetti because he was so energetic. Even in their most intimate moments, Marinetti came between them; it was clear that Papini was using her to get back at his rival.

To Mabel, Mina confessed, "I am rather blue—I've seen P again & I'm frightfully in love—& *he hates* me with a voluptuous and exotic frigidity. I do want to run away & come to New York," she continued, "but there is no way financially of settling the children—and at present *no war!* to put an end to the daily passions of life." She was so distraught over the course of the affair that she wondered "if hatred is the truth & love the lie—or whether even hatred is only jealousy." She added, "Don't ever live to see the day when the man you want sobs out the other one's name in the ultimate embrace. Philosophy is inadequate."

She needed to find a solution. Perhaps it was a matter of how one conceived of sexual desire. In the defiant mood of her manifesto, she dismissed love as the "parasitism of the weak"—another *passatista* convention. From this perspective, intercourse was just a collision of bodies. "Love with me is a mechanical interaction," she told Carl. "I can only give off what I'm absorbing." But however modern this approach might sound, it brought little satisfaction.

"Human Cylinders," a poem from the period of Mina's affair with Papini, evokes the isolation of lovers in their "mechanical" interactions:

> The human cylinders
> Revolving in the enervating dusk
> That wraps each closer in the mystery
> Of singularity
> Among the litter of a sunless afternoon
> Having eaten without tasting
> Talked without communion
> At least two of us
> Loved a very little
> Without seeking
> To know if our two miseries
> In the lucid rush-together of automatons
> Could form one opulent well-being

As in later poems that both dissect and lament the collapse of ideals, "Human Cylinders" evokes the failure of "communion," but it does so by adopting, then discarding, the vision of Futurism, which likened humans to machines.

Resorting to a familiar cure for emotional distress, Mina spent the last week of the year in bed. On December 27—her thirty-second birthday—she told Carl that she was "suffering from an unhappy love & getting quite passatist." "I am too modern to despair of the future," she went on bravely, adding, "Oh Carlo do you think there is a man in America one *could* love." There was no hope for her in Florence. "The future has ceased to be as a future," she continued. "One can only know that for the present one's heart continues to beat."

Once again careening between elation and depression, Mina told Carl the following month that she had "arrived at the *glorious* age—when the born pessimist becomes the irrepressible optimist." This self-transformation "sounds easy," she went on, "but it *meant* years of hard work—& Marinetti blithe fellow—was sent from heaven to put the finishing touch—& they say he is a brute to women!" Soon, "quite happy again," she replied to Carl's request for a letter a day that this would be costly but entertaining, "for everything takes on a fresh aspect for me daily—you'd get a collection of personal friends each one dearer than the last—with thank heavens *no* common aim!" Although Papini was still bent on misunderstanding her, she was "much too full of Marinettian vitality" to be depressed. Once she realized how proud it would make Papini if she jumped off Giotto's Tower, she decided to withhold that satisfaction. But she was, she added, "honest enough to know that the only thing that troubles me is the fear of not finding someone else who appeals to me as much."

In the meantime, Papini publicized the end of their affair in an essay called "Congedo," later translated in *Others* as "Leavetaking," although the Italian title also implies dismissal. "Love, this is not your moment," it began. Too many people had watched her "pass and pass again, shamelessly, under my window, so long and skinny in fashionable skirts." She had been too conspicuous in her pursuit, "dressed so in white and yellow, in tango and strawberry." He had shut the door against her, and now, he mused, "I can walk without second-thoughts along the empty and lunar streets, like a night policeman who doesn't think of the sorrows hidden behind the perpendiculars of the walls." From this point on, he gave her to understand, he would "police" his emotions. "Goodby for this evening and for this life," he concluded.

About the time that Papini dismissed her, Mina also began to feel "really cross" with Stephen because he refused to let her divorce him. He had further compromised her chances by telling friends that he still loved her. She had engaged a lawyer in London, but did not know how to instruct him. If Stephen kept behaving this way, she would have to prove that he had committed adultery, which would mean bringing witnesses from Florence to London, as well as paying both her English lawyer and his American associate. The answer to her prayers came when Stephen wrote that Amelia DeFries would be joining him. Since Amelia's residence in Stephen's Manhattan apartment that winter would provide the grounds for an American divorce, she could afford to be generous. "Let us all help them to defy destiny," she told Mabel.

In addition to acting as confidant, agent, and editor, Carl had taken on the role of go-between. Stephen not only claimed that Mina was the love of his life, Carl explained, but he wanted to manage her art career. At Stephen's insistence, Carl lent him the three pieces—two designs for wall decorations and *Love among the Ladies*—that Mina had given him in Florence, which Stephen placed in an exhibit at the New York Architectural League. Furious that he was posing as her agent, Mina asked Carl, "Is there no way I can *forbid* him to touch my pictures & send them to just the sort of exhibitions I'd rather *not* exhibit in?" She could no longer trust Stephen, she explained, "& that is the worst feeling one can get."

Having taken leave of Mina, Papini enacted his desire for revenge on Marinetti. The February 14 issue of *Lacerba* ran the headline FUTURISM AND MARINETTISM in extra-bold letters on page 1; in the lead article Papini denounced "Marinettism" and praised the Lacerbiani as the only true Futurists. "Marinettism," he claimed, stood for ignorance, scorn for the past, militarism, chauvinism, and contempt for women, whereas Florentine Futurism meant "superculture," scorn for the cult of the past, combatitiveness, patriotism, and sexual freedom. A case of wounded pride disguised as ideological warfare, this attack left no room for compromise.

Mina longed to discuss the situation with Mabel. "Do write to me—you are the only *woman* yet evolved," she begged. "Your intuition will tell you—that there is a state of annihilation—waiting for war," she went on. As much as she longed to see Mabel, the New York trip was impossible to arrange, and in any case, as spring approached, Florence was coming back to life. "I've got the latins in my blood," Mina confided, "and the only latin's got me in his spleen—printing Marinetti's name . . . in L'Acerba— If people only realized how much too delightful they are to be quarrelled with." She added, "I don't describe to you my utter defeat in the sex war." The European war and the "sex war" were by now so thoroughly entwined that one combat suggested the other.

Mabel's own thoughts on the subject were explored in her recent antiwar piece from *The Masses*, entitled "The Secret of War: The Look on the Face of Men Who Have Been Killing—And What Women Think About It." During the weeks with Reed in Paris after their departure from Florence, Mabel had interviewed a number of soldiers in order to grasp "the principle behind that overwhelming fact that all the nations of Europe and some of Asia and Africa were at war." She discovered the secret, she thought, in "the inconceivable, the inevitable love of—fighting itself," an age-old masculine lust that had only been intensified by this ultra-modern "machine war." (A French officer told her that in hand-to-hand combat, men would not go on "mowing each other down." But with the machine gun, he explained, "you just go on turning the handle.") Some gave patriotism as the cause, others claimed to be advancing socialism, but Mabel argued—no doubt influenced by Reed—that the real explanation lay in the ruling classes' lust for power. When she talked to the soldiers' wives, they all voiced their opposition to the fighting. In Mabel's opinion, "the only hope of permanent peace lies in a woman's war against war."

Like many in Florence, where the machine war's ravages were not yet known, Mina longed for the end of neutrality. What impressed her in Mabel's piece was her friend's allusion to the soldiers' faces—their eyes "full of light": in poems years later she would recall this image of spiritual illumination. And while she would soon change her mind, Mina did not share Mabel's pacifism. "My masculine side longs for war," she replied. Given the volatility of her opinions, she felt unsure about the women's war against war. "I may be able to decide on it—after this is all over. I think I am safe in saying that there is not a single personality in Europe that has not undergone metamorphosis during the last six months," she continued. "When the tension is relaxed shall we never revert to ourselves—shall we have become something more—or shall we find no way of fitting in anywhere?"

V I

Mina continued to identify her "masculine" side with the aggressive, action-seeking rhetoric of the Futurists and her "feminine" side with the promptings of the unconscious. In 1915, when she was writing the radically modern poetic sequence that she would call "Love Songs," the blank page became the space in which to record her fear that she would never revert to her former self. "Love Songs" began as an analysis of her "utter defeat in the sex war," as she called it, but the process of writing offered a way out of depression—through a deeper self-exploration than she had yet attempted.

Mina was reluctant to part with these poems at first. They were "rather pretty—rather mawkish—probably a little indecent," she told Carl; although her love had spent itself, she was uncertain whether to send them to New York. By summer, when she could look back on the affair in "a fine flown tranquillity of revocative retrospect," she had made up her mind to offer the first four to Alfred Kreymborg's new magazine, *Others*. Promising Carl that she would finish the full sequence, she imagined it as a chapbook: "I am soon going to write the second batch—which will be finer—the whole will make a progression of realisations—crescendo & transcendo!" The metaphor of musical form, mounting intensity followed not by a decrescendo but by a willed transcendence, made clear her desire to go through and beyond her unhappiness. Although the first poems "came straight out of my subconsciousness," she told him, she would have to think hard about the rest.

Since the demise of the short-lived *Trend*, Carl had been sending Mina's poetry to *Rogue*, a lively new magazine calling itself "the cigarette of literature." Published by Allan and Louise Norton as New York's equivalent of the London reviews of the nineties, *Rogue*'s first issue featured Wallace Stevens and Gertrude Stein; the Nortons also threatened "to publish Miss Gertrude Stein's History of a Family which is nine volumes of five hundred pages each." The magazine soon became known for its nose-thumbing stance. It poked fun at timely issues like women's suffrage—by endorsing votes for hermaphrodites—or at the war itself, which it dismissed as "silly."

In April *Rogue* ran Mina's "Sketch of a Man on a Platform," a poem which addresses Marinetti without naming him. The May 1 issue featured Walter Arensberg's poems and Mina's "Three Moments in Paris" (a three-

185

poem sequence including a revised version of "Café du Néant"), along with Carl's account of prewar life at the Villa Curonia. During its brief run, *Rogue* would publish a number of Mina's poems, her two short Futurist-inspired plays, and one of her drawings: her name would become synonymous with its reputation for sophisticated mockery.

Mina was pleased to find herself in such company. She adored Arensberg's "To a Poet," she told Carl, no doubt because of its irreverence toward God—"the great Cosmical Non-entity"—and its description of the poet, "like a naughty child / . . . Without a wedding and a little wild." She also liked the "Philosophic Fashions" by "Dame Rogue" (Louise Norton), a series of arch disquisitions on subjects like perfume, trousers, and petticoats, combining urbane wit with sexual innuendo—they had clearly been written by a kindred spirit. Once she made her way to New York, she would be among her own kind.

That spring Mina returned to the Costa, to the house next to her own, which was rented to the Vails, an expatriate American family from Paris. Although Mina had known Eugene Vail in Montparnasse art circles, she had more in common with his attractive children, Laurence and Clotilde, both in their twenties. With his flamboyant looks and high spirits, Laurence made a charming escort to the Giubbe Rosse when Mina wanted company, and he and Clotilde admired her spirit. They encouraged her to go to New York, where, they said, she would make a fortune with her designs.

Yet there were days when her optimism vanished. Often she closed the shutters and forbade the children to disturb her. When her nerves allowed, she worked on a new prose manuscript, but felt anxious about Carl's opinion of her Futurist dialogue, renamed "The Sacred Prostitute." By the time a reassuring letter arrived with a request for biographical information—Carl intended to write a magazine article about her—Mina felt well enough to reply in her triumphant vein. "Can't you write about me as a hidden wrinkle," she asked, "the only woman who has been decided enough to forgo—easy success—etc etc—untempted by the potency of beauty—who has succeeded in holding on to *herself* until she found herself all alone on the Costa—*its true!*"

Throughout the spring Papini called for war in ever more strident language. He made the case for intervention as the revolt of youth against age, progress against decadence, and heroism against cowardice. But as it has been said of such interventionist rhetoric, "underlying all these arguments, fueling the passion with which they were advanced . . . was a feverish and intoxicating feeling that the war offered a once-in-a-lifetime opportunity to destroy the Giolittian regime, to throw off the fetters of bourgeois existence, and to open the way toward some ill-defined but radically different future." War was the means to release aggressive impulses that could find no other outlet.

By this time, the political atmosphere had become so heated that all public gatherings of pro-war factions were deemed subversive. Marinetti had been arrested again for demonstrating at rallies with his fellow Futurists, and in April, with Mussolini, who had left the anti-war socialists to join the interventionists. Informing Carl of Marinetti's recent jail sentence, Mina wrote: "The Brute's been let out after 6 days—it was the first time I knew he was out of mischief—I think he's absent minded again—probably he is dreaming of becoming Emperor of Italy. He's the only one in Europe who approximates William II." She envied his opportunities for heroism, even though Marinetti's posturing sometimes struck her as "cerebral gymnastics" or as "the self-indulgent play of children."

She was also growing weary of the war. "Once having lost its 'unexpected' quality its like everything else that goes on too long," she told Carl. At other times, inflamed by the pro-war sentiment that swirled around her, Mina longed to serve her adopted country. She volunteered to work with the Italian Red Cross as soon as the government made up its mind; in the meantime, she wrote Carl, "I shall bury myself in Florence as a nurse." By late spring she was again working in a surgical hospital, "entirely devoid of sentiment—*entirely* on the chance of getting near a battlefield & hearing a lovely noise! . . . You have no idea what fallow fields of psychological inspiration there are in human shrieks & screams," she continued. "I'm so wildly happy among the blood & mess for a change & I stink of iodoform—& all my nails are cut off for operations—& my hands have been washed in iodine—& isn't this all a change." Worrying that Italy might not go to war, she added, "I will write a poem about it—& you should hear what a tramp calls the Madonna when he's having his abdomen cut open without anesthetic."

After months of hospital work, Mina doubted that she would ever see the fighting. "I am afraid," she told Carl, "in spite of my slavery & efforts it is impossible for me to get anywhere near it." Hoping that the English would offer military training to women who wanted it, she added, "I'm a *little* envious of these young men's eyes—going to the front! . . . Carlo don't you sense—what wonderful poems I could have written—round about a battle field!" In this excitable atmosphere, she longed to know how it felt to be a hero, to experience the transcendence that lit up the soldiers' eyes. Many poems from this period are colored by her frustration at having to accept the "womanly" role. "Babies in Hospital," for example, says little about the hospital and nothing about the war: a meditation on the differences between the sexes as observed in young children, the poem is in fact closer to her writings on the sex war.

Mina's brush with Futurism had brought about a political, as well as a personal, awakening. Now, unexpectedly, her exclusion from the war encouraged her to focus on the polarization of the sexes. "What I feel now are feminine politics," she told Carl, "but in a cosmic way that may not fit in anywhere." It was not clear that the female sex could be shoved in some new direction. Her belief that some innate antagonism existed between the sexes had been enhanced during her skirmishes with Marinetti and Papini: men and women were "intimate irritants," she thought, whose attraction was based on hostility. Put another way, they were "enemies whose dearest desire is to be rid of each other." And while she could not get close to the machine war, she wrote, her book would "ferret out the innards of the 'Sex War.'"

By May, as Papini exhorted readers to answer the call to arms, it seemed that prolonged neutrality would produce either revolution or civil war. The government had conducted secret negotiations committing Italy to fight Austria, but the premier lacked parliamentary approval. The return that month of D'Annunzio, a well-known interventionist, from his exile in France, was timed to coincide with the eruption of well-orchestrated demonstrations by the pro-war forces—a mixture of university students, nationalists, Mussolini's breakaway socialists, and the Futurists. Predictably, D'Annunzio's appeals to Italian national honor further heated the temperature of political debate. Following his arrival in Rome on May 12, when pro-war rioters manhandled neutralists, the deputies reversed themselves and voted for war.

By May 24, the Italian Army was on the move. Florence was full of flags, and within a few days soldiers appeared in the streets bellowing songs of farewell. In the final issue of *Lacerba* Papini crowed, *"Abbiamo vinto!"* (We won!). "This War's getting jolly serious," Mina told Carl. "We're all pervaded by a consciousness that goes beyond while intensifying the personal, and death has entirely lost its absolute quality." They were nearing a turning point. "I intuit what it quite *is* & I can't grasp," she went on. "To me it seems that the result will be so devastating in subversion of our present psyche—that those who haven't an open mind—will simply be negated." As for herself, she felt younger each day: "the vitality I learnt from Marinetti . . . has not abated. That inimitable explosive—rejuvenates his familiars," she continued, "though I think I am the only female who has reacted to it—exactly the way I have noticed men do— Of course being the most female thing extant—I'm somewhat masculine." Following this paradoxical self-analysis, she added, "Do you know, I shall be quite upset if anything happens to either of those men . . . I am approaching the predicted fruition of my life," she concluded. "I've learnt how to be happy enough to live."

True to his belief in war's purgative value, Marinetti enlisted. When asked for his thoughts on the country's future, he predicted, "Through the intense deployment of all her energies," [Italy] will finally take her true place among those countries that are alive, strong, and full of glory." He was not afraid of death, since "to die in combat would be to disappear in full apotheosis." Mina prayed for his safety: "The brute is—everyway— the angel," she told Carl. But she was even more relieved to learn that the myopic Papini had been judged unfit for service, and over the course of the summer, her elation at Italy's involvement subsided. Her father had lost money, plans to go to London were impractical, and the future was entirely uncertain. "Think of me trying to live on nothing—grandly philosophical—succeed or die," she told Carl. "I have lost my wild desire to shoot germans—my attitude toward the war has become transcendental."

Moreover, the war was "not doing many women much good," she added, thinking perhaps of herself. Preoccupied with "feminine politics" of both a personal and a general nature, Mina had, for over a year, been trying to prod Stephen into accepting a divorce. "Tell him 'that all the men I like consider me stupid & unfeminine' or too thin or anything to convince him there is no competition," she begged Carl, then added, "I only want freedom for the sake of self-respect." When her poems began appearing in the little magazines, Stephen wrote disapprovingly from New York to say that she should "study literature for a few years" before posing as a writer. He might damage her reputation as well as withholding her freedom, she worried. But her most immediate concern was his whereabouts: Stephen had gone to live in the Bahamas. "I wonder if he did it on purpose," she mused. By September, Mina understood why Carl was less active on her behalf. He had recently visited Stephen in his new home.

Mina was "beginning to feel constrained" with Carl, yet she depended on his advice. Mabel wrote infrequently; there was no one else with whom she could discuss literary matters, and she counted on him to have her work published in the right places. By September, the prolonged isolation began to tell on her nerves, but like everyone else, she informed him, she was making an effort to "hold on tight to [her] sanity till after the war."

When Mina finally heard from Mabel, she let down her guard. "I was so relieved to get a note from you," she wrote. "I thought I should never hear from you again—I am just hanging on to my sanity." The affair with Papini still distressed her: "Giovanni came within an ace of really smashing me." As for her Marinettian vitality, she went on, "I have lost what I had of it—wanting—a very cruel grubby—blind man more—still I make gymnastic efforts to recapture it—& succeed for seconds at a time. But it's the chaos of the subconscious one gets lost in." Believing that "some psychic expansion must result from this physical world-contension," she confided to Mabel that she sometimes longed to weep on her shoulder. As for Stephen, she asked, "Do you remember the American woman who met him at lunch and said—he would turn & bite the hand that fed him?"

To escape the late-summer heat, Mina took the household to Forte dei Marmi. There she read the latest *Rogue*, which reassured her about Carl's devotion as her agent. To prove his theory that the artist's eye translated things seen into formal terms, Carl explained that while "the paintings of Mina Loy seem to the beholder the strange creations of a vagrant fancy," they too had a basis in reality. In one of her canvases, he went on, "an exquisite Indian girl stands poised before an oriental palace, the most fantastic of oriental palaces, it would seem, but the artist explained to me that it was simply the façade of Hagenbeck's menagerie in Hamburg, seen with an imaginative eye." Although Carl was consorting with the enemy, he believed in her enough to want to drop her name.

Refreshed by the sea air, Mina finished the thirty-four-poem sequence of love songs, retitled "Songs to Joannes" in a characteristic impulse to conceal while also revealing the name of her difficult lover. He had already appeared in the first set as the eternal masculine:

> The skin-sack
> In which a wanton duality
> Packed
> All the completions of my infructuous impulses
> Something the shape of a man

While hardly news, the idea that women desired "all the completions" of intercourse was discussed neither in polite society nor in print. By this time, Mina's allusions to "mucous-membrane" and "saliva" in "Pig Cupid" were shocking New Yorkers, and the image of the lover's genitalia—"Something the shape of a man"—was scandalizing Amy Lowell, among others.

As yet unaware of their impact Mina told Carl that her poems were "*the* best since Sappho": "All the first were written in red hot agony—the first of the second part in the traditional recuperation in the country—& the rest—settled cerebral." She continued, "If you wanted me to be a happy woman for five minutes or more, you would get songs for Joannes published for me—all together—printed on one side of each page only—& a large round in the middle of the blank reverse of each page—one whole entirely blank page with *nothing* on it between the *first* & the second parts—(pause in between moods)—the dedication—'TO YOU.' " She corrected the typographical errors that had crept into the published versions of the first four and asked to have the full sequence appear as a supplement to *Others*. This step would mark her own leavetaking, the end of the affair with Giovanni-Joannes.

That fall, resettled in her house, Mina understood that she would have to win her freedom through her own efforts. While an English divorce was impossible under the circumstances, she could obtain an American one without Stephen's consent, but wondered how to provide for the children. "I have only one idea in my mind *make money*," she told Carl, "& can turn my hand at anything that comes along." Every few weeks, the children returned from school to discover traces of Mina's latest "invention." When she tried recipes for tempera paint using rotten eggs as the binder, the smell permeated the house. During the winter of 1915–16, she concentrated on paintings for the annual Florence exhibition but completed only one, a *Donna con bambino* (*Woman with Child*), which Boccioni called one of the most *simpatico* things in the exhibit. In the spring, when she trimmed hats as a way to prepare for the fashion business, snippets of straw, curls of ribbon, and silk petals decorated the halls. When her millinery inspiration ran out, she drew fashion covers intended for *Vogue* and designed an elegant American wardrobe to impress potential backers. The children knew their mother was in earnest when packers came for Stephen's antiques. His Jacobean chests, Queen Anne tables, and William and Mary chairs disappeared, along with the china, silver, and brassware.

At the same time, Mina worried about her literary reputation, as if replaying the psychic tangles of her student days—when her teachers' notice meant her parents' disapproval. Although writing about the sex war was bound to be controversial, it was one thing to be provocative and another to learn that some considered her writing "pure pornography." The influential Amy Lowell had threatened to withdraw her support of *Others* because of "Love Songs" and had let it be known that she despised Mina's poetry. But when Carl asked for "something without a sex undercurrent," Mina replied that she knew "nothing about anything but life—& that is generally reducible to sex!" She would have to work her way to the end of her thoughts on the subject before she could develop some other vision.

To explain her reasons for writing candidly, Mina observed, "I think the anglo saxon covered up-ness goes hand in hand with a reduction of the spontaneous creative quality—there's *nothing* covered up in Italy." In England, she went on, the modern movement stayed on the surface. "English men write about prostitutes," she went on, "& it's found daring—but we all know there are prostitutes—but nobody tries to find out how or rather express what they react to things." After all she had been through, she felt sure "that life can only evolve something more ample for us—if we help it by getting right into our emotions . . . We moderns have hardly a proscribed psychic area," she added. The range of topics was constantly expanding.

By way of expressing women's reactions, she sent him a poem entitled "Virgins Plus Curtains Minus Dots"; it probed the emotions not of prostitutes but of their near-relations, the marriageable young women of the Italian middle classes. These "virgins for sale" gaze at the street below, yearning to "wande[r] at will." However, lacking dowries ("dots" in French), they are kept at home:

> *Some   behind curtains*
> *Throbs to the night*
> *Bait   to the stars*
>
> *Spread it with gold*
> *And you carry it home*
> *Against your shirt front*
> *To   a shaded light*
> *With the door locked*
> *Against virgins who*
> *Might   scratch*

That young women not only had sexual desires but that their resentment at being treated like property might cause them to "scratch" was part of the "secret well kept" of woman's condition, whether in Catholic Italy or Protestant England.

While Mina was committed to greater honesty, she also felt nervous about its consequences. "Do you notice how frightened I get like a small child," she asked Carl, "when I have written anything I mean I feel my family on top of me." In America, she hoped, readers were more open-minded. It was disappointing to learn that the new London quarterlies featured imitation-nineties poetry, and already she felt more American than English. " 'We' are doing much better in America," she observed. "I don't believe the men in England have got any of the new consciousness about things that is beginning to formulate in some of us," she continued. "I believe we'll get more 'wholesome sex' in American art—than English after all." Yet, in her concern for her reputation, she wondered whether she *had* overstepped the bounds of decency. Sometimes she thought all Florence disapproved—"It is difficult all alone—being thought mad in this stagnant hole."

By the summer of 1916, she told Carl, she had grown "so tired of Florence that I hardly ever go outside my door." After a year of war, the best of the Futurists lacked inspiration. "They have theories & no genius to carry them out," she wrote. "The intellectuals & geniuses have all left the movement." (She did not explain that some had already been killed.) The only ones left were Marinetti and Papini, who had both come to call —on separate occasions. "Marinetti said I'm a big genius," she boasted, "& Papini has read some of my stuff—& says delightful things when he's not in a bad temper." She had taken pleasure in reading Marinetti the sections of her Futurist dialogue in which she (as Love) debated him (as Futurism) on the woman question. Marinetti was so much a part of her imagination that she found an unmistakable likeness of his head in her latest drawing. And although Papini's anger had subsided, he was still wary. "I believe he's really tried to forgive me," she wrote, "but viva Italia! & I think hes a little jealous of Songs to Joannes." He was "going to ruin himself," she feared, "getting narrower & narrower—& when I try to wake him up—he says the medicine's too strong." It was clear to her that while she was indebted to the Futurists for her own awakening, she needed to move on.

Mina spent the summer making preparations. Once she had found the solutions to her domestic problems, which included the children, she felt as if she already had put Florence behind her. Her mind was on New York, on Frances's exhibition of her Futurist paintings and Carl's growing reputation as an exponent of modern art. She was disturbed to learn that since the minor scandal provoked by the publication of her first four "Love Songs" in *Others*, Carl had not found a publisher for the rest of the sequence. Even though she was deliberately "trying to think of a subject that's not sexy to write about," she teased him, she could not find one: "When I go out to look for one—people offer me nothing else . . . The only thing that is stronger than sex—is 'snobbism' & you can't write about snobs—its *so*—snobby!"

There was, it seemed, a price to pay for writing with candor. If Amy Lowell disliked her poetry, did this mean that other moderns would reject it? Stephen had already written to say that he considered her writing so offensive, she told Carl, "that in future wherever I go I can only associate with outcasts—that it is useless for me to have my freedom." Asking him for reassurance, she added, "I've got a beautiful daughter—I can't *outcast* —what shall I do . . . I have tried my things on *ultra respectable* elderly ladies (not stupid ones of course)," she went on, "& they survive magnificently—will America be so *very* different?" Despite her fear of "outcasting," she would be sailing for New York on October 15.

As the date drew near, Mina's conflict about leaving the children with Miss Penrose, the head of the English school, became acute. Since Giles was seven and Joella nine, they would not miss her much, she told herself. They would be well looked after, and she would send for them as soon as she was making enough money.

But however rational this plan sounded, she felt more than a little guilty. It had always been difficult for her to see the children as individuals with needs of their own. Some time later, from a perspective that mingles emotional distance with artistic foreshortening, she described Joella on the eve of her departure as if her daughter were a work of art:

her forehead winged with the bluish fragility of temples shading off into the almost invisible implantation of the half golden, half curling undulation caressing her face, her forehead, that inverted base—let down the pure shaft of the nose, a pillar in the foreground of an oval. This contour, scarcely interrupted by the almost imperceptible mounts and hollows of underlying muscles, showed, with the pivoting of the head, a suspicion of concavity beneath the lovely height of the cheek; giving her that famished look of beauty ahunger for some unimaginable consecration.

However lovely, a nine-year-old girl is not a statue. This separation, which would last nearly three years despite Mina's plans, confirmed her inability to see her daughter as a child whose wish for a stable family would always be thwarted by her mother's contradictory desires.

Waiting with Joella in the passport office, Mina studied her daughter's beauty as if it held some meaning. "With the heavenly blonde allure of a Luini, the virginal sublimity of a Botticelli," she observed, "her lashes pointed upwards like a crown, she cradled in her arms, admiringly, the waxen pop-eyed prettiness of a tow-wigged doll." She could have sat for a painting of a youthful Madonna. But this small image of maternal plenitude was a temptation. "I must run away from it," Mina remembered thinking. Ambivalent feelings about mothering and being mothered—who was the parent and who was the child?—rose to the surface in a moment of panic, "that gripping panic that so long had worn on me seemed to be wringing my features in the anguish of a thousand years." Parting may have resurrected the anguish of her first memory—of exile from home and the enchantment of beauty.

Some weeks later, Mina boarded an early-morning train, the first leg of her journey from Florence to Naples, where she would embark for America. With her she carried a vision of her children: Joella "framed in the window of the railway carriage—the coiled wisps of corn-colored hair blowing about the unbelievable blue of the innocence of her eyes—the string of lapis lazuli marbles round her neck lay like a deepened reflection those eyes might have dropped there—the sun-baked muscles of my boy's sturdy legs stamping out a dance of excited farewell to one setting out on a fabulous journey." She committed them to memory while their small images receded into the past.

Interlude I

Love Songs

BY THE TIME MINA sailed for New York in 1916, she had acquired a reputation as a free-verse "radical" whose literary forms were as provocative as her thoughts on social problems. Her writing appeared regularly in the little magazines; she was widely considered one of the most enigmatic of the moderns. Depending on the critic, poetry like Mina's was either pernicious—"eroticism gone to seed"—or revolutionary—"the expression of a democracy of feeling rebelling against an aristocracy of form." *Life's* reviewer wrote that free verse was "among the most live things being done in America." After reading "Love Songs," he urged readers to try *Others*, because "a side of you that has been sleeping would come awake."

Some felt that 1916 was the year that poetry itself awoke from its slumbers. "It was the time of manifestos, movements, overnight schools, sudden departures," recalled Louis Untermeyer. "The Cubists, Futurists, Imagists, Impressionists, Vorticists had all taken a hand at rejuvenating the staid and perplexed Muse," he went on. But however much Untermeyer welcomed this awakening, he objected to "that unaffiliated group of radicals, mood-jugglers and verbal futurists," the *Other*ites. Indicting *Others* for poetic rebellion, he held up for particular scorn "Exhibit A, the first of Miss Loy's *chansons d'amour.*" She was, he felt, a notorious example of the sort of new women who, "having studied Freud, began to exhibit their inhibitions and learned to misquote Havelock Ellis at a moment's notice."

In defense of *Others*-style free verse, Kreymborg called it "nothing more nor less than the individual expression of individuals." Free-verse writers created new forms not to be contrary, he explained, but because they could no longer live with the old ones, which felt to them like fusty Victorian houses. The *vers librist* needed a new dwelling, he went on. "He wants a house . . . built of material he finds inside himself." While this airy house of poetry was being built with the aid of the many women writers "finding their most intimate expression through free verse," at the head of this "noble tribe" came Mina Loy, whose counsel to "forget that you live in houses that you may live in yourself" echoed in Kreymborg's metaphor for modernism.

The publication of *Others'* first issue in 1915, William Carlos Williams recalled, had produced "wild enthusiasm among free-verse writers, slightly less enthusiasm among Sunday Magazine Section reporters, and really quite a stir in the country at large." This unexpectedly jarring publicity had focused on "Love Songs." "Detractors shuddered at Mina Loy's subject-matter and derided her elimination of punctuation marks and the audacious spacing of her lines," Kreymborg noted. Decades later, he still felt their impact on American readers: "In an unsophisticated land, such sophistry, clinical frankness, sardonic conclusions, wedded to a madly elliptical style scornful of the regulation grammar, syntax and punctuation . . . horrified our gentry and drove our critics into furious despair."

In our era, the scandal following the publication of *Others* seems quaint, yet contemporary readers were outraged. Newspaper editors seized on Mina's poems as the latest brand of Continental vice. The *Evening Sun's* columnist Don Marquis published one of his many parodies of *vers libre* as if it were a collaborative effort by Loy, Kreymborg, and other *Otherists*: it read

> *Oh, beautiful mind,*
> *I lost it*
> *In a lot of frying pans*
> *And calendars and carpets*
> *And beer bottles****
> *Oh, my beautiful mind.*

In his next column, he claimed that "people who pretend that they are unable to understand the work of the Imagist or polyrhythmic or *vers libre* bards" were simply too lazy to heed their hidden meanings, and he quoted Mina's first "Love Song" to prove his point. Such poetry was easy, he went on. "Put into the old-fashioned verse form it would read: 'Trickle, trickle little syrup / You're a grocer's staple / Seldom, seldom seen in Yurrup.' "

For more than a year, "Yurrupean" imports like *vers libre* had to contend with Yankee ridicule. Don Marquis soon invented *vers librists* of his own. (One of his spoofs runs "You ask me, do you, what I am in Revolt against? / Against you, fool, dolt, idiot, against you, against everything! / Against Heaven, Hell, and punctuation.") Marquis also asserted wryly that when Kreymborg wrote a poem, *no one but Mina Loy knows exactly what it means, and she never tells anyone but Sadakichi Hartmann. Sadakichi Hartmann is sometimes comprehended by Ezra Pound, but never by himself. When Gertrude Stein writes a book she takes it to Stieglitz, who reads it aloud and Marsden Hartley paints a picture of the reading, and there are only three people in the world, besides us, who can look at the painting and tell Miss Stein what she thought when she wrote the book, and even after she is told she does not understand.*

Soon Don Marquis was hailing free verse as "the most glorious space-filler / ever invented by the brain of a / World-weary columnist." (Ironically, it gave him an immortality of his own—as the creator of Archy, the free-verse cockroach who typed in lower case because he could not manage the shift key.)

For perhaps the first and last time in America, poetry became a sensation. The *New York Tribune* sent its reporter Margaret Johns to the ramshackle artists' colony in New Jersey where Kreymborg published *Others*. Making much of its picturesque site, she professed surprise to find the new poetry housed in cottages, where it flourished despite the lack of modern comforts. The *Tribune*'s headlines spoofed the movement—"Free Footed Verse Is Danced in Ridgefield, N.J. Get What Meaning You Can Out of the Futurist Verse . . . It's as Esoteric as Gertrude Stein Herself"—but the article was sympathetic. It explained that *vers libre* demanded an intellectual effort: "In the new poetry there is a riddle, something to be solved. It is like . . . a Gertrude Stein rhapsody or a Schoenberg symphony." Mina's first "Love Song" was quoted at length and the significance of its white spaces mentioned, if not understood. "A notable feature of the movement," the article continued, "is the early prominence taken in it by women."

The parallel between female free-verse writers and suffragists was obvious to Mina's contemporaries: the idea of a "free footed verse" practiced by women was nearly as controversial as the suffragist challenge. Indeed, to cultural activists of the sort Don Marquis liked to satirize, sexual liberation, women's emancipation, artistic innovation, and political protest were all versions of the same impulse. When Isadora Duncan danced in New York in 1916, she seemed to express these ideals. Mabel Dodge thought her the embodiment of the *élan vital*, and the professional rebel Floyd Dell gushed, "It is not enough to throw God from his pedestal, to dream of superman and the cooperative commonwealth: one must have seen Isadora Duncan to die happily." Such unfettered movement lay behind the metaphor of "free footed verse": the image of bare feet, liberated from stiff shoes and dated choreographies, recurred whenever people discussed the new movement.

But there were those who wanted poetry conventionally housed and opposed the thought of women dancing as they pleased. Such unrestrained expression, Untermeyer insisted, produced "a perfumed and purposeless revolt," a "falsetto radicalism." Parodists mocked the Isadora-like abandon of the new verse: it was skinny, impoverished, preoccupied with sex and empty of thought. The author of "Lines to the Free Feet of Free Verse," published in the *Tribune*, argued that once poetry was set free, it became graceless and clumsy. Don Marquis chastised the free feet: "I have loved thee long, and thou hast laughed and trampled on me," then proposed that free verse be renamed "paroled," "acquitted," or "escaped." Perhaps in seriousness this time, he called for the return of *Poetry*'s Harriet Monroe, "a rather conservatively inclined chaperone of the radical brood" who would bring the wayward bards back to "rhyme, rhythm, and reason."

In this climate of opinion American readers associated Mina's writing with the projects of her fellow modernists, and her subject matter with the public soul-searching and lawbreaking of the New Woman. Not only were her poems written in "escaped" verse, but they also presented an alarming perspective—one that linked free verse to free love. Few readers, however (apart from Mabel, Frances, and Carl), could recognize in these elliptical poems the real men and women embroiled in the sex war.

Like nearly every foreign resident, Mina had been moved to write about herself through the lens of her reactions to Italy. But unlike other Anglo-Florentines, she found inspiration not in the Renaissance but in her response to the forms that, to her mind, embodied the new consciousness.

By 1912 Mina had read several of Gertrude's early manuscripts, including "Italians"—a group portrait drawn from Gertrude's summer holidays which tries to characterize a people in a series of minutely varied generalizations. Although Gertrude noted, "They are not all the same," her Italians never become individuals. Distinguished only by the extent to which they are quick, noisy, small, dark, hairy, staring, or smiling, and whether they have long fingernails, they exist as the occasion for the speaker's ruminations on similarity and difference. Of her subjects, Gertrude allowed herself two tentative statements: "It is a pleasant thing to be living among them," presumably because "they like being living"—an attitude amplified in the conclusion that Italians in general are "warmly liking being living."

In our era Gertrude's portraits seem insensitive and overly general. At the time, her contemporaries responded favorably to these studies, and to the racial pseudo-science informing them. Some years later, Mina called "Italians" the best example of her friend's Bergsonian phase. "Not only are you pressed close to the insistence of their existence," she observed, "but Gertrude Stein through her process of reiteration gradually, progressively rounds them out . . . They revolve on the pivot of her verbal construction like animated sculpture," she continued. "They are of one, infinitesimally varied in detail, racial consistency." But it was to the variations, to the differences within sameness that she responded—"the startling dissimilarity in the aesthetic denouement of our standardized biology." Peoples might be subject to fixed laws governing their actions, but within this framework one could make distinctions, each with its "aesthetic denouement."

Although Mina, too, wrote about the people around her, her vantage point was different from that of the summer visitor. After years of watching her neighbors, she was closer to them than other foreign residents could imagine in the detachment of their villas. Her sympathies went out to her female neighbors, especially to the young women pining for suitors, who would offer them only domesticity and repeated childbearing. In 1914 and 1915, while Mina was working out her ideas on "feminine politics," she was also writing a series of poems that critique the social, economic, and psychological control of women—and, through these poems on Italian women's destinies, making comparisons to her own. In these "Italian" poems, the metaphors that amused the New York journalists—the house of poetry and the wandering feet of free verse—are nuanced by their immersion in the context of her life.

Mina's "house" poems assume that women's lives will not change until they are offered alternatives to the requirements for the sex—a protective "housing" of innocence followed by its transfer into marriage. At the same time, they also explore the image of the house as a metaphor of female destiny, one in which the inner spaces of domesticity and corporeality overlap. Typically, "Virgins Plus Curtains Minus Dots" satirizes Latin attitudes toward marriageable women, who are kept at home to safeguard their one marketable commodity. These foolish virgins imagine love as "a god / White with soft wings"—a vision recalling Mina's own in adolescence—but because they lack dowries, they are little more than objects whose value resides in their remaining "intact." Romantic hopes deflate when juxtaposed to reality: "Love is a god / Marriage expensive." As they peep at the world from behind closed curtains—"Men's eyes look into things / Our eyes look out"—the parallel between the house and the female body becomes explicit.

Particular cases could illustrate general principles. "At the Door of the House" tells the story of Petronilla Lucia Letizia Felicità (to give only four of her twelve names) as the drama of "a thousand women's eyes." Like other disappointed matrons, a lady visits a voyante who sees in the Tarot cards the future the lady cannot herself envision: in these "maps of destiny," the "Man of the Heart" appears at the lady's threshold but will not come in. At the close, the lady, still "covered with tears about matrimony," keeps "looking for the little love-tale / That never came true," and the speaker distances herself from the "other" female subject—one of Mina's characteristic strategies for marking the gap between reality and illusion.

The distance between observer and subject could collapse in moments of sympathy when—as in Futurist painting—she placed herself inside the scene. "Costa Magic," one of the three poems of "Italian Pictures," tells the story of a neighboring family in its tale of a father who prevents his daughter's marriage by casting a deadly spell. (The neighbors conspire to work female counter-magic, to no avail.) This third-person account is interrupted by a first-person speaker—like Mina, a resident of the Costa—who, listening to the father's "mumbling malediction," seems to hear her husband's voice. Unlike Gertrude's distanced view of Italians, Mina's close-ups emphasize both their vitality and the costs of their "being living."

Inevitably, writing about the lives of her neighbors brought Mina back to the power imbalance between men and women. Inspired no doubt by Gertrude's portraits of artists, she chose Marinetti and Papini as the subjects of her word portraits. In "Sketch of a Man on a Platform," the speaker sizes up a public figure who, like Marinetti, possesses "absolute physical equilibrium":

> Your genius
> So much less in your brain
> Than in your body
> Deals so exclusively with
> The vital
> That it is equally happy expressing itself
> Through the activity of pushing
> THINGS
> In the opposite direction
> To that which they are lethargically willing to go.

This man rushes onto the battlefield or into the boudoir "with the same assurance of success," yet energizes all those who engage with him.

In a related poem, "One O'Clock at Night," a woman watches the Marinetti-figure spar with his "brother pugilist of the intellect." Her tone is both wry and intimate:

> Though you had never possessed me
> I had belonged to you since the beginning of time
> And sleepily I sat on your chair beside you
> Leaning against your shoulder
> And your careless male voice   roared
> Through my brain and my body
> Arguing dynamic decomposition.

The poem's ironic diction distinguishes between the man's posturing and the woman's awareness. Enacting the role of "animal woman / Understanding nothing of man," she assumes a "personal mental attitude" on awakening. Asleep, she had been "indifferent," contained within the structure of sexual difference; awake, she is aware of its effects and unsure whether to dismiss the men's sparring as "the self-indulgent play of children" or "the thunder of alien gods."

Mina's satire of Futurist attitudes would be honed and sharpened. Indeed, just a few years later in New York, she would dismiss these "sympathetic enemies" as behind the times. But in Florence, such detachment was impossible. In some moods, and some poems, Mina focused the same unsentimental gaze on Papini that she had turned on his rival. "Giovanni Franchi," completed six or seven months after the end of their affair, calls him Giovanni Bapini, the philosopher who boasts "everybody in Firenze knows me," and herself the woman who "never knew what he was." By this point, Mina was sufficiently detached to poke fun at her contradictory desires—"to be faithful to a man," "to be loyal to herself" ("She would have to find which self first"), and finally, "to find out how many toes the / Philosopher Giovanni Bapini had." It is of interest that this research is conducted in language:

> She made a moth's net
> Of metaphor and miracles
> And on the incandescent breath of civilizations
> She chased by moon-and-morn light
> Philosopher's toes.

While Bapini continues to ignore this "loy-al" woman, she cuts him down to size—in poetry, if not in life.

When it came to male avant-gardists, portraiture shaded into satire. Another poem written after the end of the affair with Papini is even more transparent. Mina's daydreams about their union took shape as "The Effectual Marriage, or The Insipid Narrative of Gina and Miovanni." The names imply an exchange of identities in which each partner is imagined through the eyes of the other, and their union resides in the daily crossing of the sexual threshold: "The door was an absurd thing / Yet it was passable / They quotidienly passed through it." Apart from Miovanni's sexual attentions, however, he remains aloof:

> In the evening they looked out of their two windows
> Miovanni out of his library window
> Gina from the kitchen window
> From among his pots and pans
> Where he so kindly kept her
> Where she so wisely busied herself
> Pots and Pans she cooked in them
> All sorts of sialagogues
> Some say that happy women are immaterial

Miovanni leaves material existence to Gina, whose function as maker of "sialagogues" (saliva-producing dishes) reduces her to the "immaterial" status of mere being.

Yet Gina recognizes her own complicity. She jots a poem on the milk bill—

> *The first strophe   Good morning*
> *The second   Good night*
> *Something not too difficult to*
> *Learn by heart.*
> *She resists the temptation to look into his mind,*
> *fearing that this might blind her*
> *Or even*
> *That she should see   Nothing at all.*

The silence indicated by the space between "see" and "Nothing" voices their estrangement, just as the airtight arrangement of the lines underscores their mutual isolation:

> *What had Miovanni made of his ego*
> *In his library*
> *What had Gina   wondered among the pots and pans*
> *One never asked the other.*

One infers that all is not wedded bliss from the poem's witty use of pedantic diction. That this is a portrait of sexual disunion is clear by the final line —printed in prose: "This narrative halted when I learned that the house which inspired it was the home of a mad woman."*

But Mina's complicated feelings about Papini could not be disposed of in satire. In oblique relation to "The Effectual Marriage," "Love Songs" holds in unresolved tension the desire for romantic love coupled with a critique of this same desire. No wonder even the most sophisticated readers of free verse did not know how to take them: "Love Songs" resembled no known lyrics by female poets. The emotions of Elizabeth Barrett Browning's *Sonnets from the Portuguese* were too carefully restrained and the sensuality of Christina Rossetti's poetry too deeply repressed to serve as models. Like other *vers librists*, Mina had to construct her form with material she had found inside herself.

From the opening of the first "Love Song," this experimental sequence of thirty-four poems is unsettling. Although the love affair seems to have taken place, the action is replayed in the present. As the speaker imagines what might have been, the reader is plunged into uncertainty. An unidentified someone speaks from an unclear location in a world unlike that of "once upon a time":

---

* Ezra Pound admired the poem so much that he reprinted his own edited version, retitled "The Ineffectual Marriage," in two anthologies of outstanding modern poetry. Pound's abbreviated version eliminates the poem's personal and geographical references, however, thereby suppressing the most autobiographical aspects of the poem.

Interlude I

> *Spawn   of   Fantasies*
> *Silting the appraisable*
> *Pig Cupid   his rosy snout*
> *Rooting erotic garbage*
> *"Once upon a time"*
> *Pulls a weed   white and star-topped*
> *Among wild oats   sewn in mucous-membrane*

Erotic fantasies jostle romantic icons; carnality replaces the god of love. There is no lyric voice, no actors or actions, no complete or completable statements. Words hover on the page like a free-floating collage whose elements stick to the surface with varying degrees of adhesiveness—or like images from the unconscious, the realm that Mina called the source of these poems.

In the second stanza, where a first-person speaker makes a tentative appearance, the difficulty of understanding what happened (the process of "silting" or appraisal) is underscored by the unreliability of perception itself:

> *I would   an   eye in a Bengal light*
> *Eternity in a sky-rocket*
> *Constellations in an ocean*
> *Whose rivers run no fresher*
> *Than a trickle of saliva*
>
> *These are suspect places*

A desiring "I" crosses with its homonym, the "eye," yet the moment of illumination passes in an instant.

In the past to which the poem alludes, sexual passion—explored in the descent from the garden of romance to the geographies of "saliva" and "mucous-membrane"—has resulted in plenitude ("Eternity in a sky-rocket"), an illumination that dissipates as soon as the "I" seeks to understand it. The wary consciousness that tries to signal across the "suspect places" of sexuality by the light of the mind declares a retreat:

> *I must   live in my lantern*
> *Trimming subliminal flicker*
> *Virginal to the bellows*
> *Of Experience*
> > *Coloured Glass*

Although this first love song positions its colors and textures like shapes in a stained-glass window, its juxtapositions more nearly resemble the shifting patterns of a kaleidoscope: meaning comes in "subliminal" flickers. And it is more than likely that behind the image of colored glass (made prominent by its setting) lay in palimpsest the brilliant shards of her first memory.

The "you" to whom the sequence is addressed appears in the next poem, but not as a public figure. Our first glimpse of the beloved comes through the speaker's eyes as she trains her gaze on his body or, more precisely, his sexual apparatus:

> *The skin-sack*
> *In which a wanton duality*
> *Packed*
> *All the completions of my infructuous impulses*
> *Something the shape of a man*
> *To the casual vulgarity of the merely observant*
> *More of a clock-work mechanism*
> *Running down against time*
> *To which I am not paced*
> *My finger-tips are numb from fretting your hair*
> *A God's door-mat*
> *On the threshold of your mind*

Sexual difference itself—the "wanton duality" of their needs and responses—may be at the heart of the last line's insurmountable division, where the woman waits on the "threshold." As in the first poem, the dominant mode is incompletion. No statement is possible until the speaker, as "wise virgin," parses the syntax of passion by the light of her lantern, the analytic "I."

Yet after such knowledge, she cannot regain the innocence of "once upon a time." The third poem imagines the lovers joined in parodic union:

> *We might have coupled*
> *In the bed-ridden monopoly of a moment*
> *Or broken flesh with one another*
> *At the profane communion table*
> *Where wine is spilled on promiscuous lips*
> *We might have given birth to a butterfly*
> *With the daily news*
> *Printed in blood on its wings*

The repeated past conditionals ("We might have coupled," "We might have given birth") at once imagine sexual fulfillment and stress its impossibility. And this restaging of intercourse—"the bed-ridden monopoly of a moment"—implies both dis-ease ("bed-ridden") and its guilt-ridden aftermath. All attempts at unpacking the poem's freighted diction become entangled in its temporality. What might have been communion becomes the coupling of "broken flesh"; what could have been regeneration defiles the spirit—the iridescent butterfly sullied with blood and newsprint.

While the last of the four "Love Songs" seems to restart the story in the land of "once upon a time," it quickly deflates this fairy-tale rhetoric:

> *Once in a mezzanino*
> *The starry ceiling*
> *Vaulted an unimaginable family*
> *Bird-like abortions*
> *With human throats*
> *And Wisdom's eyes*
> *Who wore lamp-shade red dresses*
> *And woolen hair*
>
> *One bore a baby*
> *In a padded porte-enfant*
> *Tied with a sarsanet ribbon*
> *To her goose's wings*

This dwelling is real enough and specifically Italian (a *mezzanino* is an apartment a half story up from the ground floor), but its family cannot be housed, even in the imagination. In imagery anticipating Surrealist mergings of human and non-human, the speaker evokes a nightmare made real through precise allusions to fabrics, colors, and textures—domesticity become a Mother Goose for unborn babies.

At the close of Poem IV, the "I" returns to reflect on what would have been her stance toward the "spawn of fantasy":

> *But for the abominable shadows*
> *I would have lived*
> *Among their fearful furniture*
> *To teach them to tell me their secrets*
> *Before I guessed*
> *—Sweeping the brood clean out*

The next poem of the sequence (which would not be published until 1917) made it clear that it was the lover's leavetaking, his defection to his own idea of selfhood, which left her stranded: "And I don't know which turning to take / Since you got home to yourself—first."

When the "house" of poetry overlapped with the spaces of the unconscious, it was a darker place than one would have supposed from the controversy over the airy dwellings of free verse. For Mina, the metaphor of the house held ambivalent meanings. Like the body, it was the dwelling of the soul, but a dwelling clogged with the remnants of the past, as she would later observe—"Our person is a covered entrance to infinity /

Choked with the tatters of tradition." Just as the doorway implied multiple thresholds—access to worldly experience as well as the exploration of inner spaces—so the image of the house evoked all possible modes of linkage between world and self, mind and body, sex and spirit. And although there might be specters in the shadows, this house could become as vast as the cosmos—provided one swept away "the tatters of tradition."

In a similar way, "Love Songs" offers contradictory images of psychic fulfillment. Cupid reappears as the god of love in the urban landscape of Poem V, yet he is tarnished: "One wing has been washed in the rain / The other will never be clean any more." Other winged creatures flutter through the sequence without performing their rites as emblems of the spirit. The bloody butterfly and "Bird-like abortions" of III and IV horribly deflate such associations, while the beribboned "goose's wings" of the one who "bore a baby" (in her imagination?) invite only mockery.

In the same divided state of mind, Poem VII contrasts the "scum" of the city streets invading the woman's lungs as she pursues the man to her vision of "exhilarated birds / Prolonging flight into the night / Never reaching — — —." And following her retreat to the country, where she watches the fireflies, she concludes, "Let Joy go solace-winged / To flutter whom she may concern" [XX]. The exaltation she had sought in love is out of reach.

Kreymborg read and reread Mina's poems, which he admired even when he did not understand them. "Love Songs" is now being studied as an example of modernist poetic narrative, but like Kreymborg, many readers find the sequence challenging because of the divided state of mind informing it—the multiple ironies embedded in its syntax, diction, voices, and narrative. There are still riddles to be solved: the tensions between these contradictory impulses do not yield to simple conclusions.

It is tempting, just the same, to see the illumination of orgasm as a truce in the sex war, especially when, in Poem XII, "voices break on the confines of passion / Desire   Suspicion   Man   Woman / Solve in the humid carnage." Yet the same poem that recalls the moment of "inseparable delight" asks whether the partner is "only the other half / Of an ego's necessity." The lovers stare at each other across the divide that keeps getting re-established between them: sexual bliss does not eradicate the fear that they might "tumble together / Depersonalized / Identical / Into the terrific Nirvana / Me you—you—me" without resuming their identities [XII].

When the speaker distances herself through "the traditional recuperation in the country" (as Mina told Van Vechten), she finds in nature an image of the illumination that humans attempt but seldom achieve: an "aerial quadrille" of fireflies, "Bouncing / Off one another / Again conjoining / In recaptured pulses / Of light" [XIX]. But unlike fireflies, the lovers' conjoinings produce "only the impact of lighted bodies / Knocking sparks off each other / In chaos." And while the riddle of their opposed natures may be "solved" in the moment where sexual division is overcome, this "ephemeral conjunction" results in "NOTHING." As Poem XXVII has it, "There was a man and woman / In the way." A future—Futurist?—breed of humans may welcome the chance to "clash together / From their incognitoes / In seismic orgasm." But she is stuck in the present, watching her "Own-self distortion / Wince in the alien ego" [XXIX].

"Love Songs" asks, but cannot answer, the question of discord between the sexes. The woman's energies swell while the man's diminish into "climacteric withdrawal." When she intervenes in his "insolent isolation," he rebuffs her as a "busy-body," one who asserts the importance of carnal knowledge. Both the arrangement of the lines and the insistent sound patterns of Poem XXXIII stage the impasse of their relations:

> *The prig of passion — — — —*
> *To your professorial paucity*
>
> *Proto-plasm was raving mad*
> *Evolving us — — —*

He calls her a "prig of passion" ("prig" suggesting that she is both self-righteous in her ardor and a petty thief in the service of "Pig Cupid"), while she claims she has been reduced to this posture by his emotional stinting.

"Love Songs" hints that such impoverishment has both literary and spiritual consequences. It concludes with a poem consisting of a single line: "Love — — — the preeminent literateur." Although the woman tries to dismiss romance as a self-enclosed system, the last line repeats the sequence's tendency to circle back on the past—just as, earlier, its haunted conditionals mimed her obsession with what might have been. In this one-line afterword, language winnows down to ironic spareness, and what goes unsaid outweighs what it is possible to say.

Accustomed to the sparseness of Pound and Eliot, we respond to the ways in which "Love Songs" illuminates the motions of the mind. Mina's contemporaries read her poems differently, as if their aim was to deflate romantic love by reducing it to a series of sexual skirmishes. Some, particularly her fellow modernists, surely appreciated the wit in Poem X's revision of sexual intercourse as the contest of "shuttle-cock and battle-door" (with emphasis on the embattled "door" that the "cock" would enter). While Kreymborg conceded that "it took a strong digestive apparatus to read Mina Loy," he also pointed out that once past the difficulties of her style, "the careful reader, reading many times, might have detected genuine emotions, feelings inspired by 'something the shape of a man.' "

Yet for all their emphasis on sex, these modernist love songs cannot be understood unless we put them in historical context. That is to say, into the time of the Great War. When *we* see an evocative phrase like "humid carnage" [XII], we think of sex. But Mina's contemporaries would, no doubt, have made the double association with the war's large-scale slaughter, its "human carnage." In 1915, readers would have caught the allusion in the image of a bed as a field of combat—the "counterpane" as "battlefield" where love, bloodied, tries to "counter" pain (XVII), and they would have been more disturbed than we are by a poem that begins like an aubade ("The little rosy / Tongue of Dawn") but ends with a vision of lovers as hostile machines (XXV).

These love songs are haunting not only for their exploration of sexual dissonance but because they are drenched in the atmosphere of World War I. They are a peculiar kind of war poetry. Their range of attitudes—the tonal shifts from hopefulness and anticipation through wariness and suspicion to vexation and bitterness—may all be understood as those of the outsider, the nonparticipant, the woman whose life is put on hold yet deeply affected by the collapse of civilization around her. Similarly, what now seem like hallmarks of modernist style—the ironic swerves, the impossibility of resolution, the emphasis on shards, fragments, and flickers of meaning, the distortion of time and the closing off of the future—are all historically based, in a period when Italy temporized and Europe fought its "machine war." As Samuel Hynes observes of other writing in which battles are absent but the Great War's pressure is felt, the war is present "as a state of mind, expressed in the tone, in the movement of the action, in the endings, and in a hovering preoccupation with violence and death."

Contemporary readers of "Love Songs" were disturbed by this hovering preoccupation. Looking back on the violence of reactions to "Love Songs," Kreymborg recalled that, in 1915, New Yorkers did not know what to make of poetry that was at once analytical and passionate. Progressives and nonconformists were troubled by the poems' eccentricities, but without doubt, what upset readers most was their diagnosis of sexual love as yet another casualty of war. Kreymborg was right: Mina inadvertently challenged too many pieties when she felt and wrote with "all the earnestness and irony of a woman possessed and obsessed with the sum of human experience."

PART III

THE

MODERN

WORLD

Art and anarchy are in the world for the same reasons.

—MARGARET ANDERSON, *The Little Review*

Our social institutions of today will cause future generations to roar with laughter.

—MINA LOY, *Psycho-Democracy*

10

Subversive Amusements

(NEW YORK, 1916–17)

MINA WAS NOT PREPARED to like New York. Mabel often complained of its vulgarity; other New Yorkers had fled to Florence. She imagined their home as the "den of a composite myriad-clawed human monster clutching spasmodically at the dollar," but what she saw as her ship approached the harbor took her breath away. "An architecture conceived in a child's dream" rose above the mist. Manhattan's towers shone "with the glittering clamor of a myriad windows set like colored diamonds." The brilliance of her first memory was returned to her in this vision—on a monumental scale.

I

The voyage to the New World had begun as a farewell to the Old—Florence, the Futurists, her family. As soon as the *Duca d'Aosta* left Naples, however, life aboard ship began to replicate the stratifications of terra firma. While the first-class passengers dined with the captain, Mina and the others in second class took comfort in the knowledge that their berths were vastly superior to the dormitories into which the hundreds of steerage passengers were crowded. She was the only English person on board.

Mina went ashore for the day when the *Duca d'Aosta* stopped in Sicily. She was content to stroll among the dazzling white buildings, shining like sugar in the sunlight, until a performance of traditional Sicilian marionettes reminded her of the uncertain future. As she watched the giant toy soldiers' jerky motions, the mechanism guiding their wooden arms became visible. It was, she wrote, like a glimpse of fate—"that 'wire' by which, at the

time, all the bamboozled combatants of the World War were being
'pulled.' "

Once the *Duca d'Aosta* left the coast, she could not stop worrying. They
zigzagged past German submarines on their way west. One day the captain
called the passengers on deck, gave out lifebelts, and assigned them to
lifeboats. Mina strapped on her belt as the others teased her for taking the
drill seriously. An hour later she learned that, despite the suspension of
attacks on shipping, a U-boat had been after them: the captain had called
the exercise a drill to avoid panic. Once again she had defied fate—as in
Munich, when the lamp lashed to her waist had exploded, and in Arcetri,
when the bullet from Stephen's pistol had grazed her forehead. From then
on, Mina was preternaturally alert. As they neared Gibraltar—a safe harbor
because it was British—she thought she read some meaning in the beacon's
pulses. Peering through the dark at the British Navy, she was watching a
mechanical ballet—"battleships afloat upon the waters like iron-clad swans
. . . converging in the methodic measure of a marine gavotte." They were
under the care of the British Empire, its dominion expressed in the powerful
searchlight.

Once in the Atlantic, they seemed to drift. Mina had little in common
with the other passengers, who were nearly all emigrants. The women
kept to their families, except for one spirited young person who chatted
gaily with everyone. When a rumor spread that her easy manner resulted
from her experience in the oldest profession, Mina made it a point to keep
on talking to her. She also befriended a girl from the south who was
delighted to leave her home, where at twenty-one an unmarried woman
was considered an old maid. But they shared little more than the desire
to live in a country where women had greater freedom. Finally, on October
14, 1916, the *Duca d'Aosta* entered New York Harbor.

II

By 1916 New York, the capital of modernity, had acquired a mythic status.
More than a geographical place, it was the embodiment of the new, the
site where the twentieth century was being unveiled and the frontier beyond which the future lay like terra incognita. New York soon acquired
other meanings for her: as a vortex of energy, an urban parade, an artistic
and intellectual community, and a refuge for those who, for diverse reasons,
were the outcasts of Europe. New York would allow Mina to obtain her
long-awaited divorce, and she would be happier there than ever before.
One had to live in New York, she maintained, to understand the modern
world.

Yet her American friends took the city for granted. By 1916 Mabel had
retired from her role as hostess to the Heads of Things, and while the
painter Maurice Sterne had replaced John Reed in her affections, rumor
had it that she was no happier with an artist than she had been with an

activist. That autumn Mabel was devoting herself to her latest enthusiasm, a Duncan school run by Isadora's sister Elizabeth as a model of progressive ideals. As usual, when embarking on another phase, Mabel had moved to a new setting—she was living in the country and had invited a few friends to live in her guest cottages. But Mina was not among them.

Carl Van Vechten, no longer on speaking terms with Mabel, had also gone on to other things. Following his return to New York, he had published his essays on life among the avant-gardists, quoting Leo Stein's belief that Cubism and Futurism would soon be passé. By 1916 he had abandoned the little magazines for more mainstream publications: his next book, a mix of criticism and gossip entitled *Music and Bad Manners*, had launched his reputation as a tastemaker. He maintained warm relations with Gertrude Stein, who made good copy, but saw little of Mina. She was on her own.

Of her friends from Florence, only Frances Stevens wanted to pick up where they had left off. She helped Mina find a small apartment on West Fifty-seventh Street, a few doors down the street from her painting studio. Frances had thrown herself into her career since her return. A regular at Stieglitz's gallery, she continued to paint in the Futurist manner, but had also produced cartoons, some of which were published in *Rogue*. She had recently developed a line of *objets d'art* with commercial appeal—hat rests in the form of papier-mâché heads painted with the faces of fashionable ladies and gentlemen. That year a New York gallery had shown her Futurist canvases and some war scenes. Mina's protégée knew her way around the art world.

Within a few days Frances took Mina to one of the nightly gatherings at Walter Arensberg's duplex apartment at 33 West Sixty-seventh Street. Since then, this group of expatriates and avant-gardists has become nearly as famous as its Parisian equivalent, the legendary salon of Gertrude Stein. While both were early collectors of modern art, the Arensbergs were more daring than the Steins—especially once they came under the influence of Marcel Duchamp. And although they had taken up the role that Mabel abandoned, their salon was at once more selective and more intimate than hers had been. At a time when the war preoccupied many of their guests, the Arensbergs combined emotional support with artistic patronage.

Their nightly gatherings were known for scintillating talk and racy innuendo. Witty conversation is impossible to recapture; like the bubbles in champagne, it evaporates. Yet the effect lingers in the memoirs of those who attended these soirées, a list that reads like a *Who's Who* of modernism. On any given evening the Arensbergs' guests might include Duchamp's friends from Paris: the painters Albert Gleizes; his wife, Juliette Roche; Jean and Yvonne Crotti; and Francis Picabia, as well as his wife, Gabrielle Buffet-Picabia; the composer Edgard Varèse; and the novelist and diplomat Henri-Pierre Roché. The new figures in American art and letters were also represented: at various times the salon attracted the artists Man Ray, Beatrice Wood, Charles Sheeler, Katherine Dreier, Charles Demuth, Clara

Tice, and Frances Stevens, as well as poets Wallace Stevens, Alfred Kreymborg, William Carlos Williams, writers Allen and Louise Norton and Bob Brown, and art critic Henry McBride. And then there was the Baroness Elsa von Freytag-Loringhoven—artist's model, poet, and ultra-eccentric.

Soon Mina could be found at the Arensbergs' nearly every evening— flirting with Duchamp, explaining Futurism to Kreymborg, discussing the Salon d'Automne with Juliette Gleizes or the latest fashions with Louise Norton. The topic of choice was psychoanalysis. Freud's terminology functioned like a lingua franca: neurasthenia was now called neurosis. Arensberg's friend Dr. Ernest Southard, director of the Boston Psychopathic Hospital, played the part of resident psychoanalyst whenever he came to town. Southard conversed with Duchamp on the significance of his famous *Nude*, diagnosed artists according to their preference for rounds, squares, or triangles, and encouraged the guests to tell him their dreams. Freudianism—understood to mean the lifting of repressions—seemed to sanction the racy talk prevailing between the sexes.

Since few Parisians spoke English well and fewer Americans could manage conversation, let alone innuendo, in French, Duchamp's group often kept to themselves. Bill Williams, who spoke their language passably, credited them with the perspectives that freed his mind, yet he found their worldliness intimidating: "We were not, or I wasn't, up to carrying on a witty conversation in French with the latest Paris arrivals." Similarly, although Wallace Stevens and Walter Arensberg had been friends at Harvard, their relations cooled once Stevens chided Arensberg for spending more time with the Parisians than with his compatriots. Given the language barrier, most guests gathered in one group or the other.

Mina was an exception in that she could cross linguistic and cultural lines. At first she, too, gravitated toward the French, who, she learned, did not think much of Futurism. Duchamp had been a frequent visitor to the 1912 Futurist exhibit in Paris—at a time when he was working on his *Nude Descending a Staircase*. But despite the similarities between his studies of bodies in motion and Futurist art, he disdained the Italians. They were urban Impressionists, he argued; they valued art's sensual side, and what he wanted was intellect. Varèse, who had known Marinetti in Paris, dismissed the idea of music as noise, and Gabi Picabia said that the French had rejected Marinetti because of his style—he was simply too theatrical for the ironic Parisians.

To Americans, who had never encountered Futurism up close, such discussions were academic. But they took a particular interest in Mina, who at this distance from Florence was beginning to think with greater detachment about the movement's effect upon her. (She had begun a play, entitled *The Pamperers*, in which she satirized the idea of vanguardism as a fashionable pastime.) Kreymborg urged her to translate the manifestos for a special issue of *Others*; Williams wanted to know more about Marinetti's aims. Despite their interest in Futurism, the Americans seemed mesmerized by the French, whose presence produced either Francophilia, in the case of Arensberg, or ambivalent Francophobia, in the case of Williams.

Since the Armory Show, Duchamp had become the touchstone for American attitudes toward modern art. The elegant Frenchman had made a good impression from the day he arrived. "He neither talks, nor looks, nor acts like an artist," declared *Arts and Decoration*. Nor did he voice "the time-worn disgust with America and its standards generally ladled out to this country by artists." "If only America would realize that the art of Europe is finished—dead—and that America is the country of the art of the future," he was quoted as saying, "instead of trying to base everything she does on European traditions!" Journalists cited his every word, as if he were the prophet of a new artistic vision: he was, Roché believed, as famous as Napoleon or Sarah Bernhardt.

To the Arensberg group, Duchamp was the index by which one measured sophistication. While Williams pleaded *nolo contendere* on the grounds of linguistic disability, his friend Bob Brown took Duchamp as his guru. The easygoing Brown, a prolific freelancer, contributor to the left-wing journal *The Masses*, and denizen of Greenwich Village, credited Duchamp with suggesting a way out of his career as a hack. When the Frenchman told him that he and his friends in Paris had decided to paint the first thing they saw each morning, whether an ax, a bidet, or a baby, Brown adopted this approach. Soon he was drawing word pictures of the oysters on his plate and calling them "optical" poems. Duchamp hailed him as a member of the vanguard, and Brown felt reborn.

Yet apart from Brown, few Americans could interpret Duchamp's stance. At the Arensbergs', only those who had known him in Paris saw his detachment as a pose struck for his American audience. Like a modernist Oscar Wilde, he was putting his genius into his life; like Sarah Bernhardt, the other fin-de-siècle figure he resembled, he enjoyed posing as a femme fatale. "Marcel at twenty-seven had the charm of an angel who spoke slang," recalled the young actress Beatrice Wood. "But when his face was still it was as blank as a death mask."

Both men and women saw what they wanted in Duchamp's impassive features. Arensberg had succumbed to his charm at their first meeting, after which his taste evolved in the direction of Duchamp's blend of Cubo-Futurist machine art, linguistic mystification, and esoteric sexual symbolism. When Roché told Duchamp about his affair with Beatrice Wood, the artist gave Wood the key to his studio so that she and Roché could meet there: in Duchamp's bed, they discussed "his smile, his features, and his virtues." Although Roché teased Beatrice about falling in love with their host, it did not occur to the young woman that their "divine experience in friendship" had homoerotic overtones.

By the time Mina met Duchamp, his status as a culture hero had eclipsed his notoriety as an artist. The Frenchman was as famous as Marinetti hoped to be, but without a trace of the Futurist's swagger. Mina was intrigued by his reserve. And since Duchamp's enigmatic features suggested a modernist version of her Pre-Raphaelite models, she took pleasure in sketching him. Roché thought he detected the traces of a current between them, and others believed that they were close. But Mina was reluctant to begin a relationship that would be conducted, as it were, on stage.

Moreover, it was clear to all that, while far from celibate, Duchamp planned to remain single. He lived in a bare studio with more recycled objects or "ready-mades" than furniture (Arensberg paid the rent) and earned enough for his needs by teaching French. Although the Parisians called him *le célibataire* (the bachelor), he claimed that he was not so much a misogynist as antisocial: a commitment to art meant that one chose painting at the expense of marriage. To Roché, Duchamp's opposition to bourgeois values—virginity, possessiveness, and fidelity—gave him prophetic status; his dicta on sexual freedom were the tenets of the "emotional communism" that would soon replace "capitalist" notions of love.

Each woman saw something different in him. To Beatrice Wood, who embraced the Arensberg salon as a refuge from middle-class morality, Duchamp's gaze was so penetrating that it caused her to swoon. (Her mother had allowed her to attend Gordon Craig's school until she learned that he had fathered children by several women; when Beatrice joined the New York French Repertory Company, she was chaperoned, even at rehearsals.) The bohemian education for which she longed had begun with Roché and continued with Duchamp, who told her that "sex and love . . . were two very different things." Both loved her, she believed: "The three of us were something like *un amour à trois*." But it was Marcel who appeared each night in her dreams.

While Beatrice fantasized about getting in bed with Duchamp, Elsa von Freytag-Loringhoven pursued him with the full force of her extraordinary energy. Insisting that Duchamp loved her but could not cope with her passion, she addressed their relationship in a series of dislocated poems on the war between the sexes. The man she desired was, she wrote, possessed of a "harsh mouth—harsh soul," not to mention "a frozen body." Despite her fine figure, many New Yorkers were put off by her dress: at times the Baroness was seen wearing a bustle equipped with a taillight, a brassiere made of tin cans and string, and a birdcage necklace (complete with canary), or, in a gesture toward current events, a French soldier's helmet over her vermilion crewcut. She could often be heard muttering in her thick German accent, "Marcel, Marcel, I love you like hell, Marcel."

The two Louises were more reserved. Lou Arensberg watched the more volatile members of the group: she shared neither their penchant for drink nor their need for self-aggrandizement. Lou had the self-assurance of a practical nature and a generous inheritance, which allowed her some independence from her high-strung husband. She could, on occasion, be witty. It amused the group to see Lou assuring visitors that *Princess X*, a Brancusi bronze which the Arensbergs bought at Duchamp's urging, was an abstraction with no particular meaning, when it flagrantly resembled an erect phallus. To Mina, she was "a perfect dear who, however, just could not acquire the knack of misbehaving."

Louise Norton clearly had the knack and, like Duchamp, enjoyed turning received opinion on its head. "War is silly," she declared as Dame Rogue. "Patriotism is the vice of the ages," she insisted. Claiming to notice the war simply as a source of fashion, she remarked upon the appearance of helmet-shaped hats, airplane hats, hats à la Napoleon, and Washington-Crossing-the-Delaware hats. As for the sexes, they were at odds, she said, because men were dogs and women were cats. Well-dressed men were not alluring. "The comical bifurcation of their clothes," she noted, made them look like "well-bred eels." She was a match for Duchamp, who would remember her as "the exquisite psychologist with the large hat."

Despite his admiration, Duchamp enlisted Louise in one of his favorite pastimes, setting up the opposite sex as a source of scandal. She was half aware that he was teaching her words not found in the dictionary. One day at the group's Village headquarters, the Brevoort Hotel, where the waiters were French, Duchamp encouraged her to practice her new vocabulary. Shocked to hear *gros mots* in the mouth of a lady, the waiter dropped a tray; mayonnaise splattered the guests while Marcel smiled serenely. When Gleizes warned Louise that she would be ostracized if she spoke that way in France, she understood Duchamp's game. But she forgave him: "Marcel was so charming."

Apart from Mina, the only ones to question his intentions were Juliette Gleizes and Gabi Picabia. Both had known him in Paris as a diffident young man who in no way resembled the figure he cut in New York. Beneath his charming exterior, Juliette Roche recalled, "he was always bored, he even bored himself, he had no pleasure from nature or beauty." One day he told her that without whiskey he would have killed himself. His irony, she thought, was a mask for despair, yet she admired how well it hid his depression: "He was always charming, kind, and pleasant, at least on the surface."

Gabi Picabia agreed that Duchamp's detachment was his way of coping with unhappiness: "The attitude of abdicating everything, even himself, which he charmingly displayed between two drinks, his elaborate puns, his contempt for all values, even the sentimental, were not the least reason for the curiosity he aroused, and the attraction he exerted on men and women alike." But in some ways, she remarked, he remained an adolescent: "In his obsession with virginity and other erotic matters, he was reacting to the strictness of his provincial upbringing." It disturbed him that women were in pursuit, and he shunned commitment to protect himself against the demands of female desire.

Mina's response to Marcel was complex. Here she was one of the cognoscenti. Not only had she been elected to membership in a progressive Paris salon, but she had consorted with the Futurists, who—however much Paris disdained them—were secretly admired for having stirred up European cultural politics. She had broken with her upbringing to seek a new life, much like any man, like Duchamp himself. She was critical of marriage and understood Duchamp's wish to sabotage the idea of the virgin—an icon at odds with reality given the many women yearning to be initiated into love's mysteries. And since her affair with Marinetti, she thought it only honest to call things by their names.

Yet at the same time it was distressing to see American women being taught to enact, at least in words, their loss of innocence. When Beatrice uttered the bawdy slang she had learned from Duchamp and Roché while her tutors smiled disingenuously, those who got the joke—Juliette Gleizes, Gabi Picabia, and Mina—felt compassion for her. They found themselves in an awkward situation. To protest such behavior meant that one was insufficiently liberated, yet to keep silent was to be complicit in Duchamp's reducing of these young women to purely sexual status. The effect of his "lessons" was to treat all women as brides stripped bare by the bachelor's language.*

Unexpectedly, this scenario was enacted one evening when Mina arrived with Bill Williams to find as the center of attraction a kind of *tableau vivant*. A young Frenchwoman was reclining on a divan like a virginal Olympia while the male guests took turns stroking parts of her body. Duchamp was devoting himself to her legs, which he caressed with the tips of his fingers. Williams watched the spectacle in awe: "It was something I had not seen before. Her feet were being kissed, her shins, her knees, and even above the knee, though as far as I could tell there was a gentleman's agreement that she was not to be undressed here." After looking in vain to Mina for an explanation, he kissed her, said he was leaving, and sighed, "You're all so damned sophisticated."

Williams was out of his element, but Duchamp, turning his attention to Mina, was, she wrote, "as slick as a prestidigitator—he could insinuate his hand under a woman's bodice and hug her very body without it being at all apparent." He was equally adept at insinuating racy language into a woman's ear: " 'On peut dire,' he quoted, his beautiful streamlined face pressed to mine, 'Madame, vous avez un joli caleçon de satin— On ne peut dire,' he concluded with a whimsical kiss, 'Madame vous avez un sale con de catin.' " His "contrepetteries"—spoonerisms containing obscene puns—generally turned on the revelation that beneath a lady's "pretty satin underpants" (the "joli caleçon de satin") lurked a less attractive sight, the whorish female genitalia ("un sale con de catin"). Such verbal play, or

---

* Mina's "emancipated" attitude toward marriage, as expressed in her Italian poems, was at odds with Duchamp's view despite a surface similarity. During interviews with the author, both Gabrielle Buffet-Picabia and Juliette Gleizes commented on the awkwardness of Mina's position, and their own, as French-speaking witnesses of Duchamp's linguistic sabotage.

foreplay, carried with it the understanding that it would go no further, and relied on the fact that only the sophisticates were in on the secret.

Like Mina, Williams was uncomfortable in this atmosphere. His account of the Arensberg circle—written some thirty years later—still bristles with rancor, which derived as much from the interest that he, too, took in Mina as from his feeling of inferiority vis-à-vis Marcel. These charged evenings are best memorialized in "Walter's Room," a poem by Allen Norton depicting the Arensberg salon as the place

> *Where people who lived in glass houses*
> *Threw stones connubially at one another;*
> *And the super pictures on the walls*
> *Had intercourse with the poems that were never written*
> *. . .*
> *Where nobody ever made love*
> *For all were lovers.*

Mina received a number of propositions that winter. "An instantaneous affection was fashionable," she recalled. "One heard little else than exhortations to love." But the scenarios were unchanged. While the men amused themselves by undermining established codes of behavior, the women waited. "Among these scintillating modernists whom I could accompany —led by mysterious cocktails so magically expanding our universe—into an unusual dimension," she continued, "I watched the men cooing the assertively 'modern' women into the nests of their astringent lusts, to crush them 'tomorrow' in the contracting pupils of their observant eyes." (Duchamp's penetrating gaze is evoked in her metaphor of vision as possession.) In theory, all subscribed to the code of modern love, but in practice they formed "a marionette theatre" where "interchangeable actors and audience played into each other's hands."

Instantaneous affections had to be resisted while her American divorce was in process. Mabel had finally obtained her freedom once Edwin allowed her to divorce him. Other divorces took place less discreetly. On January 26, the *Evening Sun* stunned readers with the headline "His Model and Soul Mate, Too. Artist's Infatuation for Baroness Told by Wife." A Mrs. Renée Dixon was suing for divorce from her husband, the artist Douglas Gilbert Dixon, because his attentions "had been almost completely monopolized by his poetic soulmate model, the beautiful Baroness Elsa von Freytag-Loringhoven." Within a short time Louise and Allen Norton would separate, and Louise would take up with Edgard Varèse. Lou Arensberg began thinking that she *could* misbehave: she soon acquired the knack with Roché, who explained this turn of events to Beatrice Wood only after she had married outside their circle. And as soon as Gabi Picabia left for Europe, her husband took up with Isadora Duncan. Connubial stone-throwing had begun in earnest.

Yet if marriage was passé, love among the modernists was no improvement. Mina may not have known at this point, as she waited for her divorce, that Amelia DeFries was also suing Stephen for breach of promise, a problem that he dealt with by moving to the Caribbean. According to New York law, with or without proof of adultery, Mina's action was straightforward: *he* had deserted *her* four years earlier.

Mina described her case to Bill Williams. It was only a matter of time until she would be a free woman. Given this history, Williams was surprised neither by her concern with the sex war nor by her sardonic view of marriage. At this point Mina was full of contempt for what she called "marriage boxes":

> *Oh God*
> *That men and women*
> *having undertaken to vanquish one another*
> *should be allowed*
> *to shut themselves up   in hot boxes   and breed*

III

Within the month, Alfred Kreymborg offered Mina the chance to express her anti-matrimonial convictions in *Lima Beans*, the one-acter he had written for the Provincetown Players. When he asked her to play the wife, "the super-sophisticated Mina sniff[ed] a little at the commonplaceness of the marriage theme," he recalled. Kreymborg insisted that he *had* to have her and Bill, who would play the husband, because they could speak the dialogue as rhythmical free verse. Mina agreed despite her reservations. The artist William Zorach would double as set designer and the third member of the cast, a vegetable huckster. Williams was unsure about the demands on his time, since he would have to drive to Manhattan every night after his office hours. He accepted when Kreymborg promised him "all those kisses from Mina, lovely, lovely Mina."

Soon Williams, who picked her up before each rehearsal, was entertaining thoughts of greater intimacy with the glamorous and soon-to-be-single "wife." The language of his *Autobiography* hints at these daydreams: her role becomes "the soubrette" and his "the lover." But while Williams was fantasizing about Mina, she kept things on a friendly basis, with enough flirtatiousness to make life interesting. One evening, to his surprise, "she asked me what my annual income was from my practice of medicine," a question that struck him as odd. Williams later confessed that "he had once thought he might have married the poet Mina Loy." His long-suffering wife, Flossie, replied: "She wouldn't have taken you. You didn't have enough money."

The uncertain bases for relations between the sexes were very much in question that winter, particularly in Greenwich Village. Downtown,

Freudianism had made even greater inroads, although in a vulgarized form. Among the intelligentsia, psychoanalysis and the marriage theme were so timely that they dominated the Provincetown Players' programs for 1916. The little theater group produced *Suppressed Desires*, a satire of Freudianism by George Cram Cook and Susan Glaspell, and *Enemies*, a tense marital dialogue written and acted by Neith Boyce and Hutchins Hapgood. Although Kreymborg's *Lima Beans* also sent up marriage in its stylized way —by showing a couple at odds over dinner—the play was accepted for performance only because John Reed threatened to resign from the group. Yet its zany spirit and bold uses of abstraction now seem representative of its cultural moment.

Because he wanted the actors to perform like marionettes, Kreymborg conducted rehearsals with a baton, an approach that helped Williams forget his self-consciousness and Mina her irony. The play's opening lines echoed her own satires of marriage:

> *The Wife* (wistfully whimsical)
> *Put a knife here,*
> *place a fork there—*
> *marriage is greater than love.*
> *Give him a large spoon,*
> *give him a small—*
> *you're sure of your man when you dine him.*

She began to enjoy the comic aspect of a plot that hinged on the wife's decision to serve string rather than lima beans, and to enjoy being a marionette, provided the wire-puller was as harmless as Kreymborg.

The actors' puppetlike gestures, Zorach's checkerboard kitchen set, and the vegetable-festooned curtain were nonetheless such departures from naturalism that most of the Players were baffled. Still, they "loved to eye Mina Loy" and "wagged their heads knowingly," Kreymborg noted. At the dress rehearsal, some of the group criticized the production's experimental nature. While Mina's décolletage "served to fascinate the beholders, Bill Williams's costume, a weird concoction he had designed and executed himself, met with scanty approval," Kreymborg recalled. Of Zorach's set one regular complained, "There's nothing to it," to which another replied, "It fits the play."

The cast tried not to lose heart. At tea before the opening performance, Mina arrived in high spirits, wearing the green taffeta gown, gold slippers, and pieces from her jewelry collection that comprised her costume. Among the guests was a young woman with carrot-colored braids and a prim demeanor—Marianne Moore, the other female modernist with whom Mina was always compared. Moore took note of Mina's mosaic brooch, dangling gold earrings, and ornate English rings. Although Williams recalled seeing Moore in awe "of Mina's long-legged charms" whenever they met, Moore made a sympathetic appraisal of her rival's debut: she was "very beautiful in the play, very rakish previous to the play owing to the necessity of wearing a mixed costume—some of the properties and also ordinary street clothing. She enunciated beautifully." Moore was as impressed by Mina's ideas as she was by her costume: "We discussed Gordon Craig whom she knew, George Moore, and the hollowness of fashionable life, and I thought her very clever and a sound philosopher."

That evening, however, the audience appreciated Mina's décolletage more than her philosophy. Zorach's performance enhanced the play's wackiness: looking like Harpo Marx, he ran in and out shouting, "I got toma*toes*, I got pota*toes!*" Bill and Mina did their best to imitate marionettes, holding hands woodenly and bowing in unison. But the audience wanted something more. After Bill took Mina in his arms in gratitude for the reappearance of lima beans and gave her "a glancing sort of china-doll kiss," a spectator yelled, "For God's sake, kiss her!" The play concluded with more kisses, a ceremonious shelling of lima beans, and some unanswered questions on the meaning of love. After a short silence the house burst into an uproar. While Bill and Mina jerked up and down, Kreymborg counted curtain calls. He rushed to take a bow, but fled when Zorach "sent up a huge basket bulging, not with flowers, but with vegetables."

Unlike Kreymborg, Williams considered the performance a qualified success, although, as his biographer notes, "he may have been thinking of Mina rather than the play." At least one Provincetown regular liked *Lima Beans* and observed, "Two poets and a poet painter moved and spoke in a series of rhythms so carefully worked out . . . that it seemed spontaneous play."* That winter, Kreymborg hoped to build on his connection to the Provincetown by having the work of *Others* writers performed. Soon Wallace Stevens and Williams were writing free-verse dramas, and Mina thought of staging her Italian plays, the two Futurist playlets and her satire of vanguardism, *The Pamperers.*

But if progressive Provincetowners found Kreymborg's scherzo baffling, what would they make of Futurist drama? Mina's playlets had mystified readers when they appeared in *Rogue.* The first, *Collision,* had as its single character a Marinetti-like orator but no dialogue, and a set that was supposed to vibrate as the "planes and angles of walls and ceiling interchange kaleidoscopically." Her second play, *Cittàbapini,* had characters of a kind, a "greenish man" and the "City" he seeks to possess, but like its title, an amalgam of *città* and "Bapini," the play made sense only to those who knew about her affair with Papini. That these extremely compressed scripts followed Futurist rules for the reinvention of drama might have impressed Marinetti had he read them, but no New Yorker would know what to make of a play that took a minute to perform.

---

* Most Players preferred Eugene O'Neill's *Before Breakfast,* a one-acter on the same bill as *Lima Beans* which consisted of a shrewish wife's monologue, followed by her offstage husband's slitting his throat—a depressing foil to Kreymborg's lighthearted romp.

Mina went back to work on *The Pamperers*, the most conventional of her three plays in that it had dialogue. It began with a collage of the "tag ends of overheard conversation"—of the kind frequently uttered at Mabel's salon. A member of the group—"picked people melted by a distinguished method among the upholstery"—declares dramatically, "I don't want to know anything about Marinetti but I respect him . . . I am willing to accept the creed of any man who wears a clean collar." "There are only two kinds of people in society," replies Diana, the Mabel figure, "geniuses and women." "I am the woman who understands," she purrs to her next candidate for genius status—a tramp who proposes to "make *Life* out of cigar-ends." But Diana soon turns this filthy genius into a member of the middle class, with good taste and a clean collar. If Mina's satire of patronage seemed to bite the hand that had fed it, she could reply that she was merely pointing out the hollowness of fashionable life.

I V

The Arensberg circle began planning subversive amusements on a larger scale in December, when 33 West Sixty-seventh Street became the unofficial headquarters of the Society of Independent Artists. Members of this new exhibition society ranged from the progressives George Bellows, Robert Henri, and Walter Pach to ultramodernists Man Ray, Joseph Stella, and Duchamp, but all shared a common opposition to the National Academy's tradition of juried art shows. Modeled on the Paris Société des Indépendants, the Independents endorsed the slogan "No jury, no prizes," an approach that was hardly new to the Parisians but in New York nothing short of revolutionary.

In January 1917, the new society—with Arensberg as director and Duchamp as head of the hanging committee—informed America's artists that they could exhibit two paintings at the Grand Central Palace that spring provided they paid six dollars. "New York is to have what will be the largest and most radical art exhibition ever held in America," declared the *International Studio*. "Every school of art from the most radical to the most conservative will be represented," asserted the *New York Herald*; "Cubists, futurists, post-impressionists will be there; and so will some of those who are just artists." "If the Liberty Bell were not so cracked already it should sound the glad tidings throughout the land," wrote Henry McBride, happy that young artists would be thus "enfranchised." Among the nearly two hundred female applicants for enfranchisement, Mina, Frances, Clara Tice, and Beatrice Wood made plans to exhibit.

While the Independents promised to be even more revolutionary than the Armory Show, the months before its opening passed in the shadow of far greater disruption. The Germans announced on January 31 that they would torpedo without warning all ships, including neutrals. After the sinking of the U.S.S. *Housatonic* on February 3, President Wilson severed

223

diplomatic relations, promising peace without victory. It looked as if the United States could no longer maintain neutrality. Once the Attorney General tried to curtail freedom of speech by enhancing the powers of a 1903 anti-anarchist law, foreigners began worrying about the increasingly blatant expressions of xenophobia in the country at large.

Mina also had to think about earning a living. Soon after her arrival it had become clear to her that *Vogue* was not interested in her fashion plates. She had been naïve to suppose that in Florence she could foresee what was wanted in New York. Inspired no doubt by Frances's ability to create commercial *objets d'art*, she set up a small workshop to produce "art" lampshades. At a time when U-boats were on everyone's mind, Mina began tracing silhouettes of old-fashioned sailing ships, to be attached in low relief to the shades. When illuminated, they glowed like the images in a magic lantern show: they "had a fairy-tale feeling, like their maker," recalled Juliette Gleizes. But the prospect of opening a shop evoked both her father's business acumen and her mother's aversion to trade, even though in the New World, it seemed, distinctions between "high" and "low" art no longer mattered.

About the same time, the *Evening Sun*'s reporter was pondering her next assignment. "Who is . . . this 'modern woman' that people are always talking about?" she asked. "Does she look any different looks or talk any different words or think any different thoughts from the late Cleopatra or Mary Queen of Scots or Mrs. Browning?" Since the modern woman looked, talked, and thought like Mina Loy, it appeared, the reporter arranged to meet her. Mina told the story of her life—edited to sound convincingly modern—and read aloud from *The Pamperers*. This satire, the reporter noted, was a foreign import: "The play was written over on the other side, where Modernism is said to have begun." Mina's thoughts on the contrast between the Old World and the New were also noted. Despite her reservations about Italy, she felt "respect for the nation and enthusiasm for the spirit of the soldiers," and while the political situation was grave, she was optimistic about life on *this* side, in the New World.

On February 13, when Mina's thoughts on art and life appeared in the *Evening Sun*, the paper's front page warned readers, "Decision to Arm U.S. Steamships May Bring Speedy Clash at Sea." Because Wilson's plan to arm American shipping would almost certainly cause retaliation, noted the lead column, "in the opinion of many in close touch with developments, a state of war now exists." Other articles related the fate of Allied vessels attempting to get through the blockade. A White Star steamship had just been torpedoed, the French Line would delay departures, passengers returning on the American Line were asked to release the firm of responsibility "in case of accident or untoward occurrences." American citizens were outraged to learn that German propaganda had infiltrated the home front and that it had been "abetted by prominent American pacifists, to divide public opinion in this country."

Reading the paper that day, one had the sense of a nation poised between a familiar past and a menacing future. Congress had already doubled the size of the army; preparedness groups were readying volunteers. The government had invested so heavily in war loans to the Allies that intervention looked inevitable. In the following weeks, as public opinion became increasingly bellicose, socialists, pacifists, and other dissenters had cause for concern. For the time being, Wilson temporized. By April, seven American vessels had been sunk, a German plan to foment a Mexican-American war had been uncovered, and the Russian Tsar had been overthrown. On April 6, after four days of bitter debate, Wilson declared war.

For many, America's entry into the hostilities was the occasion for rejoicing. Patriotic groups paraded up Fifth Avenue; flag-waving became a national pastime. The hastily organized Committee on Public Safety, under the direction of George Creel, worked to repress the voices of dissent that Creel had formerly encouraged as a contributor to *The Masses*. Overnight, those who showed anything less than wholehearted support for the war were deemed subversives. "War means an ugly mob-madness, crucifying the truth-tellers, choking the artists, sidetracking reforms, revolutions and the working of social forces," Reed predicted. "For many years," he continued, "this country is going to be a worse place for free men to live in."

While the fear of being choked for their art did not keep the Independents from opening four days after the declaration of war, the show's importance as the last exercise in artistic reform was obvious. In the Arensberg group's participation, the desire to *épater* the bourgeois mingled with the wish to defy warmongering. Liberal backers of the Independents had welcomed the "no jury, no prizes" idea as a breath of fresh air, but to the ultramodernists in Mina's circle, it became an excuse for artistic subversion. The group's sardonic spirit, "charged with blasphemy and harshness under the pressure of events," Gabi Picabia recalled, "manifest[ed] itself with unforeseen violence" in the actions of her husband and their friend Duchamp, who shared "a veritable genius for perturbation and polemics."

Of the two, Duchamp was the more refined. Scandal would prove his weapon of choice and perhaps his only means of voicing anti-war sentiment that spring. In the Arensberg circle, few were aware that Duchamp had twice been declared unfit for service in France because of heart trouble: at a time when able-bodied men were volunteering, he had been taken for a shirker, and it was in part for this reason that he had left Paris.* On March 27, two weeks before the opening of the Independents, Duchamp was

---

* In France, Duchamp had served one year in the military rather than the obligatory two by learning printing in order to qualify as an "art worker." *Salt Seller*, his collection of writings, includes the following note under the heading "Deferment": "Against compulsory military service: a '*deferment*' of each limb, of the heart and the other anatomical parts; each soldier being already unable to put his uniform on again, his heart feeding *telephonically*, a deferred arm, etc. *Then*, no more feeding; each '*deferee*' isolating himself" (p. 23).

again ordered to report to French authorities before being judged permanently unfit for military service. This experience no doubt revived bitter memories. In the days following his deferment, Duchamp used the Independents as an arena for acts of sabotage against all systems of classification. As head of the hanging committee, he insisted that exhibits be hung in alphabetical order. Doing away with jury selection was the first step, he argued, but now, in order to transcend the biases of those who hung the works, they needed a system based on chance.

Reactions to this innovation were mixed. "Pictures will be hung on a plan never before devised," observed the *New York Herald*. "They will be placed in alphabetical order without regard to class or artist's reputation." McBride, who applauded most of Duchamp's ideas, disapproved this time, because works of quality would be lost in the confusion. Proposing to reconcile the old approach—which grouped paintings according to affinities—with the new, he suggested that if artists would agree to a collective name change, one room could show "Jules De Pascin, John De Marin, Charles Demuth, Abram De Walkowitz, Arthur B. De Davies and Samuel De Halpert." And while Guy Pène du Bois, who would have fit into such an arrangement, respected the idea of alphabetical democracy, he felt sure that, put into practice, it would prove "a complete failure."

Those who favored Duchamp's plan trusted in the benefits of variety, randomness, and accident in art (as in life) and saw in it the means toward a fecund mix of juxtapositions. Shrewdly they explained that the alphabetical system was in keeping with the American dream of opportunity for all: by obliterating hierarchies and distinctions, it would create democracy on a grand scale. "The hanging of all works in alphabetical order, for the first time in any exhibition, will result in the most unexpected contacts and will incite every one to understand the others," argued Roché.

But it was no good thumbing one's nose at convention only to fall under other constraints. Since those whose names began with A, B, and C would have the advantage, the hanging committee decided to place the letters of the alphabet in a hat and draw to see which came first. They selected R. Not only had Duchamp done away with classifications that placed landscape artists in one room and Cubists in another, he had subverted the alphabetical determinism that decided when one would be called up, or deferred from, service—whether military or artistic. But few outside their circle grasped his subtle logic.

The proof of his ideas was the "Big Show" itself. On April 9, everyone who was anyone appeared at the Grand Central Palace for the private viewing. Large temporary screens had been set up to create the avenues down which the crowd strolled or raced to see the nearly 2,500 entries. "Two miles of paint and a sea of speculation as to where the good things may be seen without employing a guide or a bath chair," declared *International Studio*. Members of the Arensberg group caught glimpses of each other inspecting their enormous project. Mina stood in front of her painting while Duchamp and Arensberg paced up and down the aisles, and Frances made a theatrical entrance with her dog Sacha. Louise Norton amused herself by turning the canvases she did not like to the wall. That others would have liked to follow her example is clear from the remarks of art patron John Quinn, who spent the evening arguing "that the whole damn thing went on the theory that art was democratic; that it never was; that art was aristocratic; that that meant choice, fastidiousness, taste, style."

The female Independents, many of whom were showing their work for the first time, were the beneficiaries of the show's "democratic" spirit. More than a third of the 1,235 exhibitors were women. Because the exhibition began with R, many visitors stopped first at Dorothy Rice's *Claire Twins*, a portrait of two overweight women which made people laugh. Another show stopper, in part because of its size, was Gertrude Vanderbilt Whitney's memorial to the *Titanic*: this eighteen-foot classical sculpture of youth reminded visitors of the millions of lives already lost in the war. Next to Whitney's study of masculine valor, Beatrice Wood's assemblage looked positively offensive: it showed the torso of a female bather whose privates were veiled by a piece of soap. "Crowds stood in front of it, men left their calling cards, and the reviews gave it more space than that given to serious artists," she recalled gleefully.

Those who started over at A eventually found their way to L—where they encountered Mina Loy, "one of those upon whom the whirligig of fate, I mean, of course, the alphabetical hanging system, had played a scurvy trick," noted McBride. Her entry, *Making Lampshades*, hung next to one of the most sensational works in the show, a nude by George Lothrop, who had painted his Venus with almost *trompe l'oeil* illusionism and put real jewels in her hair. Mina's painting was "clever with a European kind of cleverness," McBride noted, but few saw it next to Lothrop's crowd-pleaser. When he asked why Mina didn't take off her gold earrings and pin them on her canvas, McBride continued, "Miss Loy's sad eyes flashed with opaline brilliancy for an instant and then as quickly dimmed. 'No, I could not do that,' she replied. 'It would be plagiarism.' "

Others thought that the alphabetical system had played a scurvy trick on everyone. At best, it produced a hodgepodge; at worst, an *olla podrida*, a *salmagundi*, a *bouillabaisse*. The *International Studio*'s critic dismissed the show in a revealing mix of metaphors: "The good ship Independent was wrecked on the Scylla of No Jury and the Charybdis of Alphabetical Hanging. 'Open Shop' for art is a failure and must give way to selection by jury. Some people think marriage a mistake but have never been able to supply an adequate substitute. Similarly, there is nothing to replace a jury." In his view, the ship of Art had been torpedoed by that subversive trio—modernism, trade unionism, and sexual freedom. But one could count on opposition from this bastion of conservatism.

To create dissension among the enlightened was another matter. In the days after the declaration of war and before the opening, Duchamp devised a way to test his American associates. He had long been intrigued by machines, especially those that adapted human actions to impersonal ends, but unlike Marinetti did not see machinery as a means to extend human capacity. Rather, like Picabia, he wanted to bring industrial forms into art to objectify human relations: both men were drawn to one aspect of human relations, which they depicted in a formal vocabulary of "mechano-sexual metaphors." Before leaving France, Duchamp had imagined the assemblage that would become his best-known work, *The Bride Stripped Bare by Her Bachelors, Even*, in which an amorous Bride machine keeps on disrobing while her Bachelors—marionette-like figures in the shape of uniforms—are rendered unfit to consummate marriage. By 1917, this allegory of solipsism was known to the Arensberg group, which had seen it in the studio Arensberg rented for Duchamp down the hall from his duplex.

But familiarity with Duchamp's depiction of sexual impasse could not have prepared one for the next stage of his campaign. Flanked by Arensberg and Stella, Duchamp went to the showroom of the Mott Iron Works to inspect plumbing devices. He bought a white porcelain urinal and submitted it to the Independents under the name R. Mutt, along with a Philadelphia address and the requisite six dollars. Duchamp later explained that the name, which would prove nearly as offensive as the urinal, wed the R of "richard" (French slang for moneybags) to the "Mutt" of "Mutt and Jeff," implying that this *pissotière*, as "the opposite of poverty," was a rich source of R, or "art." His close friends may have wondered whether the "richard" in question was Walter Arensberg, Duchamp's co-conspirator and patron.

Mutt's submission, entitled *Fountain*, arrived at the Grand Central Palace two days before the opening. When it was set on its pedestal like a piece of sculpture, dissension arose. Before Duchamp and Beatrice could ease it into place among the Ms, Bellows and Arensberg started arguing. Bellows, who had been in charge of hanging the Armory Show, shook his fist while Arensberg, repressing a smile, stroked the object. "A lovely form has been revealed, freed from its functional purpose, therefore a man clearly has made an aesthetic contribution," he declared. The board of directors split over Mutt's submission. The committee's conservatives, including Duchamp's friend Katherine Dreier, said that it could not be shown. On the contrary, Arensberg argued, it *had* to be shown: according to the rules, this exhibit allowed "*the artist* to decide what is art, not someone else." When the board met to resolve the crisis, Mutt's defenders lost, whereupon Duchamp and Arensberg resigned.

The society's internecine warfare made news chiefly because of Duchamp's protest. The *New York Herald* noted the board's ruling—Mutt's *Fountain* failed to qualify as art—and its supporters' objections, taking care to describe the item as "a familiar article of bathroom furniture." While the Arensberg group lamented this blow to artistic freedom, other members of the board, remembering the hysteria over the Armory Show, worried about the Independents' reputation at this critical moment, as tolerance for non-conformity evaporated. This was the kind of publicity they had hoped to avoid. Another controversial submission, a portrait of Germany's crown prince, had disappeared before the opening, presumably the victim of anti-German sentiment. Showing Mutt's *Fountain* would have been like tossing a bomb.

Although the press dropped the *Fountain* controversy once the object itself disappeared from view, reporters clamored to interview the more outspoken of the Independents. Tracked down by a reporter for *The Morning Telegraph*, Beatrice announced that she was "out for red blood." "I want to return to the ecstasy and wild imaginings of childhood," she continued.

As these remarks were not enlightening, the reporter sought out the Independent said to be the "expert"—Mina Loy. "The artist is jolly and quite irresponsible," Mina began: art was a "divine joke" which the public did not get simply because it had been trained to see things in just one way. But the artist saw each object with fresh eyes. "The artist is uneducated, is seeing IT for the first time," she continued. "The public and the artist can meet at every point except the—for the artist—vital one, that of pure, uneducated seeing. They like the same drinks, can fight in the same trenches, pretend to the same women; but never see the same thing once." Despite Mina's timely reference to the trenches, her philosophy sounded abstract, at a time when the pressures of war were mounting.

Under the headline "Your Country's Art Calls You," the *Telegraph*'s reporter compared her survey of the Independents with a trip to a recruiting station: "It must be done, but how you dread to do it." The exhibition, she noted, was "full of splendid material," but the artists were "unorganized, undrilled [and] incongruous." Other New York art critics picked up the theme. Gustav Kobbe emphasized the show's timeliness: it included paintings done in the trenches and aerial sketches by a member of the British Royal Flying Corps. Among exhibits inspired by the war, that of Frances Stevens stood out, especially since she was a woman and a Futurist. Dubbing the show "the spring offensive," McBride admitted that only one out of ten works gave offense, while other critics compared the modernists to U-boats and the Academy to "the objects to be torpedoed." A member of the American Federation of the Arts praised war as the solution to aesthetic chaos. "We need war," he fulminated; "for if war is itself a madness, it is also a cure for madness." *Vanity Fair* struck a more serious note: the Independents represented "the spirit of the greater freedom that all real Americans confidently believe will mark the end of the War."

This spirit, some observed, had begun to infiltrate the other arts. Several New York papers carried notices of a poetry reading planned in connection with the Independents. "Chance To See Live Poets," announced the *Morning Telegraph*: the event would feature "those who are writing war verse . . . classic poets, the cubist poets, futurists, vers librists and poets of other sorts." Like their confrères at the exhibition, the participants were listed in alphabetical order: they included Mary Austin, William Rose Benét, Maxwell Bodenheim, Padraic Colum, Arturo Giovanitti, Harry Kemp, Mina Loy, Allen Norton, and William Carlos Williams. Beatrice Wood joined the audience gathered on April 18 at the Grand Central Palace, along with some skeptical reporters.

The reading began badly. Poetry was governed by "rhyme, rhythm, and reason," explained the mistress of ceremonies, but "in these parlous times, rhyme and rhythm had departed and reason was on the doorstep." Following her introduction, Benét injected an energetic note with a poem on America's entry into the war, Colum offered verse that had both rhyme and meter, and Giovanitti read from his new book of poems on New York City.

Once again the victim of alphabetical order, Mina came after manly Harry Kemp, who ended his reading with "a double-barreled oath that made everybody gasp." She made her entrance a few seconds later, strode to the platform and launched into her poem without giving its title, then marched off as quickly as she had come. "Miss Loy gives us credit for a great deal of divination," observed a member of the audience. Although Mina's reading was among the most dramatic, she told Williams that his was the best. Not only was his verse "replete with hells and damns," recalled an observer, but his concluding poem "kicked rhyme and rhythm down stairs and threw reason out of the window."

It was unclear to participants and observers alike whether this reading, like the exhibit itself, was meant to educate the public, provoke it, or do both at the same time. On the one hand, the modernists relied on the audience's capacity to be shocked, but on the other, they wanted the public to appreciate them. At various times that spring, both attitudes prevailed in the Arensberg circle: the balance shifted depending on whether the more antisocial tactics of Duchamp and Picabia were in ascendance or whether more conciliatory voices made themselves heard. While everyone disparaged those who came to see live artists in action, the more reasonable argued for attempts at communication. Yet they were uncertain whether they wanted to appease the public or enrage them.

As the country geared up for war, the avant-garde stance became increasingly ambivalent. When Duchamp and Roché suggested launching a magazine to publicize their perspective, members of the inner circle had agreed to help with the venture, to be called *The Blind Man*. Arensberg again lent his duplex as headquarters; *Vanity Fair*'s editor, Frank Crowninshield, gave advice; while Mina, Roché, and Beatrice composed the articles. Just as "Russia needed a political revolution," Roché argued, "America needs an artistic one." To this end, the "no jury" rule ensured that all were represented, but more important, the alphabetical system would provoke a creative chaos—provided that painters, paintings, and public could meet without preconceptions. In this spirit, *The Blind Man* proposed itself as an artistic dating service, whose role it was to introduce the parties. Other aspects of the magazine contradicted this account of *The Blind Man*'s function. The cover, showing a gentleman in a bowler hat being led through the Independents by his Seeing Eye dog, played with the idea of official blindness: a mutt could find its way through this exhibition better than a bourgeois. One of Roché's "suggestions" was more reassuring. "To learn to 'see' the new painting is easy," it claimed, but "it is something like learning a new language."

Mina developed this theme in the concluding article, a longer version of her remarks to *The Morning Telegraph*'s reporter. The public was more intelligent than its teachers, she began: "It knew before the Futurists that Life is a jolly noise and a rush and a sequence of ample reactions." But education had placed "spectacles on wholesome eyes" by teaching people to avoid what they did not recognize: "Education in recognizing something that has been seen before demands an art that is only acknowledgeable by way of diluted comparisons." It was these unwholesome spectacles that kept the public from "seeing IT for the first time." Although Mina did not mention Duchamp's *Fountain*, her defense of the artist's unbiased eye complemented Arensberg's claim that any object, even a *pissotière*, could be a thing of beauty.

Yet the group's desire to scandalize the man in the bowler made it hard to take at face value either the magazine's stated aim or its posture of detachment. From the start, the editors imagined ways to shock the public. Beatrice wanted to parade up and down at the entrance wearing a sandwich board advertising *The Blind Man*. When this plan was vetoed, the editors tried to place the magazine with a pretty salesgirl next to the cash register. This idea was no more successful than the sandwich-board proposal. Disappointed that they had failed to provoke a scandal, the group concluded that the public's indifference resulted from the fact that no one actually read the magazine.

At the end of April, Mina, Beatrice, and Roché went to work on a second issue, planned as a defense of Duchamp's *Fountain*. In addition to their pieces, this *Blind Man* included free verse by such varied talents as Arensberg, Picabia, Demuth, Allen Norton, Frances Stevens, Erik Satie, and Bob Brown, along with reproductions of art by Duchamp, Stieglitz, Joseph Stella, and Clara Tice, prose pieces by Louise Norton and Gabi Picabia, and letters from Stieglitz and Crowninshield. This group effort may be taken to represent the Arensberg position, a mix of modernist formalism and vanguard attempts to tweak the reader's nose.

On May 5, as the second issue was about to be mailed, they hit a snag. Duchamp and Roché had asked Beatrice to take responsibility as publisher: as foreigners in a country mobilizing for war, they ran the risk of being deported through their association with a magazine that could, under the circumstances, be deemed subversive. As soon as Beatrice's father saw the issue, however, he ordered her to withdraw it from circulation. The editors had all but dared the postal authorities to come after

231

them. "Brave people who like to run risks may send to *The Blind Man* five dollars as subscription and encouragement," they announced. Beatrice might like parading as "queen of the anarchists," but she was too naïve to understand the significance of her actions. The magazine was distributed by hand and became, in Beatrice's eyes, a *"succès de scandale."*

The group had set its course for a head-on collision with orthodoxies. The cover featured another of Duchamp's mechano-sexual metaphors, the innocently drawn *Chocolate Grinder*. Opening the magazine, the reader came upon Bob Brown's "Eyes," an optical poem that played with the idea of vision. The next page showed Stieglitz's frontal photograph of *Fountain*, labeled "The exhibit refused by the Independents." Directly opposite this suggestive image, an editorial defended Mutt's right to a showing on the grounds that "He CHOSE it." In case anyone missed the point, Louise Norton offered a rejoinder to *Fountain*'s critics. Only "atavistic minds," she teased, could find this sculpture indecent, "yet to any 'innocent' eye how pleasant is its chaste simplicity of line and color!"

With this claim for its formal purity, the urinal had reached its apotheosis. Since then, much ink has been spilled on the subject of Duchamp's intentions. Already at the time of the Independents, there were, Norton observed, "those who anxiously ask, 'Is he serious or is he joking?' " Her response—"Perhaps he is both!"—comes close to identifying the reason for the anxiety provoked by this work in 1917, when ambivalence looked unpatriotic and irony seemed subversive. Duchamp's *Fountain* expressed the corrosive disillusionment we now call Dada, though the term was not yet current in New York. In their circle, Norton explained, this mood was called "blague," or sardonic joking. "There is among us today a spirit of 'blague,' " she went on, "arising out of the artist's bitter vision of an over-institutionalized world of stagnant statistics and antique axioms." Duchamp was playing a joke on a world that had put him at odds with its "antique axioms"—including the demand for seriousness in time of war.

In this same spirit, Mina's contribution to the second *Blind Man* praised the artist Louis Eilshemius—a self-styled "painter, poet, musician, inventor, linguist, mystic, educator, prophet"—whose reputation Duchamp was trying to revive in yet another joke on the art world. This American Rousseau, Mina asserted, no doubt with tongue in cheek—a "simple soul unhampered by a traditional mode of representation"—possessed the uneducated eye she had recommended in the first *Blind Man*. Eilshemius painted "instantaneous photographs of his mind" and wrote free verse of "granite simplicity," she went on. Given the nature of both his art and his poetry, it is difficult to accept claims for his brilliance—until one realizes that, like Duchamp, Mina was both serious and joking. As a critic suggests, "It is hard not to read Mina Loy's article as if her pen had been at times held by another hand"—that of Duchamp, whose voice, "sarcastic in a deadpan fashion," echoes in her own. She ended the piece with a remark that says more about Duchamp's aims than about her subject: "Anyhow,

Duchamp meditating the levelling of all values, witnesses the elimination of Sophistication."

Others among their contemporaries agreed that the group's activities —from the Independents to *The Blind Man*—sprang from a common desire to level values. Crowninshield saw this aim in a positive light when he praised the magazine's editors for fostering the art of their time, "however morbid, however hurried, however disorganized, however nerve-wracking that time may be." If, through their efforts, they succeeded in creating an art of the modern age, "even if the age is one of telephones, submarines, aeroplanes, cabarets, cocktails, taxicabs, divorce courts, wars, tangos, dollar signs," then, he wagered, people would say, "Yes, they had an art, back in New York, in the days following the Great War."

As an American for whom the ravages of the machine war were still an abstraction, Crowninshield could draw on reserves of optimism about an art of telephones, submarines, airplanes, and divorce courts. From a European perspective, Gabrielle Picabia summarized the group's activities rather differently—as a shared response to "the world's anguish that everyone consciously or not bore within himself." Such subversive amusements were, she thought, the shared symptoms of a collective "heart trouble."

11

Colossus

(NEW YORK, 1917)

THERE WERE OTHER WAYS of being modern, some more in keeping with the American penchant for activism. Members of the Arensberg circle told so many stories about a provocative newcomer that spring, Mina recalled, that "it was becoming *the thing* to make his acquaintance." Long before she met the poet and boxer Arthur Cravan, she heard about his pugilistic exploits, his claim to be Oscar Wilde's nephew, his insolent little magazine, *Maintenant*, his notoriety as the most "American" member of the Paris avant-garde, and his astounding capacity for alcohol and scandal. These contradictory tales were, she noted, "so extravagant they broke upon the mind with the rumble of a social earthquake." *Colossus*, her memoir of Cravan—written as she came to know him and after his disappearance—records his effect on her as a series of seismic shocks.

He had foisted himself upon the Paris art world before the war by flaunting his connection to "Uncle Oscar." Given the currency of the Wilde legend after the writer's death in 1900, this tie had given Cravan a cachet. But just as the Parisians doubted that the French-speaking pugilist was British, as he claimed, many doubted the veracity of his tie to Wilde—especially after reading *Maintenant*, the review that he wrote, edited, and peddled from a wheelbarrow. In one issue Cravan printed an article entitled "Oscar Wilde Is Alive!" in which he related a visit to his uncle, who was said to be composing his memoirs thirteen years after his demise. This hoax was picked up by *The New York Times*, setting the tone for any number of mystifications to come.

Before attracting the art world's attention, Cravan had made his name as a boxer. Although he earned the light heavyweight championship of France because his opponent failed to show up, he had won the respect of Montparnasse. Since the revival of the Olympic Games in 1906, the sport had been in vogue among artists and intellectuals seeking to distinguish themselves from the decadents of the previous generation. Picasso, Segonzac, and Picabia had all painted studies of boxers, and Roché, who practiced the sport, had sparred with Braque. The regulars who flocked to Van Dongen's to watch Cravan fight the black Americans on the boxing circuit did not find it odd that these exhibitions were taking place in a painter's studio: this tall, handsome "American" combined the aesthetic heritage of the poet-outcast with the brashness of modern art.

To the Parisians, Cravan's "American" qualities included his physique, his energy, his antisocial tendencies, and his posture as a "manly" man uncorrupted by the civilizing efforts of an effeminate culture. Before the war, when Americans were a curiosity, Cravan had taken as his model the macho male described in his essay "To Be or Not to Be . . . American": being American, in his view, gave one prerogatives, including the right to self-defense. "The American is feared because he knows how to box; or at least people think he does," Cravan observed. Moreover, one could be American as others were poets or painters: it was a calling. To be a really good American, one had to be tall, say little, and express disdain for women. But above all, being American meant being arrogant: "The most important thing is to have a hell of a nerve."

Not content to flout bourgeois manners, Cravan was also eager to take on the avant-garde. He had welcomed the Futurists to prewar Paris—"We like the commotion that Marinetti makes," *Maintenant* noted—and *Lacerba* had returned the favor by publicizing Cravan and his magazine. By the following year, however, Cravan was preparing to one-up the Italians, at least where sartorial innovation was concerned. He regularly accompanied the poet Blaise Cendrars and the painter Robert Delaunay to the Bal Bullier, where this avant-garde trio could be seen dancing the tango in costumes painted the colors of the rainbow. Delaunay favored a scarlet-and-green tuxedo; Cravan sported a black shirt with cutouts through which one glimpsed obscenities scribbled in red on his chest and sometimes decorated his shirttails by sitting on Delaunay's palette. The boxer's talents were as impressive as his physique, explained a friend, but his morals were those of the athletes he befriended, men "worn out by their intensive training [and] enslaved by their splendid bodies." Cravan had ended his boxing career the previous year in Barcelona—in a match with Jack Johnson, the former heavyweight champion, who knocked him out in the sixth round.

Mina could not help being curious about this phenomenon. Judging by his match with Johnson, Cravan was not much of a boxer, Gabi Picabia observed. What was worse, he often boasted of robbing a jewelry store in Lausanne, where his family lived. Cravan "was not to be trusted"; she hid her jewelry when he came to call. But despite these shortcomings, she went on, he possessed "the courteous manners of an Englishman and a certain poetic gift." He had been unhappy in Paris because, apart from his friends, the art world took him for the brute he made himself out to be. He had made important enemies by publishing a scurrilous attack on the 1914 Salon des Indépendants, which insulted the most prominent avant-garde painters and poets. Sonia Delaunay had threatened to sue, and Apollinaire had challenged him to a duel, which was canceled once Cravan offered "hypocritical excuses."

Juliette Gleizes was less charitable. Cravan's height was his only claim to grandeur, she insisted. His blond Anglo-Saxon looks were the sort common among lifeguards and footmen, and he behaved like a brute when under the influence of alcohol. His claims to superiority masked a refusal to recognize that society found him wanting: his was "the limitless existence of the failure." In her opinion, Cravan was not a true pacifist like her husband but a deserter whose existence for the past three years had been devoted to the various forms of deception he practiced to avoid the draft.

Moreover, no one knew how Cravan had made his way to New York, recalled Duchamp, whose own contretemps with the authorities failed to produce any fellow feeling for the boxer. Duchamp wondered whether Cravan's sudden appearance there in the winter of 1917 had involved forged papers. "These are things people don't talk about," he observed years later. In his view, Cravan was a peculiar character: "I didn't like him very much, nor he me." But while Duchamp was circumspect about Cravan's peculiarities, Cravan dismissed Duchamp as a poseur. This antipathy, which dated back to Paris, would be augmented by the interest that both men took in Mina.

The few Americans who had heard of Cravan took him at his own valuation. In the literary columns of the respectable *Dial*, an observer of the Paris scene noted approvingly that Wilde's nephew had not only put the idea of *pluralisme* into poetic form but also "invented the term 'machinisme,' which very appropriately characterizes the mechanical and industrial side of our life."* "Machinisme," she continued, was one of the most appealing new aesthetic philosophies, because it appealed to real life. Moreover, Cravan's "monstrous capacity of imagination" distinguished him from those who sought inspiration in the old idea of art for art's sake: "Conscious of being identical with all things, all human creatures and all animals, he also desires ubiquity and wishes that he could gobble . . . all the tempting dishes on the world's menus."

Soon after Cravan's arrival in New York, his poetry and person were celebrated in a new magazine entitled *The Soil*. From the first issue, Robert Coady, *The Soil*'s publisher and owner of the Washington Square Gallery, argued that an indigenous American art—"young, robust, energetic, naïve,

---

* The critic observed that Cravan's "machinisme" had not found favor because it was less euphonious than "dynamisme," the critical term in vogue.

immature, daring and big spirited"—already existed but had not been recognized. Taking Duchamp as his antagonist, Coady condemned the internationalism of the Independents, along with what he deemed its facile democratization, the alphabetical hanging system. Calling instead for an art that returned to the "soil" from which American experience sprang, Coady listed as examples of this native art such diverse items as the sky-scraper, the airplane, the Panama Canal, the crazy quilt, and the cakewalk, as well as icons like Jack Johnson and Charlie Chaplin. In this context, Cravan—who had shared the ring with Johnson and whose poetry exhib-ited "American" values—was made to order.

To cap *The Soil*'s first editorial, Coady quoted Cravan's invitation to the sophisticates of the art world to "chuck this little dignity of yours to the winds!" Although Cravan's gibe had been aimed at the Parisians, it applied equally well, Coady felt, to New Yorkers, particularly those avant-gardists who championed the "innocent eye" but would not stoop to be-having like children. "Go and run across fields, across the plains at top speed like a horse," Cravan advised, "skip the rope and, then, when you shall be like a six year old, you'll know nothing and you'll see the most marvellous things." In an issue of *The Soil* that featured the art of boxing, Cravan praised Jack Johnson as "a man of scandal," "eccentric," "lively, good-natured, and gloriously vain," adding that, in his view, the champion was the one U.S. citizen who deserved to be king.

Cravan exemplified Coady's belief that only unself-consciously dem-ocratic art could make contact with life in America. Before sailing to New York, he had written poetry that seemed to fulfill Whitman's poetic vision:

> The rhythm of the ocean cradles the transatlantics,
> And while the heroic express arriving at Havre
> Whistles into the air, where the gases dance like tops,
> The athletic sailors advance, like bears.
> New York! New York! I should like to inhabit you!
> I see there science married
> To industry,
> In an audacious modernity,
> And in the palaces,
> Globes,
> Dazzling to the retina
> By their ultra-violet rays . . .

Unlike Europeans, who played jokes on those they claimed to admire, Cravan saw in the New World a dazzling collage of "marvellous things."

Before meeting Cravan in person, Mina gazed at him in the pages of *The Soil*, which included photographs: one, taken in Barcelona, showed Cravan the boxer sparring with Johnson; another showed Cravan the poet lolling on a chaise longue with two Siamese cats. While the second photo made an impression on Mina, its effect was negative. The décor of the Paris studio, his expression, and the Siamese, she noted, "gave him the air of a homosexual." This man would take no interest in her; his was a mind that would "snub" her.

Mina first saw him in the flesh with Walter Arensberg at the Independents' opening. Cravan, who was six feet four, towered over her friend. Noticing that Arensberg had failed, whether on purpose or by accident, to introduce them, Mina passed by "with no premonition of the psychological infinity that he would later offer my indiscreet curiosity as to the mechanism of man." In person, he was "dull and square in merely respectable tweeds; not at all homosexual."

When she saw him next, Cravan was more than usually dull, since he was recovering from the events of the previous day. On the morning of April 19, Duchamp and Picabia had been plotting another scandal. Knowing that Cravan was to lecture at the Grand Central Palace, the two men made sure that he got drunk. Half of Greenwich Village and a large group of society matrons turned out to see the poet-pugilist discuss "The Independent Artists of France and America." Cravan arrived late and wobbled up to the platform with Duchamp and Picabia as bodyguards. He swayed from side to side, then, like a ship on troubled seas, noted a reporter, "leaned too far to port and in another moment he had dealt art a terrible blow by striking the hard surface of the speaker's table with an independence of expression plainly heard on Lexington Avenue."

Cravan proceeded to make himself comfortable. He took off his coat, which seemed natural on a spring afternoon, then removed his vest, collar, and suspenders. Although he had uttered not a word, the audience was indulgent. "Monsieur Cravan was temperamental, but of course, he was also independent," noted an observer. "Was not that the subject of his lecture?" Suddenly he began roaring so loudly that he drowned out the noise of the incoming trains. The uptown contingent looked about nervously. When Cravan started shouting obscenities, his bodyguards rushed to his side, and four private detectives jumped him. Outnumbered, he was handcuffed and dragged off to the police station. Arensberg posted bail and took him back to West Sixty-seventh Street to sleep off his exploits. That evening, Duchamp gloated, "What a wonderful lecture."

Cravan's wonderful lecture goes unmentioned in *Colossus*. But whether or not Mina was in the audience, she could not have ignored the scandal. Judging by her evasive prose, she wanted to forget that she had been present when writing about him some years later. Instead, she recalled him hunched "in sodden insolence" at the Arensbergs' the following night, when the group gathered before the Independents' costume ball. Describing this occasion, she compared Cravan to a giant she had once pitied when, "like a towering statue of animated stone, he had swayed lethargically above the spectators" in an Italian circus. No doubt because this unflattering picture of him "swaying" above the audience was too close to reality, her next sentence evokes an antique statue: Cravan's costume—a bedspread around his torso and a towel on his head—"gave the perfect construction of his face the significance of great sculpture."

Nor did Mina mention that Cravan as antique sculpture was, once again, inappropriate. Although guests had been asked to dress as schools of modern art, artists rarely followed directions: Clara Tice came as a steam radiator, and John Covert as a hard-boiled egg. In any case, the nearly two hundred guests at the ball, a war benefit, had come chiefly to see Cravan repeat the previous day's spectacle. He obliged by removing his toga before slumping down next to Mina. When he put his arm around her, his "unspoken obscenities chilled my powdered skin," she noted. Despite the perfect construction of his face, he lacked "magnetism"—in large part, it seems, because of his previous day's performance.

While Mina's presence at the ball was noted, along with the other artists in the news, the event left much to be desired as far as she was concerned. Duchamp had asked her to accompany him that night, and he remained a prominent part "of the crazy pattern round the table." Whether to make her jealous or to be contrary, he had, she wrote, been "making love right under my nose to a woman like a horse wearing a toby frill." Cravan had attempted to make contact when he saw the chance to move in on Duchamp's territory. At that moment the idea of an involvement with either man was so repellent that Mina rose and left the group. Toward morning she ran into Cravan lurching through the crowd and asking women for their phone numbers. He could not promise, he told her, but he *might* find time to call.

Cravan found it more difficult to be "American" in New York than in Paris. Although he was unemployed and followed no set routine, he would doze for hours at the Arensbergs' before jerking bolt upright and making pronouncements. On one of these occasions, when the group was discussing the war, he sat up, shouted, "They can all go to hell," and returned to his slumbers. On another, he told Mina that he had had delirium tremens. They spoke in French, the language he preferred, but his conversation consisted of little more than swear words. Despite these peculiarities, Mina drifted into a partnership with the man who had initially repelled her. They often spent the evening ensconced "in the same deep arm chair, sharing the same inverted book." One night, as they were leaving, an intelligent phrase issued from his mouth: "You had better come and live with me in a taxi-cab," he told her. "We can keep a cat."

But insults—directed at life in general—often followed Cravan's moments of tenderness. As their partnership edged into courtship, relations became unpredictable. He lacked an income and a permanent address: at various times he slept on park benches, in a shed above Pennsylvania Station, at the homes of his women friends, or at the Village apartment of Arthur Frost, a painter friend from Paris and an Independent. These irregular slumbers contributed to Cravan's lethargy. In conversations with

Mina, the problem of where to spend the night recurred with such frequency that she finally agreed to take him home the next time he asked. "I will sleep upon the table," he promised, "and I shall not trouble myself to address a single word to you."

Mina found herself daydreaming about his potential as a lover. Unfortunately, the group would know as soon as she took the decision: they were never alone. The Parisians continued to warn her against him. Despite his ambitions as a poet, he had no verbal facility, he admired Victor Hugo, he was not one of them. It was clear that Duchamp and Cravan were opposites. Marcel was all lightning wit and mercurial mood swings. Arthur was stolid. "Having nothing of the modern spirit," she reasoned, "he was at a disadvantage," and, for that reason, "might make a passable lover." And in spite of his reputation, he *was* English. One evening as he wrapped his arms around her, she discovered that he was not entirely lacking in magnetism. "All your irony is assumed," he whispered. "You really have the tender heart of the romantic. My one desire," he went on, "is to see you smile at last." But these stock phrases, generated, she thought, "by the exigencies of courtship," made her laugh. If they could arrange to drop their cynicism, she and her lumbering suitor might perhaps "leap back over the choking sophistication into the heart of innocence."

Mina's account of their first night together is tinged with the self-protective irony she had hoped to shed. After a long-winded attempt to impress her as a literary light, he asked whether he might have a bath—for a man in his circumstances a welcome luxury. Emerging from the bathroom and making his way to the bed—he had no intention of sleeping on the table—he looked, she thought, "like something escaped from the British Museum." But the coldness of his embrace made her wonder whether she had made a mistake. It was unclear how sophisticates could find their way back into innocence.

Cravan proposed to take her to the country, a more suitable setting for the cultivation of their affections. But given his lack of funds, the "country" proved to be Van Cortlandt Park in the Bronx. This sylvan setting did not allay her sense that they had been intimate without intimacy. Cravan was so convinced of his mental superiority that he did not bother to share his thoughts. "In the progression of the literary man's love affair," she noted tartly, "he finds it proper, at certain moments, to expose his intellectual isolation. Colossus, with his ingrown spirit, assumed me to be . . . outside the radius of his creative meditation." On the way home he sang vulgar French songs about prostitutes while Mina watched as "the magic carpet of the 'El' floated under the sky, trailing its shreds of iron fringe along the Avenue."

She continued to see him in spite of his faults. They tramped around the city, visited museums, and tried every form of recreation requiring no entrance fee. Cravan seemed to be searching for something in the heights and depths of Manhattan. Wandering together "in the false appealing half-lights of artificial illuminations, among the network of iron structures, the opal fountains of electric signs, upon the grating bucking trolleys, along suburban avenues and palisades," Mina discovered an urban poetry and a repertoire of images that exalted her spirit—in part, because she was sharing it with Cravan.

Yet she had few illusions about her lover. He combined the "air of a Viking" with the "repartee of a Victorian charwoman." For some time they played at modernist love, with periods of complicity, jockeying for advantage, and feigned indifference. Cravan introduced her to his other women friends, who, he said, had let themselves be seduced too quickly: he claimed to appreciate those whose psychology did not follow the norm. She decided on a new tactic—she would pay no attention when he pitted others against her. Rather than be possessive, she would refuse to play the game, "the love-racket organized at woman's expense." One day he announced that he might be falling in love with her. "You have a very fascinating way of being yourself," he told her, "but what do you get out of it? To get the benefit of experience you must let yourself go," he went on, "you should allow yourself to be passionately in love with me."

She was already half in love, but did not want to let on. Emotionally she was ready. "Songs to Joannes" had just appeared as a special issue of *Others*. They were public property. And Kreymborg had asked her to edit an issue consisting of Futurist manifestos: seeing them into print would put the past behind her. Her divorce would be final in a few months. She had not seen Giles and Joella for a year, but given that the war continued with no end in sight, it was unthinkable to bring them to America. They were, it seemed, all right without her. (Whether from a lack of concern, a suppression of feeling, or ambivalence about her role as a mother, Mina's writing from this period barely mentions the children: one can only speculate that while she missed them, she chose to subordinate their needs to her own.)

It was not easy to admit that what she wanted was Cravan. Once she could see that she *was* in love with him, this "Gargantuan boor" became a "monster as lovely as Venus." The sight of him meditating in her bath moved her to tears. She thought of writing her own Song of Solomon now that she knew what it was to love body and soul. Like a dancer, Cravan *was* his body. He identified with his physical being, which had struck her as cold but now seemed eloquent. She admired his physicality, the bone structure emerging from the compact form, his arms' "subtle contour" and the "extreme delicacy" of his wrists, tapering off into "the almost independent intelligence of his Michelangelesque hands."

She had not, however, lost her sense of humor. In her tiny apartment "it was not so easy having the place cluttered up with this sculpture of perfection, chucking off its boots with the grace of Discobolus throwing his discus." And since she had no idea whether his emotions matched her own, she sometimes felt as if she were "at the mercy of a universe of moral order conceived by man, which, whenever you come near him, turns out to be amoral chaos." Trying to regain her balance, Mina willed herself to put *him* at a disadvantage. "It occurred to me that were I on every occasion to say exactly the opposite of what I thought, Colossus would be in as great a psychological fix as any woman," she reasoned. To test this theory, she told him that they were seeing too much of each other.

Mina sensed that she was following a familiar scenario—pretending not to want her deepest wish in case it would not be granted. One day as they sat together in Central Park, she responded angrily to Cravan's disquisition on women's ideas of love. She accused him of hypocrisy: *she* had never bothered him with sentimental nonsense, but *he* had never bothered himself about her. "Your sole concern is for the effect of your Greek torso," she told him, then did an imitation of "Colossus approach[ing] the couch of a woman." Cravan burst out laughing. When he caught his breath, he studied her as if he had never seen her before. "Je t'aime," he declared, "all the other women were like butter."

From this point on, their relations changed. Cravan had laughed his old self out of existence, she believed. And as he peeled off layers of distrust, she began feeling something "so astounding, so entirely new" that it took some time to understand. "Gradually it dawned upon me that for the first time in my life I had the sense of being protected," she wrote. Was she aware of seeking in her lover the sanctuary she lacked as a child? Her memoir hints at glimpses of self-knowledge beneath layers of ambiguity: "Colossus was like a fortress which—my mind so very made up of dream-stuff, having fluttered about its menacing exterior like a bat in the dusk—should open to receive me in a spacious refuge, a world lit up with a warm unwavering light." Their love was the refuge she had sought but found neither in family nor in art.

Their circle was astonished at the change in Cravan, who suddenly behaved like a devoted husband. "He became courteous and reserved," marveled Gabi Picabia; "he was so attached to her that he seemed almost bourgeois." "No longer did he nose into the contents of ladies' pocketbooks—nor lay his giant's feet in ladies' laps," Mina recalled. "No longer did he invade drawing rooms with a sodden insolent sulk. In public he was civilized—in private, sublime." They had reached the stage of mutual adoration and spent days telling each other the stories of their lives.

Cravan, whose real name was Fabian Avenarius Lloyd, was indeed the nephew of Oscar Wilde, who had married his aunt Constance (his father's sister) when Cravan's parents, although British, were living in Lausanne. He was nearly five years younger than Mina, and his education was even more irregular, although he had attended schools in Switzerland and England. Bored by the tranquil life of Lausanne's expatriate colony, he had sought adventure, like Rimbaud, who was one of his heroes. While in his teens, he had slept under London Bridge, consorted with Berlin lowlife, and gone to sea as an engine stoker, a job that he so disliked that he jumped ship in Australia to work as a lumberjack. His relation to British society was, to say the least, eccentric.

Moreover, Cravan was an outsider who was happiest when traveling. In 1903 he made his way across the United States to California, where he picked oranges; in 1907, while Mina was settling in Florence, he was in Munich; the following year, when he was in Florence, they could have crossed paths. Starting in 1909 he had lived in Montparnasse, a few blocks away from her student haunts: if Mina hadn't gone to Italy, they could have danced together at the Bal Bullier. Through his brother Otho, an artist, he had come to know the foreigners at the Dôme, but he preferred the more literary set at the Closerie des Lilas, Symbolists and Cubists like Gleizes and Duchamp. Although he had tried desperately to win their respect, it was only with the appearance of *Maintenant* that he became a personage in the Paris art world.

Boxing, which interfered with writing, had never been more than a pastime on the way to literary fame. Cravan had taken his *nom de plume* after becoming the light heavyweight champion, a title he had indeed acquired by default. Among boxers, he particularly admired Jack Johnson, whom he had met in Paris after the American champion fled there following his conviction under the Mann Act of having transported a female across state lines for immoral purposes—a charge that many believed was trumped up in order to persecute this black man for his defiance. In those days it was "the height of fashion to pretend to be a negro," according to Cravan, who said that he often felt ashamed of being white. His regard for Johnson took the form of imitation. After the American began performing in Paris music halls—his routine included exhibition boxing, singing, and dancing—Cravan adapted this form to his own talents. But given the recent scandal at the Independents, he preferred not to attract further attention.

By May, Cravan was not only worried about his military status but suspected that he was being watched. Since America's entrance into the war, it was thought that European deserters, draft dodgers, and conscientious objectors in the United States would soon be turned over to their respective governments. Because of his birth in Lausanne, Cravan hoped that under American law he would be considered Swiss—an interpretation of his status that would allow him to benefit from that country's neutrality. To make his case he was obliged to report to the Exemption Board, and his situation was further complicated by the fact that he had recently acquired an American passport, having left his official (British) documents in Lausanne.

It was unclear, moreover, whether the Justice Department already looked with disfavor on Cravan, as Bob Brown believed, or whether it was their friendship that brought him to their attention. Brown, who came to know Cravan at the Arensbergs', thought that he had been under surveillance since the day of his lecture. Once the Committee on Public Information began checking on contributors to *The Masses*, however, Brown and his circle came under increasing surveillance; although he had resigned from the magazine, as far as Creel was concerned, once a socialist, always a socialist. Now that registration was imminent, some of Cravan's leftist acquaintances were making plans to emigrate before they could be called up.

When Mina asked Cravan how he had avoided military service so far, he explained his "arrangement": he always managed to leave a country as soon as it declared war. There was no point in registering as a conscientious objector. "I don't *object*," he insisted, since opposition implied recognition of the system. "They may *all* allow themselves to be murdered for aught I care, only they need not expect me to follow suit." The war, he predicted, would have devastating consequences—the world would go bankrupt. The only political thinker of any note was Trotsky, who had befriended him in January on the ship to New York. However, in Cravan's view, although Trotsky had called for more sweeping changes than the post-tsarist Provisional Government was prepared to make, the Russian was naïve, Mina remembered him saying. "It was useless my telling him the result of his revolution will be the founding of a red army to protect the red liberty." For while Cravan detested all forms of government, he was neither an anarchist, a socialist, nor a follower of any party. He dismissed the idea of civilization, and at the word "progress," "he loudly guffawed."

She was pleased to learn that Cravan nonetheless believed in a higher power. At this point Mina, who "imagined God, for the creative, as the ultimate function of the mind," regretted the modernists' refusal to entertain things of the spirit. Unexpectedly, the inventor of "machinisme" felt that there was more to life than the material plane. What was more, he shared her belief that geniuses—like themselves—could intuit the divine. One day Cravan remarked casually, "It is useless to discuss the nature of God—we can only know that He exists because there are passages in the Bible so sublime they could not have originated in any human brain." Unexpectedly, his beliefs accorded with her own: "I had found the one man with whom my mind could go 'the whole way.' "

She could not, however, go the whole way with him in his rejection of society. In this respect, she was one of the moderns, who "being aesthetic-moralists . . . see society as a school for the blind run by pupil teachers." Although they were trying to subvert the rules by which society functioned, except for Cravan "it has never occurred to any of us to ignore it." He was set apart, she thought, by this refusal and his contempt for warring "isms," whether artistic or ideological. "I have not fallen for their modern art," he roared, "and I will not fall for their great war." He dismissed the cerebral high jinks of Duchamp and Picabia, moreover, and swore "to 'break the face' of the modern movement." Art was "situated more in the guts than in the brain," he insisted, but apart from Rousseau, no modern artist had exhibited natural genius.

At first, Cravan's opinions struck her as the ravings of an egomaniac. But as their affair progressed, Mina began taking him at his own estimation. By summer she was seeing the world through his eyes. Sixty years later, Juliette Gleizes was still astonished that "a woman as refined as Mina Loy could fall in love with a brute like Cravan." Their mutual self-absorption struck some members of the group as a *folie à deux*, particularly when they showed up at the Arensbergs' with their imaginary children—a paper lion and tiger purchased in Chinatown and baptized "Gaga" and "Moche" ("Crazy" and "Ugly").

Their idylls were interrupted by Cravan's need to recalculate the "arrangement" by which he had thus far avoided military service. On May 18 Congress passed the Selective Service Act, requiring that all men between the ages of twenty-one and thirty-one, native and foreign-born, register for the draft. The same day, Emma Goldman's No-Conscription League held its first mass meeting at the Harlem River Casino, where volunteer soldiers chanting "The Star-Spangled Banner" interrupted when she tried to talk. Overnight, it seemed, tolerance had vanished. *The New York Times* voiced the popular sentiment when it welcomed the Selective Service Act—"a long and sorely needed means of disciplining a certain foreign element in this nation." Cravan's case came under the jurisdiction of the Exemption Board, despite his refusal to recognize its validity. Most likely because the new legislation did not go into effect until June, he left New York precipitately to travel with Arthur Frost.

In the meantime, Duchamp, who later revealed that he himself had "left France basically for lack of . . . patriotism," saw that he "had fallen into American patriotism, which certainly was worse." Despite Duchamp's avoidance of all situations requiring one to take sides, the terms of the Selective Service Act made it clear that his French exemption did not protect him: as an unmarried man of thirty, he could be drafted in time of need. And when he learned that "there were various categories, A, B, C, D, E, F, and F was foreigners" like himself, it may have seemed that the alphabet was enacting its revenge.

The Arensberg group was preparing the last of their subversive amusements. *The Blind Man* was to host another ball on May 25, in the Village. Beatrice Wood's poster—a high-stepping stick figure thumbing its nose at the bourgeoisie—set the tone. "A new fashioned hop, skip, and jump," it announced, "to be held at the Pre-historic, ultra-Bohemian Webster Hall." Guests were to come in costume and stay all night: "The dance will not end till the dawn. The Blind Man must see the sun. Romantic rags are requested. There is a difference between a tuxedo and a Turk and guests not in costume must sit in bought-and-paid-for boxes." In a gesture of support for the revolutionaries, Beatrice dressed as a Russian, but Mina's costume, a cross between a Pierrot and a lampshade, avoided political statements.

The Arensberg group gathered on the balcony. Amused by the swirl of conversation, Mina took notes. Duchamp ordered rounds of a champagne cocktail called Perfection, behaved as if he hadn't a care, and sang to the guests. When he saw that Mina was noting his every word, he asked whether she had put in his pronunciation. The outside world intruded only when the conversation turned to the likelihood of censorship, which would mean the demise of *The Blind Man*. Duchamp expressed his opinion by dropping a miniature American flag—his party favor—into his champagne and making a gesture that was praised by all but remembered differently by the inebriated guests. Wood recalled his climbing a chandelier over the dance floor, while Roché thought he had mounted a flagpole. Mina remembered Duchamp "with his robe afloat, the symmetry of his bronze hair rising from his beautiful profile, wavering as a flame, he was —actually—climbing a paper festoon hung from the top of the dome to the musicians' gallery." Leaving the others to welcome the dawn, Mina's group repaired to the Arensbergs' at 3:00 a.m. for scrambled eggs.

After their meal, Mina led four of them to Duchamp's apartment to spend what remained of the night. While she shared the bottom of his pull-out bed with the actress Aileen Dresser, Demuth draped himself across the mattress and Wood squeezed into the few inches remaining between Duchamp and the wall. When Mina's notes on the night (minus their sleeping arrangements) appeared in the final issue of *The Blind Man*, they produced "a bewildering uproar as to the base immorality of the modernists," she recalled. A country at war could not tolerate such insouciance, yet some years later it struck her that this account had been an elegy "In Memoriam of that era."

By June, war fever had contaminated the artistic and intellectual milieux. "It is a great thing to be living when an age passes," Jane Heap, editor of *The Little Review*, noted sardonically. "There is a beautiful poetic vengeance in being permitted to watch that age destroy itself," she concluded. As the bureaucracy for conscription was put in place, anarchists, socialists, and Village radicals attended more anti-draft meetings: at one of these, the crowd of five thousand, including many immigrants, was "too full for speech," Heap observed, "because of this last numbing disappointment in America." When angry servicemen charged the stage, the police did little to protect the speakers, but showed more than usual zeal in dispersing the women, who were chanting, "Down with conscription!"

Despite their pacifist sympathies, many artists enlisted in the war effort once it became national policy. Gertrude Whitney set to work on a weeklong war benefit, to be held in Greenwich Village's raffish MacDougal Alley. The wealthy sculptor hired an army of Village artisans to plaster and paint the narrow street where her luxurious quarters co-existed with the studio-stables of local artists. By June, the alley was unrecognizable: stuccoed Neapolitan façades with authentic balconies, towers, and arcades had turned it into an Italian street scene. At the opening, an expressionless Isadora Duncan made an appearance in a green toga; Clara Tice, in Neapolitan garb, sketched the notables; and the members of society mixed with Villagers while their chauffeurs waited around the corner. "Everybody in the art world was present," gushed a reporter. "Oh beautiful people, oh beautiful fête!" noted Heap with more than usual acerbity. But when real Italians from the slums below Washington Square came to gape at the crowd, they were told to move on "because this was a fête for humanity," Heap ironized, before dismissing the fiesta as "a bastard performance, a bastard street, a bastard hilarity, bastard plutocrats and bastard artists."

In Reed's view, this event was "New York's last real laugh. Within a very few months now," he warned, "the casualty lists will be appearing . . . Our streets will slowly fill with pale figures in uniform, leaning on Red Cross nurses; with men who have arms off, hands off, faces shot away, men hobbling on crutches, pieces of men. Then New York will not laugh any more." A few days later, Congress enacted the 1917 Espionage Act, its own version of the writing on the wall. Henceforth, all expressions of dissent would be seen as interference with the war effort. The Act's provisions for fines, prosecution, and, in the case of aliens, deportation sent chills down the spines of radicals. As of June 15, any dissenter could be charged with treason.

In a strange coincidence, on the same day that Congress passed the Espionage Act, Mina was summoned to appear at the Manhattan County Court House. Charging that Stephen had displayed affection for Miss DeFries and other parties, she petitioned for custody of the children and funds for their support. The judge granted Mina custody and ordered Stephen to pay twenty dollars a week and legal costs. He also ruled that she was allowed to resume her maiden name "Mina Loy," presumably without realizing that this decision would, in effect, sanction her self-renaming. Mina had not only won her independence, she had won back the name she had chosen for herself fifteen years earlier. But after four years of waiting, planning, and scheming for this moment, the event may have seemed anticlimactic.

It was no longer possible to take refuge in private life. By mid-June, more than nine and a half million men had registered. When Cravan returned from his travels, he found a note ordering him to report to the draft board. Mina accompanied him, knowing that while he would comply outwardly with regulations, his "arrangement" meant that he would resume his travels as soon as possible. But according to the law, he was not to leave the country without the Exemption Board's permission. This time he was trapped. Yet whenever "the humility of his circumstances mocked his innate sense of grandeur," Mina mused, he was most likely to "commit some magnificent recklessness." And given his lack of funds, Cravan's defiance was all the more striking, especially as *she* had "none of his recklessness, having absorbed the middle-class financial anxiety-complex which forbids one even to begin to exist without the assurance of a certain capital."

Although her lampshade business provided a modest income, Mina's lack of capital weighed on her mind. When word of her father's death at sixty-nine reached her in New York, she was shocked. Despite his limitations, he was the only family member who had taken her side: she had been his favorite, and she was now following in his footsteps, after a fashion. But she had not seen him for the past five years. In her grief, she concocted fantasies about herself as the one family member who could have saved him. "Hush Money," an unpublished story drafted about this time, tells the story of David—herself as the son (and bearer of a royal Jewish name) that her father never had: when this prodigal son returns to England, the ailing father gives David his blessing. But imaginary reconciliations could not erase her ambivalence about the legacy she would receive. Judging by "Hush Money," Mina felt obscurely that, in accepting her inheritance, she was allowing herself to be bought off by those who had let her father die—she maintained that Julia had nagged him to death—while at the same time she was relieved that her financial situation would improve.

Cravan was in and out of Manhattan all summer. In July Gabi Picabia found him a job in a rural part of New Jersey, where he worked as a translator for a philosophy professor. This unusual employment not only agreed with him but helped shield the all too noticeable Englishman from the government agents who began haunting the Village in search of draft dodgers. "I'm in my element," he told Mina. "I spend my time running, eating, and swimming, which does a brute good."

But in the hot, muggy weather and intensified pro-war atmosphere of Manhattan, few shared his well-being. A number of former leftists were exhibiting patriotic sentiments: George Bellows was drawing propaganda posters, and Floyd Dell would soon enlist, despite Reed's efforts to keep *Masses* writers from joining Creel at the Committee on Public Information. Village bars had replaced German pilsner with English ale, young women with bobbed hair exchanged their bohemian dress for Red Cross uniforms, and movie ushers took collections for war work as if they were in church. Few could afford to laugh at the *New York Evening Telegraph*'s list of "daily health hints for aliens"; it advised, "Don't whistle any popular tunes written by Irving BERLIN. . . . Don't allow your lady friends to sprinkle themselves with COLOGNE."

By August, war hysteria had invaded daily life. In bars like Sailors' Snug Harbor, Bob Brown's local, the talk was almost entirely anti-German. When Brown joined those of his friends who had not yet capitulated to patriotism, they met in the back room. Under the impression that spies were everywhere, especially among former progressives, they whispered about escape routes to Mexico, where a number of dissenters had repaired. In the meantime, they agreed, it was better to avoid such places, where conscription agents regularly turned up to check the draft cards of known radicals. Cravan had nearly been nabbed on a recent visit to Manhattan,

Brown observed, when he was heard boasting about his peripatetic existence.

Cravan's preferred method of playing it safe meant prolonged absences from New York. When his stint with the philosophy professor came to an end, he continued his travels south along the coast. By the end of August, he was "almost always in a frenzy," he told Mina, but it was a productive frenzy, one that had moved him to write. "I've seen such things," he continued. He was full of new ideas, "analogies that have started communicating with each other." Soon, he promised her, he would compose his "thing," which would help her to understand him better, to see that there was something in his nature "that couldn't be found elsewhere."

When he returned to Manhattan, she took him to meet Frances, who was proving one of her most reliable friends. Like Mina, Frances was in love. She had recently met Prince Dimitri Golitzine, the commander of the White Russian fleet and the son of the last premier under Tsar Nicholas. Given Golitzine's mission—to fight the Bolsheviks in Siberia—and Cravan's admiration for Trotsky despite his "naïveté," one wonders how these unlikely companions negotiated the subjects of war and revolution.

Mina's own views were ambivalent. On the one hand, since her year in Munich with the Baroness, she felt little fondness for the Germans, but on the other, it was unthinkable to join the anti-German hysteria that had swept the country. Turning sauerkraut into Liberty cabbage and hamburgers into Liberty sandwiches was ludicrous. In any case, her people were the "geniuses," those who rejected the bourgeois thought patterns underlying the conflict. Like them, she believed that a shift in cultural forms could change how one saw the world, that the imagination held the power to transform reality.

Yet their territory—New York, the playground of modernism—had been overtaken by the force of events. The Arensberg circle was regrouping; individual members spent as much time as they could away from Manhattan. Gabi Picabia had returned to France to see her children, Lou Arensberg was taking up with Roché, and Louise Norton was distancing herself from New York and her husband in California. Ironically, just as the group was breaking up, its female members became the "Who's Who in Manhattan": for a double-page magazine spread on the leading artistic personalities, Clara Tice had drawn thirteen of her friends, including Frances, the two Louises, and Mina—wearing a top hat and acclaimed as a "painter-poet." She had made her name as a modern among moderns, yet recognition came just as the group began to founder.

That summer, the handful of radicals who continued anti-war work did so knowing they risked prosecution. Reed rehearsed the view shared by Mina and Cravan—that the war was an occasion for capitalists to reap profits. "We always used to say certain things would happen in this country if militarism came," he observed in *The Masses*. "Militarism has come," he went on. "They are happening." As proof, Reed described recent attacks on peace rallies and raids on the Socialist Party headquarters. But the Post Office declared this issue "unmailable" under the Espionage Act, thereby setting in motion a process of official suppression. By the end of the summer, the situation was even worse. Reed called August "the blackest month for free men our generation has known." "The country has acquiesced in a regime of judicial tyranny, bureaucratic suppression, and industrial barbarism," he went on, pointing to the recent conviction of Emma Goldman, the suppression of radical journals, vigilante attacks on strikers, race riots, and the jailing of the women's suffragists protesting abuses of civil rights. After appealing the Post Office ruling, the *Masses* editors won back their mailing privileges—until a higher court reinstated the original ruling, which, in effect, meant the end of this outspoken magazine.

In the Village, rumor had it that Creel's blacklist read like the Who's Who of radicalism. Along with the usual suspects—anarchists, socialists, and any remaining Wobblies who had not been caught in the Justice Department's recent sweep—other nonconformists were said to be well represented. Of the *Masses* staff, in addition to editors Reed and Max Eastman, the cartoonists Boardman Robinson and Henry Glintenkamp, and the poet Josephine Bell, who lamented the incarceration of Goldman and Berkman in free verse, were indicted as authors of "treasonable" material.* Government agents were also keeping Isadora Duncan under surveillance, because she knew Goldman and had danced the "Marseillaise" wrapped in a red flag. Paranoia thrived, often with good reason. Bob Brown thought that his companion, Rose Johnston, was being watched as a known feminist, socialist, and pacifist, but most of all because she lived with him. Brown, Glintenkamp, and others of their friends began planning their escape to Mexico, while Cravan, in New York to say goodbye to Mina, mapped out a northerly route to freedom.

On September 1, Cravan and Frost donned soldier's uniforms and headed for New England. Cravan's letters to Mina mark their route as they hitchhiked through Connecticut, Massachusetts, Maine, and Canada, and eventually, they hoped, to Nova Scotia and Newfoundland. Cravan wrote that he longed to take her on a trip. "I am only at my best when travelling," he declared. And although he hated having to stay too long in one place, he loved her, her studio, her bathroom, and everything that reminded him of their time together. He asked her to tell the Exemption Board that he had no address but could be reached through her. In mid-September, he wrote, their efforts to sail from Nova Scotia to Newfoundland were frustrated by the authorities, who refused to let them go without the correct papers. When the Canadians proved no more cooperative than the Amer-

---

* In one of Glintenkamp's cartoons, the Liberty Bell was disintegrating, and in the other, "Conscription," two naked men were chained to a cannon; Robinson's cartoon was entitled "Making the World Safe for Capitalism."

icans, Cravan thought of returning to New York. But in the end, he apparently dumped the ailing Frost and escaped by sea, ending up on a schooner bound for Mexico.

In addition to Cravan's affairs, Mina had to take care of unfinished business of her own. Although her father's will was probated in August, she did not receive her inheritance until later. Lowy's estate was considerable: its value was estimated at more than £40,000. By the terms of his will, Julia inherited his business along with £300, while each of their daughters received legacies of £200. The remainder of the estate would be managed by the Public Trustee of England, and from these investments each received a share, which meant that Mina would soon have a small annual income.* Furthermore, her divorce decree became final on October 28. Rid of Stephen at last, she could begin to plan the rest of her life.

The question was, what did she want? Despite Cravan's declarations of love, she doubted his ability to remain faithful. In December, when he made his way to Mexico City, joining Bob Brown and the other Village renegades, he deluged her with letters: He loved her as no man had ever loved a woman. He was lost without her. He wanted to marry her. No woman could compare, none had her subtlety, her delicacy, her intelligence. He would kill himself if she did not reply. She must come as soon as possible. Despite the rumors about bombs and bandits, the trains were safe. He begged for a lock of her hair, then added, "Better yet, come with all of your hair." On the last day of the year he implored her to join him: his soul was dying. Certain that she would not come, he bade her adieu. The letter concluded, "La vie est atroce."

"Looking for love with all its catastrophes is a less risky experience than finding it," Mina noted. Unable to resist, she bought a ticket to Mexico City and boarded the train for a five-day journey to another world.

---

* The will also expressed Lowy's wish to come to rest in a Jewish burial ground—even in death, he could not comply with Julia.

12

Mexico

(1917–18)

FEW AMERICANS, and fewer modernists, knew much about Mexico in 1917. D. H. Lawrence had not yet celebrated Mexican mornings, artists had not yet colonized the hilltowns, and the myth of Mexico as unspoiled alternative to civilization had not yet taken hold. Those who ventured south of the border before the revolution had gone to make their fortunes or escape trouble. In 1913, when Mabel followed Reed there, he recalled, she had hoped to find in Pancho Villa "a sort of male Gertrude Stein, or a least a Mexican Stieglitz"; to her, all insurgents were part of "the great world-movement." By the autumn of 1917, few could afford Mabel's naïveté. In New York it was said that while the great days of the revolution had passed, anti-Americanism was rife, and scattered outlaws still took pot shots at gringos.

Even among Village radicals, few understood the course of the revolution. Thanks to Reed's reporting, everyone knew of Pancho Villa, whose stronghold in the north included cavalry troops of cowboys, bandits, and cattle rustlers. They had also heard of Villa's counterpart in the south, Emiliano Zapata, whose peasants, armed with homemade explosives, sought to take back the land from the hacienda owners. Those who followed the news remembered the American invasion of Veracruz in 1914 and Pershing's failed attempt to chase Villa across the border two years later. What captured the popular imagination, however, was not the changing course of Wilson's Mexican policy but tales of trains blown up, peasant-soldiers followed by their *soldadera* sweethearts, and Americans held for ransom by "anarchists" in woven sandals and broad-brimmed sombreros.

By the time the Constitutionalist Party established a coalition excluding the insurgents, most Americans had lost interest in Mexico—except as a haven from military service. Since the spring of 1917, relations with the United States had improved following the election of Carranza, whose insistence on Mexican sovereignty commanded Wilson's grudging respect. At the same time, Carranza was known to be pro-German. Mexican officials frequented the German Club, German officers advised the Mexican Army, and it was largely because of Carranza's stubborn anti-Americanism that the Germans had tried earlier that year to enlist Mexico's allegiance by promising the return of the lost border states. Although Carranza had disavowed this scheme, radicals contemplating trips to Mexico were told that once across the border it was safer to pose as *alemán* than to identify as American.

Mina's knowledge of the situation was slight. She was setting off as much to get away from a life that no longer sustained her as to explore new territory. Her visions of spiritual fulfillment had evaporated in the repressive atmosphere that winter, when the celestial city turned cold and gray. Shortly after her thirty-fifth birthday, one of those markers when one decides that some risks are worth taking, she had made up her mind to go.

There was little to do until they reached the border. There, one changed to the Mexican National Railways, whose armored cars and military convoys may not have been reassuring. Provided the train made its way through the northern deserts without incident, it began its climb up the hills, mesas, and mountain valleys of the Great Plateau—the land of silver mines, opals, amethysts, and crystal—and finally across a high rugged region, through the Barrientos Tunnel and down across the Valley of Mexico to the capital, beyond which loomed the snowy peaks of Popocatepetl and Iztaccihuatl. Trying to describe Mexico to Mabel, Mina could say only that it was "volcanic & feathery & altogether magnificent."

But in January 1918, the capital was another story. Foreigners escaping from northern climes were often disappointed to find that one had to struggle to keep warm, since Mexico City was nearly one and a half miles above sea level. Cravan's letters had mentioned neither the icy winter winds blowing through the broad avenues nor the countless beggars huddled in doorways. Few foreigners had ever seen such misery. A short time after Mina's arrival, a journalist observed, "Mexico City is full of starving Indians, insufficiently clad and with no shelter . . . They mutely appeal with outstretched hands and wistful eyes to the passers-by, and there are legions of them." Foreigners were equally shocked to see children wandering the streets—there was no money for teachers—and usually did not realize that less than 5 percent of the country was literate. From the English-language paper, the visitor soon learned that public services of all kinds were neglected while taxes skyrocketed. The Carranza regime's corruption was so blatant that a new verb, *carrancear*, meaning "to steal," was common usage. Apart from the officials, Mexicans had yet to see the benefits of the new constitution.

Given this situation, a tiny group of radicals—in 1917, the local Socialist Party was called the *cinco gatos* (five cats)—had begun discussing the need for a more equitable distribution of the country's assets. From 1917 until 1920, Mexico's "red years," these revolutionaries, joined by a cosmopolitan cast of Bolshevik sympathizers, organized the Mexican Communist Party. By 1918, when Mina arrived, this left-wing international was known to the Allied secret services in Mexico. Its members included the American journalists Carleton Beals and Linn Gale, as well as an outspoken contingent composed of Indian anti-imperialist M. N. Roy, American feminist Evelyn Trent Roy, Japanese Communist Sen Katayama, and Soviet envoy Mikhail Borodin. These names made up the Who's Who—or blacklist—of revolutionary politics.

At the same time, a group of lesser American anarchists, conscientious objectors, and draft dodgers had assembled in the capital, where they were known in English and Spanish alike as "slackers." Cravan's letters to Mina had also failed to mention that, upon arrival, he looked up their Village friends at the place known to all as the Slackers' Hotel. Prominent among the inmates of this down-at-the-heels mansion were Bob Brown, Rose Johnston, and "Red" Winchester, the enterprising Wobbly who acted as hotelkeeper. (Winchester brought female camp followers to prepare meals and warm the residents' beds, even though venereal disease was rampant.) Other inmates included *Masses* regulars Henry Glintenkamp and Mike Gold, who "in those days was fluctuating between literature and Marxianism, Bohemia and the class-struggle." New Yorkers played chess in their rooms, but the few Texans who had jumped the border soon left with their Mexican sweethearts. Some learned to live by their wits, as peddlers of silk stockings or prints of the Virgin of Guadalupe, while the more fortunate taught English or worked for newspapers. All lived in fear of being sent home.

The Carranza government tolerated the remarkable number of intelligence agents in Mexico at this time in order to maneuver to its own advantage. The American Departments of State, Justice, and the Treasury, as well as the army and navy, had sent spies to its neutral neighbor, in part because the German espionage service was already devoting large sums of money to operatives like M. N. Roy, whose anti-British activities they funded. (Roy and his wife lived in a mansion, where impecunious leftists were sometimes invited for a good meal.) British undercover agents, who had the advantage of having cracked the German telegraph codes, sometimes appealed to writers for help. Nonconformists whose pacifism was more intuitive than principled found themselves in a murky situation, where people were not what they seemed.

In the effort to avoid discovery, some took new names. M. N. Roy, who began life in India as M. N. Bhattacharya, had entered the United States disguised as Father Charles Martin, fled to Mexico in 1917 after his cover was blown, and there communicated with the world as Manuel Mendez. Mike Gold used his legal name, Irwin Granich, and another Bolshevik sympathizer, Charles Philips, called himself Manuel Gómez when he was not Frank Seaman. In a place where everyone had an alias, Cravan may have hoped to fit in, particularly if he could pass as *alemán*. He had already obtained a Mexican passport, which identified him—incorrectly but usefully—as Swiss. But given the surveillance of mail to the States, it was unwise to explain the details of survival as a foreigner.

Mina knew nothing of what she was getting into when she stepped off the train in Mexico City. It was a new kind of exile, one where her sophistication, beauty, and sensitivity were of little use. Because she had to rely on Cravan, moreover, the Mexican sections of *Colossus* focus almost entirely on their relationship, suggesting that she sought refuge from the charged political situation in private life. During this time, their friend Bob Brown was also observing the couple and taking mental notes for his *roman à clef*, *You Gotta Live*, in which Cravan appears as Rex, and Mina as Rita. Together, these two reconstructions of life among the slackers comprise an episodic newsreel of their year in Mexico.

Mina knew that Cravan had found work teaching at a school of physical culture. As boxing was all the rage in Mexico City, the director of the school urged him to bring Jack Johnson there for a rematch of their Barcelona bout—a project about which they both felt optimistic. What was more, Cravan insisted that he had reformed. No longer the layabout Mina had known in New York, he lived cheaply in a room near the school and led a disciplined life, spending mornings in the public library, where he read the classics, and afternoons with his pupils.

As soon as Mina had rested from her journey, they resumed their habit of spending all day in each other's company. "Our life together," she wrote, "consisted entirely in wandering arm in arm through the streets. It never made any difference what we were doing—making love or respectfully eyeing canned foods in groceries, eating our tamales at street corners or walking among weeds. Somehow we had tapped the source of enchantment." Living in the moment, they could forget both past and future—as one does in a foreign land, or in the present tense of reciprocal love.

Soon after her arrival, they decided to marry. Legalizing their union proved more difficult than making this decision, however, since it required the permission of the authorities. Someone said to find a place called Val de Graz, which sounded like a Mexican version of the Latin Quarter church of the same name.* When the only Val de Graz proved to be a bankrupt emporium where dummies in wedding gowns languished in the windows, Mina grew worried: "The formal dream of my life, a marriage of love, turning out to be true, was about to fade away because the 'wedding shop' was shut." Once a policeman pointed to the building across the street from this travesty of a church, they began negotiating the bureaucratic maze awaiting candidates for matrimony. The doctor who was to check for venereal disease failed to question "the señorita," took Cravan's word that he was in good health, but became suspicious when he produced the Mexican passport, which gave his name as Lloyd. Wasn't he English, the official asked pointedly. After Cravan explained that there were Lloyds of all sorts, like those who owned the North German Lloyd shipping line, the doctor obligingly stamped the certificate.

Their honeymoon began the night before the wedding, when they moved into their nuptial quarters. The room, the ground floor of a tenement on the road to the Guadalupe cathedral, had primitive wooden furnishings and a disturbing odor, but it possessed a saving grace, a mass of arum lilies on the patio. When Mina discovered that Cravan's ill-fitting boots had lacerated his feet, she bathed and powdered them, imagining herself as "the Magdalene in ecstatics." Her emotions, strained to an unbearable pitch during their separation, finally found release, and their embrace blotted out the squalid surroundings: "All that was left of being alive was a ferocious longing to unlock the center of oneself with the center of someone else . . . We sought the ultimate refuge of sleep in the shadow of the body of love."

In her mind's eye Mina could visualize the wedding ceremony that would embody their passion. What took place the next day was disappointing, judging by the regretful tone of her prose and the recurrence of the image that expressed her dream of fulfillment. "We both wanted to 'really' marry," she wrote, "in a rosy Mexican cathedral," which would have bestowed its "benediction." In such a site—the cathedral of Guadalupe, for instance—"in receptive aisles splashed with the wine and gold of stained-glass windows," they would have felt blessed. But church weddings were expensive. They were married on January 25 at the mayor's office, with two passersby hauled in as witnesses. Mina's account of this day is structured like one of her poems—a moment of exaltation (the stained glass) followed by her ironic acceptance of reality (the passersby). Yet through this simple rite, she felt, they acquired a "foundation."

Mina took refuge in the moving combination of tenderness and strength that she brought out in Cravan. She felt so secure in their love that she no longer cared that he had slept with countless women, or that

* An allusion to the church of Val de Grâce, whose imposing baroque interior would have offered an appropriately grand site in which to celebrate their union, is implicit in Mina's use of "Val de Graz" as the title of this section of Colossus.

he had presented his French mistress, Renée, as his wife. She had discovered his secret. "Underneath a thin Parisian crust," she remembered telling him, he was "stolid British," even "respectable." Despite his "modern" claim that there was no difference between a mistress and a wife, he was happy to have "caught" her.

They were, it seemed, a perfect match. The parallels in their lives— their irregular educations, taste for travel, distaste for the conventions— became especially striking when one considered their chosen names. "Loy" had loosened the constraints of family and established a separate identity; "Cravan" simultaneously avoided and flaunted the legend of Oscar Wilde, yet as a man of physical courage, he was the opposite of "craven." Although their French friends always called him by his *nom de plume* (*et de boxe*), Mina preferred his Christian name. What was more, she could put on his surname like a garment that had been made to order: "Loy" fit into "Lloyd" as if predestined. (Paradoxically, this surname suggested both the outcast status of his family following the Wilde scandal and the solidity of British institutions like Lloyd's of London.) By taking his name, Mina achieved what in part of herself she had always desired, an unmistakably British identity to cover the traces of Lowy-become-Loy. Henceforth, when it suited her, she could be plain Mrs. Lloyd.

As for her new family, the Lloyds, their situation was complicated. Fabian's grandfather Horace Lloyd, a counselor to Queen Victoria and a London literary light, had had two children, Constance Mary, who married Oscar Wilde in 1884, and Otho Holland, who married Fabian's mother, Nellie Hutchinson, that same year in Lausanne. By 1887, when Fabian was born, each couple had produced two male offspring, and in a strange coincidence, both Oscar and Otho had distanced themselves from their spouses. On her brother's advice, Constance took her two boys to Switzerland during Oscar's trial and changed their name to Holland. In the settlement following Nellie's divorce from Otho, she received the greater part of his fortune before remarrying a Swiss doctor, Henri Grandjean. Fabian's stepfather, an upstanding man who adored Nellie, raised him and his brother as his own sons. Fabian grew up knowing little about his father except that he was a classicist and had another family. His relations with Nellie, who regarded him with extreme distrust, had improved before he left Europe, but he was loath to offend her, since she controlled what remained of his father's legacy.

Fabian was slow to tell the Grandjeans that he was married. On January 31 he wrote that he would stay in Mexico until the summer but failed to mention Mina. His mother and stepfather learned of his new status only in April, when he asked Nellie to keep his wedding a secret because of Renée. He had married an Englishwoman who was divorced, he explained, with two children under the care of a nurse in Florence. Proud that his bride was a poet, he announced her name as "Mrs. Haweis" and explained that she used the "pseudonym Mina Loy" in her writing. The parallelisms in their family histories—divorces, expatriations, and name changes—were striking. Upon receipt of the news, however, the Grandjeans became more than usually suspicious of Fabian's motives and, for this reason perhaps, did nothing to welcome Mina into the family.

In the meantime, Bob Brown and Rose Johnston put on a celebration for the newlyweds, who were trying to live as cheaply as possible on Mina's inheritance and Cravan's irregular earnings. Of necessity, Mina, who rarely cooked anything in her life, made tortillas over a charcoal stove and, like a Mexican housewife, scrubbed their clothes in the hard water from the well in the courtyard. Within weeks of her arrival, the experimental poet had become a camp follower, "a kettle-polisher in the Slacker Army," observed Brown. (Her enemies included the insect population and the earthen floor of their room.) After several months of housekeeping, when she began to look forward to their departure, Cravan learned that he could not leave Mexico after all, because his papers were not in order.

Within a short time, it became apparent that his health was not what the doctor had thought. When he began staying in bed all day, Mina sent to the Slackers' Hotel because Cravan did not want to risk seeing another official. The Browns concluded that he was suffering from a combination of amoebic dysentery, fever, and stomach trouble. He was so weak that Mina wrote to Nellie Grandjean on his behalf. After telling her about his illness, she pleaded for copies of his birth certificate and proof of Nellie's marriage to Otho so that the British Consulate could issue Fabian a passport. Although everyone gave him up for lost, she wrote, he might recover if he could travel to a better climate.

As they waited, Cravan lay on their low couch while Mina nursed him. His illness seemed to go on forever. Listening to the whining beggars in the courtyard, she sat by his side, jotted notes about their life together, and occasionally went out to find things to amuse him. He could stare for hours at the facets in a piece of quartz: like her, he loved the brilliance of refracted light. Other times she returned with exotically named fruits— calmitos, mameys, cherimoyas, and zapotes—which seemed to ripen one moment and rot the next. They made him smile even though he could not eat them. Of an unfamiliar fruit filled with a shiny paste, he exclaimed, "This one is like the excrement of a newly born child." Life was a game, and they were still playing.

Touring the city in the blissful days after Mina's arrival, they had ignored everything but each other. Now when she went out on her own, she did not avert her gaze from the misery surrounding them. In the courtyard, just beyond the arum lilies, "crouched old hags enveloped in dark stiff folds of stuff," immobile reminders of mortality. In the street she saw beggars whose tattered clothing no longer covered their bodies. "They have no comfort of their own beauty," she wrote. "The grandfathers nurse the weak babies, kiss their ophthalmic lids. Poverty has left these men only the recompenses of women." She could bear witness to their suffering by describing exactly what she saw: "One leans praying against a wall, a naked child sits straight up between his legs, his little arms crossed on his chest as children beg here, his sleeping eyes upturned to the morning sun." Thinking of her own children perhaps, and finding it impossible to accept such misery, she visualized this child in a state of grace—"the Nirvana of infancy, the state before understanding"—as if the imagination had the power to protect the innocent. Although she had "never found such subjects as some of the unexpected types of beggars," she later told Mabel, apart from these few notes she could not put them into poems, let alone draw their emaciated bodies.*

By summer, Cravan had recovered sufficiently to think about boxing. Jack Johnson had written to say that if Cravan sent him five thousand pesetas and three first-class tickets to Veracruz, he would come to Mexico; together, they could make a fortune in boxing exhibitions. But Johnson's terms were out of the question. What was more, as Cravan may have suspected, their correspondence was being monitored by American intelligence, which took an interest in his link to the former champion. At any point the Americans might decide that a friend of Johnson's—especially one who had dodged the draft in numerous countries—was no friend of theirs. Depending on Carranza's mood, they could arrange to have him expelled from Mexico. And when a letter finally arrived from his mother, the papers required for his British passport were not included. The situation was not encouraging.

They were trying to survive under extremely difficult circumstances. Mina's funds had nearly run out by midsummer. To cut corners, they began eating breakfast every other day, and Mina flavored the old coffee grounds with orange peels. Soon they had neither orange peels nor coffee grounds and, after a few days of not eating, very little strength. They lay in each other's arms for comfort. In an uncharacteristically pessimistic mood, Cravan proposed that they kill themselves, since starving to death would not be pleasant. Although Mina was so weak that she had begun to hallucinate about all the food she had ever left on her plate, she refused to consider suicide. She was too happy. "How can we die," she recalled protesting, "when we haven't finished talking." In a similar vein, her memoirs make light of their rescue. The Browns called and noticed her protruding shoulder blades. They returned with nourishing food, and other friends offered loans.

It is tempting to imagine the Lloyds among the international group enjoying the spread at M. N. Roy's mansion. Even if invited, they might have stayed away, given that their shared vision of a better world was

---

* Loy's almost photographic approach to the Indian beggars anticipates the work of Tina Modotti, of whom Carleton Beals wrote: "She has gone into the slums of Mexico and discovered there types so terrible in their misery as to attain an Michelangelesque exaggeration."

more utopian than Bolshevik. A rumor was going round, moreover, that due to the displeasure of the established American colony slackers would soon be deported. The middle-class Americans whose families had lived in Mexico for generations already crossed the street to avoid their more disreputable compatriates, but recently, it was thought, they had protested their presence to the authorities. The slacker culture had become too visible: the English section of one of the best papers, *El Heraldo de México*, had been taken over by the radicals—including Glintenkamp and Mike Gold —who filled it with articles from *Soviet Russia Today*. A census of draft dodgers was being taken. Since the Village contingent felt like sitting ducks at the Slackers' Hotel, they talked of decamping to Veracruz. Then, if things went well, they would make their way to Buenos Aires, the latest mecca for cosmopolitan draft dodgers.

By the end of July, Cravan was back in training. After the idea of a rematch with Johnson evaporated, he agreed to let "Red" Winchester, the manager of the Slackers' Hotel, arrange his matches. In August he went ten rounds with Honorato Castro, the Mexican champion—a respectable showing for a man who was still convalescing—and put on an even better show for the reporter from a local sports magazine who came to interview him. After boasting about his European boxing career, he explained his routine—morning workouts, walks in Chapultepec Park, bed by 8:30—and said that all bets on his next match would be handled by Winchester.

Cravan did not let on that he needed to earn enough money to leave Mexico. It was clear, just the same, that he and Mina could no longer scrape by from one day to the next. She was going to have their child, and in the spring, when the baby was born, they would need to settle somewhere. There was her income from England and the house in Florence, provided Stephen allowed her to occupy it. And there were Giles and Joella, whom she had not seen for more than two years. Despite their disdain for society, they could not live entirely on their own. They came up with a plan: since Mina's papers were in order, she would leave Mexico City along with the Browns and research escape routes. Cravan would earn what he could and join her by the end of September.

On September 6 a local sports weekly, *Arte y Deportes*, announced a championship match between Jim Smith, an American known as Black Diamond, and Arthur Cravan, said to have resisted Jack Johnson for seventeen rounds. The bout, scheduled for September 15, would be held in the bullring outside town. The victor would win a gold medal, and betting arrangements, it was understood, would be made in private.

The match began well, according to *Arte y Deportes*: the crowd erupted with cheers at the sight of the two "colossi." During the first round Cravan held Smith at arm's length, apparently hoping in this way to wear out his opponent. Cravan forgot his strategy in the second round, when Smith eluded his defense and hit him with a solid right to the jaw. Cravan, in reality fighting "in a waking nightmare," Brown observed, "was knocked out, a disorganized, pulsating jelly mass." The angry crowd demanded their money back, since the entire event had taken only five minutes. Moreover, the take was so low that Winchester turned down his percentage. Although the money enabled Cravan to survive until he could face a re-match, he had hurt both his hand and his reputation. The organizers thought it best to stage the rematch elsewhere, in Veracruz or Mérida, and Brown and Winchester tried to convince Smith to take a dive so that Cravan could emerge the victor—with the understanding that they would split the take fifty-fifty.

Colossus, a fragmentary memoir at best, does not describe these matches or allude to them as the price of survival. In New York, once Mina had put Cravan's performance at the Independents out of her mind, she could think of him as an avatar of Wilde with a Greek torso and the wit to recognize her intelligence. There, he had been a boxer only in theory. But in Mexico, where no one cared that he had written poetry or published a magazine, Cravan was in danger of becoming the pug that his handlers thought him. Perhaps it was too painful to record his failures. In her responsiveness to his vulnerability, Mina accepted Cravan the "brute," whose body she loved, but she saw something more in his poignant phys-icality. "Light—passed through the poet Cravan—became brilliance," she wrote. In him, flesh and spirit were one.

Nor does her writing record Mina's response to the dazzling colors of Mexico, the riot of saints, angels, Virgins, and Saviours who populate its art, or its rich intermarriages of subtlety and garishness, spiritual and elemental, Old World and New. Living on the road to Guadalupe, where the Virgin had appeared to an Indian centuries before, she undoubtedly watched the pilgrims on their way to the shrine during festivals, when the road was lined with vendors of fruit drinks, trinkets, and religious sou-venirs. And if she followed the crowds up the hill to this rosy cathedral, she was surely touched by the image of the Virgin as an Indian, by the stained-glass window of St. Teresa, but perhaps most of all by the patch-work of *retablos*—homemade scenes of miracles wrought by the Virgin—on the the walls.* While *Colossus* is imbued with this sensuous spirituality, especially in its evocations of their love, no poems survive from Mina's year in Mexico. She "had too many other things to think of," she told Mabel.

One of these was survival: how could they arrange to get Cravan out of the country? Anxious to leave Mexico City, the Browns went to scout out Veracruz, and Mina followed within a short time. Of the two train lines, the Mexican Railway and the Interoceanic, the former was preferable, even though it took longer, because of the frequency with which the rebels

---

* Beals describes the collage of images on the sacristy walls: "Here, an auto struck by a train; the occupants, who cried out to the Virgin Guadalupe, escape unhurt; the whole episode is depicted in brusque oil on a cigar-box cover. There, a man escaping a firing squad in front of the Palacio Nacional. Here, a woman surviving a Caesarian."

destroyed tracks, cars, and bridges on the other line. The train, sandwiched between armored cars full of soldiers at the head and rear, passed Guadalupe and ascended to the highest point in the country, then made its way slowly to the *tierra fría*, the cool mountain towns whose snowy peaks looked like New England. After Orizaba, a winter resort between the *tierra fría* and the *tierra caliente*—the moist jungle and hot plains below on the way to the Atlantic—they traveled through steep, dark inclines to village stations where barefoot Indian women jumped on board to sell wreaths of gardenias, whose overpowering sweetness was all but asphyxiating. As they continued the descent, vines reached into the cars, while outside, monkeys cavorted and parrots screeched. Once sand hills became visible, and the heat, already intense, grew stifling, it was a short ride to their destination.

If life in Mexico City had its squalid side, Veracruz had a seedy charm—provided one did not mind centipedes, lizards, bats, and spiders, or the scent of gardenias mixed with the smell of decaying tropical life. A number of slackers were already encamped in shabby hotel rooms where the wallpaper hung from the walls in melancholy strips. After a stifling summer, the rainy season had arrived, bringing in its wake the *nortes*, the Mexican version of a monsoon. Between storms there was plenty to see, from the Spanish-style plaza where social life was conducted as a series of dances to the crumbling ramparts of the Renaissance castle. But the slacker population was too busy surviving to go in for tourism. They did everything from driving taxis to selling condoms, a slacker monopoly in this Catholic land. Those who had hoped to go to Buenos Aires were out of luck: the Allies were stopping all boats in the Gulf to search for deserters. The Browns decided to continue on to Salina Cruz, a Pacific port where ships bound for Peru and Chile called, although, it was said, there was "nothing of interest to the stranger."

About this time Cravan turned his luck around with a victory in Oaxaca, and Mina, then entering the middle term of her pregnancy, traveled to Salina Cruz, having equipped herself for the journey with six hard-boiled eggs. The Trans-Isthmus Railway still zigzagged from the Veracruz coast to the Pacific, but standards had declined since the Revolution. Mina found the lack of salt for her eggs more bothersome than the wooden benches, third-class compartments, and the constant bucking of the carriage. At each stop, Tehuana women boarded the cars bearing mangoes, tortillas, coffee in coconut shells, and "objects of ingenuous grace"—canes carved with Zapotec patterns, "architectural bouquets from the white fields of tuberoses shrining their coloured centers of tin foil." The vegetation was "prodigious," the jungle "turbulent" and full of a "sibilant silence." Beside the tracks Mina saw a sign—a corpse dangling from a tree. By day, barefoot soldiers rode on the roof to protect the train, but at night, when it was too dark to spot the rebels, everyone got off to sleep in the wayside villages.

Mina was taken to a primitive "hotel" by the widowed Mexican seamstress with whom she shared the eggs once salt was obtained from the Tehuanas. On hearing that she had come all the way from Europe, New York, and Mexico City, the seamstress told the story of her life, placing the emphasis on her virtuous behavior since her husband's death. Watching the woman's "fly by night amour" with another traveler unfold in the promiscuous sleeping quarters of their hotel, where thin wooden partitions barely separated the guests, Mina thought that she behaved with discretion. But the next day on the train she found herself being ignored by the seamstress, who preferred the company of her protector to that of an inconvenient and possibly censorious witness. While Mina prided herself on her "modern" behavior—"with the snobbishness of those who under-standing all things forgive all things"—she had failed to see herself through the seamstress's eyes. She was, after all, a *gringa*.*

Mina rejoined Cravan and their friends in Salina Cruz, where he had made his way separately, along with Winchester, the young American pacifist Owen Cattell, and a Swedish friend. Former residents of the Slack-ers' Hotel had drifted to this torrid coastal town in hopes of making their way to Buenos Aires. "Someone said living was cheap there, meat only five cents a pound, drinks good, and a regular flourishing Parisian nightlife with cabarets, Pigalles, and girls," recalled Brown. And so many orders for war supplies were being filled in Argentina that it would be easy to find work. With what remained of his boxing proceeds, Cravan paid off his debts and took up a collection from his friends to purchase the boat in which they intended to sail to Chile. "They would all meet again at the foot of the towering Andes," Brown expected, "under better conditions."

There was little to do in Salina Cruz, which resembled a frontier town unexpectedly grown up by the Pacific. Situated in the half circle formed by the bare hills and the shoreline of the Bahía Ventosa (Windy Bay), it was swept by stiff offshore breezes. Small craft were often blown out to sea, and the tides were said to be treacherous. Newly arrived slackers had requisitioned the best hotel and chosen as their headquarters the rick-ety shack called Otto's Bar—which the owner, an enterprising German-American, stocked with beer from the foreign ships that came to port. Otto paid no attention to the bursts of fighting that broke out sporadically between the rebels in the hills and the government forces. Unlike Veracruz, Salina Cruz was neither picturesque nor hospitable. Its inhabitants, like Otto inured to the fighting, retreated behind steel shutters whenever they heard gunshots.

The Lloyds settled at the hotel before looking for a boat. Within a short

---

* In Mexico, Mina's worldliness—acquired with difficulty and as a form of self-protection—sometimes screened her from the reality of others' lives. Despite moments of fellow feeling, when she saw the poorest Mexicans, especially the Indians, as people like herself, she never entirely threw off the pseudo-scientific beliefs about "inferior" races on which the British sense of superiority rested. Similarly, her hostility toward the middle class (particularly the petit bourgeois) continued unabated.

time, Cravan became feverish again and had to stay in bed while Mina nursed him. Brown remembered watching him turn on her: she was too much the long-suffering heroine, he needed to be alone, "away from all these savages, draft dodgers, everybody." Cravan's mood improved as soon as his health began to mend, and he talked impatiently of leaving. Worried that the secret police knew of their plans to go to Argentina, the slackers decided to split up. To safeguard Mina's health and that of the baby, she would travel on a passenger ship; the Browns would make their way by land through Central America; and Cravan, Winchester, Cattell, and their Swedish friend—all lacking the necessary papers—would sail to Chile. In the meantime, Cravan kept Mina's fare in cash rather than use a money order, which could have tipped off the authorities. Insofar as his plans can be reconstructed from Mina's surviving letters and Brown's account, Cravan probably fixed up his small craft in Salina Cruz with the idea of selling or trading it for a larger vessel in Puerto Angel, a few days up the coast. On this larger boat he would return to Salina Cruz to pick up his friends, then all four would slip away.

When the rainy season came to an end, Cravan poked around the docks until he found the boat he wanted. "Because of a hole stove in its hull, he bought it cheap," Brown recalled. The Browns watched him go down to the pier each day to fit the boat for its voyage, while Mina, dressed in sailor's pants, cooked their meals and sewed the sail at her camp under a nearby tree. As they transformed the old craft into a primitive yacht, their work became play; too far away to hear each other, they banged on their implements with whatever came to hand, hammer or wooden spoon, and soon devised "a primitive system of signals to keep in close communion," Brown wrote. When Cravan ran one of these signaling devices up the mast, he was ready to set sail.

He was so excited that he decided to test the boat that same day. While Mina waved from the pier, a breeze caught the sail and Cravan set off. She watched the boat rush toward the open sea and the sail dip out of sight. As his friends waited nervously for him to return from Puerto Angel, she grew worried. After several days, when there was still no sign of him, Mina became so frightened that she could neither speak nor move. She waited for him on the beach, wrapped up in his coat. But Cravan did not return. She never saw him again.

The Browns coaxed Mina back to her room by telling her that such behavior was not good for the baby. She stayed there for days and talked of keeping things as they were until he reappeared, while the Browns looked after her. When she started knocking on the bed frame to send him a message, they began to doubt her sanity. The shock had been too great. With the money that had been set aside, they booked a berth on a Japanese ship bound for Chile, put her on board, and made plans to rendezvous in Valparaíso. They would cross the Andes together and make their way to

Buenos Aires as planned. There, Mina could find out what had happened and see to her future.

The coastline receded as she sailed west into the Gulf, as Cravan had done. She was traveling without a guide or companion. There was no foundation after all, no terra firma, only the tossing of the waves and the "heavy leaden color" of the "surly" sea.

13

Dislocations

AS THE SLACKERS plotted their escape routes, the cataclysm that had dislocated their lives was drawing to a close. On November 11 the Armistice was signed—soon after Cravan's disappearance, and following four years of hostilities with more than eight million dead. Mina did not hear the news until the end of her sea voyage; in the meantime, her emotional and spiritual displacement more than equaled her discomfort. She was carrying Cravan's child, but the future she had imagined with him had evaporated.

I

Sailing from Salina Cruz to Valparaíso one traveled south so long that days and weeks began to blur. One enchanting name followed the next— Nicaragua, Costa Rica, Panama, Ecuador. Once the ship left the open sea to follow the coast, the Andes offered a diversion to those with an eye for shape and color. Some days their jagged shapes were shrouded in mist; on others they rose so high that their peaks disappeared in the clouds. Attentive passengers could tell time by their colors—mauve and beige at midday, crimson and lavender in the evening, iridescent at dawn. There was no getting away from them. "To the astonished traveler," a contemporary noted, "the stately procession of mountains, its colors like streaming banners in the changing light, muffled and revealed by the passing clouds, seems to march day after day beside him, as if to prepare his mind and emotions for a proper and ceremonious entrance into this strangest of tropics." The Southern Hemisphere became real when hundreds of small islands gleaming with what looked like rock crystals (huge lumps of guano) came into view. Soon they caught sight of treeless ports, beyond which, people said, there were cities full of oleanders, olives, and Inca ruins.

Mina found more to interest her in the other passengers than in the scenery. The most picturesque part of the ship was the steerage. Hundreds of Japanese immigrants on their way to pick rice in Peru were crowded into a "horrible hole—with a yellow forest of wooden beams in it—supporting wooden berths," she recalled. Yet it was "a dainty fairyland—while they inhabited it": encamped on their mats with domestic utensils arranged about them, these meticulous travelers turned the steerage into home. Across the gap of their differences, Mina fancied that she understood them. Compared to the other passengers, the Japanese were "so civilised" that she could only "look on the word *savage* as a synonym for European imbecility—in applying it." But the European costumes they put on as they approached Callao, their destination, made them ill at ease. "There is a relationship between their souls & bodies & customs that transcends anything we can show," she mused, and this relationship had come unhinged. While she did not make the connection, Mina's diagnosis applied as well to herself.

At Callao, ships like theirs waited in the harbor for the small boats that took cargo, animate and inanimate, to the port. Travelers with energy to spare visited nearby Lima, but most, enervated by weeks on shipboard, wandered about the docks, gazing at the surprising mix of races at work there. When they set off again along the stark coastline, the procession of mountains resumed in alternating stripes of gray, white, and lavender. The only change in the scenery occurred when dark clouds of birds surrounded the ship in search of the anchovies swarming in the current, then lay upon the water. But Mina had neither the naturalist's eye nor the self-forgetfulness of the rapt traveler. This endless voyage—exceeding any she had taken—was an emblem, an allegory of her estrangement.

During the last week at sea, the Pacific seemed to extend itself indefinitely. More than five thousand miles from New York and just halfway down the coast of Chile, one saw only "sculptured mountains and this sea so deep that for miles and miles there is not a single breaker," a traveler observed, before adding, "But seeing is a matter of the mind as well as of the eye." They called at last at Arica and Iquique, both important in the Chilean nitrate trade. When Rose Brown met Mina's ship at Valparaíso a few days later, it was clear to her that Mina's suffering had deepened. She looked older and seemed utterly alone.

After a year in Mexico and a month at sea, it was surely a shock to find herself in an outpost of the British Empire. With its English-trained navy, English business firms, and residents named Smith and Jones, Valparaíso struck travelers as a Latin version of an imperial colony, a dream version of "home." Beginning with the Valparaísan method of disembarking, everything was strange. Because docks could not be built in the deep waters, passengers were lowered into the small craft that met liners, while their captains shouted in a tangle of languages their fees, advantages, and ties to local hotels. "It seemed perilous enough to go into those little dancing boats," recalled Duchamp's friend Katherine Dreier, who disembarked at Valparaíso that autumn. "To have one's precious belongings of trunks and hand bags lowered by ropes from the big ocean liner seemed almost overwhelming."

Once this transfer was accomplished, a single woman invariably noticed that she was in an awkward situation. "South America does not believe in women traveling alone, unless it is to join their husbands," observed Dreier, who, like Mina, planned to continue to Buenos Aires. As Mrs. Lloyd, a married Englishwoman expecting a child, Mina was afforded more respect than the long-suffering Dreier, yet her reunion with the Browns was not an unalloyed pleasure. While she could rely on Rose's practical nature, her friends could not help reminding her of Salina Cruz. Rose did what she could to shield Mina from the resident slackers, who were already speculating that Cravan had sailed to Tahiti—the first in a series of myths and legends that would grow up about him.

Valparaíso was only a stopping point. Mina and Rose began the long uphill train ride to Santiago, where the Browns had alighted until they could earn enough to settle in Buenos Aires. The trades open to slackers in Valparaíso came under the heading of war work: Bob Brown had decoded export-import cables, others sewed military uniforms or furnished the naval cadets with condoms. Bob was earning good wages in Santiago. Having capitulated to the Creel Bureau at last, he had signed on with its Chilean branch and was now "pimping for the Compub," as he noted with his usual irony. His job—providing German atrocity stories to the newspapers—was one he viewed with disgust, especially when it involved "photographs freshly faked every day in Washington." But given the choices, he explained, he "had hardened himself to the work of peddling lies."

Mina went on to Buenos Aires by train, a trip that had been possible since the recent completion of the tunnel linking Chile to Argentina. From Santiago one ascended to the town of Los Andes to spend the night before an early-morning departure on the narrow-gauge railway something like a streetcar. Seeing the sheer, almost perpendicular Andes up close reinforced their grandeur, recalled Dreier, who in painterly fashion noted their brilliant oranges, purples, and browns and observed of the isolated hamlets, "One was struck with the courage of the settlers, so far from what once had constituted their home." While the mountain goats put travelers in mind of Switzerland, these icy peaks were more remarkable than anything in Europe.

Although passengers were told that they would cover the 888 miles between Santiago and Buenos Aires in a day and a half, objective measurements like these could not begin to trace the spiritual meaning of such displacements. When Mina finally reached Buenos Aires, she was five months pregnant and could not accept the thought that Cravan would not return. On November 3 she informed Nellie Grandjean of her address there and included a letter for Fabian, in case he got in touch. On December 9 she wrote Nellie again to ask once more for Fabian's papers, because she was expecting their child. Soon after the new year, she sent Nellie another letter addressed to Fabian, naming him her children's guardian and giving her address in Florence. The Grandjeans ignored these requests, since in their view it was more than likely that the couple had never even married.

One can only guess at Mina's mental state once it became clear that Nellie was not going to respond. Perhaps an instinctive need to protect the baby took over. Perhaps as Mrs. Lloyd it was not hard to find help in the English community. Some years later, Mina told Joella that she had lived as the guest of the British consul in Buenos Aires. She may have found comfort in the existence there of a large English colony, with English papers, clubs, and other institutions. But judging by her letters to her mother-in-law, questions of home—the inner face of travel—were never far from her mind.

In addition to the sense that a new era had begun, for herself and for the world, she had to contend with culture shock. Americans and Europeans were often disoriented on arrival in a world turned upside down, where the new year began in midsummer, but during Mina's stay, the pervasive social unrest in Buenos Aires enhanced the impression of displacement. On January 9 a one-day general strike was called so that workers could attend the funeral of strikers who had been killed at a nearby iron-works. After shots fired on the crowd caused more deaths, the strike was extended. Overnight most of the city was placed under military guard; civilian militias formed as rumors of Bolshevist agents spurred attacks on the Jewish population, many of them Russian-born. While to Dreier it was "a marvelous experience to have lived through the Great Strike," for a woman in the final term of pregnancy, it must have been a nightmare.

The strike was followed by an event that looked like its dream image—Mardi Gras. Less than a month after barricading their property against the "Reds," the citizens of Buenos Aires flocked to the streets in brilliant costumes, tossed streamers with abandon, and flirted across the social lines that some had died to protect. Women did as they pleased behind the security of their masks, and the poor drove their wagons down the elegant streets. Because "Wilson the just" was then at the height of his reputation, a float bearing Uncle Sam met with wild applause. "The Spirit of Freedom takes a peep at the world of Buenos Aires and beckons Youth to follow," noted an optimistic Dreier.

While the spirit of freedom beckoned in Buenos Aires, the postwar peace conference was meeting in Versailles. The victorious nations had already adopted Wilson's "Fourteen Points" as a basis for negotiation: these included open diplomacy, "absolute freedom of navigation," the elimination of trade barriers, and an international commitment to arms reduction and national self-determination. The newspapers emphasized the President's call for a democratic world revolution along with his plan for a peace-keeping force, the League of Nations. It was a time when imaginative remappings of the world seemed possible.

Inspired no doubt by Wilson's idealism, as well as by her talks with Cravan about their future, Mina composed her own fourteen-point program, which she called "International Psycho-Democracy." She addressed herself not to questions of governance—politicians could take care of these things—but to the spirit of postwar life. Wilson proposed to make the world safe for democracy; Mina wanted "TO MAKE THE WORLD FIT FOR HUMANITY." A shift in human consciousness could now take place, she wrote, provided the world accepted certain principles, including the institution of "a Psycho-Democratic press" with the means to "propagate enthusiasm for constructive social ideas by constantly stimulating our imagination." The time was ripe to envision a "constructive pacifism"—a platform that transcended conscientious objection and guaranteed "the prestige of all logical idealists, including those who are too superior to fight!"

Mina was to redraft this tract, which had special significance for her, several times over the next few years. A blend of utopian vision and special pleading, "International Psycho-Democracy" adapted Wilson's rhetoric to Cravan's ethics while celebrating the idea of "intellectual heroism." The world exploited the artist, Cravan had insisted; now it was "time for the Artist to exploit the world." But if artists were to help in the reconstruction of society, it was also time to stop thumbing their noses at it.

Coincidentally, Buenos Aires had recently become an outpost of the Arensberg circle, whose épatiste spirit Mina now questioned: Duchamp, Dreier, and the Browns were all in residence there during the winter of 1919. The year before, as American military participation intensified, Duchamp had decided to absent himself from New York, and within a few months Dreier followed him to Argentina. Duchamp was indignant on her behalf. "The insolence and stupidity of the men here is insane," he wrote the Arensbergs. The capital was so provincial, its inhabitants so ignorant of modern art, and its atmosphere so unlike that of New York that there was little for him to do but play chess: "The outside world has no interest for me other than its transposition into winning or losing positions." Strangely, he and Mina did not meet. When the Browns told him of Cravan's disappearance, Duchamp relayed the news to the Arensbergs as a consequence of war, like his own transformation into a chess maniac.

While Duchamp immersed himself in gamesmanship, Mina made up her mind to go home. By March she was cabling her mother—her only recourse once it was clear that the Grandjeans would not help. England was all that she had rejected in fifteen years abroad—its class system, its suspicion of everything artistic or intellectual, its anti-Semitism, and its xenophobia. Yet her mother country offered refuge. And in another, less accessible part of herself, she must have longed for a reconciliation. There had been too many losses—her father, Cravan, their future. She could not go ahead without going back into the trouble that she and Julia shared.

On the voyage home Mina had ample time to ponder her repatriation. The ship called at Rio de Janeiro after making its way north through the Atlantic without incident, the fear of German submarines having been put to rest. Rio's spectacular bay "further reduced Europe to a greyish patch," Mina noted. If the voyage south had shaken her sense of direction, the voyage north was disorienting in a different way. They were traveling from the New World to the Old, an itinerary that seemed to unfold backwards.

I I

Arriving in England shortly before her April due date, Mina set foot in her own corner of the grayish patch at a volatile stage of postwar reconstruction. The government was finding it difficult to preside over the transition to peacetime, and many, poor and privileged alike, feared that the country faced, at best, a period of upheaval; at worst, a revolution.

Before concerning herself with the health of the nation, Mina took in the changes in her family. In the years before the war, as Sigmund Lowy's condition worsened, Julia had become the dominant partner. As her daughters reached adulthood, her circumstances improved. Although Mina's first union had been unconventional, she had married into a good family, and while Dora remained single, she never became as strong-headed as her older sister. Julia's dreams were fulfilled in her youngest. In due course, Hilda married and bore three children, all with conventional names: nothing in the next generation hinted at exotic origins. A few years before Sigmund's death, they had moved to the town of Simpsfield, in Surrey. While Julia was more secure as a wealthy widow than at any point in her life, Mina's impression of her domain—the house was called Burnside—can only be imagined. Perhaps the shift in the family dynamics allowed a truce between mother and daughter.

The baby, a girl, was born on April 5, 1919, and registered as Jemima Fabienne Cravan Lloyd, the daughter of Fabian Lloyd, poet. Julia could not have guessed that in calling her baby Jemima, Job's firstborn, Mina was passing on her secret identity as the first child of a persecuted father. But she surely found it odd that Mina not only refused to baptize the baby in England but insisted on holding the ceremony later that year in Geneva—at the home of her friend George Herron, now famous in Europe as Wilson's spokesman.

Life at Burnside was restful but restrictive. After the extremes Mina had endured, the settled routines of a London suburb must have seemed unreal. There, it was barely apparent that England was undergoing a transformation, while in London everyone talked about reconstruction—although there was little agreement on the meaning of the word. To some it meant the return of the class privileges that had prevailed before the

271

war, while to others it meant a more democratic society. A Reconstruction Ministry had already produced official reports; thinkers as varied as Bertrand Russell, H. G. Wells, and lesser-known social visionaries had published books and pamphlets with titles like *After the War, Peace and Victory*, and *New Science, New Freedom, New Outlook*. Mina's "International Psycho-Democracy" resembles these speculations in a general way, especially its call for "the reconstruction of our conception of social institutions."

By the spring of 1919, however, reconstruction had become an irony for much of the population. The Reconstruction Ministry was disbanded, its ideals reduced to slogans: ads for a patent medicine urged British subjects to "first Reconstruct Your Nervous System" before launching the new era. To demobilized soldiers, many of them disabled, reconstruction meant return to social neglect that no amount of tonic could cure. To the workers, who had enjoyed wartime wages, it was unthinkable to return to the past, and to the many women who had worked for the first time, it was equally unthinkable to renounce their independence; yet within a year's time, three-quarters of them had lost their jobs. And while females over thirty won the right to vote, *The Times* worried about the more than one million "surplus women"* (its formula for their preponderance), who now needed something other than marriage to occupy them.

If Mina considered settling in England, she no doubt realized that despite her New York reputation, at home she was just another "surplus woman." Boasting to Mabel that she had turned down "a splendid job in London," she made it clear that she had lost interest in England. She disliked the prevailing mood of disenchantment—people "bawling about reconstruction & everybody with their mouths gaping & looking vacant." Nor did she share the alarm of those who thought their lives threatened by Bolshevism, said to be spreading across Europe like an infectious plague.

Struggling with her own version of shell shock, Mina could not tolerate confusion in others. In the Bolshevist "bogey" she saw a failure of nerve, and in the country's isolationist turn a failure of vision. Those who bemoaned "little England" refused to see the big picture. Still clinging to the illusions that had sent young men to war as if to the playing fields, the English imagined the future in terms of the past. But once the Versailles Peace Treaty jettisoned most of Wilson's program in favor of a vindictive settlement, it was impossible not to think that millions had died in vain.

Mina had always fluctuated between skepticism and derision in response to the gap between official pieties and wartime realities. Her tone turned savage that spring as her New World optimism gave way to the bitterness of repressed grief. Her few poems from this period are corrosive. In "The Dead," the victims of war ("we") rage at the living ("you"):

---

* While a new law allowed women to become lawyers, architects, judges, or Members of Parliament, this patchy liberalization affected only those with the means to avail themselves of such opportunities.

We have flowed out of ourselves
Beginning on the outside
That shrivvable skin
Where you leave off

Of infinite elastic
Walking the ceiling
Our eyelashes polish stars

Curled close in the youngest corpuscle
Of a descendant
We spit up our passions in our grand-dams

Fixing the extension of your reactions
Our shadow lengthens

In your fear

In the past the dead had taken into themselves the "irate hungers" of the living; now, eluding their grasp, they "splinter into Wholes." "Our tissue is of that which escapes you," they taunt, "Birth-Breaths and orgasms / The shattering tremor of the static / The far-shore of an instant." In 1919 the poem all but shouted *J'accuse* at the war's survivors. Decades later, its caustic blend of grief and rage is still unsettling, particularly if one reads the poem as a draft of the epitaph that Mina could not write for Cravan.

That spring, even as she tried to face the idea of his death, she continued to hope he was alive. Gambling that Nellie Grandjean knew more than she was letting on, Mina cabled Lausanne to ask for his address. But her mother-in-law wired back that she had no news of her son's whereabouts. In June, when Fabienne was three months old, Mina had had enough of "home." As the signatory powers ratified the covenant of the League of Nations, Mina and Fabienne were on their way to Geneva, its future home.

III

England was Julia's country, Switzerland was Fabian's. Mina's first impression of the country she had once disdained was enthusiastic. "Switzerland—can one believe it—is the only decent country in Europe now," she told Mabel. The federation was orderly, prosperous, and, above all, unscathed by war. "One feels a great sense of relief," she went on. Although she had not seen Giles and Joella for three years, she delayed the trip to Italy until the end of summer, when Fabienne would be less likely to suffer from the heat.

In Geneva Mina renewed her friendship with George Herron, who

273

had moved there from Florence after his wife's death. His new marriage was a success, she told Mabel, and their old friend was revered for his integrity and vision. Throughout the war Herron had maintained a vast correspondence with editors, labor leaders, socialists, and pacifists, while also serving as a spokesman for the idea of a World Federation. His ability to interpret Wilson's policies to Europeans had earned him the respect of citizens and officials alike. Now, despite the harsh terms adopted at Versailles, Herron urged ratification of the Treaty. "I would not choose a raft as a permanent foundation, or as a safe and happy mode of traversing the seas," he explained. "But if the ship had gone down and there were naught else to cling to, I would stay with the raft." The Treaty was acceptable because of the raft—the League of Nations.

Herron's equanimity was inspiring. And his personal vision—Geneva as the world capital—cloaked his millenarianism in practical form. When Mina asked him to be Fabienne's godfather, he accepted and offered his home for the ceremony. Herron's guidance helped her to acknowledge the loss of Cravan by linking it to his survival in their child, just as the conclusion of the war shortly before the baptism marked the beginning of the future—in an uncanny correspondence between her inner and outer worlds. Under the rubric devoted to the city's foreign colony, *La Tribune de Genève* reported "the baptism of the daughter of Mr. and Mrs. Fabian Lloyd (the poets Arthur Cravan and Mina Loy)," adding, "Only the immediate family attended because of the recent death of Fabian Lloyd." The infant was baptized by a Protestant pastor and named, the paper noted, by "her illustrious god-father, professor George Davis Herron." Under the circumstances, Mina's choice of Herron as Fabienne's spiritual guide was especially meaningful—he stood in a paternal relation not only to the baby but also to Mina and those of her generation who remained internationalists.

Through him Mina met others who envisioned the future as she did. The Women's International League for Peace and Freedom had recently moved to Geneva. That summer Mina spent much of her time at the League's Maison Internationale, a graceful eighteenth-century building whose windows looked across the lake to the Alps. At tea in the Maison's walled garden, she met kindred spirits, idealists who, despite the Bolshevist "plague," foresaw a future based on cooperation. The Europeans had hoped "that the young & vital America—was going to brush away the cobwebs" from which the Old World could not extricate itself, she told Mabel. Although Wilson's failure had bred despair, she remained hopeful, having "experienced so much & such hitherto undiscovered kinds of people and circumstances that I can see nothing but the world as a whole."

In an optimistic mood, Mina redrafted her blueprint for world peace. The Geneva version began confidently: "The satisfaction of living is in projecting reflections of ourselves into the consciousness of our fellows." It followed that success could be measured by one's ability "to externalise our soul, that others may hear our word & see our light." Although this talent was the natural possession of the genius, under Psycho-Democracy everyone would learn "to realise his own particular form of crystallized personality." The Geneva draft implied that a select group of geniuses (like herself and Cravan) would by virtue of their example "consciously direct evolution," thereby eliminating "psychic death"—the nonrecognition of the other's humanity—which Mina believed to be at the base of all antagonisms.

Like the first draft, this version was untroubled by practical considerations. The method by which the genius would teach the masses to project their particular forms of crystallized personality was not specified, nor were the political underpinnings of Psycho-Democracy spelled out. With the skepticism of hindsight, one may wonder whether she had not stayed too long in the walled garden of her mind. Yet at the time, when visionary schemes abounded, Mina's might not have seemed farfetched. Her Geneva acquaintances approved of the plan, she told Mabel: "Professors seem to understand it more sympathetically than most people."

By the end of summer, Mina felt ready to approach Cravan's family. In a letter to Nellie Grandjean she announced the birth of Fabienne, their presence in Geneva, and her intention to stop in Lausanne on the way to Florence. After receiving this news, Cravan's mother decided that it would be easier to play dead in her summer home and left Dr. Grandjean to deal with their intrusive "daughter-in-law." Although he received her with skepticism, Mina made a good impression. She was elegantly dressed, had a distinguished manner, and offered to produce proof of her wedding. By the time she left for Italy, however, he had come to the conclusion that she was as untrustworthy as Fabian: there was nothing artless about her.

I V

Mina's enthusiasm evaporated following her return to Florence nearly three years after her departure in 1916. The city was still in the grip of summer. Entire families lay on the dusty paving stones at night to escape their airless dwellings; she could see into a neighboring couple's flat, where scenes of lovemaking alternated with violence. The Futurists were right. Florence was *passatista*. Geneva's serenity had directed her mind toward the future, but in Florence the narrow streets led back to the past.

If Florence was unchanged, her own travels had taken her so far that she seemed to look back on her life from a distance. Her reunion with the children did not avoid a certain awkwardness: Giles and Joella, thrilled to greet their mother, were nonetheless puzzled by her after three years. And while they were delighted with their baby sister, they were both confused by Mina's stories about Cravan. She had informed them of her marriage and sent pictures of her new husband, but letters arrived infrequently, and it was not clear what had become of him. It was even more disconcerting

275

to be asked to adjust to a person with strong views. With their parents gone away to places they could barely find in the atlas, they had grown accustomed to the gentle reign of the servants and the distant benevolence of the residents.

The children had, in their own way, grown up. At ten Giles was a sturdy boy who won medals at the Sporting Club, showed no inclination to follow his father's example at the tea table, and was not averse to coming home covered in mud. He was "rather an enigma," Mina thought, fancying that she saw in his behavior some of the manipulative "Haweis strategies." Joella, on the other hand, was a model *jeune fille*. Having attended a German kindergarten, a Christian Science school, and Miss Penrose's Academy, an institution frequented by the children of foreign residents, she hoped to study classics at the Italian *ginnasio*. For the past three years she had spoken mostly Italian, with Giles and their friends and with Giulia, who had brought up the children as her own—to the extent of taking them home to the country for the holidays. Giulia had, moreover, trained Joella in the feminine arts: at twelve she composed the family menus, selected her own wardrobe, and had chosen her new school. In manners and outlook she was a European child.

While Mina always maintained that children flourished in the company of servants, it shocked her to see Joella grown, as she put it, so old-fashioned. Failing to consider the effect of her words, she interfered with her daughter's accomplishments. Joella was to practice a more streamlined script—her decorative Italian hand was old-fashioned, Mina insisted—and forget her attraction to Catholicism, Giulia's religion. Her disposition was "heavy," she complained. She should be more like the American girls, more modern. Unaware how much her daughter yearned for her love, Mina urged her to be independent: she should invent stories to make herself interesting. She might, for instance, say that Papini was her father. It did not occur to her that, at twelve, one does not want to stand out, particularly in ways that are socially shocking. Too absorbed in her visionary schemes to empathize with her child, Mina noted with the detachment of a stranger, "Joella it is said is going to be a great beauty."

Her preference was clear. "Those Lloyds had great charm—which the baby has inherited," she told Mabel. Fabienne was "flawless & tremendously interested in the world." Although she "cl[u]ng to dear old Giulia like a limpet," Mina added, she was still "the most self contained infant I have ever seen." In the opinion of Leo Stein, who had just returned from New York, Fabienne was exceptional. "If she continues as she is doing now," he predicted, "she will do very well."

Like Mina, Stein was disillusioned with Florence. While he was interested in the causes of conflict—personal and global—after years of psychoanalysis he felt reluctant to involve himself with anything more demanding than his own psyche. One of the most significant changes he had undergone in New York was his realization, as a result of treatment, that he no longer felt angry at Gertrude, who had spent the war years in Paris and seen service as an ambulance driver. From his new perspective Leo looked back on the past as "a prolonged disease, a kind of mild insanity."

While few residents were as detached as Leo Stein, for some the conflict had been little more than an inconvenience. At first the owners of villas had discussed politics with lofty detachment, occasionally inviting convalescent British officers to tea. (Only the exuberant Braggiottis had gone so far as to welcome truckloads of American soldiers to their villa.) To those whose wealth guaranteed isolation, Florence had remained relatively untouched until the end of 1917, when thousands evacuated from the north were billeted there after the rout at Caporetto. Pillars of Anglo-Florence had mobilized to help the evacuees, of whom a resident observed naïvely, "Those who suffered most were perhaps the women who had owned palaces and country estates and who were now in mud-stained dresses."

Of Mina's friends, those who had suffered the most were the Braggiottis. Unable to regain her health after her ninth pregnancy ended in a miscarriage, Lily had died the previous April, just as Mina was settling in Surrey for the birth of Fabienne. True to Lily's philosophy, she had spent each day with a healer and refused medical care until the end. Her death came soon after Easter: at the funeral, Isidore Braggiotti had read her favorite passage from the Bhagavad Gita and told the children that her spirit had gone to another realm. Inconsolable without her, he planned to return to Boston. The villa Braggiotti was strangely gloomy when Mina went to say goodbye.

Most English residents had returned to the tranquil pattern of prewar life—meetings at Doney's, teas at one another's villas—but many now looked to Spiritualism for guidance. People exchanged the names of Tarot readers, psychics, and spiritual healers. Soon after her return Mina picked up the study that Mabel had sent her in 1913, Frederic Myers's *Human Personality and Its Survival of Bodily Death*. But after perusing this massive study, she told Mabel, she understood that "scientific dissertations fall flat—because they lack the element of taking risks—that art & life have." She had just put the finishing touches on her own philosophy of personal regeneration, called Auto-Facial-Construction—a method of physiognomic renewal which she planned to teach "when not drawing or writing about art."*

When it came to communication, she preferred direct contact with

---

* Mina proposed to teach "men or women who are intelligent . . . to become masters of their facial destiny." While other methods for dealing with the ravages of time "have compromised our inherent right not only to *be* ourselves but to *look like* ourselves," Auto-Facial-Construction showed the middle-aged how to express "the youth of our souls." Those for whom appearance counted most—"the society woman, the actor, the actress, the man of public career"—were urged to apply: "The initiation to this esoteric anatomical science is expensive but economical in result, for it places at the disposal of individuals a permanent principle for the independent conservation of beauty" (Auto-Facial-Construction).

psychics. "I have come across some extraordinary clairvoyants," she continued, whose methods were "entirely & *continuously* relied on, to be compared to calling upon information by telephone." (Whether they shed light on Cravan's disappearance was not disclosed.) And since she rarely spoke of him to English people (they disapproved of slackers), Mina thought she was being snubbed by the Anglo-Florentines, who also wondered whether she had really remarried. It was galling to find herself as sensitive to their opinions as when she had first arrived.

People had stories to tell about the end of the war. At the news of the Armistice, bells rang all over Florence and everyone embraced. Within a few days, however, unrest broke out along class lines. There was talk of a renegade Socialist named Mussolini, whose youth squads were staging violent run-ins with his former allies. The Socialist authorities seemed unable to deal with increasing inflation and unemployment. During the war they had governed some regions as Socialist fiefs, controlling labor and agriculture through their ability to call strikes, but in the aftermath of victory they had lost the ability to govern.

Moreover, the country had been unprepared for demobilization. The soldiers returned to find that not only was there no work but they were being blamed for the postwar morass. Italy had won the war, as D'Annunzio was fond of saying, but lost the peace. Soon bands of dissatisfied nationalists—called *arditi* (shock troops), *squadristi* (gangs), and *fascisti* (patriotic groups)—were holding battles with the Socialists, in which patriotic fervor and postwar disgruntlement combined in a particularly violent form. These warring factions could be told apart chiefly by their dress. The *arditi* wore black, the nationalists and liberals wore blue and gray, and the Socialists waved red flags to show their support for Bolshevism.

As these groups battled one another, the government's laissez-faire attitude had created the ideal climate for Mussolini. Earlier that year he had formed an alliance with Marinetti, whose *fasci futuristi* supported Mussolini in their shared opposition to labor and government. The war, they argued, had demonstrated the moral grandeur of Italian patriotism. And unlike the Socialists, they embraced returned soldiers—"the proletariat of the trenches." In Tuscany this social cleavage had become more alarming than the war itself. When the peasantry revolted the previous year against the system of land tenure, middle-class Florentines had formed an Alliance for Civil Defense; impatient with the Alliance's law-abiding ways, a gang of university students, Futurists, and ex-soldiers then founded the local *fascio*, one of the most violent in Italy. No doubt for this reason, Papini was living in the mountains. Said to be writing the life of Christ, he had regained his faith after removing himself from the fray.

The zeal with which the Florence *fascio* attacked strikers, internationalists, and anyone said to be lacking in patriotism inspired Mussolini to convene the national Fascist Congress there a month after Mina's return. City officials were noticeably anxious about the outcome of a conference featuring Mussolini and Marinetti: having written the program that would become the basis of the new party, Marinetti was at the height of his influence, yet differences were already apparent in the two men's approaches. When Mussolini hailed Fascism as the heir to the Roman Empire, the Renaissance, and the Risorgimento, Marinetti grew impatient. Emphasizing a more Futurist line, he urged the abolishment of the parliament and the Vatican and called for lessons in patriotism rather than Latin and Greek. In the postwar world, he argued, Italy would make its reputation "by the indisputable force of its creative geniuses."

Marinetti's speeches were widely publicized, and his presence in Florence impossible to ignore. If Mina saw him again, she did not mention it, yet his rhetoric echoed that winter as she again rewrote "Psycho-Democracy." Whatever turn he took, she remained grateful to him for forcing her to link art with life—to imagine that what she wrote might make a difference. And although she had become a convinced internationalist, while he remained a nationalist, both thought politics too important to be left to politicians. In spite of their differences, Marinetti's call—"Power to the artists!"—was resonant with Mina's own demand for "government by creative imagination."

That autumn, given the political vacuum, it seemed that poets might become the acknowledged legislators. Within weeks of Mina's return, D'Annunzio, a war hero with a following of legionnaires, invaded the Istrian city of Fiume, which many Italians saw as theirs despite the contrary dispositions at Versailles. D'Annunzio drafted a modern constitution, won the support of diverse political groups, and formed an "anti–League of Nations" composed of those who had done badly at Versailles. Inspired by his daring, Marinetti and Mussolini ran for office in Milan, where they were defeated and sent to jail for antisocial agitation. Undaunted, Marinetti proclaimed that artists rather than politicians would save Italy and foresaw its future glory under "the proletariat of the gifted."

v

In Mina's view, the adventures of both D'Annunzio and Marinetti amounted to little more than swashbuckling. Yet she, too, wanted to believe that the gifted could influence the future. Apart from a few poems and the drafts of "Psycho-Democracy," however, she had written little since her departure from New York. The Andes, the newest New World in Argentina, her disappointing return to postwar Europe—none of this lent itself to poetic form. She had, as she told Mabel, had too many other things to think about—including love, death, birth, and survival. In Florence, where the servants saw to everything, she polished the one piece of writing in which she could express, however obliquely, the vision of postwar life she had imagined with Cravan.

When poets set themselves up as rulers, it became possible to think that "government by creative intuition" could be realized. By the end of 1919 the program that began in Buenos Aires as a fourteen-point outline had grown into an eight-page pamphlet entitled *Psycho-Democracy, a movement to focus human reason on The Conscious Direction of Evolution.* Modern life, it argued, was based on the beliefs of a powerful minority: the one real difference was "between the dominator and the dominated," who, despite sporadic rebellions, were easily assimilated into the dominant group.

The political impasse, Mina went on, could be explained by "the tendency of human institutions to outlast the psychological conditions from which they arose." From a more advanced perspective (hers and Cravan's) it seemed obvious that "social institutions of today will cause future generations to roar with laughter." The masses still worshipped flags, uniforms, marches, and parades (as they were doing in Fiume), yet the *"belligerent masculine* social ideal" was absurd, and the problem with pacifism was that it offered no alternative to this militarist "rhythm." To fill the void, Mina invited potential psycho-democrats—"the thinker, the scientist, the philosopher, the writer, the artist, the mechanic, the worker" —to join in promoting *"a new social symbolism, a new social rhythm, a new social snobbism."* Together they would replace outworn institutions by substituting "consciously directed evolution for revolution, *Creative Inspiration for Force,* Laughter for Lethargy, Sociability for Sociology, Human psychology for Tradition."

Mina had *Psycho-Democracy* privately printed in Florence before sending it off as a New Year's greeting to Herron, Van Vechten, Mabel, and others who might appreciate its blend of the spiritual and political. (The Grandjeans also received a copy.) Her itinerary since 1918 was noted in its sites of composition—"Mexico. Buenos Aires. Surrey. Geneva. Florence." Few readers knew its relevance or understood the private significance of Mexico as starting point. Yet Cravan's words echo in the tract's mixed appeal to autocratic and democratic sentiments, and the past two years' pattern of bliss, alienation, and loss is discernible in its pronouncements. Indeed, the psycho-democrats resemble the ideal selves that she and Cravan had seen in each other.

At this point Mina identified the outer world with her inner states, and recent history with her own. As things stood, she concluded, Europe was little more than a set of "inhibitive social and religious precepts that ordain that man must suffer." When she turned to her surroundings, the suffering became apparent: she had only to look out her window. Reverting to the precise social observation she had practiced in Mexico, she also composed a verbal street scene, entitled "Summer Night in a Florentine Slum." This pendant to *Psycho-Democracy* compares her neighbors' values to the aestheticism that had once nourished her sense of superiority: the view from her window revealed working-class Florentines sprawled on the Costa "in what they could manage of earthy abandon" while the local freaks—the dwarf news vendor, the witch, and the legless woman—dealt as they could with their lives.

Unexpectedly, "Summer Night in a Florentine Slum" ends with Mina's reflections on the self-absorption in which she and Stephen had once been enveloped. Turning from her "inopulent neighborhood," the narrator draws "English chintz curtains scattered with prevaricating rosebuds." Inside, her gaze is returned by a picture on the wall, Beardsley's well-known portrait of Mademoiselle de Maupin as a cross between the dandy and the femme fatale. From Mina's more "modern" perspective, the mocking image that Stephen had revered as the epitome of Decadence was another untruth, like the prevaricating rosebuds.

"O Hell," a poem also composed at this time and published as a coda to "Summer Night in a Florentine Slum" expresses even more poignantly Mina's longing for personal and social regeneration:

> To clear the drifts of spring
> Of our forebear's excrements
> And bury the subconscious archives
> Under unaffected flowers

Europe was, she told Mabel, "an hereditary disease." To cure herself, she went on, she would return to New York, "the only spot I have ever had to say a thank you to" because of the happiness she had known there. Giulia opposed Mina's departure, thinking more seriously than her employer perhaps of the three children's welfare. But after watching Mina smash all the dishes, Giulia reluctantly agreed to let her sail in March.

14

Postwar Despairing

(NEW YORK, 1920–21)

MANHATTAN WAS FAR LIVELIER than Florence, but the mood had changed. Americans were wary of foreigners, anti-Bolshevist hysteria had replaced anti-German sentiment, and the term "radical," which three years earlier evoked a harmless crackpot, now conjured up a bomb-throwing terrorist. Similarly, since the country's turn inward, "international" was taken to mean "anti-American." Congress had rejected both the Versailles Treaty and the League of Nations, and Wilson had suffered a stroke that left him unable to govern, let alone curtail his Attorney General's attacks on "undesirables." By 1920, thousands had been arrested, and many deported on the *Buford*, or the "Soviet Ark"—the most notorious of whom was Emma Goldman. Finding that he had popular support, Attorney General Mitchell Palmer stepped up his raids to forestall a predicted May Day coup. That spring, a friend of Mina's recalled, progressives were in the throes of "postwar despairing."

I

On Mina's return, she found that little was as she had imagined it. Still other changes had dampened her circle's spirits. Prohibition had been in force since January: while alcohol could still be had, its quality had declined. A depressed Henry McBride was uncertain whether, in this mood, the twenties would proceed "with enough approximation to the old life to permit the arts to exist." And the change in the atmosphere had taken the sparkle out of the Arensbergs' evenings. Even before Prohibition, the nightly festivities had frayed their marriage, which all but unraveled during

Louise's affair with Roché. The couple had patched things together since then, but Louise was concerned about Walter. Despite Prohibition, he was not only drinking too much but was mismanaging both her fortune and his own.

When Mina reappeared at West Sixty-seventh Street, Louise was already planning to leave New York. She and Walter were in low spirits following the death of Ernest Southard, whose role as the group's resident Freudian had provided many hours of entertainment. "We could have spared anyone of our circle of friends better than Ernest," Louise told Roché, taking care to inform him that she would be gone when he came to town. The Arensbergs' decision to travel in the West would mean the dispersion of the group. McBride was convalescing in the country after a nervous collapse, Beatrice Wood had dropped out of sight, Louise Norton Varèse no longer frequented their circle, the Gleizes and Picabias had gone back to Paris. Telling Roché of Mina's return, Louise added, "Everything is very quiet since prohibition came in—and we seem to be growing old and sober."

Of the French contingent, only Duchamp remained. He had reappeared in January with a gift for his patron, a sealed glass vial filled with air from Paris, which Arensberg unveiled whenever the yen to *épater* bourgeois callers overcame him. But as McBride observed of these occasions, "The only drawback to *épaté*-ing the bourgeois is that half the time they don't know when they are *épaté*-ed." Along with his Paris air, Duchamp brought tales of Dada, the new anti-art movement which made it impossible for anyone, even the bourgeois, to miss its intent. Founded during the war in Zurich, this nihilistic assault on meaning itself had spread to Germany and, in the past year, to Paris. Picabia had been particularly receptive. He and his new friends André Breton and Louis Aragon welcomed the "Grand Dada," Romanian poet Tristan Tzara, to their circle of artists and writers. But while the Parisian Dadaists considered Duchamp a kindred spirit, he had distanced himself from the movement by returning to New York.

Arensberg, on the other hand, was eager to sign on. That winter Tzara was publicizing Dada's international cast with official lists of adherents, the movement's "Présidents" and "Présidentes." Among the English-speaking Dadaists he included Charlie Chaplin, Mabel Dodge, Alfred Stieglitz, Arthur Cravan, and Mina Lloyd [sic]. Hoping for a fresh source of scandal at a dull time, Arensberg pressed Tzara to bring the Dadaists to New York. "I can't tell you how happy America would be to have you transplant the center of the world," he wrote, but he could not predict "the form of hospitality which the guardians of free speech would extend to you." Later that spring, Arensberg made it clear that an irruption of Dadaists would be a diversion. "Your adventures with the New York police," he told Picabia, "would make the history of Cravan at the Independents a very pale affair."

Mina did not comment on Walter's enthusiasm, nor did she remark on Cravan's posthumous enrollment among the Dadaists. Finding his name and her own in their latest manifesto could not have given her much pleasure when the enigma of his disappearance still haunted her. And reading Cravan's words—or those attributed to him posthumously—in the movement's magazine could only have caused pain. Without consulting her, the Parisians had put obscenities in his mouth. Cravan had predicted that he would become a legend, but he would not have wanted it to occur under the imprint of Picabia's latest fad.

Duchamp, as intent as Cravan on going his own way, was dividing his time between chess and his work on his Bride machine, now renamed *The Large Glass*. He saw few people apart from Man Ray and Katherine Dreier. This incongruous trio was organizing another society for the promotion of modern art. Although the project was less outrageous than the 1917 Independents—it was to be the precursor of New York's Museum of Modern Art—he could not resist the urge to stamp it with his own version of Dada humor. After several attempts at naming the new group, Duchamp talked Dreier into calling it Société Anonyme, which Man Ray had proposed because he took the phrase to mean "anonymous society"—until Duchamp explained that it was the French equivalent of "incorporated."

On April 30 the remnants of the Arensberg circle turned out for the opening of the Société Anonyme, Inc.—"Inc., Inc." to the cognoscenti. The exhibition included works by Man Ray, Picabia, Morton Schamberg, and Joseph Stella, which were all but overshadowed by Duchamp's décor: he had covered the floor with gray ribbed rubber. This odd surface had been chosen, McBride suggested, "with the idea of insuring a firmer foothold for tottering Academicians." In this setting, he continued with a touch of his prewar zest, they were sure to encounter "performances of some of the most wilful, eccentric, daring, amusing, irreverent and powerful artists."

No doubt because the Arensbergs were leaving, Mina established herself downtown, in the Village, where willful, eccentric, and daring performances were never lacking. A number of prewar institutions—the Provincetown Playhouse, Polly's Restaurant, the Brevoort Hotel—were unchanged. In compliance with Prohibition, however, the saloons were boarded over. The teashops that had replaced them were advertised in the Village handbooks that had proliferated since the war—like high rents and the influx of tourists, signs of the area's commercialization.

Settled in rooms on Bedford Street, Mina took stock of her situation. Cravan's disappearance was no longer her private mystery. And while it was more than likely that he had drowned, she was not yet ready to accept this as fact. She made inquiries with the State Department and the British Secret Service, which, she suspected, had taken an interest in him. But from what she could glean from their reports, traces of his movements were fragmentary at best. His passport had been recorded in Salina Cruz; he was known to have traveled with the young American pacifist Owen

Cattell; there were scattered reports of his drowning. But there was no certainty, no closure.

About this time, some have speculated, Mina went back to Mexico. It is true that she often told her friends of her belief that Cravan was alive: if, as she suspected, he was languishing in a Mexican jail, he might be found and released. William Carlos Williams listened sympathetically to Mina and tried years later to reconstruct what he could of her account of their life together. Cravan had "bought and rebuilt a seagoing craft," he wrote, "got into it to try it out in the bay," while Mina "watched the small ship move steadily away into the distance. For years she thought to see him again," he concluded. It seemed possible "that he might be on some island, or in the prisons of one of the numerous countries at war," recalled Gabi Picabia, to whom Mina also told her story; she "looked for him after the Armistice in every possible place of this kind," yet despite these efforts, it became "evident that the mystery surrounding the end of this amazing figure w[ould] never be cleared up."*

Whether or not Mina returned to Mexico, or whether she went there in her imagination, no trace of this journey remains—except for "Mexican Desert," a poem whose cadences are saturated with loss:

> The belching ghost-wail of the locomotive
> trailing her rattling wooden tail
> into the jazz-band sunset . . .
> The mountains in a row
> set pinnacles of ferocious isolation
> under the alien hot heaven
>
> Vegetable cripples of drought
> thrust up the parching appeal
> cracking open the earth
> stump-fingered cacti
> and hunch-back palm trees
> belabour the cinders of twilight . . .

This shorthand travel diary lacks human actors, but in a striking reversal of the modernist aesthetic that saw humans as machines, a female locomotive grieves like an unquiet ghost. The sunset's failure to illuminate and the mountains' isolation both refer back to the speaker, who, like the landscape, appeals in vain. The elliptical conclusion—of journey and poem—implies that there was no end to her emotional "belabouring."

---

* On June 18, 1920, Van Vechten wrote to Mabel Dodge as follows: "Ducie [sic] is seeking her husband in all the jails—as a possible haul-in by the U.S. government as a spy or an embusqué [draft-dodger] or something. He went across a lake in a boat & was supposed to have been drowned but perhaps not, thinks Ducie. Others—some others—prefer to believe that marriage appalled him & that he has disappeared."

As Mina struggled with the conflict between the wish to find Cravan alive and the need to mourn his death, the Dadaists began turning him into the legend that would, in time, overlap with her memories. Increasingly, successive avant-gardists claimed him as one of their own. The young Parisian Philippe Soupault had already composed a mock epitaph, which appeared that June in Breton's magazine *Littérature*. "The pushcart vendors have emigrated to Mexico," Soupault began with an nod to *Maintenant*'s method of distribution. "Good old boxer," he continued, "you died down there / You don't even know why / You yelled louder than all of us in the palaces of America / and all the cafés of Paris." From Mina's perspective, this epitaph came too soon, and what was worse, Soupault, who knew her husband only by reputation, saw him as a loudmouth boxer. Someone who had known him as she had might write a fitting epitaph, but it would take decades until she could complete the psychic travail required for such a poem.

II

While Bill Williams listened patiently to her stories, his sympathy had limitations. Writing from Washington, where she was consulting the intelligence services, Mina asked him to call again and promised not to talk politics. The issue of the day—whether enough states would ratify the Nineteenth Amendment, women's suffrage—may have been the one that she promised not to mention, since Williams's support was lukewarm. Women should have the vote if they wished, he conceded, but he did not understand why they cared. Politics was not easily ignored in the Village, however. Although the May Day coup had not materialized, vigilantes were raiding the homes of suspected radicals, and when the anarchists Sacco and Vanzetti were charged with the murder of a Massachusetts paymaster, many artists and intellectuals rose to their defense. Mina still hoped that *Psycho-Democracy* would rally the like-minded. Disappointed to learn that Mabel had not understood it, she did not let on that the tract was a disguised memorial to her life with Cravan.

While it was difficult to avoid such topics when Williams came to call, they could always discuss another kind of politics, the shifting trends of the literary world. Writers tended to identify with the magazine that published their work. *Others*, Mina learned, was no more. Williams and Kreymborg had been estranged since *Lima Beans*, when Kreymborg began neglecting the magazine to devote himself to his plays. Despite its rousing debut, *Others* had failed after several years of sporadic publication, and Williams was disturbed by the current emphasis in experimental circles on formal beauty at the expense of content. To be modern, he insisted, poets had to tackle contemporaneity, however dispiriting. But after the demise of *Others*, no one had stepped forward to take its place. Irving Granich, calling himself Mike Gold since his return from Mexico, was carrying on

Reed's work at *The Liberator*, which had replaced *The Masses*. But his politics were too identifiably Bolshevik to make common cause with aesthetic radicals, and since the war, these groups had parted company.

For a time Williams looked to the latest incarnation of *The Dial*: this literary institution had taken a modern turn under the new owners, James Watson and Scofield Thayer. It had seemed as if the magazine would publish the sort of poetry that Williams favored; what was more, contributors were paid. But by 1920 the *Others* group was not speaking to Watson and Thayer because of their shabby treatment of the poet Emanuel Carnevali, whose article on Papini they had commissioned, then refused. (Since Papini's conversion to Catholicism, his work had appeared, often in Carnevali's translation, in *Vanity Fair* and *Others*, which published "Leavetaking," his veiled farewell to Mina.) Rather than submit to *The Dial*, one *Other*ite declared, he and his friends would "remain perpetually aloof from the whole papier-mâché turmoil."

The only magazine to enter the fray was *The Little Review*. The editors, Jane Heap and Margaret Anderson, had settled in the Village in 1917. Their refusal to follow anyone's taste but their own had resulted in the magazine's suppression on charges of pornography, although many thought its real offenses were its anti-war stance and defense of Emma Goldman: the item in question, a story by Wyndham Lewis, had been more striking for its pacifism than for pornographic content. Until recently Ezra Pound had played a major role as the magazine's London editor and discoverer of geniuses, such as the Irish writer James Joyce. Since 1918, Heap and Anderson had been running sections of *Ulysses*—despite interference by the postal authorities—and they had just published Williams's prose "Improvisations." Given their emphasis on the new women writers—Djuna Barnes, Mary Butts, and Dorothy Richardson—they would, most likely, be receptive to Mina.

Through Williams's association with the magazine, he had, however, collided with more experimental energy than he could handle—in the person of Elsa von Freytag-Loringhoven—in Anderson's view "the only figure of our generation who deserves the epithet extraordinary." Despite readers' expressions of outrage, *The Little Review* was also running her nearly incomprehensible poetry, including a free-verse homage to Duchamp. When Williams visited the magazine's office the previous year, he had noticed another of the Baroness's tributes to Duchamp, an assemblage which to his eye resembled "chicken guts." Inquiring about the creator of this work, he learned that she was temporarily incarcerated at the Women's House of Detention. Soon after bailing her out, Williams realized that he had taken Duchamp's place in her affections. When she tracked him to New Jersey, shrieking "Villiam Carlos Villiams, *I vant you*," their farcical courtship concluded with her return to jail.

Williams's attitude toward the Baroness mingled embarrassment, disgust, and the sense that he had missed the chance to learn something extraordinary. In the Village, she was considered New York's answer to Tristan Tzara, "the only one living anywhere who dresses dada, loves dada, lives dada." In her own person, explained John Rodker, *The Little Review*'s new foreign editor, the Baroness enacted a momentous artistic communion: "In Elsa von Freytag-Loringhoven," he declared, "Paris is mystically united [with] New York." The magazine had not only been prescient in the matter of *Ulysses* but it was, the editors boasted, "the first magazine to reassure Europe as to America, and the first to give America the tang of Europe." Having decided that Mina, too, had the tang of Europe, they invited her to join their contributors.

With the Arensbergs away, Mina gravitated toward the subset of Village intellectuals in which women prevailed—in their overlapping roles as writers, editors, and organizers of the informal salons characterizing literary life. With these women she could talk politics whenever she wished and receive the emotional support she craved in this dark period. Mina often visited Heap and Anderson at their Eighth Street apartment, where the living room's black walls, magenta floor, and oversize divan suspended from the ceiling provided a theatrical backdrop to discussions of official prudery. From there it was a short walk to Lola Ridge's more ascetic rooms, where poets read their work and anyone from the fiery Russian Mayakovsky to reserved Marianne Moore might show up. Like Mina, Ridge was an immigrant (Irish-born, she had lived in Australia and New Zealand). Having dedicated her life to the new verse and the revolution, she had kept *Others* going after Williams pronounced it dead. But despite their anarcho-feminist sympathies, she and Mina had little in common—perhaps because, in Ridge's view, the more overt social content in a poem, the better.

It was experimental prose rather than radical content that came under attack when *The Little Review* next ran into trouble with the law. *Ulysses* had been running in its pages for nearly three years when the district attorney persuaded John Sumner, head of the New York Society for the Prevention of Vice, to file a complaint. The crisis began when the daughter of a prominent New York lawyer showed her father the issue containing the Nausicaa episode, in which Leopold Bloom fantasizes erotic communion with Gerty McDowell: the obscurity of the prose did not conceal the fact that at the end of the episode, Bloom found fulfillment in autoeroticism.

"*The Little Review* has been arrested," Mina told Mabel. A hearing at the Jefferson Market police court would allow the magistrate to decide whether the episode was, as Sumner charged, "so obscene, lewd, lascivious, filthy, indecent and disgusting, that a minute description of the same would be offensive to the Court." On the appointed day, Mina and the *Review*'s other supporters formed a cheering section. The novelty of the situation—stylish women from the Village defending art in a courtroom full of plainclothesmen and prostitutes—was not lost on the participants.

"We looked *too* wholesome in Court representing filthy literature," Mina noted.

Those present at the scene interpreted it according to their lights. To John Quinn, the magazine's long-suffering attorney, Heap, Anderson, and their supporters looked guilty, "as though a fashionable whorehouse had been pinched and all its inmates hauled into court." Quinn, who represented the magazine chiefly to defend Joyce, shared the common assumption that women were either innocents or tarts. To Jane Heap, their legal problems resulted from this very way of thinking, which caused men like Sumner to want to protect "our young girls" from any reference to sex. Her view was more realistic, she claimed. "Men think thoughts and have emotions about these things everywhere," she noted, but seldom did they do so "as delicately and imaginatively as Mr. Bloom." After studying Joyce's prose, the magistrate heard Quinn. The episode could do no harm, he claimed: one would either fail to grasp its meaning or, grasping it, be amused or bored. But Quinn was not persuasive. Since anyone could understand "the episode where the man went off in his pants," the magistrate ruled, the charge was warranted.

The defendants were released pending trial, and the magazine's next issue, planned to feature Mina and the Baroness, became a defense of Art. It was more important to honor "a great artist's freedom to write as he pleases," the editors stated, than to respect "Mr. Sumner's freedom to suppress what he does not know to be a work of Art." In the same vein, Heap condemned the hypocrisy of invoking "the mind of the young girl" to enforce "denial, resentment and silence about all things pertaining to sex." "The Nausicaa episode," she went on, related "the simplest, most unpreventable, most unfocused sex thoughts possible in a rightly-constructed, unashamed human being," and its suppression would result in an America of "facsimile women and stereotyped men." Packing the issue with writing that was bound to be provocative, Heap and Anderson ran a story entitled "The Bomb Thrower," a Dada novel supplied and, some said, written by Pound, Djuna Barnes's tale of a "depraved" love affair, Robert McAlmon's animadversions in favor of "life," and the last episode of *Ulysses* to appear pending trial.

In this context, the contributions of Mina and the Baroness were counterweights to the demand for facsimiles and stereotypes. Man Ray's portraits of them, taken for this issue, form a striking contrast: while the Baroness contrived to look bourgeois in her dark dress and beads, Mina eyed the reader warily from beneath the brim of her mannish hat. But their perspectives were complementary, especially their critiques of male avant-gardists. Those in the know read the Baroness's poems as a series of ripostes to Williams, while those who had followed the succession of artistic "isms" saw in Mina's free-verse satire "Lions' Jaws" her farewell to Futurism.

"Lions' Jaws" was in some ways the antidote to the elegiac mood of

"Mexican Desert." The poem defied the conventions for poetry by women while also bringing news from distant aesthetic battlegrounds. Just as the Futurists had staged ritual murders of their precursors, so the Dadaists had taken to denouncing D'Annunzio and Marinetti. In their view, Futurism was just another grab at power. In a similar spirit, Mina's verse portrait of three Italian writers—"Gabrunzio" (D'Annunzio), "Raminetti" (Marinetti), and "Bapini" (Papini)—disdains their "manoeuvres" in the modern manner. But unlike the Dadaists' attacks on predecessors, this satire was voiced by a woman, the anagrammatically named "Nima Lyo, alias Anim Yol, alias Imna Oly," also described as "secret service buffoon to the Women's Cause."

"Lions' Jaws" evokes the decadent *mise-en-scène* with which Gabrunzio mesmerized admirers, then deploys a satire of Futurism from the perspective of one who has seen it at close range. Because Gabrunzio is known for his love affairs, the poem hints, his disciple Raminetti tries to "wheedle" his way into the heart of the "excepted" (exceptional) woman; the scholarly Bapini, in turn, gets close to Raminetti due to some erotic charge between them. But to Imna Oly, neither man is credible. Raminetti, astride "a prismatic locomotive / ramping the tottering platform / of the Arts," is a traveling salesman with "novelties from / Paris in his pocket," and once absorbed in his rivalry with Raminetti, the high-minded Bapini cannot refrain from penning obscenities.

Although "Lions' Jaws" dispatched Mina's relations with the Futurists, few readers understood its allusions to these literary "lions." Yet even if one knew little about Futurism, the poem's final section, "Envoi," made its point: vanguard maneuvers produced little of value. Wittily, Mina linked Marinetti's "short sentences" to his jail terms, scoffed at Papini's recent appearance in *Vanity Fair*, and scorned the damage done to "Imna Oly" through her involvement with "these amusing men." Even if some claimed that she was "not quite a lady," she had turned the tables on these "Latin litterateurs."

As a contributor to *The Little Review*, Mina soon came under attack as well. Reviewing Kreymborg's *Others Anthology for 1919*, John Rodker observed that the magazine had suffered "a distinct falling off." "All these folks seem to think poetry is a polite after dinner amusement like musical chairs," he noted. While there were exceptions to the general mediocrity —Mina Loy's "distinguished effort" and Marianne Moore's "rich pyramids"—Mina was, in his view, "the only poet in this bag who is really preoccupied with that curious object THE SOUL." For this reason, it pained him to admit "that since the last 'Others' she appears to have lost [her] grip."

When the editors gave Mina the right of reply, she composed a defense of American poetry against "English" ears. Rodker had assimilated American poets to the Georgians, who had "nothing to say," she argued. It was "more difficult by far for American[s] to say nothing," she continued, "when there is so much to be said." Moreover, she rejected the misogynistic terms of Rodker's praise. "Never mind what the women want," she hissed. Their duel continued in the next issue. "My own pet serpent turns upon me," Rodker lamented, to which Mina replied that he was acting like a snake charmer "parr[ying] his pet snake's indulgence." The dispute ended on a friendly note. "As one European to another," she quipped, "Mina Loy salutes you." It was, after all, a family affair.

III

By autumn, Williams had lost faith in *The Little Review*. It devoted too much space to Continental fads, and too little to Americans. Savoring the tang of Europe was all right provided it did not mean that only the French had something to say. Williams had recently met Robert McAlmon, a brash Westerner who thought it time to launch a magazine favoring the American vernacular. Together they drafted a manifesto. "We will be American," it read, "because we are of America": their venture, to be called *Contact*, would feature work that made "the essential contact between words and the locality that breeds them." The tone of the manifesto betrays Williams's defensiveness about Dada, the import which, in his view, was dazzling his peers. This "latest development of the french soul," he feared, would be imitated in New York "without there being—we venture to say—any sense whatever of its significance." America seemed to offer good soil for this "French orchid," since it was "a bastard country where decomposition is the prevalent spectacle." But because America's "local conditions" differed from those that had spawned Dada, America's "decomposition" had to be expressed in "local terms."

Throughout the autumn Williams was searching for alternatives to Dada's nihilism. Duchamp's group—Arensberg, Picabia, Bob Brown, and Mina—represented one pole of the avant-garde, as demonstrated in *The Blind Man*. But however stimulating, theirs was not a path that he could follow. If Mina's cosmopolitanism formed one extreme, Marianne Moore's reclusiveness suggested another. "In contradistinction to their south," he wrote, her "austerity of mood" defined true north. Mina flashed across the sky like an erratic meteor while Marianne stayed home, finding there "sufficient freedom for the play she chooses." Increasingly, it was by her fixed star that Williams would set his course.

When Williams published these remarks in 1920, he was already embroidering a theme that he had helped to develop: the poetic rivalry between two distinguished women poets. During Mina's first stay in New York, he claimed, Marianne was the only one whose poetry she had feared. Underscoring this point, he added that both had achieved "freshness of presentation, novelty, freedom, [and a] break with banality," but had done so "by divergent virtues." From then on, he always described them as each other's foils.

Ironically, any rivalry that may have existed between the two women no doubt developed from their male colleagues' insistence on their divergences. By 1920 it had become a commonplace to compare them. In one of Pound's *Little Review* columns, he had invented a term to describe their sort of poem—"logopoeia," or "the poetry of ideas." Evoking neither beautiful images nor noble sentiments, such poetry, he argued, was "a dance of the intelligence among words and ideas." Pound also supposed that like Marianne, Mina was a college graduate, the kind of woman who read French poetry and exemplified what he called "le tempérament de l'américaine." This temperament expressed itself in "a mind cry, more than a heart cry"—a type of writing so cerebral that he had difficulty grasping how it came to be written by these two "girls," with (or without) benefit of college degrees.

That same year in *The Egoist*, T. S. Eliot had developed this comparison at Mina's expense. Given the existence of two intelligent women poets, the article implied, Eliot felt called upon to rank one above the other. Although some of Mina's poems were "extremely good," her "oeuvre" was slight; he taxed her, moreover, with "abstraction." Soon Pound would issue a rejoinder. While both women had, he supposed, been "subject to something like international influence, there are lines in [Loy's] 'Ineffectual Marriage' perhaps better written than anything I have found in Miss Moore."

Comparison of their writing led inevitably to comparison of their persons. In this respect the girlish Marianne, whose most striking feature was her carrot-colored hair, often braided in a crown on top of her head, was at a disadvantage. Noticing her "in awed admiration of Mina's long-legged charms" or "with her mouth open" when Mina appeared at a literary event in a leopardskin coat, Williams guessed that she felt awkward in the presence of the better dressed, more worldly and socially adept Mina Loy.

Characteristically, Moore said little on the subject of her glamorous rival. When Moore's friend Hilda Doolittle (the poet H.D.) asked what she knew about Mina, Moore described their first meeting four years earlier, when she had thought her "beautiful," "rakish," and "clever"—high praise from this exacting judge of style. She had not seen Mina since her performance in *Lima Beans*, Moore continued, and while she was still "considered very beautiful" by those who knew her, she did not pronounce herself on the subject. Noting that Mina had married "a prize-fighter and editor," she related their story as she understood it, which involved Mina's living "in Tahiti or one of the South Sea Islands" until her husband's death by drowning. (This account conflates Stephen's travels with those of Cravan.) Moore closed her letter by quoting McAlmon. " 'To tell the truth,' he said, 'I used to see [Mina] in a restaurent [sic] before I knew who she was and I thought, 'she has good features, a fine nose and beautiful eyebrows,' but I didn't think she was beautiful and I wouldn't have cared if I had never seen her again.' " Cagily, Marianne avoided giving her own opinion.

Nor did she let on that she had written a poem about Mina or, more precisely, about Mina's image in literary circles, which she read at one of Lola Ridge's evenings. The poem, "Those Various Scalpels," studies its subject from a distance, starting with the éclat of her conversation—"those / various sounds consistently indistinct, like intermingled echoes / struck from thin glasses successively at random." Turning to her coiffure (Mina's hair was often arranged in a chignon of the sort Moore could not manage), the poem likens it to "the tails of two / fighting-cocks head to head in stone— / like sculptured scimitars repeating the curve of your ears in / reverse order." Her eyes were "flowers of ice and snow / sown by tearing winds on the cordage of disabled ships"—perhaps an allusion to her bereavement.

In the next section Moore's subject is seen in a characteristic pose— one hand raised in "an ambiguous signature," the other bristling with "a bundle of lances all alike, partly hid by emeralds from Persia / and the fractional magnificence of Florentine / goldwork." Finally, her dress, "a magnificent square / cathedral tower of uniform / and at the same time diverse appearance" is heard to rustle, like moiré silk perhaps, "in the storm of conventional opinion." Are these feminine arts "weapons or scalpels," the poem asks. Made brilliant "by the hard majesty of . . . sophistication," the instruments with which this woman confronts her fate are, it hints, "more highly specialized than components of destiny itself."

Moore admired Mina's artful self-presentation, it seems, but she also thought her "hard," more analytic than experience warranted. If Mina grasped the wit with which Marianne had composed her portrait, she did not comment. Returning the favor, she drew Marianne not in words but on paper—with the cartwheel hat that hid her braided crown and was to become her own "signature." (Mina's two portraits evoked Marianne's sartorial oddity and emotional reserve, but they did not penetrate beneath the surface.)

Judging by McAlmon's account, either he did not inform Moore of the extent of his interest in Mina and their "rivalry" or she had, in her characteristic way, understated his opinions in her letter. While the two women watched each other from a distance, McAlmon was studying their interactions that winter for future use as literary material. Within months of the events he witnessed, McAlmon had drafted *Post-Adolescence*, his *roman à clef* of Village literary life in which Williams figures as Jim Boyle, Mina as Gusta Rolph, Moore as Martha Wallus, and McAlmon himself as the observer-narrator, Peter. The plot, a string of episodes in Peter's literary apprenticeship, includes his meetings with Gusta, either alone or with other members of their circle such as Martha Wallus, to whom she often compares herself.

McAlmon's alter ego declares his "decided leaning" for Gusta toward the end of the novel, during a drunken reverie. In earlier scenes he admires "her straight Greek profile," while also noting the toll taken by "pallor and nervous tiredness." "She must have been wonderfully beautiful a few years back," he thinks, soothing her vanity after hearing her story of a millionaire who supported a writer who was losing his sight and her wish to contact this millionaire because she is losing her complexion. Daydreaming about Gusta alone with "the hard brilliance of her own mentality," he notes that she cares too much about being clever: "The dazzle of her own wit meant more to her" than "depth of insight." McAlmon's fictionalized portrait of Mina that winter evokes, as Moore's poem could not, "the impression of real discouragement, almost despair" he felt when they were together.*

In January, Mina and McAlmon called on Marianne at the Village apartment where she lived with her mother. Just before this visit—as restaged in *Post-Adolescence*—Gusta tells Peter how unhappy she has been and wonders how Martha (Marianne) manages her life. Speculating about her on their way to St. Luke's Place, Gusta surmises that her spinsterly ways must be due to "some suppression or cowardice." Given the widespread myth of their poetic rivalry, *Post-Adolescence* suggests, the two women could not help being self-conscious in each other's presence. Martha greets her guests graciously, however, and tells Gusta that she has wanted to talk with her because of her poetry. After Martha admits that her employment as a librarian keeps her from writing, Gusta replies, "You observe things too uniquely to let any paid job interfere," before adding tartly, "though I presume you believe in self-discipline and duty more than some of us."

The contrast between Mina's emancipation and Marianne's reserve was not lost on McAlmon. Unlike Williams, he saw his two friends not as opposites but as temperaments peculiar to these women: despite his "decided leaning" toward Mina, she could not serve as his model. The first issue of *Contact* featured, in addition to the editors' manifesto in favor of the "local," Williams's plea to Moore to "save us! / Put us in a book of yours," and Mina's study of her home ground, "Summer Night in a Florentine Slum." The second issue ran "Those Various Scalpels," which read—provided one knew its subject—like a delicate gloss on Mina's prose and person.

Despite the positioning of their names within a rivalry invented and staged by their male associates—Pound, Eliot, Williams, and McAlmon—Mina and Marianne maintained a wary respect for each other. Moore's only published mention of Mina's poetry places it in the context of the avant-gardists' *vers libertine*. Recalling the "sliced and cylindrical, complicated yet simple use of words by Mina Loy," Moore aligned her writing with that of Walter Arensberg and Gertrude Stein. Mina was, in other words, an internationalist of the kind promoted in *The Little Review*, where Moore did not wish to appear. Mina, equally circumspect although less

---

* About this time McAlmon also wrote "A Poetess," most likely a prose portrait of Mina Loy: its subject is "a malnutrite saint politician, bitter through never having received purification [who] writes songs from the urge within her . . . She does not want sympathy, and the cold purity of understanding chills her to the marrow."

generous, committed herself to print only once on the subject of her rival. While Marianne wrote "amusingly," Mina noted, and had produced "at least one perfect poem," her writing "suggest[ed] the soliloquies of a library clock."

Of the women in their circle, Mina preferred the dashing young reporter Djuna Barnes. Barnes, a quintessential Village bohemian known for her sardonic poetry and drawings, earned her living by commenting on cultural trends—she had interviewed everyone from the labor leader Mother Jones to Stieglitz. Recently she had written some dreamlike plays, three of which were performed that year at the Provincetown Playhouse. Although Barnes had long wanted to meet Mina, she was ill at ease when introduced: as re-created by McAlmon, this scene takes place in a smoky Sixth Avenue café where bootlegged liquor is served in coffee cups. Beryl (Djuna) and Peter discuss Gusta's character while waiting for her. Her poetry is "mostly about ideas," he thinks, but she has "a romantic soul" beneath her veneer of sophistication. "She doesn't sound a hell of a lot different from the rest of us," Beryl replies, "except I suppose she's more of a lady than I am."

Soon after meeting, the women compare notes about love. "My mind will keep wondering about that husband of mine," a dejected Gusta explains, "whether he's really drowned or not. If it had only been my first husband," she adds, "so he couldn't pester me about the children." When Beryl asks whether her children were "accidents," Gusta replies that she had wanted the third one "because I liked her father so much. The other two," she continues, "I rather wanted because I detested their father so much, and thought they'd keep me from reflecting on that all the time." It had taken years to break away from their "conventional English environment," she continues. Beryl, equally disillusioned, runs through the list of men she has supported. (Djuna was having an affair with Laurence Vail, Mina's young friend from Florence, at the time.) "We'll have to form a union of women to show the men up," Gusta retorts, "and make ourselves exhibits A and B."

At another meeting the women tease each other like old friends. Gusta is "her own original portrait of the artist," Beryl declares. Between rounds of Asti Spumante, Gusta keeps insisting that she is "finished." The war, you know," she explains, "waiting three years for my husband, and coming here expecting to find him only to find that he was drowned." Unaware that McAlmon was taking notes on the conversation, Mina sank deeper into melancholy. When Djuna took her leave, McAlmon noted, "With her went most of the expressive life in the room."

Mina rose to the occasion in Djuna's company. Despite the ten years' difference in their ages, they saw the world the same way and liked each other's sense of style. (Recalling Djuna's "regal bearing" and "supreme elegance of clothing" decades later, Mina remarked on her gift for friendships that were "entire loyalties.") After noticing the two women, Man Ray asked to photograph them at his new Village studio. "They were stunning subjects," he wrote, and the contrast between them "made a fine picture." Dressed as each other's foil—Mina in beige and Djuna in black —they posed as if oblivious to the camera: the double portrait suggests their affinity, as well as the awareness that friendship was an artful composition.

During the winter Mina's depression worsened as prospects for regeneration, both personal and social, evaporated. McAlmon noted her self-absorption. She had begun writing about Cravan and could not stop talking about him. He was a "biological mystic," a man who could think with each part of his body. Her love for him was obvious. But she felt ashamed, McAlmon thought, of her inability to go forward. A man has an easier time than a woman, Gusta tells Peter: in the end, she is defeated by life "whether she cares about others' opinions or not." And however confidently she rejects the past, it keeps on functioning inside her or else catches up with her through the accidents of fate.

What remains of her correspondence from this period confirms McAlmon's portrait. "My health is very smashed up & I don't know what will be next," Mina wrote, daydreaming about a visit to Mabel in Taos, where she lived with her latest husband, Tony Luhan, a full-blooded Indian. By January Mina had lost all hope of finding Cravan, she told Nellie Grandjean, who became more cordial after Mina sent a copy of her marriage certificate to Lausanne. While she could not help thinking that the best part of herself had gone down with Cravan, she continued to hope that he was alive. (Joella was told to consult the Tarot reader, in case she had new information.) At the same time Mina became more than unusually anxious as her funds diminished along with her prospects.

In December Mina auditioned for a part in Laurence Vail's *What D'You Want?* which was to run through January at the Provincetown. The Players were full of excitement over the first bill of the season, which featured Eugene O'Neill's new play, *The Emperor Jones*; it had been so successful that it was going to Broadway. The second bill—including Vail's curtain-raiser and another O'Neill play—was sure to attract attention. And it was no doubt amusing to find her young friend making his name as a Village bohemian. Vail had changed little since his family lived in Mina's house before the war: his long blond hair, French accent, and high spirits had made his reputation even before he became Djuna's lover.

Although *What D'You Want?* takes place in that quintessential American setting the drugstore, the play has an unusual premise. Along with their milkshakes, customers are granted the fulfillment of their dearest wish: Vail was satirizing both American puritanism and the quasi-Freudian vogue for the shedding of inhibitions. Cast in a role that in no way resembled her debut in *Lima Beans*, Mina was to play Esther, a "drab" spinster. Fearing that "what one wants in one's heart may not seem . . . respectable," Esther realizes that what she wants is a bohemian like Vail—"his hair long and seldom brushed." While one can only speculate about Mina's thoughts each night as she turned herself into a caricature of an old maid, her decision to list herself on the playbill as Imna Oly, her anagrammatic pseudonym, suggests that what she wanted was to distance herself from this part.

The program ran from December 27—Mina's thirty-ninth birthday— through January 27. By mid-January, when the Players talked of taking both plays to Broadway to capitalize on the success of *The Emperor Jones*, Mina could bear New York no longer. Many of her friends were anxious to move on. McAlmon talked of shipping off to China despite his commitment to *Contact* and the reinvigoration of American poetry. Others spoke of Europe, where one could live on a modest income. Mina cabled to London for money and eked out the days until the funds arrived, when she left for a rest cure at the Rose Valley sanatorium in Pennsylvania. Once there, she replied to Nellie Grandjean, who had asked repeatedly whether Fabienne might spend the summer with her. Mina had suffered too much to put pen to paper, she explained. And while she was glad that the Grandjeans cared for Fabi, she could not say whether she would send her to visit. The little girl was a comfort to her, she continued, but at the same time, her resemblance to her father was heartbreaking.

Too unhappy to complete the novel she had begun about Cravan, she did little but rest. Her sense of being "finished" pervades the wintry vision of "Poe," an address to the poet of despair written, most likely, about this time:

> *a lyric elixir of death*
> *embalms*
> *the spindle spirits of your hour glass loves*
> *on moon spun nights*
>
> *sets*
> *icicled canopy*
> *for corpses of poesy*
> *with roses and northern lights*
>
> *where frozen nightingales in ilex aisles*
> *sing burial rites*

Poe had asserted (in his melancholy "Philosophy of Composition") that "the death of a beautiful woman is, unquestionably, the most poetical topic in the world." Mina's sardonic reply suggests that women appear in Romantic poetry not in their own right but as "corpses of poesy," the silenced objects required by Poe's vision. But while her ironic "hommage" to Poe and his descendants critiques this vision by reversing the power dynamics—positioning a female voice in response to a male perspective—

it also betrays her state of mind. As in "Mexican Desert," Cravan goes unmentioned. Yet the death of the male muse was, at this point, her own most poetical topic.

IV

On her return to New York in March, Mina found that she had missed the events of the season. The *Little Review* trial had taken place the previous month, with an excitable group of reporters crowded into the courtroom along with an even more excitable group of avant-gardists, for whom the notion of genius itself was on trial. Quinn's strategy—he began with a lecture on Joyce's genius—was deemed irrelevant. Witnesses for the defense contradicted each other by claiming either that *Ulysses* was too obscure to be corrupting or urging that the Gerty McDowell episode be read as a revelation of the subconscious, a tactic which backfired when the judge told the witness to "speak plain English" rather than a jargon that sounded like "Russian."

The trial kept reverting to the problematic status of language, especially when used to evoke feelings that were not to be mentioned in the presence of those who provoked them—the ladies. The district attorney's request to have the questionable passages read aloud was denied on the grounds that they would offend Miss Anderson, who, the judge argued, could not have understood what she published. The passages were read nonetheless, and the newspaper accounts played into the prosecution's hands: the observation that the issue was "a too frank expression concerning a woman's dress" seemed to prove the point—writing about a woman's underpants unveiled what ought to remain covered. The editors were fined and ordered to cease publication of Joyce's novel.

As the *Little Review* crowd watched the trial, Williams, Moore, and McAlmon played their parts in another drama, not without its farcical aspect. Within a few weeks of her visit to New York with her companion H.D., the English writer Bryher proposed to McAlmon. Soon it became known that Bryher was the daughter of Sir John Ellerman, the wealthiest man in England. It was a marriage of convenience, Williams thought, an arrangement that bought Bryher's emancipation from her family. Given Bryher's love for H.D., not to mention the newlyweds' incompatibilities, they would surely divorce after a decent interval. Henceforth, Williams told their friends, the groom should be known as Robert McAlimony.

One can only speculate about the effect of McAlmon's change of fortune on Mina. It may have seemed as if he, rather than she, had received the check from the millionaire who took pity on writers. Following the rest cure in Rose Valley, her spirits lifted. Feeling more able to face the facts of Cravan's disappearance, she bombarded the intelligence services with telegrams. Through a member of the British Secret Service with contacts in Mexico, she told Nellie Grandjean, she learned that from what they knew of the case, Cravan and his friends had either been blown out to sea or else "murdered if they were blown ashore . . . those boys could not have been in Salina Cruz without the British S.S. keeping an eye on them," she went on, "so we may hear *something*."

Of Mina's old circle, only Duchamp and Man Ray continued their tradition of subversive amusements. During another visit to Ray's studio, she and the photographer contrived a piquant idea for Mina's next portrait. Turning her head to the right and closing her eyes, she struck the profile pose of a nineteenth-century beauty, much like the *Evening Sun*'s portrait for her 1917 interview. This time, in a parody of "art" photography, Man Ray replaced her candelabrum earring with his darkroom thermometer. Although Mina went along with the joke, one wonders whether she saw in this self-consciously modern pendant a comment upon her emotional temperature. Since the mercury remained at the bottom of the "earring," it is possible that, from his perspective, she had gone cold with the loss of Cravan. In a way, Man Ray's portrait was as objectifying as his nude photographs of the Baroness, and the joke, quite possibly, was on his subject.

It was in this equivocal spirit that Man Ray and Duchamp had recently effected Duchamp's transformation into his alter ego, Rrose Sélavy. Although Rrose—Duchamp in women's clothing—existed only in Man Ray's photograph, Duchamp's persona allowed him to adopt a female identity whose punning name barely concealed the motto "Eros, c'est la vie." Here, as in Mina's portrait, the joke was on the woman, whose "femininity" was false. Through Rrose, Duchamp hinted that if gender was as fraudulent as his masquerade, then both sexes functioned in ambiguity. But the message was too subtle to make much of an impression.

From Paris, Tzara was still trying to promote a New York branch of Dada. Apart from the *Little Review* crowd, New Yorkers had not taken to a movement that few understood, despite the newspapers' efforts to publicize it. "Enter 'Dadaism' Very Latest Fad," proclaimed *The World* in December. "Not Being Definable, Even by Its Apostles, Its Vogue Seems to Be Assured," the paper continued. Heralding the movement's arrival in America, the article claimed that Dada was "so many leagues ahead of the other conceits of the ultra-modernists that post-futurism, vers libre and psychoanalysis are lucid by comparison." " 'Dada' Will Get You If You Don't Watch Out," warned the *Evening Journal* a month later, after asking members of the Société Anonyme to define the foreign import. Dada meant "irony," Dreier explained, but was contradicted by Duchamp, who said it meant "nothing." Perhaps best suited to the paper's readers was Man Ray's account: Dada "consists largely of negations," he explained. The tail end of the earlier vanguards, it was "a state of mind."

This state of mind, it was hoped, would prevail during the Société Anonyme's first Dada soirée, appropriately scheduled for April 1. The evening began with a declaration by a woman in a lace-curtain shawl who claimed that the first Dadaist had been Swinburne. In her opinion, Dada not only lacked originality but she doubted whether anyone could say "what these dreadful pictures on the wall mean, if they mean anything at all." It took the intervention of a philosophy professor to elucidate their meaning, "thus bringing the evening to a safe and sane conclusion," noted an observer. While it is tempting to imagine Mina in the audience with Duchamp, Man Ray, and the other members of their circle, anyone who had attended a Futurist *serata* would have found the evening rather tame.

The event failed to convey the essence of Dada, which was neither safe nor sane. The organizers had planned to give this task to the artist Marsden Hartley, who was scheduled to address the topic. In a version of his lecture, entitled "The Importance of Being 'Dada,' " Hartley called Dada "the first joyous dogma . . . invented for the release and true freedom of art." Art appreciation was "a species of vice" in a country that cared above all for business, he continued; Dada was the "hobby-horse" (another of the term's meanings) on which the artist rode away from art's "idolaters." It was a sympathetic assessment, but one that may have fallen on deaf ears.

Recalling Mina's role at the Independents, the organizers invited her to educate the public. The Société's next event was a symposium, a form more congenial to the American temperament, and its subject, Gertrude Stein, was sure to excite attention, since the press had already dubbed her the Mama of Dada. On April 30, Mina, Henry McBride, Marsden Hartley, and a Mrs. Charles Knoblauch assembled to discourse on and recite examples of Steinese. No reports of this "Evening with Gertrude Stein" survive, unfortunately, especially given the participation of Mrs. Knoblauch, who before her marriage had been the recipient of Gertrude's attentions in the triangular love affair later transposed into her lesbian novel *Q.E.D.*

Dada, it seemed, was no respecter of persons. In breaking down the barriers between public and private, it encouraged artists to remake their identities in such a way as to mock the notion of identity itself—as Duchamp had done. After the publication of *New York Dada*'s single issue—with Rrose on the cover—Mina found allusions to her own life hidden in its pages. Asserting the linkage between Paris and New York through his new persona, Duchamp as Rrose gazed at the reader from a perfume bottle on which his remade likeness had been pasted, along with the inscription "NEW YORK–PARIS." McBride took this to mean that America had a special place in the movement. While "they say in Europe that we are all dadas over here," he wrote, Duchamp was "a genuine Dadaist, if not the first and original one." The magazine dealt with the issue of originality by including a letter from the Grand Dada himself: Dada belonged to all, Tzara proclaimed, "like the idea of God or of the toothbrush." In this spirit, Man Ray recalled, articles were left unsigned, "to express our contempt for credits and merits."

Despite Dada's bow toward anti-authoritarianism—making anyone's merits fair game—the magazine's third page may have seemed to Mina like a low blow. Under the headline PUG DEBS MAKE SOCIETY BOW, an anonymous article in mock journalese announced that Mina would preside over a Madison Square Garden coming-out party in the form of a boxing match between the painters and "pug-debs" Stella and Hartley. Before introducing her "protégés," the article went on, she would release flocks of trained butterflies to flutter through the Garden before landing on the spectators' heads. Although no doubt intended to spoof American culture, the article did so by mocking Cravan—and by implication, Mina's love for him.

The last page of *New York Dada* featured Man Ray's latest portrait of the Baroness, wearing only her jewelry, as Dada's "naked truth." A month earlier, her accusations of masculine "brutality" had been directed at Williams in *The Little Review*; this critique mingled private griefs with denunciations of the poet as the exemplar of the American male's cowardice. But if Mina felt any sympathy for the Baroness, her unlikely ally in the sex war, she did not say so, nor did she comment on her own appearance in the magazine. Despite McBride's enthusiasm—"It was inevitable," he wrote, "that some manifestation of the dadaists would occur in New York"—*New York Dada* failed to provoke a scandal. As Williams had foreseen, Dada, "the small, sweet forget-me-not of the war," did not take hold. Attempts to nurture Dada in America, Man Ray recalled, were "as futile as trying to grow lilies in a desert."

Mina was more absorbed in efforts to earn a living that spring than in her friends' antics. It was a difficult time for artists; even those who had found work at the advertising agencies that sprang up after the war were being laid off. About then, Frances Stevens returned from Russia full of moneymaking schemes. She and Mina would act as agents in the sale of some valuable tapestries that had come her way. As reputable artists with European credentials, they would surely find buyers, and Mina could use her commission to bring the children to New York.

After several months, it was clear that this scheme was unlikely to succeed. "Different things turned up which promised the chance of making some money," Mina wrote Nellie Grandjean, who had inquired about her plans. "But America is in a state of tension financially," she went on. "The big collectors of pictures & tapestries have stopped collecting on account of the heavy income tax—& on the other hand the big antique dealers make it impossible to make private sales." And she had spent what remained of her income searching for Fabian. "I could never have been at peace," she continued, "unless I made every effort—especially as we had hoped that he was in prison & thought we might get him released . . . if he had only been alive."

In the meantime, Mina sent her work to anyone who might be inter-

ested, starting with *The Dial*. Increasingly, the magazine was being identified with a measured kind of modernism, leaving more experimental work
to *The Little Review* and free-spirited publications like *Broom* and *Playboy*. In
March, Thayer and Watson had run Moore's review of Eliot's essays, which
showed her support for his view of literary tradition. Although it was
rumored that Thayer was courting the skittish Marianne, whose writing
appeared regularly in *The Dial*, Thayer's partiality did not prevent him from
taking an interest in Mina. He chose *The Pamperers*, her satire of vanguardism, to initiate the magazine's "Modern Forms" section, featured her drawings, including a stylized *Girl with Red Hair* and a watercolor of two dancers,
and over the next few years published several of her poems. Thayer's
decision to take both "Mexican Desert" and "Poe" suggests his response
to her bereavement.

At the opposite end of the spectrum, the Village publisher Egmont
Arens also took an interest. A Bolshevik sympathizer, Arens had recently
launched *Playboy* as "a passing record of those who are ALIVE NOW"); he
listed Blake, Whitman, and Jesus Christ among the magazine's "sponsors"
and featured D. H. Lawrence's defense of free verse—"the insurgent naked
throb of the instant moment"—at a time when many were returning to
traditional forms. The May 1921 issue featured a play by Djuna Barnes, a
war story by Richard Aldington (H.D.'s estranged husband), and another
of Mina's portraits, showing the three Graces with bobbed hair posing in
empty modernist space. The following month Arens suspended publication
until he could assemble the funds to continue. In the meantime, he gathered
an impressive group of essays, poems, and illustrations by such varied
talents as Edmund Wilson, Elinor Wylie, Dorothy Parker, and Maurice
Sterne. Mina's new prose piece, "Preceptors of Childhood," was featured
in the gala issue with which he resumed publication. In this mélange
of modernist art and satire, Mina's evocation of youth struck an unusual
note.

Attempting for the first time to write about herself as the product of
a particular time and place, she devised a strategy to distance herself from
the subject—her childhood—by naming her heroine Maraquita. While this
device gives "Preceptors of Childhood" an air of objectivity, the perspective
is, nonetheless, that of the author: the "preceptors" have the names of her
own governesses. ("Preceptors" begins "Lilah was pale, and Maraquita
loved her. She read her 'Peep of Day,' a pretty book about a pretty man,
that made her cry. Maraquita's introduction to crying without being hurt
for it.") Representative of an era when radicals looked to psychoanalysis
as the means of self-transformation, "Preceptors" was a departure for her
and would lead, within a few years, to the self-probing of "Anglo-Mongrels
and the Rose."

While good for Mina's reputation, these publications did not advance
her plan to bring the children to New York. After the tapestry scheme fell
through, she turned to another artistic outlet. The Arensbergs' friend Louis

Bouché, a painter who had studied at Colarossi's, had recently been put in charge of the Belmaison Gallery in Wanamaker's department store. This luxurious showplace allowed him to exhibit the best of the new work, both American and foreign. After taking several of Mina's drawings, Bouché arranged to have them publicized in a new magazine, *Art Review*: included were one of her most accomplished portraits—showing two gypsies and a young girl—and a series of heads inspired by Joella, which the magazine ran under the title "Three Studies by an Unusual Artist, Mina Loy."

Joella, who was nearly fourteen, wrote frequently from Florence with news of Giles and Fabienne, the many visitors who looked in on them, and her hopes for the future. Thinking she would like to be a dancer, she asked whether Mina could send her to the Ruth St. Denis school in America. English residents in Florence, it was clear from her letters, had seen to it that she was taken in hand during Mina's absence. But despite their attentions, Joella wanted her to come home.

Nellie Grandjean also wrote of her interest in Fabienne, now that she accepted the toddler as her legitimate, and only, grandchild. That year she had traveled to Florence to see Fabian's daughter for herself. Giulia was a perfect governess and Fabienne an affectionate baby who was adored by her siblings, she noted in an account of this visit; adding that they were probably better cared for by the servants than by their mother. To Nellie's repeated requests to have Fabienne spend the summer, Mina replied that she could not separate her from Giulia but would bring her to Lausanne herself the following Christmas. While foreigners who had known Mina in pre-war Florence shared Nellie's opinion of her failings, they agreed that Joella needed the guidance of a mother, however unconventional. A concerned resident who came to New York that spring made a point of telling her that, of the three children, Joella needed her the most.

Unaware that her mother-in-law did not think much of her maternal instincts, Mina wrote to Lausanne about her plans to return to Florence in July. She was turning over in her mind various projects for the future and hoped to educate Fabienne as Cravan wished, which meant teaching her "to speak French as he did." She had come up with a solution: she would bring the entire household to Paris, where she would open a restaurant with Estere as cook, "& pay her a third of the profits—to keep her interested." Since everyone was going into business, this would entail no loss of status.

Mina had understood that Nellie would be concerned about a loss of standing, but did not anticipate that her mother-in-law was even more cautious where money was concerned. Assuming that she could speak her mind, Mina mentioned the three thousand francs remaining in Cravan's bank account. "Would you be so good as to try to get it so that I can start the cook in this restaurant for Fabienne's sake," she wrote. "I know he would want me to have it for Fabienne," she continued confidently. The details were all worked out. Estere's relatives would do the work; the business would stay in the family. "I am anxious about it as it is so easy for families with small incomes to become submerged after this war," she entreated, "and so important for daughters especially not to be at the mercy of poverty, don't you think so?"

The Grandjeans did not think much of Mina's scheme, nor were they moved by her entreaties. Not only did the three thousand francs remain in the account, but her mother-in-law ensured that at the proper time the bank would release the funds only to Fabienne. Mina would have to manage on her own.

Soon after this rebuff, Mina received a greater shock. Joella wired from Florence that Stephen had passed through town and taken twelve-year-old Giles with him to live in the Caribbean. Everything had happened very quickly. Although Joella and Giulia thought it wrong for Stephen to take Giles without telling Mina, they had been powerless against him. Moreover, Stephen had made it clear that because the deed to 54 Costa San Giorgio was in his name, he could dispose of it as he pleased.

In despair, Mina turned to Mabel. Would she help with the restaurant scheme, Mina pleaded; it would allow her "to keep the children & myself without the daily anxiety." The letter continues:

I suppose this is a ridiculous thing to ask after all these years—but I was so wondering what to do next. Haweis has been to Florence & taken the boy & the house away from me. I have suffered so much since the war to keep them going. I want to be free of worry—& work. I have so much accumulated that is bursting for expression—it is getting unbearable. Would you lend me a thousand dollars to be paid back in two years—to help me start a restaurant. When once I have got it going I shall have some time and peace. I have not been able to get along in the commercial field in New York because I cannot understand their distinctions between one nothingness and another. I've had a hell of a time off and on the last few years—it has fired my imagination . . . Moose—if you find it in your heart to help me—at this dark homeless moment—please send me the word yes—by deferred cable to "Cooks" Fifth Ave. I am trying to get over as soon as possible to Joella—and it would be such a comfort to know there was any chance for me.

This *cri de coeur* proved no more successful than her letter to Nellie Grandjean. Still wondering what to do, Mina decided to return to Europe. She would salvage what remained of her life in Florence and move to Paris.

Among her friends, the exodus had already begun. Man Ray and Duchamp left for Paris in June, and Djuna was packing her trunks. McAlmon had migrated there from London with the intention of starting an English-language press. What Williams feared was now taking place. The idea of contact with "local conditions" as the means to revive American letters was evaporating. The younger artists all talked of Montparnasse, where the mores and the exchange rate were said to be favorable. Everyone agreed that they did things better in Paris. Art was honored, Prohibition unthinkable, and all the greats—Joyce, Picasso, Pound, and Stein—were in residence.

If the younger generation sought exile as a form of salvation, Mina sailed to Europe in a different frame of mind. Her return would mark the end of her hopes for another way of life, one that was more open, generous, and modern. Ironically, she learned just before leaving New York that a revised version of *Psycho-Democracy* would appear that summer in *The Little Review*. The fulfillment of her wish—the publication of her plan for a world made safe by, and for, geniuses—would come too late. In the postwar world what counted was business. It was pointless to form a group of artists for peace, and in any case, all the geniuses were leaving for Paris.

15

Europe without Baedeker

(FLORENCE—BERLIN, 1921–23)

"IF YOU COME TO FLORENCE," Mina wrote to Scofield Thayer, "do find your way to my roof." From there, she continued, "like Satan, I can tempt you with an extensive panorama . . . of the past." New York—however depressing—had strengthened her conviction that Italy was mired in the old ways of thinking. People would always disapprove of her and of her writing in a backwater like Florence. And if they insisted on gossiping about her unconventional ways, she might as well play the part. Within weeks of her return, the children were packed off to the seacoast for the summer and Mina was on the train to Paris.

I

Despite Mina's prejudice against Florence, many changes had occurred there since the war. Visitors now came not so much for the art or the language, a resident noted, "but because Florentine society was expansive without being expensive." No longer obliged to take tea with the dowagers of villadom, the younger set danced the fox-trot at the newly opened nightclubs. And while titles, especially foreign ones, were still respected, tolerance for eccentricities had, if anything, grown. To the London literati who came there in increasing numbers, it seemed as if "every other member of the foreign colony had had a purple past." But to Mina, the Anglo-Florentines—however tolerant—still inhabited the previous century.

The political situation was more unstable than in 1920, when she had left for New York. Bolshevik sympathizers attacked the trains; strikes erupted all over the country; hand grenades went off in the streets during the Fascists' combats with the Socialists. Moreover, the Fascists were winning the battle for Florence, where they had gained support among university students and the middle classes. They not only broke the strikes that were paralyzing the economy, their supporters argued, but they planned to prevent future disruption by forming their own labor organizations.

Although most foreigners stayed aloof from politics, others, like Janet Ross, said that the Fascists had saved Italy from Bolshevism. They lowered their voices when discussing the situation, and, when speaking of Mussolini, referred cautiously to Mr. Brown. Young Fascists had been known to break into people's villas in search of funds, and already the faithful servants from before the war seemed to have been replaced by a less submissive breed. In town, squadrons of men swaggered through the streets in homemade uniforms, all waving the flags of their insignia. An unrepentant Socialist had recently been beaten to death.

While Mussolini was letting these groups do as they pleased, it was rumored that he would control them when it came time to make his move. In October this analysis proved correct, when Mussolini formed the National Fascist Party, an organization meant to appeal to respectable citizens. Within a short time, it numbered two million members, and was said to be well funded, armed, and disciplined. Nonetheless, while the foreigners found themselves speaking more often of Mr. Brown than of each other's peccadillos, many thought that politics would have little effect on them: they would cultivate their gardens as they had always done.

Uncertain that she had anything left to cultivate—Stephen still threatened to sell the house out from under her—Mina had no desire to remain in Florence. She was so angry at Stephen for taking Giles that rage, rather than sorrow, erupted when she spoke of her son, dismissing him as a "Haweis." Joella could write to them if she wished, but Mina refused to do so. She had to look to their future, which meant going to Paris to see whether the restaurant scheme was feasible, whether Cravan's friends and the Dadaists could be counted on to "boom it."

That summer in Paris, Mina caught up with Bob McAlmon and Djuna Barnes. McAlmon had spent the spring with Bryher's family before escaping to the French capital, where he befriended James Joyce; he hoped to begin an international edition of *Contact* soon, in London or in Paris. Once settled on the Left Bank, Djuna kept running into New Yorkers. Sherwood Anderson and the editorial staff of *Broom*—Kreymborg, the young writer Harold Loeb, and their wives—were all staying at her hotel. When not café-hopping with McAlmon, she took refuge in her favorite churches, Notre-Dame and St.-Germain-des-Prés. If Paris was "the magnet that drew writers toward the knowledge of their minds," as she later observed, it was in the church of St.-Germain-des-Prés that she gained the serenity to explore her own.

Assessing her friends' responses to Paris on her return home, Mina told Thayer that they were each "reacting in their different ways." Yet all

believed in the artist's need to express his vision, whatever the consequences. Since the *Little Review* trial, Joyce was the archetype of the genius
made to suffer for his courage. Mina's letter to Thayer included a recent
poem, "Apology of Genius," written from this perspective:

> Ostracized as we are with God
>> The watchers of the civilized wastes
>> reverse their signals on our track
>
>> Lepers of the moon
>> all magically diseased
>> we come among you
>> innocent
>> of our luminous sores

More spiritual apologia than apology, the poem assumes the antagonism
between the "we" and the "you" employed in "The Dead."

From this perspective, "you" includes all those who guard the
"wastes" of culture against "us," the geniuses:

>> We are the sacerdotal clowns
>> who feed upon the wind and stars
>> and pulverous pastures of poverty
>
>> Our wills are formed
>> by curious discipline
>> beyond your laws
>
>> You may give birth to us
>> or marry us
>> the chances of your flesh
>> are not our destiny—
>
>> The cuirass of the soul
>> still shines—
>> And we are unaware
>> if you confuse
>> such brief
>> corrosion with possession

The poem read like the anthem of a generation desperate to jettison family
ties—"the chances of your flesh"—along with the previous century. The
scorn with which these "corrosive" contacts are dismissed gave Mina's

credo a self-consciously modern tone, despite its romantic conclusion, which likens the creative power of genius to that of the divine:

> *In the raw caverns of the Increate*
> *we forge the dusk of Chaos*
> *to that imperious jewelry of the Universe*
> *—The Beautiful—*

> *While to your eyes*
> *A delicate crop*
> *of criminal mystic immortelles**
> *stands to the censor's scythe.*

Following its 1922 publication in *The Dial*, "Apology of Genius" would be seen as a defense of modern art's creations, the "criminal mystic immortelles" of the final lines.

Although this vanguard stance may strike us as grandiose, it took courage to resist the censors of the imagination, as the *Little Review* trial had shown. During the summer of 1922, the avant-garde rose to the magazine's aid with contributions for the autumn issue, a protest against censorship. Photographs of Brancusi's sculptures were scattered through its pages, as if these ultra-modern shapes voiced an implicit defiance of prudishness. The editors reaffirmed their internationalism by including Pound's homage to Brancusi, a poem in German—still a suspect tongue—and Picabia's invitation to the advanced thinkers of the world to destroy "everyone and everything" in the name of renewal. Following these defiant words, they ran "Psycho-Democracy," its pages interspersed and in a sense illustrated with Brancusis.

One of these pictures caught Mina's eye. It showed the sculptor's studio and a recent creation, *Golden Bird*: this gleaming brass shape transposed into three-dimensional form the soul's gestures at transcendence. Moved by the correspondence between their visions, she praised the sculptor as another modernist genius. In "Brancusi's Golden Bird" his studio is the realm where miracles like this sculpture are made by a "patient peasant God":

> *This gong*
> *of polished hyperaesthesia*
> *shrills with brass*

* While "immortels" in the masculine plural often designates the "immortal" members of the Académie Française, Mina's usage suggests that she was anglicizing the feminine plural "immortelles," the common name in French of a number of everlasting dried flowers such as edelweiss, or *immortelle des glaciers*, which—like the production of the avant-garde—outlast attempts to "scythe" or destroy them.

as the aggressive light
strikes its significance

The immaculate
conception of the inaudible bird
occurs
in gorgeous reticence — — —

The poem claimed a status for the artist outside, and beyond, the world's turmoil, in a place where what counted was "the Alpha and Omega / of Form." With this poem, Mina turned from her engagement with the postwar world to the private space of formal perfection.

Unlike their expatriate counterparts, the Italian literati were still enmeshed in the consequences of the war. Since Marinetti's defeat in the 1919 elections, his alliance with Mussolini had frayed; although he had published a political program the following year, the Futurists were no longer at the forefront of radical struggle. Marinetti had recently quit the Fascist Party to devote himself to his writing and his young wife, a decision which earned the scorn of his former allies. Papini had long since made a strategic withdrawal from public life and adopted the stance of the former atheist turned believer. With the 1921 publication of his life of Christ (it would be translated into twenty-five languages), his political fortune was assured. Having settled the score with Marinetti by rewriting the history of Futurism to his advantage, Papini was enjoying his status as "the greatest national genius of Italy"—in the words of his translator, Emanuel Carnevali. And having finally overcome the stigma of his lowly origins, Papini was on the way to becoming one of Fascism's best-known intellectuals.

In November, when it was clear that Mussolini could no longer be ignored, Mina returned to Paris, motivated as much by her dislike of Florence as by Italy's turn toward Fascism. There she renewed her friendship with Gertrude Stein and collaborated with Djuna on an interview with Joyce for *Vanity Fair*. They recognized the writer as soon as he approached their table at the Deux Magots: the man who, in Djuna's eyes, "has been more crucified on his sensibilities than any writer of our age" bore himself with a discouraged air. No ordinary sadness, she observed, his was "the weariness of one self-subjected to the creation of an over abundance in the limited." While Joyce talked, Mina drew him with his head resting on his hand, the profile pose that Djuna thought his "most characteristic . . . turned farther away than disgust and not so far as death."

Mina continued to draw as they discussed the "great talkers"—who spoke the language of Sterne, Swift, and Oscar Wilde, Joyce explained, as if they were schoolgirls. Over time, she and Joyce would themselves speak "of rivers and of religions," of churches, music, and women, Djuna recalled. "About women he seems a bit disinterested," she noted, adding slyly, "Were I vain I should say he is afraid of them, but I am certain he is only a little skeptical of their existence." Just the same, Joyce was a good companion, "for he is simple, a scholar, and sees nothing objectionable in human beings if they will only remain in place."

Contrary to expectations, Joyce was proving "the most gentle of geniuses," Mina observed in a letter to Nellie Grandjean. Now that *Ulysses* was to appear in France, its author was the "God of Paris." She had seen a good deal of him, she went on, and had "a most happy time." Moreover, Gertrude Stein, for whom Mina expressed equal admiration, had been "very admiring of Cravan." It did not take much skill at reading between the lines to see that to Mina's mind, her place was with the geniuses, and in Paris.

Yet her plans for the future were still uncertain. On her return to Florence she saw that she had bungled the opportunity for a rapprochement with the Grandjeans, who had been expecting her to bring Fabienne to Lausanne for the Christmas holidays. There, she was to have met her mother-in-law at last, as well as Fabian's brother Otho and his wife, Olga Sacharoff, but she had returned to Italy too late to make the trip. Hoping that her mother-in-law would be understanding, Mina wrote to ask whether Otho and Olga might find her a room in Barcelona, where they were living for the winter months—since she hoped to make their acquaintance while preparing a set of drawings for an exhibition. Fabienne liked to draw, she added, and had "an excellent musical ear like her dear dear Father."

Far from endearing her to Nellie Grandjean, this letter speeded up the process of estrangement already in the making. Nellie concluded that Mina was impulsive and pretentious, as demonstrated in her remarks about the geniuses. Furthermore, her letters—written in pencil on whatever came to hand—were incoherent, and her plans for the future illogical. Requests for help with lodgings only proved the point: she was becoming a burden. When her mother-in-law declined to come to her assistance, Mina's desperation grew. McAlmon had said that the exchange rate in Germany and Austria was so favorable that the longer one stayed in these countries, the cheaper life became. The household would remove to Austria for the summer, she announced; her income would go farther there while she decided what to do next. Unaware that Cravan's mother had turned against her, she wrote again to ask whether Otho, now relocated in Paris, might find her an apartment. After some time, she understood that despite the Grandjeans' affection for Fabienne, no help was forthcoming from Lausanne.

II

Toward the end of spring, Mina traveled with Joella, Fabienne, and Giulia to Mariahilfburg, a pilgrimage center near Vienna. Refreshed by the mountain air, Mina read, watched the throngs of pilgrims in their special crowns, and played with Fabi while Joella went mountain climbing. Although prices were lower in Austria than in Italy, they kept rising from one week to the next. Those who held hard currency, pounds or dollars, found that they could live well, for the time being.

Mina decided to take Joella in hand. Her outlook was old-fashioned, Mina kept saying, as if this were Joella's fault. During her mother's absences, she had been brought up by the servants and the English residents. At fifteen Joella was an innocent *jeune fille* who soaped herself under her nightgown when bathing, as Giulia had taught her. She liked order in her life and hoped to return to Florence to continue at the *ginnasio*, where she was learning Latin and would soon begin Greek. In Mina's view, her plans were hopelessly bourgeois. Exposure to genius would provide the antidote.

In this spirit Mina had Joella read to her after their daily walks and told her to ask the meanings of unfamiliar English terms (Joella's first language was Italian). After an hour of reading John Addington Symonds's *Renaissance in Italy*, Mina scolded her for not inquiring about the vocabulary. When Joella said that she understood the hard words because they resembled Latin, Mina was astonished and perhaps a little jealous; *she* had not studied the classics. Joella should learn Russian, Mina insisted; "come the revolution," she could make herself understood. But it was pointless to prolong her studies past fifteen, the age when *she* had left school. Men did not marry intellectual women, she went on, and in any case, no one looked her best in glasses.

In Mina's haphazard manner, she was providing Joella with a new way of looking at life. That summer they spent some weeks in Vienna because Mina wanted to see Scofield Thayer, who was undergoing psychoanalysis with Freud.* (Oppressed by his responsibilities at *The Dial*, Thayer had considered hiring her as his aide.) Until his breakdown in 1925, Thayer's enthusiasm for the new German literature would result in the magazine's featuring such outstanding but little-known writers as Thomas Mann, Arthur Schnitzler, and Hugo von Hofmannsthal, as well as the equally unfamiliar artists Gustav Klimt, Oskar Kokoschka, and Egon Schiele. His co-editor complained about printing so much "Teutonic stuff," however, and the New York staff rejected an essay that Thayer had obtained from Freud.

Mina was eager to meet the great man. When she and Joella joined Thayer at the theater one evening, they were introduced to his other guests, Freud and his daughter Anna. Possibly at Thayer's suggestion, Freud agreed to sit for his portrait. Mina drew him in profile, against a black background from which his forceful head emerged as if disembodied—a portrait of pure thought. Freud was—one gathers from the portrait's em-

---

* Thayer, a wealthy Harvard aesthete with socialist leanings, lived apart from his wife, whose love affair with E. E. Cummings he had encouraged; during this period, Thayer courted Marianne Moore without success. Thayer suffered from paranoia and psychosexual problems that caused his relations with women to founder.

phasis on his "Semitic" profile—the type of intellectual Mina associated with Judaism. Some years later, she observed that there had been two messiahs, one Christian and the other Jewish. "When the Gentile world required a Saviour they nailed up the Christ," she wrote. "When it required a second Saviour to counteract the effects of the first, Freud was at its service."

Although Mina did not pursue the idea of treatment, her meetings with Freud had an impact. They discussed her belief that each person repeated an expressive gesture in art, as in life: one wonders whether she saw her reaching for the unattainable stained glass as her own. While Freud sat for his portrait, he studied her stories—whose veiled autobiography no doubt revealed her preoccupations. After reading "Hush Money," the story of David's reconciliation with his dying father, Freud pronounced it "analytic"—ambiguous praise in that it implies a tendency to overintellec-tualize. Mina's choice of this story suggests that she saw Freud as a father figure, a counterweight to the claims of Christian correctness. "A Jew today wears his intellect as the Christian his coronet," she later observed.

After Vienna she went to Berlin. Among her friends from New York, Djuna, Marsden Hartley, and McAlmon had all described the city as one where the arts were as lively as the nightlife and the cost of living negligible. The young writer Matthew Josephson had settled in Berlin because he could afford to live in a palatial apartment and publish *Broom*—by the autumn, he had replaced Kreymborg—for practically nothing. Moreover, the atmosphere was wildly stimulating, a mix of postwar reconstruction and vibrant modernity. Even more than Paris, Berlin was the place everyone was watching, "some with dread, some with hope," the Russian émigré Ilya Ehrenburg recalled, because it seemed that "in that city the fate of Europe for the next decades was being decided."

Mina had also heard of a nearby institution for young ladies that might cure Joella of her provinciality. After the war Isadora Duncan's sister Elizabeth had opened a school in Potsdam, where her pupils studied Duncan technique in the hope of joining Isadora's company. But Joella was far from enthusiastic; she had made plans to stay with friends from Florence on her return. Mina was adamant. She would spend the winter nearby, in Berlin, and Joella would visit on the weekends, "to see how the mad people lived." Mina enrolled Joella at the Duncan school, installed Giulia and Fabienne nearby, and set out to explore Berlin.

There, people spoke of the abortive 1918 German revolution as if it had just occurred. For a few months, when it had looked as though Germany might go the way of Russia, many artists and intellectuals had supported the revolution, some even going so far as to back the extreme left wing's efforts to sabotage the new republic. By February 1919, however, after the assassinations of the "Bolsheviks" Rosa Luxemburg and Karl Liebknecht, the national assembly had convened at Weimar and founded a new government. The political turmoil of the past four years had affected the artists, who, like their counterparts in Russia, were trying to adapt modern forms to postwar society. Already the arts school in Weimar was being reorganized along more egalitarian lines. While the fine and applied arts would receive equal emphasis, both would be subordinated to the idea of rebuilding implicit in the school's new name, Bauhaus: the cathedral of socialism, it would offer technical training and artistic inspiration.

This utopian vision had not yet influenced the appearance of Berlin. The city's depressing slums, peeling façades, and gray stone walls, along with its omnipresent advertisements and garish electric signs, gave it the look of "Everyman's City of modern times," Josephson recalled. Yet despite its ugliness, visitors all felt the "dreadful fascination of the place," he noted, since "part of the population [was] half-famished, the other wallowing in fleshpots." The economic crisis resulting from the Versailles Treaty's harsh terms had completed the process of social upheaval begun during the war. Everything, and everyone, was for sale. Prostitutes of both sexes, transvestites, and traders in cocaine or contraband haunted the streets. The city, Josephson wrote, "showed us human creatures with souls laid bare, a people brutalized, as in the steel-hard drawings of George Grosz, or utterly forlorn, as in the pictures of Käthe Kollwitz." This desperate situation had already inspired much fiercely expressive political art.

By 1922, German artists were addressing themselves to the problems of postwar society, and suggestions were circulating among the foreigners to form an "international organization of creative persons of revolutionary outlook." Left-leaning Germans talked of setting up a constructivist international in Berlin, where an exhibition of the new Russian art was drawing crowds. Following their summer encampment in the Tyrol, Tzara and the Dadaists had met with the exiled Russian abstractionists in Weimar. It was a time when creative persons of progressive outlook could envision themselves, and their art, making a difference, when intellectuals identified the transformative power of the imagination with the process of revolution.

At the same time, Berlin was also full of foreigners taking advantage of the nightlife, the inflation, and the air of perpetual crisis. An international crowd gathered each night at the Romanisches Kaffeehaus on the Kurfürstendamm, Josephson noted, people "with long hair, short hair, or shaven skulls, in rags or in furs." (George Grosz often came dressed as a cowboy.) In different corners of the vast café, one heard conversations in Russian, Hungarian, or American English. From there, groups went on to drink cheap champagne at garishly decorated nightclubs, where young women writhed to imitation jazz. Mina tired of the nightlife, Josephson recalled, unlike McAlmon, who was bent on experiencing everything.

At the opposite end of the spectrum from McAlmon's crowd were the political exiles. Among the most famous of the many anarchists, Bolsheviks, and socialists were Emma Goldman and Alexander Berkman, who had left Russia the year before and settled in Berlin. Goldman was working on the book she intended to call "My Two Years in Russia"—which would appear the following year, to her dismay, as *My Disillusionment in Russia*. Her disillusionment was personal as well as political; she was not only depressed but felt that she could no longer rely on Berkman. Despite Mina's sympathy, their acquaintance did not develop into friendship, perhaps because Mina found Goldman, and Bolsheviks in general, lacking in humor. ("Moral, social, and intellectual supremacy is the sense of humour," she insisted.) And when Joella expressed her admiration of Berkman, Mina retorted, "The only man you like is a murderer!"

The most noticeable group of foreign nationals were the Russians—émigrés who had escaped the revolution as well as a number of Soviet citizens disenchanted with the government's new plans for industrial design. Their names read like a roll call of the Russian avant-garde. The abstract artist Lissitzky was designing Constructivist covers for *Broom*, Kandinsky had stopped in Berlin on his way to the Bauhaus, the writers Ehrenburg and Gorky were in residence, the sculptor Archipenko had opened a drawing class, and the poets Mayakovsky and Marina Tsvetaeva had recently joined the sizable Russian enclave.

The most notorious Russian in Berlin was the poet Sergei Esenin, Isadora Duncan's handsome young husband. Stories about the Duncan-Esenins, as they wished to be called, had acquired the quality of legend. The previous year, at the invitation of the Commissar of Education, Isadora had founded the school of her dreams in Moscow. Russia was the only nation that cared about art, she insisted; there she had put behind her the "Inequality, Injustice and the brutality of the Old World." By the end of 1921, however, the Russians could no longer afford to support her school. Isadora had stayed in Moscow nonetheless, because she had fallen in love with Esenin.

Despite the differences in age (Isadora was forty-five and Esenin twenty-seven), upbringing (his family were peasants), and worldly experience (she believed in free love; he was, in this respect, more conventional), they had married so that he could accompany her on her next American tour. When Mina arrived in 1922, they were honeymooning at the Adlon, the best hotel in Berlin, and Esenin was living up to his reputation as author of *The Hooligan's Confession*. Although both spouses drank to excess, Esenin's violence alarmed Isadora's friends. But she was so much in love that she forgave him. "He is a genius," she insisted, "and marriage between artists is impossible."

Full of sympathy for Isadora, Mina considered her marriage to Cravan so exceptional that she could not imagine life with another. Shortly after settling in a modest pension, however, she met a young Russian poet in the Duncan-Esenin circle with whom she began to be seen. While nothing is known about this man except that he was desperately poor, it seems possible that in some way he reminded her of Cravan. When they began living together, Joella recalled, some were shocked because of the difference in their ages. (Had they stayed at the Hotel Adlon and lived on the scale of the Duncan-Esenins, this discrepancy would, no doubt, have been excused.) Given what was going on around them, the scandal of their relations was of no great matter. In Mina's view, they could set their own standards. "There are only two kinds of people in society," she observed (echoing Diana in *The Pamperers*), "geniuses and women."

Most foreigners liked being shocking. The Dadaists had directed Josephson to a hotel near the zoo where he and his wife stayed until they discovered that it was a *maison de passe*. Malcolm Cowley, another young American writer in Berlin, enjoyed the hotel's lurid atmosphere so much that he invited friends and acquaintances there to see the looks on their faces. At one of his dinner parties, Mina appeared, "all unsuspecting," Josephson recalled, with "her lovely golden-haired daughter." This "droll" situation, he continued, provided "a bright note for us in the rather grim Berlin scene."

The scene was enlivened by the constant flow of visitors from Paris. So many Americans turned up that it seemed like an artistic migration. Djuna, the American sculptor Thelma Wood, Man Ray's assistant Berenice Abbott, McAlmon's friends from Montparnasse, Heyward and Mariette Mills, and Marsden Hartley, who often appeared in evening dress with an orchid pinned to his lapel, all took up residence at various times. Hartley, a covert homosexual, had abandoned his usual restraint and was "luxuriat[ing] in orchidean emotions," McAlmon noted, but Djuna avoided the city's hectic nightlife, except to store it in her mind as literary material.

With Joella busy at the Duncan school, which included a program of academic studies, Mina settled down to her new routines. After the young Russian poet disappeared from her life as mysteriously as he had entered it, she started drawing classes with Archipenko and began an essay on the significance of Gertrude's prose. Josephson asked her for work for *Broom* —he and his co-editor, Harold Loeb, classed Mina's writing with that of Eliot, Joyce, and Moore—but she told him that she had nothing ready for publication.

Forgoing the aimless nightlife, she often dined with the Josephsons and their guests, young Americans associated with the magazine or visitors from Paris. One evening she met McAlmon's friends Jacques Rigaut and André Germain: Rigaut, a Dadaist dandy, and Germain, the wealthy backer of *La Revue Européenne*, inquired eagerly about Cravan, whose exploits had become legend in Paris. "Mina gave us a fascinating account of this celebrated character," Josephson recalled, "deliver[ing] it in her most studied duchess manner," while in the street young proto-Nazis shouted their determination to "cut the throats of forty million Frenchmen next time." Perhaps her own losses seemed less overwhelming in this crazed atmosphere.

Increasingly, the Cravan legend served to screen her emotions and define her public persona. "Der Blinde Junge" ("The Blind Youth"), a poem from this period, evokes the subject of loss with much bitterness. As in her other postwar poems, it is addressed obliquely—in this case through the image of a blind street musician in Vienna. The opening lines assess the youth as if he symbolized a culture devastated by its own folly:

> The dam Bellona
> littered
> her eyeless offspring
> Kriegsopfer
> upon the pavements of Vienna
>
> Sparkling precipitate
> the spectral day
> involves
> this visionless obstacle
>
> this slow blind face
> pushing its virginal nonentity
> against the light
>
> Pure purposeless eremite
> of centripetal sentience
>
> Upon the carnose horologe of the ego
> the vibrant tendon index moves not
>
> since the black lightning desecrated
> the retinal altar
>
> Void and extinct
> this planet of the soul
> strains from the craving throat
> in static flight upslanting

Still other losses are hidden in this portrait. The poet's own sense of deprivation hides in the figure of war as a cruel mother ("The dam Bellona") and in the youth's "craving," with its echo of Cravan's name. To varying degrees, all were casualties of war, or *Kriegsopfer*.

Refusing the comforts of self-pity nonetheless, the poem, whose German title suggests its precise time and place, trains its scorn on those responsible for the losses. As in other poems energized by her contempt for society, "Der Blinde Junge" ends with a change of tone: while its conclusion reads like satire, the poem gestures at the spiritual realm. The youth exemplifies holiness defiled—his skull, the "planet of his soul," his blindness, the "desecrat[ion"] of his "retinal altar"; moreover, meaning glimmers through his broken music:

Listen!
illuminati of the coloured earth
How this expressionless "thing"
blows out damnation and concussive dark

Upon a mouth-organ

The geniuses of Europe—its "illuminati"*—are summoned to an unlikely church, whose music arises from a lowly harmonica. The poem challenged readers in its time and is still difficult in ours, no doubt because satire and elegy assume different emotions, yet here combine to suggest the extremity of the period and the hope of some larger vision.

Finding inspiration in unexpected places, Mina also completed an essay on the spiritual significance of Gertrude's prose—her *Geography and Plays* had just been published with an introduction by Sherwood Anderson. "The work of Gertrude Stein consists in a rebuilding, an entirely new recasting of life," Anderson explained, praising her linguistic vigor at a time when words were devalued. But he said little about her building materials, nor did he discuss the dismantling of syntax, punctuation, and sentence structure that preceded these recastings. This work, and its implications, became Mina's subject.

In her view, Gertrude's reconstructions comprised a philosophy of consciousness as revolutionary as Bergson's. Recalling "the austere verity" of her prewar prose, which reminded Mina of Ecclesiastes, she noted that her friend had moved from this first phase, the analysis of " 'Being' as the absolute occupation," to a more "impressionistic" one, which involved a telescoping of time and space, subject and object. In Mina's reading of "A Sweet Tail, Gypsies" (included in *Geography and Plays*) Gertrude depicted a gathering of gypsies as Picasso might have done, by breaking up the pictorial planes and emphasizing each detail. Through this process, she gave "fresh significance to her words, as if she had got them out of bed early in the morning and washed them in the sun." Her friend had once described the goal of Cubism, Mina went on, as the process of "deconstruction preparatory to complete reconstruction of the objective." Gertrude's prose enacted this same process, which could be "disconcerting" to the reader. Although "one had to go into training to get Gertrude Stein," Mina concluded, the rewards were worth the mental push-ups.

In this perceptive study of Gertrude's writing, Mina was also expressing her own ideas about modernism. Its intent, she wrote, was "to track intellection back to the embryo," to try to know "what would we know about anything" when seeing it for the first time. The attainment of such

---

* The term "illuminati" was used by a number of unorthodox groups (including Freemasons and Rosicrucians) whose claims to spiritual enlightenment earned the condemnation of religious institutions like the Catholic Church. In Mina's usage, it suggests that the enlightened are, paradoxically, blind to common suffering—a theme she would increasingly take up.

knowledge had long been the goal of religion, she believed, but given "the bankruptcy of mysticism," the search "had devolved upon abstract art." Modernism was both a way of treating subject matter and a philosophy— "a prophet crying in the wilderness of stabilized culture that humanity is wasting its aesthetic time."

What is most striking in Mina's account of modernism is her belief that the postwar world needed a democratic approach to art, one that took beauty out of the museum and made it available to all. "Modernism has democratized the subject matter and la belle matière of art," she noted. "Through cubism," she went on, "the newspaper has assumed an aesthetic quality, through Cézanne a plate has become more than something to put an apple upon, Brancusi has given an evangelistic import to eggs, and Gertrude Stein has given us the Word, in and for itself." In this quasi-theological view, a democratized culture was indispensable to the work of reconstruction. But in 1922, few could devote themselves to Gertrude's and Mina's grail—"the Word, in and for itself."

By November, after his triumphant march on Rome, Mussolini had formed a new government. In Berlin even the most apolitical foreigners found their lives changed when the French occupied the Ruhr Valley to protest the Germans' cessation of war payments, which had the immediate effect of cutting off coal supplies. "One becomes peculiarly sensitive to political developments when, as a result of them, a boiler blows up in the cellar and central heating is off for the rest of the winter," Josephson observed dryly. What was more, inspired no doubt by the Fascists, bands of hooligans and proto-Nazis had taken to venting their rage both day and night. The outside world no longer felt safe.

One by one, Mina's friends were leaving Berlin. While the Duncan-Esenins had gone to the United States, most people talked of returning to France: the political situation was stable there despite the higher cost of living. Even for those who had enjoyed the all-night parties, random affairs, and drug-induced dreams, McAlmon noted, "the innumerable beggars, paralytics, shell-shocked soldiers, and starving people of good family became at last too violent a depressant." Having received a settlement of seventy thousand dollars from Lord Ellerman, he was ready to begin his publishing career in Paris. His new press, to be called Contact Editions, would begin with a book of Mina's poems, provided she put them in order. In the meantime, he would travel.

While McAlmon could go where he pleased, the map of Mina's future—her place on the "colored earth"—could be redrawn only in Paris. There she would be in the company of friends, her poems would appear, and she could become reacquainted with the painters she had known in Montparnasse and through the Salon d'Automne, where she might show her new drawings. Anyone who mattered was already there—Brancusi, Duchamp, and Man Ray, Gertrude and Joyce, Pound and Tzara, and she could expect a welcome from Jacques Rigaut and André Germain, as well as from Cravan's friends. According to Josephson, recently returned from France, Cravan was the idol of the former Dadaists, who, under the command of André Breton, were calling themselves Surrealists and delving into their unconscious minds for the sake of art. The Josephsons would soon be leaving; *Broom*'s endowment had dried up, and they were tired of living "as if the sheriff were expected to come in at any moment and foreclose the mortgage."

Mina's path was clear. With Mussolini in power and the house in Stephen's hands, there was no going back to Florence. Leaving Joella at school and Fabienne with Giulia, in the spring of 1923 Mina followed her friends to Paris, where, Josephson recalled, they were surprised to see people smiling.

16

Being Geniuses Together

(PARIS, 1923–27)

IN 1923 MINA'S POEMS traveled more than she did. With her manuscript in his valise, McAlmon raced from Venice to Rome to Capri, where he completed the novel in which she appears as the dispirited Gusta Rolph. After a sojourn in Florence, he stopped to see Ezra Pound in Rapallo—with her poems still in his luggage. McAlmon's devotion to her manuscript no doubt impressed another of Pound's guests, Ernest Hemingway, whose own suitcase, containing almost everything he had written that year, had been left at a Paris train station. When McAlmon offered to publish his remaining stories, Hemingway declared himself "pleased to be part of a series of books by such expatriates as Marsden Hartley, Mina Loy, and William Carlos Williams." McAlmon's plan—to "bring out works by various writers who seem not likely to be published by other publishers"—was realized at last with the appearance of Hartley's verse, Hemingway's stories, a book of prose and poetry by Williams, and Mina's first volume.

I

The manuscript that traveled around Europe with McAlmon was published as *Lunar Baedecker* (with his spelling error a part of its identity). The title evoked the old-fashioned, opinionated, and reliable Baedeker, the handbook familiar to all European travelers. Whatever country it described, Baedeker's reassuring format—red cloth jacket, marbled edges, cream pages, and elegant maps—implied that one was in good hands: its authoritative tone lulled the traveler into accepting the author's tastes and prejudices. Mina's addition to the series charted the landscape of the artistic imagination, where the sights were the commonplaces of a tradition that, like Baedeker, predated the century.

Yet *Lunar Baedecker*'s perspective was self-consciously modern. Mina had divided her poetry into two sections, the first entitled "Poems 1921–1922," the second "Poems 1914–1915." The book's internal structure evoked the distance she had covered. Judging as much by what was omitted as by what was included in her guide to aestheticism, she preferred to forget some of these journeys. Of the sixty-two poems published in the past ten years, a small but distinctive oeuvre of the kind T. S. Eliot had been waiting for, she included only half. Marianne Moore's well-known caveat "Omissions are not accidents" comes to mind when one realizes that Mina omitted ten early poems and twenty-one "Love Songs." In writing the history of her imagination, she was also revising the past.

The volume and first section both begin with the title poem's introduction to the moon of literary tradition—a figure "pocked with personification." The poem's mannered tone, vocabulary, and sound patterns underscore its critique of the decadent tradition from which it arises:

> *A silver Lucifer*
> *serves*
> *cocaine in cornucopia*
>
> *To some somnambulists*
> *of adolescent thighs*
> *draped*
> *in satirical draperies*
>
> *Peris in livery*
> *prepare*
> *Lethe*
> *for posthumous parvenues*

At the same time, "Lunar Baedecker" deploys its short, jazzy stanzas in a recognizably modern landscape—amid the "Delirious Avenues" and "Stellectric signs" of a metropolis. In the city's glaring light, both the moon and the poetic tradition over which it presides are passé:

> *A flock of dreams*
> *browse on Necropolis*
>
> *From the shores*
> *of oval oceans*
> *in the oxidised Orient*

> *Onyx-eyed Odalisques*
> *and ornithologists*
> *observe*
> *the flight*
> *of Eros obsolete*

It was an arresting start for a volume proposing itself as a guide to the modernist mindscape.

To the young American poets who had formed their taste by reading *Others*, *Lunar Baedecker* was a revelation. Yvor Winters found in its title poem an "ominous grandeur"—the result, he thought, of its litany of images "frozen into epigrams." One handled such poetry, he added, as one would a rosary in which the string was frayed but the beads "spectacular." From Winters's response to her poems, it is clear that while *we* might attend to the poem's "spectacular" verbal surface, his generation read differently. Attuned to a mental universe inhabited by Heaven and Hell, God and Lucifer, they saw in Mina's rosary a yearning for spiritual solace.

In this reading, each poem was linked to the next in a devotional pattern. After "Lunar Baedecker" came "Apology of Genius," a poem that was "in itself a proof of genius," according to Winters—"a genius that rises from a level of emotion and attitude which is as nearly common human territory as one can ever expect to find in a poet." Whether her poetic subject was understood as the soul or as the subconscious, he went on, one could not help noticing in her treatment of it "a strange feeling for the most subterranean of human reactions." Read this way, "Apology of Genius" resembled "a stone idol become animate." Of the book as a whole, he concluded, "She moves like one walking through granite instead of air."

Writing in the United States, Winters did not observe that *Lunar Baedecker* had cultural aims as well. If the book was a rosary, it was also a series of transits through the stages of an argument. The next poem, "Joyce's Ulysses," treats its subject as a test case for the stand taken in "Apology of Genius." The 1922 Paris publication of *Ulysses* had been an event of great significance, celebrated by English and French literati alike. But while Mina's tribute to Joyce signaled her support, the poem's prominence in *Lunar Baedecker* also aligned her work with his. Both were eccentric to English tradition by virtue of birth and exile, and Joyce was a kindred spirit, whose novel fired "pandemoniums / of Olympian prose" at "England / the sadistic mother":

> *Hurricanes*
> *of reasoned musics*
> *reap the uncensored earth*

323

The loquent consciousness
of living things
pours in torrential languages

The elderly colloquists
the Spirit and the Flesh
are out of tongue — — —

As *Ulysses* reveals the mystery of "The word made flesh," its author becomes godlike, at once the "rejector—recreator" of language and the illuminator of European culture's "sub rosâ."

This "sub rosâ"—with its echoes of the subconscious, the improper, the illicit—undergoes a witty transformation in the volume's fourth poem, "English Rose." A rose "of arrested impulses," this blossom clings to "the divine right of self assertion":

Early English everlasting
  Rose
    paradox-Imperial
trimmed with some travestied flesh
tinted with bloodless duties   dewed
with Lipton's teas
and grimed with crack-packed
herd-housing
petalling
the prim-gilt
penetralia

The rose, of course, bears an unmistakable resemblance to Mina's image for her mother, whose domestic sway is compared to that of the British Empire. "English Rose" also relates the Empire's decline from glory, its shriveling into a "Conservative Rose / storage / of British Empire-made pot-pourri / of dry dead men." In this tart satire of her mother's "self pruning" and her country's "paralysis," Mina dismissed an England "whirling itself / deliriously around the unseen / Bolshevik."

Alternative values are proposed in the first section's remaining poems on society's rejects, its freaks, outcasts, and artists. Included in this section are three poems—"Der Blinde Junge," "Crab-Angel," and "Ignoramus"— in which compassion overlaps with rage at a society that will not recognize their quest for transcendence. In the same spirit, Mina's poetic tributes to Poe, Brancusi, and Wyndham Lewis gesture toward an elsewhere within artistic form. "The Starry Sky," a poem written like a meditation on a painting by Lewis, ushers the reader into "the cyclorama of space" inhabited by his abstractions:

Enviable immigrants
into the pure dimension
immune   serene
devourers of the morning stars of Job

Jehovah's seven days
Err in your silent entrails
Of geometric Chimeras

The Nirvanic snows
Drift
To sky worn images

Like Lewis's painting, the poem restages Genesis in the fourth dimension—the "austere theatre of the Infinite."

In a prescient essay on modernist abstraction composed at this time, Mina noted her belief that what mattered was not the subject of a work but the "map of the artist's genius"—the design giving the poem, sculpture, or painting its "singularity." Each formal creation, she argued, had within it an intelligence, its "God in the machine." Just as the compositions of Joyce and Lewis exteriorized their mental maps, her poetic homages attempted to convey the "purely metaphysical structure" of their creations.

If "Poems 1921–1922" charted the shapes of modern consciousness through its own rejections and re-creations, "Poems 1914–1915" outlined the personal itinerary that had preceded this map-making. *Lunar Baedecker's* progress backward through the remaining "Love Songs" to the few prewar poems still included drew on Mina's poetic record as an archive, exhuming some poems and leaving others underground. Compared with the 1917 "Songs to Joannes," *Lunar Baedecker's* version (retitled "Love Songs") is a résumé. Most references to Italy have been omitted, as well as clues to the lovers' identities. The tone is detached, the emphasis placed not on their skirmishes but on the theme of romantic illusion. In the same revisionary spirit, the second grouping of earlier work included only two Parisian poems, three "Italian Pictures," "Sketch of a Man on a Platform," and "Parturition." (The other Italian poems, especially those inspired by her engagement with Futurism, were judged unworthy of inclusion.) The volume ends with the allegory of the poet's rebirth in "Parturition." With this curious conclusion, Mina's guide to the modernist imagination circled back to its beginnings.

II

By the time *Lunar Baedecker* appeared, Mina was forty. It no doubt seemed odd to find herself living in a small apartment a few doors down the street from the rue Campagne Première studio she had shared with Stephen twenty years earlier. But if the street was full of painful memories—her marriage, the death of Oda Janet—now, even more than before the war, Montparnasse was the nexus of artistic energies.

Mina returned to Paris in 1923 to find it full of Americans. Expatriates of long standing surveyed the newly arrived from the terraces of the Dôme and the Rotonde, the cafés at the hub of Montparnasse that served as mailing address and social center. At first she stayed at the Hôtel Namur in the rue Delambre, up the street from the Dôme and near her first Paris lodgings with Eva and Mrs. Knight. (Because of the postwar housing shortage, foreigners generally lived in hotels until an apartment came their way.) Man Ray had lived and worked in one of the rue Delambre hotels until his success as a photographer allowed him to move to a studio on the rue Campagne Première, and when McAlmon was in town, he stayed there because of the location's proximity to the cafés and his tendency to pack his bags at any moment. (McAlmon behaved, Joyce noted, as if he was always about to "run up to Iceland or down to Zanzibar for a few minutes.")

For writers with children or for those whose lives were less volatile than McAlmon's, hotel life was unsatisfactory: it offered no facilities for housekeeping. Expatriate society was divided into those who had apartments and those who did not. The few that became available were relet even before their tenants had vacated. People without connections were at a loss, since news of vacancies often came through acquaintances. Through Man Ray or perhaps Joyce, Mina sublet the tiny rue Campagne Première apartment used intermittently by the Irish writer James Stephens, and soon thereafter found an apartment of her own at number 11.

The building, an unimpressive apartment house with mansard windows, was distinguished only by its location halfway between the boulevards Montparnasse and Raspail. Mina's lodgings were next door to Chez Rosalie, the crèmerie that had inspired her short-lived restaurant scheme. Unlike most places where art students gathered before the war, Rosalie's had survived the area's modernization. The tiled floor, wooden tables and benches, and menu were unchanged. The Italian proprietor, who had been Whistler's model and Modigliani's patron, still cooked for those who liked *cuisine familiale* and not for tourists (a typical menu listed "oeuf mayonnaise," beef stew, and crème caramel). At the other end of the street, near the Raspail Métro station, Man Ray's studio seemed almost luxurious. After photographing Joyce, Stein, Picasso, and Matisse, he had become known as a portraitist of geniuses. His financial success set him apart from his compatriots; he enjoyed the "modern comforts"—a bathroom, heat, and electricity—of the lavishly decorated Art Nouveau building at 31 *bis*, where he worked and lived with the notorious artist's model Kiki.

Relieved to have found shelter near friends, Mina rented her apartment despite its lack of comforts and its wallpaper, an orange pattern with silver moons and green palm trees. What was worse, the owner refused to let her repaper. Once again coaxing the sublime from the ridiculous, she devised a solution to this aesthetic nightmare. After gluing sheets of soft gray paper together, she pinned this floating wall cover to the ceiling and fastened it with blue paper stars. The effect was ethereal, a setting for reverie.

In this dreamy atmosphere, Mina received a shock which plunged her deeper into the melancholy that had shadowed her since the war. Although Giles had written from his new home in Bermuda, Mina refused to answer his letters. He had not written in some time, moreover, because she failed to tell Stephen of her move to Paris. For this reason, a letter informing her of Giles's illness (a rare kind of cancerous growth) arrived with some delay, as did the news of his death at fourteen. Stephen had written to a mutual friend in Florence, who relayed his letter to Paris that autumn. "Tell Dusie, if you ever find out where she is," it read, that Giles "lived finely and died bravely, loved and respected by everybody who had anything to do with him." In his final months, he noted, the boy suffered so from Mina's rejection that he could not write. Giles did not see "why her dislike for me should affect her love for him," Stephen remarked, adding that he planned to put the house up for sale. He could not see living there again.

Mina wired for Joella, who by this time had adapted to life at the Duncan school and was about to leave for London to help open a new branch. At sixteen Joella had developed a practical turn of mind. She looked forward to her new occupation as a gymnastics teacher, the post with which she was to be entrusted. But Mina would not hear of her becoming a teacher; it was an occupation which, in her eyes, doomed one to bourgeois status. She needed her in Paris. They would comfort each other, Joella could study at the Sorbonne, and they would prepare the apartment for Giulia and Fabi, who would follow later.

Mina dealt with her son's death as she had with Cravan's. Her inability fully to acknowledge the loss, let alone her role in Giles's estrangement, allowed her to go on, but although she still looked remarkably youthful, something in her went rigid, Joella thought, expressing itself in recurrent neurasthenia. Any mention of Giles or Cravan could set off an attack of nerves or cause the return of mysterious pains. And while Mina found relief in talks with Mrs. Ramsey, the Christian Science practitioner, she considered the daily lessons "too boring," she told Joella, herself a faithful follower of Science. Sometime later, after reading a letter from a stranger who had written Joella about Giles's last weeks, Mina was so disturbed that she threatened to jump out the window. She turned not to Mrs. Ramsey but to her teenage daughter, on whom she relied as if she were an adult. Her losses had caught up with her, Joella thought. With mixed feelings, she agreed to sleep in Mina's bed to keep her from harming herself.

To the friends who met her in the cafés, bookshops, and expatriate salons, Mina's gaiety of spirit successfully masked her grief. She became an indispensable member of the cosmopolitan set that McAlmon called, with some irony, the geniuses—a group comprised of British and American writers, their French counterparts, and assorted Dadaists or Surrealists. Mina's vivacity was remarked upon by all. To the younger generation she was legendary—"a Juno" to the Surrealist Jacques Baron, "a regal English lady with romance in her eyes" to Glenway Wescott, an American writer who claimed to be half in love with her. Wescott, who listened sympathetically to Mina's accounts of life with Cravan, observed later of his generation and Mina's alike, "We were all bewitched by the forms of fiction."

Except in tête-à-têtes with sympathizers like Wescott or at home, however, she kept her sorrow to herself. During the winter of 1923—a season of modernist reunions—Mina's social calendar was a Baedeker of expatriate Paris. She was, McAlmon recalled, one of the luminaries often seen at Mariette Mills's studio on the rue Boissonade. "When Picabia, Léger, Brancusi, Mina Loy, Marcel Duchamp were there to dinner," he wrote, "there was brighter and more intelligent conversation than one was apt to get elsewhere in Paris." She also dined at Brancusi's, where he cooked peasant-style on a brazier while guests sat on chairs hewn from blocks of wood. One evening, Jane Heap, Margaret Anderson, Tzara, and Mina had themselves photographed with Brancusi to celebrate their reunion as the Paris branch of *The Little Review*. Her old friends Jules Pascin and Hermine David invited her to a banquet for McBride. One of the most extravagant events of the season, it began at Pascin's Montmartre studio, progressed to Montparnasse, and moved eventually to a restaurant near the Bal Bullier—with a variety of spouses, models, and children in tow.

The inner circle met infrequently at such places. Like Mariette Mills, Gertrude Stein entertained at home. Almost as soon as Mina was settled, she called on her old friend, whose Saturday evenings were attracting even greater numbers than before the war. Gertrude observed with characteristic understatement, "We were glad to see Mina whom we had known in Florence." But she was, most likely, even gladder to learn that Mina had written an essay about her. Still bitter about the lack of interest in her work despite the recent publication of *Geography and Plays*, Gertrude had been cultivating the poet Jean Cocteau, who had not, however, replied to her suggestion that he review the book. Given Mina's literary connections, *her* essay on Gertrude might actually appear.

Gertrude was also glad when Mina appeared one Saturday with McAlmon, whose publishing company made him a person of interest. Mina's friends made a favorable impression on each other at first. Gertrude pronounced McAlmon "very mature and very good-looking," while McAlmon, who had been expecting an expatriate Amy Lowell, was surprised to find her "almost shy"—no doubt because he was a publisher. After discussing their mutual passion for Trollope, McAlmon left thinking that "one could become quite fond of Gertrude Stein if she quit being the oracle." Although McAlmon never overcame his wariness around oracles, he agreed to publish *The Making of Americans*, a decision he would regret once Gertrude began interfering in the editorial process. He would prove one of her most astute critics, but Mina, still certain that those who counted were geniuses and women, remained faithful to her belief in the importance of her friend, who was both.

Gertrude was, in Mina's opinion, as central to the spirit of modern literature as Madame Curie to modern science, as she stated in the short poem that accompanied her essay:

> *Curie*
> *of the laboratory*
> *of vocabulary*
> > *she crushed*
> *the tonnage*
> *of consciousness*
> *congealed to phrases*
> > *to extract*
> *a radium of the word*

The poem elevated Gertrude to Mina's pantheon while also hinting that women had much to gain from the explosion of "consciousness / congealed." And more forcefully than her other poems on the subject of genius, it voiced her sense that the aim of modernism was to release this untapped energy.

By 1923 it had become a commonplace to associate the two women's names as exponents of the modern. That autumn, the *New York Tribune* featured Djuna Barnes's drawings of *Three American Expatriates*, Mina, Marsden Hartley, and Gertrude—whom the paper dubbed the "spiritual mother of all the modernists." After meeting Mina at one of Ford Madox Ford's parties, Janet Flanner, *The New Yorker*'s Paris correspondent, dismissed her writing as "Gertrude Steinish." Glenway Wescott, on the other hand, felt honored when Mina not only befriended him but presented him at the rue Fleurus, to Gertrude's approval.

Those who, like McAlmon, failed to grow fond of Gertrude often gravitated to the other leading expatriate center, Sylvia Beach's bookshop and lending library, Shakespeare and Company, on the rue de l'Odéon. There the genius of the house was Gertrude's rival, Joyce. As the library's first annual subscriber, Gertrude had been on cordial terms with Beach and her companion, Adrienne Monnier, whose French bookshop across from Shakespeare and Company drew young French writers, and both women had gone out of their way to introduce her to literary figures like Tzara.

But when *Ulysses* appeared under Beach's imprint, Gertrude informed her that she would not be renewing her subscription.

Despite her ties to Gertrude, Mina remained on excellent terms with Beach—as a subscriber, one of the authors whose books were on display, and a member of the group that Beach called "the Crowd." A brisk, practical woman, Beach responded to Mina's charm. "We had three raving beauties in 'the Crowd,' " she observed in her memoirs, "all in one family, which was not fair." Mina, Joella, and Fabi "were so lovely," she went on, "that they were stared at wherever they went." While Beach thought that "Mina would have been elected the most beautiful of the three" had they been asked to vote, Joyce favored Joella, for her fair complexion and golden hair. Mina "wrote poetry whenever she had time," Beach added in an afterthought.

Implicit in Beach's recollections is the sense that Mina was not a serious writer, an attitude that emerges in her description of Mina's domestic ambience a few years later. "When you went to Mina's apartment you threaded your way past lamp shades that were everywhere," Beach observed. "Her hats were very like her lamp shades," she went on, "or perhaps it was the lamp shades that were like hats." Beach had, nonetheless, put her finger on Mina's problem—on the one hand, the distraction resulting from being doubly gifted; on the other, the need to apply herself despite her scorn for commerce. From her own perspective as a businesswoman, Beach was sympathetic, yet faintly amused by Mina's situation.

It was a short walk from the rue de l'Odéon to the rue Jacob in St.-Germain-des-Prés, where Natalie Barney's salon attracted even more visitors than Shakespeare and Company; there, one had the impression of having gone back to the turn of the century. Although Barney, an American heiress, had presided over her salon since the 1900s, Mina did not make her acquaintance until the 1920s; during her student days, they had moved in different worlds. Natalie had acquired legendary status in prewar French literary circles as Rémy de Gourmont's "Amazone"—the sobriquet alluded to her prowess as an equestrienne while also hinting at her amorous conquests. Barney was frank about being a lesbian, but unlike Stein and Beach, who both maintained monogamous relationships, she behaved like a female Don Juan. She was "charming," Beach recalled, "all dressed in white and with her blond coloring, most attractive." "Many of her sex found her fatally so," she added slyly.

Fond of boasting that she had the most respectable of bad reputations, Natalie was also renowned for her salon. Cocteau, D'Annunzio, Gide, and Rilke had all enjoyed her conversation along with her cook's excellent pastries, and during the twenties many English and Americans—Berenson, Isadora Duncan, Eliot, Hemingway, Fitzgerald, and occasionally Gertrude—were seen mingling with French literary lights at the rue Jacob. Barney, an observer noted, arranged her Friday evenings to illustrate the old-fashioned pact between "elegance and letters." An admirer of Oscar

Wilde, she cared above all for style and enjoyed the company of those who reflected hers back to her. Mina's cultivated manners, accent, and Anglo-Florentine patina appealed to her, as did the story of Cravan, whose status as Wilde's nephew gave Mina added glamour. And with the publication of *Lunar Baedecker*, Mina's reputation was made where Natalie was concerned. Yet despite her prestige, Mina remained, in Natalie's opinion, "an ethereal being, one who was forever distracted from the common lot through her own development and through the shocks she had received."

While Natalie liked people who lived up to their legends, there were those for whom her salon was more apt to provoke giggles. When Sherwood Anderson came to one of her Fridays, he grew increasingly uncomfortable as he watched a number of tall women in monocles reciting verses about love as practiced on the island of Lesbos, where Natalie had tried to found an artists' colony in Sappho's honor. Americans and Parisians alike gossiped about her intimates, who sometimes danced with each other; William Carlos Williams, whom Pound brought to the rue Jacob during a visit to Paris, relished the apocryphal story about a male guest whose response to these women was to exhibit his penis. But if some shunned Natalie because of her reputation, her financial independence allowed her to do as she pleased.

Pound, who was more sophisticated than Williams where sexual mores were concerned, was impressed by Natalie's ability to compose in French as well as her devotion to literature. After attempting to modernize her fin-de-siècle English, he gave up the attempt, because she lacked the discipline to put her prose through the process of revision. Reviewing her *Pensées d'une Amazone* for *The Dial*, he complimented her for publishing "with complete mental laziness a book of unfinished sentences and broken paragraphs which is, on the whole, readable and is interesting as documentary evidence of a specimen liberation." About the time that Mina met her, Pound enlisted Natalie in a scheme called "Bel Esprit." They proposed to offer shares in a venture whose aim it was to relieve writers of financial worries, "a sort of consumers' league to pay for quality rather than quantity in literature." Natalie raised a large sum with the intention of bestowing it upon Eliot and Paul Valéry, but neither was interested. Their effort reinforced Mina's sense that artists deserved the support of the rich, and despite its failure, Natalie's prestige grew among those who saw that she liked being a patron—provided it was with style.

The role of patron could be a thankless one, however, as the novelist Ford Madox Ford discovered. Visiting Paris that autumn, when few outlets for experimental writing appeared with regularity, he concluded that expatriate life could be invigorated by someone with his experience. (Although Heap and Anderson had settled in France, *The Little Review* came out infrequently, *The Dial*'s modernism had limitations, and *Broom* had gone under.) Ford convinced himself that he was the one to "start a centre for the more modern and youthful of the art movements with which in 1923 the city, like an immense seething cauldron, bubbled and overflowed." When John Quinn arrived in October, the brain trust of Anglo-American modernism—Pound, Ford, Joyce, and Quinn—gathered in Pound's studio to discuss the idea of an international monthly under Ford's editorship.

Ford's prospectus announced the new magazine's aims. They were twofold: "the major one, purely literary, conducing to the minor, the disinterestedly social." Like Contact Editions, *The Transatlantic Review* proposed to publish those who confounded the establishment. But it would do so, Ford went on, with the hope of "introducing into international politics a note more genial than that which almost universally prevails." His aim was to point the way toward "a state of things in which it will be considered that there are no English, no French—for the matter of that, no Russian, Italian, Asiatic or Teutonic—Literatures: there will be only Literature." If ever this came to pass, he went on, "we shall have a league of nations no diplomatists shall destroy."

While Ford's idealistic vision of literature's diplomatic mission appealed to the more progressive expatriates, the word went round the cafés that a new magazine was to appear, and what was more, it paid. Writers studied Ford's prospectus as if it were a set of guidelines. After rehearsing his achievements as editor of *The English Review*, where he had published D. G. Rossetti, Henry James, Joseph Conrad, and D. H. Lawrence, Ford explained that his new monthly would feature the moderns, Joyce, Cummings, Eliot, McAlmon, and "Miss Mina Loy." And he had "no party leanings" apart from sympathy for a view "so fantastically old fashioned as to see no salvation save in the feudal system as practised in the fourteenth century—or in such Communism as may prevail a thousand years hence."

Despite Ford's commitment to experimentation, his literary program was as undefined as his politics. "Preliminary Number," a collection of the kinds of writing likely to appear in the review, was distributed about the same time as Ford's brochure. Although it began defiantly with four uncapitalized and unpunctuated poems by E. E. Cummings (his name had not yet shed its capitals), a footnote stated sheepishly that while the editor did not object to poems with initial capitals, "none has however either reached him or attracted his attention of late." To suggest the sort of verse that might attract his attention, the "Preliminary Number" included two of Pound's Cantos and a new poem of Mina's entitled "Marble":

> *Greece has thrown   white shadows*
> *sown*
> *their eyeballs with oblivion*
>
> *A flock of stone*
> *Gods*
> *perched upon pedestals*

> *A populace*
> *of athlete lilies*
> *of the galleries*
>
> *scoop the façades of space*
> *with spiral curves*
> *of idol substance*
> *in the silence*
>
> *A colonnade*
> *Apollo haunts Apollo*
> *with the shade*
> *of a lost hand*

Although unpunctuated, "Marble" seemed more accessible than Cummings's poems, since it alluded to art of the kind that one could see at the Louvre. Yet a careful reader could have noticed in "Marble" the cold beauty that Winters had discerned in "Lunar Baedecker." Once again, Mina moved through her thoughts as if walking through granite; like the gods on their pedestals, her images had turned to stone. The poem implied an emotional impasse. For this reason, perhaps, it was not reprinted in the magazine's first issue.

Ford's editorial decisions did not limit his social relations. Mina often joined him at the review's Thursday teas on the Ile St.-Louis, where she met the flocks of admiring writers who climbed the rickety stairs to the balcony of the barnlike vault Ford shared with the printer William Bird. Since Ford liked to encourage the young, his Thursdays were informal affairs where anyone might show up. Charmed by the old-fashioned manners of the young English poet Basil Bunting, Ford's overworked and underpaid assistant, Mina urged him to take his poetry seriously. The crowds were even greater at Ford's studio on the boulevard Arago. "In Montparnasse, if you gave a party," recalled his companion, the artist Stella Bowen, "you could not hope to know more than half the people who came."

Mina brought Joella to these gatherings in the belief that she furthered her daughter's education by introducing her to geniuses. Social graces could be acquired in cafés and cocktail parties just as well as in Florence, she explained. One should know how to talk to all levels of society. Within a short time Joella knew everyone—from Man Ray and Kiki to Pound, McAlmon, Gertrude and Alice, Brancusi, Ford, and Hemingway, whose newborn baby, Bumby, she was taken to admire. Observing Joella's poise at one of his Thursdays, Ford said that she must have her own "at home" when she grew up, but McAlmon, who also thought her one of the Crowd's beauties, noted her belief that few of them "were getting any satisfaction out of being 'intellectual.' "

Joella was determined to avoid the self-inflicted suffering that seemed to her to shape the lives of her mother and her mother's friends. Most of them failed to understand that strength of character mattered more in life than being "intellectual" or "amusing," she later reflected. At the time she was chiefly annoyed that Mina had brought her to Paris under false pretenses: she was not to study at the Sorbonne after all. Feeling rebellious, she scanned the want ads, but soon understood that while she was willing to work, she lacked qualifications. What was worse, Mina would not hear of her daughter seeking employment. (When Mariette Mills suggested that Joella learn typing, she protested that no child of hers would become a secretary.)

Mina was bringing up Joella as if she herself were her own mother. Despite her lectures on the need to be "modern," the contradictions of her upbringing had emerged in her attitude toward the next generation. Mina explained sexual matters without embarrassment, yet told Joella that while she wanted her to understand the sexual banter that prevailed in their Crowd, she was not to let this knowledge show. In her "dowager duchess manner," Mina warned Joella against the French and the Italians—seducers all—and insisted that despite their friendship with the Joyces and her own poem on *Ulysses*, she was not to read that "immoral" book. Joella was to remain a *jeune fille*, make a good marriage, and provide for Mina in her old age.

The examples of marriage one saw in their Crowd were less than reassuring. If, as people whispered, McAlmon's had never been consummated, he made up for his disappointment—with both men and women. And despite Pascin's determination to keep Hermine David from divorcing him over his relations with their friend Lucie Krogh, Hermine spent many afternoons at Mina's in tears. Of the younger generation, Laurence Vail had just married an American heiress named Peggy Guggenheim. Having satirized the craze for wish fulfillment in *What D'You Want?*, Vail found some of his own fulfilled, since Peggy was both wealthy and indulgent about his friendships with women like Mina and Djuna, who, he insisted, would set a good example for his bride.

But the Vails spent much of their time at drunken parties, and while Peggy looked elegant in her Poiret gowns, Laurence claimed to despise her for being middle class and Jewish. At first Peggy accepted his view of her limitations along with his plans for her income. Since she had no talent of her own, he insisted, she should subsidize those who did: her protégés were to include *The Little Review*, the photographer Berenice Abbott, Emma Goldman, Djuna Barnes, and Mina.

Whenever the Vails tired of Paris, they asked friends to join them in the country. Mina spent most of the summer of 1923 in their Normandy villa, along with Peggy's cousin Harold Loeb, Man Ray and Kiki, and Laurence's sister Clotilde and her lover, Louis Aragon. Two years later, Peggy bought a house in the South of France in the village of Prasmousquier (her mother called it "Promiscuous"), whose literary associations—Cocteau had lived there with his lover Raymond Radiguet—gave the house cachet. That summer Mina and the girls were among Peggy's first guests. Mina amused herself by painting her bedroom walls with a fresco of dancing lobsters and mermaids but dwelled on her unhappiness since Cravan's disappearance.

As a marriage, the Vails' was a model of what not to do. Peggy kept checking her accounts as if she had to watch every penny, while Laurence complained of her stinginess. And like Mina, he loved to contradict people. "When you walk into a room," he insisted, "*always* disagree": a contrarian attitude made one more "amusing." While he enjoyed the company of artistic women, he saw his wife as a *tabula rasa* in need of instruction and, more often than not, an "idiot." Vail's cruelty was, moreover, an attitude common in the Crowd toward those whose lack of verbal agility made them seem "heavy," or "not one of us."

At this time, Vail was composing *Murder! Murder!* a *roman à clef* in which Mina, or some aspects of her, appears as Miriam Oon, Peggy as Polly, and Vail as the aptly named Martin Asp. Miriam is an "intelligent, intolerant, tall" woman who had once been "sympathetic" toward Martin but whose eyes have lately narrowed with "suppressed rage." And while she is generous to outcasts, Martin observes, she avoids involvement with those around her: "Miriam, notorious for her sympathetic attitude towards unusual strangers, attractive waiters, pittoresque beggars, sweet drunkards, has little respect for the misfortunes and enthusiasms of her friends." Yet, the narrator asks, "can one blame her if she is unable to extend her notorious sympathy to those bores who think their catastrophes are worth her own?" Vail's portrayal of Mina as Miriam (the prophetess and proto-feminist of Jewish tradition) suggests that, to his eyes, her self-absorption was excessive and her rehearsal of her catastrophes tiresome.

With the exception of Vail, members of the Crowd were generally charmed by Mina's high spirits. McAlmon, who invited her to all his gatherings, recalled her presence at the high point of an especially hectic Quatorze Juillet celebration: "Jane Heap and Mina Loy were both talking brilliantly: Mina, her cerebral fantasies, Jane, her breezy, traveling-salesman-of-the-world tosh." Neither quite made sense, he added, but no one cared. "Conversation is an art with them," he went on, "something entirely unrelated to sense of reality or logic." McAlmon assembled another party, including Mina, Bryher, Mary Butts, and the Hemingways, to meet the novelist Dorothy Richardson and, when Bill and Flossie Williams visited Paris the following year, organized a banquet in their honor to which he invited Mina and Joella, Sylvia Beach and Adrienne Monnier, the Fords, the Joyces, Aragon, and Harold Loeb. When Duchamp and Man Ray turned up as well, the New York and Paris avant-gardes were reunited in an evening of songs and banter—in which Mina's brilliance outshone her despair.

One night Harriet Monroe, the editor of *Poetry*, joined McAlmon at the Strix, the Crowd's new headquarters. Monroe was sipping Madeira, he recalled, when Mina appeared, looking "too beautiful for description." Others joined them—Pound, Jane Heap, the Vails, and Tzara—but it was Mina's charm, Monroe observed, that provided the evening's "gayety and color . . . I may never have fallen very hard for this lady's poetry," she continued, "but her personality is irresistible." At the same time, beneath Mina's effervescence Monroe detected the same note of desperation she felt in her verse. Mina's gaiety resulted from "the worldly-wise conquest of many despairs," she concluded, in the issue of *Poetry* that recounted her Montparnasse adventures. Monroe's review of *Lunar Baedecker* described its "bitter humor" and "satiric *moues*" as if speaking of the author. While Mina simply meant to "épater les bourgeois," Monroe went on, "her utterance is a condescension from a spirit too burdened with experience to relax the ironic tension of her grasp." Yet her toleration of her lot struck Monroe as "the shadowed under-side of the saint's ecstatic sensuality." Mina's poetry lacked magic, she concluded, but it was of interest because it showed "a modern temperament" dealing with the ravages of the spirit.

A few months later, reviewing the first books published under the Contact imprint, the English poet Edwin Muir took McAlmon to task for advancing his authors' experimentalism as the cause of their neglect. *Lunar Baedecker* was "arresting" just the same: it was "the surprise of the bunch." But like Monroe, Muir had reservations about Mina's "philosophic" tendencies. Distinguishing between the "intellectual artist" (who looks at life "as if he were responsible for it, and does not rest until he has given it a rational form") and the "cerebral artist" (who "intellectualises life without . . . coming to conclusions"), Muir argued that McAlmon's list included too many of the latter. "Where Mrs. Loy is good she is not cerebral," he concluded, "and where she is cerebral she is not at all good."

Lunar Baedecker made such an impression that he elected to review it again. Muir, an autodidact with a spiritual inclination and an experience of exile, was more attuned than Monroe to Mina's idiosyncrasies. "There are things in this volume worthy of the highest praise and the severest blame," he began. Among those things that he found blameworthy was Mina's use of a vocabulary smattered with ill-digested classical and scientific allusions—the sort of English spoken by poorly educated colonials eager to make an impression. Yet, he continued, "when she is original, she achieves effects which astonish us by their intensity." "Der Blinde Junge" was not only sincere but "full of a literary finesse dictated directly by its sincerity." Moreover, Mina's description of Leopold Bloom—"Don Juan / of Judea / upon a pilgrimage / to the Libido"—was a splendid example of her wit, "which, like her vision, is unique."

Because of their independence of mind, both Monroe and Muir saw in Mina's poetry the thirst that Monroe called the "underside" of spirituality and Muir called mysticism. To those who saw art's formal processes as modernism's proper concern, the soul was not a legitimate topic. But to Muir, whose modernism was eclectic, formal perfection did not exclude spiritual seeking. Mina was, he thought, "a mystic of a very peculiar kind, a negative mystic, the chief fruit of whose mysticism is an acridly intimate awareness of the flesh." She seemed "perplexed" by the senses. "When she is moved by pity," he added, "the sense of metaphysical obscenity is not far away; but that obscenity is the complement of her subconscious, helpless mysticism." Of all those writing about her poetry at that time, and perhaps since then, Muir best captured the tension between the two poles of her vision, the spiritual hunger that he called mysticism and the contempt for a world where things did not turn out as imagined. This tension produced flashes of unusual intensity, he thought: when they came, "she is so genuine that her utterance arrests us."

Depending on one's temperament, Mina's ability to stop the reader in his tracks was either arresting or disturbing. When the Paris *Tribune* sent the journalist Eugene Jolas to interview her in 1924, he pronounced himself honored to meet "a writer who works with almost Stoic slowness, Miss Mina Loy, author of that strangely cryptic *Lunar Baedecker*." Of all her poems, the most famous was "Brancusi's Golden Bird," which "made a profound impression." Written before she had actually met the sculptor, Jolas went on, the poem illustrated the "intuitional approach." The interview gave the last word to Mina, who observed epigrammatically, "One must have lived ten years to write a poem."

Soon Mina was expanding her thoughts on the sources of modern poetry. What began as an epigram grew into an essay written for publication in *Charm*, a magazine combining photographs by Man Ray with reports on French culture by Djuna Barnes. Modern poetry was a distinctly American product, she argued, a linguistic compound of time pressures, jazz rhythms, and immigrant inflections. "It was inevitable," she went on, "that the renaissance of poetry should proceed out of America, where latterly a thousand languages have been born, and each one, for purposes of communication at least, English—English enriched and variegated with the grammatical structure and voice-inflection of many races, in novel alloy with the fundamental time-is-money idiom of the United States." This novel alloy was, moreover, a democratic medium.

This composite language is a very living language, it grows as you speak. For the true American appears to be ashamed to say anything in the way it has been said before. Every moment he ingeniously coins new words for old ideas, to keep good humor warm. And on the baser avenues of Manhattan every voice swings to the triple rhythm of its race, its citizenship and its personality.

337

In America, she went on, "the mind has to put on its verbal clothes at terrific speed if it would speak in time."

The remainder of the essay was devoted to those whose verbal clothes fit their minds—Pound, Williams, Cummings, H.D., Marianne Moore, and Laurence Vail—each of whom had written "one or two perfect poems." What was more, Mina claimed, that each of these writers had developed an individual metric proved the point of the free-verse revolt—that modern verse was conceived as "the chart of a temperament . . . the spontaneous structure of a poet's inspiration."

V

By 1925, when this essay appeared, Mina's own sources of poetic inspiration had run dry. Following the publication of *Lunar Baedecker*, her autobiographical epic, "Anglo-Mongrels and the Rose," had appeared in sections—first in consecutive issues of *The Little Review* and then in McAlmon's 1925 compilation, *Contact Collection of Contemporary Writers*. She had, for the time being, stopped charting her temperament in verse and, while it is impossible to know for certain, may have turned to *Colossus* and the early drafts of her veiled autobiography.

Whenever one medium no longer felt satisfactory, Mina tried the other. It was one of her enduring complaints that she never knew whether to develop an idea with a pen or with a paintbrush. She showed one painting at the 1923 Salon d'Automne: entitled *Marchands de New York* and listed for sale at two thousand francs, it has—like most of her art—disappeared. Two years later she turned to *la décoration* (interior decoration), the newest branch of the applied arts as practiced in Paris, where a *décorateur* could market imaginative designs with commercial appeal.

Lacking the means to start a business, Mina made the best of her situation by spending Sundays at the Marché aux Puces. The Porte de Clignancourt flea market, at that time not a setting frequented by the bourgeoisie, became for her the equivalent of the Bon Marché and the Galeries Lafayettes. These expeditions gave her the occasion to form her daughters' taste. Whenever Fabi and Joella accompanied Mina, they learned which colors went together and how to recognize quality. One had to buy the real thing, a piece of old lace, she explained, or something funny, but nothing from a department store. On these expeditions through the cast-off treasures of previous centuries, she bought Louis Philippe frames for a fraction of their worth and began collecting old liqueur bottles in fantastic shapes in the hope that once she had enough, their value would increase. Mina had "a distinct talent for inventing fantasies," McAlmon thought, even if they were "slightly overcerebral."

Her latest fantasy, devised to earn the money for a larger apartment, crossed the traditional still life with Cubist collage. She cut leaf and petal shapes from colored papers, layered them to form old-fashioned bouquets, and arranged these pressed flowers in découpé bowls and vases painted with meticulous attention to surface texture. These "arrangements" were then backed with gold paper and set in Mina's flea-market frames: instant antiques, they looked expensive but were made from the cheapest materials. She had created a medium that lived beyond its means.

Family and friends were enlisted in the effort to produce more bouquets once it became clear that they were salable. Mina justified the hours Joella spent painstakingly cutting out petals as the next phase of her aesthetic education. The Vails took Mina's inventions with them to New York, Peggy arranged for exhibitions at galleries and department stores, and Laurence produced a name for them—"Jaded Blossoms." The exhibit's title, a reviewer noted, "does scant justice to Mrs. Loy's very charming handicraft and painting." The overall effect was "quaint," he continued, and Peggy was to be congratulated for "acting as horticultural curator." *The New York Times*, on the other hand, liked the title and mentioned that the artist was "a poet as well as a designer." Her version of the pressed-flower keepsake fit perfectly with the current vogue for stylized patterns, and despite the gallery commissions, she made a profit.

Peggy also placed Mina's drawings in a Long Island gallery. The exhibition, which included portraits of Assagioli, Marinetti, Papini, and Gertrude, was accompanied by an unsigned "Introduction," which hinted that some mystique surrounded the artist. "The name she uses is an assumed one," it claimed, "adopted in a spirit of mockery in place of that of one of the oldest and most distinguished families of England." In this joke on the Americans, who would be intrigued by the note of mystery, one hears the scornful tone of Laurence Vail. Still, the prices were low for an artist said to be "one of the most advanced of the modernists," and the drawings, which have also disappeared from sight, presumably sold. The Vails had shown what could be done with a European background and an imagination.

In the meantime, the Exhibition of Decorative and Industrial Arts, which was to run from April through October, was opening in Paris. The first international exhibition to have as its raison d'être the applied arts, it came at a period of French preeminence in Art Deco, as both the dominant style and the genre were called. Although a show of this kind had been planned since 1913, it was not until 1925 that the European participants had recovered sufficiently from the war to undertake such a project. French manufacturers had voiced such hostility toward their German counterparts that none was represented: the exhibition was to revive the prestige of France.

The importance accorded *la décoration* was clear from the scale of its grounds, which stretched from the Esplanade des Invalides on the Left Bank across the pont Alexandre-III to a sizable area of the Right Bank, including the Grand Palais and the banks of the Seine. Visitors window-shopping their way across the bridge, where luxury boutiques displayed examples of the new spirit, soon understood that this exhibition was meant to appeal to persons of means. Unlike Bauhaus artists attempting to wed good design to mass production, these artists combined expensive materials—incised crystal and glass, inlaid woods, gleaming metals, rich fabrics and tapestries—with a vision of a life lived by the happy few.

While Mina studied the displays, Joella spent much of her time that summer wandering around the showgrounds with their paying guest, a school friend. Mina's New York success made the idea of going into business look feasible, provided she could market her inventions. The most striking blend of art and industry in the show, some thought, was the collaboration between Sonia Delaunay and the couturier Jacques Heim; her *simultanés*, geometric patterns printed in dazzling hues, were used in everything from "simultanist" shoes and fabrics to a pair of pajamas for Tristan Tzara. Their boutique showed that, with the help of a businessman, a fine artist could become a successful designer.

Mina also studied the work of the *verrier* Lalique, featured throughout the exhibition. Lalique's large-scale decorative designs in glass—wall panels and shimmering fountains—adorned several French national displays and were also housed in their own pavilion, where the firm's perfume bottles, vases, and table lamps demonstrated the adaptability of the material to mass production. While Lalique displayed a variety of fixtures, their *bibelots lumineux* (illuminated figurines or statuettes) captured Mina's interest. Made of opaline, an opaque glass in tones of white or blue, these designs featured female figures in Isadora-type draperies, whose folds were illuminated when the light came on. These luminous objects brought matter to life, their opalescent glass translated the shimmer of the fin-de-siècle into modern form. While Delaunay's Cubist-inspired *simultanés* were striking, Lalique's art spoke to Mina's imagination.

Since her New York lampshade business had been moderately successful a decade earlier, she thought of modernizing her designs. Two styles were apparent at the exhibition. The first, purely decorative in its concern for ornamentation, employed the rounded forms of the Art Deco rose, a motif found in decorative panels and friezes as well as fabrics, glass, and ceramics. The design studios at the Bon Marché and Galeries Lafayette department stores had printed these stylized flowers in vivid colors, for use in fashion and decoration alike. By 1925, however, the sheer number of Art Deco roses had produced a reaction. The alternative style (called L'Esprit Nouveau) favored geometric abstractions. Influenced by Constructivism and Cubism, it offered a colder, more technically perfect look, combining simplicity of form with richness of finish. A careful observer at the exhibition could have foreseen that while the first approach to decoration was at its height, the "new spirit" was about to banish the Art Deco rose.

Disregarding this trend, Mina began turning her antique bottles from the flea market into lamps: these amusing shapes could also serve as a poor man's version of a more costly fashion. Originally designed as containers for liqueurs, they had, until recently, been distributed by wine merchants as Christmas presents. Mina's collection housed every conceivable shape, from a female figurine bearing a circus on her head to a miniature version of the column in the Place Vendôme; there were crayfish, butterflies, peacocks, clowns, and a range of mythological and historical personages, including Bacchus, Lafayette, and Napoleon. She had only to work out the wiring and find shades to complement these ingenious bases.

Mina was a genius, Peggy exclaimed. She should sell her creations, she went on. With the profits, she could devote herself to poetry. When Mina replied that she had often thought of something along these lines but lacked capital, Peggy offered to back her in whatever project she devised: lamps in the shape of glass figurines would do nicely. Flush with the success of the Jaded Blossoms, the two women entered into a peculiar partnership, in which no binding contract existed. Given Mina's mood swings and resentment of the rich, not to mention Peggy's tactlessness, the enterprise was unlikely to prosper. And since neither could recognize, let alone admit, her shortcomings, each would blame the other for misunderstandings.

Peggy put everything in Mina's name to avoid French taxes. Mina swallowed her disappointment when her partner asked her to use her own funds for initial purchases, since Peggy expected the franc to fall and thought that, by waiting, she would end up with more to invest. After cashing in her savings at 100 francs to the pound, Mina's resentment grew as she watched the franc fall to 250 to the pound, as Peggy had predicted. Their collaboration had begun badly. Mina became even more alarmed when Peggy bought the lease on an expensive Right Bank shop where she planned to sell antiques along with Mina's lamps. Disheartened by the thought of her partner's taking an active role, she told herself that given the location, on the rue du Colisée between the Champs-Elysées and the rue du faubourg St.-Honoré, things might go well. Far from leaving artistic matters to Mina, Peggy also had plans for the décor: the shop's central partition had to come down, and the cracked enamel walls had to be repaired. After Mina had funds advanced from London to purchase the electrical fixtures, wiring, and supplies, Peggy reimbursed her, but said that the sum would have to do. She had just given most of her income to the striking English trade unionists.

That summer, Mina recalled, "Jo and I were ditched with a dirty shop in the most fashionable quarter of Paris." Working by themselves, they took down the partition, prepared the walls, and furnished the shop. While Joella did the heavy work, Mina experimented with different ways of hiding the cracked enamel, eventually devising an elegant solution which, like most of her inventions, required hours of work executed, preferably, by someone else. She showed Joella how to rub lead dust into the walls, a technique that created a silvery background for the lamps but was not only laborious but potentially toxic. They sat on the floor and made lampshades as a rest from their labors. Joella, who at seventeen adored her mother and, like Peggy, thought her a genius, did not complain, although her health suffered from the long days spent indoors so as to have the shop ready by autumn.

Peggy wrote from Prasmousquier to ask why they had not opened, adding that people thought Mina a poor businesswoman. When Mina explained to her friend Heyward Mills that they had to do everything themselves because they lacked capital, he advanced the funds needed to open in September and volunteered business advice. Soon so many customers appeared that their stock was exhausted. It looked as if she might be a success after all. Mina was easily unnerved, however, especially by wealthy patrons. When Peggy's mother came to check on the new business, she criticized the lampshades and told Mina to lay in a supply of colored scarves from the Galeries Lafayette as a sideline. Mina said nothing, remembering Peggy's promise that her family would bring customers. Tensions increased after Peggy's return, when she repaid Mills but accused Mina of disloyalty for involving him in the business. She had "heaps of money," Peggy insisted, and would give Mina carte blanche.

Peggy's account of their partnership reads like high comedy. "For the opening of the shop," she wrote, "we allowed my mother to invite her lingère to exhibit some underwear at the same time, as we then thought to make some money; this upset Mina so much that she refused to be present at the vernissage. We also sold some hand-painted slippers made by Odile (Clotilde Vail) and later we gave Lorenz (Laurence) an exhibition of his paintings* . . . The lampshade shop was very successful once I got rid of the underwear." However comical this affair sounds years later, Peggy's obtuseness about the underwear hurt Mina's pride and subverted her sense of herself as an artist. Despite these inauspicious beginnings, business prospered. The lamps attracted customers who preferred more traditional décor to the "new spirit."

Soon Mina turned her attention from the base of the lamp to the shade. Although she claimed to dislike Art Nouveau (which she associated with Stephen), several designs harked back to prewar motifs. One of her most popular, *La Galère*, showed an old-fashioned schooner whose sails stood out from the shade in billowing relief; when the lamp was turned on, it appeared to set sail. She also created shades made of opalescent papers layered one over the other, which looked opaque but became translucent when illuminated. Light filtered through a double shade of opaline papers to illuminate the outer surface of *Les Vagues* (*Waves*), and a similar device created the shadowplay of *Les Poissons* (*Fish*), a green cellophane shade

---

* Vail's paintings may be those shown in a photograph of Mina and Peggy at the "Galeries Mina Loy," as the shop is called in the invitation to his exhibit—to which Tristan Tzara contributed a mock appreciation that mingles surrealistic imagery and pompous rhetoric.

doubled so that the inner layer's patterns projected onto the outer surface, evoking the blurry transparency of water in reflected light.

Mina turned next to the illuminated globes she called *mappemondes* (world maps) and *globes célestes* (celestial globes). These were made by transferring antique maps onto glass balls into which bulbs had been inserted. As a slight concession to the recent emphasis on "modernist" furnishings, she devised *Les Etoiles*, a series of matching shades in the shape of stars for wall sconces and ceiling lights. (Despite their geometric look, these folded parchment constructions also suited more traditional decorative schemes.) Believing her destiny "ravelled up somehow with the lunar globe" (as she told the artist Joseph Cornell years later), Mina was again charting her temperament: her celestial globes and star shapes seemed to have materialized from the pages of *Lunar Baedecker*.

Indeed, to those who knew her poetry, Mina's lamps transferred its images to an earthly plane. The starry skies and cosmic reaches of her poems, their slow transit through states of being, their concern with the liberation of form could all be rendered through design, just as the contemplative unfolding of her verse could be conveyed in the transformation scenes of these devices. Her increasingly abstract meditations on the theme of creativity (and creation) could be dramatized in the play of light and shadow—the moment of revelation when a *mappemonde* was lit from within. God of her universe, she was creating stages on which to replay the divine *fiat lux*.

These creations were advertised in the trade magazines under the name "L'Ombre féerique." The phrase played on the meaning of the word *féerie*, which suggests the world of supernatural beings and the spectacular presentation of that world by means of poetic illusion. For her customers Mina's "fairy shadows" evoked the enchantments of childhood—the ephemeral charm of the kaleidoscope or magic lantern—while for their creator, one senses, they also evoked the childhood memory of sunlight streaming through colored glass. Few, if any, of her "fairy shadows" have survived, however, since Mina's materials—cellophane, opaline, and cutouts—were extremely fragile. Both their delicacy and their lack of durability were consequences of her vision, a subtle art of fleeting illuminations.

The critic for the design review *Art et Industrie* noted perceptively in the shop's first season that unlike other lighting fixtures on the market, Mina's were not intended for mass production: hand-made, they could be adapted to suit the particular room they were to ornament. "In order to obtain a harmonious ensemble," he went on, "it was necessary to create models that have the appearance of great lightness." Mina's success in this difficult art, he concluded, was shown by the fruits of her labors, "lampshades whose fairylike shadows transform the décor and domesticate dreams." More delicate and far more fragile than the Jaded Blossoms, they seemed as light as the air. Characteristically, she was fabricating illusions.

VI

The practicalities of producing these illusions devolved, in large part, upon Joella, whose sunny temperament kept the business running. At nineteen she had become her mother's right hand, managing the shop by day and working with Mina at night. Whenever finances allowed, Mina hired helpers, including two Romanian girls recommended by Brancusi. Soon she was spending most of her time in the Montparnasse workshop she called her "factory," located in an alley off the avenue du Maine, where Vail had his studio. She spent her days there supervising the Frenchwomen who assembled the lamps while Joella ran the shop.

By all accounts, her daughter made a charming forewoman. Her blond braids coiled over her ears gave her an old-fashioned air; her Florentine accent and manners charmed the British clientele, who, increasingly, sought out Mina's lamps for their country houses. One day Joella looked after an English visitor who required twelve lampshades made to order with a particular kind of boat—intended, she learned, for the Mountbattens, relatives of the British royal family. Once Joella bobbed her long hair, members of the Crowd noticed that she was becoming a woman. Joyce still thought her the beauty of the family, and Natalie Barney commented on her radiance. She was "the most marvellous *jeune fille* in all the world," in McAlmon's opinion. Joella had reached the age when *jeunes filles*, and their mothers, began thinking of marriage.

Few suitors presented themselves. While the French and Italians were out of the question, the young English and Americans in their circle were equally unsuitable. Wescott often called, but it was obvious that, in addition to being homosexual, he had a crush on Mina. Basil Bunting frequently dropped in for tea, but he, too, was "at least half in love" with Mina, Bunting recalled, and liked to sit watching her as she talked about Cravan, a subject that came up in the presence of young admirers. Bunting was so struck by her beauty, "a dark, melancholy beauty that didn't sentimentalise itself," that he evoked it from memory some years later in an ode dedicated to Mina and her sorrows:

> *Oval face, thin eyebrows wide of the eyes,*
> *a premonition in the gait*
> *of this subaqueous persistence*
> *of a particular year—*
> *for you had prepared it for preservation*
> *not vindictively, urged*
> *by the economy of passions.*
>
> *Nobody said: She is organising*
> *these knickknacks her dislike collects*
> *into a pattern nature will adopt and perpetuate.*

The intricate network of flea-market finds that filled her apartment found its way into the "knickknacks," and Cravan's fate echoed in the "sub-aqueous persistence / of a particular year." Not only did they share an affinity, Bunting recalled, but Mina let him imagine that she enjoyed his attentions.

One day Ford, whose habit it was to send Bunting to meet friends at train stations, ordered him to the Gare de Lyon to greet Joella with a bouquet on her return from holidays. From then on, the young man found himself "split, as it were, between mother and daughter." Bunting took every opportunity to call, until it occurred to him that Ford had concocted the plan as a way of ridding Mina "of my altogether too young attentions. I felt as much attached to her as ever," he went on, "but it was Joella I now wanted to make up to." Next Ford threw a party intended, Bunting thought, to give him the occasion to woo Joella. But the young man, who could not dance, spent the evening glowering at her partner, Tristan Tzara. Mina tried to make up for the evening by inviting him to a gala at the American Embassy. "I had had enough drink already to set free my taste for mischief," Bunting recalled in a letter that must be quoted at length:

When I came in some American lady, goodness knows who, introduced me to a very august looking female sitting with another like her in full evening regalia with a very cutaway bodice. She was said to be the wife of the missionary bishop of somewhere or other. As she held out her hand for it to be kissed in the French fashion I reached beyond it and scooped her exuberant bosom out of its corsage. Scandal. She, however, seemed to like it, set about drinking a great deal, and was presently doing cartwheels on the dancing floor. The scandal of the bishopess (or whatever you call her) was at its worst just as Mina Loy and Joella arrived.

Joella told him to leave, and he slunk off "in disgrace." When sober, he was so worried that Mina and Joella were angry that he left Paris without saying goodbye. The incident is recalled at the end of Bunting's ode to Mina: "Very likely I shall never meet her again / or if I do, fear the latch as before."

McAlmon took on Ford's role as matchmaker. One evening at the Vails', he introduced Julien Levy, a handsome young Harvard graduate who had heard about Mina from Duchamp, his traveling companion on the boat to France. With Man Ray's help, Julien hoped to make experimental films rather than enter his father's New York real-estate business. He was, by his own account, "ripe to be deeply impressed"—especially when whisked off by his new friends to a gathering that included such legends as Hemingway, Pound, Cocteau, and a portly Isadora Duncan lying on a couch that was all but hidden by her robes. Suddenly the crowd welcomed "little Joella." They treated her like a child, but to Julien's eyes she was "a mature and competent young woman." Their courtship took place, he wrote, "across the mysterious and miniature Isle St. Louis, down the steps of the embankment, and along the Seine, back into the sequin luster of some café or brasserie," in churches and concert halls, parks and doorways: "It was the loveliest time of the year in the world's loveliest city."

While he was in love with Joella, the young American responded equally to Mina's charms. Julien was, moreover, the most eligible of the sensitive young men who were often drawn to her—the impoverished Russian, Wescott, Bunting—and whose attentions in some way elicited memories of Cravan. His description of Mina in 1927 suggests both his fascination with her and the erotic charge between them. At forty-four, he wrote, she looked "exceptionally young, almost blond, because her grey bobbed hair held so much vivacity as to be ageless." "Her hips were capable," he went on, recalling a visit to her workshop, "and she came toward me brandishing the gun of a compressed-air brush—a Diana, bold and aggressively intelligent, and in great disarray." Her life struck him as the stuff of legend—her Victorian upbringing, the Italian years, the cult of Cravan, and little Fabienne, who looked like "some small mythological beast, only half human, a very young centaur or Minotaur."

Julien's susceptibility to Mina's habit of seeing her life as a legend was at its height at twenty-one; he would remain in her spell for decades. Joella, Mina, and Fabi all seemed more glamorous than American females, and their life offered what he had been seeking since the death of his mother, like Mina another "elusive, beautiful woman." When Julien asked Mina for Joella's hand, she refused at first, insisting that Joella was needed to run the shop. "If you disrupt our precarious affairs, we must all eat nothing but stardust," he remembered her saying. In June, Mina gave her consent, even though Joella had not yet made up her mind. If she married Julien, she would have to live in New York, and they would be dependent upon the Levys, who, it appeared, were wealthy (although not on the scale of the Guggenheims), but decidedly Jewish and middle class. While Joella returned Julien's affection, she did not know whether she wanted to share his life. Julien's father, who wanted his son to marry someone of his own class and religion, made inquiries about the "Lloyds." After coming to Paris to meet Mina and Joella, Edgar Levy was reconciled to the match and promised to help both the young couple and his new relation.

The wedding took place in August, at the mairie of the Fourteenth Arrondissement, where Mina's marriage to Stephen had been celebrated two decades earlier. Although both Joyce and Brancusi were invited as witnesses, Brancusi arrived alone, bearing his wedding present, an oval-shaped brass entitled Le Nouveau-Né (The Newborn). To win his father's consent, Julien wrote, he had to abandon "my European life and dreams, my unmaterialized prospects in the cinema," and begin his apprenticeship in real estate. No one seems to have thought of what Joella was giving up. Her father-in-law paid for her trousseau—from Lanvin and Molyneux—as well as the couple's Italian honeymoon and passage to New York on the

Ile de France. It was obvious that in worldly terms, Joella had made a good match, and friends hinted that Mina could do worse than to consider a closer connection to Edgar Levy. Yet in Le Havre, as she watched Joella and Julien sail away, she could not help thinking that she had been abandoned.

Interlude II

Anglo-Mongrels

MINA NOW FOUND HERSELF ALONE with eight-year-old Fabienne, who thus far had been brought up by others—Joella, Giulia and her sister Estere. Since she had moved to Paris, Mina's involvement in Fabi's life had consisted largely of the fairy tales Mina invented for her, their games, and their joint appearances at the Crowd's gathering places, where the little girl's shyness grew in response to the admiration she received. Certain that Fabi had inherited Cravan's genius as well as his looks, Mina believed that her nature would express itself of its own accord. Fabi was a child who seemed to have more in common with the animals she adored than with other human beings—or with Mammà.

Mina's educational theories emphasized the importance of languages and of the imagination's need to develop unimpeded. Consequently, Fabi had grown up speaking both Italian and French, her father's tongue, and being allowed to do as she pleased, an approach that compensated for the rigors of Mina's childhood as well as illustrating her belief that geniuses deserved special treatment. In 1922, after enrolling Joella in the Duncan school, Mina had settled Giulia and her charge nearby—where Fabi was to absorb the school's progressive spirit along with some German. Since then, Mina had been pondering the conditions for the breeding of geniuses.

During the mid-1920s, Mina was transposing the story of her own childhood into "Anglo-Mongrels and the Rose," the indignant long poem begun, most likely, during her Berlin winter, when individual neuroses seemed like symptoms of societal breakdown. While *Psycho-Democracy* looked to a new awareness to replace the mindset that had caused the collapse of Europe, "Anglo-Mongrels" examined the "long nightmare" of the past—Europe's and her own. Mina returned to first principles in the initial segment of this free-verse epic, published in the spring of 1923. (Because it was initially published in three parts—in *The Little Review* and McAlmon's *Contact Collection*, "Anglo-Mongrels" was published as a whole only after her death.) Starting with the story of her father as Exodus, the wandering Jew, Mina constructed an auto-mythology in which themes of language learning, aesthetic sensibility, and exile arose naturally from her forebears' characters and backgrounds.

In the poem's first section, Exodus's cultivated mind loses ground to British pragmatism. His languages (Hungarian, German, and Hebrew) are replaced by the "stock quotations" he learns, to make his way in London, and his inarticulate yearnings—"the dumb philosophies / of the wondering Jew"—reduced to an obsession with his physical body, "target of his speculation." His social status is evoked with characteristic irony, aimed at Exodus as well as the world he hopes to conquer:

> The highest paid   tailor's
> cutter in the "City"
> Exodus   Lord Israel
> nicknamed   from his consummate bearing
> his coaly eye
> challenging   the unrevealed universe
> speaking fluently   "business-English"
> to the sartorial world
> jibbering   stock exchange quotations
> and conundrums of finance

Yet success comes at the cost of spiritual alienation: "Exodus knows / no longer father / or brother / or the God of the Jews."

Her father's desire to possess "the culture / of his epoch" is dramatized in the second section, "English Rose"—a longer version of the poem that appeared the same year in *Lunar Baedecker*. While the shorter version ends with a satire of postwar England, the "Anglo-Mongrels" version goes on to satirize the contradictions of her parents' courtship:

> She
>   simpering in her
>   ideological pink
> He
>   loaded with Mosaic
>   passions that amass
>   like money

Once wed, the English rose (whose name alternates between Alice and Ada) defends herself against his passions with her ideological thorns.

In the last section to appear in *The Little Review*, "Ada Gives Birth to Ova," Mina staged her own appearance in the world as an embryonic consciousness or seedling. The poem posits Ada's lack of sexual fulfillment as the reason for her dislike of Ova, her firstborn:

> *Her face*
> *screwed   to the mimic-salacious*
> *grotesquerie of a pain larger than her intellect*
> *— —They pull*
> *A clotty bulk of bifurcate fat*
> *out of her loins*

In the poem's imaginative metaphysics, the soul acquires individuation by being trapped in its body: a traveler "from back of time and space," it becomes a clot of flesh, "A breathing baby / mystero-chemico Nemesis / of obscure attractions." And as a "Anglo-Israelite," Ova's only birthrights are her grandmothers' curses—until one of them declares, "Behold my gift / The Jewish brain!"

In 1923, when the first three sections of the poem appeared, a reader of *The Little Review* might have thought Mina was replying to T. S. Eliot on his own terms. The year before, "The Waste Land" had been hailed as the exemplar of postwar sensibility as well as a new kind of social critique. Like Eliot's satiric poem, "Anglo-Mongrels" uses verbal fragmentation, juxtaposition, wit-play, rapid shifts of linguistic level ("low" forms such as journalism and vulgar speech side by side with learned terms) to construct a modern poetic language, its "dictionaries of inner consciousness." And despite its didacticism, the full version of "Anglo-Mongrels" also includes lyrical moments, such as the brief, moving poem that evokes Ova's sense of oneness with the cosmos, "Illumination." The sequence employs a counter-poetics that has come to seem the hallmark of modernism but introduces something new: Mina's awareness of herself as a mixed being, an "Anglo-Mongrel."*

The poem's third section, published two years later, examines the links between art and temperament. The remaining poems brim with resentment, no doubt because Haweis and Cravan appear in them as representatives of opposed aesthetics—and as if their characters had been formed by the age of five. "Enter Esau Penfold" portrays Stephen as the "Infant Aesthete" of his mother's treatise (Mina's send-up of Mrs. Haweis's *Chaucer for Children*), the child who not only lives in the best part of town but is "singled out / by British culture." In contrast to the Penfolds', Ova's house (Mina

---

* When the first section of "Anglo-Mongrels" appeared in *The Little Review*, Ezra Pound expressed his approval of Mina's new form, the "free-verse novel."

demeaned her West Hampstead address by placing it in "Kill-burn") is decorated with Victorian pomp, the gaudy atmosphere in which her budding consciousness develops.

Mina's private mythology emerges in the stanzas alluding to her first memory: "The prismatic sun—show / of father's physic bottle / pierced by the light of day / extinguishes! / as she is carried away." But her enduring complaint, that she had lost touch with her soul when denied these "sudden colours," is meaningful only to those who know her accounts of this ur-moment. Lines on Ova's entrance into language are more successful:

> The child
> whose wordless
> thoughts
> grow like visionary plants
>
> finds
> nothing objective new
> and only words
> mysterious
>
> Sometimes a new word comes to her
> she looks before her
> and watches
> for its materialization

The word that materializes in the next lines is "diarrhea." Hearing what sounds to her like "iarrhea," two-year-old Ova connects it to the birth of her sister: the "embodied" word, full of contradictory associations to shimmery green hues, becomes a "colour-fetish" to the inarticulate child.

The process by which such associations accrete is described in the poem's recipe for modernism—"this fragmentary / simultaneity / of ideas." This lapidary formula justifies the excremental vision of the entire sequence as well as introducing the next section, in which Esau's sensibility is contrasted to Ova's in an extended simile:

> As the arrested artists
> of the masses
> whose child faces
> turned upon Beauty
> the puny light
> of their immobile recognition
> made moon-flowers out of muck
> and things desired
> out of their tenuous soul-stuff

Until the Ruling Bluff
demanded a hell-full
of labor
for half a belly-full

So did the mongrel-girl
of Noman's land
coerce the shy Spirit of Beauty
from excrements and physic

While Esau of Ridover Square
absorbs the erudite idea
that Beauty IS nowhere

Few moon-flowers blossom in the rest of the sequence. Religion becomes one form of escape from Noman's land (in the tale of "the gentle Jesus"), but it is the infant Colossus who embodies the cure for Esau's decadence and Ova's "Christian introspection."

In our time, despite claims for "Anglo-Mongrels" as "one of the lost master-poems of the 20th century," it is of interest chiefly as one of Mina's most polished attempts to understand her background—"to arrive through a patient voyage of elucidation, at the point of departure." The poem uses logopoeia as a battering ram—an approach that softens only in lines on Ova's spiritual yearnings. Although Mina intended to trace the germination of modern consciousness, the poem impressed a contemporary reader as an "out-of-date 'modernist' platitude." It was a piece of writing, John Collier noted in *The New Age*, "in which the terminology is so stilted, so consciously artificial, that one concludes that by some monstrous exertion of faith, or self-hypnotism, its accumulator has come to regard the result of her labours as poetry." After putting so much of herself into the poem, it was no doubt infuriating to Mina to read that it had "nothing but faith and pomposity."

While Collier savaged "Anglo-Mongrels," he did so from an anti-modernist, anti-expatriate stance. Of the other contributions to the *Contact Collection*, he remarked that Djuna Barnes's prose was "strained," Hemingway's "arid," and a fragment of what would become *Finnegans Wake* "tortuous" and "complicated." (About Gertrude Stein's depictions of "being," he observed, "There is no adequate comment.") Mina could tell herself that Collier was one more narrow-minded Englishman, writing in a country "as discouraging as her climate." Not only had McAlmon devoted a major portion of the anthology to her work, but it was where it belonged—among the geniuses (other contributors included H.D., Dorothy Richardson, and Ezra Pound).

And in any case, "Anglo-Mongrels" had produced spin-offs: the infant aesthetes demanded lives of their own. Because of the poem's reception perhaps, Mina turned to prose as the medium for the lives of Penfold and

Colossus. While these unpublished manuscripts cannot be dated with certainty, it is likely that during the mid-twenties Mina revised parts of *Colossus*, the "novel" begun in New York but left unfinished. As for the Esau Penfold / Stephen Haweis material, still in fragmentary form, it may have been drafted at this time to illustrate the genteel tradition upon which Colossus made his assaults. As in "Anglo-Mongrels," the dominant note in Mina's portraits of each husband is intensely personal—in Stephen's case, a withering scorn equaled only by her rage at her mother; in Cravan's case, a passionate love including expressions of a humor rarely shown in her other writing. If Stephen represented all that Mina despised about British culture, Cravan, by contrast, inspired her to remark that "falling in love is the trick of magnifying one human being to such proportions that all comparatives vanish."

But these unfinished manuscripts could not adequately explain the flowering of consciousness. Mina returned to her point of departure, the tale of Ova's dawning consciousness, but approached it this time in prose, a medium better suited to depicting the experience of "being both liberated and trapped" in individuality. *The Child and the Parent*, one of the most readable of her unpublished autobiographical prose works, largely avoids the animus directed at stand-ins for real people (like Esau Penfold)—perhaps because it is a meditation on the mystery of embodiment.

The Child and the Parent begins with the metaphor of a bird alighting as a symbol of the soul's appearance in the world. Whether understood as the Holy Ghost or as consciousness, Mina wrote, this "feathered metaphor" presents "an image of our animation," making palpable "the roving passage of the intellect between the known and the unknown." The first three chapters lay out a theory of infantile self-awareness as "cosmic memory" and as a vision of the world undifferentiated from the self. Later, the voice shifts to that of a particular "I" as theory cedes to tales from infancy—the time, Mina wrote, when, "like Adam from Eden, Lucifer from heaven," she was " 'cast out.' " (The punctuation hints that her "casting out" parodies the prototypical falls of the Bible.) The loss of the child's sense of oneness with the world is completed, finally, with the imprint on its mind of the parental "no," setting up the internalized dualities, "affirmation and opposition; creation and destruction; God and the Devil." From this point on, the intellectual pendulum swings inexorably in the "to-and-fro . . . of positive and negative." And while this formula was universally valid, Mina believed that her hybrid status had enhanced the general tendency to think in opposites.

The remainder of *The Child and the Parent* emphasizes one half of her hyphenated being: the psyche of the Victorian woman masquerading as an "utter Christian." Through a series of poetic metamorphoses, the "feathered metaphor" of "The Child" (Part I) becomes the caged bird of "The Parent" (Part II). In a painterly chapter entitled "Ladies in an Aviary," Julia and her contemporaries are birdlike creatures with rustling bustles and pouting bosoms. Inside their cages (which resemble their corsets), they practice looking demure while awaiting suitors, of whom they will inquire in fluttering tones, "What would you like us to be?" The men respond by dangling the sweets of marriage as their only possible escape.

Mina's aviary, a cross between Kate Greenaway and Burne-Jones, has the allegorical quality of Pre-Raphaelite painting. "Fixed in the center of the aviary is a fancy tree," she wrote, "giving inmates the illusion that they are at large, and an observer the impression of its being doubly familiar, for with maidens perched on each branch with plumage outspread as they sit at easels or embroidery frames, it has a somewhat genealogical aspect; while we distinctly perceive a serpent coiled about its stem." As long as the maidens pass their time in sedate pursuits, they remain unaware of the serpent. But if they cause a disturbance, the serpent's hiss brings on the blight of "impurity" to which these creatures are susceptible. It is understood, moreover, that this blight produces "spiritual moulting," and that she who tastes the fruit of the tree will disappear into the streets, "down through the social oubliette."

For those who achieve the married state, the picture is only slightly less somber. The imagined sweets lose their savor after the ceremony: "They have reaped no harvest of promised ecstasy; they are like earth become excruciatingly conscious of the tilling." Similarly, the "marble halls" of marriage prove to be "another bird cage—or brick box." For this reason, the disappointed birds-turned-matrons vent their frustration on the figure who haunts their psyches, the fallen woman. They rule the domestic sphere while she acts out their fantasies: "The streets were the unknown, the track on which the erotic revelation paced."

Mina's vision of "the cage that confined the women of the eighties," her mother's generation, is strangely moving. The birds in the trees are figures from the nursery world. Their wayward sisters, who eat of the apple, are the femmes fatales of the decadents. The starkness of these alternatives suggests a secular allegory of the battle between good and evil. But while scorn for Victorian women overlaps with sympathy for their predicament, in the end they are blamed for having swallowed "the sugar of fictitious values." "To understand all is to forgive all," Mina told Julien when he complained to her of his family. Yet where Julia was concerned the maxim did not apply.

The Child and the Parent gave her parents' generation "a more lucid existence than they had at the time," Mina believed, in that she was writing as a "transcendental observer." Godlike in her detachment, she had only to "lift a 'feeling' out of the past to find that this long buried impression [was] still so distinct that after re-experiencing it" she could "submit it to mental analysis, just as a poet reproduces an impression with an *exact* word." This analysis helped her to see the woman's "plot" as the impasse of "an eroticism seldom discharged, an idea that is never defined, an outreaching taking no contact."

Her most philosophical and intensely imagined meditation on the sources of her unhappiness, *The Child and the Parent* concludes with a hymn to genius—the medium by which the world is to attain a more advanced state of consciousness. Although our potential is infinite, Mina wrote, "our restricted and utilitarian consciousness, into which our blind back pushes us through the window of our eyes, is a little front garden for us to potter about in." The genius expressed himself by "advancing, ever so slightly, the fence that hems his garden in, to enclose a hitherto unfound flower." Mina's "immortelles" and "moon-flowers" were discoveries of this kind (unlike the English Rose, which required fences), and she was convinced that her own wildflower, Cravan's daughter, would flourish provided she was not hemmed in. Through her, the "mongrel-girl / of Noman's land" would transcend her hybrid nature.

PART IV

"YOU SHOULD HAVE DISAPPEARED YEARS AGO"

How far *my mind had traveled never to come to the* beginning *of any route.*

—MINA LOY, *Insel*

Making art in America is about saving one's soul.

—CHARLES SIMIC, *Dime-Store Alchemy: The Art of Joseph Cornell*

17

The Widow's Jazz

(PARIS, 1927–36)

SOON AFTER THE DEPARTURE of Joella and Julien in 1927, Mina's letters to the "children" began mixing whimsical advice with complaints about business, finances, and isolation. Impressed with the scale on which newlyweds lived, Mina imagined a war between the mismatched china she had sent them from the Marché aux Puces and their Wedgwood, which was surely "unaccustomed to keeping low company." In another of these missives, after warning Joella not to let their architect "build the water closet in the ice box," she declared herself "all out of motherly advice" and added, "I'm more in need of some myself."

For the past four years, Joella had been her mother's source of emotional balance. Mina missed her calm optimism and disciplined work habits. She asked Joella to "treat" the shop through Christian Science so that she could repay Peggy Guggenheim, who had her "in such a corner," she wrote, that their partnership was "leading straight to suicide." By the end of September, Mina was so confused about what was owed to whom that she not only threatened to sell the shop but told Joella that her apartment was about to be seized. She would have turned to Edgar Levy but feared he would think her "a designing adventuress." Her life thus far had been a "stupid muddle of poverty and tragedy," yet it had developed her mind: "I have disgraceful moments of conceit when I feel as though *I know it all*."

But knowing it all did not keep her from giving way to despair. Whether because she believed that the apartment would be seized or because she could not bear to be alone, Mina took to sleeping in the "factory." Friends thought her behavior odd but concluded that she should do as she pleased; in accordance with her educational theories, Fabi was attending school in the country and spent most of her time with the gamekeeper at whose home she boarded. Fabi "adored" her, Mina wrote, but was happier living this way than in Paris.

Mina dealt with her depression by turning to old friends. Hermine David and Djuna were sympathetic, but had sorrows of their own—Pascin had left Hermine for Lucy Krogh, and Thelma Wood's infidelities were making Djuna miserable. Natalie Barney tried to comfort Mina without saying "I told you so" when she regretted her decision to let Joella marry Julien. She was, she told them, "the most isolated godforsaken creature in Paris." And her thoughts kept turning to Cravan, who had said that she was "too intelligent to have real friends." He had understood her because they were both sports of nature, mutations whose characters could not be explained by their progenitors. Nine years after his disappearance, Mina addressed him directly in a poem entitled "The Widow's Jazz":

> Cravan
> colossal absentee
> the substitute dark
> rolls to the incandescent memory
>
> of love's survivor
> on this rich suttee
>
> seared by the flames of sound
> the widowed urn
> holds impotently
> your murdered laughter

"Your marriage turning out so full of happiness for you both is the first thing that has gone right in my life," she told Joella. But however much she delighted in news from the "children," their bliss conjured up her own lost happiness.

I

Of her group, Natalie was the only one to have "gotten more out of life than it actually possesses," as she was fond of saying. While her conquests were legion, she maintained close relations with former loves and invited them to her salon. "You never knew whether her friends were there because they were writers or because they were lesbians," a guest recalled. In 1927 she was organizing a salon for women writers to bring together her French friends and their English-speaking counterparts. The Académie des femmes was an implicit critique of the Académie Française, whose members—the *immortels*—were male, but she intended nonetheless to adapt its rituals to her *immortelles*. Like the Academicians, these "representatives of contemporary, cosmopolitan writing" (as Natalie called her friends, protégées, and lovers) were each presented by a member of the group, and one could expect them to declaim in the style of the *diseuse*—a parlor version of the great tragediennes. Natalie's Académie was to be a glamorous throwback to the fin-de-siècle.

One of the first programs featured Gertrude Stein, despite the fact that her style in no way resembled Natalie's. Gertrude's fame was on the rise following her recent speaking engagements at Oxford and Cambridge, and because Mina's *Transatlantic Review* piece on her had been well received, Natalie entrusted her with the introduction. The program took some planning. The young composer Virgil Thomson set some of Gertrude's work to music, Natalie translated parts of *The Making of Americans*, and Mina wrote in French for the benefit of the Parisians. On the appointed day, Gertrude watched the proceedings with an unblinking gaze. Her prose had been misread because of her genius, Mina began, but despite this lack of appreciation, she kept on writing. This "prophetess" had shown the way to the younger writers who "dug in her manuscripts for all sorts of riches" long before her recognition by "good old conservative England." She was unknown in France, Mina continued, because her gospel resisted translation—into French or English. By making the language sound foreign, she had destabilized the belief that there was a native tongue.

This observation applied to Mina as well. She would soon observe that she had always approached English as if it had to be reinvented. "I was trying to make a foreign language," she wrote, "because English had already been used." This effort had been complicated by her liking for "far-fetched" terms, which "must have dated from a time when from lack of experience I had so little to say." It was a relief to find herself "free to use a little plain English." In 1927, however, Mina believed that Gertrude had accomplished in prose what she was trying to do in poetry—she had estranged English from itself and made it read as if it were in translation.

To Natalie's way of thinking, Mina's estrangement had already transposed her writing and her person into another dimension. For this reason, when planning a program in Mina's honor, she also invited Elisabeth de Gramont, whose down-to-earth ways contrasted with Mina's volatility. On May 6 Mina rehearsed with a trainer, Natalie recalled slyly, "as boxers do." Following her introduction, she stood with downcast eyes. She had forsaken her solitude at Natalie's insistence, she whispered, professing amazement at finding herself before the guests. She could bring herself to speak only because some found beauty in her verse. Following these rather disingenuous remarks, Mina read "The Widow's Jazz" as if in a dream—until she reached its impassioned address. "Husband / How secretly you cuckold me with death," she called out, a cry that reverberated in the muffled salon. Then she withdrew into herself.

It was this characteristic retreat, Natalie believed, that produced the "prismatic poetry" through which Mina escaped into the fourth dimension.

"We were pleased to return to the material world," she noted, "after these voyages with our guide to the moon." Decades later, Natalie's preciosity seems either endearingly arch or faintly ridiculous. Yet such differences of tone are *une question d'époque*, a matter of an era's self-understanding. Although Natalie behaved like a period piece, she liked to think that a woman's identity was shaped by her performances.

At the same time, Natalie's private behavior was scandalous. While the grand style was *de rigueur* at the Académie des femmes, in more intimate moments these same friends often descended to bawdy teasing. Once Mina began to feel comfortable with Natalie, she enjoyed playing the role of token heterosexual, often reporting her sallies to the children. During a sale at Jean Patou's, Natalie had announced to Mina that she "couldn't stand the smell of all those women." When Mina replied, "Why, darling, I thought you'd love it," Natalie said no, "one at a time, and I like to choose mine." Later, in cahoots with Natalie, Mina claimed to have fallen for Thelma Wood, Djuna's lover. Soon they had Djuna believing that Mina not only returned Thelma's affections but wanted to live with them in a ménage à trois. In some moods she was the ethereal spirit of her public performance, but in others, she could be as ribald as the occasion warranted.

Despite her refusal to "convert," Mina joined Natalie's inner circle. Her new friends included one of Natalie's most piquant loves, Dolly Wilde, who was not only Oscar's niece but looked like him. ("I am more Oscar-like than he was like himself," she was fond of saying.) While their love affair was full of drama—Dolly drank to excess and used cocaine—it encouraged both women to act out their fantasies: Dolly came to a party dressed as Oscar, accompanied by Natalie as a *femme de lettres*. Dolly had also inherited her uncle's wit. Friends jotted down Dolly's *bons mots*, but her exchanges with Mina, regrettably, went unrecorded. One can imagine them discussing the Wildes: of the younger generation, Dolly and Fabian had been the most marked by their uncle's legend. And since Dolly loved "Wildean tales," she no doubt appreciated the story of Mina's life with her cousin, from unlikely beginning to uncertain end.

Increasingly, Mina socialized with Natalie, Djuna, and their circle. In Natalie's view, each woman had her myth: *she* was the Amazon, Dolly was "Oscaria," Djuna a female Rabelais with "a mid-Victorian heart," and Mina a fugitive spirit on the verge of quitting the world of appearances. To envision them in this way was to give her friends the power they lacked in the practical realm. "It is a good idea to believe in the mystery of woman," she was heard to say, "since in doing so, one creates it."

Natalie's awareness of her role in cultivating this mystery is apparent in Djuna's portrait of her circle, *Ladies Almanack*. Written in 1927–28, the period in which Joella married and Mina joined Natalie's salon, this guide to expatriate lesbian life has the teasing tone of the Académie des femmes in its private moments. (Djuna was one of Natalie's intimates and may have been her lover; the two read each other's manuscripts and discussed such works as Proust's *A la recherche du temps perdu*—whose depiction of lesbianism they criticized.) *Ladies Almanack* was intended, Djuna observed, as "neap-tide to the Proustian chronicle, gleanings from the shores of Mytilene, glimpses of its novitiates, its rising 'saints' and 'priestesses.' " Written for "a very special audience," it recounts the life of "Dame Evangeline Musset": the audience in question, Natalie's intimates, recognized her in Dame Evangeline and themselves in her converts.

A pastiche in the spirit of Joyce—had he written as a lesbian—*Ladies Almanack* crossed the book of saints with the old-fashioned chronicle. On its cover, equestriennes gallop after their leader, in whose features one discerns Natalie's likeness. The preface is a flashback to Evangeline's birth: her parents expected a boy, but when "she came forth an Inch or so less than this, she paid no Heed to the Error." About her proclivities, Evangeline asks her father, "Am I not doing after your very Desire, and is it not the more commendable, seeing that I do it without the Tools for the Trade, and yet nothing complain?" When her chronicle begins, the author notes, Dame Musset has "come to be a witty and learned Fifty," and is "so wide famed for her genius at bringing up by Hand, and so noted and esteemed for her Slips of the Tongue that it [has] finally brought her into the Hall of Fame."

Following this tribute, the almanac proper (or improper) begins with the month of January, where Mina appears as Patience Scalpel. Patience, the author notes, "was of this Month, and belongs to this Almanack for one Reason only, that from Beginning to End, Top to Bottom, inside and out, she could not understand Women and their Ways." To Women in the know, the joke was obvious. A Capricorn, Mina illustrated this sign's intellectuality, and her refusal of Women's Ways made her seem cold. Moreover, her surname (perhaps an allusion to Moore's "Those Various Scalpels") implied that her wit was "as cutting in its Derision as a surgical Instrument."

Mina's talent for dissection emerges in her character's rejection of Sapphism. Women are too much alike, Patience argues, for her to see "what it is in the Whorls and Crevices of my Sisters so prolongs them to the bitter End. Do they not have Organs as exactly alike as two Peas," she goes on, "and are they not eclipsed every so often with the galling Check-rein of feminine Tides? . . . In my time," she continues, "Women came to enough trouble by lying abed with the Father of their Children"—an understatement for one who knew Mina's life. January concludes with her defense of the means by which the species perpetuates itself:

"Methinks," she mused, her Starry Eyes aloft, where a Peewit was yet content to mate it hot among the Branches, making for himself a Covey in the olden Formula, "they love the striking Hour, nor would breed the Moments that go to it. Sluts!" she said pleasantly after a little thought, "Are good Mothers to supply them with Luxuries in the next

*Generation; for they themselves will have no Shes, unless some Her puts them forth!
Well I'm not the Woman for it! They w[i]ll have to pluck where they may. My Daughters
shall go amarrying!"*

While some consider Patience the author's voice, the book's playful tone
makes it pointless to ask where Barnes stood. It is clear, nonetheless, that
Ladies Almanack includes dialogue that embroiders on actual conversations.
During the time that Djuna was writing, Mina's daughter *had* gone "amarrying" and was awaiting the arrival of the next generation, begotten according to the "olden Formula." Natalie hated the thought of Joella's going
through this "unnecessary experience," Mina wrote; whenever Natalie
asked "how she was bearing up," Mina boasted of her happiness.

For this reason, perhaps, Patience continues to spar with Evangeline.
In March, when the Women declare men useless except "for carrying of
Coals" and "lifting of Beams," Patience insists that having two sexes makes
life interesting. If men did not exist, she scolds, lesbians would not be "half
so pleased" with themselves, since "Delight is always a little running of
the Blood in Channels astray!" By May, her voice has lost its edge. While
she holds forth "in that divine and ethereal Voice for which she was noted,
the Voice of one whose Ankles are nibbled by the Cherubs," Dame Musset
brings Doll Furious (Dolly Wilde) "to a certainty"—a lusty demonstration
of what it is that "women see in each other."

Patience gives ground in the month of August. "Though it is sadly
against me to report it of one so curing to the Wound as Patience Scalpel,"
the narrator notes:

*yet did she (on such Evenings as saw her facing her favorite Vintage, for no otherwise
would she have brought herself to it), hint, then aver, and finally boast that she herself,
though all Thumbs at the business and an Amateur, never having gone so much as a
Nose-length into the Matter, could mean as much to a Woman as another.*

But Evangeline will have none of it, asking Patience what can she "know
about it, who have gentlemaned only?"

Djuna was having fun at Mina's expense. Not only does Patience
imbibe a fair amount of "her favorite Vintage" throughout the year but,
once under the influence, renounces her opposition. Following Joella's
departure, Mina's turn to her women friends—and a more frequent con-
sumption of "Vintage"—made it possible to think that she, too, could
follow Evangeline. While Djuna may have been taking revenge for the
night when Mina claimed to be in love with Thelma, the month of October
gives Patience the right of reply. "God help us!" she declares after draining
her glass, "not one good hammer-throwing, discus-casting coxy Prepuce
amongst you!"

Despite Mina's feelings of abandonment, the business prospered. Her employees proved efficient at their tasks; orders came in from England and America, *Art et Industrie* featured her work and gave her free publicity by offering one of her lamps to the winner of their design contest.* At the height of her success, during the winter of 1927–28, she employed half a dozen "factory" workers, and while her most popular design, the illuminated globe, sold for two thousand francs (about one hundred dollars), she could not turn them out fast enough.

Mina was also developing new designs. She began making shades with a type of strong but malleable cellophane called Crystal Lux. Within a short time she also discovered a new synthetic called Rhodoid, which could be shaped to the simplified floral forms she had in mind. During the winter she devised lamp bases featuring different flowers made of Rhodoid. In one, a water lily floating in a glass ball cast reflections on its transparent shade, and in another, calla lilies with filaments concealed in their pistils emerged from a base that looked like a vase until the light came on. Major French firms—Lanvin and the lighting company France Danube—expressed interest in these striking models, and from New York, both Macy's and Wanamaker's placed orders. She was on the way to becoming a success.

At the same time, however, French designers were abandoning naturalistic forms in favor of clean geometric lines. This aesthetic not only wed practicality to elegance but also allowed manufacturers to employ the techniques of mass production. *Lux*, a design review concerned with the science of lighting, welcomed this approach, one which saw the artist as an engineer rather than a craftsman. While Mina experimented with Crystal Lux and Rhodoid, her competitors began using more durable materials—brushed metal, marble, alabaster, and molded, etched, or engraved glass —in the Cubist-inspired designs which, increasingly, appeared in the shops and magazines. Mina's "greatest hero" was Henry Ford, she told Julien, but she could not imagine engaging in mass production.

Mina's craftsman-like aesthetic was a streamlined version of Art Nouveau, despite her professed dislike of this style. For that reason, her designs appealed to those who were not prepared to adopt the severe chic of the new furnishings. In 1928, when Mina's rivals were showing *bibelots lumineux,* her floral bouquets and celestial globes offered a reasonably priced alternative. She would soon abandon lampshades, she told the "children," and concentrate on a line of *"imageries lumineuses,"* art objects such as a cherub with a light on its back, to be suspended from the ceiling. She was also working on glass sun and moon shapes, to be cast using molds made

---

* In New York, five of Mina's most popular designs were reproduced in the July 1927 issue of *Arts and Decoration* (p. 56): the article "Prize Lamp Shades from Nina Loy of Paris [sic]" noted that they had "received the highest honors at a recent exhibition of interior decoration in Paris"—a claim which has proved impossible to verify.

from old carvings. But until she could spare the money to patent these models, she preferred not to show them.

Mina's letters to New York explored, as tactfully as possible, the idea that Edgar Levy might buy out Peggy Guggenheim. His father was not a man "who would amuse himself at my expense," she told Julien, as the Vails had done. Not only was Peggy an impossible business partner, she explained in a letter to Edgar, but the Vails' behavior was too unconventional. "They are scandalizing the most outré of the bohemians," she continued, "and their children are being brought up in a manner that frightens me—on Fabi's account." To help disentangle the business, Edgar offered to loan Mina ten thousand dollars, which would allow her to buy out Peggy. Her acceptance hints that Edgar's generosity was already being repaid in Julien's marital bliss. "I am sure that you like myself are getting 'spiritual comfort' out of the fact that our dear children are making each other happy," she wrote. "Let me add gratefully that your kind help has had a great effect on my health and nerves," she told Edgar. "I feel *safer*," she added, safe enough to admit that her distress of recent few months had been a "nervous breakdown," which she had not mentioned in order not to frighten Joella.

With the Vails out of her life, the thought that her designs were being stolen still preyed on her mind. "The French idea of business is the infringement of other people's copyrights," she told Edgar. Her glassmakers had sold the calla-lily design to France Danube, she believed, and the mapmakers had done the same with her antique world and celestial maps, which had begun turning up around Paris in poorly made copies. By the spring of 1928, when Mina became embroiled in lawsuits to prevent imitators from marketing her designs, she was obsessed with the thought that everyone stole from her, from her employees at the "factory" to her trusted accountant. And even though a sizable amount of Edgar's loan went for legal consultations, her designs kept showing up in unexpected places: an artisan at the annual Foire de Paris was selling versions of her ship lampshades, and her representative, she felt, had taken the molds for her glass sun and moon. Her trusted forewoman was practicing a subtle form of black magic against her, and the workers sold trade secrets to other firms as fast as they learned them.

Although Mina's accounts of these commercial dramas suggest a touch of paranoia, as with many obsessives, she had reason to be worried. Because the designs were made by hand of inexpensive and widely available materials, they were easily copied once one understood her methods of production. Ironically, the same qualities that gave her lamps their charm made them impossible to protect. Mina had foreseen what would become popular, but given her disdain for business and her conviction that some *homme de confiance* should attend to practical matters, she left herself open to the abuses that seemed increasingly to befall her.

The birth of Mina's first grandchild in July—a strapping boy—provided her with a reason to forget her woes. She cabled merrily, "Clever Joella Granny Aunty dancing with joy." After many exchanges of letters about names, his parents called him Javan, which Mina had found in the Old Testament, although she preferred Mino, for the Renaissance sculptor, Mino da Fiesole, and for herself. In August, once passage had been arranged by the Levys, she and Fabi were on their way to New York.

From the start, the children consulted Mina on nearly every phase of their life together. As the arbiter of style, she helped decorate their apartment as if it were her own. Paint colors, wall finishes, and all design features were submitted to her; the scheme had to be altered until it met with her approval. The young couple asked what she thought of the Levys and how to distance themselves from this tightly knit family, on whom they were financially dependent. Accustomed to frank discussions with her on all aspects of behavior, they even recounted the details of their erotic life, praising Mina for having imparted the secrets of female arousal and fulfillment.

While in their eyes she could do no wrong, Julien in particular was under his mother-in-law's spell. "Your approval is what we most care to cherish," he told her. Julien often seemed more her child than Joella: was not their kinship marked by the similarity of their surnames, Lowy and Levy? Hoping to do some writing of his own, he asked permission to use Loy as his *nom de plume*—a request which Mina granted immediately because it gave her such pleasure. In him she had an adoring son-in-law, and one whose strong family feeling, which Mina associated with Jewish culture, embraced her own. What was more, Julien was so much in awe of Cravan that he had expressed his homage by shaving his head in the summer, as Cravan had done. If this was not sufficient proof of his love, his embrace of Christian Science made him the complete Loy-alist, as he was fond of saying.

On her return to Paris, where no one cherished her or needed her approval, Mina's mood darkened. The only solace in her "lonely & unprotected" state came from the Christian Science practitioner, whom she saw once a week. "My life since I saw you has been one fearful hell," she complained to the children. Despite her resolve not to notice her birthday, Mina became unusually depressed soon after turning forty-seven. "If you and Jo are the happiest people in the world," she wrote, "I certainly am the most unhappy." In January, when the temperature dropped below zero and the heating system failed, her annual winter flu overcame her, she wrote, in reaction to the "intensity of thinking—the body gets tired in place of the mind."

Convinced that as a foreigner she would never succeed in commerce, Mina decided that the business was too expensive to run. If she sold it, she could buy an inexpensive apartment for herself and Fabi where she could paint and write. She had lost touch with herself during the last three years, she believed, when attending to the shop. "The effort to concentrate on something in which one takes no interest, which is the major degradation of women," she observed, "gives pain so acute that in magnifying a plausible task to an inextricable infinity of deadly detail, the mind disintegrates." Furthermore, after three years of being "shut up alone with the lower classes," she was "almost demented"—her Bolshevik leanings having evaporated once she found herself in the role of employer. She had no one to talk to but the accountant, whose chief interest was her ledger: "You can imagine a poet wanting to learn about accounts!"

Her spirits lifted as the weather improved. When Djuna urged Mina to move to her own building, she used what remained of Edgar's loan as a down payment on an apartment, which she took sight unseen. This impulsive decision made sense, she explained to the Levys: "Djuna said I wouldn't be so madly lonely if I lived near her where she could run in & see me." She had often visited Djuna at the rue St.-Romain, a quiet street near the Bon Marché department store and St.-Germain-des-Près. The previous spring, she and Fabi had spent hours at Djuna's helping to hand-color fifty copies of *Ladies Almanack*. Because the book was censorable, Djuna decided not to identify herself as author; it seemed prudent, as well as amusing, to call herself a "A Lady of Fashion." It is easy to visualize Mina, Djuna, and Fabi bent over the bound copies, to imagine Mina's smile as she shaded the figure of Patience Scalpel, and Djuna's pleasure at seeing Fabi, who looked like a young Thelma, filling in the outlines with her colored pencils. Djuna was Mina's closest friend, and she looked forward to life in the rue St.-Romain.

Once the apartment came vacant, Mina was happy to see that as well as having modern comforts, it was light and airy, even "cheerful." Her decorative scheme featured her portraits of Cravan, antique bottles in every room, and, soon, her paintings. The large entrance hall was "*divinely* furnished," she wrote, with flea-market finds, and her metal dining-room chairs, originally designed as porch furniture, were painted in pastel hues. While their new interior resembled "the shabby seaside lodging of fifty years ago," Mina joked, the effect was tasteful. All in all, it made "quite a home."

Soon Mina was consoling Djuna, whose relations with Thelma had reached another crisis. While Djuna often ran down to Mina's apartment to vent her feelings, she kept away from the specifics of Thelma's betrayal because of Fabi, who had not yet been informed of the ways of "Women." Djuna sometimes read to Mina from her new manuscript (*Nightwood*), the intensely poetic love story inspired by Thelma, which, Mina recalled, poured over her "with a sensation of beauty such as I never received from any unison of words." But despite Mina's declarations of sympathy, Djuna spent more time with her lesbian friends, who, she explained, could "really understand." When Djuna decided go back to New York, Mina felt that she, too, had been betrayed—her response whenever the person on whom she depended became unavailable. And although she agreed to act as her

Mina Loy and William Carlos Williams in Lima Beans, *Alfred Kreymborg's "scherzo for marionettes," as staged at the Provincetown Playhouse, December 1916*

Who's Who in Manhattan: *drawing by Clara Tice,* Cartoons, *August 1917. At the center: Mina Loy, wearing a top hat and identified as a "Painter-Poet"; below: Frances Stevens, "Futurist Painter and Horsewoman"; to the left: Louise Norton, "Writer"*

Mina Loy and Djuna Barnes: photo by Man Ray, New York, c. 1920.
"They were stunning subjects—I photographed them together and the
contrast made a fine picture," Man Ray recalled

Robert McAlmon
at Shakespeare and Company,
Paris, c. 1925

Man Ray: drawing by Mina Loy,
inscribed "Never say I dont love you"
(Collection of Roger L. Conover)

Arthur Cravan, Paris (published in The Soil, *April 1917)*

The Crowd outside The Jockey, Paris, c. 1923, including in front row: Man Ray, Mina Loy, Tristan Tzara, Jean Cocteau; second row: Kiki, Jane Heap, Margaret Anderson, Ezra Pound

Little Review *reunion, Paris, c. 1923: Jane Heap, Mina Loy, Ezra Pound*

"Globe céleste,"
lamp by Mina Loy, c. 1927

"Les Etoiles,"
ceiling light and wall sconces
by Mina Loy, c. 1927

*Mina Loy and Peggy Guggenheim at 52, rue du Colisée shop, c. 1927, with
Mina's lampshades and Laurence Vail's paintings*

Julien Levy, New York, c. 1930

Richard Oelze with self-portrait

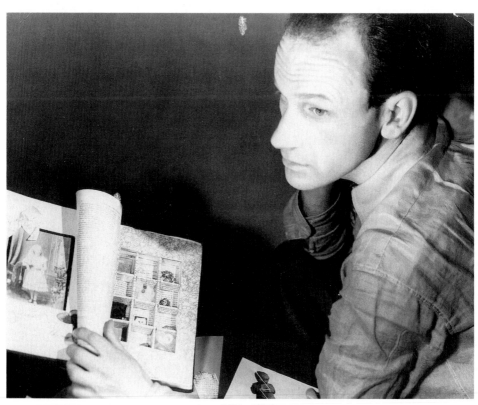

Joseph Cornell with box, c. 1940

Mina Loy's assemblages, 1950s, as photographed in her Stanton Street apartment: (above) Marcel Duchamp inspects Bums Praying; *(below)* Househunting *with David Mann, Duchamp, and Alex Bossom*

(above) No Parking: *photo by Berenice Abbott; (inset) Mina Loy,*
Aspen, 1957: photo by Jonathan Williams. At Mina's request, Williams
cropped this photograph to show only her eyes on the jacket of
Lunar Baedeker & Time-Tables

friend's rental agent, from Djuna's perspective, Mina proved too "starry" to attend to the matter.

In the summer, her worries multiplied. Fearing that she would be unable to sell the business let alone keep her own apartment, Mina begged Joella and Julien to "treat" her situation. Despite his conversion to Christian Science, Julien's "fine Jewish compassion," along with an occasional check, had kept her from feeling that the past three years had been wasted. In some way he had taken her father's place. But even with his support, she did not know how much longer she could go on. "Anything nice that could happen seems to be in another universe," she complained.

Her social life was at a low ebb. Lacking the confidence to see acquaintances, she often turned down invitations, and when she managed to appear at the rue Jacob, Natalie scolded her for running away from the people she had brought to meet her. Of her old friends, Man Ray was absorbed in his romance with the beautiful Lee Miller, a young American model who had become his assistant; Duchamp, after a disastrous marriage to Lydie Sarrazin, an heiress Picabia had chosen for him, was living with Mary Reynolds; and Laurence Vail had begun an affair with the writer Kay Boyle following Peggy's departure to England with John Holmes, her new lover. Laurence and Kay were moving to the South of France with their respective children. Except for fixtures like Natalie, Gertrude, and Alice, everyone seemed to have left Paris or to be thinking of doing so.

By 1929 it felt like the end of an era. "What Paris had once offered was no longer there," McAlmon concluded. Taking a good look at his fellow expatriates at a New Year's Eve party, he muttered, "They're wraiths, all of them." In October, the news of Wall Street's collapse hit expatriates and Europeans alike. Within a fortnight, Jacques Rigaut, the Surrealist who admired Cravan and called suicide a "vocation," proved his point by shooting himself in the head, and two months later Harry Crosby, whose guests had struck McAlmon as wraiths, committed suicide in New York. Their deaths seemed symbolic of the spiritual crisis shadowing the economic *crise* discussed in the papers.

As if they had known something was wrong, Jane Heap and Margaret Anderson had just brought out the "suicide" issue of *The Little Review*. "The revolution in the arts, begun before the war, heralded a renaissance," Heap began, at a time when "so-called thinking people" were hoping for "a new world order." Despite her devotion to making *The Little Review* the organ of this renaissance, she now saw that it was pointless to try "to reform or reorganize the world-mind" by publishing a magazine. "The world-mind has to be changed," Heap went on, "but it's too big a job for art." Anderson, on the other hand, had lost interest because she was seeking "illumination" rather than reform. As a final gesture, the editors sent a questionnaire to sixty "thinking people," asking them to focus on what was to be done.

The list included everyone who had helped define what it meant to be modern, and the responses were as varied as the contributors. To one of the most stimulating questions—"What is your world view? (Are you a reasonable being in a reasonable scheme?)"—McAlmon replied, "The world is reasonable . . . but something's wrong"; Janet Flanner concluded that while *she* was reasonable, the others were mad. Natalie was reluctant to reply, not wanting to leave "definite mind-marks," but Djuna said only that the questions did not interest her. Others said that they could not come up with a "world view." Emma Goldman, who had been living in the South of France on a stipend from Peggy Guggenheim, was perhaps the most disillusioned; to the question "Why do you go on living?" she replied, "I suppose because my will to Life is stronger than my reason."

Given the gloomy feeling that year and Mina's habitual depression, her replies were unexpectedly positive. To the question "What should you most like to do, to know, to be? (In case you are not satisfied)," she replied, "Quite satisfied" and declined the opportunity to "change places with any other human being" on the grounds that there was "no room." Asked what she feared, she answered fear itself (anticipating F.D.R.). Her "weakest characteristic" was her compassion, her "strongest" her "capacity for isolation." (She disliked her "inability to live without sleep.") And concerning her worldview, she mused, "I am reasonable and the scheme may catch up with me." To the query "What has been the happiest moment of your life?" she replied, "Every moment I spent with Arthur Cravan." To its corollary, "the unhappiest," she answered, "The rest of the time."

That autumn, during an extended European vacation with Julien, Joella began to suspect that her mother was going through the change of life. Soon their affectionate concern helped Mina forget her miseries. She and Julien understood each other so well, she thought, that she must be "his cousin some millions of times removed." But as soon as they left, Mina returned to her worries. Certain that she and Fabi would find themselves "in the gutter" if she could not make the next mortgage payment, she put the shop up for sale well in advance of the lucrative holiday season. Nineteen twenty-nine was, however, an unusual year. Shortly after the stock-market collapse in October, businesses catering to the tourist and luxury trades began to show the effects of the *crise.* Jewelers, antiques and art dealers, and hotelkeepers were all losing money, and Mina worried that the business would stay on the market indefinitely. When Julien wired the funds for her payment, she thanked him for saving her life.

Increasingly, Mina turned to her son-in-law for help and advice. He began sending a regular "allowance" even though the shop had found a buyer, whose down payment was sufficient to keep her solvent. When it finally sold in March (for 75,000 francs, or about $170,000 at today's rate), Mina's mood improved considerably, and she was cheered by the arrival of Joella's second baby, a boy. But to a letter congratulating her for surrounding herself with males, Mina added an alarming afterthought: "I am going to form a suicide club for the 'saved,' " she wrote. Joella and Julien were sufficiently worried to wire their reply. She had "no mind, no character," she responded. She had been "joking," and while she did not need to be saved, she felt bound to accept the "allowance" because of Fabi. Julien was becoming the *homme de confiance* she had wished for, but at the cost of a curiously triangulated relationship between the children and herself.

More than her son-in-law, she wrote, Julien was her son. He wrote to her "loy-ally," while Joella did not. He knew how her mind worked and understood her dark humor. What was more, he was devoted to Fabi. Soon after his marriage, Mina had asked him to be Fabi's guardian. "All you have to do is take my allowance to the keeper of the Zoo," she teased, "and ask him to board Fabi on it—she'd stay put, all right! And my ghost would not haunt itself with her possible complexes." He appreciated both her irony and the seriousness of the request. "We think she's a pretty good creature and are delighted that she would tolerate us," he replied. Mina began sending Julien copies of her writing and seeking his advice on literary matters.

By April, Mina had found "perfect peace," she wrote, in the form of a Breton servant woman who not only cooked and cleaned but was "intelligent," "humane," and picturesque: this "heavenly ambassador" arrived every morning in a starched Breton cap and bodice. While Mina was enjoying the ministrations of this devoted servant, she complained nonetheless of feeling "like an escaped lunatic when I talk to anyone." People always asked about her work, but for the time being she could not think of doing any. Her "three years of torture" at the shop had left her vacant. Unless Julien told her what to do, she wrote, she might vanish into Natalie's fourth dimension. "Too old for love, too young for death" (she was forty-eight), she could now contemplate her life with detachment.

Although the deaths of Rigaut and Crosby, both fixtures in expatriate circles, had been shocking, they had not touched Mina deeply, as she had meant to imply in her jest about the suicide club for the saved. In June, when she learned that Pascin had slit his wrists, it was different. He had been half in love with her in prewar Montparnasse, and although his emotional life was in permanent disarray, he was one of her oldest friends. All the galleries closed for his funeral, and the procession was so large that it stopped traffic. Mina's memorial is entitled, simply, "Jules Pascin":

> So this is death—
> to rise to the occasion
> a shadow
> to a shadowy persuasion
>
> Pascin has passed
> with his affectionate swagger

his air
of the Crown in the role of jester

The poem evokes Pascin's "immaculate leer" and "satyric spirit"—a neat combination of "satyr" and "satire"—as well as the sleazy atmospheres he loved to paint:

Pascin has ceased
to flush with ineffaceable bruises
his innubile Circes

ceased to dangle
demi-rep angels
in tinsel bordels

Silence bleeds
. . .
The seeds of his sly spirit
cast to posterity
in satyric squander

In their last conversation, she told Julien, Pascin had said that her poems were the equal of Valéry's. In her own way, she was repaying the compliment.

III

From 1929 until 1931, Fabi spent much of her time at home; she had lessons but rarely attended school. This situation did not strike either of them as odd, no doubt because up to that point her education had been irregular. Persuaded that children learned nothing in the public schools, Mina had previously enrolled Fabi at church-run establishments and later at boarding school. She had done well in their orderly atmosphere, in part because of her drawing ability and gift for languages. But as soon as Fabi adjusted to one school, Mina found reasons to try another. Fabi developed a dread of being *la nouvelle*, since new girls were regularly shunned. Between bouts of convent education, she lived *en pension* in the country, where she gave free rein to her love of animals. But by 1929 Mina's loneliness was so great that she kept Fabi at home and took her to the "factory" as a substitute for school.

Mina encouraged her to learn as many languages as possible. As a young child, Fabi spoke Italian and French, the two languages in which she conversed with Joella, then picked up German in Potsdam. When she was seven, Mina began teaching her English by telling stories first in French and, whenever Fabi asked to hear them again, in English. Fabi learned to pronounce *crocodile* in her mother's tongue when Mina told her a story about a "funny" mama who "loved to see the children 'express' themselves." ("As she had nothing to do but ring for the maid to clear up after them," the story continues, "there was really no reason why they should not.") After adopting a detoothed crocodile who was also tailless, this progressive family attached a Christmas tree to his rear, then took him to entertain the children of the poor, to whom they distributed presents. Along with English pronunciation, Fabienne was being taught a certain vision of childhood. "In this democratic household," the story goes on, "all who chose to come and live there were sure to be accepted on terms of perfect equality." Soon the mother was lifting her reptilian boarder onto her lap, only realizing who he was "when she found that most of the Crocodile was still sitting on the floor." By the end of the story, the crocodile has received an education, and the children make a fortune showing him at a fair.

In this idealized Victorian household, self-expression is valued as much as formal knowledge. Perhaps for this reason, Mina insisted that Fabi's drawing talent must be nurtured whether she liked it or not. Since her natural ability would improve with practice, Mina believed, she used every tactic, from brainwashing to bribery, to make her daughter draw. But the effort required was too great, she told Julien. ("My next job is lion tamer for a rest," she added.) When Fabi learned that her aunt Olga Sacharoff, Uncle Otho's wife, taught in Montparnasse at the Académie de la Grande Chaumière, she begged to be allowed to take lessons there. Mina refused, claiming that instruction would kill her imagination, and in any case, Olga and Otho were bourgeois. During the years that she stayed at home, Fabi produced an impressive number of drawings as well as the occasional poem, yet longed for the kind of education which even the crocodile had not been denied.

Although Mina could be tyrannical about the need for self-expression, on other matters she was neither practical nor firm. She sympathized with Fabi, particularly when she noticed that her daughter was lonely. Although the apartment was small, she let her keep pets—birds in fanciful cages, which Fabi liked to draw, Samoyed dogs, hamsters, and a monkey, who moved to the zoo during the winter when the building lacked heat. No stranger to artistic eccentricity, Ezra Pound visited one day with two small tortoises for Fabi and instructed her to tickle their stomachs with a toothpick. And when they had rows, Mina tried to make up by bringing Fabi flowers or a new hamster.

Fabi was a lively, imaginative child who spent much of her time alone. Mina liked to think that her pets, imagination, and Christian Science sufficed to keep her from suffering: she told her there was "no substance in matter" when she shut her thumb in a door. Along with her other coping mechanisms, Fabi learned not to complain, although it struck her as odd that someone who adhered to her mother's faith should believe in spirits, or claim, as Mina did, that she had been driven from Florence by ill-wishers. (She would soon call this tendency Mina's "persecution complex.")

When Fabi expressed the desire to know her maternal grandmother, Mina overcame her reluctance and sent her to England. Julia Lowy looked and sounded distinguished but was not, Fabi reported; furthermore, she was in the habit of shrieking at her maids. Her Aunt Dora, still unmarried, sometimes visited them in Paris. Unlike her own career, Mina explained, Dora's had come to nothing because Julia had succeeded in "smashing her nerves." When Fabi asked to have singing lessons—her voice was "small" but pleasant—Mina told her to visit Dora's voice teacher, then living in Paris, and say that she should teach her for free, a strategy which required more nerve than Fabi could summon. But whenever Mina spoke of Cravan, she told her mother that she did not want to hear about him.

In 1931, when Fabi was twelve, she persuaded Mina that she not only had to go to school but must attend an institution with standards. She chose the school herself: the Collège Sevigné, the oldest private school for girls in Paris, was not only serious about teaching but had a cosmopolitan student body composed of the daughters of Sorbonne professors, prominent French Jews and Protestants, and expatriate families. The school was so well known that its fiftieth-anniversary celebration was held at the Sorbonne—an event of such solemnity that even Mina was impressed. Fabi did so well at the Collège that her teachers encouraged her to take the daunting French baccalaureat exams several years in advance.

As Fabi began to find herself, Mina's vagueness—the self-absorption Djuna called her "starriness"—only increased. This, combined with her habit of criticism, made it hard for those closest to her, yet even the butts of her irony found her irresistible when she was being charming. Fabi and one of her classmates, an American named Sheila Carroll whose mother enjoyed being a bohemian, decided that year that they would like a family Christmas rather than a restaurant dinner—despite the fact that neither of their mothers did much cooking. Mina agreed, as long as the twelve-year-olds saw to the preparations. When their mothers sent them out to buy a bottle of sherry, they misunderstood and returned with Cherry Heering, only to be sent back to the shop, which reopened once they banged on the metal shutters. Despite the scolding they received from the shopkeeper, the girls had done the right thing: while they cooked, their mothers polished off the sherry. Dinner appeared hours later. Mina pronounced it "not bad, though not quite what it should be," and they burst into tears. (Characteristically, she went in search of presents.)

Apart from Djuna, Natalie, and Mina's immediate family, few people knew of her absorption in the voluminous manuscript she called her "novel." In the years following her release from the business, she rewrote this *roman à clef* from several perspectives and under several titles, most of which fictionalize, very lightly, her childhood, student days, and education in vanguardism. Watching Fabi develop from a young child into a teenager with ideas of her own had prompted her to analyze her own development. The result—a book that had, she told Julien, grown increasingly "fat"— told the story of her escape from Julia's assault on her nerves while laying the blame for her problems at her mother's door. Although Mina had, she believed, "been carefully brought up to be a thoroughgoing neurotic," she had escaped "the logical dénouement of lunacy through the indefatigable optimistic helping hand of C.S." (and though she did not mention it, a little sherry).

After reading Mina's "novel" in its different versions, one comes away with the impression that the author's animus against her parents provided the source of her rebellious energy. Her infancy, she noted in one of the more polished versions, *Islands in the Air*, was the time "when like Lucifer from heaven I was 'cast out' of perfection." (Although she was repeating the sentiment voiced in *The Child and the Parent*, in this version she aligns herself unambivalently with the devil.) In some moods, Mina saw Julia not so much as a wrathful god but as a woman of another generation. But as she re-created her mother's tirades, the Voice blew through her "like an ungovernable wind," and Julia's "vocal shrapnel" revived old wounds. Like much autobiography, Mina's "novel" was shaped by the need to compose a self for whom she could feel compassion.

Goy Israels, a version drafted most likely during the 1930s, represents Mina's attempt to analyze the Jewish half of her "bi-spirited" self. As "Goy Israels," her own character's name, implies, she saw herself from both parents' perspectives. Until Hitler's rise to power, her internalized anti-Semitism had kept her from facing this aspect of her split heritage. As the Third Reich's racial policies became common knowledge, she sought to understand what it had meant to be half Jewish. Her father had been "an unbeliever" yet had boasted of his "pedigree," which in his view went "back into the past for over three thousand years." He was, she thought, a natural aristocrat whose superiority showed in his intellect as well as his status as one of the chosen. Yet having deposited his progeny "in a protestant nest," he had created in her a new kind of being—"a wanderer infinitely more haunted than the eternal Jew: a bi-spirited entity." For this reason, her mind always spun in "disparate orbits—its functioning a mental gymnastics more challenging than either Torah or catechism."

Like many of her era, Mina largely accepted the nineteenth-century racialism, or pseudo-science, which not only assigned to different races innate characteristics but assumed that these were genetically determined. At the same time, she was also aware that generalizations about "the English" or "the Jews" were meaningful only up to a point: "So is every race at long distance uniform as distinct from other races; yet in every race at close-up there is infinite variety." What counted was one's perspective, the angle and distance from which one studied the question. Yet as *Goy Israels* makes clear, Mina continued to believe that (unlike herself) Jews were clever with finance, brilliant mathematicians all, and so intellectual that they had no time for make-believe. Their survival after centuries of persecution could be explained only by their belief in themselves as the chosen people: "continuing in this worship this race survives, for the sole reason that once it has got an idea into its head that idea is im - poss - i - ble to dislodge."

Mina also believed that "every scion of every race has a racial memory." As a secular Jew, her father had urged her and Dora "to enter the promised land, imposing the obligation of his pedigree upon them—to inherit the earth." Yet although his daughters had inherited this genetic reminiscence of his race's glories, far from giving them comfort, it made worldly success a "fulfillment of duty." In the end, what mattered was the cost of salvation. As her mother's child she was—at least in theory—among the elect. As her father's child she was, from his perspective, one of the chosen people, and from her mother's, one of the damned. The impossibility of her situation had come home to her one day at a birthday party when she tried to befriend "a little golden-haired girl who looked like an angel" but proved to be Jewish and unconcerned about salvation. Had Mina, as nominal Christian, "stolen this salvation from this Jewess—or was this salvation like Mother-love so torturous [sic] that the Jew preferred hell?" Unable to resolve the paradox of her mixed being, *Goy Israels* finally posits a God unimagined by Jew or Christian: "the invisible dancing-master destiny" who has chosen her to do His most difficult steps on her own.

IV

While Mina wrote her way through personal and "racial" history to understand her origins, she was also probing similar ideas in paint. "The two, writing and painting, go together with me," she told Julien. When "inhibited" in her writing, she noted, "I couldn't get free in my painting either"; conversely, progress in one medium helped with the other. If writing led back to the subconscious archives, painting probed abiding questions about the nature of form. "I realize that there is something of the drop of water torture on the scalp inherent to my way of progressing through my thought," she wrote, "but that cannot be eliminated."

For the time being, Julien was fascinated by Mina's progress through her thought and more than willing to put up with its meanderings. "Does form result from seeing unform repeatedly," she scrawled on the new manuscript she sent him; entitled "Mi and Lo," it was a philosophical dialogue, she explained, between two parts of herself—Mi(na) Lo(y). To Lo's thesis—that "the intellect of man is an instrument for imposing form upon phenomena"—Mi replied that form had not begun with man but was a sign deployed by the intellect "on its march upon the illimitable." Although this reinvention of the Platonic dialogue provided Mina with a forum in which to stage her debate with herself, it remained abstract.

The same concerns could, she decided, be worked out more concretely in art. Of the paintings begun in this period, she wrote: "I felt, if I were to go back, begin a universe all over again, forget all form I am familiar with, evoking a chaos from which I could draw forth incipient form, that at last the female brain might achieve an act of creation." Soon after her liberation from her shop she began a series of meditations on the theme of "incipient form." Against background washes painted in ethereal gray-blues floated imaginary beings—wraithlike human profiles emerging from snail shells, disembodied cherub heads with wings, an oyster-woman and her companion, a butterfly-woman, and a variety of mixed-species "sunset-creatures." In other paintings, the imagery of *Lunar Baedecker* took shape, and elemental forces seemed to burst upon consciousness as if for the first time. The brooding atmospheres and almost weightless line of these visions gave the best in the series a haunting quality, as if Blake's drawings had been redone by a disciple of Cocteau—who unexpectedly believed in God.

Mina was now having "a lovely time," she told Julien. She had "won back enough energy to desire to express—and some inkling of what I want to express—which I had thought had been knocked out of me." Her return to painting came at a propitious moment. With the proceeds of the trust fund left by his mother, Julien planned to start a gallery featuring the latest in modern art. He not only needed Mina's advice about the Surrealists but intended to give her a one-woman show. In Paris with Joella during the summer of 1931, Julien saw the paintings of Salvador Dali, not yet known outside Surrealist circles, and bought the canvas called *The Persistence of Memory*, renamed by the Levys *The Limp Watches*. It is tempting to imagine its effect on Mina when Julien took the painting to her apartment. In years to come, they often discussed Dali's motivation: was it black magic, drugs, or, as Dali was fond of saying, delirium?

With this purchase, the gallery's direction was set: it became the New York showcase for Surrealism. By 1932, in addition to Dali, the roster included Max Ernst, Cocteau, Duchamp, Man Ray, Alexander Calder, and an unknown who came in because he liked what he saw there—Joseph Cornell, the shy collagist and maker of boxes. To this provocative list, Julien added the neo-romantic Russian painter Eugene Berman and his brother Leonid, as well as Juan Gris, Magritte, Tchelitchew, de Chirico, Leonor Fini, and Frida Kahlo, to name only a few of his artists. He went to Paris on business each summer, accompanied every other year by Joella, and Mina agreed to become his Paris representative, an arrangement that not only brought her out of herself but to her mind justified the monthly "allowance" on which she depended.

Moreover, in Julien's view, whether or not his mother-in-law was painting, Mina was herself a work of art. Not only was her novel on a par with *Ulysses*, he believed, but her daily life demonstrated a kind of genius. Mina's household, "always in a state of delicate equilibrium between threadbare poetic freedom and aristocratic elegance," was the perfect location for his own "balancing act between America and Europe." To some,

Mina's apartment seemed threadbare, but to Julien it was a "fairyland dream." The panes of her sitting room's glass doors were covered with squares of colored cellophane, and the crumbling plaster concealed beneath scraps of silver paper arranged in the floral patterns of her Jaded Flowers. Fabi's bird cages served as room dividers, their wire and wicker shapes like filigree apartment houses. After Maurice Grosser, an American artist on Julien's roster, visited Mina with his friend Virgil Thomson, he baptized her aesthetic "the prickly Baroque." But to Julien, "this abundance of subtle, casual visual experience was a banquet for which I had been starved."

Because Julien had been also starved for an alternative to the work ethic, he liked to think that Mina's way of life offered "an encounter with beauty that had no practical, moral, or prestige implications whatsoever." Her poverty was relative—more a matter of penny-pinching—but it embarrassed her, he observed years later, and kept her from seeing old friends like Man Ray and Duchamp. "Mina hated being poor," he insisted, "and she had a hard time making the best of it." At the time, Julien's romantic view of artists in general and his mother-in-law in particular blinded him to her unhappiness.

During these years Julien combined gallery trips to Paris with his latest project, a series of short experimental film portraits of artists in action. He planned to show Brancusi, Léger, Max Ernst, and Mina, all in their natural environments. Ernst chose as his setting the Crosbys' luxurious moulin at Ermenonville, where he staged an ambiguous scenario in the empty swimming pool. Mina, on the other hand, asserted with much bitterness "that her true environment should be a dustbin." Julien filmed her at the Marché aux Puces, sleuthing for the treasures she made from other people's castoffs. "Your poverty is really luxury," he told her with the innocence of a young man endowed with a trust fund.

Despite his marital happiness, Julien was tempted by the thought of an affair with a beautiful and unobtainable woman—a fantasy which, in Surrealist circles, was treated with the utmost respect. Although it is unclear to what extent Mina encouraged Julien to act out this fantasy, she took an interest in his love life, even defending him once his waywardness disturbed his marriage. By 1932 Lee Miller had left Man Ray, who was said to be inconsolable and in possession of a revolver. Eager to prove that he could attract such a beauty, and the leading lady in Cocteau's film *The Blood of a Poet*, Julien told himself before their first rendezvous that they would have a pleasant night together if he could charm her. "And so it proved," he observed discreetly years later. At the time, when staying at Mina's apartment, he showed no discretion whatsoever.

Unperturbed by her son-in-law's behavior, Mina accompanied Lee and Julien to an underground cinema for a clandestine showing of *L'Age d'Or*, Luis Buñuel's provocative anti-bourgeois film, which had been banned by the French censors. When right-wing groups in the crowded theater began denouncing the Surrealists, Julien expressed surprise that in France artistic events generated such passion. Despite, or perhaps because of, the film's shocking images and the uproar it created, Mina urged Julien to show it in New York. That summer, when the heady mix of extramarital love, clandestine art, and political protest proved particularly exciting, Julien was sorry to return to America.

Whenever possible, he arranged to bring souvenirs of his Parisian life home with him. To Joseph Cornell he gave the antique puzzle boxes and watch parts in old containers he had unearthed at the flea market with Mina. In a few weeks Cornell returned to the gallery with a collection of small objects in glass balls and boxes utilizing these French treasures, which Julien included in his Surrealist show.

Mina's most recent paintings, Julien believed, would have a similar effect, importing his Parisian life into an American setting. To inform New Yorkers about her artistic lineage, he had "Lunar Baedeker" printed on the catalogue for her 1933 exhibition. "Mina Loy is so distinguished on the left bank of the Seine for her poems and her paintings that everything she does merits attention and gets it," the *New York Evening Sun* noted. "Miss Loy does not paint measurable facts but immeasurable feelings," it went on. "Those who respond to Blake and Arthur Rimbaud and other such mystics may also come to terms with Miss Loy," it concluded, adding, "No others need apply." The critics agreed that her paintings had "the same imaginative feeling" as her poems: one called the exhibition "a sort of sonnet sequence, in which the general poetic mood seems more important than any of its component parts."* Generally speaking, the critics were right. As component parts, the paintings were enigmatic, and for this reason, perhaps, failed to sell. As a poetic atmosphere, however, they made an impression on those who were spiritually inclined, like Cornell. But the timing was wrong, Julien concluded. By 1934 the fashion had changed and everyone was "crazy for pictures which are 'féerique' and candy box and magical."

Mina's *féerique* manner had more admirers in Paris than in New York. As Julien's representative, she was not only someone to be treated with care but proof that, although American, her son-in-law understood the artistic psyche. Julien told her to be on the lookout for anyone whose work had the impact of Dalí's and, because he was drawn to Surrealism, asked

---

* The "News and Gossip" columnist for *Creative Art* was enthusiastic but said nothing about her art: "Mina Loy, who is having her American premiere at Julien Levy's Gallery, is in Europe as distinguished as a person as she is as a painter. She was one of the early innovators of *vers libre*. Her apartment is one of the most stylish in Paris, a fact in which she takes especial pride, since not an item in it costs more than ten francs, everything having been bought at 'The Flea Market.' She was the wife of Arthur Cravan (Fabian Lloyd), who was a ringleader of dadism and is still regarded by the surrealists with veneration as their guiding spirit. She is, so I am told by Harry Streeter, who was one of that crew in his Paris days, a person of noble loveliness. She is also the mother of Mrs. Julien Levy, which is a lovely thing all by itself." One suspects that this information was supplied by Julien, who may also have told Mina to backdate her 1933 paintings (several are misdated 1902 and 1903), to enhance their value.

her to keep in touch with Breton, who had reasons of his own for courting Cravan's widow. Hoping to persuade Mina to let him publish Cravan's surviving manuscripts, Breton was deferential. In private, Mina remarked that Breton had "the expression of an outrageous ram," while his wife resembled "a reanimated mummy of an Egyptian sorceress." "People who get mixed up with black magic do suddenly look like death's heads," she went on. (Max Ernst looked like "a skull with ligaments still attached with the false eyes of an angel.") The Surrealists were, she thought, "expressive of their art, which after all takes the sort of shapes which would seethe out of the cauldron over which a wizard hangs." Although Mina could not understand why misunderstandings arose whenever she handled payments to these "wizards," she liked being Julien's agent, a position that brought her out of herself and gave her status in the art world.

In this positive state of mind, Mina was less self-conscious about her fear that she had wasted her talents. Moreover, the early thirties were a difficult period for everyone. She found that she could comfort friends whose sufferings resembled her own: after Pascin's suicide, Hermine David often visited the rue St.-Romain or took Mina and Fabi to her favorite restaurant, where they joined Pascin's mistress, Lucy Krogh, and her son, who was Fabi's age. (One wonders whether seeing the grandson of Christian and Oda Krogh revived memories of Oda Janet and the Colarossi days.) Although they had all suffered losses of a dramatic kind, the old sparkle returned at these reunions. Mina and Fabi joined Hermine and her friend Marc Chagall one evening at the Dôme when Chagall was chaffing Hermine about her attraction to Catholicism. "Hermine," he teased, "when you're an old nun, pining away in a convent, I will be fêting the gals in the bordellos." Brancusi often stopped to take Mina to the movies. Together they discovered the "Thin Man" series and Mina's "namesake," the glamorous Myrna.

Of the old crowd, only Gertrude and Alice, Natalie and several of her "Women," and Djuna remained. They called on Mina's day—Thursday afternoon, a school holiday and a time when Fabi could be made to polish the brass doorknobs, spray the potted palms with cologne, and serve lemonade. During the early thirties, Mina joined Djuna and Natalie on a trip to the South of France, and in 1934 returned to Florence for a last look at the Costa San Giorgio. (Florence looked "more magnificent—though less secure," she told Carl Van Vechten, with whom she was again corresponding. "Mussolini—Mousie to his pals," she went on, "has dressed the giovanotti [boys] in such alluring travestie that one feels it would be unfortunate to be a girl"—an impression she had often had in Italy.) During this visit, she struck an old friend as "vague and quite unbalanced," no longer the self-possessed artist she had known in the teens. And although Kay Boyle wrote to say that she and Laurence Vail would love to have her stay in their new home near Nice—they had been discussing Mina's "glorious, sharp, miraculous work" with Bob Brown, who lived nearby—Mina declined the invitation.

Nor did she wish to see friends from the Arensberg circle like Juliette Gleizes and Gabi Picabia. Perhaps they reminded her too much of Cravan, or possibly their less than laudatory comments on his prewar behavior made them seem unsympathetic. At a time when the Surrealists kept inflating the myth of Cravan as their precursor, Mina worried about the legend that had grown up about him. He had "taken on an immortality as an evergrowing myth," she wrote, but it was hard to accept those aspects of the myth that escaped her control. When, for example, the story of his disappearance was told in a way that implied his wish to leave her behind, she went into a rage. After Gabi Picabia published a memoir of Cravan that was largely complimentary but expressed doubt about the reasons for his disappearance, Mina cut her dead.

When "The Widow's Jazz" appeared in a new review called *Pagany* in 1931, Mina had all but ceased writing poetry and, on Julien's advice, was again revising her novel. The free-verse movement of the teens had evaporated, he wrote; its time had come and gone. "My 'poetry' had nothing to do with that movement," she protested: she had turned to verse after hearing someone say that "one should write as one feels." After that, she went on, "I tried to forget that I had ever in my life read anything & see if I could let out that natural expression that must be innate to all mankind." Although she had found her "rhythm of expression," it had come as a surprise when the Americans decided that she "knew the way to write vers libre." Only once she had written "Apology of Genius," she continued, did she find that she was really interested in poetry. Now that she was painting and writing prose, this interest had subsided.

v

On the lookout for the next genius, Julien asked Mina to contact the German Surrealist painter Richard Oelze. Oelze had been living in Paris since 1933, but few outside the Surrealist inner circle—Breton, Dali, and Oelze's compatriot Max Ernst—knew much about him. Described as an introvert, and possibly a drug addict, Oelze piqued her curiosity. When she finally met him, this tall, threadbare eccentric elicited her compassion—in her own estimate, her weakest feature. Oelze suffered from a number of ills—an inability to communicate (he spoke only German), poverty, isolation, and semi-starvation. He saw himself as a character by Kafka. Although younger than Mina by eighteen years, he was, she observed, "strangely pitiable in a premature old age." She began noting down their conversations, her thoughts on his character, and the psychic phenomena that flourished during their acquaintance. A "congenital surrealist," he was good material.

Oelze opened up to her, in part because Mina spoke German. While

381

his background was of interest—he had lived in Berlin—she felt an affinity with this "uncommon derelict" that transcended biography. At first, she was taken with the idea that, although "economically nude," he approached survival as a creative act. And despite Oelze's "nonsensical manner of being alive," he had a kind of elegance. She was the only one who understood him, he insisted, the only one with whom it was possible to discuss *Die nackte Seele*, the naked soul. His own was so delicate, she thought, that it had a hard job holding his body together.

Mina was flattered yet disconcerted when she next saw Oelze: "He greeted me with the relief of an object which, having fallen apart, should chance upon its other half." Although he was so emaciated that he seemed on the verge of dematerializing, some mysterious force emanated from him. He was hard to resist. Despite his peculiarities, he possessed a distinction of the kind she had always hoped to find, she wrote, in someone "who, like myself, had 'popped up' from nowhere at all—as if all my life I had lacked a crony of my 'own class.' "

His artistic vision also resembled hers. She was "an extraordinarily gifted woman," he told her after gazing at her blue paintings. When she finally visited his studio, it struck her that Oelze had already painted the incipient forms of which she had only dreamed. Like herself, he had "visualized the mists of chaos curdling into shape," but he had pushed this idea further than she had taken it. His pictorial universe contained biomorphic shapes in constant metamorphosis. Looking at his canvases was, moreover, like looking into his mind. Oelze's "half formulated concepts" generated paintings, she wrote, in which "glaucous shades dissolved and deepened into the unreal tides of an ocean without waves." His hallucinatory landscapes, which populate the nightmare space of German Romanticism with Surrealist forms, are to this day disturbing—no doubt because, as Mina saw, they depict forms that are "at once embryonic and precocious."

Insel, the novella into which Mina transposed her friendship with Oelze, is structured as a series of walks, visits to cafés and studios, and discussions of the sort that comprised their acquaintance. The narrator—who scouts for a New York gallery when she is not writing a novel—expresses some concern about her attraction to Insel [Oelze]. She finds herself "giving in to a dislocation of my identity" in his presence, yet this "perilous" behavior is justified, she thinks, by the result—"a revelation of what supremely lovely essence was being conveyed to me by this human wreck." By the end of *Insel*, the reader, whose own tolerance for dislocations of identity it tests, is less certain that the experiment has been worthwhile.

As an account of its author's psychic state, *Insel* is a revealing document. Before long, the narrator invites her new friend to dinner, telling herself that in her role as gallery "tout," she is simply "feeding a cagey genius in the hope of production." "*Sterben—man muss*" (One must die),

382

he keeps repeating gloomily, as if his tendency to dematerialize will be perfected in death. "If Insel committed suicide—I could share in that too," she muses, a thought which brings "a flowering peace." But despite its appeal, she fights her inclination to follow his lead.

After inviting him to live in her apartment while she is away, she returns to find him taking up more room in her psychic space than in the physical world. In this respect, the artist is the ideal tenant: "The flat seemed emptier for his being there." He is drawn to death, perhaps, because his medium is absence. Staring raptly at the portrait of Colossus, who is mentioned as the flat's other inhabitant, he claims him as a soulmate: "We would have been as one."

It is difficult not to see *Insel* as Mina's search for another soulmate in Oelze, who combines the roles of psychic double and substitute lover/son. This affair of the mind fails after the narrator reproaches the artist for using her loan to "barricade" himself with his *Mädchen*, habituées of the Dôme and ladies of the night. When she sees that they share little but their former intimacy, the narrator realizes that something like this had happened before. In his distress at having his psyche invaded, she recalls, Geronimo [Papini] had chided her, "You just walk into a man's brain, seat yourself comfortably in an armchair to take a look around—afterwards, you write down all you have found there." As in the affair with Papini, Mina would convert an aborted relationship into fictional form, where she could have the last word. "How goes the book," Insel asks in the final scene. "Vainly imagining that I had criticized my last incompletion," the narrator replies, "wonderfully." Their relationship, and the novel, conclude with Insel's expression of gratitude.

In the novel, the narrator's triumph demonstrates that she was not, as Mina secretly feared, a clochard or a madwoman. Moreover, *Insel*'s conclusion—in which the narrator bids the painter farewell after he voices the desire to "come home" to her—neatly reversed the collapse of their "understanding." In Mina's notes to herself, however, the collapse of their bond brings her sorrow. "I saw why Insel and I had that fundamental understanding—clochard to clochard—of those who are fated to failure," she wrote. Despite her "primordial affinity with a presumed madman," she went on, "I had failed to establish any reality between [him] and myself."

In October 1936, after the failure of their friendship, Oelze made his way to Switzerland. He had spent three years as *persona non grata* in France, the country to which he had fled on the last train from Berlin before the closing of the border. Once in Germany, Oelze would again become an undesirable because of his Bolshevik past. Although *Insel* mentions his "anguish," it does so in passing—when he agrees to tell the story of his life if she will "get [him] to America." It is clear that while Oelze yearned for a kindred soul, he also saw Mina as his ticket to New York: when he expressed the wish to explore Manhattan, she noted, he seemed to be praying.* But this theme is not developed. Whether because Mina completed *Insel* in America or because she told it as an allegory of artistic ripening, she underplayed Oelze's plight.

Yet the syntactic and psychic explorations pursued in the novel convey a sense of emergency, of pressures felt but deflected into another arena— where after embarking on "the whole itinerary of Good and Evil," as Mina called her acquaintance with Oelze, she emerged the victor in a struggle that was no less real to her for being psychic.

---

* After mentioning Insel's "ardent yearning to flee to New York from a threatening war" (p. 63), the narrator turns from the idea of war to imagining flimsy skyscrapers as a Surrealist might paint them.

18

Promised Land

I

Oelze had dematerialized from her life in much the way that he came into it. But he had left a trace of himself. His most recent canvas, *Expectation*, remained in her apartment, where it communed with the portrait of Cravan and haunted Mina. "Whenever I'm in the room with it," she wrote, "I catch myself looking at that sky—waiting for something to 'appear.'" Unlike most of Oelze's paintings, where embryonic forms crawl through pre-human dreamscapes, *Expectation* is inhabited by men and women dressed in the bowler hats, turbans, and furs of the bourgeoisie. Yet, despite their urbane appearance, these citizens wait at the edge of a wilderness beneath the ominous sky that drew Mina's gaze. She saw herself in "the commonplace back of a woman watching for signs on his painted firmament." The woman was waiting for something to appear, but whatever it was, the menacing clouds implied, it would not be for the good. Oelze's canvas was, Mina wrote, a "chart of unarrival."*

Seen from our perspective, the years of *Expectation*'s composition—1935 to 1936—are almost palpable in the brooding backs of Oelze's subjects. It was obvious that war was in the offing by this time, and only a question of when it would break out. From our perspective, these Magritte-like figures suggest the refugees already streaming into France from Germany or, soon thereafter, deportees on their way to the death camps: while Hitler

---

* *Expectation* is in the collection of the New York Museum of Modern Art, as are another of Oelze's paintings, *Daily Torment*, and a drawing, *Frieda*, based on a character in Kafka's *The Castle*.

had not yet made known the means by which he hoped to obtain *Lebensraum*, few doubted that he would act on his intentions. Oelze, doubly displaced when painting *Expectation*, had suffused the canvas with a premonition of things to come.

His painting was like himself, Mina thought. At first glance it looked perfectly ordinary, yet she had the eerie feeling "that any moment it will light up." Since 1934, her letters to the children had been full of references to the "end of the world" atmosphere prevailing in Paris. That year, the so-called Rome Protocols had established an understanding among Italy, Hungary, and Austria aligning these countries with Germany. The Germans had left the League of Nations, and both they and the French were rearming, while the British "appeased" Hitler in the hope of avoiding hostilities. At first Mina refused to take the threat of war as seriously as Brancusi, who, she told Julien, believed that "this is the end of everything." In her opinion, the European governments were "whipping up the war scare to keep their populations quiet in face of the financial impasse." (Her prose shows her tendency to express herself as if in translation: "in face of" being an anglicized form of *en face de*, or "facing.") By mid-1935, the consensus was "that we are bound for war"—whether in twelve or in eighteen months no one could say. Having been urged to "clear out," Mina was now sufficiently concerned to ask whether she should send Fabi to New York.

After looking into the idea of renting or selling her apartment, Mina learned that she not only owed a large sum for its maintenance but that apart from the German Jewish refugees appearing in increasing numbers, no tenants could be found. "Really everything is rather depressing," she wrote—after waking one night to the sound of German and "thinking it was Hitler." To Julien's objections that the common people did not understand politics, she replied, "Every grocer's son & femme de ménage's husband knows when they are calling up troops on the frontier—one gleans a little that never gets into the papers." The entire male populace, she added, took the war for granted. The Germans were not only "the most virile race," but more important, "they have suffered too much." And this time it was unlikely that they would "solve things by a revolution." In the same letter she mentioned that friends had said to go to New York while it was possible: "We would be safer in America *however poor*." She added, thinking perhaps of Oelze, "I really believe if the world were run by a handful of irresponsible artists—who liked negroes & 'bad' women & slept all the morning—provided they had no political leanings, we should be much better off."

In December 1935, as Hitler prepared to occupy the Rhineland—and after consultations with a clairvoyant and a palm reader—Mina sent Fabi to New York to live with Joella and Julien. Although Mina rarely mentioned the danger to herself, the idea of her Jewishness preoccupied her, especially as she worked on *Goy Israels*. Because Jews had more family feeling than Christians, she told Julien, her "Jewish blood" kept her "longing for relations," and she feared that the "world crisis" would be blamed on the Jews. The American Consulate had just repatriated hundreds of citizens; the general feeling was that "the world [was] shaking to pieces." What was more, Mina's banker had told her that the safest place to keep her money was in her stocking. "When there are no more banks," she wrote hopefully, "currency will have lost its significance."

In 1936, after Hitler announced that the Germans needed "additional living-space," Joella and Julien made arrangements to bring Mina to New York. She sold her apartment at a loss, left the life she knew best—having lived in Paris for twenty years all told—and was now as unsure of her expectations as the refugees in Oelze's disconcerting canvas.

II

Looking down at the dock where Joella and Fabi awaited her, Mina was surprised that "they looked so much a part of a generation" unlike her own. Fashionably dressed, particularly by European standards, her daughters seemed to have stepped out of the pages of *Vogue*. At twenty-nine, Joella was handsome in an unfamiliar and mature way, and Fabi nearly unrecognizable, having been transformed from a gawky sixteen-year-old into "a composite evocation of all the current types of beauty," Mina noted, "with the added depth of something Colossus had bequeathed to her." She took it amiss, however, that her daughters dressed in black, "that colour I alone could not wear." As if their clothes declared their independence, she continued, "they were thus cut off from me—& yet it was a consolation."

If Mina was shocked by the change in her daughters, they were astounded at the change in her. She had always seemed younger than her age, but at fifty-four she looked older. Their beautiful mother had suffered a *coup de vieux*, a dramatic onset of aging's most visible signs. Her hair had gone white; she walked with a defeated air.

Acting as Julien's Paris representative had given Mina a life, one in which she moved easily and knowledgeably. There, she was an expatriate—one of the geniuses. In New York she was just another refugee. Full of memories of the Arensbergs', *Others*, but, most poignantly, of Cravan, she was unprepared for the pace of Manhattan. And if she had had any expectations about advising Julien, she saw that she was not needed at the gallery. Although Mina had been an asset in Paris, she was now a poor relation. "Promised Land," her account of the period after her return to New York, is depressing to read. In this ironically named section of her ongoing autobiography, Joella appears as Alda, Fabi is Sophia (the name Mina often gave herself in accounts of life among the Futurists), and Julien is Aaron, the biblical figure who helped lead the Jewish people out of captivity. More than ever, in a situation where she felt powerless, writing provided the space in which to revise reality.

She lived with the "children" until the apartment that Joella had found for Mina and Fabi was ready. Having given birth to Jonathan, her third son, the year before, Joella had her hands full. By 1937 Julien's drinking, combined with his affairs with other beautiful and talented women—his need to sow his wild oats, as he put it—had placed such a strain on their marriage that the tension was palpable. But Mina's self-absorption kept her from sympathizing with Joella. In despair over the failure of her "affinity" with Oelze, her lost soulmate, Mina felt estranged from her daughters and imagined herself a burden. She was in no position to appreciate that while preoccupied with her own life, Joella was doing what she could—while growing increasingly concerned that her mother *had* gone mad, as she often said in her letters. Mina was so unhappy in this new setting, she wrote in "Promised Land," that "it seemed like the end of my life."

From 1937 until the early '40s, Joella recalled, Mina was "at her maddest." Joella arranged parties in her honor, to which she invited her friends from New York and Paris, but after hours of preparation Mina would refuse to appear, claiming it was too difficult to make herself presentable. And while Joella could not ignore her threats to put her head in the oven or jump out the window, she resented the atmosphere of psychic emergency with which her mother surrounded herself. She derived some comfort from the Christian Science practitioner to whom Joella took her in desperation, who told her that Mina's problem was "selfishness."

Once Fabi and Mina moved to their own apartment, Fabi developed her own techniques for coping with her mother. As the decision to give Fabi the name she used for herself suggests, Mina felt closer to her than to Joella. Despite her belonging to another generation, she was Cravan's daughter and had many of Mina's gifts. After her arrival in New York the year before, Joella had shown her sister's fashion designs to a *Vogue* editor, who promised Fabi a job provided she went to art school. (Fabi's plans to take the French baccalaureat exam had been abandoned when Mina packed her off to New York.) Fabi studied at the Parsons School of Design during the day and attended classes at the Art Students League at night until 1938, when she ran out of funds. By then, Mina's British income had dwindled to forty dollars a month: the Public Trustee had disposed of Sigmund Lowy's international stocks and invested in utilities and war bonds, whose value had fallen. Although Parsons offered Fabi a scholarship, she dropped out to become a wage earner.

She found work as a model for a designer who made clothes for celebrities like Katharine Hepburn, a position that allowed her and Mina to maintain appearances. After the firm's unexpected closure, Mina began worrying how they would live, let alone pay the gas bill. She proposed to find a job, but Fabi pointed out that in a depression, with her white hair and lack of training, she would have a hard time getting employers to take her seriously. And in New York, her European background counted for nothing. It was pointless to dwell on the past, she insisted: Mina's "sentimentality" stood in her way. Americans "despise sentiment," Sophia [Fabi] maintains in "Promised Land." "They have nicknamed it sentimentality," she continues, "because they can't recognize it." While Mina wallowed in nostalgia, people striving to keep their businesses alive tried not "to feel anything."

By 1938 Joella's personal situation was difficult. Separated from Julien, she had taken a job as an interior decorator at Saks Fifth Avenue—as Joella Lloyd. (When Mina learned that Joella went under the name she had told her to use in Paris, she was miffed. "It's not your name," she told her with no sense of contradiction.) Mina had taken Julien's side. A woman should do anything to save her marriage, she told Joella, unconcerned that her own behavior failed to illustrate this maxim. Yet even before their separation, Julien had begun to regret his susceptibility to Mina's charm as well as his commitment to her support. The novel in which he had once believed as devoutly as if it had been written by Joyce had, by 1938, been rejected by all the publishers to whom he had shown it. It occurred to him that this unfinished masterpiece served as an excuse for Mina to get money from him, since the day when he promised to look after her while she completed it.

Mina found Julien's defection the greatest loss of all. Aaron [Julien] had come to her in Paris, she recalled in "Promised Land," and declared with great feeling, "I want to take the place of the son you lost—to *be* your son." She had been proud that he wanted to take care of her, "as if he had in some way held me a little responsible for his happiness." To be told that her book was an excuse, that she had been doing "nothing" for the past ten years, was unbearable. "Now I had lost my beautiful Jewish son," she went on, "my only concrete link with one of my races—to neither of which I 'belonged.'" "In a strange country," she continued, "I really was all alone."

With a great deal on her mind, Joella had less time for Mina, who relied almost entirely on Fabi despite her belief that her younger daughter was a free spirit. Fabi did what she could. Despite her irregular schooling, she found a summer job at the 1939 New York World's Fair by claiming to be a college graduate. In the autumn she took another temporary position at Lord and Taylor. Her lack of qualifications inevitably translated into low wages and little hope for advancement. That year, when Natalie Barney paid them an unexpected visit, she was distressed to learn that Mina could not afford a refrigerator. A few days later, after one appeared on their doorstep, Fabi was so pleased that she wrote a poem in praise of their glistening icebox. But Mina, whose "starriness" had increased under the circumstances, failed to write Natalie to thank her, whether from sheer forgetfulness or from embarrassment over the decline in her fortunes.

Mina's state of mind worsened as her confusion about her daughters' lives increased. Again insisting that Joella should do anything to keep her husband, she took Julien's side once her daughter began divorce proceedings. Faced with this inexplicable attitude, Joella stopped trying to make Mina understand. Soon they were not speaking. And although Mina's health was deteriorating, she did nothing until Fabi insisted she see a doctor, who diagnosed her complaint as a duodenal ulcer and prescribed changes in diet, rest, and medication, which, as a Christian Scientist, Mina was loath to take.

Joella, who had replaced Julien as Mina's financial support, arranged for her to spend the summer of 1940 in Connecticut with her three grandsons, a cook, and a nurse. The country air and the attention brought Mina out of herself, and the German nurse, one of the many refugees Joella was helping at the time, entertained her. Mina held séances, amused the boys with ghost stories from Florence, and taught them to use a Ouija board. Accustomed to European ways, which Joella preferred to American childrearing practices, the boys accepted their grandmother's eccentricities. But they were surprised when Mina gave Javan a leaf as a birthday present: they much preferred the teddy bear–sized suit of armor that Fabi made for Jerrold. Because Mina found the children tiring, she spent much of her time alone—drinking tea, playing solitaire, and doing crossword puzzles.

On her return to Manhattan, Mina announced that she and Fabi would make ends meet by selling their designs to decorators. Her outlook somewhat improved after her rest cure in the country, she prepared maquettes of window displays for department stores and encouraged Fabi to put the finishing touches on the "show valise" in which she was to take her own designs to fashionable companies. But no one wanted the window displays, and Fabi encountered few favorable responses. Once Fabi found a secretarial job, they were able to make ends meet. She talked her way into a position with Dr. Sandor Rado, head of the New York Psychiatric Institute, by claiming to be an English major from Vassar, the alma mater of Mary McCarthy, one of his most famous patients. (Since her English was better than Rado's, she could edit his lectures perfectly well without benefit of a degree.) Given his interest in literary matters and women's neuroses, Rado was in a position to help with Mina's habitual depression, although his thoughts on the female castration complex would have disqualified him, had she known them.

Too often, Fabi came home from work to find the telephone cut off because her mother had forgotten to pay the bill. Mina was also given to announcing that they had to commit suicide because there was no more gas, a threat that became so familiar that Fabi stopped paying attention until the afternoon when she returned from work to find the curtains drawn; by that time, Mina had forgotten her threat. Calendar time also seemed to lose its meaning. Mina phoned Fabi at work on April 5, 1940, to say that the electricity had been cut off. When Fabi replied, "Oh, what a treat, for my twenty-first birthday," Mina said vaguely, "Oh yes, dear, is it your birthday?" After buying herself a record as a present, Fabi persuaded a pawnshop owner to rent her an old-fashioned Victrola. That evening Mina and Fabi sat in the dark, listening to music by candlelight.

Despite her low spirits, Mina continued to think that the better firms would buy her designs. During the summer in Connecticut, she had invented three alphabet games that combined her feeling for letters as objects with lives of their own and her dissatisfaction with the moralizing alphabets of the Victorians. The first, "Build Your Own Alphabet," was housed in a box containing the pieces with which the twenty-six letters were formed: made of inexpensive plastic, these pieces were to be laid on a board "during the process of Alphabet Construction." The accompanying script for the teacher or "older playfellow" in charge might seem repetitive, but "it is this repetition," she explained, "that, I found in my own experience, fixes the letters so easily and firmly in the budding mentality." The child was won over as soon as the teacher revealed the "magic" that could be performed as one letter turned into another. In a variant, "The Alphabet That Builds Itself," the inner surfaces of the letters were fitted with magnets, affording "the small student" the thrill of seeing each block spring together when assembled. In a third version, the blocks opened to reveal pop-out toys whose initials corresponded to the letters. But F.A.O. Schwarz, to whom Mina sent her designs, failed to take an interest.

As in Paris, but on a more reduced scale, Mina devised ways to put inexpensive materials to good use. She often bought individual cigarettes in her effort to stop smoking and imagined a new kind of perfume bottle made with the glass containers in which they were sold. She cut the tubes to various lengths, filled them with colored waters, and tied them with a gold band: the result, "Pipes of Pan," was to be her most marketable design. Mina sent Fabi to show her invention to the director of Helena Rubinstein's cosmetic company, who promised them one hundred dollars but changed the name to "Syrinx." Hoping to follow up on her success, Mina sent him several lines of poetry intended for the publicity campaign: "Fragrance is harmonious on the air / as music is a fragrance to the ear / The very silence of Perfume offsets its subtlety." But neither her association of the two Rubinsteins, Helena and Arthur, nor her idea about the silence of perfume appealed to him as much as her inexpensive and easily produced design.

When the check arrived, Mina told Fabi that their luck was changing. She set to work on a new design, a powder compact to be called "French Window": beneath the top's golden shutters, one saw the shimmering mirror that popped up as the compact opened. (Although New York manufacturers were unlikely to catch the allusion, Mina's "French Window" echoed the windowlike *Fresh Widow* construction made by Duchamp's alter ego Rrose Sélavy two decades earlier.) But like most of her inventions, "French Window" did not sell.*

---

* Mina also designed a long brush with a curved handle for cleaning "modern (French) windows," as well as knitting needles "with inches & inch divisions printed upon them"—some of the more practical ideas she registered with a notary during the 1940s.

Moreover, without an understanding of modern business methods Mina was incapable of producing these designs. The only recourse, she thought, was to register her ideas with a notary in an effort to protect them before finding interested parties. With Fabi, Mina also imagined a doll called "Crybaby," whose tears came from a reservoir in her back, but she could not obtain a patent: several years later, their idea appeared on the market as Tiny Tears. When she finally sold another model, a compact in the shape of a poodle, this success confirmed her view that Americans lacked taste. Fabi sold her jewelry designs to Elizabeth Arden, which also bought some of Mina's remaining antique bottles to give as Christmas presents. Mina alternated between optimism about their talents and despair over their finances.

In the fall of 1940 Mina and Fabi moved to a large rooming-house apartment on Lexington Avenue near Fifty-fifth Street. Although they had to share a double room and use the common kitchen, the location was promising, and their quarters almost lived up to the idea that it was a "decorator apartment." Of the other tenants, the most interesting proved to be the woman Mina called Madame de Beauté, an elegant but slightly suspicious saleswoman at Saks, and Eliza MacCormack, an aspiring actress who also worked as a model and appreciated Fabi's ability to cook satisfying dinners with little more than boiled potatoes. Eliza wondered what Mina did all day apart from her trips to the corner for cigarettes and her occasional visits to a friend across the street, the lighting expert Richard Kelly.

After a winter in these shared lodgings, they discovered bedbugs. The three women took refuge at Richard Kelly's until they could move into the cheap apartment Fabi found for them on East Thirteenth Street, near Union Square. The front room was large enough for Eliza and Fabi, and the back room had a skylight that made it seem like a painter's studio. Although located above a cigar factory, the apartment's general effect was cheerful, until winter arrived. Mina had the front room painted a brilliant pink, a color she associated with Fabi. Their lone gas radiator gave them headaches, which were marginally preferable to the bone-chilling temperature when it was turned off. Fabi was happy living down the street from Irene Klempner, a friend from the World's Fair: since Irene's capable mother—known as Klemp—cooked for her two daughters, son-in-law, Fabi, and Eliza in the evening after her day job in a hospital, Klemp's became an extension of their apartment. But Mina rarely joined them.

She no longer cared about the conventions, Eliza thought, if they had once mattered to her. Mina went to sleep wrapped up in her robe on the couch and, just as she seemed not to notice what she ate, showed no concern about housekeeping. One day after a bag of sugar fell over on the kitchen table, sugar began trickling to the floor, a grain at a time. When Eliza said that they should remove the sugar pyramid before the cockroaches discovered it, Mina protested, "Oh leave it there, it's so lovely the

392

way it is." But despite her habits, Eliza thought, Mina was not senile, only eccentric and somewhat "dotty."

On the rare occasions when Mina told Eliza about Cravan, it was as if he had just disappeared from her life. She spoke at length and with great feeling about his physique: he "had the most beautiful body in the world." But when she explained his disappearance by saying that one day he swam out from the shore into the ocean and disappeared, Fabi took Eliza aside and told her not to believe anything her mother said. Eliza felt how fresh the loss was for her and respected her reticence. Mina's way of seeing things impressed her, as did her insights into human behavior. When discussing relations between men and women, Mina insisted that what mattered was lovemaking. If that went well, everything else would follow. She told Eliza that Joella and Julien, then going through the process of divorce, had been "such beautiful children when they met and had a beautiful love, but they tired of it." But while she spoke of sex in the language of her time, Mina could also be frank. When Eliza asked Mina to look at her modeling portfolio, she was startled to hear her exclaim, "What a face, it's as cold as a refrigerator!" Years later, she saw what Mina meant, but still felt the sting of Mina's observation.

While Mina no longer complained about living in poverty, her indifference did not extend to Fabi's welfare, and she could not understand her daughter's lack of interest in a modeling career. "Fabi is so beautiful but she hates showing it," Mina fretted. She had inherited Cravan's looks but did not want to "use" them—although, like her father, she enjoyed pretending to be someone else. Mina also worried ineffectually about Fabi's health and tried to cajole her into taking her childhood tonic (hot consommé with milk). She no doubt understood that while her daughter's erratic education had not prepared her for adulthood, she was doing her best to adjust to New York. But at twenty-two Fabi had already exchanged roles with her mother, wrapping her shawl around her and putting her to bed with a cup of hot milk. Despite her preference for escapades, she had to be the practical one.

III

America's entrance into the war in December 1941 shocked Mina out of her vagueness. A decade after all but abandoning poetry to immerse herself in her novel, she composed a poem of praise, "America * A Miracle," which salutes the United States as "a stroke of genius." Recalling her first glimpse of Manhattan, she described a city conceived by sheer willpower:

> *your soaring architecture*
> *rose from the aboriginal grass*
> *of a virgin continent*

> *in a grandeur*
> *of windowed cliffs*
>
> *to spangle days*
> *with microscopic suns*
> *or flag the coded beauty*
> *of their mazda blaze*
> *as night comes*

The poem's inflated rhetoric conveys the strength of her desire to think that in the New World, Europe's "discard sons" were not only relieved of their past but conjoined to form "an instant giant / democratically / their old tears derelict in the Atlantic." And because this "avenger" was mightier in moral force than Germany's "mechanized monster," it would prevail.

In this patriotic spirit, she composed a poem the following year, inspired, most likely, by discussions with her grandson Javan, an air force pilot. "Aviator's Eyes" locates a renewed spiritual vision in the voyages of America's war pilots, who "never efface their far focus."

> *Aviator's eyes*
> *have indrawn the horizon*
> *of drifting heaven*
>
> *Aviator's eyes*
> *on arrow excursion*
> *into profusion of distance*
> *beyond our residence*
>
> *fly an illusion of unmoving motion*
> *into dissolving fortresses of cloud*
> *intrude upon the jewel of the rainbow*

These young heroes, she believed, saw into the celestial realms that she inhabited in her imagination.

About this time, when the Allies had not yet begun their counter-offensive, the American Surrealist magazine *View* asked a number of writers—including Mina, William Carlos Williams, and Marianne Moore—to address not the war itself but civilization's drift "towards the unknown." To the question "What do you see in the stars?" Marianne replied succinctly, "Hope," while Mina expatiated, "Our need of an instrument analogous to, yet the inverse of a telescope, which would reduce to our focus the forms of entities hitherto visually illimitable, of whose substance the astronomical illuminations are but the diamond atoms and electrons." She yearned to see (as aviators did) that "profusion of distance beyond our residence."

Mina's patriotic "starriness" did not, however, keep her from imagining inventions suited to the war effort. She proposed to adapt her most successful lampshade design to the concerns of the day by replacing its sailing ship with an airplane whose windows lit up when one turned on the light. She also imagined a curtain design on which "airplane sky writing" was represented with V shapes formed by pleats or ruches of material, suggesting either the "V for Victory" or a "loop trailing behind a speeding airplane." Another of her dress-for-war schemes, which no doubt called to mind the Futurists' "anti-neutralist" clothing, described a dress material with an "all over design of polka dots among which certain dots differing in colour or tone from the others form Victory V." But however timely, these ideas did not translate into commercial terms.

Like her alphabet games, another invention for children held some potential. A year before the country's entrance into the war, she conceived of an educational gift with applications "in all branches of Defense work." The idea was simple: engineers would designate parts needed in their systems of production which "could be shaped, stamped out, finished, or made entirely by boys in their play-rooms or work-shops." The materials, along with the necessary tools, would be prepared in kits, to be sold as gifts for "intelligent handy boys" desirous of contributing to the war effort. "Such 'Defense Sets,' " Mina imagined, "would be more sought after than any construction toy; their possession and utilisation would enormously foster the boys' budding patriotism, in giving it a practical outlet, & allowing them to contribute to the building up of American defense." As originator of the plan, she desired only "some remuneration & small royalties." The remaining profits would go to the country's defense, the Red Cross, "or as they sufficiently accumulated, be distinctly appropriated to the production of some important engine of defense such as a plane."

While Mina focused on inventions, Fabi dealt with the fact that it was becoming increasingly difficult to find employment as a British subject. Her languages and draftsmanship finally stood her in good stead when she applied for a position with British counterintelligence, which included translating documents from French and preparing false identity papers. Asked to copy a twenty-dollar bill, she executed the task so convincingly that an unsuspecting office worker changed it without hesitation. (These results seemed ironic under the circumstances.) Soon she was forging signatures equally well, a talent developed no doubt during the forced drawing sessions of her childhood. While Fabi's income made daily life more comfortable, she and Mina watched every penny, and Fabi spent evenings at home reweaving her co-workers' stockings on a small machine designed for the purpose.

Work of this kind was encouraged as part of the war effort. By 1943, propaganda had become as important as defense work, and Americans who uttered unpatriotic sentiments were denounced with as much vigor as two decades earlier. During the summer, when Ezra Pound was indicted for making anti-U.S. broadcasts, a New York reporter interviewed Mina about her old friend. Trying to understand how the man described as "the greatest single influence on American poetry" could betray his country, he summed up Pound's career as if it had led to his current status. Mina offered an explanation of Pound as a faddist. In Paris he was always talking about endocrine glands, she recalled; "one of his friends said he had brought from America the faults of America, and none of the virtues." Unable to explain his behavior to her own satisfaction, she added, "He was a sensitive man who didn't think other people were sensitive."

As her young roommate Eliza understood, the same could be said of Mina in some moods, especially in periods of intense concentration. On the rare occasions when Mina invited Eliza into her room, she was allowed to peek at her inventions, provided she promised not to tell anyone about them. At work on still other ideas, Mina was obsessed with the thought that they, too, would be stolen. At various points, she devised new lampshades—one in the shape of a swan made of bent tubing, another decorated with down blown onto the shade to form flowers in relief. Solving old problems long after they ceased to matter, she came up with an idea that she could have utilized in her Paris business—a synthetic called Chatoyant, described as "a new structural combination of materials for use in manufacture" combining brilliant-colored foil with plastic or glass to create silvery or cloudy surfaces. One of her most ingenious ideas, Chatoyant— as defined in Webster's dictionary, the term meant "having a changeable lustre or colour like that of a changeable silk or a cat's eye in the dark"— harked back to her love of the shimmering, opalescent effects of the fin-de-siècle, yet tried, as in many of her designs, to modernize this passé aesthetic.

From her rare visits to Mina's room, Eliza understood that she was also working on a noncommercial project incorporating sections from the Sunday color comics, which she clipped and saved in special envelopes. Mina intended to arrange them in collage form, she hinted, to demonstrate unfolding patterns in spiritual development. She had chosen this medium so that the man in the street could understand. Living near Union Square, she had begun to think of how to translate the high cultural forms understood by the enlightened for the benefit of the urban crowds she saw hurrying by each day. Rather than update "Psycho-Democracy," she was adapting the "funnies" to a serious purpose.

Although no trace of this collage project survives, it was undoubtedly related to a series of jottings from this period—written, Mina noted, to "pacify the intellectual consternation, stunning as an explosion, before the unprecedented inhumanities of Axis warfare." What was needed was for thought to begin again "with the simple relation of savage apprehension of the Macroscopic presence—modified in some divinely decreed manner by its lengthy civilized apprenticeship"—by which she meant a return to the "primitive" idea of the divine, reformulated in a "civilized" manner.

"By ignoring the Consciously Creative Power where from all phenomena within, & beyond our range of response, derive," she argued, "modern intellection" had reached an impasse. The Occident's mistaken belief in the concrete world as the sole reality was being demonstrated, moreover, in daily reports of mass destruction.

People did not recognize the spirit, she thought, simply because it was invisible: "It is because of the infinite obviousness of God that he escapes man's narrow attention." To those who had seen the light, it was obvious that spirit not only existed but governed the visible world from within. What was more, the enlightened were under the obligation "to impart to others the formula for its inducement." It is hard not to conclude from a reading of Mina's religious writings—where she often sounds like her own Mary Baker Eddy—that during the 1940s, believing herself one of the illuminati, she hoped to impart to others her formula—"that Christ meant what he said." In a time of world strife, this message was available "for the relief of desolation—for those who have arrived at the end of all things of the intellect—as an antidote to extinction."

At the same time, her notes also suggest that Mina was struggling with the contradiction between her lifelong desire to be set apart from the crowd and her heightened need for human solidarity. In them, she spoke as "an observer from some cosmic distance" but also as a Christian certain that "our real dilemma [i]s our desperate determination to establish our identity apart from the general mass." The illuminati were obliged to transmit their wisdom, she wrote, in order to send the "Deific electricity coursing through a circle of mentalities, all concentrated on a like aspiration." By connecting *"all men* as one whole one circle," the brotherhood of man could be realized.

This tension between solipsistic isolation and fraternal inclusiveness is depicted more concretely in her most successful poems from the 1940s, where imagined contact with others provides solace. In "Mass Production on 14th Street," the speaker observes "the unique unlikeness of faces" in the crowds thronging through Union Square:

> *Ocean in flower*
> *of closing hour:*
>
> *Pedestrian ocean*
> *whose undertow,*
> *the rosy scissors of hosiery*
> *snips space to a triangular racing lace*
>
> *in an iris circus of Industry.*
>
> *As a commodious bee*
> *the eye*

> *gathers the infinite facets*
> *of the unique unlikeness*
> *of faces . . .*

As in Pound's famous impression of urban masses, "In a Station of the Metro," the crowd is described in floral metaphors. In Mina's poem, its feminine nature is emphasized by pointillist dots of color, the "audacious fuchsia / orgies of orchid / or dented dandelion" of light summer dresses. Although this bouquet of workers and shopgirls merges into an "everywoman," the "Femina / of the thoroughfare," the multilayered pun covertly asserts the observer's identity (Fée Mina) with the observed. Also present in the Dickinsonian image of the "commodious bee," she takes nourishment from the scene while gathering "the infinite facets" of this image: "carnations / tossed at a carnal caravan / for Carnaval."

The ambivalence of Mina's feelings about her place in city life emerges more clearly in the two-part structure of "On Third Avenue," also from this period. In the first section, the speaker wills herself to vanish into the crowd:

> *So disappear*
> *on Third Avenue*
> *to share the heedless incognito*
>
> *of shuffling shadow-bodies*
> *animate with frustration*
>
> *whose silence only potence is*
> *respiration . . .*

In this down-at-heels landscape, the poor remain "hueless," until "Time, the contortive tailor," clothes them in "an eerie undress / of mummies / half-unwound." (The images of Time the tailor and his "sweat-sculptured cloth" give her father's trade a human context, albeit an ironic one.)

In the second section, which begins "Such are the compensations of poverty / to see," the speaker nonetheless finds beauty in the glitter of "a ten-cent cinema" and "the brilliancy / of a trolley / loaded with luminous busts." The poem ends in meditation on these ephemeral, and freely available, urban images:

> *lovely in anonymity*
> *they vanish*
> *with the mirage*
> *of their passage.*

Set apart from those she observed, she willed herself to be one of them.*

Preoccupied perhaps with the mirage of her own passage, Mina learned that year, as she neared sixty, of her mother's death. Although she continued to blame Julia whenever she felt caught in the trap of circumstances, her mother appeared one night in a dream, she told Joella (to whom she was again speaking), and said of their lifelong misunderstanding, "Now what was all that nonsense? That was stupid!"

IV

Typically, Mina was trying to let go of the past while holding on to it. Reticent with old friends, she spoke briefly of her health to McAlmon when he visited on the way to the Southwest, but let on that she was writing again. While he wanted to see her poems, he remarked, "these are bad days for publishing." Americans had, in his opinion, "reverted completely to the conventional stereotyped, mediocre mind thing." McAlmon sent news of Mariette Mills and Kay Boyle, still in Europe, mentioned his own attempt to recover from a collapsed lung, and hoped that Mina was "feeling as well as these days let us." After Peggy Guggenheim returned to New York, she bought one of Mina's Oelze drawings for $150, which Mina spent in an attempt to patent an invention. Occasionally Mina made up her mind to attend one of Peggy's parties, but changed her mind at the last minute.

She preferred the informal gatherings at the Gotham Book Mart, a meeting place for intellectuals and artists and a treasure house of banned books, little magazines, and experimental authors. There she met writers who recognized her name but had not known her at the height of her beauty—although the owner, Frances Steloff, remembered Mina from progressive circles in the Village. Frances, who was five years younger but a great deal more active, observed how much they had in common: like Mina, she was self-taught. She had become a champion of the avant-garde, founded the James Joyce Society, and was a student of Oriental religions. In Mina, she believed, she had met a kindred spirit. Mina's visits to the Gotham included hours in the occult section, where she and Frances discussed their latest readings. But despite their shared interests and the admiration of her young acquaintances at the bookstore, Mina seemed embarrassed by her age, appearance, and reduced social status.

Through Steloff, Mina met another kindred spirit, the reclusive young photographer Clarence John Laughlin. Like herself, Laughlin admired the writings of Charles Fort, whose visionary *Book of the Damned* had been a revelation when it appeared in the 1920s. Fort, a philosopher and theorist, posited the idea of the cosmos as a living entity whose laws evolved as

---

* "Mass Production on 14th Street" and "On Third Avenue," both written in 1942, share the democratizing impulse of W. C. Williams's *Paterson* (1946); when asked by James Laughlin, the head of New Directions and Williams's publisher, to comment on her old friend's poem, Mina praised its analysis of "the components—indigenous & historical—of an unwitting majority."

the need arose; this notion had appealed to many at the time and provided countless ideas for science-fiction writers. When Laughlin declared Fort "the William Blake of our time," Mina agreed. Laughlin was in his own way a poet among photographers. Julien had included his photographs in a 1940 show, but his haunting portraits of vanishing urban scenes remained unknown. In a phrase that Mina could have written, Laughlin called the old-fashioned mannequins he had photographed in a shop window "phantoms out of the fourth dimension." Surprised to find that he shared so much with someone from another era, Laughlin nonetheless felt that while he was trying to look *"through reality,* and into the past," Mina wanted to see the future.

After Julien moved to the Village, Mina saw more of him and his new wife, the young artist Muriel Streeter. Muriel looked up to Mina and appreciated her open-mindedness. But once she learned that a mutual attraction had always existed between Mina and Julien, she concluded that Mina was a "complicated person." Mina spoke frequently of Cravan and sometimes of Giles, and appeared to feel their losses keenly. At the same time, Muriel thought, she alternated between periods of vagueness and moments of ironic playacting. "It was hard to tell when Mina was serious," she added. And although she was still handsome in her sixties, she seemed insecure, especially in the presence of friends from the art world.

After knowing her for some years—during and after the war—Muriel decided that Mina felt divided between pride in her Jewishness and a fear of being thought Jewish, an ambivalence which to her eyes touched on anti-Semitism. (During these years, Mina asked Julien to look into the idea that there was a higher rate of mental instability among Jews.) She was also torn between her otherworldly spirituality, associated with Christian Science, and the deep worldliness that expressed itself as cynicism. Sensing "much mystery and frustration about her," Muriel wondered why Julien's father did not do something for her. "She carried off her declining years as she could, under the circumstances," Muriel added.

Julien assured Mina of his abiding affection and tried to help when she would let him. After arranging for the sale of her remaining antique French bottles to the appropriately named Julian Lamp Shop, he promised to forgo his agent's commission if she would once again entrust him with the new draft of her novel, called *Islands in the Air.* He had been sending her recent poems to various magazines, but they remained unpublished. Like McAlmon, Julien was discouraged about the literary world. "I fear that we are today much worse off than your 'lepers of the moon,' " he told Mina. "We have become quite indigestible and incommunicable (even between ourselves)," he added. With Muriel, he celebrated Mina's naturalization as an American in 1946—a happy occasion to which she wore a wine-red robe and a cape. But despite Julien's standing invitation to his new home and gallery openings, Mina found it increasingly difficult to make the effort.

With many Surrealists exiled in New York during the war, Julien's influence as the movement's apostle was at its height, and his gallery a focal point of art-world politics. Since Mina's return, he had shown Dali, Tchelitchew, Frida Kahlo, Leonor Fini, the Bermans, Joseph Cornell, Oelze, Roberto Matta, Dorothea Tanning, and Max Ernst, among others. Marcel Duchamp, once again a New York resident, acted as advisor, designed announcements, and, although he had renounced painting, occasionally let Julien show his work. Duchamp saw Mina chiefly at the gallery. He still admired her and thought everything she did, whether with paint or in words, "sensitive and original," but it was hard to be close to her, he felt, because she was full of self-pity. Mina dwelt in the past, some thought, because there was little to take its place.

After Breton's arrival in 1941, when he started organizing the exiled Surrealists, Julien's gallery became a Duchamp-Breton stronghold. Soon Breton was holding Surrealist meetings in the back room of a bar on Eighth Street and stirring up controversy about the correct line under the circumstances. Although Charles Ford had published a Surrealist issue of *View* and devoted another to Max Ernst, Breton considered the magazine an impure branch of the movement and soon began his own magazine, *VVV*, published in French as well as in English.* He had nothing but scorn for New Yorkers who took Surrealism to mean Salvador Dali, whom he dismissed as "Avida Dollars."

Intending to write a definitive account of the movement's history, Breton persuaded Duchamp to ask Mina for Cravan's unpublished writings, a series of notes that she had kept since his death. Mina was reluctant to part with them and continued to think that Cravan would have disapproved of his posthumous enrollment in the movement. ("Nothing would have enraged him more than to be appropriated by the Surrealists," she wrote.) In 1942, however, she decided to let the notes appear in *VVV* provided Breton presented them properly. Jointly, as the pope of Surrealism and Cravan's widow, *they* would grant the faithful a glimpse of his genius. Breton outdid himself. Expressing gratitude to "Mme. Mina Loy, for her contribution of these very important unpublished NOTES," he declared that they were not only of "great historic interest" but that their publication revealed "the atmosphere of pure genius, a genius unrefined—*à l'état brut.*" More than any other, he went on, the name Arthur Cravan brought back the heroic era of Cubism and Futurism, when Apollinaire, Picasso, Duchamp, Picabia, and Cravan dominated the scene. Cravan, always at odds

---

* John Bernard Myers, *View*'s managing editor, noted: "Breton is not altogether convinced that *View* is up to his standards. At best, he has tolerated it. He does not, for instance, much approve of neo-Romantics like Berman, Leonid, Berard, Tchelitchew or Parker Tyler. It is also to be remembered that Breton is a snob and thinks Americans are essentially crass and somewhat childish."

with the others, had been the most intransigent. This incarnation of Rimbaud's famous mot "Il faut être absolument moderne" had been murdered in Mexico, he added, no doubt at Mina's behest—she not only preferred this version of the story but it also fit into the hagiography Breton was constructing. Twenty-five years after his disappearance, Cravan had undergone the Surrealist equivalent of canonization.*

Having relaxed her grip on the past while also retaining a measure of control over the story that obsessed her, Mina found it possible to contribute to a special issue of *View* in Duchamp's honor. When Charles Ford asked to reprint "O Marcel" from *The Blind Man*, she agreed, provided he include the note she had written to commemorate that era. Recalling the night of the Blindman's Ball, when Duchamp had "let fall his favor, a miniature American flag, into his champagne," she re-created the scene as if it had just happened. Ford printed the note because of its precise detail, but also because he saw Mina as a legend, like Cravan, Duchamp, and their mutual friend, Djuna Barnes. Mina's poetry had always seemed "mediumistic, as if spoken from another world," he thought, but he wondered about her state of mind at this time and tried to imagine the cost of appearing in public once "her consciousness had gone inward."

As Mina withdrew into her private world, Joella and Fabi continued to provide for her. By the time Joella's divorce became final, Mina still did not understand that her own attraction to Julien (along with her self-interest in urging Joella to marry him) had helped to destabilize the young couple. And although she had always blamed her parents for failing to give her an education, she had, in effect, repeated this pattern with her daughters, who were nonetheless supporting her and themselves at a difficult time.

In 1944 Fabi married Hans Fraenkel, whom she dubbed "the Frenchman" because he wore a beret and appreciated French culture. Fraenkel, who was a number of years older than Fabi, was a German who had escaped to the United States after serving in the French Foreign Legion. Following their marriage, Mina joined them in their two-story brownstone on East Sixty-sixth Street, which included a ground-floor sitting-room apartment for her. Fraenkel and Mina got on well because he understood her need for privacy and did not mind the omnipresent clutter of clippings and objects. "She was quite removed from everyday life," he thought, "lost in her own mythology." She rarely left the house and sometimes refused to open the door. She might make an appearance at their parties, looking otherworldly in white face powder and flowing dark red robes. When they persuaded her to accompany them to openings at Peggy Guggenheim's, where one saw Duchamp, Ernst, Virgil Thomson, and, occasionally, Djuna, Mina floated through the room as if unaware of what was happening. By the mid-forties, she seemed to inhabit another world.

---

* In 1946 Duchamp stated before a notary public—presumably at Mina's request—that he "knew [Cravan] well and only death could be the cause of his disappearance."

At the same time, the poet Kenneth Rexroth began lobbying to get her poetry back into print, a project that would occupy him for decades. In his view, she was a major modernist presence. "There is no question but what she is important," he insisted in *Circle*, a literary review of the 1940s: "No one competent and familiar with verse in English in this century would dream of denying it." Taking up the old comparison of her poetry with Marianne Moore's, he argued against T. S. Eliot and in favor of Mina. "Her material is self evidently more important than Miss Moore's, and treated with great earnestness, never with Miss Moore's dehydrated levity," he went on. Rexroth's estimate of her work, the most perceptive since Edwin Muir's 1923 review of *Lunar Baedecker*, continued in this vein:

> She writes of the eternal platitude: the presence or absence of sexual satisfaction; and of the results: recreation, marriage, procreation; sterility, disorder, death . . . As one reads of Mina Loy's babies, one's sphincters loosen. Her copulators stay copulated. Miss Moore, of course, is interested in establishing public privilege for a special and peculiarly impoverished sensibility. One thing has never reared its ugly, funny, lovable little head in the garden of cast iron mignonettes which is her eminent domain. Mina Loy, in her best known work, dipped her pen in the glands of Bartholin,* and wrote.

"Erotic poetry is usually lyric," he went on. "Hers is elegiac and satirical . . . She commonly transforms the characteristic envy of little girls into the superciliousness of an unhappy suffragette." Her poetry made people uncomfortable, he thought. But precisely *because* it was challenging—"tough, forthright, very witty, atypical, anti-rhetorical, devoid of chi-chi"—it was what the world of letters needed at a time when poetry seemed as anaesthetized as Eliot's patient "etherised upon a table."

Despite the general impression that Mina had disappeared into the fourth dimension, she summoned up her repartee in a letter to Rexroth a year after his article appeared to tease him about the "cast iron mignonettes." "Now you will understand why I have been neglected," she wrote. "I am one of those who can't write letters. The more pleasure the letter I *receive* gives to me, the less am I able to answer it.. . . . If Marianne Moore were not good you could not have wrapped her in so perfect a phrase," she continued, insisting that poetry could be inspired by emotions that were "erotic," in her case, or "monastic" in Moore's. It did not matter, provided one was "creative." But she could not remember who had published her poems nor could she help Rexroth with the bibliography he requested.

About the same time, several younger writers called to pay their respects. Henry Miller, visiting in New York from California, persuaded Mina to dine with him one evening. "It seemed to me that I was talking to 'an

---

* Two glands, one on either side of the vaginal orifice, which secrete lubrication, they were named after Caspar Bartholin, a seventeenth-century Danish physician.

old soul' that night," he told her, before adding, "I don't believe there is anything you wouldn't understand." That evening Miller also brought Gilbert Neiman, a young poet and translator who had admired Mina's poetry since college. Neiman was visiting from Hollywood, where he was friendly with Peggy Guggenheim's sister Hazel, Man Ray, and Max Ernst, who by the early 1940s had formed an avant-garde outpost in Los Angeles. When Neiman begged Mina to send him her poems, she sensed in him an agent like Carl Van Vechten or another "son" like Julien. "Only two people have ever written poetry in the present—you and Hart Crane," Neiman wrote. "I think if a book of yours would come out, it might show that the Western World can still work." She should "give up the children," he added, and join him, Henry Miller, and their wives in Big Sur on the Pacific coast. When Mina expressed doubt about her ability to adapt to California, Neiman scolded: *"Don't be afraid of anything! . . .* That spirit of the eternal rebel is probably stronger in you now," he went on, "than it was when you were in the height of the *sangsara."** Age did not matter, he insisted, as long as one had "Poetic Imagination."†

V

Of Mina's male admirers, the one whose presence in her life meant the most in these years was Joseph Cornell. It had seemed as if they already knew each other when Julien introduced them. On Cornell's side, this affinity dated back to 1931, when he first entered the gallery. After showing Julien his collages and asking whether they resembled the work of Max Ernst, Cornell voiced his fear of Surrealism's "deviltry," adding that in his religion, Christian Science, "evil doesn't exist." On learning that Julien's wife and mother-in-law were followers of Science, the normally reticent Cornell opened up. What *he* hoped to do, he explained, was to practice "white magic." Through Cornell's encounter with the one art dealer in New York who practiced Science, he had also met, at least in spirit, the woman whose flea-market finds would inspire his boxes. As a tribute to Mina's role in his imagination, Cornell sent her a small box containing "the delicious head of a girl in slumber," a silver ball, and one of "witch's blue," which she kept in her Paris apartment until, on a whim, she gave it to Oelze.

Years before Mina's return to New York, Cornell had made her acquaintance more directly, through her paintings. When he saw her canvases at Julien's gallery in 1933, their blue backgrounds mingled in his mind with

---

* *"sangsara"*: samsara (misspelled by Neiman): in Hinduism and Buddhism, the cycle of birth, suffering, death, and rebirth.

† In 1961, when Neiman was editing *Between Worlds*, a review of experimental and progressive writing in several languages, he introduced Mina to a new generation of readers as "the sibyl of the century" and featured her late poems along with work by Cocteau, Prévert, Mayakovsky, William Carlos Williams, and Robert Creeley.

404

his "canvassing experiences in strange out of the way parts (of Long Island and Brooklyn)," leaving such "indelible impressions" that they remained with him a decade later. These memories had become "a kind of essence," he continued, "evoking at times certain commonplace experiences with amazing vividness and unbelievable pleasure." Now that they were acquainted in life as well as in art, Cornell associated their friendship with a "feeling of familiarity in strange places."

Moreover, as the author of *Lunar Baedecker*, Mina was an emissary from the rich European culture whose relics Cornell cherished. Since Baedekers were a major source of the imagery that comprised his constructions, the idea of a guide to the moon held a special appeal. Like Mina, he loved old sky maps covered with astrological signs, and it became apparent that they were both Capricorns. Not only did they share this cerebral sign, but he understood Mina's belief that her character was lunar. When Cornell rose before dark to read his daily lesson in Science, seeing the moon, he told Mina, made him think of her.

Among the network of images, ideas, and beliefs linking them, the most important, from Cornell's perspective, was Christian Science. Cornell adhered more faithfully to the schedule of daily and weekly readings in *Science and Health*, but felt nonetheless that Mina understood the spiritual context in which his art had evolved. "My Science and healthy thoughts about the unconscious in Surrealism (about which I know nothing) combined to give me extraordinary emotions," he told her. "Maybe Breton has splendid visions," he added, "but one doubts it from the way that he holds his pipe." Although Surrealism had been a revelation, by the 1940s Cornell was on another path.

In his practice of white magic as antidote to Surrealism—which was to inspire new creative efforts in Mina—each poetic image had a spiritual meaning. Like her, he thought in constellations of ideas, networks of mutually illuminating forms and phrases. But before these webs of connections could take shape in the boxes he made for those who inspired him, they had to travel through his "chambers of imagery," the mental maps that gradually came to life as one luminous image attracted another.

Mina's images began showing up in Cornell's mind-maps during this period, when he often visited during escapes to Manhattan from his home on Utopia Parkway in Queens. On a hot summer day in 1943, after lunch at her apartment, they talked all afternoon. He derived so much benefit from her "wise and comforting thoughts," he told her, that he wished "that all the details of your interesting conversation could stay with me as much as the spirit of it does." She had told him about a book she thought he would like, *Le Grand Meaulnes* (translated as *The Wanderer*). The mysterious château of Alain-Fournier's novel had impressed him so deeply in Mina's retelling that when he awoke the next morning to the sound of doves, their cooing, he wrote, "seemed to transform the hazy outlines of their adopted home into what seemed for the moment the 'pinkish' atmosphere of the château." "Were it not for daylight saving (or wartime as it is now called)," he continued, "I'd be back in that wonderful atmosphere I have floating around somewhere in the back of my subconscious." Promising to bring Mina "a little piece" at their next meeting, he expressed his gratitude in a thank-you note decorated with cutout figures glued onto blue paper, a delicate homage to her blue atmospheres.

Mina's presence in Cornell's mental chambers became more pronounced after he finished *The Wanderer*. That fall he wrote of his desire to discuss the book with her again and began a series of enchanted châteaux and palaces, all variations on the mysterious Domaine, where the novel's hero discovers love. This series of boxes poses the central problem of the novel and of Cornell's art: supposing one can capture the atmosphere of the past, can its enchantments also be recovered? In *The Wanderer* the narrator grasps the reasons for the hero's departure after searching through "old boxes full of piles of old letters and yellowed photographs" and inhaling their perfume, which awakens "memories and regrets." Like the narrator, who reconstructs events from cast-off records, Cornell was trying to evoke the perfume of another era—alluding enigmatically to "memories and regrets" in ways that Mina could understand.

By introducing her shy friend to the novel's spiritual meaning, Mina had helped him find his way into a particularly creative mindset. Soon Cornell was asking her for pictures of herself for his "romantic museum," another chamber of images he planned to assemble. After hearing about Mina's art-student days, he wanted to borrow photographs of her as a young woman, "especially delightful items like the Munich mardi-gras. I've thought about you many times," he added, "especially when we first moved and the glamour of novelty made things seem brighter."

Soon Cornell had completed a box on the theme of the enchanted castle and was starting another. *Castle*, finished in the summer of 1944, may be the box he described, then showed, to Mina: an eighteenth-century French château whose severe architecture occupies almost all the space in its box, its darkened windows emphasizing the sense of loss typical of the series. But as Mina alone would understand, *Castle* also evokes Meaulnes's first glimpse of his enchanted domain—at a time when "no one had replaced the panes in the windows, leaving black holes in the walls." Unlike his later palaces, *Castle* is denuded of human presence.*

When at work on this series, Cornell worried about the ethics of his borrowings from other sources, literary and visual. Concerned that he was engaged in theft, he discussed these fears with Mina. "You have a way of making things your own," she told him. "You can't help making beautiful things," she went on, admonishing him to "stop analyzing so much"—

---

* Cornell's diary entry for March 1944 connects his interest in an unpublished novel supposedly akin to *Le Grand Meaulnes*, a recent visit to Mina, and his attendance at Christian Science lectures to the start of his "new palace," possibly the one later titled *Castle* (reproduced in McShine, ed., *Joseph Cornell*, p. 8).

advice she might have given herself. Although she understood his desire to find meaning in his appropriations, she told him not to worry about doctrinal implications. What he did was "not pilfering," since the process of election and relocation made these images his own. Moreover, she wanted him to create "an object of magnitude: the Kingdom of Heaven."

Cornell shrugged off her suggestion, however, and kept making palaces, sometimes adding tiny figures in dance costumes from the ballets to which he was devoted, *Ondine*, *Swan Lake*, and *Sleeping Beauty*. In 1945, after completing *Portrait of Ondine* (a box containing images of his favorite ballet character), he invited Mina to visit this imaginary "friend" in her installation at the Museum of Modern Art. He also wondered whether he might be allowed to call during the Christmas season: "Maybe I'd find a piece of my beloved marzipan in the cupboard and a spot of tea."

By this time Mina had taken her place in his mental galaxy, the slow process of accretion that Cornell called "a type of image-search akin to poetics." During this period he was thinking about how to put her in his next installation, which would include portraits of romantic feminine presences. After seeing her 1933 exhibition, he had made a box for Mina as Julien first knew her, in Paris: using one of Man Ray's photographs, which shows her gazing enigmatically at the camera while holding a gloved hand to her chin, Cornell had recessed the image beneath a layer of glass shards. But this icy image was unsuitable because it predated the growth of their friendship. Nor did the photograph she sent, herself as an art student in an oversized hat, correspond to his mental image.* To show Mina what he wanted, he sent her a picture of Beatrice Webb, along with "another Webb, Mary," he wrote, "which also reminds me of the Saturday afternoon luncheon (summer 1943) when you acquainted me with Precious Bane"— the other book she had mentioned on the day she discussed *The Wanderer*. Mina had entered into his "web" of distinguished women.

Cornell also hinted at his association of Mina with Mary Webb's novel of English country life in his 1946 exhibition, "Romantic Museum, Portraits of Women, Constructions and Arrangements." Although he filed her photograph with those of the actresses and dancers in his private museum, it was not included in this public version. But the lines from *Precious Bane* at the end of the catalogue alluded delicately to their friendship:

The past is only the present become invisible and mute; and because it is invisible and mute, its memoried glances and its murmurs are infinitely precious. We are to-morrow's past. Even now we slip away like those pictures painted on the moving dials of antique clocks—a ship, a cottage, sun and moon, a nosegay. The dial turns, the ship rides up

---

* Cornell kept in his files, possibly for future use, a photograph of the mantelpiece in Mina's rue St.-Romain apartment labeled "Paris, 1920's." It showed, in evocative juxtaposition, an owl statue, a harlequin figure, several old-fashioned toys, a figurine in a long robe, and a tiny Madonna in a bird cage.

and sinks again, the yellow painted sun has set, and we, that were the new thing, gather magic as we go.

Through her wise counsel, Mina was helping him to go on gathering magic.

Much of the time, Cornell was unable to speak about the "profounder cross-currents of emotion and significance." Because Mina understood how his mind worked, he wrote to her again that year about a particularly moving "lesson in INSPIRATION." On the side of an old delivery truck he had noticed an *enseigne* (using the French term rather than the commonplace "sign" gave it an evocative power): it showed fish painted in "colours that make one think it might at one time have been a bright decalcomania." As interesting as this sign was in its own right, its peeling paint allowed a glimpse of another image below, "the black lettering of a former, less picturesque version of trade-mark." Although the effect was "shabby and uninspired," he had suddenly remembered seeing the same *enseigne* two years earlier." Finding it again, he grasped its import—"that it is possible to see 'lightning strike in the same place' more than once."

Trying to express this revelation was "a little more difficult." The image and his thoughts about it, he continued, seemed "so evanescent and nebulous that I have never even mentioned the trifle to anyone." As if they had been enjoying tea and marzipan, he asked her, "Terms like 'evanescent' and 'nebulous' are defeatist, are they not, to those who like ourselves are tortured most of the time by their reality?" Although he had "paid a pretty high price" for such experiences, they still served as "weapons against discouragement." At a time when Mina, too, had need of such weapons, her friendship with Cornell was her most fulfilling relationship. New York was not the promised land, but she had formed a bond with the man she considered "one of the angels."

19

The Compensations of Poverty

(NEW YORK, 1948–53)

AS MINA WITHDREW FROM SOCIETY, her daughters' lives were changing. After Joella's divorce in 1942, she became engaged to Herbert Bayer, an Austrian artist who had studied and taught at the Bauhaus. Bayer, a handsome man with a precise, geometric style and a love of order, was the antithesis of the emotional disarray with which Mina and her friends surrounded themselves. Soon after their marriage in 1944, the Bayers moved to Aspen, Colorado, a dilapidated mining town which Bayer's friend and employer, Walter Paepcke, head of the American Container Corporation, intended to restore. In Paepcke's view, Aspen was perfectly situated to support a European-style ski resort combined with a center for artistic and intellectual inquiry. When he asked Bayer to take charge of redesigning the town, Herbert and Joella saw the move as their opportunity for a fresh start and relocated there with Joella's three sons. By 1948 they had also found a beau for Fabi, by this time separated from Hans Fraenkel. During a visit to Aspen, Fabi found that she liked the town and her beau, the architect Fritz Benedict, so much more than anything in New York that she, too, decided to begin life again in Aspen.

Although Fraenkel agreed to let Mina stay on at East Sixty-sixth Street, Fabi and Joella were anxious to see her settled in a place of her own. Fabi's friend Irene Klempner, whose apartment had been Fabi's second home during the early forties, suggested that Mina might feel comfortable in her mother's communal household on Second Street. Mina had always liked "Klemp" and in many respects was happier downtown, near the Village. Since Klemp's young boarders seemed adaptable, she would fit in, provided she did not mind living near the Bowery. Despite her misgivings about one household member, a temperamental Japanese woman, Mina's initial visit went well. She decided to move there in the new year: there was no clear alternative, and her daughters were both intensely involved in the renovation of Aspen.

In 1949, after Fabi's divorce became final, she sent Mina a peony-pink announcement of her marriage to Fritz Benedict, which stated that she had been given away by her mother, "Mrs. Fabian Lloyd." But in the midst of her new life, Fabi still worried about Mina's welfare. Trying to lure Mina to Aspen for the summer, she recounted her domestic life and described all the clothes she was making for her. She wanted Mina to think seriously about moving West, perhaps to Big Sur, near Henry Miller and Gilbert Neiman. "Life among people who admire your poems," she wrote, "and in pretty surroundings, instead of Second Street, would be much more agreeable."

Klemp had gone out of her way to tell the household that Mina was special. Robert Lindsay, an acting student who lived there at that time, recalled her telling the boarders before Mina's arrival that she was "a very distinguished lady, someone who is known all over the world and herself knows everyone." When introduced, Lindsay was struck by Mina's regal bearing, her elegance, and, most of all, her eyes. He took an instant liking to her, which he felt she returned.

"Your mother seems to like her Bowery home," Irene told Fabi the day after her move. "She and Klemp 'darling' each other. They swell with each other's pride—drink tea and coffee—hold court like the red queen and the white queen," she went on. In this Alice in Wonderland atmosphere, she noted, "great names fly—artistic ideas and examples are the stuffy air you breathe." But while Klemp enjoyed teasing "the Duchess," not everyone took to Mina's aristocratic ways. The Japanese boarder took an immediate dislike to her: Mina not only returned her sentiments but made matters worse by mentioning the "yellow peril." Irene's letter about Mina's new home ended on a discouraging note: "It feels like Alice down there—only more so," she told Fabi. "Under foot is anything from sleeping bums on the stairs to frantic cats—the kitchen is the court—and the dishes pile up and the grease collects, and poor Sakiko (co-tenant with Klemp) works and finds she has a cardiac condition—fish heads lie around the floor—no one cares except to keep the guy next to him toeing the mark! It's a jungle," she concluded, "it's the home of your mother and mine."

When Sakiko found that she could no longer put up with Mina, she had to be kept from going at her with a pair of scissors. Mina enjoyed the scuffle, some thought, especially when Sakiko shrieked, "You Anglo-Saxon." (Although this epithet had been intended as an insult, Robbie Lindsay saw that Mina liked being identified in this manner.) After the scissors incident, Klemp decided that the household would be better off without Sakiko, whose financial problems accentuated her instability. She was replaced by a young artist named Stephen Ferris, who, like Robbie, saw in Mina the kind of person he had always admired. But just as their domestic tensions began to ease, Klemp received an eviction notice. After only six months on Second Street, Mina was about to be homeless.

To her daughters' surprise, she elected to stay with the household when they moved three blocks farther south, to 5 Stanton Street. Robbie had found a three-story house to rent for $175; because it had eight rooms, each with a fireplace, everyone could live there in a more stable and comfortable fashion. Originally a one-family townhouse, it had a garden in the back and two basements, as well as the original beams and timbers. Klemp occupied the first-floor bedroom, next to the living room, and Mina had the second floor. A law student named Leo Samiof joined the group, and a succession of female boarders inhabited the remaining rooms. Klemp was the glue that kept the group together, Robbie thought, not only because she earned a good salary as a nurse, but because she liked mothering her eclectic family.

While Klemp continued as matriarch, Mina amused herself in the role of Duchess. Even after months of daily life together, the boarders remained in awe of her. Her unruffled air of respect for her opinions impressed young Americans who were still unsure of themselves. They admired the ease with which she talked to the Italian shopkeepers in the neighborhood, but most of all, they were impressed with her self-assurance. No one found it odd that all her clothes were the same color, a dark wine red—although it was rumored that she dyed her underwear in the privacy of her room. The household approved of her eccentricities, whether they involved going to the store with her maroon coat tossed over her nightgown or carrying tin cans, egg crates, and banana peels up to her room. When Mina came down to the common quarters, a visitor recalled, "you knew that you were in the presence of 'somebody.' "

There were, nonetheless, exceptions. Those who admired Mina saw themselves as the cognoscenti, Leo Samiof believed, and considered him the resident philistine. Mina could be snobbish, he felt, and more than a little anti-Semitic. She took no interest in people who did not measure up to her standards. Leo preferred Klemp. Rather than lecturing them on aesthetics, she looked after the boarders and never seemed to notice that Mina and her admirers took advantage of her good nature.

One would like to know what the neighborhood made of this unusual family. The surrounding streets were inhabited by Sicilians, and it was said that the area was under the control of the Mafia. Their neighbors were "touchy people if you were nosy but otherwise left you alone," Samiof recalled. "No one ever mugged us," he added, "because we minded our business." Across the street from Klemp's house, Al's Bar served as the local hangout; an exception to the all-Italian commercial network, it was owned by five Jewish brothers who had acquired real estate on the street. One met the more prosperous derelicts at Al's. For their benefit, he poured the remains of customers' drinks into a slop, from which he ladled refreshments, and combined the roles of godfather and banker, keeping the bums' earnings on deposit and doling them out for necessities.

To the residents of Klemp's house, the derelicts were fellow humans down on their luck. Used to seeing groups of men slumped in doorways, passing cheap wine in paper bags, or stretched out on the sidewalk, Mina and Klemp pronounced them harmless. The bums took good care of them when the women went out at night, demonstrating a gallant humor even in their weakened condition. One day when Mina was sketching a derelict sprawled on the pavement, his companion asked boozily, "Is that your girlfriend?" On another occasion, after a bum lurched at Mina and Stevie from a doorway, his companion slurred, "Leave them alone, they're ours."

From Mina's perspective, the bums represented her lifelong fear of "outcasting." To most people they were human wreckage, indistinguishable in their grime and degradation, but in her eyes they were individuals with habits and histories. Within weeks of her move to Stanton Street, she had made friends with the regulars and introduced them to members of the household as "Red" or "Whitey." Observing these new friends on a daily basis, she sent brief reports to her daughters: "Today is quite hot— all the bums are extra-exhausted—the Bowery is fascinating." Joella and Fabi were less than pleased with the idea of their mother, who was by this point nearly seventy, living in such circumstances.

When Mina's nephews came to visit, they understood the pleasure she took in her surroundings. Pointing out the "beauty" in the derelicts' faces, she sketched them from her window and sent them on errands so that she could give them a quarter. After one man thanked her, said he'd get himself a sandwich, then headed straight for Al's, Mina said tolerantly, "Yes, I know, a glass sandwich." Because she sometimes gave the men bottles of wine on the understanding that the empties would be returned for her collection, some of them also called on her at home. But they made no claims beyond the occasional quarter and accepted her as their local Duchess.

It was difficult for her daughters to admit that Mina was happy living so close to the Bowery. There, only the Italians criticized her for befriending the bums, whom they despised; but as she understood their point of view, their disapproval did not trouble her. Her chief concern was the loss of her looks. Whenever she gave the residents to understand that she had been a great beauty, Lindsay reassured her that she was still very handsome. "She was full of life, warmth when she chose, and she had a stunning wit," he recalled. "She had everything going for her," he added, "but she didn't know it." Her vision of herself in these years is revealed in a poem entitled "An Old Woman":

> Years like moths
> erode internal organs

412

hanging or falling
in a spoiled closet.

Does your mirror bedevil you?
Or is the impossible
possible to senility?

How could the erstwhile
agile and slim self—
that narrow silhouette—
come to contain
this huge incognito—
this bulbous stranger
only to be exorcised by death?

The past had "come apart," events were "vagueing." Her former self, the slender nude of Stephen's photographic studies, the agile image of Man Ray's portraits, was now an "incognito."

During Mina's years on Stanton Street, her days were much alike. After early-morning tea in the kitchen, she went back to her room. It was so full of her collections that one could barely squeeze in, Lindsay observed, and the other residents were not allowed inside. Whenever they caught glimpses of her rags, bottles, clothespins, and egg crates, they whispered about Mina's plans for her "trash." Gradually they came to understand that she was assembling "objects"—three-dimensional constructions. They were not important, she said, just things she did to amuse herself. Hoping to be invited in for a better look, they loitered on the second floor by her room, where, Lindsay felt, "things were happening."

Occasionally her domestic circle was given to understand that she had written a poem. Through Henry Miller's friend Gilbert Neiman, who had taken on the role of Mina's informal agent, three poems appeared in *Accent*, along with the work of Bill Williams. Both had contributed work with Jewish themes. Mina's, entitled "Hilarious Israel," pondered the survival of the Jews through their "self-sought anaesthesia": addressing a master of ceremonies from the Yiddish theater then flourishing nearby as a "Phoenix of Exodus," she was also speaking to a part of herself. Similarly, another poem included in *Accent*, "Aid of the Madonna," evoked Mina's lasting attraction to Madonna figures as "aeon-moments of motherhood," a nostalgic vision of a plenitude she had longed for but not experienced.

The third poem, "Chiffon Velours," expressed her sense of the spirit hidden in earthly things by focusing its sympathetic gaze upon an old woman in the street. "She is sere," it begins:

413

Her features,
verging on a shriek
reviling age,

flee from death in odd directions
somehow retained by a web of wrinkles.

The site of vanished breasts
is marked by a safety pin.

Rigid
at rest against the corner-stone
of a department store.

Hers alone to model
the last creation,

original design
of destitution.

Clothed in memorial scraps
skimpy even for a skeleton.

Trimmed with one sudden burst
of flowery cotton
half her black skirt
glows as a soiled mirror;
reflects the gutter—
a yard of chiffon velours.

The woman's presence in the world is recorded with dignity, and in the final stanza transformed in the gutter's "soiled mirror," where her "memorial scraps" glow and shimmer.

Although Mina alluded to some new poems she was writing, when in company, she devoted her verbal talents to the *New York Times* crossword puzzles and weekly Double-Crostic. Apart from the newspapers, she read only metaphysical treatises. Soon after her move to the Bowery, Joella had sent her Joel Goldsmith's *The Infinite Way.* Goldsmith, who was born Jewish but turned to Christian Science, had left the Mother Church after many years as a practitioner: in Joella's view, he had streamlined the teachings of Science. "He agrees with you that C.S. practitioners are not healing any more," she told Mina, and spoke enthusiastically of her classes with him in San Francisco. After reading Goldsmith's book, Mina requested more of his writings. She found comfort in his idea of God's infinite "supply" and his belief that it was reproduced within the individual like "an infinite

414

storehouse." She began writing and phoning him herself for consultations. Soon she looked only to Goldsmith.

Mina guarded her spiritual life as carefully as her objects. The residents did not share her vision; Klemp was too busy for metaphysics. When depressed, Mina usually wrote to Joella, complaining about her health, the inventions she hoped to have patented, and her sense that she was a burden. Goldsmith could "show you a way where you can be active," Joella replied, urging Mina to forget her inventions. "You are not a burden to us as long as you are not a burden to yourself," she added. Goldsmith advised travelers on the road to the "Kingdom" to start their journey by freeing the mind. "We share our unfoldments, our experiences, and our spiritual resources," he explained. "We would not withhold any of these from each other."

In the effort to unburden herself, Mina reread Cravan's letters. His tattered correspondence gave off an "an uneasy mist." She generally told people that he had been murdered—an account of his disappearance which ruled out the idea of his leaving her—but she would never know what really happened. After thirty years, she was finally able to acknowledge the air of unreality clinging to their story and, in the poem entitled "Letters of the Unliving," his death:

> *The present implies presence*
> *thus*
> *unauthorized by the present*
> *these letters are left authorless—*
> *since the inscribing hand*
> *lost life— — —*

"Well chosen and so ill-relinquished," it continues, "the husband hearts-ease" suffered "death's erasure," yet his words remain. Riddling its way through this enigma, the poem asks whether one who "has ceased to be" ever existed, whether she "still has being" when he is not there to address her.

> *I am become*
> *dumb*
> *in answer*
> *to your dead language of amor*
> *. . .*

> *O leave me*
> *my final illiteracy*
> *of memory's languor*

415

my preference
to drift in lenient coma
an older
Ophelia
on Lethe

What began as a process of unburdening had created another myth—Cravan the murdered prince and Mina his consort. Unable to accept the mirror's "bulbous stranger," she would continue to drift as she saw herself in her mind's eye, an "older" Ophelia.

That winter, nonetheless, reassured by Goldsmith as well as by her new family, Mina was more energetic than she had been in years. Sitting around the kitchen table with Robbie and Stevie, who both worshiped her, she talked about her life in Paris and Florence, the Salon d'Automne, her friendships with Gertrude and Marcel, and sometimes of Cravan, whom she called "a beautiful poet and the amateur boxing champion of France." Impressed to know that a man could be "beautiful," Robbie encouraged her to talk about him and, in general, adopted her opinions on life and art. Although the others roared with laughter, he did not protest when Mina asked him to let down his pants because she wanted to draw his bottom. Whatever she did, he believed, was its own justification, but he wondered how she had had the courage to defy convention.

While Mina seemed reluctant to discuss her childhood, she was curious about her young friends' lives. They had a better chance of doing what they wanted because they were Americans, she told them. Moreover, they were fortunate to have been born in a classless society, where working women could buy copies of designer clothes at places like Klein's department store. Pleased to have taken American citizenship, she declared emphatically, "I'm an American!" when they remarked on her British ways.

Mina had the best of both worlds in this unprecedented domestic arrangement. As the Duchess, she was treated with respect and given everything she needed. Left to her own devices, she ate little more than Rice Krispies, sweets, and numerous cups of strong, heavily sugared tea. (Leo Samiof pretended not to notice when she finished the fruit pies stored in the refrigerator.) Otherwise she depended on Klemp's provisions from the hospital and looked forward to evenings when she or Stephen Ferris prepared dinner for all. During the day, she did as she pleased. The household saw that "the class thing," as they put it, mattered a great deal after Robbie's English friend, who was working-class, took offense at Mina's posh accent. From that point on, he recalled, they "looked daggers at each other."

Despite this glimpse into inherited antagonisms, Lindsay thought of Mina as "a dear strong woman and a loyal friend, with courage and integrity," who taught him to see the beauty in their shabby neighborhood.

One afternoon she showed him how the play of light transformed the old brick buildings; another time she pointed to the many shades of red concealed in their gray surroundings. Mina found treasures in things others thought sordid, he recalled, like the spirituality in the haggard faces of the bums. She saw what others never noticed.

"Property of Pigeons," a poem composed at this time, hints that the divine light reveals itself to a vigilant eye. While most people thought of pigeons as pests, Mina saw in them creatures of mixed being like herself, city dwellers much like their human neighbors:

> Pigeons arise,
> alight
> on vertical bases
> of civic brick
>
> whitened with avalanches
> of their innocent excrements
> as if an angel had been sick
>
> all that is show to us of bird-economies,
> financeless,
> inobvious as the disposal
> of their corpses.

These emblems of the spirit are imagined with such thoughtful attention to the details of their embodiment—"their striped crescendos / of gray rainbow," "their claws, a coral landing-gear"—that they come to represent the intertwining of body and soul. This richly contemplative poem also meditates on verses from the Sermon on the Mount—"Behold the fowls of the air: for they sow not, neither do they reap, nor gather into barns; yet your heavenly Father feedeth them." But one needed to be in the state of spiritual receptivity that Mina had imparted to Robbie to grasp the meaning of her observations concerning the habitats and "economies" of the pigeons, a variant of the "feathered metaphor."

By this time Mina moved more easily in the realm of metaphor than in the social world. When visitors called, her routine was turned upside down: because her objects took up all the space in her room, she received those who were not family members in Klemp's quarters. Members of the household tiptoed around when Djuna, long since a recluse, came to see Mina and listened in awe when they overheard Mina discussing the "Infinite Way" with Frances Steloff. Berenice Abbott also visited, and occasionally Duchamp came to call. But since visits from old friends were visibly upsetting, they stayed out of the way.

Sometimes Mina informed the household that James Laughlin or Sidney Janis had requested the pleasure of her company. Arrangements would be made for her to occupy the bathroom, where she could wash her long white hair; her young friends did last-minute errands. But as the hour approached, she often found the prospect too daunting. And when she did manage to go uptown, she generally arrived at the end of the party. Conscious of her age and embarrassed at the thought of seeing those who had known her at the height of her beauty, she found it increasingly difficult to leave the Bowery. She didn't want people to know where she was, she told her housemates, who took the explanation at face value.

Near the close of 1949, Mina made an exception when Cornell invited her to his December exhibition, an *Aviary* at the Egan Gallery. His installation of twenty-six bird cages included cutouts of birds in their habitats, which comprised carefully mounted mirrors, springs, and sets of drawers in luminous containers. The critics responded favorably to Cornell's apparent move in the direction of formalism. "These new works of sunbleached and whitewashed boxes," *Art News* noted, "have a strict honesty, a concentration on texture and ordering of space, that raise them far above the older, velours-lined jobs." The reviewer did not mention that although sparer in execution than his earlier boxes, Cornell's aviary was no less illustrative of his preoccupation with the soul. On entering the gallery, Mina saw that his dovecotes were mute gestures at transcendence, earthly habitations for the spirit such as she imagined for her own feathered metaphors.

She was so deeply moved by Cornell's *Aviary* that she started writing a prose appreciation, something she had not attempted since her essay on Gertrude Stein. Like that piece, "Phenomenon in American Art" conveys the impact of her encounter with another's imagination. This aviary was, Mina wrote, a "sublime entertainment." A cloister tactfully constructed of wood so as "to retain the entity of seedling, of branching, of foliage," it offered its inhabitants a "consolatory shade" while also hinting that the bird's nature was celestial. During her visit to the gallery, Brancusi's *Golden Bird* had come, or flown, to mind: "It was a long aesthetic itinerary from Brancusi's Golden Bird to Cornell's Aviary. The first is the purest abstraction I have ever seen," she went on, "the latter the purest enticement of the abstract into the objective." Cornell had succeeded in enticing an abstract idea—the soul—into "objective" or "composite" form following its long banishment from modernist art. (The Surrealists' return to representational form, Mina thought, had been too severely limited by their shallow conception of reality to let them speak of such matters.)

Entering Cornell's gallery, she felt, was like going to church: one entered the realm of silence—"that atmosphere of enduring elevation one's mind inhales on entering certain ancient European Cathedrals." His "optic music" was soothing as a Bach chorale. But while his birds were "songsters of silence," they were also "descendants of the Holy Ghost." More than an exhibition, *Aviary* was a revelation. Mina mailed the essay to Cornell, who replied that he was "overwhelmed by [her] winged words."

Mina was, of course, hinting at her own concerns in the essay. By this time, she was writing a long narrative poem about the Bowery and had already asked Robbie to check certain details, such as the exact term for the bums' favorite beverage—a cheap red wine which, he learned, was known as "creepy Pete." Her housemates listened to Mina's successive drafts as she worked on the poem, taking care to include the same degree of precision that gave "Property of Pigeons" its verisimilitude. The poem, entitled "Hot Cross Bum," was to be a tour of the neighborhood led by a detached yet sympathetic observer.

The poem's speaker, in the role of tour guide, presents the Bowery as a zone existing somewhere beyond the city dweller's consciousness. A kind of urban hell, it is nonetheless the bums' "sanctuary," a place where

> *Faces of inferno*
> *peering from shock-absorbent*
> *torsos*
>
> *alternate with raffish saints'*
> *eleemosynary innocence*

These "blowsy angels" work out their own approach to salvation in "a Brilliance all of bottles." (The image of the colored bottles suggested that Mina imagined their visions to resemble her own.)

The narrator also observes the derelicts' failings as they assault passersby. One rails learnedly at the world:

> *graduate of indiscipline*
> *post-graduate of procrastination*
>
> *a prophet of Babble-on*
> *shouts and mutters*
> *to earless gutters*

Noting that the "dole / of pity" cannot endow them with "that inborn fortune / self control," the speaker refuses to sentimentalize the outcasts.

The poem's next section narrates an incident that had recently taken place. A member of the charity profession, "some passing church / or social worker," informed the Catholic order assigned to the Bowery that he had commandeered "a certain provision / of hot-cross buns." In a parodic communion, these buns replace the wafers, and "creepy Pete" stands in for the libation. Moreover, the priests' "egoless eagerness" is matched by the "impious" mysticism of the bums, "shrunken illuminati / sunken / rather than arisen."

419

"Hot Cross Bum" turns sardonic in the remaining stanzas' extended comparison of a funeral leaving the church to the processional of garbage trucks in its wake. Once their "Dust to dust" rites are complete, disorderly elements remain. The bums continue to dream in their "communal cot" while one of their number pursues his "ignis fatuus," an imaginary love beneath him on the sidewalk. Yet despite her sarcasm, the derelicts stirred Mina's compassion, for she understood their "divers failures / to fit personality / in envelopes of rigidity." At the same time, she measured the distance across which she observed them and counted as an "inborn fortune" her ability to express herself, and, in this instance, to see her Bowery Baedeker published in Laughlin's highly regarded *New Directions* annual.

While writing "Hot Cross Bum," Mina was also constructing Bowery scenes with materials which, like her poetic images, were taken from the street. Like Picasso's collages, Mina's assemblages were incongruous couplings of commonplace objects, and like Duchamp's ready-mades, they seemed to thumb their nose at middle-class culture. But unlike either of these innovative recyclers, Mina brought to her shabby materials an acute sense of the cost involved for those who searched the garbage cans: rather than posing as outsiders, as the avant-garde had done, they actually lived at the bottom of the heap. And though Cornell's assemblages had inspired her to evoke the spirit in bric-a-brac, by using junk rather than the scraps of European culture he favored, she was dethroning the idea of art's *belle matiere*—unseating an art whose status relied on its superiority to humbler forms of expression.*

Having herself dropped out of the enlightened circles to which she had once aspired and then joined, Mina now had little interest in the New York art world's formalism, which at this time saw spiritual matters as intrusions into art's proper concerns. In these new works, she was reflecting on her own perspective, that of a person of higher status looking from her window at the derelicts below. But to understand her constructions, one had to see through her eyes. When she showed the bums in low relief, she mocked an artistic trend that made it unthinkable to treat subjects of such low status that they went "on relief." And while her objects adopted the outsider stance of the Salon des Refusés, her refuse was recombined not to assail artistic convention, as Duchamp had done, but to make it more responsive. As a name for these disturbing objects, she proposed "Refusees" —a punning blend of *refuse*, *Refusés*, and *refugees*, which summed up her long itinerary from West Hampstead to the Bowery. Later, quoting a phrase from her own poem, she would suggest another name—"the compensations of poverty."

---

* Mina's assemblages also illustrated Joel Goldsmith's belief in "the flow of giving": by finding the spirit in matter and offering it to the world in the form of art, one might experience the return of grace, or spiritual "supply."

While the members of her household were unaware of Mina's lifelong preoccupation with "outcasting," they were, nonetheless, her perfect audience, and they felt honored when invited into her room to see her objects. One of the most imaginative, some thought, was called *No Parking*. It recreated the scene outside their door one day when the contents of a garbage can spilled onto the pavement where derelicts dozed with beatific expressions. One had to look closely to see its most unexpected element: a butterfly whose wings were made from a flattened paper cup and whose body consisted of the metal spiral from a vacuum can—discards resurrected as a celestial messenger.

Still other images from "Hot Cross Bum" came to life in *Communal Cot*, Mina's modernization of the twelve apostles. Gazing down at it, one saw small figures stretched or curled up on the pavement, their bodies contorted and their faces appealing upward. But unlike Cornell, whose boxes had inspired her, Mina infused these assemblages with disturbing emotions. The careful observer of *No Parking* and *Communal Cot* could not help feeling assaulted by the contrast between the delicate modeling of the derelicts' features and the squalor of the materials used to depict them. While these objects were intended to be seen from above, others were head-on confrontations. In *Bums in Paradise*, the household recognized local derelicts: Mina had used them as models for the ragged men shown at prayer around a jukebox that resembled a cathedral window. Similarly, in *Christ on a Clothesline*, they recognized the tubercular, Scandinavian fisherman who hung around the Bowery. Mina had chosen him as the model for Jesus, she explained, because of his trade and his emaciation, but as he posed, his expression had become ecstatic at the idea of the money he was earning.

Surely the most disturbing of the series, *Christ on a Clothesline* places the viewer on the roof of a Bowery tenement. Against a hyperreal background of fluttering laundry and shabby brick buildings, an almost weightless Christ dangles from a clothesline. His body held fast by clothespins, his long, muscular arms beseech the viewer, who is put in the position of an awkward passerby. Although one senses that his spirit is on the verge of departing, the cadaverous face looks straight at the viewer. Mina had put her outrage at the world's injustices into this accusatory figure—the culmination of a series of similar figures, from the blind young street musician in Vienna to this savage version of the "gentle Jesus" she had sought in her childhood.

Concerned about her constructions' frailty—like the subjects depicted, her materials had all lived previous lives—Mina experimented with different glues in an effort to fix paper cups, rags, and clothespins to the surfaces. Realizing that these works were fragile, she asked Berenice Abbott, whose studio was nearby, to photograph them. When Abbott suggested that she think about an exhibition, Mina became interested in the idea, but at the same time wondered whether anyone who did not know the Bowery as she did could understand them. But while the irony of making art under such conditions was on her mind, she hoped to complete the series, Abbott thought, to demonstrate her belief that vision was itself a form of salvation.

On the morning of December 27, 1952, Mina told Robbie and Stevie that she was seventy. This declaration came as a shock. She never mentioned her age and had let it be known that she did not celebrate birthdays. In a retrospective mood, she had been working on a construction that summed up years of trying to understand the costs of "outcasting"—living in a way that did not "fit in anywhere," except on Stanton Street. Entitled *Householding*, this mixed-media assemblage differs in feeling and perspective from everything else she made while living near the Bowery.

Householding shows the head and bust of a woman modeled in flesh tones on cardboard and drawn with Pre-Raphaelite delicacy. Against a mottled background, where broken images of Italianate buildings hover, the woman sees in her imagination all the places where she has lived. Above her head, in a concave aureole or crown, are gathered her domestic objects: a ball of yarn stuck with miniature knitting needles, doll-sized dishes, a teapot, a ladder, and a laundry basket—all of them surmounted by a clothesline to which items of clothing are attached with tiny pins. The most personal of Mina's constructions, *Householding* seems to offer a glimpse into her soul.

As retrospective in its own way as *Christ on a Clothesline*, this image of a woman's indwelling expresses an entirely different set of moods and emotions. Although *Householding* evokes the idealized woman of Botticelli or Burne-Jones, it discards their settings to display her in her own space, dreaming of her life. This construction summed up Mina's turn from the tradition that had shaped her vision, particularly when it came to the representation of a woman's life, and gave shape to the poignancy of her lifelong flight from and quest for a sense of belonging. The fragility of daily life is reflected in its materials, moreover, as if they embodied her fears about age and vulnerability. For she was aware that she, too, could become as "unhoused" as her Bowery neighbors.

In these years Joel Goldsmith continued to offer spiritual comfort. Joella sent copies of his writings and tried to comply with Mina's requests for prayers and "demonstrations" on her behalf. Goldsmith's words brought "great spiritual uplift and the real sense of Presence," Mina told him; she found solace in his belief that, as an artist, she was peculiarly sensitive to "the overshadowing presence of the Spiritual Universe." He would keep his "spiritual eye" on her, he wrote, until she "received the realization of complete freedom." This watchfulness had its price, however: the number of "enclosures"—checks made out to her spiritual guide—began to add up.

Mina was still trying to understand the effects of her divided heritage. Glimpses of this process exist in her unpublished essay "History of Religion and Eros," and in her scattered notes on various spiritual traditions. Although she continued to think that Jews were more intelligent than other people, she could not rid herself of prejudice when it came to interactions with immigrants on the Lower East Side. And while she took an interest in the newly established state of Israel, she expressed the fear that the Jewish nation might turn into a priest-run theocracy like the Vatican. Her absorption in spiritual matters was accompanied by a deep suspicion of religious orthodoxies.

In 1950, a group of left-wing lay Catholics moved around the corner to a genteel brick building on Chrystie Street, where they ran a soup kitchen, housed as many homeless people as they could, and published *The Catholic Worker*: the magazine, whose title alluded to the Communist *Daily Worker*, was already notorious for its pacifist, anarchist, and "personalist" interpretation of the Word. Mina and Dorothy Day, the group's mainstay, had been acquaintances in the Village decades earlier, when Dorothy worked for the *Masses*, and had seen something of each other when Mina acted at the Provincetown. Since then, Day's conversion to spiritual witness and community service had set her and the group at odds with the Church and, in particular, its local representative, the Archbishop of New York.

Mina was struck by their way of living a radically Christian life. She subscribed to their paper and may even have found inspiration in its black-and-white woodcuts, which showed the destitute of all races at supper with Jesus or depicted Him on the same breadline one saw from the corner of Stanton and Chrystie. Day's column in the *Worker* read like a neighborhood gossip column with a spiritual perspective. "Let us be fools for Christ," she was heard to say. "Let us recklessly act out our vision, even if we shall almost surely fail, for what the world calls failure is often, from a Christian viewpoint, success." While the details of Mina's interest in the Catholic Worker movement are not known, she took its presence nearby as support for the view that art was another way to evoke "the overshadowing presence of the Spiritual Universe."

"In Extremis," an unusually direct poem from Mina's Bowery years, voices her absorption in the idea of spiritual witness:

> *Show me a saint who suffered in humility;*
> *I will show you one and again another*
> *who suffered more and in deeper humility*
> *than he.*
>
> *I who have lived among many of the unfortunate*
> *claim that of the martyr to have been*
> *a satisfactory career, his agony*
> *being well-advertised.*

Is not the sacrifice of security to renown
conventional for the heroic?
The common tragedy is to have suffered
without having "appeared."

In both poems and constructions she had been trying to make common suffering "appear"—although society preferred it to remain invisible.

Mina's metaphysical bent did not keep her from seeing the precarious humor of life on the Bowery. In September 1953 she apologized for again misplacing Joella's monthly check, explaining that she had hidden it behind a picture on the mantelpiece in April and rediscovered it five months later. In the same letter, she told Joella that recently, as she was walking down the Bowery, her handbag had slipped from her arm without her noticing. One of the bums "picked it up & brought it to me *intact*! I gave him a whole dollar," she added. "*But* to prove the truth of Bowery tradition," she went on, another bum immediately followed me home with the complaint that *he* had found my bag but the other bum had snatched it away from him."

Given Mina's increasingly absentminded approach to practical matters, stories like those related in this letter heightened her daughters' concern. To make things worse, after Klemp lost the lease on 5 Stanton Street, the members of the household began looking for separate apartments. Alex Bossom, the owner of Al's Bar and several buildings on the block, found places across the street for Klemp and Mina, at numbers 16 and 18. Out of respect for Mina, the household moved her belongings piece by piece. "It was quite a business to take all her stuff there," one of them recalled, "since she had so many little things, all kinds of eggshells. You had to be very careful with every object, or piece of junk."

Joella and Fabi worried that without Klemp's stabilizing influence, not to mention her dinners, Mina would suffer, and Fabi renewed efforts to bring her to Aspen. Whenever Mina agreed to visits in the past, Fabi had explained each step of the long train trip and promised her quantities of rag, cardboard, broken glass, and egg crates. But Mina had always canceled these carefully planned visits once it came time to leave. This time Fabi announced that she would arrive in December, pack Mina's materials, and take her and her objects to Colorado.

20

Aspen

(1953–66)

ASPEN WAS ENJOYING a modest revival in 1953 but in no way resembled the cosmopolitan center it would become. Arriving there in late December, Mina saw the town under a blanket of snow. The brightly painted Victorian houses had lost their outlines; the trees were indistinct blurs. After Manhattan's narrow canyons and the Bowery's brick tenements, this unfamiliar Western scene stretched for miles across a high plateau, beyond which the mountains loomed like brooding presences.

At first, exhausted by the trip and the change in altitude, Mina stayed inside her small apartment. Because none of Aspen's buildings was higher than two stories (except for the landmark Hotel Jerome), she had an uninterrupted view across the minuscule town to the mountains. After Manhattan, Aspen felt open, spacious, and airy, but she was unsure how long she wanted to stay there. Once paths were cleared outside, she began taking walks. The ubiquitous miners' cottages, many trimmed with Victorian gingerbread and stained glass, caught her eye, as did the winter sunlight streaming through the old glass bottles aligned in windows. The miniature town favored the Victoriana of her childhood, but in this new light, even familiar details looked fresh.

To New Yorkers, Colorado's remoteness presented either an exhilarating prospect or an alarming challenge. Aspen had only one paved street and little in the way of modern plumbing or sewerage at this time. The downtown measured three blocks by four, and its buildings were scattered among vacant lots. During the decades of Aspen's decline following the collapse of the silver boom, a number of houses had deteriorated or had been carted away to make additions to other dwellings. The remaining

Victorians had spacious yards lined with cottonwoods and aspens. The small town was full of light, especially in autumn, when a golden sheen lit the valley.

In the 1950s Aspenites in Levi's and work shirts still rode their horses into town. The area's ranchers lived as they had always done and tried to ignore Paepcke's efforts to turn their town into a center for "the whole man," as he was fond of saying. Western dress suited the climate. In good weather the streets were covered with the earth from the never-ending excavations for pavements and sewer lines, and during the spring thaw the melted snow flowing through these mounds created rivers of mud. These public-works projects were begun with so little foresight, some complained, that the newly paved streets were often dug up and paved over again. (People told the story of a New Yorker who abandoned her heels in the first few weeks of the muddy season.)

Aspen's population, about nine hundred, all told, was a heterogeneous mix of ranchers, sheepherders, artists, intellectuals, and self-declared free spirits who enjoyed the town's seedy charm. Everyone mingled, longtime residents recall. When it was time to celebrate a birth or a wedding, they borrowed each other's gloves to dress for the occasion. Mina soon attracted attention. She was "a person you'd notice walking down the street," they said, "a handsome woman who wore eccentric clothes." At a time when most people dressed Western-style, Mina wore trailing robes of velvet or brocade and wrapped her head with scarves or turbans pinned with antique brooches. While the locals wondered whether she bought these clothes at the thrift store, her tattered elegance delighted those who saw Aspen as a bohemian haven. Surprised to learn that she was the mother of Joella and Fabi, who, along with their husbands, were among the town's most prominent residents, the more artistically inclined were also intrigued because Mina was a poet and had lived in Paris. When they noticed her picking up trash in the alleys, they decided that she was more than a little "fey." Mina made such a strong impression that four decades later local memories of her are still vivid.

At first she lived across the hall from Fritz and Fabi and above Fritz's office. This location meant that she could dine with the Benedicts, but that she opened her door (out of curiosity and boredom) whenever their bell rang. When she moved with them to their new house on Red Mountain, she felt so isolated that her daughters moved her back into a larger apartment in the building where she had lived before. Its light front room became her studio, and the middle room, her bed-sitting room. In theory, her living arrangements could be tidier this way, since cardboard boxes, tin cans, and eggshells had a way of piling up while she was thinking of how to use them. Concerned about the accumulation of trash, Joella suggested keeping art supplies separate from living quarters. But Mina would not allow her scrap piles to be touched.

By the following year, it was obvious that she no longer saw Aspen

426

as a place she was visiting. Joella continued to pay the rent on the Stanton Street apartment in case Mina wanted to go home, but while she often complained of the isolation or wished that she could see Djuna Barnes, Cornell,* and friends from the Bowery, she did not fancy the train trip. The mountain air agreed with her, moreover, and she had begun taking an interest in local history and politics, which Aspenites were only too glad to relate.

During the 1880s, the time of Aspen's boom, the town had been discovered by Jerome Wheeler, who built the hotel named after him as well as the opera house. After the country went off the silver standard, the town's economy collapsed. Sixty years later Paepcke was reviving Aspen through the related activities of his enterprises, the Aspen Skiing Corporation, the Aspen Company, and the Aspen Institute for Humanistic Studies. Although the town had made a modest recovery, its essential character had not yet changed.

In all seasons the Hotel Jerome served as social center. Its dark wood panels, gleaming bar, and silvered mirrors looked like a set for a film of Aspen in its heyday. Visitors gathered there in the late afternoon to rub shoulders with the Austrian and Swiss ski instructors, or to get a glimpse of movie stars like Gary Cooper, attracted by the town's reputation as a European-style ski resort. There one saw the new elite, the friends and associates of Walter Paepcke.

As the town's major landowner, Paepcke behaved, some thought, like an hereditary monarch. "If the royal family had a prime minister," a local reporter noted, "he was Herbert Bayer." Impressed with Bayer's Bauhaus training, Paepcke had entrusted him with the restoration of old Aspen as well as with the guidelines for new construction. Unlike the imitation Swiss chalets and pseudo-Victorians proposed by lesser architects, Bayer's clean designs were compatible with the miners' cottages. But while his opera house restoration retained the best of its motifs and colors, the remodeled Hotel Jerome—painted in shades of gray trimmed with "Bayer" blue— jostled the sensibility of the locals, who preferred the original brick red. Moreover, when Paepcke offered free paint to homeowners, all but one of them refused, believing that the colors would have to be approved in advance by Bayer.

Locals and those who did not see themselves as part of the elite congregated across the street from the Hotel Jerome at the Epicure, where a Danish couple sold pastries and served light meals during the day. "The place to find someone if you couldn't reach them on the phone," one

---

* "It's nearly 2 years since they whisked me up here," Mina informed Cornell. "I am not at my ease here," she went on, "but the altitude is stimulating—sometimes surprising. When I arrived my hair stood on end and crackled with electricity, the metal utilities give electric shocks under one's fingernails—The Radio is a volley of shots except at night—& in the streets mostly all there is to walk on are 3 cornered stones." The letter also voiced her fear that Cornell had been "displeased" with her constructions, although "one man said he's seen the God in them."

regular recalled, the Epicure became one of Mina's favorite haunts, especially after the new owner planted a garden. Younger residents thought the Epicure "very bohemian," because the European population and local artists gathered there, but also because the owners prepared birthday cakes to order, tinting them blue if that was what one fancied. Although Mina felt out of place at the Jerome, she was always welcome at the Epicure.

During the fifties, the town's social life featured ladies' auxiliary meetings and fund drives along with the music festival and institute lectures: in the *Aspen Times*, accounts of the Rodeo Queen contest appeared next to articles on Goethe. But while some saw Aspen as a fertile mix of small-town life and cosmopolitan culture, others resented the Paepcke "invasion." And although most Aspenites were grateful for the improvement in living standards brought by Paepcke's enterprises, "a kind of bewilderment" often accompanied their gratitude, a local historian noted. "Occasional visitors who came for fishing, hunting and sight-seeing had always been part of the Aspen picture," she continued, "but to have the whole town taken over by outlanders and foreigners was another matter."

The interests of Aspen's various populations were not easily reconciled. Disagreements arose between the organizers of the summer concerts and the rodeo—a conflict known as "Music vs. Manure." Paepcke's vision—"great books, great men, and great music"—deserved the town's support, asserted Mortimer Adler, a University of Chicago professor and part of the Institute's brain trust. More representative of efforts to negotiate a truce, the Masque and Music Club staged a Western operetta in the opera house: set in a dude ranch, it featured a romantic plot in which several "Dudines" competed for the attentions of the corral boss, among them Fabienne Benedict in cowboy clothes. The Chamber of Commerce would soon resolve the "Music vs. Manure" debate by scheduling rodeos and stock-car races so as not to conflict with the Festival, thus creating a summer season that ran from May through September.

Fabi and Joella were increasingly involved in the phases of Aspen's resurgence, from refurbishing the Hotel Jerome to the large-scale projects of the Institute, and Herbert also relied on Joella's help in his many projects for Paepcke's Container Corporation. When she and Herbert moved out of town, Joella and Fabi decided to hire a companion for Mina, someone who could come a few hours each day. Mina scrutinized one of the first candidates for the job, a high-school student named Esther Jane Herwick, and told her tartly that although she was young, they could give it a try. Each day after school Esther went to Mina's apartment to make tea, prepare her evening meal, and tidy the premises as best she could.

To their mutual surprise, the fifteen-year-old schoolgirl and her seventy-five-year-old charge became friends. Esther, whose family believed in Christian charity, was careful not to disturb Mina's piles of trash and accepted the strange diet she required because of her false teeth and digestive problems. She prepared puddings, wheat germ, and the alarming mixture of raw liver ground up and blended with grapefruit juice on which Mina depended, and enjoyed grooming Mina's long white hair or rubbing her feet with wheat-germ oil to alleviate the dryness brought on by the climate. While it was clear to her that Mina had once been a beauty, Esther admired her as she was.

Despite her increasing frailty and arthritic hip, Mina refused assistance when bathing until she could no longer manage on her own. When she told Esther not to look at her ugly body, the girl replied that everyone was beautiful in God's eyes. From then on Mina placed her full trust in her young companion. She asked how Esther's parents had taught her compassion, as well as their thoughts on sex, religion, and one's spiritual obligations to others—as if she were reliving her upbringing with this young girl whose background was so different from her own, and wondering, perhaps, what course she would have taken had she followed her parents' precepts.

Esther became so fond of her charge that she often stayed until Mina fell asleep. Whenever Fabi and Joella traveled, Esther stayed in Mina's studio among the canvases and eggshells. She liked to gaze at Mina's "suffering souls," as she called her constructions; their "mystical" expressions made her think that they were the derelicts Mina often talked about. The young girl also marveled at the transformation of her trash. What began as "a mess" in the early stages would come together at the end, when the tin cans and eggshells vanished into the composition. Once she could see these projects through Mina's eyes, she understood her choosiness: the right eggshells, used texturally in a figure's clothing or as part of the earth, became unrecognizable.

When Mina fully accepted the idea that she was now an Aspenite, she began a new series about the area's prospectors and miners, incorporating the copper plates and metal scraps she had salvaged. The faces in these new constructions resembled her suffering souls, but the series became a memorial to all those who had sought their fortunes, and lost their lives, in Colorado. What was more, she told Esther defiantly, she planned to sign these objects "Mina Loy, I'm a litterbug."*

In addition to explaining her artistic aims, Mina also spoke with much emotion of her life with the avant-garde of London, Paris, and New York. But she talked with even greater feeling of her sympathy for the outcasts and the homeless people often found in these places. "I learned so much from her—culture, sympathy, and kindness," Esther recalled. "I had heard about the winos but I didn't know that they were real, just as I'd heard

---

* Mina's Aspen constructions, the Western equivalent of her Bowery series, were kept in storage for many years and are now in private collections in Maine and Colorado.

about the other half but had no idea how they live—until I knew Mrs. Lloyd." She was the most imaginative person Esther had ever known. "I loved her dearly," she told a visitor thirty years later.

During the years in which Mina relied on Esther's affection, she seemed content. She had a companion who did not tire of her stories and was happy to keep her secrets. Esther inspired such confidence that Mina entrusted her with her personal mail and with the small sums of money she kept in various hiding places. Despite her fears about privacy, Mina was perfectly lucid, Esther thought. She recalled events in the distant and recent past with clarity and was amused to learn that some thought her "dotty." Although she wrote little apart from the occasional letter, she worked regularly on her constructions and no longer spoke of returning to New York. When Mina finished work for the day, she and Esther had tea at the Epicure; the rest of the time, she smoked, read, played cards, and gazed out the window at the mountains.

Despite their busy lives, Fabi looked in every morning to see how Mina was doing, and Joella called frequently. Apart from the family, Mina had few visitors. Another paid companion was found for her after Esther's family left Aspen in 1959: Billie Brondizi, a part-time model at a local art school who looked and behaved like a gypsy, also became devoted to Mina but soon proved too much of a free spirit for the job.

Local intellectuals and artists took to calling on Mina once they learned who she was. When an aspiring young writer named Norris Taylor came to discuss poetry, he was amused to see that while they drank tea and ate gingersnaps, Mina kept the door ajar because of her "gentleman caller." Martie Sterling, another young writer who was running a ski lodge, wanted to meet Mina because of her interest in the expatriates. During her visits, Mina received in bed, propped up on pillows. When Martie asked her about Ernest Hemingway, Martie's idol, Mina sat straight up, glared at her guest, and asked why she was wasting time on that "pompous boor." She spoke with affection of Gertrude, Djuna, and their friends, but complained of being left alone. Aware that her daughters had busy lives, she asked out loud, "But why should I expect them to spend so much time with me when I spent so little time with them?" And in the middle of talking about other subjects, she asked plaintively about Cravan, "Why was I never able to find him?" Her moods swung between self-accusation and self-pity, Martie observed; her spirit had not come to rest.

Although Joella tried to include her in social events, Mina either bristled at her suggestions or apologized for being a burden. Herbert Bayer showed little affinity for his mother-in-law's meandering conversation, while Fritz Benedict seemed more at home with her and understood her feeling for Fabi. At their parties, where she caused a stir because of her appearance, Mina often looked forlorn or angry, and few knew what to say to her. At one of these gatherings Mina asked defiantly whether anyone had a cigarette—despite her daughters' efforts to persuade her to stop smoking. A guest offered her one that had been hand-rolled, explaining that it was "tea," to which she replied blithely, "Oh, I've smoked *that* before!" Everyone was amused, except Joella and Fabi.

On one of these occasions, Mina met the French Abstract Expressionist Yvonne Thomas, a friend of Duchamp's. As a European of another era, Mina was out of place, Yvonne thought; she was ill at ease in a provincial town where most people thought her odd. When they met again, Mina harked back to the time of her friendships with Duchamp and the Arensbergs and kept bemoaning the present. Yvonne sensed a contradiction between her bohemianism and her rigidities. Mina had yearned all her life for something unattainable, she thought, although she was unsure whether she had wanted social success or artistic recognition. And while Yvonne shared many of Mina's opinions, she was surprised how strongly she held them.

When Yvonne took her to lunch one rainy afternoon, Mina was wearing a pair of gold shoes, an unusual choice given her arthritis, the weather, and the mud running through the streets. They jumped over the rivulets, laughing as they went; at lunch, the return of Mina's gaiety led to the subject of Marcel's antisocial pranks. Later, sitting on Mina's balcony and gazing at the sky, they asked each other what she saw in the clouds. When a mock argument began about whose shapes were preferable, Mina insisted that hers were superior. Yvonne enjoyed her company but felt that her certainties masked a deep dissatisfaction.

Over the years James Laughlin had kept in touch with Mina after publishing her long poem "Hot Cross Bum." Through Laughlin, who continued to publish Pound and Williams when they were out of fashion, the young poet and publisher Jonathan Williams wrote to her in 1957 during a trip to Colorado: having just read Rexroth's article on Mina's "extreme exceptionalism," he wondered whether she might allow him to issue an edition of her poems. Williams was surprised to receive a wire summoning him to the Hotel Jerome, but found it impossible to comply after a snowfall blocked the mountain passes. When he made his way to Aspen, after presenting his credentials as the head of Jargon Press to Joella and Fabi, he called on Mina—"still a distinguished and handsome woman," he thought, who was delighted to learn that Pound and Bill Williams were both alive. She was very much interested in his proposal but no longer had copies of *Lunar Baedecker* or her other publications to give him.

After months of research, Williams prepared a version of some poems from *Lunar Baedecker*, to which he added sections of "Anglo-Mongrels" and several of Mina's "contemplative" poems. This new collection excluded "English Rose," "Der Blinde Junge," "O Hell," and "Poe"—among her most savage denunciations of society—and nearly all the poems from "Anglo-Mongrels" that were about her parents (the sequence having been retitled "The Anglo-Mystics of the Rose"). The manuscript concluded with

seven "later poems," including one ambiguously titled "Revelation"—
which calls Christ's agony on the Cross the time "when Genius / disillusioned comprehends / —the incommensurable idiocy— / as you would
say— / sin—of the world." Of this last group, perhaps the most moving
in its blend of painterly, spiritual, and worldly concerns is "Omen of
Victory":

> Women in uniform
> relaxed for tea
> under the shady garden trees
> discover
> a dove's feather
> fallen in the sugar.

After noting the many typographical errors in the 1923 Contact edition,
Williams proposed emendations and established the manuscript that appeared in 1958 as *Lunar Baedeker & Time-Tables*. It is unclear whether Mina
approved its many changes. Because of her limited energies and desire to
finish her constructions, Fabi and Joella did most of the final reading.

Having told Williams that she "never was a poet," Mina was, nonetheless, pleased with the result. *Lunar Baedeker & Time-Table*'s publication
—"a real EVENT, like the opening of King Tut's tomb," Rexroth observed—was heralded by the poets who introduced the book, Bill Williams,
Rexroth, and Denise Levertov. Speaking for his generation, Williams began,
"Mina Loy was endowed from birth with a first rate intelligence and a
sensibility which has plagued her all her life facing a shoddy world. When
she puts a word down on paper it is clean," he went on, but this "clean-
liness" had frightened her readers. In his opinion, the hallmark of her style
was its directness, "in which she is exceeded by no one." Contemporary
poets would do well to adopt her "delicate if sardonic humor."

To Levertov (who, like Mina, grew up in England), Mina's name was
"long-familiar, legendary," and her spirit one of "electrifying truthfulness."
While she also noted Mina's "appetite for sounds," it was her honesty that
impressed the younger poet: "Bite on it," she observed, "you'll break your
teeth." The ferocity of Mina's desire for the truth was not widespread in
England, Levertov noted tactfully. "The idealism and bevelled edges of
most educated English people," she felt, made them resistant to "hard
substance and close scrutiny." But it was just this quality in Mina's writing
that made her important for younger poets, since its value was "indivis-
ibly—technical and moral."

In addition to the remarks of Williams, Levertov, and Rexroth—his
1944 article was excerpted in the introductory material—her new publisher
also included "testimonies" from Henry Miller, Edward Dahlberg, Walter
Lowenfels, Alfred Kreymborg, and Louis Zukofsky on the back cover. *Lunar
Baedeker & Time-Tables* was "news of the utmost importance," Kreymborg

declared. That Mina remained a poet decades after dropping out of sight, Zukofsky noted, was proof of her significance. These blurbs pale next to Miller's encomium: hers was "an interplanetary voice whose subtle vibrations only faintly pierce our smug-laden atmosphere." If no one in Aspen knew who she was, this book brought proof that among the literati she was, as Dahlberg put it, one of modern poetry's "tutelary Muses."

Mina did not feel up to making the trip East for the publication party, held in New York at the Martha Jackson Gallery in December 1958, nor could she bear the thought of seeing people who had known her decades earlier. During the party she telephoned from Aspen to talk to the guests, among them Kay Boyle and Bob Brown, but scolded Jonathan Williams for not taking the trouble to hang her Bowery constructions at the gallery, where they belonged. ("Miss Loy says she is a painter," a reporter noted a few years later in the *Aspen Times*, though everyone liked to think of her as a poet.)

When it became apparent that no one but Rexroth would review *Lunar Baedeker & Time-Tables*, Williams complained to Mina that there was "no winning in this country." He supposed that he must be *"persona non grata"* with the literary establishment. In reply, Mina suggested a strategy for dealing with poetry's difficulties. "The best way to conquer is to wear as helmet: *a smile*," she wrote. "I don't agree that there is no winning in this country," she went on. "Change from *Persona Non Grata* to Persona Good Grinner—now don't hate me!!!" She looked forward to his next visit, when she would discuss with him "the right design for your face-armour. Now don't let this seem merely an encouragement to relax," she concluded; "it is entirely for friendliness between poetry and the world."

By 1959, when Mina was dispensing this whimsical advice, she had reason to be cheerful. She had just had her first one-woman show in New York, where her "Refusees" not only received critical attention but found buyers. Since 1953, when she left the Bowery on what she thought would be a brief trip to Aspen, the constructions had been wrapped in plastic in her Stanton Street apartment—under the care of Alex Bossom, the proprietor of Al's Bar, and her friend from Klemp's, Stevie Ferris. In the months following her departure, Stevie contacted galleries on her behalf and was present when Cornell came to inspect the series in the hope that it might suit his gallery. Cornell was so overwhelmed by her objects, Stevie reported, that he retreated into the kitchen, where he whispered that given their material condition, his dealer would not want them. Since then, Julien had also tried to arrange a show, he informed Mina during one of her bouts with depression, "because you have a Soul and deserve to be cheered." Nothing came of his efforts until 1958, when he, Duchamp, and David Mann, a young art dealer, went to Stanton Street. Everything in her apartment was neat, even the dust, Julien reported, and they all agreed that her "angel-bums" were "marvelous." Mann decided on the spot to give her a show, and neither Julien nor Marcel wanted a commission, he

433

teased; they were both happy to be her agents because they were "in love with Mina Loy."

The following year Mina's constructions were crated and taken to the Bodley Gallery on East Sixtieth Street, an odd setting for these fragile depictions of homelessness. In the exhibition catalogue Julien called her "an English poetess of a vanishing generation" whose knowledge of the Bowery was visible in these "contrary pictures": "lyric in their drabness, whole in their fragmentation," they glorified "the aristocrats of the dispossessed" with "Victorian sugar." Duchamp noted, more succinctly, "MINA'S POEMS À 2½ DIMENSIONS: HAUTS-RELIEFS ET BAS-FONDS, INC., MARCEL DUCHAMP (ADMIRAVIT). In praising her "poems in two and a half dimensions," Duchamp gave these "high reliefs" and "lower depths" his imprimatur.

In April Mina called to speak to the friends who attended her opening—the guest list included Julien, Marcel, Cornell, Bob Brown, Hans Fraenkel, Stevie Ferris, Kay Boyle, Peggy Guggenheim, and Frances Steloff, as well as Alex Bossom and his lady friend, who, Julien thought, resembled Mae West. To everyone's surprise, Djuna appeared, although she had become so reclusive that she rarely left her apartment. The event was "very glamorous and satisfying," Julien told Mina: they drank champagne, spoke admiringly of Mina's art, and, in some cases, made purchases. Of all the works shown, Peggy preferred *Househunting*, Mina's most personal construction, and took it with her to Venice to install, ironically, in her palazzo.

Mina's opening was "gay and exciting," Frances Steloff remarked, a reunion of the old avant-garde at a time when many of their number were frail, out of touch, or reluctant to attend social gatherings. Frances placed the construction called *No Parking*, which showed the bums around a brimming garbage can, in the Gotham Book Mart's window, where she was also featuring *Lunar Baedeker & Time-Tables*. The display "attracted a good deal of attention," she wrote.

Few critics shared the enthusiasm of Mina's friends. As David Mann feared, in 1959—when Abstract Expressionism ruled the art world—Victorian sugar was unlikely to please. "The alliance between Dada and social comment is downright sinister," declared *The New York Times*. "Theatrical trappings dripping with sentimentality," agreed *Art News*. In *The New Yorker*, Robert Coates, a friend from Paris, admitted that he preferred Duchamp's title to Mina's, since her constructions emphasized "the Lower Depths." "For all their grim subject matter," Coates went on, "the mood of the show is tender, and in its own uninsistent way, extremely moving." But Mina's art was so unusual that it was hard to classify. Of all the reviews, the most sympathetic to her vision appeared in *Arts*, whose critic did not seem to care that Mina was neither a formalist nor easily classified. Through her constructions one saw the Bowery "in terms of heaven and hell," this reviewer noted. *No Parking*'s butterfly arising from the trashcan spoke for the show, she went on: "That image, the plea of discarded life to be reanimated, inspires all of these works, in which the common becomes triumphant through a spiritual effort."

Whatever Mina thought of her reviews, she was more than pleased when she received a check from David Mann for the constructions that sold—at two thousand dollars apiece, the sum was more than gratifying. And her dealer expressed his gratitude for having been allowed to show them. Because he did not have her "double gift," he wrote, he was unable to say what he felt about such "moving and genuinely beautiful objects," but he considered it a privilege to represent her: while the critics had not understood, her art had "the melange of ugliness, beauty, humanity and that wonderful banality that the really great human utterance[s] always have." Within a short time, an article entitled "The Rediscovery of Mina Loy and the Avant-Garde" appeared in a literary review, and through the efforts of Duchamp, Mina received the Copley Foundation Award for Outstanding Achievement in Art. There remained some hope of friendliness "between poetry and the world."

Although Mina had always walked around the Bowery, it was hard for her to negotiate Aspen's streets, which at various times were full of snow, broken asphalt, and potholes. By the late fifties she stopped appearing at the Epicure and spent nearly all her time at home. She agreed to cortisone injections for her chronic back and hip pain, despite her belief that Christian Science did more than doctors. And while she allowed Dr. Crandall, a trusted local physician, to treat her for the borderline diabetes that developed with age, she also made it clear that she required the care of her favorite practitioner in New York. As Mina's telephone bills mounted—she also made long calls to Djuna and other friends there, informing them that life in Aspen was not to her liking—Fabi came up with a way to deal with the expense and comfort her mother at the same time. After telling Mina about an unusually gifted practitioner in a nearby town, she mentioned that this woman, who was hard to reach by phone, had agreed to call Mina when she found the time. Mina was so pleased to hear from her—Fabi with her voice slightly altered—that she told everyone how helpful she was.

Mina's health deteriorated despite these consultations, and she welcomed Dr. Crandall's visits once she began spending most of her time in bed. He found her alert and argumentative but prey to obsessions. She spoke repeatedly of Cravan and said that what she wanted most of all was to look as she had in her youth. Although "she didn't always make sense," he admired her spirit. Soon after her eightieth birthday, her daughters concluded that Mina should no longer live alone. She was forgetful, failed to take her medicine, and had no appetite. Mrs. Bibbig, a German woman who took boarders—mostly young children—in her two-story Victorian, agreed to look after Mina. She could live upstairs with her own sitting room, and her peculiar diet posed no problems.

Mrs. Bibbig had difficulty getting Mina to eat, nonetheless. In 1964, when she was eighty-two, Dr. Crandall noted, she had lost her "usual sparkle." But as soon as he persuaded her to go into the hospital, her spirit returned. She ordered the nurses around, told one of them to her face that she would look much better without glasses, and dismissed the new color television sets because the colors were wrong. (She preferred black and white.) Somewhat improved after a short stay in a nursing home, Mina returned to Mrs. Bibbig's, where Dr. Crandall noted general deterioration, a lack of appetite, and, more disconcertingly, given her character, "no particular desires." She had lost weight and her delicate bones dominated her face. Although Mina felt her age, she was unreconciled to it.

During the summer of 1964, Jonathan Williams often called with the poet Ronald Johnson. Mina's coquetry had returned when Williams took her photograph for *Lunar Baedeker & Time-Tables*: she stared straight at the camera with a mischievous expression, and, when shown the result, declared, "Only the eyes are left." (Williams respected her wishes by cropping the photograph to emphasize the ferocity of her gaze.) In their company she talked of the Provincetown Players, *Others*, *The Little Review*, and Paris, often interspersing her reminiscences with complaints about Aspen. Her spirits revived when they gave her news of old friends like Pound and Williams.

In 1965, while Jonathan Williams was the Institute's Poet in Residence, Robert Creeley and Paul Blackburn, two younger poets who were not well known, visited Aspen. Like Williams, whom they had known at Black Mountain College, they were not attracted to the academic poetry favored by the "new critics": their circle of poets, which included Denise Levertov, Charles Olson, and Robert Duncan, admired work with a mixture of tones and a certain wryness at the expense of the self. Blackburn particularly liked the note of seriousness shot through with irony in Mina's poems, and he was curious about her reputation as a recluse. With Robert Vas Dias, director of the Aspen Writers' Workshop, he visited Mina at Mrs. Bibbig's and taped their interview. (Creeley was to have joined them but became ill at the last moment.)

Mina was touched that they had come to see her but quite unlike the recluse they were expecting. At eighty-two she had the presence of a much younger woman. Her mind went in tracks that the average person might find hard to follow, Vas Dias thought, but she was perfectly clear provided one grasped her allusions. "She wandered off the track occasionally," he recalled, "but her wanderings were quite intelligible to us." She was so happy to see them that she became "charmingly loquacious." At first, given the presence of the tape recorder, Mina worried about her dentures: should she speak with or without them, she asked her guests. The new set was a failure. When she wore them for long, she complained, "they make me deaf and they bite my tongue." (It was worse when she took them out, since they sat in their glass and stared at her.) The story of her teeth, pulled out one by one until none remained, was like the story of her life, she remarked: "Everything happened to me like that."

Along the track of memory, these painful losses led to a much greater one. Her husband had been a poet, she explained, and had disappeared mysteriously with the money she gave him. After relating the tale of their brush with starvation ("A man looks better when he's starving than a woman does," she commented), Mina claimed that the mystery had been cleared up when she heard from a Christian Science practitioner the story of a man much like him who had been killed for his money in Mexico— an explanation that seemed reassuring because it meant that "he hadn't tried to shove me off." Of Christian Scientists, she added, "They always seem to put you right."

With the story of Cravan resolved to her satisfaction, she returned to the subject of marriage later in their visit. Her first husband had been "the shortest man," she said vehemently, a "little dwarf" with whom she had arranged to "get married but not be married"—to avoid going back to her parents. This husband (in their interview he remains nameless, as if she had lost interest in him and was unaware that he still lived in the Caribbean) was distinguished only by his dwarfishness and his famous name. He had an inferiority complex, she explained, to which she responded by "trying to look as if I liked and respected him." She was always kind to this man, she went on, but "managed to get rid of him" before marrying his antidote, whose massive physique she still admired. (Cravan was "perfectly solid everywhere, his legs in the same proportion.") "Everything has been funny in my life," she concluded, "but it wasn't funny losing him."

Once Mina felt at ease with her callers, she allowed Blackburn to prod her into reading from *Lunar Baedeker & Time-Tables*. Speaking tremulously at first and stumbling over the difficult words, she rediscovered her poems, but it was as if someone else had written them. Praising "Parturition" ("a good poem"), she liked her description of labor and chuckled at her fondness for "long, long words." Remembering that "Pig Cupid" had been notorious in its time, she pronounced its sexual images "clever," even "quite good," and recalled them as the reason she was thought "frightfully immoral"—an accusation that still appeared to rankle. After reading more "Love Songs" and savoring their wit, she asked coquettishly, "Don't you think I must have been awfully wicked?"

Rediscovering her glee at being "immoral," she told them that the editors of *The Little Review* had been "horrified" by her reputation until they met her, when they began "clamoring" for her work. "I suppose I sounded as if I were rather pugnacious," she mused. "I wasn't at all," she went on. "I'd only written these things for the sake of the sounds." Poems like "Costa San Giorgio" were transpositions of reality—the poem re-created her street "exactly as it was." Similarly, "Jules Pascin" evoked the artist's drawings, just as "Joyce's Ulysses" described his prose. When she read this poem with precision and vigor, her callers were amused by her disdain for "England / the sadistic mother" and the zest with which she evoked Bloom's "pilgrimage / to the Libido." Of Joyce, her ally in immorality, she chortled, "He did frighten everybody, didn't he!"

As she read her poems, the circumstances of their composition—the old battles and opponents—came to life again, along with her self-confidence. "I don't think it matters how many poems you wrote, do you?" she asked Blackburn. People were always going to the bookshops and asking for *Lunar Baedeker & Time-Tables*: it ought to be reprinted, she thought, since she did not have it in her to write anymore. She could, on the other hand, imagine painting—for the Salon d'Automne. "I'd love to be able to send them one more picture before I die," she said with a sigh. After she'd boasted of the prices fetched by her constructions, her thoughts wandered back to her 1912 one-woman show in London and the duchess who had taken a fancy to her. Her pride in these accomplishments still intact, she wondered how she had ever written anything. "I must have remembered something I learned in a former life," she mused, "because I learned nothing here."

This interview, punctuated by worries about her teeth, age, and "wickedness," as well as the opinions—both critical and admiring—of her family, provides the last portrait of Mina in old age. Antagonists like Julia and Stephen had diminished in importance: her mother had become "this woman shrieking and driving us cracked with her bad temper," and her husband "this dark-haired dwarf." Old grudges, except for a generalized one against society, lacked their intensity. Her Jewish ancestry came up obliquely, when she misunderstood Blackburn's allusion to the Jutes (she heard the term as "the Jews") as predecessors of the "English"—a race to which she had never belonged, she let on. What remained unclouded by age or doubt was her conviction that in "Apology of Genius" she had written "one of the great poems of the world," and that she might just be, as a correspondent had alleged, "the greatest poet that ever lived." (Or was it, she wondered, "the greatest woman poet.")

So frail that she required the attendance of a children's nurse, Mina believed in herself. A few weeks later, confirmation of her importance to the younger experimentalists arrived in the form of a message from Vas Dias, quoting a letter he had received from Robert Creeley. After listening to their interview, Creeley had written, "She is a very great poet, and of such an order of woman there would never be quite another like her."

Of all the correspondence Mina received after the publication of *Lunar Baedeker & Time-Tables* in 1959, a letter that arrived with its own illustration showed that the younger generation also understood her spiritual longings. From Our Lady of Gethsemani monastery came a postcard of a carved wooden angel in flowing robes, its hand outstretched in blessing. This Madonna-like image accompanied a note from Thomas Merton, the author, scholar of Zen Buddhism, and Trappist monk. "Dear Mina Loy," it began,

Thanks to J. Laughlin I have been reading your Lunar Baedeker *and after I told him how much I liked it he said I must tell you also. Which puts you in the curious situation of receiving a fan letter from a Trappist. Do you mind? I would not want this letter to sound silly.*

Merton listed among his favorite poems "Apology of Genius"—it was "tremendous," he thought, "very clean, very ascetic," and, moreover, "very healthy. . . . You will say perhaps that they were all written a long time ago," he went on, "and that it is too late to tell you this. But they were not written a long time ago at all. They are as if they had not been written. As if they *were* all by themselves."

Merton also admired "Joyce's Ulysses," the section of "Anglo-Mongrels" about the "Infant Aesthete," and "Italian Pictures," although he asked, "Weren't you hard on nuns?" And the fleeting visions at the close of "On Third Avenue"—the box-office goddess and the "trolley / loaded with luminous busts"—reminded him of the only things he could remember that were "sympathetic about New York." He also liked the poems he would be expected to like, those with religious themes, "above all the terribly poignant one" about the contradictions of her religious background. After thanking Mina for writing in the first place and for allowing her poems to be republished, Merton offered "a gesture of gratitude and friendship":

First I shall send you this angel which I like, and an offprint of an article which is just something to send you. And then beside that, which is perhaps better, I will often remember you when I say Mass, for I am a priest too as well as a monk, and this is one of the things I am able to do for you that perhaps another might not be able to do. And again, I can ask God to bless you, which I do also. So may you be blessed, and be at peace, and be glad that many people love you in heaven and on earth, among them, and in all of them Christ.

A fan letter from a Trappist was exactly what Mina wanted, especially one signed "cordially yours in Christ." Her poems had found their reader. Her soul had touched another's, who saw through age and infirmity to the ardent girl she had been, and who, moreover, blessed her.

One hopes that Merton's angel stayed within sight as Mina's strength declined. Hospitalized again in 1966, she was found to have advanced spinal osteoarthritis. Despite her fragility, the doctor thought her "feisty" for a woman of eighty-three; when he spoke of his wife's pregnancy, she snorted, "Oh how unimaginative!" Observing that she was unusually alert, he noted generalized weakness and memory loss, stomach cramping, and poor appetite. Soon she had to be readmitted. As Joella sat by her side in the hospital, Mina took her hand, kissed it, and whispered, "I never knew what you were." This recognition came not long before her death—of pneumonia—on September 25.

Memorial services were held in Aspen at Christ Episcopal Church, a curious compromise for the child of a mixed marriage who had explored the New Thought and Eastern religions before settling on Christian Science—without abandoning her hope for revelation. On such occasions it is customary to read from the poet's work. Mina had left no epitaph, nor did any one poem suggest itself.

Several meditations on mortality were found among her papers, along with a prose *pensée* that reads like a spiritual autobiography. To the question "What value does death give life?" she answered that the idea of death made living bearable. "For many, their manner of being alive is an impossible situation," she observed. "Caught in the trap of circumstances their condition would be unimaginable were it not for the one way out." All are taught to fear death, but while this fear "a little enfeebles our delight" in the midst of life, death was but "an innocuous disaster."

The house of self, the mansion of the ego, were illusions, as were all attempts to understand our place in the scheme of things. "We are but a ramshackle edifice around an eternal exaltation," she mused, "a building in which the moralities are a flight of stairs whose bases dissolve in the wake of our ascension . . . We wonder if Life is fleeting and escaped us while we essayed to reason it out," she went on, "or whether Life is static while we absent-mindedly shamble past it." These questions remain unanswered. "Being alive is a long time while so little comes within reaching-distance," the passage concludes—but more than anything one might say, "Being alive is a queer coincidence."

NOTES

BIBLIOGRAPHY

ACKNOWLEDGMENTS

INDEX

Notes

The bulk of the Loy papers—correspondence, manuscripts, drafts, and personal papers—are in the Collection of American Literature, Beinecke Rare Book and Manuscript Library, Yale University. Where no archival reference for quotations in the text is given in the notes, all material comes from this generous source. Loy papers in other libraries, private collections, or in the Loy family estate are denoted by the name of the university or collection; information on the location of specific collections appears in the acknowledgments. Unverified or speculative information, including dates, is contained in brackets. No date is indicated by "n.d."; no page number by "n.p." Unless otherwise indicated, all translations are my own.

   The Last Lunar Baedeker, the 1982 collection of Mina Loy's poetry and prose edited by Roger L. Conover (Highlands, NC: Jargon Society), is referred to as *TLLB*. Loy's autobiographical manuscript, *Islands in the Air*, is referred to as *Islands*. A list of Loy's publications appears at the beginning of the Bibliography.

   To minimize repetition, references to other works cited more than once in the notes have been kept brief. When more than one work by an author has been cited, the short title as well as the author's name is given; when only one work by an author has been cited, the author's name is given. Published works for which full references appear in the Bibliography are referred to by the author's name; unpublished works and correspondence are referred to by the author's initials.

Archives are abbreviated as follows:
AAA: Archives of American Art, Smithsonian Institution. Louis Bouché papers; Joseph Cornell papers
BOR: Barràs collection
CBC: Carolyn Burke collection
COL: Columbia University Library, Special Collections. Stephan Haweis papers
JLE: Julien Levy Estate
MLE: Mina Loy Estate
PC: Private Collection
ROD: Musée Rodin Archives
ROS: Rosenbach Museum & Library, Philadelphia. Marianne Moore papers
YCAL: Collection of American Literature, Beinecke, Yale University. ML papers; ML correspondence
   with Mabel Dodge Luhan, Alfred Stieglitz, Gertrude Stein, Scofield Thayer, and Carl Van Vechten,
   in their respective collections; Hapgood family papers

Notes

UCLA: University of California, Los Angeles, University Library, Special Collections. Kenneth Rexroth papers

Names are abbreviated as follows:
AC: Arthur Cravan
ADF: Amelia DeFries
CB: Carolyn Burke
CVV: Carl Van Vechten
DB: Djuna Barnes
EP: Ezra Pound
FB: Fabienne Benedict
FTM: Filippo Tommaso Marinetti
GBP: Gabrielle Buffet-Picabia
GP: Giovanni Papini
GS: Gertrude Stein
HPR: Henri-Pierre Roché
JB: Joella Bayer
JC: Joseph Cornell
JG: Juliette Gleizes
JL: Julien Levy
JW: Jonathan Williams
LN: Louise Norton
LS: Leo Stein
LV: Laurence Vail
MD: Marcel Duchamp
MDL: Mabel Dodge Luhan
ML: Mina Loy
MM: Marianne Moore
MR: Man Ray
NBH: Neith Boyce Hapgood
NCB: Natalie Clifford Barney
NG: Nellie Grandjean
RMcA: Robert McAlmon
SH: Stephen Haweis
WCA: Walter Conrad Arensberg
WCW: William Carlos Williams

Introduction

page
vi Footnote: Myrna Loy, in James Kotsilibas-Davis and Myrna Loy, *Myrna Loy: Being and Becoming* (New York: Knopf, 1987), p. 42.

Prologue

3 "was the nearest": Stephen Graham, quoted in Irving Howe, *World of Our Fathers* (New York: Harcourt Brace Jovanovich, 1976), p. 42.

3 "I felt grateful": Stella Petrakis, quoted in Chermayeff et al., *Ellis Island* (New York: Macmillan, 1991), p. 43.

4 "No inordinately": ML, "Alda's Beauty," pp. 10–11, MLE.

4 On Stevens, see Francis Naumann, "A Lost American Futurist," and Carolyn Burke and Naomi Sawelson-Gorse, "In Search of Frances Simpson Stevens," both in *Art in America*, April 1994, pp. 104–15, 136, 141.

5 "shuddered at Mina" to "expressing herself freely": Kreymborg, *Troubadour*, pp. 235–36.

6 "Not only do we": Don Marquis, "A Key to the New Verse," *New York Evening Sun*, July 24, 1915, p. 6.

6 "A touch of purple": Djuna Barnes, "Becoming Intimate with the Bohemians," *New York Morning Telegraph*, November 19, 1916, sec. 2, p. 1.

6 "imaginary conversation": L[ouis] U[ntermeyer], *Poetry*, November 1916, p. 109. Muna Lee's rhymed verse appeared in *Poetry* at this time.

6 "swill poetry": T.N.P., "The Conning Tower," *New York Tribune*, August 13, 1915, p. 7.

6 "utter nonchalance" to "offensive": Kreymborg, *Our Singing Strength*, pp. 488–89.

7 "Never shall I forget": Wiliams, *Autobiography*, p. 147.

7 "drinking intelligentsia": Louise Varèse's phrase in *Varèse*, p. 127.

7 Footnote: Conrad Aiken, *Skepticisms: Notes on Contemporary Poetry* (New York: Knopf, 1919), pp. 162, 241.

7 "much of the expression": Hapgood, *A Victorian in the Modern World*, p. 341.

8 "women are the cause" to "talking about": Anon., "Do You Strive to Capture the Symbols of Your Reactions?," *New York Evening Sun*, February 13, 1917, p. 10, the source of subsequent quotations.

8 The Baroness: As described by Djuna Barnes in "How the Villagers Amuse Themselves," *New York Morning Telegraph*, November 26, 1916, sec. 2, p. 1.

1 / The Bud beside the Rose

Except where indicated, prose quotations from ML are from *Islands* and lines of poetry from "Anglo-Mongrels and the Rose."

14 Footnote *: Marion Milner, *On Not Being Able to Paint* (Oxford: Heinemann, 1989), pp. 11–12.

14 Footnote †: See D. W. Winnicot, *Playing and Reality* (London: Tavistock, 1971).

16 "not only were": Trudgill, p. 20.

22 "how easy it would be" to "better than this": Mortimer, Favell Lee Bevan, *The Peep of Day*, 3rd ed. (New York: American Tract Society, 1849), pp. 18, 196–97.

22 "All the streets": ML, "Preceptors of Childhood," p. 12.

23 "curative colour": ML, "Anglo-Mongrels."

26 "was a great scold": *Islands*, p. 29, where ML replaces the X in "Xantippe" with a Z. As the many rhyming alphabets in which the letter X is accorded to Xantippe all mention her scolding, I have been unable to identify Mina's.

29 "at the western foot," "populous vulgarity": Thompson, *Hampstead*, pp. 375, 371.

30 Footnote: As cited in Davidoff, p. 116.

31 " 'Where on earth's your modesty' ": ML, *Goy Israels*, fragments.

2 / The Worst Art School in London

Except where indicated, quotations from ML are from *Islands*.

35 "It was with": Virginia Woolf, *The Three Guineas* (New York: Harbinger, 1966), p. 38.

35 "of recalling to her remembrance": Phillis Browne, *What Girls Can Do*, pp. 239–40; cited in Yeldham, p. 34.

36 "In these happy times": *Pall Mall Gazette*, November 12, 1888, p. 5; cited in Yeldham, p. 35.

36 "the royal road" to "difficulties of art": *Pall Mall Gazette*, October 19, 1888, p. 6; cited in Yeldham, p. 35.

36 "women have created nothing": George Moore, *Modern Painting*, 1893, cited in Nunn, p. 235.

36–37 schools open to women: See Mackenzie, especially Chap. 1, "Design Education for Women."

37 "My opinion": Cited in Davidoff, p. 95.

37 "the lesser territories": Bell, p. 55.

38 Footnote: See Macdonald, pp. 30–35.

38 "the worst art school": ML, *Goy Israels*, fragments.

40 1893 Royal Academy directive: Cited in Sidney C. Hutchison, *The History of the Royal Academy, 1768–1968* (London, Chapman & Hall, 1968), p. 143.

42 "a beautiful romantic dream": Burne-Jones, "The Garden of Hesperides," cited in Farr, p. 53.

42 Footnote: Andromeda as an example of the "invitation to rape" depiction of the female nude is discussed in Dijkstra, p. 109.

42 "It was almost a crime": Gertrude Massey, *Kings, Commoners, and Me*; cited in Yeldham, pp. 34–35. See Yeldham on the 1885 newspaper controversy about the nude in art and its "immoral effect . . . on the rising female generation."

43 "a world in which": Bell, p. 68.

45 "subsisting, like monkeys": John, p. 31.

45 "exclaimed when he visited": Holroyd, p. 66.

45 "not only were his drawings": Rothenstein, Vol. 1, p. 333.

47 "the right side": ML, *Goy Israels*, p. 93.

3 / Jugendstil

All quotations from ML are from *Islands*, Chap. X, "Munich."

54 "the ones who": This opinion is voiced by the drawing master in a *Simplicissimus* cartoon, as cited by Radycki, p. 12.

56 Footnote *: Reventlow as cited in Weiss, *Kandinsky*, p. 155, n. 2. On the Von Richthoven sisters, see Green, passim.

56 Footnote †: On this movement, see Weiss, *Kandinsky*, pp. 124–25, 212, and figs. 113a, 113b, 114, and 115.

61 "If only the Munich bourgeoisie": Hermann Obrist, cited in Jelavich, "Munich," p. 23.

61 "a rejuvenation": Jelavich, "Munich," p. 21.

62 Bruno Paul: This cartoon is reprinted in Weiss, *Kandinsky*, p. 89.

63 "Under the rule" to "victory": Jelavich, *Munich*, pp. 147, 149.

64 cabaret song: This song is cited in German in ML, "Munich," p. 154.

4 / La Ville Lumière

Except where indicated, all quotations from ML are from the drafts and fragments of *Esau Penfold*.

67 "flashing black eyes": "Two Englishmen in the Latin Quarter," *Pall Mall Gazette*, January 1904, ROD.

68 "He had a famous name": ML taped interview with Paul Blackburn and Robert Vas Dias, August 1965, CBC; also in Archive for New Poetry, University of California, San Diego.

68 "I went home": Ibid.

68 "An invalid chair": ML, *Islands*, fragments.

68 "a sort of moral sewer": ML, *Goy Israels*, fragments.

69 "As sometimes" to "core of a metropolis": ML, *Islands*.

69 "normally British" to "exist incognito": ML, *Islands*, fragments.

70 "with a Voice": ML, *Islands*.

70 "that of remaining calm": ML, *Islands*, fragments.

70 "In the first years": Lady Kathleen Kennet (who studied at the Slade and then at Colarossi's), in *Self-Portrait of an Artist* (London: John Murray, 1949), p. 23.

71 "a shimmering transformation": ML, "Alda's Beauty."

71 "That the life": Clive Holland, "Lady Art Student's Life in Paris," *International Studio*, 1903–4, pp. 225–26.

72 "There's a childish joy": Modersohn-Becker, p. 173.

74 "the female student": Maximilienne Guyon, "L'Avenir de nos filles," *L'Académie Julian*, December 1903, p. 3.

74 "arranged to satisfy": M. A. Burke, p. 31.

75 "an atmosphere of impeccable": *L'Académie Julian*; cited in Catherine Fehrer, "New Light on the Académie Julian," *Gazette des Beaux-Arts*, 1984, p. 212.

75 "as if they hadn't seen": Modersohn-Becker, p. 350.

75 "mystery of color": Woods, p. 108.

75 Miss Bates: This story is told in an unpublished manuscript by Alice Woods Ullmann, "Paris-Chizzy," p. 234, PC.

75 "His force": Lilian Whiting, *Paris the Beautiful* (Boston: Little, Brown & Co., 1908), p. 377.

76 "things you do not learn": Alice Woods Ullmann, p. 232.

76 "What seems simply rowdy": Modersohn-Becker, p. 170.

76 "without as much": Alice Woods Ullmann, p. 231.

77 "so perfect": SH, *Memoir*, COL (title is in singular).

78 Crowley in Paris: Information from Francis King, *The Magical World of Aleister Crowley* (New York: Coward, McCann & Geoghegan, 1978).

78 "no young thing": Hamnett, p. 31.

80 "students and artists": Modersohn-Becker, p. 192.

81 "for making a decorative appearance": Woods, p. 122.

86 "If we did not make out well together": SH papers, "Arr. Mss.," Notebooks, 1963, COL.

86 "If anyone": ML, *Islands*, "Munich," p. 140.

86 "horrible parents": ML interview with Blackburn and Vas Dias.

5 / "Café du Néant"

Except where indicated, all quotations from SH are from his *Memoir*.

88 "radiant, beautiful wife" to "her husband": SH, "Love Letters to Dead Ladies," pp. 14, 16, 60, COL, in which Haweis insists that Mina was a virgin when they married.

89 "the head of a sallow crow": ML, *Esau Penfold*, fragments.

91 "the most exquisite study": *Pall Mall Gazette*, January 2, 1904, n.p.

91 "aroused the enthusiasm": Anna, Countess of Brémond, "The Rodin Picture by Stephen Haweis and H.A.V. Coles," *American Register*, n.d., n.p., ROD.

94 "was all he needed": Auguste Rodin, "Testament pour les jeunes artistes," *L'Art*, 1967, p. 209.

94 "how well the very principle": Roger Marx, *Gazette des Beaux-Arts*, 1904, p. 461.

94 "a vision of the world": Teodor de Wyzwa, "Berthe Morisot," 1907 Salon d'Automne catalogue, pp. 251–54.

94 "intimate little scenes": Cited in M. A. Burke, p. 44.

97 "the confused order": Elie Faure, Salon d'Automne catalogue, 1905.

97 "in a spirit of mockery": *Bulletin of the Mattatuck Historical Society* (April 1925), n.p.

97–98 "because they dressed so differently": Lydie LeSavoureux interview with CB, June 7, 1977.

98 "She had a way": ML, *Esau Penfold*, fragments.

98 "foolish-looking mother": Luhan, *European*, pp. 340–41. The painting, now lost, was last in MDL's Taos, NM, house.

99 "a riot of color": Claribel Cone, cited in Mellow, p. 103.

100 "reminiscences of Whistler": François Monod, *Art et Décoration*, 1905, p. 206.

100 "Mlle Mina Loy": Paul Jamot, "Le Salon d'Automne," *Gazette des Beaux-Arts*, December 1906, p. 484.

101 "One feels": Paul Jamot, *Le 4eme Salon d'Automne*, 1906, p. 11.

101 "mysterious and perverse": André Peraté, "Les Salons de 1907," *Gazette des Beaux-Arts*, July 1907, p. 66.

101 "With you": SH, "Love Letters," pp. 16, 11.

102 Footnote *: Janis and Blesh, *Collage* (Philadelphia: Chilton, 1967), p. 21.

102 Footnote †: *Who's Who in Paris, 1953–54* (Paris: Editions Jacques Lafitte, 1954), p. 537.

103–4 "presented himself" to "financial situation": ML, *Esau Penfold* fragments. On SH's conviction that this was not his biological child, see the following, all in SH papers, COL: "Love Letters," p. 64, on the death of his offspring by Mina; correspondence from Sir Gerald Kelly to SH, June 10, 1964: "I understand from your letter of the 11th April that . . . your wife had a daughter with her medical student and that she was called Joella"; correspondence from Renée Chipman to Mrs. Philip Roosevelt, February 3, 1969, quoting SH's belief that he had no living descendants; correspondence from Mrs. Philip Roosevelt to Renée Chipman, May 15, 1969: "There seems to be no family descendant of any sort." See also SH's notebooks, "Arr. Mss." Notebooks, 1963, the passage beginning "I had lost my own wife to a lover, who really loved her . . . a penniless French medical student." I am aware that ML's descendants do not hold this view.

6 / Anglo-Florence

Except where indicated, all quotations from SH are from *Memoir*.

106 "the only Italian city" to "Germans": Acton and Chaney, p. 30.

107 "like a fat, old George Sand": Luhan, *European*, p. 337.

107 "An atmosphere": Acton, *Memoirs*, p. 9.

107 "the[ir] sublime, unconscious arrogance": Arnold Bennett, "Night and Morning in Florence," *English Review*, 1910, pp. 444, 455, 451.

108 "more or less" to "commonplace": Berenson, as quoted in Secrest, pp. 93, 221–22.

109 "even putting in the blemishes": Luhan, *European*, p. 246.

109 "it was as if": Acton, *Memoirs*, p. 65.

109 "they gathered round them": ML, "Piero and Eliza."

109 "One would have thought": Luhan, *European*, p. 246.

109 "on his well-dusted anecdotal shelves": ML, *Esau Penfold* fragments.

109 "naïve priggish volumes": Acton, *Tuscan Villas*, p. 12.

109 "*Bisogna begonia!*": Origo, p. 128.

110 "Deprived of her art": ML, *Esau Penfold* fragments.

110 "serious": Gordon Craig, quoted in Edward Craig, p. 228.

111 "aura of moral sultriness": Berenson, quoted in Secrest, p. 283.

112 "But the fighting": Rothenstein, Vol. II, pp. 122–25.

112 "nothing": This incident is related in Secrest, p. 282.

112 Footnote: Berenson, quoted in Secrest, p. 57.

113 "a rare and blessed frankness": Santayana, pp. 224–25.

113 "discussed and rediscussed": Luhan, *European*, pp. 189–90.

113 "We both had": Shaw, pp. 90–91.

113 "But is it not beautiful": Craig, as quoted in Luhan, *European*, p. 347.

113 "My confusion": ML, *Brontolivido*, "Geronimo," the source of all subsequent quotations from ML in this chapter.

116 Sinara: MDL noted that the name was pronounced with the accent on the second syllable; Luhan, *European*, p. 340.

116 "by giving me": SH papers, Arr. Mss., Notebooks, 1963.

117–18 "a tall very slim woman" to "his family": JB memoir, MLE.

7 / Delightful Dilettanti

Except where indicated, all quotations from MDL are from *European*.

119 "of shilly-shallying shyness" to "alive": ML to CVV, CVV papers, YCAL.

120 "a fleshy odalisque": Blanche, p. 272.

120 "absolutely hopeless": Ross, as quoted in Secrest, p. 282.

120 "Mabel Dodge made friends": Mary Berenson's comment is noted on her copy of Luhan, *European* at I Tatti. I am grateful to Naomi Sawelson-Gorse for this information.

120–21 "stuffed with things": Unless otherwise noted, all quotations from ML in this and subsequent paragraphs are from "Mabel."

121 "I can be a Manet": MDL as quoted in Blanche, p. 271.

122 "strung on the continuous flux": ML, "Gertrude Stein," *Transatlantic Review*, 1924, p. 305.

122 SH self-portrait: In MDL papers, YCAL.

123 "In pretending" to "etiquette": Unless otherwise noted, *Esau Penfold* fragments is the source of all subsequent quotations from ML in this chapter.

124 "fasten their right to exist": ML, "The colonial lady artist."

124 "When we see": Luhan, *Movers*, p. 393.

124 "We must look": BB, as quoted in Secrest, pp. 111, 188.

124 "The parents": Acton, *Memoirs*, p. 10.

125 "Self-expression": Ibid.

125 "naked devils": This anecdote is related in Gloria Braggiotti, *Born in a Crowd* (privately printed, 1968), pp. 17–19.

126 "the hors d'oeuvres": *The Standard*, May 24, 1910, n.p.

126 "the seed-plot": *The* (London) *Times*, May 24, 1910, n.p.

127 "London may be unaware": Arnold Bennett, *New Age*, December 8, 1910, as cited in Hynes, *Edwardian Turn*, p. 332. This section is indebted to Hynes's account of Post-Impressionism's impact in London.

127 "or compel[led] them": Walter Sickert, "Post-Impressionists," *Fortnightly Review*, January 1911, as cited in Hynes, *Edwardian Turn*, p. 333.

127 "a widespread plot": Robert Ross, *Morning Post*, November 7, 1910, as cited in Frances Spalding, *Roger Fry: Art and Life* (London: Granada, 1980), p. 136.

127 "the rejection": Wilfred Blunt, *My Diaries* (New York: Knopf, 1921), p. 330, as cited in Hynes, *Edwardian Turn*, p. 329.

127 "The Post-Impressionists": Christina Walshe, *Daily Herald*, March 25, 1913, as cited in Spalding, p. 139.

127 "the rebels of either sex" to "mere representation": These remarks, the first in Frank Rutter, *Revolution in Modern Art* (1910), the second in C. L. Hind, *The Post-Impressionists* (1911), are cited in *Post-Impressionism*, p. 182.

127 "To be able to speak": Roger Fry, as cited in Spalding, p. 140.

127–28 "At a time": Spalding, *Vanessa Bell* (New York: Ticknor & Fields, 1983), p. 91.

128 "a revolution in his soul": SH, "Paul Gauguin," *International Studio*, 1921, p. xciii.

129 "a friendship with her": Toklas, pp. 76, 77.

129 "among the very earliest": Stein, *Autobiography*, in *Selected Writings*, p. 124.

130 "I am writing": Stein, *The Making of Americans*, in ibid., p. 261.

130 "Mina Loy equally interested": Stein. *Autobiography*, in ibid., p. 124.

130 "bottom nature": Gertrude Stein, "The Gradual Making of *The Making of Americans*," in ibid., p. 243.

131 "Dear Gertrude Stein": ML to GS, December 2, 1911, GS papers.

131 "walking as it were": Brooks, p. 255.

131 "I have not gotten religion": Leo Stein, *Journey into the Self* (New York: Crown, 1950), p. 65.

132 "like a light": Georgina Jones, quoted in Veysey, p. 254.

132 "falling on good soil" to "beautiful": Paramananda, quoted in Sister Devamata, Vol. I, p. 207.

133 "those who": Ibid., p. 213.

133 "*Why* are there": MDL to GS in Gallup, p. 53.

133 "to find out": Gertrude Stein, "Portraits and Repetition," in Patricia Meyerowitz, ed., *Writings and Lectures* (Baltimore: Penguin, 1974), p. 109.

133–34 "The Portrait of Mabel Dodge at the Villa Curonia": The full text is included in Stein, *Selected Writings*, pp. 527–30.

134 "thanks from both of us": SH to GS [Fall 1912], GS papers.

134 "To Gloria": ML, "Mabel."

135 "notes to my beloved": ADF to SH, n.d. Unless otherwise noted, all subsequent quotations from ADF and SH are from their correspondence, CBC.

135–36 "The Seven Ages of God": SH arranged for a private printing of this pamphlet, dated December 12, 1912.

138 "The emotions of these painters": Robert Ross, *Morning Post*, November 7, 1910, p. 3, as cited in Hynes, *Edwardian Turn*, p. 330.

138 "The Directors": *The Studio*, 1913, p. 159.

138 "both dainty and strong": *Morning Post*, October 14, 1912, n.p.

138 "met bigwigs": SH to MDL, n.d., MDL papers.

139 "Ducie Haweis & I": Draper is quoted in a letter by MDL to GS, in Gallup, p. 65.

140 "a marvellous draughtsman": ML to MDL [1913], MDL papers.

140 "What on earth": ML to MDL [1913], MDL papers.

141 "not to the savages": SH to GS [1912], GS papers.

141 "I would like Dusie": SH to MDL [1912], MDL papers; all subsequent quotations in this chapter are from this source.

8 / Risorgimento

Except where indicated, all quotations from ML's letters are from the MDL papers, and all quotations from MDL are from *Movers*, which includes her "Speculations, or Post-Impressions in Prose."

143 "painfully seeking simplicity": SH, "Paul Gauguin," p. xciii.

144–45 "uprush" to "intensified glow": Frederic W.H. Myers, *Human Personality and Its Survival of Bodily Death*, Vol. 1 (New York: Longman's, Green & Co. 1903), pp. 71, 77, xxix, and passim.

145 Footnote: Hynes, *Edwardian Turn*, p. 139.

145 "*Who* is Gertrude Stein?": MDL to GS, January 27, 1913; as cited in Rudnick, p. 68.

147 "with his flowing hair": Acton, *Memoirs*, p. 46.

147 "Mother Goose": Luhan, *European*, p. 347.

148 "You have your children": JB interview with CB, February 5, 1978.

148 Paterson pageant: See Rosenstone, pp. 126–27, for an account of the affair in which Mabel's role is minimized.

149 "She had some bad qualities": CVV, Oral History Research Office, p. 147, as cited in Rudnick, p. 107.

149 "almost everyone": Draper, p. 121.

149 "*Please* come down": MDL to GS [1913], YCAL, as cited in Rudnick, p. 95.

149–50 "a real picture": John Reed, as cited in Rosenstone, p. 139.

150 Reed's play is reprinted in Luhan, *Movers*, pp. 222–27.

150 "Each artist": ML as quoted in Van Vechten, *Peter Whiffle*, pp. 124–25, 176, 178.

150 "has really turned language": Van Vechten, "How to Read Gertrude Stein," in *Trend*, August 1914, pp. 553–57.

152 "Futurism could only": Aldo Palazzeschi, cited in DeMaria, p. xiii.

152 "*new forms of art*": Antonio Gramsci, "Marinetti the Revolutionary," in *Selections from Cultural Writings*, eds. David Forgacs and Geoffrey Nowell-Smith (Cambridge, MA: Harvard University Press, 1985), p. 51.

152 "You must convince yourself": Marinetti, as cited in *Futurism 1909–1919* (Edinburgh: Scottish Arts Council, 1972), p. 69.

152 "We will sing" to "funerary urn": Marinetti, "The Founding and Manifesto of Futurism 1909," in Apollonio, pp. 22–23.

152 "All is conventional" to "emotional ambience": "Futurist Painting: Technical Manifesto 1910," ibid., pp. 27–31.

153 "render the sum total" to "modern sensation": "The Exhibitors to the Public 1912," ibid., pp. 45–50.

153 "to insert ourselves": Carrà, "Piani plastici come espansione sferica nello spazio," *Lacerba*, March 15, 1913, p. 52.

153 "the continuity of life": Marinetti, "Technical Manifesto of Futurist Literature," in *Selected Writings*, p. 84.

153 "the economic defense": Marinetti, "Programma politico futurista," *Lacerba*, October 15, 1913, pp. 221–22.

154 "Each one of us" to "it must be": ML, *Brontolivido*, "Gloria."

154 "Futurism has made people laugh": Papini, "Il significato del futurismo," *Lacerba*, February 1, 1913, p. 22.

154 "his restless silence": ML, *Brontolivido*, "Gloria."

155 "the most important" to "our great country": *Lacerba*, December 1, 1913, p. 273.

155 "the most important demonstration": "Esposizione di Pittura Futurista di *Lacerba*," catalogue as reprinted in *Esposizioni futuriste*, ed. Piero Pacini (Florence: Studio per edizioni scette), n.d., p. 5.

155 "free of any": *Lacerba*, December 1, 1913, p. 273.

156 "Things were said": Francesco Cangiullo, "La Battaglia di Firenze," in *Sipario*, December 1967, as cited in Kirby, p. 14.

156 "Your frenzied behavior": FTM, as quoted in *Lacerba*, December 15, 1913, p. 282.

156 "The only argument": FTM, as cited in Francis Simpson Stevens, "Today and the Futurists," *The Florence Herald*, December 27, 1913, p. 2.

156 "In a city": Papini, "Contro Firenze," *Lacerba*, p. 286.

156 "that she felt": ML, as quoted in Stevens, "Today and the Futurists."

156 "overflowing vulgarity": *Lacerba*, p. 281.

156 "this bombastic superman": ML, *Brontolivido*, "First Costa Visit."

156 "as the divine reservoir": Marinetti, "Against *Amore* and Parliamentarianism," in *Selected Writings*, p. 72.

157 "musical neurasthenia": Marinetti, "Down with the Tango and Parsifal," ibid., pp. 69–70.

157 "artists obsessed": "Futurist Painting: Technical Manifesto 1910," in Apollonio, pp. 30–31.

157 "a sentimental, decadent": Marinetti, "Down with the Tango," *Selected Writings*, p. 69; translation modified.

157 "His tactile adroitness" to "way before": ML, *Brontolivido*, "First Costa Visit."

158 ML's manuscript of "The Prototype" is in the MDL papers.

159 ML's manuscript of "There Is No Life or Death" in the Stieglitz papers, YCAL, differs slightly from the version as published in the April 1914 issue of *Camera Work* (p. 18).

161 "Lust, like pride": Valentine de St. Point, "Futurist Manifesto of Lust," in *Futurismo & Futurismi*, p. 504.

161 "Having had to accept": ML, *Brontolivido*, "Geronimo."

162 "the cloaks of religion": Papini, *Un Uomo finito*, pp. 95–96.

162 "My own ugliness": Papini, "Brutezza," cited in Ridolfi, pp. 144–45.

162 "Ugliness makes for timidity": Papini, *Passoto remoto*, p. 229; cited in Ridolfi, pp. 106–7.

162 "I too have been in love": Papini, *Un Uomo finito*, pp. 127–28.

163 "It was one thing": Richard Drake, "Introduction," in Aleramo, p. xxiii.

163 "beautiful lady friends": Ardengo Soffici, *Lacerba*, January 15, 1914, p. 30.

163 "very modern Englishman": *San Francisco Examiner*, December 14, 1913.

163 "Savonarola from Tahiti": Francis McComas, "Art in San Francisco," *San Francisco Examiner* [January 1914], n.p.

163 "not intellectual enough": ML to SH, March 22, 1914, MDL papers.

164 "You are a busy little mystic": ML, *Brontolivido*, "First Costa Visit."

164 "Here she was": Ibid.

9 / Futurist Wars

Unless otherwise indicated, all quotations from ML's letters to MDL and CVV are from their respective archives.

165 "where everything seemed": ML, *Brontolivido*, "First Costa."

165–66 Sprovieri recollections: Giuseppe Sprovieri, interview with CB, July 14, 1985.

166 "a urinal of flesh" to "same room with it": ML, *Brontolivido*, "Rome."

167 "to metallize": Marinetti, "La Declamazione dimanica e sinottica," in Francesco Cangiullo, *Piedigrotta*, reprinted ed. (Florence: S.P.E.S., 1978), pp. a–e.

167 "a man who": ML, *Brontolivido*, "Rome."

168 "what Marinetti could do": Wyndham Lewis, *Blasting and Bombadiering*, rev. ed. (Berkeley: University of California Press, 1967), p. 33.

168 "an intellectual Cromwell": Wyndham Lewis, in *New Weekly*, May 30, 1914, pp. 328–29.

168 "the commercial acquiescence": FTM and C.R.W. Nevinson, "Vital English Art," in *Lacerba*, July 15, 1914, pp. 209–10.

169 "superior barbarism" to "cynicism": This polemic was published in *Lacerba*, 1914: Papini, "Il Cerchio si chiude," February 15, pp. 49–50; Boccioni, "Il Cerchio non si chiude," March 1, pp. 67–69; and Papini, "Cerchi aperti," March 15, pp. 83–85.

169 "The artistic and literary world": Papini, in *Lacerba*, March 15, 1914, p. 95.

169 "to disintegrate things": Royal Cortissoz, in *Camera Work*, 1913, p. 43.

170 "My own spirit" to "all immovable 'movements' ": Papini in *Lacerba*, 1914: "Spiegazioni," May 15, p. 148; "Volubilità," July 1, pp. 193–94; "Gli amici," August 1, pp. 225–27.

171 "Mrs. Haweis" to "her present lover": Neith Boyce Hapgood, "August 1914," p. 4, Hapgood family papers YCAL.

171 "the protest of Milan" to "it is noisy": LS quoted in Van Vechten, *Sacred*, p. 116.

171 "strange and very ugly youth": Van Vechten, *Peter Whiffle*, p. 175.

171 "Just think": MDL, quoted in Van Vechten, *Sacred*, p. 118.

171 "I'm glad": MDL, in ibid., pp. 119–20.

172 "After the war": LS quoted in Van Vechten, *Music After the Great War* (New York: Schirmer, 1915), p. 3.

172 "entirely out of harmony": Van Vechten, *Sacred*, p. 132.

173 "She says he believes": Hapgood, "August 1914," p. 10.

173 "We are doomed" to "person alive": Ibid., pp. 8, 6, 16.

173 "as she tramped": Van Vechten, *Sacred*, p. 130.

173 "get jobs from": MDL, quoted in Hapgood, "August 1914," p. 13.

173 "These days": Van Vechten, *Sacred*, p. 132.

173–74 "You've got" to "one love": ML, *Brontolivido*, "Vallombrosa."

174 "fighting like wolves" to "rather sordid": Hapgood, "August 14," pp. 17, 18.

174 "There will be a peasant uprising": Marchese Salimbeni, quoted in NBH, "War Time," p. 14.

175 "everything about them": Balla, "Futurist Manifesto of Men's Clothing," in Apollonio, pp. 132–34.

175 "expressions of timidity": Balla, "Il Vestito antineutrale," in *Ricostruzione futurista dell'universo*, exhibition catalogue (Turin: Galleria D'Arte Moderna, 1980), p. 307.

175 "creative genius": Marinetti, "Sintesi futurista della guerra," in *Futurismo & Futurismi*, p. 489.

176 "manifesto-writing painter": G. C. Cook, Chicago *Evening Post*, September 25, 1914, p. 7. I am grateful to Steven Watson for bringing this article to my attention.

176 "pretty that has grown too old": ML, *Brontolivido*, "Mezzanino."

177 "the younger men" to "taken up the pen": Van Vechten, *Trend*, November 1914, pp. ii, 101.

178 "Man can manage everything": SH, in "Current Cant," *Trend*, October 1914, p. 144.

178–79 "her actual state": Marinetti, "Against *Amore* and Parliamentarianism," in *Selected Writings*, pp. 73–75.

179 "The feminist movement" to "pressure of life": ML, "Feminist Manifesto," MDL papers; this text differs from the version in *TLLB*.

180 "empire of the spirit": Papini, "La Vita non è sacra," *Lacerba*, October 15, 1913, pp. 223–25.

180 "little Milanese demonstration": Papini, "*Lacerba*, il Futurismo e *Lacerba*," *Lacerba*, December 1, 1914, p. 325.

180 "a loophole whereby" to "the sex-war": ML, *Brontolivido*, fragments.

181 "a truly modern aesthetic" to "brand name": Papini, "*Lacerba*, il Futurismo e *Lacerba*," *Lacerba*, pp. 32–24.

181 "Powerful as this indictment": Flint, in Marinetti, *Selected Writings*, p. 22.

183 "Love, this is not your moment": Papini, "Leavetaking," *Others*, July 1919, pp. 20–21. Given the essay's date of composition, description of its subject's distinctive clothing, and verbal echoes in ML's "Love Songs," I identify her as the woman to whom "Leavetaking" is addressed.

184 *Futurism and Marinettism*: Papini, *Lacerba*, February 14, 1915, p. 149.

184 "The Secret of War": Mabel Dodge, *The Masses*, November 1914, pp. 8–9.

185 "to publish": *Rogue*, March 15, 1915, p. 14.

186 "To a Poet": Walter Arensberg, *Rogue*, April 1, 1915, p. 6.

186 "underlying all these arguments": Wohl, p. 168.

187 "cerebral gymnastics": ML, "One O'Clock at Night."

188 "intimate irritants": ML, "Pazzarella," pp. 7, 31.

188 "Through the intense deployment": FTM, quoted in Serge Basset, "Les Futuristes et la guerre," *Le Petit parisien*, July 27, 1915; cited in Lista, *Marinetti et le futurisme*, p. 218.

189–90 "the paintings of Mina Loy": Van Vechten, *Rogue*, August 1, 1915, p. 14.

Notes

190 *simpatico*: Umberto Boccioni, "L'Esposizione invernale d'arte di Firenze," *Gli Avvenimenti*, February 6–13, 1916.

193–94 *"her forehead"* to *"fabulous journey"*: ML, "Alda's Beauty," MLE.

Interlude I / Love Songs

195 "eroticism gone to seed": Untermeyer, p. 192.

195 "the expression" to "come awake": J. B. Kerfoot, as quoted in *Others*, November 1915, n.p.

195 "It was the time of manifestos": Untermeyer, pp. 187, 183, 185, 192.

195 "nothing more": Kreymborg, "Vers Libre," *New York Morning Telegraph*, August 8, 1915, p. 5. Kreymborg noted that Mina's poetry "falls under the influence of Marinetti."

196 "wild enthusiasm": W. C. Williams, "The Great Opportunity," *The Egoist*, September 1916, p. 137.

196 "Detractors shuddered": Kreymborg, *Troubadour*, pp. 235–36.

196 "In an unsophisticated land": Kreymborg, *Our Singing Strength*, p. 489.

196 *"Oh, beautiful mind"*: Don Marquis, *New York Evening Sun*, June 29, 1915, p. 10.

196 "people who pretend" to "Yurrup": Ibid., June 30, 1915, p. 10.

196 "You ask me": Ibid., July 8, 1915, p. 10.

197 *"no one but Mina Loy"*: Ibid., July 24, 1915, p. 6.

197 "the most glorious space-filler": Ibid., March 3, 1916, p. 10.

197 "In the new poetry": Margaret Johns, *New York Tribune*, July 25, 1915, sec. III, p. 2.

197 "It is not enough": Floyd Dell, "Who Said That Beauty Passes Like a Dream," *The Masses*, October 1916, p. 27.

197 "a perfumed and purposeless revolt": Untermeyer, p. 192.

198 "Lines to the Free Feet": L.W.D. *New York Tribune*, June 29, 1915, p. 7.

198 "I have loved thee long": Marquis, *New York Evening Sun*, March 25, 1916, p. 6.

198 "a rather conservatively inclined chaperone": Ibid., September 12, 1915, p. 8.

198 "They are not" to "liking being living": Stein, *Geography*, pp. 48, 51, 64.

198 "Not only are you": ML, "Gertrude Stein," *Transatlantic Review*, p. 306.

202 Footnote: "The Effectual Marriage" is included in Ezra Pound, *Instigations* (New York: Boni and Liveright, 1920), p. 240, and *Profile: An Anthology Collected in 1931* (Milan: John Scheilwiller, 1932), pp. 67–68.

202 sequence of thirty-four poems: After the appearance of the first four "Love Songs" in 1915, the full text was published two years later as a special issue of *Others*, retitled "Songs for Joannes." Because Loy again used "Love Songs" for the abbreviated version of the sequence included in *Lunar Baedecker*, I use this title except when referring to the 1917 edition in historical context.

205 "Our person": ML, "O Hell."

206 On "Love Songs," see my articles, Kouidis, and Rachel Blau Duplessis, " 'Seismic Orgasm': Sexual Intercourse, Gender Narratives, and Lyric Ideology in Mina Loy," in Ralph Cohen, ed., *Studies in Historical Change* (Charlottesville: University of Virginia Press, 1992), pp. 264–91.

207 "it took a strong digestive apparatus": Kreymborg, *Our Singing Strength*, pp. 488–89.

208 "as a state of mind": Hynes, *A War Imagined*, p. 136.

208 "all the earnestness": Kreymborg, *Our Singing Strength*, p. 488.

10 / Subversive Amusements

211–12 "den of a" to "marine gavotte": ML, "Alda's Beauty," MLE.

214 "We were not": Williams, p. 137.

214 Information on MD and Futurism: GBP interview with CB, April 9, 1980.

215 "He neither talks": "A Complete Reversal of Art Opinions by Marcel Duchamp, Iconoclast," *Arts and Decoration*, September 1915, pp. 427–28.

215 "the time-worn disgust": "French Artists Spur on an American Art," *New York Tribune*, October 24, 1915, sec. 4, pp. 2–3.

215 "If only America": "The Iconoclastic Opinions of M. Marcel Duchamps [sic] concerning Art and America," *Current Opinion*, November 1915, p. 346; cited in Tashjian, p. 50.

215 "Marcel at twenty-seven": Wood, *I Shock Myself*, pp. 22–23. (Duchamp was actually twenty-nine when Wood first met him.) On Duchamp's androgynous appeal, see also Watson, pp. 274–75.

215 "his smile": Roché, p. 94.

215 "divine experience": Wood, *I Shock Myself*, p. 25.

216 "emotional communism": Roché, p. 53.

216 "sex and love": Wood, *I Shock Myself*, pp. 24–25.

216 "harsh mouth": Freytag-Loringhoven, "Metaphysical speculation-logic-consolation concerning love to a flame-flagged man," *The Little Review*, May 1919, p. 71.

216 "Marcel, Marcel": EvFL, quoted in Louis Bouché, "Oral History," AAA.

217 "a perfect dear": ML, *Colossus*, MLE, p. 5.

217 "War is silly" to "of the ages": Louise Norton, "Dame Rogue's Review," *Rogue*, June 15, 1915, p. 4.

217 "The comical bifurcation": Norton, "Trouser Talk," *Rogue*, April 15, 1915, p. 15.

217 "the exquisite psychologist": Marcel Duchamp, *Salt Seller*, p. 178.

217 "Marcel was so charming": Louise Norton interview with CB, March 21, 1982.

217 "he was always bored": JG interview with CB, April 15, 1977.

217 "The attitude of abdicating everything": GBP, in Motherwell, p. 260.

217 "In his obsession": GBP interview with CB, April 22, 1977.

218 "It was something": Williams, p. 141.

218 "You're all so damned sophisticated" to "con de catin' ": ML, *Colossus*, pp. 9–10.

219 "Walter's Room": Norton's poem appeared in *The Quill*, June 1919, pp. 20–21.

219 "An instantaneous affection": ML, *Colossus*, pp. 4, 12, 10.

219 "had been almost completely monopolized": *New York Evening Sun*, January 26, 1917, p. 16.

220 "marriage boxes": ML, "Anglo-Mongrels."

220 "the super-sophisticated Mina": Kreymborg, *Troubadour*, p. 309.

220 "all those kisses": Kreymborg, cited in Mariani, p. 140.

220 "she asked me": Williams, pp. 138–39.

220 "he had once thought": Charles Tomlinson, "Some American Poets: A Personal Record," *Contemporary Literature*, Summer 1977, pp. 300–1.

221 "loved to eye Mina Loy" to "It fits the play": Kreymborg, *Troubadour*, pp. 309–10.

221 "of Mina's long-legged charms": Williams, p. 146.

221–222 "very beautiful": MM to H.D., January 11, 1921, ROS.

222 "a glancing sort": Williams, p. 139.

222 "sent up a huge basket": Kreymborg, *Troubadour*, p. 311.

222 "he may have been thinking": Mariani, p. 141.

222 "Two poets": Edna Kenton, cited in Sarlós, p. 70.

223 "tag ends" to "cigar-ends": *The Pamperers*, published in *The Dial*, July 1920, pp. 65–78; inaugurated the magazine's "Modern Forms" section but was never performed.

223 "New York is to have": *International Studio*, April 1917, p. lxviii.

223 "Every school of art": Gustav Kobbe, "What Is It? 'Independent Art,' " *New York Herald*, April 1, 1917, sec. 3, p. 12.

223 "If the Liberty Bell": Henry McBride, *New York Sun*, January 21, 1917, cited in Watson, p. 380, n. 121.

224 "had a fairy-tale feeling": JG to CB, April 5, 1977.

224 "Who is" to "of the soldiers": *New York Evening Sun*, February 13, 1917, p. 10.

225 "War means an ugly mob-madness": John Reed, "Whose War?" *Masses*, April 1917, p. 11; cited in Rosenstone, p. 265.

225 "charged with blasphemy": JBP, in Motherwell, p. 13.

226 "Pictures will be hung": Kobbe, "What Is It?"

226 "Jules De Pascin" to "a complete failure": McBride and Pène du Bois, cited in Naumann, "The Big Show," Pt. II, p. 50.

226 "The hanging of all works": Roché, *The Blind Man*, April 19, 1917, p. 3.

226 "Two miles of paint": *International Studio*, May 1917, p. xcix.

227 "that the whole damn thing": Quinn to EP, May 3, 1917, John Quinn Memorial Collection, New York Public Library; cited in Watson, p. 315.

227 "Crowds stood": Wood, *I Shock Myself*, p. 32.

227 "one of those": McBride, pp. 123–24.

227 "The good ship Independent": W. H. De B. Nelson, "Aesthetic Hysteria," *International Studio*, June 1917, pp. cxxi–cxxii.

228 "mechano-sexual metaphors": I borrow this phrase from Hughes, p. 52.

228 R to "art": Duchamp, quoted in Otto Hahn, "Passport No. G255300," *Art and Artists*, July 1966, p. 10; cited in Camfield, "Marcel Duchamp's Fountain," Kuenzli and Naumann, eds., p. 69.

228 "A lovely form": WCA, quoted in Wood, *I Shock Myself*, p. 29.

228 "a familiar article": Unsigned review, "His Art Too Crude for Independents," *New York Herald*, April 14, 1917, p. 6; cited in Camfield, p. 88, n. 16.

229 "out for red blood": Wood, quoted in Theodora Bean, *The Morning Telegraph*, Sunday Magazine, Sec. 2, April 15, 1917, p. 1. I am grateful to Francis Naumann for bringing this article to my attention.

229 "The artist is jolly": ML, quoted in ibid.

229 "It must be done": Ibid.

229 "the spring offensive": McBride, cited in Naumann, "The Big Show, Part Two."

229 "We need war": Duncan Phillips, "Fallacies of the New Dogmatism in Art," *The American Magazine of Art*, December 1917, p. 44; cited in Naumann, Part 2.

229 "the spirit of": *Vanity Fair*, cited in Naumann, Part 2.

229 "Chance To See Live Poets": [N.Y.] *Morning Telegraph*, April 18, 1917.

230 "rhyme, rhythm" to "out of the window": "Poets in Spring Orgy of Verse and Not an Editor on the Job," *The Globe and Commercial Advertiser*, April 19, 1917, p. 6: I am grateful to Joe Skokowski for bringing this article to my attention.

230 "Russia needed": Roché, *The Blind Man* 1, p. 6.

231 "To learn to 'see' ": Ibid., p. 5.

231 "It knew before": ML, *The Blind Man* 1, p. 7.

232 "Brave people": *The Blind Man* 2, p. 16.

232 "*succès de scandale*": Wood, *I Shock Myself*, p. 32.

232 "atavistic minds": Norton, *The Blind Man* 2, pp. 5–6.

232 "painter, poet, musician" to "granite simplicity": ML, "Pas de Commentaires! Louis M. Eilshemius," *The Blind Man* 2, pp. 11–12.

232 "It is hard": Thierry de Duve, "Given the Richard Mutt Case," in de Duve, ed., *The Definitively Unfinished Marcel Duchamp* (Cambridge, MA: MIT Press, 1991), p. 201.

233 "however morbid": Crowninshield, *The Blind Man* 2, p. 10.

233 "the world's anguish": GBP, in Motherwell, p. 259.

11 / Colossus

Unless otherwise indicated, all quotations from ML are from the unpublished manuscript of her memoir *Colossus*. This chapter also draws on information contained in Arthur Cravan, *Oeuvres*, and Maria Lluîsa Borràs, *Arthur Cravan*.

235 "The American is feared": Fabian Lloyd, "To Be or Not to Be . . . American," *L'Echo des Sports*, June 10, 1909, reprinted in Cravan, pp. 122–24.

235 "We like the commotion": Cravan, *Maintenant*, April 1912, reprinted in Begot, p. 31.

235 "worn out by": Blaise Cendrars, *Le Lotissement du Ciel*, in *Oeuvres Complètes*, Vol. 6 (Paris, Denoël, 1961), p. 512.

235 "was not to be trusted": GBP interview with CB, April 2, 1977.

236 his only claim to "of the failure": JG interview with CB, April 15, 1977.

236 "These are things": MD, quoted in Cabanne, p. 53.

236 "invented the term": Amelia von Ende, "New Tendencies in French Poetry," *The Dial*, 1914, pp. 283–85.

236–37 "young, robust": Robert Coady, *The Soul*, December 1916, p. 3.

237 "chuck this little dignity": Arthur Cravan, *The Soil*, April 1917, p. 162.

238 "leaned too far" to "subject of his lecture": "Independents Get Unexpected Thrill," *The Sun*, April 20, 1917, p. 6.

238 "What a wonderful lecture": MD, quoted by Gabrielle Buffet-Picabia, "Arthur Cravan and American Dada," in Motherwell, p. 16.

242 "He became courteous": GRP interview with CB, April 15, 1977.

243 "the height of fashion": Fabian Lloyd, "To Be or Not to Be . . . American," AC in Begot, pp. 124, 103.

244 "situated more in the guts": Arthur Cravan, *Maintenant*, March–April 1914, reprinted in Cravan, p. 71.

245 "a woman as refined as Mina": JG interview with CB, April 15, 1977.

245 "a long and sorely needed": *The New York Times*, June 10, 1917, n.p.; cited in Wexler, p. 227.

245 "left France": MD, quoted in Cabanne, p. 59.

246 "with his robe afloat" to "of that era": ML, "O Marcel" (notes), in *View*, March 1945, p. 51.

246 "It is a great thing" to "bastard artists": Jane Heap, "Push-Face," *The Little Review*, June 1917, pp. 4–7.

247 "New York's last real laugh": John Reed, *New York Mail*, June 13, 1917; cited in Rosenstone, pp. 267–68.

247 *re* ML divorce: Information from "Mrs. Haweis in Divorce Suit, Accuses Mate," n.d., SH papers, and ML divorce papers, MLE.

248 "I'm in my element": AC to ML, July 20, 1917, in Cravan, p. 156.

248 "daily health hints": "Greene's Set of Dont's," quoted in *Cartoons*, June 1917, p. 860.

249 "almost always in a frenzy": AC to ML, August 26, 1917, in Cravan, p. 157.

249–50 "We always used to say": John Reed, "Militarism at Play," *The Masses*, August 1917, pp. 18–19.

250 "I am only at my best": AC to ML, in Cravan, p. 161; the letter continues: "When I have to stay too long in the same place, I become almost imbecilic."

250–51 *re* AC's itinerary: AC's recently discovered correspondence with the journalist and playwright Sophie Treadwell, also a member of the Arensberg circle, suggests that he may have returned to New York in October before going to Mexico. I am grateful to Naomi Sawelson-Gorse for informing me of this correspondence in the Sophie Treadwell papers, University of Arizona, Tucson.

12 / Mexico

Unless otherwise indicated, all quotations from ML, apart from her correspondence with MDL, are from *Colossus*.

252 "a sort of male Gertrude Stein": John Reed to Eddy Hunt, December 16, 1913, quoted in Rosenstone, p. 151.

253 "volcanic & feathery": ML to MDL, c. 1920.

253 "Mexico City": *New York Sun*, January 29, 1918, cited in Ronald Atkins, *Revolution! Mexico 1910–1920* (New York: John Day, 1970), p. 308.

254 "in those days": Beals, *Glass Houses*, p. 36.

257 "Mrs. Haweis": Cravan's letters appear in translation in Borràs, p. 213.

258 "a kettle-polisher": Brown, p. 144.

258–59 "This one is like" to "before understanding": ML, *Colossus* fragment, CBC.

259 Footnote: Carleton Beals, "Tina Modotti," *Creative Arts*, February 1929, cited in *Frida Kahlo and Tina Modotti*, exhibition catalogue (London: Whitechapel Art Gallery, 1982), p. 31.

259 *re* American intelligence: This correspondence is mentioned in Roberts, pp. 207–8.

260–61 "in a waking nightmare": Brown, p. 146.

261 *re* fifty-fifty split: See ibid., pp. 146–48, 244; this boxer may have been Smith.

261 "Light—passed through": ML, *TLLB*, p. 320, and see also her description of him as *"un brute mystique . . . at once le dieu qui se conserve et le fou qui s'évade,"* pp. 318, 319.

261 Footnote: Beals, *Mexican Maze*, p. 59.

262 "nothing of interest": T. Philip Terry, *Terry's Guide to Mexico*, rev. ed. (Hingam, MA: R. C. Terry, 1947), p. 861.

262–63 "objects" to "forgive all things": ML, "Transfiguration."

263 "Someone said" to "better conditions": Brown, pp. 245, 248.

264 "away from all these savages": Ibid., p. 246.

264 "Because of a hole" to "in close communion": Ibid., pp. 248, 249.

265 "heavy leaden color": From ML's description of her trip, as given in Brown, p. 377. Brown's account is the only eyewitness record available: while fictionalized, it is generally reliable, since much of it can be confirmed by outside evidence. Significant information about the circumstances of Cravan's disappearance is also contained in ML's letters to Nellie Grandjean, which are quoted, although in excerpted form and in translation, in Borràs: if and when the originals become available, it may be possible to reconcile discrepancies between Brown's and ML's versions. But given that ML's account changed over time, the exact details may never be known.

13 / Dislocations

Unless otherwise indicated, all quotations from ML are from her correspondence with MDL.

266 "To the astonished traveler": Agnes Rothery, *South America* (Boston: Houghton Mifflin, 1930), p. 3; also the source of this paragraph's descriptions of the Andes.

267 "But seeing is": Ibid., p. 128.

268 "It seemed perilous": Dreier, p. 5.

268 "pimping for the Compub": Brown, pp. 373, 371, 372.

268 "One was struck": Dreier, p. 10.

269 "a marvelous experience": Ibid., p. 186.

269 "The Spirit of Freedom": Ibid., p. 286.

270 "TO MAKE THE WORLD" to "to fight!": ML, "International Psycho-Democracy," unpublished version in MDL papers.

270 "time for the Artist": AC as quoted by ML, *TLLB*, p. 318.

270 "The insolence" to "losing positions": MD, November 8, 1918, and January 10, 1919, in Naumann, "Marcel Duchamp's Letters to Walter and Louise Arensberg," Kuenzli and Naumann, pp. 209, 212, and see also MD's letter of June 15, 1919, which notes that ML "hadn't heard from Cravan since he left Mexico," p. 218.

272 Footnote: See Hynes, *A War Imagined*, pp. 361–62.

274 "I would not choose": George Herron, *The Defeat in the Victory*, pp. 19–20; cited in Briggs, p. 163.

274 "the baptism": *La Tribune de Genève*, n.d. [c. July 1919], CVV papers.

274–75 "The satisfaction" to "psychic death": "Psycho-Democracy" fragment dated "Geneva 1919," CBC.

277 "a prolonged disease": LS to GS, December 14, 1919, in Leo Stein, p. 78.

277 "Those who suffered most": Lina Waterfield, *Castle in Italy* (New York: Thomas Y. Crowell, 1961), p. 168.

279 "by the indisputable force": FTM, cited in Schneider, p. 271.

279 "Power to the artists!": Marinetti, "Beyond Communism," in Marinetti, *Selected*, p. 155 (translation modified).

279 "the proletariat of the gifted": Ibid., pp. 156–57.

14 / Postwar Despairing

Unless otherwise indicated, quotations from ML are from her correspondence with MDL.

282 "postwar despairing": McAlmon and Boyle, p. 1.

282 "with enough approximation": Henry McBride, "The Walter Arensbergs," *The Dial*, July 1920; reprinted in McBride, p. 158.

283 "We could have spared": Louise Arensberg to HPR, April 3, 1920, Roché papers, Humanities Research Center, University of Texas, Austin.

283 "The only drawback": McBride, "The Walter Arensbergs," p. 157.

283 "I can't tell you" to "pale affair": Arensberg's letters to Tzara and Picabia are cited in Naumann, "The New York Dada Movement," p. 145.

284 Cravan's posthumous words: This apocryphal text, "Dada," appeared in *Dada* 6, 1920, cited in Cravan, p. 215.

284 "with the idea of insuring": Henry McBride, "News and Views on Art," *New York Sun and Herald*, May 16, 1920, sec. 8, p. 3.

285 "bought and rebuilt": Williams, p. 141.

285 "that he might be": GBP in Motherwell, p. 17.

285 Footnote: CVV to MDL [Sterne], *Letters of Carl Van Vechten*, ed. Bruce Kellner (New Haven: Yale University Press, 1987), p. 33.

286 "The pushcart vendors": Philippe Soupault, "Epitaphe," *Littérature*, June 1920; reprinted in Cravan, p. 215.

287 "remain perpetually aloof": Maxwell Bodenheim to Conrad Aiken, December 17, 1919; cited in Mariani, pp. 170–71.

287 "the only figure": Margaret Anderson, *My Thirty Years' War* (New York: Horizon Press, 1969), p. 177.

287 "chicken guts": Quotations in this paragraph are from Matthew Josephson, pp. 75, 76. See also Williams's fictionalized account of his relations with the Baroness, "The Three Letters," *Contact*, 1921, pp. 10–13.

288 "the only one": Jane Heap, *The Little Review*, Spring 1922, p. 46.

288 "In Elsa": John Rodker, *The Little Review*, July–August 1920, p. 33.

288 "the first magazine": Editorial comment, September–December 1920, p. 2.

288 "so obscene": Sumner's affidavit is cited in Bryer, p. 158.

289 "as though a fashionable whorehouse": John Quinn to EP, October 21, 1920; as cited in B. L. Reid, *The Man from New York* (New York: Oxford University Press, 1968), p. 448.

289 "Men think thoughts": Jane Heap, "Art and the Law," *The Little Review*, September–December 1921, p. 6.

289 "the episode": Magistrate Corrigan, cited in Bryer, p. 158.

289 "a great artist's freedom": Margaret Anderson, "An Obvious Statement," *The Little Review*, September–December 1921, p. 11.

289 "the mind of" to "stereotyped men": Heap, "Art and the Law," pp. 6, 7.

290 "a distinct falling off": John Rodker, "The 'Others' Anthology," *The Little Review*, September–December 1920, pp. 56, 55.

290–91 "nothing to say" to "much to be said": ML, "John Rodker's Frog," *The Little Review*, September–December 1920, p. 57.

291 "My own pet serpent": John Rodker, "To Mina Loy," *The Little Review*, January–March 1921, p. 44.

291 "As one European": ML, *The Little Review*, January–March 1921, p. 45.

291 "We will be American": *Contact*, December 1920, p. 1.

291 "the essential contact": Williams, *Contact*, December 1920, p. 10.

291 "In contradistinction" to "divergent virtues": W. C. Williams, *Kora in Hell*, in Williams, *Imaginations* (New York: New Directions, 1970), p. 10.

292 "logopoeia": Ezra Pound, "A List of Books," *The Little Review*, March 1918, pp. 57–58.

292 "extremely good": T. S. Apteryx [Eliot], "Observations," *The Egoist*, May 1918, p. 70.

292 "subject to": Ezra Pound, *Instigations* (New York: Boni and Liveright, 1920), pp. 239–41.

292 "in awed admiration": Williams, *Autobiography*, p. 146.

292 "with her mouth open": Williams, *Selected Essays* (New York: New Directions, 1969), p. 292.

292 "beautiful": MM to H.D., January 11, 1921, ROS.

293 "Those Various Scalpels": Moore thought well enough of this poem to include it in *Observations* (1924), *Selected Poems* (1935), and the definitive edition of her poetry, *Complete Poems* (New York: Macmillan and Viking, 1967), pp. 51–52.

293 "decided leaning" to "almost despair": McAlmon, *Post-Adolescence*, pp. 25, 74.

294 Footnote: Robert McAlmon, *A Hasty Bunch* (Carbondale: Southern Illinois University Press, 1977), p. 275.

294 "some suppression" to "some of us": McAlmon, *Post-Adolescence*, pp. 68–76.

294 "sliced and cylindrical": Moore, *The Complete Prose of Marianne Moore*, ed. Patricia C. Willis (New York: Viking, 1986), p. 121.

295 "amusingly": ML, *Charm*, April 1925, p. 17.

295 "mostly about ideas" to "exhibits A and B": McAlmon, *Post-Adolescence*, pp. 14–17.

295 "her own original portrait" to "in the room": Ibid., pp. 59–62.

295 "regal bearing": ML to James Mechem, September 17, 1960.

296 "They were stunning subjects": Man Ray, p. 98.

296 "biological mystic": The phrase "biological mystic" comes from ML's notes on AC, *TLLB*, p. 317.

296 "whether she cares": McAlmon, *Post-Adolescence*, pp. 20–21.

298 "speak plain English": Judge at *Little Review* trial, quoted in Bryer, p. 161.

298 "a too frank expression": "Improper Novel Cost Women One Hundred Dollars," *The New York Times*, February 22, 1921, p. 13; cited in Bryer, p. 162.

299 "murdered": ML to NG [Spring 1921], "Red House," BOR. Roger L. Conover graciously supplied me with copies of ML's correspondence held in this collection.

299 "so many leagues": "Enter 'Dadaism' Very Latest Fad," *The World*, December 26, 1920, p. BM7.

299 "consists largely": MR, cited in " 'Dada' Will Get You If You Don't Watch Out," *New York Evening Journal*, January 29, 1921; cited in Naumann, "The New York Dada Movement," p. 146.

300 "what these dreadful pictures": Claire D. Mumford, cited in Naumann, "The New York Dada Movement," p. 146.

300 "the first joyous dogma": Marsden Hartley, "The Importance of Being 'Dada,' " *Adventures in the Arts*, cited in Naumann, "The New York Dada Movement," p. 146.

300 *Q.E.D.*: On the affair, see Leon Katz, "Introduction," in Gertrude Stein, *Fernhurst, Q.E.D. and Other Early Writings* (New York: Liveright, 1971).

300 "they say in Europe": Henry McBride, "New York Dada Review Appears in New York," *New York Herald*, April 24, 1921, sec. III, p. 11, cited in Naumann, "The New York Dada Movement," p. 147.

300 "like the idea of God": Tristan Tzara, *New York-Dada*, p. 2; reprinted in Motherwell, p. 216.

300 "to express our contempt": Man Ray, p. 101.

301 "brutality": "Thee I Call 'Hamlet of Wedding-Ring,' " *The Little Review*, January–March 1921, pp. 48–52.

301 "It was inevitable": McBride, "New York Dada Review."

301 "the small, sweet forget-me-not": W. C. Williams, *Contact*, June 1923, p. 1.

301 "as futile as": Man Ray, p. 101.

301 "Different things": ML to NG [Spring 1921], BOR.

302 "the insurgent naked throb": D. H. Lawrence, "The Poetry of the Present," *Playboy* (1919), p. 8.

302 "Lilah was pale": ML, "Preceptors of Childhood," *Playboy*, March 1923, p. 12.

303 *re* ML portraits: ML's untitled drawing of two gypsies and a girl appeared in *Art Review*, October 1922, p. 15; *Three Studies* appeared in *Art Review* December 1922, p. 17.

303 NG's account of her Florence visit: as excerpted in Borràs, p. 235.

303–4 "to speak French" to "don't you think so?": ML to NG [Spring 1921], BOR.

15 / Europe without Baedeker

306 "If you come": ML to Scofield Thayer, *Dial* / Thayer Papers, September 19, [1921,] YCAL. Quotations from ML to Thayer in subsequent paragraphs are from this letter.

306 "but because" to "purple past": Acton, *Memoirs*, p. 102.

307 "the magnet": Djuna Barnes, "Lament for the Left Bank," *Town and Country*, December 1941, p. 92.

310 "the greatest national genius": Carnevali to Carl Sandburg, *Voglio disturbare l'America* (Florence: La Casa Usher, 1980), p. 106.

310 "has been more crucified" to "remain in place": Djuna Barnes, "James Joyce," *Vanity Fair*, March 1922, pp. 65, 104.

311 "the most gentle" to "dear Father": ML to NG [January 1922], BOR.

312 "Teutonic stuff": Watson, cited in Thayer's letter to Kenneth Burke, in Joost, p. 190.

313 "When the Gentile world" to "his coronet": ML, "Notes on Jews."

313 "some with dread": Ilya Ehrenburg, *Memoirs: 1921–1941* (New York: World, 1963), p. 16.

313 "to see how the mad people lived": ML quoted in JB interview with CB, October 2, 1991.

314 "Everyman's City" to "Käthe Kollwitz": Josephson, pp. 196, 194.

314 "international organization": Quotation and information in this paragraph from Willett, p. 77. Josephson notes that Lissitzky and Moholy-Nagy left the conference when its chair, Theo van Doesburg, failed to heed their protests against the presence of the Dadaists, "a purely *destructive* element, while they were resolved to *construct* the shining new cities of the future," pp. 210–11.

314 "with long hair": Josephson, p. 195.

315 "Moral, social, and intellectual supremacy": ML, "Lady Asterisk."

315 "The only man": JB interview with CB, October 2, 1991.

315 "Inequality, Injustice": Isadora Duncan, *My Life* (New York: Liveright, 1972), p. 359.

315 "He is a genius": Duncan, *Isadora Speaks* (San Francisco: City Lights, 1981), p. 104.

316 "There are only two kinds": ML, in JB's autograph book, p. 1.

316 "all unsuspecting": Josephson, p. 193.

316 "luxuriat[ing]": McAlmon and Boyle, pp. 96–97.

316 "Mina gave us": Josephson, p. 202.

316 satire and elegy in "Der Blinde Junge": For an especially sensitive reading of the poem, see Thom Gunn, "Three Hard Women: H.D., Marianne Moore, Mina Loy," in *Shelf Life* (Ann Arbor: University of Michigan Press, 1993), pp. 33–52.

318 "the austere verity" to "in and for itself": ML, "Gertrude Stein," *Transatlantic Review*, 1924, pp. 305, 427–30; unless otherwise indicated, all quotations in these paragraphs are from this source.

318 "deconstruction preparatory": GS quoted in ML, "Phenomenon in American Art," Joseph Cornell Papers, AAA.

319 "One becomes": Josephson, p. 201.

319 "the innumerable beggars": McAlmon and Boyle, p. 98.

320 "as if the sheriff": Josephson, p. 238.

16 / *Being Geniuses Together*

321 "pleased to be": Ernest Hemingway, cited in Smoller, p. 116.

321 "bring out works": McAlmon, Contact Editions circular [Darantière, 1923].

323 "ominous grandeur" to "instead of air": Yvor Winters, "Mina Loy," *The Dial*, June 1926, pp. 496–99.

325 "map of the artist's genius": ML, "The Metaphysical Pattern in Aesthetics."

326 "run up to Iceland": James Joyce to RMcA, cited in Smoller, p. 77.

327 "Tell Dusie": SH to Ethel Harter, New Rochelle, August 5, 1923, MLE.

327 "too boring": JB interview with CB, April 18, 1981; also the source of subsequent information in this paragraph.

328 "a Juno": Jacques Baron interview with CB, August 1, 1977.

328 "a regal English lady": Glenway Wescott interview with CB, August 28, 1977.

328 "When Picabia": McAlmon and Boyle, p. 111.

328 "We were glad": Gertrude Stein, *Autobiography* in *Selected*, p. 188.

328 "very mature": Ibid.

329 "almost shy": McAlmon and Boyle, pp. 205.

329 "spiritual mother": "Book News and Reviews," *New York Tribune*, November 4, 1923, p. 17.

329 "Gertrude Steinish": Janet Flanner, quoted in Brenda Wineapple, *Genêt: A Biography of Janet Flanner* (New York: Ticknor & Fields, 1989), p. 68.

330 "We had three" to "like hats": Beach, p. 113.

330 "charming": Ibid., p. 114.

330 "elegance and letters": Huddleston, p. 168.

331 "an ethereal being": Barney, p. 172.

331 "with complete mental laziness": Ezra Pound, "Paris Letter," *The Dial*, October 1921; cited in Wickes, p. 160.

331 "a sort of consumers' league" Ezra Pound, "Paris Letter, *The Dial* [1923], cited in Wickes, p. 161.

331–32 "start a centre": Ford Madox Ford, *It Was the Nightingale* (London: Heinemann, 1936), p. 285.

332 "the major one" to "a thousand years hence": F. M. Ford, *Transatlantic Review* prospectus, cited in Poli, pp. 37–40.

332 "none has however": F. M. Ford, *Transatlantic Review*, Preliminary Number, cited in Poli, p. 42.

333 "In Montparnasse": Stella Bowen, *Drawn from Life* (London: Virago, 1984), p. 120.

333 "were getting any satisfaction": McAlmon and Boyle, p. 226.

334 "intellectual" to "dowager duchess manner": JB interview with CB, October 2, 1991, the source of information in these paragraphs.

335 "When you walk" to "not one of us": LV quoted by Sindbad Vail, interview with CB, April 18, 1985.

335 "intelligent, intolerant" to "worth her own?": Laurence Vail, *Murder! Murder!* (London: Peter Davies, 1931), pp. 27, 15, 252.

335 "Jane Heap": McAlmon and Boyle, p. 37.

336 "too beautiful": Ibid., p. 224.

336 "gayety and color" to "a modern temperament": Harriet Monroe, "Guide to the Moon," *Poetry: A Magazine of Verse*, October–March 1923–24, pp. 100–3, 95.

336 "arresting" to "not at all good": Edwin Muir, "Readers and Writers," *The New Age*, January 31, 1924, pp. 164–65.

336–37 "There are things" to "arrests us": Edwin Muir, "Recent Verse," *The New Age*, March 6, 1924, p. 223.

337 "a writer who works": Eugène Jolas, "About Creative Work," Paris *Tribune*, July 20, 1924, as cited in Hugh Ford, ed., *The Left Bank Revisited* (University Park: Pennsylvania State University Press, 1972), p. 97.

337–38 "It was inevitable" to "a poet's inspiration": ML, "Modern Poetry," *Charm*, April 1925, pp. 16–17, 71.

338 "a distinct talent": McAlmon and Boyle, p. 163.

339 "does scant justice": *New York City Record* [April 1925], n.p.

339 "a poet as well": *The New York Times*, April 19, 1925, sec. 9, p. 11.

339 "The name she uses": *Bulletin of the Mattatuck Historical Society*, April 1925, n.p.

341 "Jo and I": ML to JB and JL, JLE. Unless otherwise indicated, this correspondence is the source of information concerning ML's partnership with PG.

342 "For the opening": Guggenheim, p. 58.

343 "ravelled up": ML cited in JC to ML, July 3, 1951, in Cornell, p. 175.

343 "In order to obtain": "Les Abat-Jour de Mina Loy," *Art et Industrie*, January 1927, pp. 42–43.

344 "the most marvellous *jeune fille*": RMcA quoted in Julien Levy, p. 33.

344–45 "at least half in love" to "in disgrace": Basil Bunting to CB, July 3, 1980. Bunting's "Ode 17," dedicated to ML, is included in his *Complete Poems* (Oxford: Oxford University Press, 1944), p. 95.

345–46 "ripe to be" to "elusive, beautiful woman": Julien Levy, p. 43.

346 "If you disrupt": ML, quoted in ibid., p. 35.

Interlude II / Anglo-Mongrels

Unless otherwise indicated, all quotations from ML are from her unpublished manuscript *The Child and the Parent*.

351 Footnote: Pound as cited in J. J. Williams, *Ezra Pound in Paris and London* (University Park: Pennsylvania State University Press, 1990), p. 326.

353 "one of the lost master-poems": Jerome Rothenberg, *Revolution of the Word: A New Gathering of American Avant-Garde Poetry 1914–1945* (New York: Seabury, 1974), p. 57. Two recent readings

include Melita Schaum, " 'Moonflowers Out of Muck': Mina Loy and the Female Autobiographical Epic," *Massachusetts Studies in English* 10 (1986); and Keith Tuma, "Anglo-Mongrels and the Rose," *Sagetrieb* 11 (1992).

353 "out-of-date": John Collier, "Contemporaries," *The New Age*, August 6, 1925, p. 165.

353 "as discouraging as her climate": ML, *Esau Penfold*.

354 "falling in love": ML, *Colossus*.

356 "moon-flowers," "mongrel-girl": ML, "Anglo-Mongrels and the Rose."

17 / The Widow's Jazz

Unless otherwise indicated, all quotations from ML are from her correspondence with JB and JL, JLE; all quotations from JL to ML are in MLE.

360 "gotten more": NCB, as cited by Mary Blume, "Natalie Barney, Legendary Lady of the Rue Jacob," *Réalités*, February 1966, p. 201.

360 "You never knew": Virgil Thomson interview with CB, June 6, 1977.

361 "prophetess": ML, "Speech for Natalie's," NCB archives. Doucet.

361 "as boxers do": Barney, p. 172.

361 "prismatic poetry": Ibid., p. 174.

362 "We were pleased": Ibid., p. 175.

362 "It is a good idea": NCB, quoted in Berthe Cleyrergue interview with CB, April 5, 1977.

363 "neap-tide": Barnes, Foreword, *Ladies Almanack* (New York: Harper & Row, 1972).

363 "a very special audience": DB to NCB, May 16, 1963, Barnes Papers, McKeldin Library, Special Collections, University of Maryland.

363 "she came forth" to "Hall of Fame": Barnes, pp. 7, 8, 9.

363 "was of this Month" to "surgical Instrument": Ibid., pp. 11, 12.

363–64 "what it is" to "*go amarrying!*": Ibid., pp. 12, 13.

364 "for carrying" to "see in each other": Ibid., pp. 24, 30–31.

364 "Though it is" to "gentlemaned only": Ibid., p. 50.

364 "God help us!": Ibid., p. 67.

367–68 "The effort to concentrate" to "disintegrates": ML, *Insel*, pp. 39–40.

368 "with a sensation of beauty": ML to James Mechem, September 17, 1960.

369 "What Paris had once offered": McAlmon and Boyle, pp. 309, 328.

369 "The revolution" to "a job for art": Jane Heap, *The Little Review*, May 1929, pp. 5–6.

369–70 *The Little Review* questionnaire, May 1929, pp. 52, 33, 17, 37.

370 ML reply to *The Little Review* questionnaire, May 1929, p. 46.

373 "funny" to "on the floor": ML, "The Crocodile without Any Tail."

374 Christmas dinner: Information from Sheila Carroll, interview with CB, March 25, 1979.

375 "when like Lucifer": ML, *Islands*, p. 23.

375 "bi-spirited" to "Torah or catechism": ML, *Goy Israels*, pp. 41, 101.

375 "So is every race" to "to dislodge": Ibid., pp. 40, 39.

376 "every scion" to "dancing-master destiny": Ibid., pp. 118, 46, 146.

377 "I felt": ML, *Insel*, p. 37.

377 "always in a state": Julien Levy, pp. 118–20.

378 "the prickly Baroque": Virgil Thomson interview with CB, June 6, 1977.

378 "this abundance" to "whatsoever": Julien Levy, p. 120.

378 "Mina hated being poor": JL interview with CB, August 22, 1977.

378 "that her true environment" to "luxury": Julien Levy, p. 149.

379 "Mina Loy is" to "need apply": "Attractions in the Galleries," *New York Evening Sun*, February 4, 1933, p. 9.

379 "the same imaginative feeling": "Briefer Comments on Current Art Exhibitions in New York," *New York Herald Tribune*, February 5, 1933, sec. VII, p. 10.

379 "a sort of sonnet sequence": "Around the Galleries," *Art News*, February 4, 1933, p. 6.

379 Footnote: "News and Gossip," *Creative Arts*, February 2, 1933, p. 87.

380 "the expression of" to "a wizard hangs": ML letter to FB, n.d., MLE. This letter served as a draft

for the "letter to a friend" included in *Insel*, pp. 21–22, where Breton is called Moto and, thanks to a creative typographical error, Ernst is "Sex"—no doubt miscopied from the Beinecke typescript, p. 3.

380 "Hermine": Marc Chagall, quoted by FB in letter to CB [1990].

380 "Mussolini": ML to CVV, December 26, 1934.

380 "vague and quite unbalanced": Ethel Harter letter to JB, February 22, 1937, MLE.

380–81 "glorious, sharp": Kay Boyle to ML, April 16, 31, MLE.

381 "taken on an immortality": ML, *Insel*, p. 160. Unless otherwise indicated, the quotations in subsequent paragraphs are from *Insel*.

383 "I saw why" to "and myself": ML, "Promised Land," CBC.

18 / Promised Land

Unless otherwise indicated, all quotations from ML are from her correspondence with JB and JL, JLE; all quotations from JL to ML are in MLE.

385 "Whenever I'm": ML letter fragment to FB, c. 1936,. CBC.

385 "the commonplace back": ML, *Insel*, p. 176.

386 "that any moment": ML letter fragment to FB, c. 1936, CBC.

387 "they looked" to "a consolation": ML, "Promised Land," the source of quotations from ML in subsequent paragraphs.

388 "at her maddest": JB interview with CB, December 16, 1979.

389 *re* NCB refrigerator story: FB to CB, September 30, 1988.

391 *re* ML's alphabet games: "Alphabet games," YCAL, "Inventions"; all quotations from ML in this paragraph are from ML to F.A.O. Schwarz, August 6, 1940, with her address listed as the Julien Levy Gallery.

391 "Fragrance is harmonious": ML to Horace Titus, July 15, 1940.

392–93 "Oh leave it" to "hates showing it": ML, quoted in Eliza MacCormack Feld, interview with CB, April 30, 1989.

394 ML, WCW, MM: Quotations from "Towards the Unknown," *View*, February–March 1942, p. 10.

395 "airplane sky writing" to "Victory V": ML, "Design for Curtain," "Designs," registered December 26, 1941.

395 "in all branches" to "such as a plane": ML, "Idea to be submitted," December 17, 1940, CBC. Mina sent herself this form in a registered letter covered with wax seals, as if these official-looking procedures would not only protect her idea but guarantee its success.

396 "one of his friends": ML, quoted in George H. Tichenor, "This Man Is a Traitor," *PM*, August 13, 1943, p. 3.

396 "a new structural combination" to "in the dark": ML, "*Chatoyant*" brochure, "Inventions," n.d.

396 "pacify the intellectual consternation": ML, "Notes on Religion," *Sulfur*, Fall 1990, p. 13.

396 "with the simple relation": ML, "The Revolution in Revelation."

397 "It is because": ML, "Notes on Religion," p. 14.

397 "to impart to others": ML, "History of Religion and Eros."

397 "that Christ meant": ML, "Note on Religion," p. 14.

397 "an observer": ML, "History of Religion and Eros," p. 3.

397 "our real dilemma": ML, "Notes on Religion," p. 15.

397 "Deific electricity": ML, "History of Religion and Eros," p. 8.

399 Footnote: ML to James Laughlin, June 5, 1948.

399 "these are bad days": RMcA to ML, January 28, 1941, MLE.

399 ML–Steloff friendship: Information from Frances Steloff interview with CB, December 9, 1977.

400 "the William Blake": Clarence John Laughlin interview with CB, September 27, 1981.

400 "phantoms" to "into the past": Laughlin, "Victorian Phantasms," *Clarence John Laughlin* (Tucson: Center for Creative Photography, 1979), n.p.

400 "complicated person" to "under the circumstances": Muriel Streeter interview with CB, February 28, 1982.

401 "sensitive and original": MD quoted by Teeny Duchamp, interview with CB, August 15, 1977.

401 Footnote: John Bernard Myers, "Interactions"; "A View of 'View,' " *Art in America*, Summer 1981, p. 85.

401 "Mme. Mina Loy": André Breton, Introduction to Cravan's "Notes," in *VVV*, June 1942, p. 55.

402 "mediumistic": Charles Henri Ford interview with CB, March 23, 1982.

402 "She was quite removed": Hans Fraenkel interview with CB, August 30, 1978.

402 "There is no question" to "chi-chi": Kenneth Rexroth, "Les Lauriers Sont Coupés," *Circle*, 1944, pp. 69–70.

403 "Now you will understand": ML to Rexroth [1945], Rexroth Papers, U.C.L.A.

403–4 "It seemed to me": Henry Miller to ML [1945], MLE.

404 "Only two people" to "give up the children": Gilbert Neiman to ML, November 23, [1945,] MLE.

404 *"Don't be afraid"* to *"Poetic Imagination"*: Gilbert Neiman to ML, n.d., MLE.

404 Footnote †: Gilbert Neiman, *Between Worlds* 1:2 (1961), unnumbered page (inside cover).

404 "deviltry" to "white magic": JC, quoted in Julien Levy, p. 78.

404 "the delicious head": ML, *Insel*, p. 168.

405 "canvassing experiences": "to strange places": JC to ML, November 21, 1946, MLE.

405 JC's association of ML and moon: JC to ML, July 3, 1951, in Cornell, p. 175.

405 "My Science": JC to ML, November 21, 1946, MLE.

405 "wise and comforting" to "a little piece": JC to ML, August 1, 1943, MLE.

406 "old boxes": Alain-Fournier, Part III, sec. 12, p. 294.

406 "especially delightful items": JC to ML, October 18, 1943, MLE.

406 "no one had replaced": Alain-Fournier, Part I, sec. 13, p. 75.

406–7 "You have a way" to "not pilfering": ML to JC, AAA, roll 1058.

407 "an object of magnitude": ML, "Phenomenon in American Art," p. 4.

407 "friend" to "spot of tea": JC to ML, December 4, 1945, MLE.

407 "a type of image-search": Joseph Cornell, *Portrait of Ondine*.

407 "another Webb, Mary": JC to ML, n.d., MLE.

408 "profounder cross-currents" to "weapons against discouragement": JC to ML, January 21, 1946, MLE.

408 "one of the angels": ML, quoted in John Bernard Myers letter to CB, August 10, 1981.

19 / *The Compensations of Poverty*

Unless otherwise indicated, all quotations from FB and JB to ML, or from ML to others, are from correspondence in MLE.

410 "Life among people": FB to ML, February 17, 1949.

410 "a very distinguished lady": Robert Lindsay interview with CB, June 14, 1978, the source of all subsequent quotations from Lindsay.

410 "Your mother": Irene Klempner to FB, n.d.

411 "you knew that": Louise Lilienfeld interview with CB, August 10, 1981.

411 "touchy people": Leo Samiof interview with CB, August 28, 1978, the source of all subsequent quotations from Samiof.

412 "Today is quite hot": ML to JB, May 16, 1951.

412 "Yes, I know": ML, quoted by Jonathan Bayer, interview with CB, July 13, 1977.

414 "He agrees with you": JB to ML, April 12, 1949.

415 "show you a way": JB to ML, May 6, 1949.

415 "We share": Goldsmith, p. 152.

417 *re* "Property of Pigeons": I am grateful for Jim Powell's fine reading of this poem, in "Basil Bunting and Mina Loy," *Chicago Review*, Winter 1990, pp. 6–25.

418 "These new works": Thomas B. Hess, *Art News*, January 1950, p. 45.

418 *re* "Phenomenon in American Art": This text exists in several versions, the most complete being ML's manuscript in the JC papers, AAA, roll 1965—the source of all quotations.

419 "overwhelmed": JC to ML, November 29, 1950.

422 "spiritual eye": Joel Goldsmith to ML, November 20, 1950.

423 "Let us be fools" to "success": Dorothy Day, quoted in Dwight MacDonald, "Profiles," *The New Yorker*, October 4, 1952, p. 40.

424 "It was quite a business": Nora Temple interview with CB, February 5, 1989.

20 / Aspen

Unless otherwise indicated, all correspondence to ML is in MLE.

426 "a person you'd notice": Dorothy Kelleher, interview with CB, October 27, 1988.

426 "a handsome woman": Robert Marsh, interview with CB, September 10, 1988.

427 Footnote: ML to JC, September 26, 1955, JC papers, roll 1055.

427 "If the royal family": Clifford, p. 24.

427 "The place to find someone": Jonny Larrowe, interview with CB, October 14, 1988.

428 "a kind of bewilderment": Caroline Bancroft, *Famous Aspen* (Denver: Golden Press, 1954), p. 51.

428 "great books": Mortimer Adler, *Aspen Times*, April 13, 1950, p. 1.

428 "Dudines": *Aspen Times*, December 7, 1950, p. 4.

428 Esther Jane Herwick: Quotations and information in subsequent paragraphs from Esther Jane Herwick Jowell interview with CB, October 30, 1988.

430 "gentleman caller": ML, quoted in Goodie Tayler, interview with CB, October 29, 1988.

430 "pompous boor" to "find him?": ML, quoted in Martie Sterling interview with CB, October 29, 1988.

431 "Oh, I've smoked *that*": ML, quoted in Robert Marsh interview with CB.

431 Yvonne Thomas: Information in subsequent paragraphs from Yvonne Thomas interview with CB, August 6, 1988.

431 "still a distinguished": Jonathan Williams, "Things Are Very Far Away," *The Nation*, May 27, 1961, pp. 461–62.

433 "Miss Loy says": Kathleen Martin, "Mina Loy, Poetess, at 83," *Aspen Times* [1966].

433 "no winning": JW to ML, May 29, 1959.

433 "The best way": ML to JW, June 3, [1950,] cited in Williams, "Things Are Very Far Away." The idea of "face-armour" recalls ML's 1919 brochure, *Auto-Facial-Construction*.

433 "because you have a Soul": JL to ML, n.d.

434 "very glamorous": JL to ML, n.d.

434 "gay and exciting": Frances Steloff to ML, May 14, 1959.

434 "The alliance": Stuart Preston, "Public and Private Worlds of Artists," *The New York Times*, April 19, 1959, sec. 2, p. 17.

434 "Theatrical trappings": E[dith] B[urkhardt], *Art News*, April 1959, p. 59.

434 "the Lower Depths": Robert Coates, "The Art Galleries," *The New Yorker*, April 25, 1959, p. 100.

434 "in terms of heaven": A[nita] V[entura], "Mina Loy," *Arts*, April 1959, p. 58.

435 "double gift" to "always have": David Mann to ML, May 26, 1959, March 18, 1959.

435 "The Rediscovery of Mina Loy": This article, by Samuel Morse French, appeared in *Wisconsin Studies in Contemporary Literature* 2 (1961).

435 "she didn't always": Dr. Jack Crandall, ML's Aspen physician, interview with CB, October 29, 1988; subsequent quotation and medical information from this source.

436 "Only the eyes are left": ML, quoted by Ronald Johnson, interview with CB, November 13, 1988.

436 "She wandered": Robert Vas Dias, interview with CB, July 9, 1982.

436 "they make me deaf" to "the greatest woman poet": All quotations from ML are from her interview with Blackburn and Vas Dias, CBC. A copy of the interview is lodged in the Archive for New Poetry, University of California, San Diego.

438 "She is a very great poet": Robert Vas Dias to ML, August 23, 1965, which cites Creeley's letter to Vas Dias.

438–39 "Dear Mina Loy" to "cordially yours in Christ": Thomas Merton to ML, August 24, 1959.

439–40 "I never knew": ML, quoted in JB interview with CB, April 7, 1979.

440 "What value": ML, "Towards the Unknown," *View* (February–March 1942), p. 10.

440 "We are but": ML, "Notes on Existence," *TLLB*, p. 313. In a series of notes on spirituality entitled "The Revolution in Revelation" (included in "Notes on Metaphysics"), ML calls intellectual understanding "an eternal stairway on which each step as you ascend from it ceases to be." A similarly worded passage appears at the end of "Being Alive," Part XII of *The Child and the Parent*.

Bibliography

Published Works of Mina Loy

POETRY

"Aid of the Madonna." *Accent* 7 (1947), p. 111.

"Anglo-Mongrels and the Rose"; Part One, *The Little Review* 9 (Spring 1923), pp. 10–18; (Autumn–Winter 1923–24), pp. 41–51; Part Two, *Contact Collection of Contemporary Writers* (Paris: Three Mountains Press, 1925), pp. 137–94. Cambridge, MA: Exact Change, 1996.

"Apology of Genius." *The Dial* 73.1 (July 1922), pp. 73–74.

"At the Door of the House." *Others: An Anthology of the New Verse*, ed. Alfred Kreymborg (New York: Knopf, 1917), pp. 64–66.

At the Door of the House (Northampton, MA: Aphra Press, 1980). Limited edition.

"Aviator's Eyes," in Larry Krantz, "Three Neglected Poets." *Wagner Literary Magazine* (Spring 1959), pp. 52–63.

"Babies in Hospital." *Rogue* 3.2 (November 1916), p. 6.

"The Black Virginity." *Others* 5 (December 1918), pp. 6–7.

"Brancusi's Golden Bird." *The Dial* 73.5 (November 1922), pp. 507–8.

"Café du Néant." *International* 8 (1914), p. 255. As second part of "Three Moments in Paris." *Rogue* 1.4 (May 1, 1915), pp. 10–11.

"Chiffon Velours." *Accent* 7 (1947), p. 112.

"The Dead." *Others for 1919*, ed. Alfred Kreymborg (New York: Nicholas Brown, 1920), pp. 112–14.

"The Effectual Marriage." *Others: An Anthology of the New Verse*, ed. Alfred Kreymborg (New York: Knopf, 1917), pp. 66–70. Poem excerpted as "Ineffectual Marriage," in Ezra Pound, ed., *Profile: An Anthology Collected in MCMXXXI* (Milan: John Scheiwiller, 1932).

"Ephemerid." *Accent* 6 (1946), pp. 240–41.

"Faun Fare." *Between Worlds* 2.1 (Fall–Winter 1962), pp. 28–30.

"Giovanni Franchi." *Rogue* 3.1 (October 1916), p. 4.

"Hilarious Israel." *Accent* 7 (1947), pp. 110–11.

"Hot Cross Bum." *New Directions* 12 (1950), pp. 311–20.

"Human Cylinders." *Others: An Anthology of the New Verse*, ed. Alfred Kreymborg (New York: Knopf, 1917), pp. 71–72.

"Idiot Child on a Fire Escape." *Partisan Review* 19 (1952), p. 561.

"Impossible Opus." *Between Worlds* 1.2 (Spring–Summer 1961), pp. 199–200.

"In Extremis" [YCAL manuscript title], published as "Untitled" in *Between Worlds* 2.1 (Fall–Winter 1962), p. 27, and as "Show Me a Saint Who Suffered" in *TLLB*.

"Italian Pictures." *Trend* 8.2 (November 1914), pp. 220–22.

"Lady Laura in Bohemia." *Pagany* 2.3 (Summer 1931), pp. 125–27.

The Last Lunar Baedeker, ed. Roger L. Conover (Highlands, NC: The Jargon Society, 1982; and Manchester: Carcanet, 1985).

"Lion's Jaws." *The Little Review* 7.3 (September–December 1920), pp. 39–43.

The Lost Lunar Baedeker, ed. Roger L. Conover (New York: Farrar, Straus & Giroux, 1996).

"Love Songs." I–IV in *Others* 1 (July 1915), pp. 6–8. As *Songs to Joannes*, *Others* 3 (April 1917), entire issue. In abbreviated form as "Love Songs" in *Lunar Baedecker*.

Love Songs (Northampton, MA: Aphra Press, 1981). Limited edition.

Lunar Baedecker (Paris: Contact Publishing Co., 1923).

Lunar Baedeker & Time-Tables (Highlands, NC: Jonathan Williams, 1958).

"Marble." *Transatlantic Review*, preliminary number c. November 1923.

"Mexican Desert." *The Dial* 70.6 (June 1921), p. 672.

Mina Loy (Lympne, Kent: Hand and Flower Press, 1984).

"Negro Dancer." *Between Worlds* 1.2 (Spring–Summer 1961), p. 202.

"O Hell." *Contact* 1 (December 1920), p. 7.

"Parturition." *Trend* 8.1 (October 1914), pp. 93–94.

"Perlun." *The Dial* 71.2 (August 1921), p. 142.

"Photo After Pogrom." *Between Worlds* 1.2 (Spring–Summer, 1961), p. 201.

"Poe." *The Dial* 71.4 (October 1921), p. 406.

"Property of Pigeons." *Between Worlds* 1.2 (Spring–Summer 1961), pp. 203–4.

"Sketch of a Man on a Platform." *Rogue* 1.2 (April 1, 1915), p. 12.

"There is no life or death." *Camera Work* 46 (April 1914), p. 18.

"Time-Bomb." *Between Worlds* 1.2 (Spring–Summer 1961), p. 200.

"To You." *Others* 3 (July 1916), pp. 27–28.

"Virgins Plus Curtains Minus Dots." *Rogue* 2 (August 15, 1915), p. 10.

Virgins Plus Curtains (Rochester, NY: Press of the Good Mountain, 1981). Limited edition.

"The Widow's Jazz." *Pagany* 2.2 (April–June 1931), pp. 68–70.

PROSE

"Aphorisms on Futurism." *Camera Work* 45 (January 1914), pp. 13–15.

Auto-Facial-Construction (Florence: Tipografia Giuntina, 1919).

Colossus, excerpted and edited by Roger L. Conover, in *Dada/Surrealism* 14 (1985); reprinted in *New York Dada*, ed. Rudolf E. Kuenzli (New York: Willis Locker & Owens, 1986), pp. 102–19.

"Gertrude Stein." *Transatlantic Review* 2 (1924), pp. 305–9, 427–30.

"In . . . Formation." *Blind Man* 1 (April 10, 1917), p. 7.

Insel, ed. Elizabeth Arnold (Santa Rosa, CA: Black Sparrow, 1991).

"John Rodker's Frog." *The Little Review* 7.3 (September–December 1920), pp. 56–57.

"Modern Poetry." *Charm* 3.3 (April 1925), pp. 16–17, 71.

"Notes on Religion," ed. Keith Tuma. *Sulfur* 27 (Fall 1990), pp. 13–16.

"O Marcel—otherwise I Also Have Been to Louise's." *Blind Man* 2 (May 1917), pp. 11–12. Reprinted in *View* 5.1 (March 1945).

The Pamperers. *The Dial* 69.1 (July 1920), pp. 65–78. Reprinted in *Performing Arts Journal* (1985).

"Pas de Commentaires! Louis M. Eilshemius." *Blind Man* 2 (May 1917), pp. 11–12.

"Preceptors of Childhood: or The Nurses of Maraquita." *Playboy* 2.2 (1923), p. 12.

Psycho-Democracy (Florence: Tipografia Peri & Rossi, 1920). As "Psycho-Democracy: A Movement to Focus Human Reason on the Conscious Direction of Evolution," in *The Little Review* 8.1 (Autumn 1921), pp. 14–19.

"Questionnaire." *The Little Review* 12 (May 1929), p. 46.

[Reply to John Rodker, "To Mina Loy."] *The Little Review* 7.4 (January–March 1921), pp. 44–45.

"Street Sister." *That Kind of Woman: Stories from the Left Bank and Beyond*, ed. Bronte Adams and Trudi Tate (London: Virago, 1991), pp. 41–42.

"Summer Night in a Florentine Slum." *Contact* 1 (December 1920), pp. 6–7.

"Towards the Unknown." *View* 1 (February–March 1942), p. 10.

Two Plays ["Collision" and "Cittàbapini"]. *Rogue* 1 (August 1, 1915), pp. 15–16.

TRANSLATIONS

Aires 9 (Haute-Loire, France, 1989): "Letters of the Unliving."

Artes 2 (Helsingborg, Sweden, 1992): "Feminist Manifesto," "Crab-Angel."

Arthur Cravan, *Oeuvres* (Paris: Gérard Lebovici, 1987): *Colossus*.

Le Baedeker lunaire (Paris: La Différence, 1995). Bilingual edition.

IF 2 (Marseilles, 1993: "The Starry Sky of Wyndham Lewis," "Mexican Desert," "Poe," "Chiffon Velours," "Omen of Victory," "Aviator's Eyes," "Transformation Scene," "The Widow's Jazz," "Lions' Jaws," "The Effectual Marriage."

Le Nouveau Commerce 71/72 (Paris, 1988): "The Dead," "Lunar Baedeker," "Joyce's Ulysses," "Chiffon Velours," *Two Plays*.

Poeti nel Deserto: Basil Bunting e Mina Loy, ed. Carlo Anceschi (Reggio Emilia: Edizioni Diabasis, 1993): "Apology of Genius," "Lunar Baedeker," "Der Blinde Junge," "At the Door of the House," *Love Songs*, "Property of Pigeons," "Aid of the Madonna," "Show Me a Saint Who Suffered," "Child Chanting."

Portrait de l'Artiste en Tête de Mort [*Insel*] (Paris: La Différence, 1995).

ART

"Les Abat-Jour de Mina Loy." *Art et Industrie* (January 1927), pp. 42–43.

"Consider Your Grandmother's Stays," *Rogue* 3.2 (November 1916), p. 7.

[Drawing.] *Art Review* (October 1922), p. 15.

"Les Eclairages de Mina Loy." *Art et Industrie* (February 1928), p. 37.

[Florence Williams.] Drawing dated May 29, 1924. First published in *William Carlos Williams Newsletter* 2.2 (Fall 1976), p. 6.

"James Joyce." *Vanity Fair* 18 (March 1922), p. 65.

"Prize Lamp Shades from Nina Loy of Paris." *Arts & Decoration* (July 1927), p. 56.

"Teasing a Butterfly." *Paintings, Drawings and Sculptures from the Julien Levy Collection* [catalogue]. New York: Sotheby Parke Bernet, 1981.

"Three Studies by an Unusual Artist, Mina Loy." *Art Review* (December 1922), p. 17.

"Two Water-Colours." *The Dial* 70.4 (April 1921), n.p.

[Watercolor.] *Playboy* 1.7 (May 1921), p. 22.

[Woman Weaver.] Drawing c. 1925. First published in *HOW(ever)* 2.4 (1985), p. 11.

"Women in a Carriage." Pen and ink/watercolor. First published in *Arthur Cravan: Poetita e Boxidor*. Exhibition catalogue. (Barcelona: Palau de la Virreina, 1992), p. 106.

Additional drawings, paintings, sculpture, and lampshades by Mina Loy are reproduced in *The Last Lunar Baedeker*. See also Marisa Januzzi's annotated bibliography, including a complete chronological listing of Loy's published work and references to her by contemporaries, critics, and scholars, in *Mina Loy: Woman and Poet*, eds. Maeera Schreiber and Keith Tuma (Orono, ME: National Poetry Foundation, 1996).

Selected Bibliography

Harold Acton. *Memoirs of an Aesthete*. London: Hamish Hamiliton, 1984.

———. *Tuscan Villas*. London: Thames & Hudson, 1973.

———. and Edward Chaney. *Florence: A Traveller's Companion*. New York: Atheneum, 1986.

Alain-Fournier. *Le Grand Meaulnes*. Paris: Emile-Paul, 1913.

Sibilla Aleramo. *A Woman*. Berkeley: University of California Press, 1980.

Umbro Apollonio. *Futurist Manifestos*. London: Thames & Hudson, 1973.

Dore Ashton. *A Joseph Cornell Album*. New York: Viking, 1974.

Elizabeth Aslin. *The Aesthetic Movement, Prelude to Art Nouveau*. New York: Frederick A. Praeger, 1969.

Ronald Atkin. *Revolution! Mexico 1910–1920*. New York: John Day, 1970.

Neil Baldwin. *Man Ray, American Artist*. New York: Clarkson N. Potter, 1988.

Djuna Barnes. *Ladies Almanack*. Paris: Printed for the Author and sold by Edward W. Titus, 1928.

Natalie Clifford Barney. *Aventures de l'Esprit*. Paris: Emile Paul, 1929.

Martin Battersby. *The Decorative Twenties*, rev. by Philippe Garnier. New York: Whitney Library of Design, 1988.

Sylvia Beach. *Shakespeare and Company*. New York: Harcourt Brace, 1956.

Carleton Beals. *Glass Houses*. Philadelphia: Lippincott, 1938.

———. *Mexican Maze*. Philadelphia: Lippincott, 1931.

Quentin Bell. *Victorian Artists*. Cambridge, MA: Harvard University Press, 1967.

Arnold Bennett. "Night and Morning in Florence," *English Review* V (June 1910), pp. 442–55.

Jacques-Emile Blanche. *Portraits of a Lifetime*. London: Dent, 1937.

Maria Lluîsa Borràs. *Arthur Cravan: Una Biografia*. Barcelona: Quaderns Crema, 1993.

Eve Borsook. *The Companion Guide to Florence*. London: Collins, 1988.

Randolph L. Braham, ed. *Hungarian-Jewish Studies*, Vol. I. New York: World Federation of Hungarian Jews, 1966.

Mitchell P. Briggs. *George D. Herron and the European Settlement*. Palo Alto: Stanford University Press, 1932.

Van Wyck Brooks. *The Dream of Arcadia, American Writers and Artists in Italy*. New York: Dutton, 1958.

Bob Brown. *You Gotta Live*. London: Desmond Harmsworth, 1932.

Jackson R. Bryer. "Joyce, *Ulysses*, and *The Little Review*," *South Atlantic Quarterly* 66.2 (1967), pp. 148–64.

Gabrielle Buffet-Picabia. *Aires Abstraites*. Geneva: Pierre Cailler, 1957.

Carolyn Burke. "Accidental Aloofness: Barnes, Loy, and Modernism," in Mary Lynn Broe, ed., *Silence and Power: Djuna Barnes, a Reevaluation*. Carbondale: Southern Illinois University Press, 1990.

———. "Getting Spliced: Modernism and Sexual Difference," *American Quarterly* 39.1 (1987), pp. 98–121.

———. "The New Woman and the New Poetry: Mina Loy," in Diane Middlebrook and Marilyn Yalom, eds., *Coming to Light: American Women Poets in the Twentieth Century*. Ann Arbor: University of Michigan Press, 1985.

———. "Without Commas: Gertrude Stein and Mina Loy," *Poetics Journal* 4 (1984), pp. 43–52.

Mary Alice Burke. *Elizabeth Nourse, 1859–1938: A Salon Career*. Washington, D.C.: Smithsonian, 1983.

Gertrude Bussey and Margaret Tims. *Pioneers for Peace, Women's International League for Peace and Freedom 1915–1965*. London: Allen & Unwin, 1965.

Pierre Cabanne. *Dialogues with Marcel Duchamp*. New York: Viking, 1971.

Jenni Calder. *The Victorian Home*. London: Batsford, 1977.

Anthea Callen. *Women Artists of the Arts and Crafts Movement, 1870–1914*. New York: Pantheon, 1979.

Montgomery Carmichael. *In Tuscany*. London: John Murray, 1906.

Susan P. Casteras. *Images of Victorian Womanhood in English Art*. Rutherford, NJ: Fairleigh Dickinson University Press, 1987.

———. *The Substance or the Shadow: Images of Victorian Womanhood*. New Haven: Yale Center for British Art, 1982.

Peggy Clifford. *To Aspen and Back*. New York: St. Martin's Press, 1980.

A.O.J. Cockshut. *The Unbelievers, English Agnostic Thought, 1840–1890*. New York: New York University Press, 1966.

Joseph Cornell. *Jospeh Cornell's Theater of the Mind*, ed. Mary Ann Caws. New York and London: Thames and Hudson, 1993.

Edward Craig. *Gordon Craig*. London: Victor Gollancz, 1968.

Arthur Cravan [Fabian Lloyd]. *Oeuvres*, ed. Jean-Pierre Begot. Paris: Gérard Lebovici, 1987.

Jean-Paul Crespelle. *La Vie Quotidienne à Montparnasse à la Grande Epoque, 1905–1930*. Paris: Hachette, 1976.

Irene Dancyger. *A World of Women*. Dublin: Gill and Macmillan, 1978.

Lenore Davidoff. *The Best Circles: Women and Society in Victorian England*. Totowa, NJ.: Rowman and Littlefield, 1973.

Luciano DeMaria, ed. *Per Conoscere Marinetti e il Futurismo*. Verona: Mondadori, 1973.

Helen Deutsch and Stella Hanau. *The Provincetown: A Story of the Theatre*. New York: Russell & Russell, 1972.

Sister Devamata. *Swami Paramananda and His Work*. La Crescenta, CA: Ananda Ashram, Vol. 1, 1926; Vol. 2, 1941.

Bram Dijkstra. *Idols of Perversity: Fantasies of Feminine Evil in Fin-de-Siècle Culture*. New York: Oxford University Press, 1986.

Muriel Draper. *Music at Midnight*. New York: Harper & Brothers, 1929.

Katherine Dreier. *Five Months in the Argentine: From a Woman's Point of View, 1918 to 1919*. New York: Frederic Fairchild Sherman, 1920.

Marcel Duchamp. *Salt Seller: The Writings of Marcel Duchamp*. New York: Oxford University Press, 1973.

Alistair Duncan. *Art Nouveau and Art Deco Lighting*. London: Thames and Hudson, 1978.

Carol Dyhouse. *Girls Growing Up in Late Victorian and Edwardian England*. London: Routledge and Kegan Paul, 1981.

David Edstrom. *The Testament of Caliban*. New York: Funk and Wagnalls, 1937.

Dennis Farr. *English Art, 1870–1940*. New York: Oxford University Press, 1984.

F. P. Fletcher-Vane. *Walks and People in Tuscany*. Florence: Dominican Press, 1908.

Hugh Ford, *Published in Paris: American and British Writers, Printers and Publishers in Paris, 1920–1930*. New York: Macmillan, 1975.

Catherine Foster. *Women for All Seasons: The Story of the Women's International League for Peace and Freedom*. Athens: University of Georgia Press, 1989.

Futurismo & Futurismi. Exhibition catalogue. Milan: Bompiani, 1986.

Donald Gallup, ed. *The Flowers of Friendship: Letters Written to Gertrude Stein*. New York: Knopf, 1953.

Lloyd P. Gartner. *The Jewish Immigrant in England, 1870–1914*. London: Allen & Unwin, 1960.

Marcel Giry. "Le Salon d'Automne de 1905," *L'Information de l'Histoire de l'Art*, 1968, no. 1, pp. 16–25.

Clarissa Catherine Goff. *Florence and Some Tuscan Cities*. London: Black, 1905.

Joel S. Goldsmith. *The Infinite Way*. San Gabriel, CA: Willing Publishing, 1976.

Deborah Gorham. *The Victorian Girl and the Feminine Ideal*. Bloomington: Indiana University Press, 1982.

Martin Green. *The Von Richthofen Sisters: The Triumphant and Tragic Modes of Love*. New York: Basic Books, 1977.

Peggy Guggenheim. *Out of This Century*. Garden City, NY: Doubleday, 1980.

Nina Hamnett. *Laughing Torso, Reminiscences of Nina Hamnett*. New York: Roy Long and Richard R. Smith, 1932.

Hutchins Hapgood. *A Victorian in the Modern World*. New York: Harcourt Brace, 1939.

Charles Harrison. *English Art and Modernism, 1900–1939*. London: Allen Lane, 1981.

Fraser Harrison, *The Dark Angel, Aspects of Victorian Sexuality*. London: Sheldan Press, 1977.

Mary Eliza Haweis. *Beautiful Houses*. New York: Scribner's, 1882.

Eric Hobsbawm. *The Age of Empire, 1875–1914*. New York: Pantheon, 1987.

Clive Holland. "Student Life in the Quartier Latin, Paris," *The Studio* 27 (October 1902), pp. 33–40.

Bevis Hollier. "The St. John's Wood Clique," *Apollo* (June 1964), pp. 490–95.

Michael Holroyd. *Augustus John: A Biography*. New York: Holt, Rinehart & Winston, 1975.

Sisley Huddleston. *Paris Salons, Cafés, Studios*. New York: Blue Ribbon Books (J. B. Lippincott), 1928.

Robert Hughes. *The Shock of the New*. New York: Knopf, 1991.

Sidney Hyman. *The Aspen Idea*. Norman: University of Oklahoma Press, 1975.

Samuel Hynes. *A War Imagined, The First World War and English Culture*. New York: Atheneum, 1991.

———. *The Edwardian Turn of Mind*. Princeton, NJ: Princeton University Press, 1968.

Holbrook Jackson, *The Eighteen Nineties: A Review of Art and Ideas at the Close of the Nineteenth Century*. New York: Knopf, 1912.

Edouard Jaguer. *Richard Oelze*. New York: Lafayette Parke Gallery, 1991.

Peter Jelavich. *Munich and Theatrical Modernism: Politics, Playwriting, and Performance, 1890–1914*. Cambridge, MA: Harvard University Press, 1985.

—————. "Munich as Cultural Center: Politics and the Arts," in *Kandinsky in Munich, 1886–1914*. Exhibition catalogue. New York: The Solomon Guggenheim Museum, 1982, pp. 17–26.

Augustus John. *Chiaroscuro: Fragments of an Autobiography*. New York: Pellegrini and Cudahy, 1952.

John Arthur Johnson. *Jack Johnson Is a Dandy: An Autobiography*. New York: Chelsea House, 1969.

Nicholas Joost. *Scofield Thayer and The Dial: An Illustrated History*. Carbondale: Southern Illinois University Press, 1964.

Matthew Josephson. *Life Among the Surrealists*. New York: Holt, Rinehart & Winston, 1962.

Friedrich Katz. *The Secret War in Mexico*. Chicago: University of Chicago Press, 1981.

Michael Kirby and Victoria Nes Kirby. *Futurist Performance*. New York: PAJ Publications, 1986.

Virgina M. Kouidis. *Mina Loy, American Modernist Poet*. Baton Rouge: Louisiana State University Press, 1980.

Alfred Kreymborg. *Lima Beans*, in Kreymborg, *Plays for Poet-mimes*. New York: The Other Press, 1918.

—————. *Our Singing Strength: An Outline of American Poetry, 1620–1930*. New York: Coward-McCann, 1929.

—————. *The Troubadour: An Autobiography*. New York: Boni and Liveright, 1925.

Rudolf E. Kuenzli and Francis M. Naumann, eds. *Marcel Duchamp, Artist of the Century*. Cambridge, MA: The M.I.T. Press, 1991.

Harriet Lane Levy. "Reminiscences," unpaginated manuscript, Bancroft Library, University of California, Berkeley.

Julien Levy. *Memoirs of an Art Gallery*. New York: Putnam's, 1977.

Vivian David Lipman. *A Social History of the Jews in England, 1885–1950*. London: Watts, 1954.

Giovanni Lista. *Marinetti et le Futurisme*. Lausanne: L'Age d'Or, 1977.

Harold Loeb. *The Way It Was*. New York: Criterion, 1959.

Mabel Dodge Luhan. *Edge of the Taos Desert: An Escape to Reality*. Albuquerque: University of New Mexico Press, 1987.

—————. *European Experiences* (Vol. 2 of *Intimate Memories*). New York: Harcourt Brace, 1935.

—————. *Movers and Shakers* (Vol. 3 of *Intimate Memories*). New York: Harcourt Brace, 1936.

Stuart Macdonald. *The History and Philosophy of Art Education*. London: University of London Press, 1970.

Tessa MacKenzie. *The Art Schools of London*. London: Chapman and Hall, 1895.

Robert McAlmon. *Being Geniuses Together*. London: Secker & Warburg, 1938.

—————. *Post-Adolescence*. Paris: Contact, 1923; reprinted and ed. by Edward N. S. Lorusso, University of Mexico Press, 1991.

————— and Kay Boyle. *Being Geniuses Together, 1920–1930*. London: Hogarth, 1984.

Henry McBride. *The Flow of Art: Essays and Criticisms of Henry McBride*, ed. Daniel Cotton Rich. New York: Atheneum, 1975.

Hugh McLeod. *Class and Religion in the Late Victorian City*. London: Croom Helm, 1974.

Kynaston McShine, ed. *Joseph Cornell*. Exhibition catalogue. New York: The Museum of Modern Art, 1980.

Man Ray. *Self-Portrait*. Boston: Little, Brown, 1963.

Paul Mariani. *William Carlos Williams: A New World Naked*. New York: McGraw-Hill, 1981.

Filippo Tommaso Marinetti. *Selected Writings*, ed. R. W. Flint. New York: Farrar, Straus & Giroux, 1972.

Alice Goldfarb Marquis. *Marcel Duchamp: Eros c'est la vie*. Troy, NY: Whitson Publishing, 1981.

James R. Mellow. *Charmed Circle: Gertrude Stein & Company*. New York: Avon, 1975.

John Milner. *The Studios of Paris: The Capital of Art in the Late Nineteenth Century*. New Haven, CT: Yale University Press, 1988.

Paula Modersohn-Becker. *Paula Modersohn-Becker: The Letters and Journals*, eds. Gunter Busch and Liselotte Von Reinken. New York: Taplinger, 1983.

Favell Lee Bevan Mortimer. *The Peep of Day, or, A Series of The Earliest Religious Instruction The Infant Mind is Capable of Receiving*. New York: American Tract Society, 1849.

Robert Motherwell. *The Dada Painters and Poets*. New York: Wittenborn, Schultz, 1951.

John Bernard Myers, "Interactions: A View of 'View,'" *Art in America*, 69.6 (1981), pp. 81–92.

Francis Naumann, "Cryptography and the Arensberg Circle," *Arts Magazine* 51.9 (1977), pp. 127–33.

———. "The Big Show: The First Exhibition of the Society of Independent Artists," *Art Forum* 17: Part I (February 1979), pp. 34–39; Part II (April 1979), pp. 49–53.

———. "The New York Dada Movement: Better Late Than Never," *Arts* 54.6 (February 1980), pp. 143–49.

———. "Walter Conrad Arensberg: Poet, Patron, and Participant in the New York Avant-Garde, 1915–1920." *Philadelphia Museum of Art Bulletin* 76.328 (1980), pp. 1–32.

Ralph Nevill. *Days and Nights in Montmartre and the Latin Quarter.* New York: George H. Doran, 1927.

C.R.W. Nevinson. *Paint and Prejudice.* New York: Harcourt Brace, 1938.

Pamela Gerrish Nunn. *Victorian Women Artists.* London: The Women's Press, 1987.

Iris Origo. *Images and Shadows: Part of a Life.* New York: Harcourt Brace Jovanovich, 1970.

Philippe Ortiz. "Avis aux gens scandalisés." Exhibition catalogue, Frances Simpson Stevens paintings, Braun Galleries, New York, March 8–27, 1916.

Swâmi Paramananda. *Vedanta in Practice.* Boston: The Vedanta Centre, 1917.

Hélène Pinet. *Les photographes de Rodin.* Paris: Musée Rodin, 1986.

———. *Rodin, sculpteur et les photographes de son temps.* Paris: Philippe Sers, 1985.

Bernard T. Poli. *Ford Madox Ford and the Transatlantic Review.* Syracuse, NY: Syracuse University Press, 1967.

Post-Impressionism, Cross Currents in European Painting. Exhibition catalogue. London: Royal Academy of the Arts / Weidenfeld and Nicolson, 1979.

J. Diane Radycki. "The Life of Lady Art Students: Changing Art Education at the Turn of the Century," *Art Journal* 42.1 (1982), pp. 9–13.

Kenneth Rexroth. "Les Lauriers Sont Coupés," *Circle,* 1.4 (1944), pp. 69–72.

Roberto Ridolfi. *Vita di Giovanni Papini.* Verona: Mondadori, 1957.

Randy Roberts. *Papa Jack, Jack Johnson and the Era of White Hopes.* New York: The Free Press, 1983.

Henri-Pierre Roché. *Victor.* Paris: Centre National d'Art et de Culture Pompidou, 1977.

Robert A. Rosenstone. *Romantic Revolutionary: A Biography of John Reed.* New York: Vintage, 1981.

William Rothenstein. *Men and Memories.* New York: Tudor [1937].

Lois Palken Rudnick. *Mabel Dodge Luhan: New Woman, New Worlds.* Albuquerque: University of New Mexico Press, 1984.

Maurice Sachs. *The Decade of Illusions: Paris 1918–1928.* New York: Knopf, 1933.

Ernest Samuels. *Bernard Berenson: The Making of a Connoisseur.* Cambridge, MA: Belknap Press, 1979.

George Santayana. *Persons and Places.* New York: Scribners, 1944.

Robert Károly Sarlós. *Jig Cook and the Provincetown Players.* [Amherst:] University of Massachusetts Press, 1982.

Martica Sawin. "Aux Etats-Unis." *La Planete affolée, Surréalisme, Dispersion, et Influences, 1938–1947.* Exhibition catalogue. Paris and Marseilles: Flammarion/Musées de Marseille, 1986.

Frank Scarlett and Marjorie Townley. *Arts Décoratifs: A Personal Recollection of the Paris Exhibition.* London: St. Martin's, 1975.

Herbert W. Schneider. *Making the Fascist State.* New York: Oxford University Press, 1928.

Meryle Secrest. *Being Bernard Berenson: A Biography.* New York: Holt, Rinehart & Winston, 1979.

Peter Selz. *German Expressionist Painting.* Berkeley: University of California Press, 1957.

Martin Shaw. *Up to Now.* London: Oxford University Press, 1929.

F. Berkeley Smith. *How Paris Amuses Itself.* New York: Funk and Wagnalls, 1903.

Sanford Smoller. *Adrift Among Geniuses: Robert McAlmon.* University Park: Pennsylvania State University Press, 1975.

Walter Shaw Sparrow, ed. *Women Painters of the World.* London: Hodder and Stoughton, 1905.

Sandra Leonard Starr. *Joseph Cornell, Art and Metaphysics.* New York: Castelli, Feigen, Corcoran, 1982.

Francis Steegmuller, ed. *"Your Isadora": The Love Story of Isadora Duncan and Gordon Craig.* New York: Random House, 1974.

Gertrude Stein. *Geography and Plays.* Boston: The Four Seas Co., 1922.

———. *Selected Writings.* New York: Vintage, 1972.

473

Leo Stein. *Journey into the Self*. New York: Crown, 1950.

Dickran Tashjian. *Skyscraper Primitives: Dada and the American Avant-Garde*. Middletown, CT: Wesleyan University Press, 1975.

Hilary Taylor. "If a Young Painter Be Not Fierce and Arrogant, God . . . Help Him: Some Women Art Students at the Slade, c. 1895–9," *Art History* 9.2 (1986), pp. 232–44.

T. Philip Terry. *Terry's Guide to Mexico*, rev. ed. Hingham, MA: R. C. Terry, 1947.

F.M.L. Thompson. *Hampstead: Building a Borough, 1650–1964*. London: Routledge and Kegan Paul, 1974.

Paul Thompson. *The Work of William Morris*. London: Quartet Books, 1977.

Alice B. Toklas. *What Is Remembered*. New York: Holt, Rinehart & Winston, 1963.

Eric Trudgill. *Madonnas and Magdalen: The Origins and Development of Victorian Sexual Attitudes*. London: Heinemann, 1976.

Louis Untermeyer. *American Poetry Since 1900*. New York: Henry Holt, 1923.

Laurence Vail. *What D'You Want?* unpublished typescript, n.d.

Carl Van Vechten. "Once Aboard the Lugger, San Guglielmo," *Trend*, 8.1, pp. 13–24.

———. *Peter Whiffle*. New York: The Modern Library, 1929.

———. *Sacred and Profane Memories*. New York: Knopf, 1932.

Louise Varèse. *Varèse: A Looking-Glass Diary*. New York: Norton, 1972.

Laurence Veysey. *The Communal Experience: Anarchist and Mystical Counter-Cultures in America*. New York: Harper & Row, 1973.

Diane Waldman. *Joseph Cornell*. New York: George Braziller, 1977.

Lina Waterfield. *Home Life in Italy*. London: Methuen, 1908.

Steven Watson. *Strange Bedfellows: The First American Avant-Garde*. New York: Abbeville Press, 1991.

Mary Webb. *Precious Bane*. New York: Dutton, 1926.

Peg Weiss. "Kandinsky in Munich: Encounters and Transformations," in *Kandinsky in Munich, 1886–1914*. Exhibition catalogue. New York: The Solomon Guggenheim Museum, 1982, pp. 28–82.

———. *Kandinsky in Munich: The Formative Jugendstil Years*. Princeton, NJ: Princeton University Press, 1979.

Jacqueline Bograd Weld. *Peggy, the Wayward Guggenheim*. New York: Dutton, 1986.

Alice Wexler. *Emma Goldman: An Intimate Life*. New York: Pantheon, 1984.

George Wickes. *The Amazon of Letters: The Life and Loves of Natalie Barney*. New York: G. P. Putnam's, 1976.

John Willett. *Art and Politics in the Weimar Period*. New York: Pantheon, 1978.

William Carlos Williams. *The Autobiography of William Carlos Williams*. New York: Random House, 1951.

Robert Wohl. *The Generation of 1914*. Cambridge, MA: Harvard University Press, 1979.

Beatrice Wood. *I Shock Myself: The Autobiography of Beatrice Wood*, ed. Lindsay Smith. San Francisco: Chronicle Books, 1988.

———. "I Shock Myself: Excerpts from The Autobiography of Beatrice Wood," *Arts*, 51.9 (1977), pp. 134–39.

Alice Woods. *Edges*. Indianapolis: Bowen-Merril, 1902.

Charlotte Yeldham. *Women Artists in Nineteenth Century France and England*. New York and London: Garland, 1984.

Acknowledgments

A great many people have contributed to this book. It could not have been written without the generosity, patience, and trust of Joella Bayer and Fabienne Benedict, who graciously shared their memories and granted unlimited access to their mother's papers. To them I owe a profound debt of gratitude. I am also deeply grateful to Samuel Hynes, who first told me about Mina Loy; the late Kenneth Rexroth, whose stories brought her era to life; Roger L. Conover, her editor and staunch fellow Loy-alist; and Naomi Sawelson-Gorse, for unfailing research wizardry and support.

It is a great pleasure to acknowledge the contributions of all those who helped with memories, letters, interviews, hospitality, and conversation. In England: Jonathan Bayer, the late Basil Bunting, Edward Craig, the late Richard Ellmann, Eric Hobsbawm, Bea Howe, Audrey Mason, the late Lee Miller, the late Nigel Nicolson, Richard Shone, Charles Tomlinson, Robert Vas Dias, Michaela Watt.

In France: Jacques Baron, André Bay, Jenny Bradley, the late Gabrielle Buffet-Picabia, Berthe Cleyrergue, Denise Detragiache, Teeny Duchamp, Gladys Fabre, Pierre Georgel, Florence Gilliam, the late Juliette Gleizes, the late Maria Jolas, the late Lydie Le Savoureux, the late Juliet Man Ray, the late Edouard Roditi, the late Philippe Soupault, Deidi Von Schaewen, Kathe Vail, and the late Sinbad Vail.

In Italy: the late Sir Harold Acton, Luigi Baldacci, Alessandro Bonsanti, Ester Coen, Giulia and Giuseppe DiPietro, Piero Ferrucci, Ian Greenlees, Drusilla Gucci, the late Peggy Guggenheim, Luce Marinetti, Piero Pacini, Stanislau Paszkowski, the late Giuseppe Sprovieri, and Mary Swisher.

In the United States: the late Berenice Abbott, Elizabeth Aley, the late Djuna Barnes, Javan Bayer, Jessica Benedict, Clurrie Bennis, the late Kay Boyle, Joseph Brewer, Donna Britten, Kurt Brown, the late Susan Jenkins Brown, Mary Denman Capouya, Sheila Carroll, William Copley, Karen Chamberlain, Morrill Cody, Dr. Jack Crandall, Robert Creeley, Dorothy Danieli, Elsa deBrun, Gloria Braggioti Etting, Bonnie Evans, the late Spencer Evans, Patrick Farrell, Eliza MacCormack Feld, Stephen Ferris, Deborah Fine, Charles Henri Ford, Hans Fraenkel, Cyril Galitzine, Donald Gallup, Natalie Goff, Betty Grindley, Maurice Grosser, Mary Hayes, George Hitchcock, Dr. Harriet Hunter, Rosalind Jacobs, Elizabeth Jakab, Ronald Johnson, the late Matthew Josephson, Esther Jane Jowell, the late Philip Kaplan, Jacques Kayaloff, Penelope Kenez, Emeric Kurz, Eyre de Lanux, Joni Larrowe, the late Clarence John Laughlin, James Laughlin, Jerrold Levy, the late Julien Levy, Bob Lewis, Louise Lilienfeld, Robert Lindsay, David Mann, Paul Mariani, Robert Marsh, Jay Martin, James Mechem, John Bernard Myers, Edward Naumberg, Charles Norman, Hank O'Neal, Luba Paz, Bill Potts, Leo Samiof,

Acknowledgments

Muriel Streeter Schwartz, Margie Sloan, Dr. Eugene Smith, the late Frances Steloff, Martie Sterling, Jim Tait, Goody Taylor, Lyle Taylor, Yvonne Thomas, the late Virgil Thomson, Carol Tinker, Clover Vail, the late Louise Varèse, Carol Vesecky, Ann Waldron, the late Glenway Wescott, Martha Ullman West, Jonathan Williams, Beatrice Wood.

Special thanks are due to Francis Naumann and Steven Watson, whose encyclopedic scholarship and rich perspectives on modernism have enriched my own, as well to Marisa Januzzi, Loy-alist extraordinaire. It is also a pleasure to acknowledge the aid of my fellow scholars and writers Jane Augustine, Neil Baldwin, Elyse Blankley, Jay Bochner, William Bohn, Maria Borràs, Mary Lynn Broe, Michael Davidson, Hugh Ford, Theodora Graham, Louis F. Kannenstine, Edmund Keeley, Kevin Killian, Virginia Kouidis, Gary Lease, Glen MacLeod, Julie Martin, Charles Molesworth, Robert Sarlós, David Sweet, Steve Taubenek, Peg Weiss, and George Wickes.

I am most grateful to my agents, Georges Borchardt and Cindy Klein Roche, and to Jonathan Galassi, Paul Elie, and Lynn Warshow at Farrar, Straus & Giroux for their sympathetic readings and editorial advice. Draft portions of the manuscript were also read by Noel Riley Fitch, Kathleen Fraser, Sarah Friedlander, Susan Gevirtz, John Jordan, Alfred Katz, Emily Leider, and Alicia Ostriker: their counsel on matters of style and interpretation has been invaluable. Diane Johnson offered wise suggestions at an early stage; Deborah Baker's generous reading of the penultimate draft convinced me that Mina Loy's life was taking shape. Jeanne and Ross Dunn helped me see the creative spirit in Christian Science; Laura Kalpakian provided energizing critiques and a week of writers' camp; William Rubel gave sound advice whenever it was needed; Karen Zukor gave *Househunting* new life. Poppy Burke, my daughter, grew up with Mina as part of the family, and Terry Burke, my husband, provided constant perspective and support, not to mention countless readings of the manuscript— only occasionally losing patience with its author or subject.

I have been fortunate to have help with research and manuscript preparation from Jane Arons, Faith Beckett, Andrea Corbett-Grant, Frances Dougherty, Nicole Kosanke, Jill Pearlman, Alyssa Post-lethwaite, Valerie Ross, Joe Skokowski, and Miriam Wallace, who will recognize their contributions in these pages. I am more grateful than I can say to Jane Bostwick, whose patient scrutiny of old newspapers at the New York Public Library unearthed treasures.

I have benefited from the guidance of curators and librarians and would like to thank, in particular, Patricia Willis of the Collection of American Literature, Beinecke Rare Book and Manuscript Library, Yale University, as well as all her highly competent, good-humored staff. Thanks are also due to Robert J. Bertholf, The Poetry/Rare Books Collection, University Libraries, State University of New York at Buffalo; Dr. Bauer, Stadtarchivs, Munich; Karen Drickamer, Special Collections, Morris Library, Southern Illinois University; Christian Ducluzeau, Centre Pompidou; Ann Ferrante, Archive of American Art; Eleanor Gehres, Denver Public Library; Evelyn Greenwald, Southern California Answering Network; Philippe Grunchec, Ecole Nationale Supérieure des Beaux-Arts; Linda Roscoe Hartigan, National Museum of American Art; Lee Johnson, Archivist, The First Church of Christ, Scientist, Boston; Farida Kassim, Institute for Advanced Study; Marge Klein, Philadelphia Museum of Art; Patrick T. Lawlor, Rare Book and Manuscript Library, Columbia University; Dr. Richard Lemp, Münchener Stadtbibliothek; Leslie Morris, Rosenbach Museum and Library, Philadelphia; Hélène Pinet, Musée Rodin, Paris; David Rundle, The British Institute of Florence; Barbara T. Ross, The Art Museum, Princeton University; Rosella Todros, Biblioteca Marucelliana, Florence; Elizabeth S. Wrigley, The Francis Bacon Foundation, Claremont, CA.

I am grateful to the Interlibrary Loan staff at U.C.S.C. for years of book searches, as well as to the following for help with research: The John Hay Library, Brown University; Commerce Graphics; Special Collections, University Library, University of Delaware; The Huntington Library; University Library Archives, University of Illinois at Urbana-Champaign; Special Collections, University Library, University of California, Los Angeles; Special Collections, McKeldin Library, University of Maryland; Metropolitan Museum, New York; National Archives, Washington, D.C.; Manuscripts and Archives, New York Public Library; Special Collections, Rutgers University Library; Marquand Art Library and Special Collections, Princeton University; the San Francisco Public Library; the Humanities Research Center, University of Texas; the Tate Museum, London; the Victoria and Albert Museum, London; the Worcester Art Museum, Worcester, MA.

I also wish to thank the American Council of Learned Societies for a Grant-in-Aid, the National

Endowment for the Humanities for its support in the form of a Summer Stipend and a Fellowship for Independent Study and Research, and the Humanities Division of the University of California, Santa Cruz, for generous assistance of all kinds.

Grateful acknowledgment is made to Roger Conover, and the Estate of Mina Loy for permission to quote from Loy's published works, unpublished manuscripts, and correspondence; to the Collection of American Literature, Beinecke Rare Book and Manuscript Library, Yale University, for permission to quote manuscript material from the Mina Loy and Hapgood family papers, as well as Loy's correspondence with Mabel Dodge Luhan, Alfred Stieglitz, Gertrude Stein, Scofield Thayer, and Carl Van Vechten, in their respective collections; to the Rare Book and Manuscript Library, Columbia University, for permission to quote from the Stephen Haweis papers; to Marianne Moore Craig, Literary Executor for the Estate of Marianne Moore, for permission to cite Marianne Moore's letter to H.D. of January 11, 1921; to Scribner, a division of Simon and Schuster, Inc., for permission to quote from Marianne Moore, *The Collected Poems of Marianne Moore*, copyright 1935 by Marianne Moore, renewed 1963 by Marianne Moore and T. S. Eliot; to Solo Syndication for permission to quote from *You Gotta Live*, by Bob Brown; to Oxford University Press for permission to quote from *The Complete Poems of Basil Bunting*, 1994; to the Estate of Basil Bunting for permission to quote from an unpublished letter to the author of July 3, 1980; to the Authors League Fund, Literary Executor of the Estate of Djuna Barnes, for permission to quote from *Ladies Almanack*; and to the Merton Legacy Trust for permission to quote from the unpublished letter from Thomas Merton to Mina Loy of August 24, 1959.

Photographs have been reproduced with the kind permission of Berenice Abbott/Commerce Graphics Ltd. (*No Parking*); the Artists Rights Society (Fabienne Lloyd; Mina Loy and Djuna Barnes); Joella Bayer (Loy family; Haweis family; Loy assemblages); the Rare Book and Manuscript Library, Columbia University (frontispiece; Loy nude); Roger L. Conover (*L'Amour dorloté par les belles dames*; Loy drawing of Man Ray); Michael Duncan (*La Maison en papier*); Lafayette Parke Gallery (Richard Oelze); Lydie Le Savoureux (Steven Haweis and Loy; Haweis); Jerrold Levy (Julien Levy); Luce Marinetti (F. T. Marinetti); the National Archives (The Crowd outside The Jockey; *Little Review* reunion); the National Museum of American Art, Smithsonian Institution (Joseph Cornell); Ana Paszkowski (Giovanni Papini); Rare Books and Special Collections, Princeton University Libraries (Robert Mc-Almon); the Collection of American Literature, Yale University (Loy drawing of Haweis; Mabel Dodge; Loy drawing of Carl Van Vechten); and Jonathan Williams (Loy in Aspen). All other photographs are from my own collection.

While every effort has been made to trace copyright holders, I would be grateful to hear from those who may have escaped my notice.

Index

Index